BETWEEN WORLDS

BETWEEN WORLDS

A Reader, Rhetoric, and Handbook

■ ■ ■

SUSAN BACHMANN
El Camino College

MELINDA BARTH
El Camino College

HarperCollins*College*Publishers

Senior Editor: Patricia A. Rossi
Developmental Editor: Marisa L. L'Heureux
Project Editor: Marina Vaynshteyn
Design Supervisor: Alice Fernandes-Brown
Cover Design: Kay Petronio
Art Studio: Academy ArtWorks, Inc.
Electronic Production Manager: Angel Gonzalez Jr.
Desktop Administrator: LaToya Wigfall
Manufacturing Administrator: Alexandra Odulak
Electronic Page Makeup: Paul Lacy/LaToya Wigfall
Printer and Binder: RR Donnelley & Sons Company
Cover Printer: The Lehigh Press, Inc.
Cover Art: The glass spheres on the cover, photographed by Claire Garoutte, are
the work of Seattle glass artist Dale Chihuly. They are up to 42 inches in diame-
ter and are called "Niijima Floats" (1992) after the island near Tokyo where
glassblowers once made balls for Japanese fisherman to keep their nets afloat.
Mr. Chihuly recalls that when he was a child he found the fishermen's floats on
the beaches near his home in Tacoma, Washington.

For permission to use copyrighted material, grateful acknowledgment is made
to the copyright holders on pp. 567–570, which are hereby made part of this
copyright page.

Between Worlds: A Reader, Rhetoric, and Handbook
Copyright © 1995 by HarperCollins College Publishers

Library of Congress Cataloging-in-Publication Data
Between worlds: a reader, rhetoric, and handbook / [compiled by]
Susan Bachmann, Melinda Barth.
       p.   cm.
  ISBN 0-673-46884-4
  1. College readers. 2. English language—Rhetoric.
3. English language—Grammar—Handbooks, manuals, etc.
I. Bachmann, Susan. II. Barth, Melinda.
PE1417.B43 1995
808'.0427—dc20   94-9459
                                                CIP

94 95 96   9 8 7 6 5 4 3 2 1

To the men in our lives:
Ron, Dylan, and Evan Barth
and
Walter, Ryan, and Adam Gajewski

Contents

■ ■ ■

PART TWO ▪ THE RHETORIC 301

Chapter 8   Revising an Essay 349

PART THREE ■ THE HANDBOOK 499

Chapter 12 Understanding Common Errors 513

Chapter 13 Understanding Punctuation 531

Preface

Between Worlds is a reader, rhetoric, and handbook that offers students and instructors a variety of materials that support their writing courses. A diverse reader with thematically arranged selections includes writing prompts that encourage students to write about each reading in isolation as well as in relation to other texts. A concise rhetoric and handbook follow the reader. They are designed to help students through every aspect of the writing process and through some of the most common writing assignments, including the research paper. Although each section of this textbook can be used independently, both instructor and student will find the cross-referencing of material between the reader and the rhetoric an advantage for teaching and learning.

THE READER

All the readings in this text reflect the conflicting realms—the "between worlds"—in which most of us live. Like us, the individuals in these readings are caught between balancing the burdens of work and school, satisfying family obligations and meeting personal needs, and defining oneself while relating with others. These "others" may be from different generations and cultures, may be the opposite sex, or may have diverse self-perceptions and values. Rather than focusing on the extremes of these experiences or on their exclusivity, we include readings that explore the overlapping worlds where most of us find ourselves.

The between-worlds experience is the substance of our five reading chapters: "Between Generations," "Between Genders," "Between Cultures," "Between Perceptions," and "Between Values." In the reader we have included numerous selections so that instructors can vary their readings (if they prefer) without changing books each semester, and so that students may be inspired to read unassigned material.

Each chapter contains essays, short stories, and poems that are deliberately paired or grouped to prompt critical thinking, class discussion, and focused writing. The writing topics encourage students to use multiple materials and genres for support and to see how the concerns expressed in an essay can be succinctly captured in a poem or illustrated in a short story. The essays are of varying complexity and length, from documented analytical studies to shorter pieces that have appeared in periodicals. All the readings relate to our theme.

Each reading is followed by questions ("Thinking About the Text") so that students can review the content of the piece prior to class discussion. In addition, "Writing from the Text" sections provide students with writing topics for each individual work. Most valuable of all for the college writer are the writing assignments ("Connecting with Other Texts") that link related readings in each chapter *and* throughout the book. Students have the opportunity in the connecting assignments to examine multiple perspectives critically and then use diverse materials to support their points in papers. Also, because students may be using more than one source, they will have practice incorporating ideas and documenting them before a longer research paper is assigned. In addition to those topics that relate to readings in the text, we have also included assignments that will send students to other sources—including research in the library—for longer, more developed papers.

THE RHETORIC

We have designed the rhetoric as a *focused guide to the entire writing process.* In order to demonstrate a process students might use when writing a college essay, we follow several writers through multiple stages of various assignments. Therefore the rhetoric can be used by the instructor or stand on its own as a how-to for the students. Because we recognize that writing is a discovery process, we emphasize the following: numerous prewriting strategies; practical advice for considering audience; ideas about arrangement, outlining, drafting, and revision; and tips for constructing and revising the thesis. In the rhetoric we show that writing is not a step-by-step process; it involves concurrent and recursive activities.

An important part of the rhetoric is a guide to developing specific assignments. We discuss strategies and methods for writing papers commonly assigned in college courses and provide discussion, models, and exercises for each. We teach how to write an in-class essay. We also explore the techniques of professional writers and examine how they use multiple strategies to analyze and argue their points. Many of our examples draw from themes, works, and assignments in the reader.

Although early in the rhetoric we introduce the skills necessary for incorporating others' ideas and words in shorter papers, we devote an entire chapter to the research paper. This chapter includes instruction and an annotated student paper that is a response to a between-worlds topic. We also provide a clear guide to MLA and APA documentation. Throughout the rhetoric, we offer plenty of illustrations and practice exercises to reinforce our conviction that we learn to write by actually writing . . . and rewriting.

THE HANDBOOK

We are convinced that control of grammar and punctuation gives the writer power over ideas and audience. Therefore the handbook is intended to empower students but not overwhelm them. We briefly explain how sentences work so that students can better organize and revise their writing. Then we focus on the most common errors—the "terrible ten"—that persistently appear in student writing. We include a list of margin symbols for this correction guide so students can interpret their instructors' comments.

We also focus on understanding punctuation and word choice to help students become efficient editors of their work. In addition, we have an alphabetical list of words that are confused or misused by many writers. The handbook is designed to help students write, revise, and edit essays and understand their instructors' comments and corrections.

APPLAUSE

This textbook could never have been written without the help of many people who have been particularly supportive and generous with their time as we worked on this book. A superb librarian, Judy Harris, searched computer screens and stacks to find what we needed. We are especially grateful to Rïse Daniels and Bill Bachmann for their talented teamwork on this book and for putting aside their own projects when we needed their expertise. Over the years, colleagues at El Camino College, Marymount College, the State University of New York at Buffalo, the University of Wisconsin at Madison, the University of Illinois at Champaign, and California State University at Dominguez Hills have shared teaching strategies and writing ideas that inspired portions of this book. Nancy Hennessy Swanby meticulously prepared parts of the manuscript. Shannon Paaske worked energetically to help us meet our deadline, and we are pleased that some of our other students—Bruce Halling, Tim Hogan, and Mary Miller—also became published writers with the printing of this text. Our students merit hearty applause.

Special thanks must go to a number of fine reviewers who brought insights from their teaching to improve our efforts in creating this text. We wish to thank these supportive critics: Chris Anderson, Oregon State University; Richard Batteiger, Oklahoma State University; Joseph Boles, Northern Arizona University; Patricia Bridges, Mount Union College; Bruce E. Coad, Mountain View College; Lynda R. Corbin, San Diego Mesa College; Timothy Dekin, Loyola University of Chicago; William D. Dyer, Mankato State University; Gabrielle Gautreaux, University of New Orleans; Patricia H. Graves, Georgia State University; Stephen Hahn, William Paterson College; Aija Hoover, Odessa College; Ellen Redding Kaler, University of Kansas; Phoebe Mainster, Wayne State University; Jack Miller, Normandale Community College; Jane Bowman Smith, Winthrop University; Carol Wershoven, Palm Beach Community College; and Elizabeth Wood, Santa Barbara City College.

We are grateful to our new friends at HarperCollins: Patricia A. Rossi, senior acquisitions editor, who was immediately and continuously enthusiastic about our project; and Marisa L. L'Heureux, developmental editor, whose judgment, support, and sense of humor helped us revise and improve this book.

Finally, we want to try to thank the men in our lives who lived *Between Worlds* with us. Walter and Ron rescued us from computer chaos and kept our children from feeling they had been banished to another world. Ryan and Adam and Dylan and Evan helped as well—sometimes with hugs, often with humor, and occasionally by simply disappearing! Other family members and friends sent us relevant articles, offered their help, and understood when we turned down invitations and did not answer letters or phone calls. They all believed this project was worth their being temporarily "displaced" . . . and we applaud their willingness to live "between worlds" with us.

Susan Bachmann
Melinda Barth

I

THE READER

■ ■ ■

The readings in this text have been chosen to reflect the interests of college students like you, who are juggling school and work as well as balancing social lives and family expectations. The selections have been arranged thematically into five chapters. These chapters describe the multiple worlds that all of us live in and the tensions that pull us between the realms of generations, genders, cultures, perceptions, and values. We chose these readings to stimulate your thinking so that you can write meaningful essays—the goal of your composition course.

Each chapter contains many essays, some short stories, and a poem or two, all arranged to parallel or contrast with each other. After each reading you will find a section called "Thinking About the Text." These questions were designed for you to use as a study review prior to class and for small-group discussions during class. We follow these questions with "Writing from the Text," a section of writing assignments that spring from the readings and from your own experience. These topics may be assigned by your instructor, or they can be used for practice writing in a journal. You will find help for writing these assignments in the rhetoric portion of this text.

A third section, "Connecting with Other Texts," will help you if your instructor asks you to compare two or more readings in this book. Some assignments in this section will encourage you to find extra material in the library, and these assignments can be used if your instructor assigns a paper that requires research. You will find instruction on how to write research papers of various lengths in the rhetoric portion of this text.

Some of the authors in this book are caught between generations and, like you, are trying to understand themselves in relation to parents and grandparents. And just as you are examining the roles that define your gender, many of these authors argue for a reexamination of those roles that limit the lives of people of both sexes. Whether you are a newcomer to the United States, a second- or third-generation American, or a settled citizen, you may find that these writers describe what you have experienced living between cultures. Your perception of who you are inevitably is colored by others' images of you. Yet your desire to be perceived as an individual, rather than a stereotype, is also the experience of many college students and of the authors who write about being between perceptions. The selections in the final chapter encourage you to think about your values—something you probably have done more seriously since you started college. You may want to examine the ideas of the authors in this last chapter in order to reassess your own convictions.

I

Between Generations

■ ■ ■

In our opening essay, Ellen Goodman quotes André Malraux's belief that "without family" the individual "alone in the world trembles with the cold." The family often nurtures its members and tolerates differences and failings that friends and lovers cannot accept. But as you may realize from your own experiences and observations, people also tremble with fear or anxiety even within the family unit. The writers in this chapter show the family as a source of both nurturing and trembling.

As they illustrate the resilience within families, three writers show the problems caused by substance abuse. Sherwood Anderson somehow "discovers" his father, while Scott Russell Sanders loses his father to alcoholism and John Leonard loses his brother to drugs.

If you have a strong bond with a grandparent, you will value Eric Marcus' essay and appreciate the friendship and understanding he gains when he tells his grandmother his truth. The conflicts between generations can be both instructive and humorous, as you will see in the short stories by Anne Tyler, Toni Cade Bambara, and Amy Tan. And the relationship between generations can also be powerfully positive, as Mary Miller shows in her essay about mothering and as Richard Wilbur illustrates in his poem about fathering.

Perhaps you have seen that families can be the source of some of our funniest experiences. If so, you will enjoy Laura Cunningham's narrative that shows a grandparent and grandchild enriching each other's lives and thriving under one roof. And you may be amused to read in William Aiken's essay the revelations of a father who fears that he has not "turned out right" in the eyes of his grown children.

Your awareness of gaps between generations, as well as a deeper sense of family connection, may inspire your own writing. The essays, short stories, and poems in this chapter attest to the will of the human spirit to mitigate family tension, to smile at some of the chaos, and to survive and thrive from one generation to the next.

THANKSGIVING
Ellen Goodman

A journalist who has worked for *Newsweek,* CBS, NBC, and a number of metro-politan newspapers, Ellen Goodman (b. 1941) has written a widely syndicated col-umn from her home paper, the *Boston Globe,* since 1967. Goodman won the Pulitzer Prize in 1980 for distinguished commentary. Her subject matter is diverse, and her responses are entertaining. As Diane McWhorter of the *Washington Journal-ism Review* has said, Goodman "attacks controversies from abortion to housework to Alexander Solzhenitsyn with the combined grace and grit of a paratrooper." Goodman's own comment about her work is that she writes about "more impor-tant questions than the average columnist." She asserts that it is "much more important to look at the underlying values by which this country exists . . . the vast social changes in the way men and women lead their lives and deal with each other, [and] about children" than to write about the "trivia," like politics, that other columnists write about. The essay included here, on the importance of family in our lives, is characteristic of Goodman's concerns. The piece was first published in the *Boston Globe* in 1980.

1   Soon they will be together again, all the people who travel between their own lives and each other's. The package tour of the season will lure them this week to the family table. By Thursday, feast day, family day, Thanksgiving day, Ameri-cans who value individualism like no other people will collect around a million tables in a ritual of belonging.

2   They will assemble their families the way they assemble dinner: each one bear-ing a personality as different as cranberry sauce and pumpkin pie. For one dinner they will cook for each other, fuss for each other, feed each other and argue with each other. They will nod at their common heritage, the craziness and caring of other generations. They will measure their common legacy . . . the children.

3   All these complex cells, these men and women, old and young, with different dreams and disappointments will give homage again to the group they are a part of and apart from: their family. Families and individuals. The "we" and the "I." As good Americans we all travel between these two ideals. We take value trips from the great American notion of individualism to the great American vision of fami-ly. We wear out our tires driving back and forth, using speed to shorten the dis-tance between these two principles.

4   There has always been some pavement between a person and a family. From the first moment we recognize that we are separate we begin to wrestle with aloneness and togetherness. Here and now these conflicts are especially acute. We are, after all, raised in families . . . to be individuals. This double message follows us through life. We are taught about the freedom of the "I" and the safety of the "we." The loneliness of the "I" and the intrusiveness of the "we." The selfishness of the "I" and the burdens of the "we."

5   We are taught what André Malraux said: "Without a family, man, alone in the world, trembles with the cold." And taught what he said another day: "The denial of the supreme importance of the mind's development accounts for many revolts

against the family." In theory, the world rewards "the supreme importance" of the individual, the ego. We think alone, inside our heads. We write music and litera- ture with an enlarged sense of self. We are graded and paid, hired and fired, on our own merit. The rank individualism is both exciting and cruel. Here is where the fittest survive.

6   The family, on the other hand, at its best, works very differently. We don't have to achieve to be accepted by our families. We just have to be. Our membership is not based on credentials but on birth. As Malraux put it, "A friend loves you for your intelligence, a mistress for your charm, but your family's love is unreason- ing: You were born into it and of its flesh and blood."

7   The family is formed not for the survival of the fittest but for the weakest. It is not an economic unit but an emotional one. This is not the place where people ruthlessly compete with each other but where they work for each other. Its busi- ness is taking care, and when it works, it is not callous but kind.

8   There are fewer heroes, fewer stars in family life. While the world may glorify the self, the family asks us, at one time or another, to submerge it. While the world may abandon us, the family promises, at one time or another, to protect us. So we commute daily, weekly, yearly between one world and another. Between a life as a family member that can be nurturing or smothering. Between life as an individ- ual that can free us or flatten us. We vacillate between two separate sets of demands and possibilities.

9   The people who will gather around this table Thursday live in both of these worlds, a part of and apart from each other. With any luck the territory they travel from one to another can be a fertile one, rich with care and space. It can be a place where the "I" and the "we" interact. On this day at least, they will bring to each other something both special and something to be shared: these separate selves.

THINKING ABOUT THE TEXT

1. What is the central contradiction or paradox that Goodman expresses in "Thanksgiving" about Americans' coming together for this yearly celebration?

2. In what ways are we "raised in families . . . to be individuals"? In what way is the family also the center of "revolt," as André Malraux might express it?

3. On what principle is our membership in the family based, according to Goodman? On what does she insist it is *not* based?

WRITING FROM THE TEXT

1. Describe some unique aspect of yourself that has developed because you were "raised" or nurtured by your family.

2. Goodman writes that on Thanksgiving, people who "live in both worlds"—the world of the individual and the family world—meet and

"interact." Write a descriptive scene of your family life and let the account *show* the interaction of the "I" and the "we." Discover a focus point about your being "a part of" and your being "apart from" your family as you develop your narrative. Conclude with that focus expressed as a thesis.

3. Write a brief analysis of a family that you know, focusing on the non-merger of individuals and the failure to create a family life.

4. Consider one of Goodman's statements, like "We are . . . raised in families . . . to be individuals," or "We don't have to achieve to be accepted by families. We just have to be." Show how one of these statements is or is not valid for defining your family life.

CONNECTING WITH OTHER TEXTS

1. Use any of the *Between Worlds* depictions of family, including "The Girls' Room" (p. 63), "The 'Perfect' Misconception" (p. 58), or "On Being a Cripple" (p. 203), to write an essay that focuses on the positive qualities of family life. Use the texts for examples and specific support.

2. Use any of the *Between Worlds* depictions of family, including "Under the Influence" (p. 11), "Discovery of a Father" (p. 6), "Two Kinds" (p. 49), "Where Are You Going, Where Have You Been?" (p. 124), and "The Bridge Poem" (p. 196), to focus on the negative characteristics of family life. Use the texts for examples and specific support.

DISCOVERY OF A FATHER
Sherwood Anderson

Sherwood Anderson (1876–1941) worked as a newsboy, paint manufacturer, house painter, and stable groom before he became a writer. The literary legend is that in 1913, Anderson walked out of his managerial job at a paint factory and abandoned his family in order to devote his life to writing. His work experiences and rejection of middle-class life and values are reflected in his writing, where psychological motivation and emotional intensity are more important than plot. His best-known works include the novel *Winesburg, Ohio* (1919) and several autobiographical accounts—*A Story Teller's Story* (1924); *Tar: A Midwest Childhood* (1926); and *Memoirs* (1939), from which this piece is taken.

1   One of the strangest relationships in the world is that between father and son. I know it now from having sons of my own.

2   A boy wants something very special from his father. You hear it said that fathers want their sons to be what they feel they cannot themselves be, but I tell

you it also works the other way. I know that as a small boy I wanted my father to be a certain thing he was not. I wanted him to be a proud, silent, dignified father. When I was with other boys and he passed along the street, I wanted to feel a glow of pride: "There he is. That is my father."

3 But he wasn't such a one. He couldn't be. It seemed to me then that he was always showing off. Let's say someone in our town had got up a show. They were always doing it. The druggist would be in it, the shoe-store clerk, the horse doctor, and a lot of women and girls. My father would manage to get the chief comedy part. It was, let's say, a Civil War play and he was a comic Irish soldier. He had to do the most absurd things. They thought he was funny, but I didn't.

4 I thought he was terrible. I didn't see how Mother could stand it. She even laughed with the others. Maybe I would have laughed if it hadn't been my father.

5 Or there was a parade, the Fourth of July or Decoration Day. He'd be in that, too, right at the front of it, as Grand Marshal or something, on a white horse hired from a livery stable.

6 He couldn't ride for shucks. He fell off the horse and everyone hooted with laughter, but he didn't care. He even seemed to like it. I remember once when he had done something ridiculous, and right out on Main Street, too. I was with some other boys and they were laughing and shouting at him and he was shouting back and having as good a time as they were. I ran down an alley back of some stores and there in the Presbyterian Church sheds I had a good long cry.

7 Or I would be in bed at night and Father would come home a little lit up and bring some men with him. He was a man who was never alone. Before he went broke, running a harness shop, there were always a lot of men loafing in the shop. He went broke, of course, because he gave too much credit. He couldn't refuse it and I thought he was a fool. I had got to hating him.

8 There'd be men I didn't think would want to be fooling around with him. There might even be the superintendent of our schools and a quiet man who ran the hardware store. Once, I remember, there was a white-haired man who was a cashier of the bank. It was a wonder to me they'd want to be seen with such a windbag. That's what I thought he was. I know now what it was that attracted them. It was because life in our town, as in all small towns, was at times pretty dull and he livened it up. He made them laugh. He could tell stories. He'd even get them to singing.

9 If they didn't come to our house they'd go off, say at night, to where there was a grassy place by a creek. They'd cook food there and drink beer and sit about listening to his stories.

10 He was always telling stories about himself. He'd say this or that wonderful thing happened to him. It might be something that made him look like a fool. He didn't care.

11 If an Irishman came to our house, right away Father would say he was Irish. He'd tell what county in Ireland he was born in. He'd tell things that happened there when he was a boy. He'd make it seem so real that, if I hadn't known he was born in southern Ohio, I'd have believed him myself.

12 If it was a Scotchman, the same thing happened. He'd get a burr into his speech. Or he was a German or a Swede. He'd be anything the other man was. I

think they all knew he was lying, but they seemed to like him just the same. As a boy that was what I couldn't understand.

13   And there was Mother. How could she stand it? I wanted to ask but never did. She was not the kind you asked such questions.

14   I'd be upstairs in my bed, in my room above the porch, and Father would be telling some of his tales. A lot of Father's stories were about the Civil War. To hear him tell it he'd been in about every battle. He'd known Grant, Sherman, Sheridan, and I don't know how many others. He'd been particularly intimate with General Grant so that when Grant went East, to take charge of all the armies, he took Father along.

15   "I was an orderly at headquarters and Sam Grant said to me, 'Irve,' he said, 'I'm going to take you along with me.'"

16   It seems he and Grant used to slip off sometimes and have a quiet drink together. That's what my father said. He'd tell about the day Lee surrendered and how, when the great moment came, they couldn't find Grant.

17   "You know," my father said, "about General Grant's book, his memoirs. You've read of how he said he had a headache and how, when he got word that Lee was ready to call it quits, he was suddenly and miraculously cured."

18   "Huh," said Father. "He was in the woods with me.

19   "I was in there with my back against a tree. I was pretty well corned. I had got hold of a bottle of pretty good stuff.

20   "They were looking for Grant. He had got off his horse and come into the woods. He found me. He was covered with mud.

21   "I had the bottle in my hand. What'd I care? The war was over. I knew we had them licked."

22   My father said that he was the one who told Grant about Lee. An orderly riding by had told him, because the orderly knew how thick he was with Grant. Grant was embarrassed.

23   "But, Irve, look at me. I'm all covered with mud," he said to Father.

24   And then, my father said, he and Grant decided to have a drink together. They took a couple of shots and then, because he didn't want Grant to show up potted before the immaculate Lee, he smashed the bottle against the tree.

25   "Sam Grant's dead now and I wouldn't want it to get out on him," my father said.

26   That's just one of the kind of things he'd tell. Of course, the men knew he was lying, but they seemed to like it just the same.

27   When we got broke, down and out, do you think he ever brought anything home? Not he. If there wasn't anything to eat in the house, he'd go off visiting around at farm houses. They all wanted him. Sometimes he'd stay away for weeks, Mother working to keep us fed, and then home he'd come bringing, let's say, a ham. He'd got it from some farmer friend. He'd slap it on the table in the kitchen. "You bet I'm going to see that my kids have something to eat," he'd say, and Mother would just stand smiling at him. She'd never say a word about all the weeks and months he'd been away, not leaving us a cent for food. Once I heard her speaking to a woman in our street. Maybe the woman had dared to sympathize

with her. "Oh," she said "it's all right. He isn't ever dull like most of the men in this street. Life is never dull when my man is about."

28   But often I was filled with bitterness, and sometimes I wished he wasn't my father. I'd even invent another man as my father. To protect my mother I'd make up stories of a secret marriage that for some strange reason never got known. As though some man, say the president of a railroad company or maybe a Congressman, had married my mother, thinking his wife was dead and then it turned out she wasn't.

29   So they had to hush it up but I got born just the same. I wasn't really the son of my father. Somewhere in the world there was a very dignified, quite wonderful man who was really my father. I even made myself half believe these fancies.

30   And then there came a certain night. Mother was away from home. Maybe there was church that night. Father came in. He'd been off somewhere for two or three weeks. He found me alone in the house, reading by the kitchen table.

31   It had been raining and he was very wet. He sat and looked at me for a long time, not saying a word. I was startled, for there was on his face the saddest look I had ever seen. He sat for a time, his clothes dripping. Then he got up.

32   "Come on with me," he said.

33   I got up and went with him out of the house. I was filled with wonder but I wasn't afraid. We went along a dirt road that led down into a valley, about a mile out of town, where there was a pond. We walked in silence. The man who was always talking had stopped his talking.

34   I didn't know what was up and had the queer feeling that I was with a stranger. I didn't know whether my father intended it so. I don't think he did.

35   The pond was quite large. It was still raining hard and there were flashes of lightning followed by thunder. We were on a grassy bank at the pond's edge when my father spoke, and in the darkness and rain his voice sounded strange.

36   "Take off your clothes," he said. Still filled with wonder, I began to undress. There was a flash of lightning and I saw that he was already naked.

37   Naked, we went into the pond. Taking my hand, he pulled me in. It may be that I was too frightened, too full of a feeling of strangeness, to speak. Before that night my father had never seemed to pay any attention to me.

38   "And what is he up to now?" I kept asking myself. I did not swim very well, but he put my hand on his shoulder and struck out into the darkness.

39   He was a man with big shoulders, a powerful swimmer. In the darkness I could feel the movements of his muscles. We swam to the far edge of the pond and then back to where we had left our clothes. The rain continued and the wind blew. Sometimes my father swam on his back, and when he did he took my hand in his large powerful one and moved it over so that it rested always on his shoulder. Sometimes there would be a flash of lightning and I could see his face quite clearly.

40   It was as it was earlier, in the kitchen, a face filled with sadness. There would be the momentary glimpse of his face, and then again the darkness, the wind and the rain. In me there was a feeling I had never known before.

41   It was a feeling of closeness. It was something strange. It was as though there were only we two in the world. It was as though I had been jerked suddenly out of myself, out of my world of the schoolboy, out of a world in which I was ashamed of my father.

42   He had become blood of my blood; he the strong swimmer and I the boy clinging to him in the darkness. We swam in silence, and in silence we dressed in our wet clothes and went home.

43   There was a lamp lighted in the kitchen, and when we came in, the water dripping from us, there was my mother. She smiled at us. I remember that she called us "boys." "What have you boys been up to?" she asked, but my father did not answer. As he had begun the evening's experience with me in silence, so he ended it. He turned and looked at me. Then he went, I thought, with a new and strange dignity, out of the room.

44   I climbed the stairs to my room, undressed in darkness and got into bed. I couldn't sleep and did not want to sleep. For the first time I knew that I was the son of my father. He was a storyteller as I was to be. It may be that I even laughed a little softly there in the darkness. If I did, I laughed knowing that I would never again be wanting another father.

THINKING ABOUT THE TEXT

1. Describe Anderson as a young boy. What are his expectations for a father? Are they reasonable? Do you empathize with him? Why or why not?

2. Focusing on the father, specify at least four different scenes that explain why the son "had got to hating him."

3. Contrast the son's view of his father's tall tales with the adults' view of this storytelling. Why do the adults like his father even though they "knew he was lying"?

4. How is the father different at the pond? List all the elements from the pond scene that dramatize Anderson's "conversion" from hating his dad to respecting him. Discuss the boy's new sense of identity. How do the concepts of baptism and being reborn apply here?

WRITING FROM THE TEXT

1. Write an essay contrasting Anderson's view of his father *before* the pond scene with his changed attitude *after* their swim. Analyze the son's "conversion." Has the father really changed? Support your claims with details from the story.

2. Describe a relationship of your own in which an adult or loved one seemed the opposite of what you wanted or needed. Include incidents,

as Anderson does, that show your disappointment or frustration. (See "Narrative," pp. 382–389.)

3. Focus on a significant event in your own life that helped you see yourself differently or that changed your attitude about someone close to you. Show the before-and-after change.

CONNECTING WITH OTHER TEXTS

1. Compare "Discovery of a Father" and "Under the Influence" (below) and analyze the differences in the two fathers' alcoholic behavior, as well as the differences in the writers' concerns with alcoholism. What do you think accounts for the differences in attitude and tone between the two?

2. Read other Sherwood Anderson stories from his *Memoirs* or from *Winesburg, Ohio* and analyze his depiction of adolescence or of the pressures and restrictions in a small-town society.

UNDER THE INFLUENCE
Scott Russell Sanders

A Cambridge University graduate, an American university professor, and a writer of fiction, short stories, and a novel as well as biographical and personal essays, Scott Russell Sanders (b. 1945) views the diversity of his literary work as an integration of the issues within his life. He describes that life as divided between the study of arts and science, but when he writes fiction, he poses the questions of the scientist. These questions, and those about the way people live and about family and generational relationships, are the subject matter of his work. The piece here was written as a history of his family coming to terms with the father's alcoholism. The essay was first published in *Harper's Magazine* in November 1987.

1   My father drank. He drank as a gut-punched boxer gasps for breath, as a starving dog gobbles food—compulsively, secretly, in pain and trembling. I use the past tense not because he ever quit drinking but because he quit living. That is how the story ends for my father, age sixty-four, heart bursting, body cooling, slumped and forsaken on the linoleum of my brother's trailer. The story continues for my brother, my sister, my mother, and me, and will continue as long as memory holds.

2   In the perennial present of memory, I slip into the garage or barn to see my father tipping back the flat green bottles of wine, the brown cylinders of whiskey,

the cans of beer disguised in paper bags. His Adam's apple bobs, the liquid gurgles, he wipes the sandy-haired back of a hand over his lips, and then, his bloodshot gaze bumping into me, he stashes the bottle or can inside his jacket, under the workbench, between two bales of hay, and we both pretend the moment has not occurred.

3   "What's up, buddy?" he says, thick-tongued and edgy.

4   "Sky's up," I answer, playing along.

5   "And don't forget prices," he grumbles. "Prices are always up. And taxes."

6   In memory, his white 1951 Pontiac with the stripes down the hood and the Indian head on the snout lurches to a stop in the driveway; or it is the 1956 Ford station wagon, or the 1963 Rambler shaped like a toad, or the sleek 1969 Bonneville that will do 120 miles per hour on straightaways; or it is the robin's-egg-blue pickup, new in 1980, battered in 1981, the year of his death. He climbs out, grinning dangerously, unsteady on his legs, and we children interrupt our game of catch, our building of snow forts, our picking of plums, to watch in silence as he weaves past us into the house, where he drops into his overstuffed chair and falls asleep. Shaking her head, our mother stubs out a cigarette he has left smoldering in the ashtray. All evening, until our bedtimes, we tiptoe past him, as past a snoring dragon. Then we curl fearfully in our sheets, listening. Eventually he wakes with a grunt, Mother slings accusations at him, he snarls back, she yells, he growls, their voices clashing. Before long, she retreats to their bedroom, sobbing—not from the blows of fists, for he never strikes her, but from the force of his words.

7   Left alone, our father prowls the house, thumping into furniture, rummaging in the kitchen, slamming doors, turning the pages of the newspaper with a savage crackle, muttering back at the late-night drivel from television. The roof might fly off, the walls might buckle from the pressure of his rage. Whatever my brother and sister and mother may be thinking on their own rumpled pillows, I lie there hating him, loving him, fearing him, knowing I have failed him. I tell myself he drinks to ease the ache that gnaws at his belly, an ache I must have caused by disappointing him somehow, a murderous ache I should be able to relieve by doing all my chores, earning A's in school, winning baseball games, fixing the broken washer and the burst pipes, bringing in the money to fill his empty wallet. He would not hide the green bottles in his toolbox, would not sneak off to the barn with a lump under his coat, would not fall asleep in the daylight, would not roar and fume, would not drink himself to death, if only I were perfect.

8   I am forty-four, and I know full well now that my father was an alcoholic, a man consumed by disease rather than by disappointment. What had seemed to me a private grief is in fact, of course, a public scourge. In the United States alone, some ten or fifteen million people share his ailment, and behind the doors they slam in fury or disgrace, countless other children tremble. I comfort myself with such knowledge, holding it against the throb of memory like an ice pack against a bruise. Other people have keener sources of grief: poverty, racism, rape, war. I do not wish to compete to determine who has suffered most. I am only trying to understand the corrosive mixture of helplessness, responsibility, and shame that I

learned to feel as the son of an alcoholic. I realize now that I did not cause my father's illness, nor could I have cured it. Yet for all this grownup knowledge, I am still ten years old, my own son's age, and as that boy I struggle in guilt and confusion to save my father from pain.

9   Consider a few of our synonyms for *drunk:* tipsy, tight, pickled, soused, and plowed; stoned and stewed, lubricated and inebriated, juiced and sluiced; three sheets to the wind, in your cups, out of your mind, under the table; lit up, tanked up, wiped out; besotted, blotto, bombed, and buzzed; plastered, polluted, putrefied; loaded or looped, boozy, woozy, fuddled, or smashed; crocked and shit-faced, corked and pissed, snockered and sloshed.

10   It is a mostly humorous lexicon, as the lore that deals with drunks—in jokes and cartoons, in plays, films, and television skits—is largely comic. Aunt Matilda nips elderberry wine from the sideboard and burps politely during supper. Uncle Fred slouches to the table glassy-eyed, wearing a lampshade for a hat and murmuring, "Candy is dandy, but liquor is quicker." Inspired by cocktails, Mrs. Somebody recounts the events of her day in a fuzzy dialect, while Mr. Somebody nibbles her ear and croons a bawdy song. On the sofa with Boyfriend, Daughter Somebody giggles, licking gin from her lips, and loosens the bows in her hair. Junior knocks back some brews with his chums at the Leopard Lounge and stumbles home to the wrong house, wonders foggily why he cannot locate his pajamas, and crawls naked into bed with the ugliest girl in school. The family dog slurps from a neglected martini and wobbles to the nursery, where he vomits in Baby's shoe.

11   It is all great fun. But if in the audience you notice a few laughing faces turn grim when the drunk lurches onstage, don't be surprised, for these are the children of alcoholics. Over the grinning mask of Dionysus, the leering face of Bacchus, these children cannot help seeing the bloated features of their own parents. Instead of laughing, they wince, they mourn. Instead of celebrating the drunk as one freed from constraints, they pity him as one enslaved. They refuse to believe *in vino veritas,* having seen their befuddled parents skid away from truth toward folly and oblivion. And so these children bite their lips until the lush staggers into the wings.

12   My father, when drunk, was neither funny nor honest; he was pathetic, frightening, deceitful. There seemed to be a leak in him somewhere, and he poured in booze to keep from draining dry. Like a torture victim who refuses to squeal, he would never admit that he had touched a drop, not even in his last year, when he seemed to be dissolving in alcohol before our very eyes. I never knew him to lie about anything, ever, except about this one ruinous fact. Drowsy, clumsy, unable to fix a bicycle tire, balance a grocery sack, or walk across a room, he was stripped of his true self by drink. In a matter of minutes, the contents of a bottle could transform a brave man into a coward, a buddy into a bully, a gifted athlete and skilled carpenter and shrewd businessman into a bumbler. No dictionary of synonyms for *drunk* would soften the anguish of watching our prince turn into a frog.

13   Father's drinking became the family secret. While growing up, we children never breathed a word of it beyond the four walls of our house. To this day, my

brother and sister rarely mention it, and then only when I press them. I did not confess the ugly, bewildering fact to my wife until his wavering and slurred speech forced me to. Recently, on the seventh anniversary of my father's death, I asked my mother if she ever spoke of his drinking to friends. "No, no, never," she replied hastily. "I couldn't bear for anyone to know."

14   The secret bores under the skin, gets in the blood, into the bone, and stays there. Long after you have supposedly been cured of malaria, the fever can flare up, the tremors can shake you. So it is with the fevers of shame. You swallow the bitter quinine of knowledge, and you learn to feel pity and compassion toward the drinker. Yet the shame lingers and, because of it, anger.

15   For a long stretch of my childhood we lived on a military reservation in Ohio, an arsenal where bombs were stored underground in bunkers and vintage air-planes burst into flames and unstable artillery shells boomed nightly at the dump. We had the feeling, as children, that we played within a minefield, where a heed-less footfall could trigger an explosion. When Father was drinking, the house, too, became a minefield. The least bump could set off either parent.

16   The more he drank, the more obsessed Mother became with stopping him. She hunted for bottles, counted the cash in his wallet, sniffed at his breath. Without meaning to snoop, we children blundered left and right into damning evidence. On afternoons when he came home from work sober, we flung ourselves at him for hugs and felt against our ribs the telltale lump in his coat. In the barn we tumbled on the hay and heard beneath our sneakers the crunch of broken glass. We tugged open a drawer in his workbench, looking for screwdrivers or crescent wrenches, and spied a gleaming six-pack among the tools. Playing tag, we darted around the house just in time to see him sway on the rear stoop and heave a finished bottle into the woods. In his good-night kiss we smelled the cloying sweetness of Clorets, the mints he chewed to camouflage his dragon's breath.

17   I can summon up that kiss right now by recalling Theodore Roethke's lines about his own father:

> *The whiskey on your breath*
> *Could make a small boy dizzy;*
> *But I hung on like death:*
> *Such waltzing was not easy.*

Such waltzing was hard, terribly hard, for with a boy's scrawny arms I was trying to hold my tipsy father upright.

18   For years, the chief source of those incriminating bottles and cans was a grimy store a mile from us, a cinderblock place called Sly's, with two gas pumps outside and a mangy dog asleep in the window. Inside, on rusty metal shelves or in wheez-ing coolers, you could find pop and Popsicles, cigarettes, potato chips, canned soup, raunchy postcards, fishing gear, Twinkies, wine, and beer. When Father drove anywhere on errands, Mother would send us along as guards, warning us not to let him out of our sight. And so with one or more of us on board, Father

would cruise up to Sly's, pump a dollar's worth of gas or plump the tires with air, and then, telling us to wait in the car, he would head for the doorway.

19   Dutiful and panicky, we cried, "Let us go with you!"

20   "No," he answered. "I'll be back in two shakes."

21   "Please!"

22   "No!" he roared. "Don't you budge or I'll jerk a knot in your tails!"

23   So we stayed put, kicking the seats, while he ducked inside. Often, when he had parked the car at a careless angle, we gazed in through the window and saw Mr. Sly fetching down from the shelf behind the cash register two green pints of Gallo wine. Father swigged one of them right there at the counter, stuffed the other in his pocket, and then out he came, a bulge in his coat, a flustered look on his reddened face.

24   Because the mom and pop who ran the dump were neighbors of ours, living just down the tar-blistered road, I hated them all the more for poisoning my father. I wanted to sneak in their store and smash the bottles and set fire to the place. I also hated the Gallo brothers, Ernest and Julio, whose jovial faces beamed from the labels of their wine, labels I would find, torn and curled, when I burned the trash. I noted the Gallo brothers' address in California and studied the road atlas to see how far that was from Ohio, because I meant to go out there and tell Ernest and Julio what they were doing to my father, and then, if they showed no mercy, I would kill them.

25   While growing up on the back roads and in the country schools and cramped Methodist churches of Ohio and Tennessee, I never heard the word *alcoholic,* never happened across it in books or magazines. In the nearby towns, there were no addiction-treatment programs, no community mental-health centers, no Alcoholics Anonymous chapters, no therapists. Left alone with our grievous secret, we had no way of understanding Father's drinking except as an act of will, a deliberate folly or cruelty, a moral weakness, a sin. He drank because he chose to, pure and simple. Why our father, so playful and competent and kind when sober, would choose to ruin himself and punish his family we could not fathom.

26   Our neighborhood was high on the Bible, and the Bible was hard on drunkards. "Woe to those who are heroes at drinking wine and valiant men in mixing strong drink," wrote Isaiah. "The priest and the prophet reel with strong drink, they are confused with wine, they err in vision, they stumble in giving judgment. For all tables are full of vomit, no place is without filthiness." We children had seen those fouled tables at the local truck stop where the notorious boozers hung out, our father occasionally among them. "Wine and new wine take away the understanding," declared the prophet Hosea. We had also seen evidence of that in our father, who could multiply seven-digit numbers in his head when sober but when drunk could not help us with fourth-grade math. Proverbs warned: "Do not look at wine when it is red, when it sparkles in the cup and goes down smoothly. At the last it bites like a serpent and stings like an adder. Your eyes will see strange things, and your mind utter perverse things." Woe, woe.

27   Dismayingly often, these biblical drunkards stirred up trouble for their own kids. Noah made fresh wine after the flood, drank too much of it, fell asleep without any clothes on, and was glimpsed in the buff by his son Ham, who Noah promptly cursed. In one passage—it was so shocking we had to read it under our blankets with flashlights—the patriarch Lot fell down drunk and slept with his daughters. The sins of the fathers set their children's teeth on edge.

28   Our ministers were fond of quoting St. Paul's pronouncement that drunkards would not inherit the kingdom of God. These grave preachers assured us that the wine referred to in the Last Supper was in fact grape juice. Bible and sermons and hymns combined to give us the impression that Moses should have brought down from the mountain another stone tablet, bearing the Eleventh Commandment: Thou shalt not drink.

29   The scariest and most illuminating Bible story apropos of drunkards was the one about the lunatic and the swine. We knew it by heart: When Jesus climbed out of his boat one day, this lunatic came charging up from the graveyard, stark naked and filthy, frothing at the mouth, so violent that he broke the strongest chains. Nobody would go near him. Night and day for years, this madman had been wailing among the tombs and bruising himself with stones. Jesus took one look at him and said, "Come out of the man, you unclean spirits!" for he could see that the lunatic was possessed by demons. Meanwhile, some hogs were conveniently rooting nearby. "If we have to come out," begged the demons, "at least let us go into those swine." Jesus agreed, the unclean spirits entered the hogs, and the hogs raced straight off a cliff and plunged into a lake. Hearing the story in Sunday school, my friends thought mainly of the pigs. (How big a splash did they make? Who paid for the lost pork?) But I thought of the redeemed lunatic, who bathed himself and put on clothes and calmly sat at the feet of Jesus, restored—so the Bible said—to "his right mind."

30   When drunk, our father was clearly in his wrong mind. He became a stranger, as fearful to us as any graveyard lunatic, not quite frothing at the mouth but fierce enough, quick-tempered, explosive; or else he grew maudlin and weepy, which frightened us nearly as much. In my boyhood despair, I reasoned that maybe he wasn't to blame for turning into an ogre: Maybe, like the lunatic, he was possessed by demons.

31   If my father was indeed possessed, who would exorcise him? If he was a sinner, who would save him? If he was ill, who would cure him? If he suffered, who would ease his pain? Not ministers or doctors, for we could not bring ourselves to confide in them; not the neighbors, for we pretended they had never seen him drunk; not Mother, who fussed and pleaded but could not budge him; not my brother and sister, who were only kids. That left me. It did not matter that I, too, was only a child, and a bewildered one at that. I could not excuse myself.

32   On first reading a description of delirium tremens—in a book on alcoholism I smuggled from a university library—I thought immediately of the frothing lunatic and the frenzied swine. When I read stories or watched films about grisly metamorphoses—Dr. Jekyll and Mr. Hyde, the mild husband changing into a werewolf, the kindly neighbor inhabited by a brutal alien—I could not help but see my

own father's mutation from sober to drunk. Even today, knowing better, I am attracted by the demonic theory of drink, for when I recall my father's transformation, the emergence of his ugly second self, I find it easy to believe in being possessed by unclean spirits. We never knew which version of Father would come home from work, the true or the tainted, nor could we guess how far down the slope toward cruelty he would slide.

33   How far a man *could* slide we gauged by observing our back-road neighbors— the out-of-work miners who had dragged their families to our corner of Ohio from the desolate hollows of Appalachia, the tightfisted farmers, the surly mechanics, the balked and broken men. There was, for example, whiskey-soaked Mr. Jenkins, who beat his wife and kids so hard we could hear their screams from the road. There was Mr. Lavo the wino, who fell asleep smoking time and again, until one night his disgusted wife bundled up the children and went outside and left him in his easy chair to burn; he awoke on his own, staggered out coughing into the yard, and pounded her flat while the children looked on and the shack turned to ash. There was the truck driver, Mr. Sampson, who tripped over his son's tricycle one night while drunk and got mad, jumped into his semi, and drove away, shifting through the dozen gears, and never came back. We saw the bruised children of these fathers clump onto our school bus, we saw the abandoned children huddle in the pews at church, we saw the stunned and battered mothers begging for help at our doors.

34   Our own father never beat us, and I don't think he beat Mother, but he threatened often. The Old Testament Yahweh was not more terrible in His rage. Eyes blazing, voice booming, Father would pull out his belt and swear to give us a whipping, but he never followed through, never needed to, because we could imagine it so vividly. He shoved us, pawed us with the back of his hand, not to injure, just to clear a space. I can see him grabbing Mother by the hair as she cowers on a chair during a nightly quarrel. He twists her neck back until she gapes up at him, and then he lifts over her skull a glass quart bottle of milk, and milk spilling down his forearm, and he yells at her, "Say just one more word, one goddamn word, and I'll shut you up!" I fear she will prick him with her sharp tongue, but she is terrified into silence, and so am I, and the leaking bottle quivers in the air, and milk seeps through the red hair of my father's uplifted arm, and the entire scene is there to this moment, the head jerked back, the club raised.

35   When the drink made him weepy, Father would pack, kiss each of us children on the head, and announce from the front door that he was moving out. "Where to?" we demanded, fearful each time that he would leave for good, as Mr. Sampson had roared away for good in his diesel truck. "Someplace where I won't get hounded every minute," Father would answer, his jaw quivering. He stabbed a look at Mother, who might say, "Don't run into the ditch before you get there," or "Good riddance," and then he would slink away. Mother watched him go with arms crossed over her chest, her face closed like the lid on a box of snakes. We children bawled. Where could he go? To the truck stop, that den of iniquity? To one of those dark, ratty flophouses in town? Would he wind up sleeping under a railroad bridge or on a park bench or in a cardboard box, mummied in rags like the

bums we had seen on our trips to Cleveland and Chicago? We bawled and bawled, wondering if he would ever come back.

36   He always did come back, a day or a week later, but each time there was a sliver less of him.

37   In Kafka's *Metamorphosis,* which opens famously with Gregor Samsa waking up from uneasy dreams to find himself transformed into an insect, Gregor's family keep reassuring themselves that things will be just fine again "when he comes back to us." Each time alcohol transformed our father we held out the same hope, that he would really and truly come back to us, our authentic father, the tender and playful and competent man, and then all things would be fine. We had grounds for such hope. After his tearful departures and chapfallen returns, he would sometimes go weeks, even months, without drinking. Those were glad times. Every day without the furtive glint of bottles, every meal without a fight, every bedtime without sobs encouraged us to believe that such bliss might go on forever.

38   Mother was fooled by such a hope all during the forty-odd years she knew Greeley Ray Sanders. Soon after she met him in a Chicago delicatessen on the eve of World War II and fell for his butter-melting Mississippi drawl and his wavy red hair, she learned that he drank heavily. But then so did a lot of men. She would soon coax or scold him into breaking the nasty habit. She would point out to him how ugly and foolish it was, this bleary drinking, and then he would quit. He refused to quit during their engagement, however, still refused during the first years of marriage, refused until my older sister came along. The shock of father-hood sobered him, and he remained sober through my birth at the end of the war and right on through until we moved in 1951 to the Ohio arsenal. The arsenal had more than its share of alcoholics, drug addicts, and other varieties of escape artists. There I turned six and started school and woke into a child's flickering awareness, just in time to see my father begin sneaking swigs in the garage.

39   He sobered up again for most of a year at the height of the Korean War, to cel-ebrate the birth of my brother. But aside from that dry spell, his only breaks from drinking before I graduated from high school were just long enough to raise and then dash our hopes. Then during the fall of my senior year—the time of the Cuban Missile Crisis, when it seemed that the nightly explosions at the munitions dump and the nightly rages in our household might spread to engulf the globe— Father collapsed. His liver, kidneys, and heart all conked out. The doctors saved him, but only by a hair. He stayed in the hospital for weeks, going through a with-drawal so terrible that Mother would not let us visit him. If he wanted to kill him-self, the doctors solemnly warned him, all he had to do was hit the bottle again. One binge would finish him.

40   Father must have believed them, for he stayed dry the next fifteen years. It was an answer to prayer, Mother said, it was a miracle. I believe it was a reflex of fear, which he sustained over the years through courage and pride. He knew a man could die from drink, for his brother Roscoe had. We children never laid eyes on doomed Uncle Roscoe, but in the stories Mother told us he became a fairy-tale

figure, like a boy who took the wrong turn in the woods and was gobbled up by the wolf.

41   The fifteen-year dry spell came to an end with Father's retirement in the spring of 1978. Like many men, he gave up his identity along with his job. One day he was a boss at the factory, with a brass plate on his door and a reputation to uphold; the next day he was a nobody at home. He and Mother were leaving Ontario, the last of the many places to which his job had carried them, and they were moving to a new house in Mississippi, his childhood stomping ground. As a boy in Mississippi, Father sold Coca-Cola during dances while the moonshiners peddled their brew in the parking lot; as a young blade, he fought in bars and in the ring, winning a state Golden Gloves championship; he gambled at poker, hunted pheasant, raced motorcycles and cars, played semiprofessional baseball, and, along with all his buddies—in the Black Cat Saloon, behind the cotton gin, in the woods—he drank hard. It was a perilous youth to dream of recovering.

42   After his final day of work, Mother drove on ahead with a car full of begonias and violets, while Father stayed behind to oversee the packing. When the van was loaded, the sweaty movers broke open a six-pack and offered him a beer.

43   "Let's drink to retirement!" they crowed. "Let's drink to freedom! to fishing! hunting! loafing! Let's drink to a guy who's going home!"

44   At least I imagine some such words, for that is all I can do, imagine, and I see Father's hand trembling in midair as he thinks about the fifteen sober years and about the doctors' warning, and he tells himself, *Goddamnit, I am a free man,* and *Why can't a free man drink one beer after a lifetime of hard work?* and I see his arm reaching, his fingers closing, the can tilting to his lips. I even supply a label for the beer, a swaggering brand that promises on television to deliver the essence of life. I watch the amber liquid pour down his throat, the alcohol steal into his blood, the key turn in his brain.

45   Soon after my parents moved back to Father's treacherous stomping ground, my wife and I visited them in Mississippi with our four-year-old daughter. Mother had been too distraught to warn me about the return of the demons. So when I climbed out of the car that bright July morning and saw my father napping in the hammock, I felt uneasy, and when he lurched upright and blinked his bloodshot eyes and greeted us in a syrupy voice, I was hurled back into childhood.

46   "What's the matter with Papaw?" our daughter asked.

47   "Nothing," I said. "Nothing!"

48   Like a child again, I pretended not to see him in his stupor, and behind my phony smile I grieved. On that visit and on the few that remained before his death, once again I found bottles in the workbench, bottles in the woods. Again his hands shook too much for him to run a saw, to make his precious miniature furniture, to drive straight down back roads. Again he wound up in the ditch, in the hospital, in jail, in the treatment center. Again he shouted and wept. Again he lied. "I never touched a drop," he swore. "Your mother's making it up."

49   I no longer fancied I could reason with the men whose names I found on the bottles—Jim Beam, Jack Daniel's—but I was able now to recall the cold statistics

about alcoholism: ten million victims, fifteen million, twenty. And yet, in spite of my age, I reacted in the same blind way as I had in childhood, by vainly seeking to erase through my efforts whatever drove him to drink. I worked on their place twelve and sixteen hours a day, in the swelter of Mississippi summers, digging ditches, running electrical wires, planting trees, mowing grass, building sheds, as though what nagged at him was some list of chores, as though by taking his worries upon my shoulders I could redeem him. I was flung back into boyhood, acting as though my father would not drink himself to death if only I were perfect.

50   I failed of perfection; he succeeded in dying. To the end, he considered himself not sick but sinful. "Do you want to kill yourself?" I asked him. "Why not?" he answered. "Why the hell not? What's there to save?" To the end, he would not speak about his feelings, would not or could not give a name to the beast that was devouring him.

51   In silence, he went rushing off to the cliff. Unlike the biblical swine, however, he left behind a few of the demons to haunt his children. Life with him and the loss of him twisted us into shapes that will be familiar to other sons and daughters of alcoholics. My brother became a rebel, my sister retreated into shyness, I played the stalwart and dutiful son who would hold the family together. If my father was unstable, I would be a rock. If he squandered money on drink, I would pinch every penny. If he wept when drunk—and only when drunk—I would not let myself weep at all. If he roared at the Little League umpire for calling my pitches balls, I would throw nothing but strikes. Watching him flounder and rage, I came to dread the loss of control. I would go through life without making anyone mad. I vowed never to put in my mouth or veins any chemical that would banish my everyday self. I would never make a scene, never lash out at the ones I loved, never hurt a soul. Through hard work, relentless work, I would achieve something dazzling—in the classroom, on the basketball court, in the science lab, in the pages of books—and my achievement would distract the world's eyes from his humiliation. I would become a worthy sacrifice, and the smoke of my burning would please God.

52   It is far easier to recognize these twists in my character than to undo them. Work has become an addiction for me, as drink was an addiction for my father. Knowing this, my daughter gave me a placard for the wall: WORKAHOLIC. The labor is endless and futile, for I can no more redeem myself through work than I could redeem my father. I still panic in the face of other people's anger, because his drunken temper was so terrible. I shrink from causing sadness or disappointment even to strangers, as though I were still concealing the family shame. I still notice every twitch of emotion in those faces around me, having learned as a child to read the weather in faces, and I blame myself for their least pang of unhappiness or anger. In certain moods I blame myself for everything. Guilt burns like acid in my veins.

53   I am moved to write these pages now because my own son, at the age of ten, is taking on himself the griefs of the world, and in particular the griefs of his father. He tells me that when I am gripped by sadness, he feels responsible; he feels there

must be something he can do to spring me from depression, to fix my life. And that crushing sense of responsibility is exactly what I felt at the age of ten in the face of my father's drinking. My son wonders if I, too, am possessed. I write, therefore, to drag into the light what eats at me—the fear, the guilt, the shame—so that my own children may be spared.

54   I still shy away from nightclubs, from bars, from parties where the solvent is alcohol. My friends puzzle over this, but it is no more peculiar than for a man to shy away from the lions' den after seeing his father torn apart. I took my own first drink at the age of twenty-one, half a glass of burgundy. I knew the odds of my becoming an alcoholic were four times higher than for the children of nonalcoholic fathers. So I sipped warily.

55   I still do—once a week, perhaps, a glass of wine, a can of beer, nothing stronger, nothing more. I listen for the turning of a key in my brain.

THINKING ABOUT THE TEXT

1. What are the behavior characteristics of Sanders' alcoholic father? Find descriptions from the essay that specifically show his habits.
2. How does the father's alcoholism affect each family member?
3. Why do you imagine Sanders has written this essay? What is his emotional position or stance as both a son and the writer of the essay?
4. What kind of man was Greeley Ray Sanders? Find specific examples of his character in the text. What can you infer about him?

WRITING FROM THE TEXT

1. Make a list of specific behavior traits of Sanders' father. Use this list to write an essay on the characteristics of an alcoholic.
2. Write an essay that describes the effects on family members of living with an alcoholic. Cite specific examples from the text in your essay. Use Sanders' work as a model for writing memorable, vivid description.

CONNECTING WITH OTHER TEXTS

1. In "The Only Child" (p. 22), John Leonard describes his brother as he is and as he was. In what ways can Leonard's experience with a mentally ill brother be compared with Sanders' experience with an alcoholic father? Write an essay that compares the men's experiences.

2. Do research to learn something about the programs that work with the children of alcoholic parents. Use this material to write a descriptive analysis of these programs.

THE ONLY CHILD
John Leonard

After studying at Harvard University and Berkeley, where he received his B.A. in 1962, John Leonard (b. 1939) worked as a book reviewer, a producer of dramas and literature programs, a publicity writer, a staff writer for the *New York Times,* and a cultural critic for *Variety.* Leonard intends his writing to ask moral questions: How do you want your children to grow up? What do you think is decent and fair? Who are your friends, and why? His work included here, from *Private Lives in The Imperial City* (1976), probes family tensions and concerns.

1   He is big. He always has been, over six feet, with that slump of the shoulders and tuck in the neck big men in the country often affect, as if to apologize for being above the democratic norm in size. (In high school and at college he played varsity basketball. In high school he was senior class president.) And he looks healthy enough, blue-eyed behind his beard, like a trapper or a mountain man, acquainted with silences. He also grins a lot.

2   Odd, then, to have noticed earlier—at the house, when he took off his shabby coat to play Ping-Pong—that the white arms were unmuscled. The coat may have been a comment. This, after all, is southern California, where every man is an artist, an advertiser of himself; where every surface is painted and every object potted; where even the statues seem to wear socks. The entire population ambles, in polyesters, toward a Taco Bell. To wear a brown shabby cloth coat in southern California is to admit something.

3   So he hasn't been getting much exercise. Nor would the children have elected him president of any class. At the house they avoided him. Or, since he was too big to be avoided entirely, they treated his presence as a kind of odor to pass through hurriedly, to be safe on the other side. They behaved like cats. Of course, he ignored them. But I think they were up to more than just protecting themselves from his lack of curiosity. Children are expert readers of grins.

4   His grin is intermittent. The dimples twitch on and off; between them, teeth are bared; above them, the blue eyes disappear in a wince. This grin isn't connected to any humor the children know about. It may be a tic. It could also be a function of some metronome made on Mars. It registers inappropriate intervals. We aren't listening to the same music.

5   This is the man who introduced me to the mysteries of mathematical science, the man I could never beat at chess, the man who wrote haiku and played with computers. Now there is static in his head, as though the mind had drifted off its signal during sleep. He has an attention span of about thirty seconds.

6   I am to take him back to where he lives, in the car I have rented in order to pretend to be a Californian. We are headed for a rooming house in one of the beach cities along a coast of off-ramps and oil wells. It is a rooming house that thinks of itself as Spanish. The ruined-hacienda look requires a patio, a palm tree and several miles of corrugated tile. He does not expect me to come up to his room, but I insist. I have brought along a six-pack of beer.

7   The room is a slum, and it stinks. It is wall-to-wall beer cans, hundreds of them, under a film of ash. He lights cigarettes and leaves them burning on the windowsill or the edge of the dresser or the lip of the sink, while he thinks of something else—Gupta sculpture, maybe, or the Sephiroth Tree of the Kabbalah. The sink is filthy, and so is the toilet. Holes have been burnt in the sheet on the bed, where he sits. He likes to crush the beer cans after he has emptied them, then toss them aside.

8   He tells me that he is making a statement, that this room is a statement, that the landlord will understand the meaning of his statement. In a week or so, according to the pattern, they will evict him, and someone will find him another room, which he will turn into another statement, with the help of the welfare checks he receives on account of his disability, which is the static in his head.

9   There are no books, no newspapers or magazines, no pictures on the wall. There is a television set, which he watches all day long while drinking beer and smoking cigarettes. I am sufficiently familiar with the literature on schizophrenia to realize that this room is a statement he is making about himself. I am also sufficiently familiar with his history to understand that, along with his contempt for himself, there is an abiding arrogance. He refuses medication. They can't make him take it, any more than they can keep him in a hospital. He has harmed no one. One night, in one of these rooms, he will set himself on fire.

10   He talks. Or blurts: scraps from Oriental philosophers—Lao-tzu, I think—puns, incantations, obscenities, names from the past. There are conspiracies; I am part of one of them. He grins, winces, slumps, is suddenly tired, wants me to get out almost as much as I want to get out, seems to have lapsed in a permanent parenthesis. Anyway, I have a busy schedule.

11   Well, speed kills slowly, and he fiddled too much with the oxygen flow to his brain. He wanted ecstasy and revelation, the way we grew up wanting a bicycle, a car, a girlfriend. These belonged to us by right, as middle-class Americans. So, then, did salvation belong to us by right. I would like to thank Timothy Leary and all the other sports of the 1960's who helped make this bad trip possible. I wish R. D. Laing would explain to me, once again and slowly, how madness is a proof of grace. "The greatest magician," said Novalis, "would be the one who would cast over himself a spell so complete that he would take his own phantasmagorias as autonomous appearances."

12   One goes back to the rented car and pretending to be a Californian as, perhaps, one had been pretending to be a brother. It is odd, at my age, suddenly to have become an only child.

THINKING ABOUT THE TEXT

1. Discuss how each "telling detail" about Leonard's brother provides a glimpse of his early promise. Then explain how these same details now underscore his sad transformation.

2. Why does Leonard's brother feel his life-style and room are "making a statement"? What type of "statement" does the author feel his brother is making?

3. In this autobiographical essay, Leonard, a New Yorker, can only "pretend to be a Californian." Find details that illustrate what California represents for him.

4. Who or what does Leonard seem to blame for his brother's experimentation with drugs? Why? What is Leonard's implied thesis?

5. Discuss all possible meanings of the title. Why does Leonard wait until the end to focus on it?

WRITING ABOUT THE TEXT

1. Write an essay contrasting Leonard's recollection of his brother before taking drugs with his perception of him now.

2. If drug addiction or mental illness has plagued any members of your own family, write an essay that illustrates an important insight you have learned from this experience.

3. Find a photograph that shows you with one or more of your siblings. Write an analysis of your relationship with your brother and/or sister based on the dynamics that you perceive in the photograph.

CONNECTING WITH OTHER TEXTS

1. Write an essay comparing Sanders' description of his alcoholic father ("Under the Influence," p. 11) with Leonard's description of his brother. Where do the two authors' experiences link, and where do they diverge?

2. Using "The Only Child," "Thanksgiving" (p. 4), and "When Parents Don't Turn Out Right" (p. 67), write an essay describing and analyzing the positive and negative aspects of family members reuniting and discovering how they have changed.

IGNORANCE IS NOT BLISS
Eric Marcus

A graduate of Vassar and Columbia, Eric Marcus (b. 1958) is a journalist who has published articles and book reviews on a variety of subjects. He was a contributing editor of *The Hip Pocket Guide to New York*. His books include *Making History: The Struggle for Gay and Lesbian Equal Rights, 1945–1990; An Oral History*; and *Is It a Choice? Answers to 300 of the Most Frequently Asked Questions About Gays and Lesbians*. Marcus lives in New York, where he volunteers as a peer counselor at Identity House and works as an associate producer for "Good Morning America." The essay included here originally appeared in *Newsweek*, "My Turn," July 5, 1993.

1 Sam Nunn didn't need to hold Senate hearings to come up with his "don't ask, don't tell" solution for handling gays in the military. If he'd asked me, I could have told him this was exactly the policy some of my relatives suggested years ago when I informed them that I planned to tell my grandmother that I was gay. They said, "She's old, it'll kill her. You'll destroy her image of you. If she doesn't ask, why tell?"

2 "Don't ask, don't tell" made a lot of sense to these relatives because it sounded like an easy solution. For them, it was. If I didn't say anything to my grandmother, they wouldn't have to deal with her upset over the truth about her grandson. But for me, "not telling" was an exhausting nightmare, because it meant withholding everything that could possibly give me away and living in fear of being found out. At the same time, I didn't want to cause Grandma pain by telling her I was gay, so I was easily persuaded to continue the charade.

3 If I hadn't been close to my grandmother, or saw her once a year, hiding the truth would have been relatively easy. But we'd had a special relationship since she cared for me as a child when my mother was ill, and we visited often, so lying to her was especially difficult.

4 I started hiding the truth from everyone in 1965, when I had my first crush. That was in second grade and his name was Hugh. No one told me, but I knew I shouldn't tell anyone about it, not even Hugh. I don't know how I knew that liking another boy was something to hide, but I did, so I kept it a secret.

5 I fell in love for the first time when I was 17. It was a wondrous experience, but I didn't dare tell anyone, especially my family, because telling them about Bob would have given me away. I couldn't explain to them that for the first time in my life I felt like a normal human being.

6 By the time I was an adult, I'd stopped lying to my immediate family, with the exception of my grandmother, and told them that I was gay. I was a second-rate liar so I was lucky that Grandma was the only person in my life around whom I had to be something I wasn't. I can't imagine what it's like for gays and lesbians in the military to hide the truth from the men and women with whom they serve. The fear of exposure must be extraordinary, especially because exposure would mean the end of their careers. For me, the only risk was losing Grandma's love.

7   Hiding the truth from her grew ever more challenging in the years that followed. I couldn't tell her about the man I then shared my life with. I couldn't talk about my friends who had AIDS because she would have wondered why I knew so many ill men. I couldn't tell her that I volunteered for a gay peer-counseling center. I couldn't talk to her about the political issues that most interested me because she would have wondered why I had such passionate feelings about gay rights. Eventually I couldn't even tell her about all of my work, because some of my writing was on gay issues. In the end, all we had left to talk about was the weather.

8   If being gay were only what I did behind closed doors, there would have been plenty of my life left over to share with my grandmother. But my life as a gay man isn't something that takes place only in the privacy of my bedroom. It affects who my friends are, whom I choose to share my life with, the work I do, the organizations I belong to, the magazines I read, where I vacation and what I talk about. I know it's the same for heterosexuals because their sexual orientation affects everything, from a choice of senior-prom date and the finger on which they wear their wedding band to the birth announcements they send and every emotion they feel.

9   So the reality of the "don't ask, don't tell" solution for dealing with my grandmother and for dealing with gays in the military means having to lie about or hide almost every aspect of your life. It's not nearly as simple as just not saying, "I'm gay."

10   After years of "protecting" my grandmother I decided it was time to stop lying. In the worst case, I figured she might reject me, although that seemed unlikely. But whatever the outcome, I could not pretend anymore. Some might think that was selfish on my part, but I'd had enough of the "don't tell" policy, which had forced me into a life of deceit. I also hoped that by telling her the truth, we could build a relationship based on honesty, a possibility that was worth the risk.

11   The actual telling was far less terrifying than all the anticipation. While my grandmother cried plenty, my family was wrong, because the truth didn't kill her. In the five years since, Grandma and I have talked a lot about the realities of my life and the lives of my gay and lesbian friends. She's read many articles and a few books, including mine. She's surprised us by how quickly she's set aside her myths and misconceptions.

12   Grandma and I are far closer than we ever were. Last fall we even spent a week together in Paris for her birthday. And these days, we have plenty to talk about, including the gays in the military issue.

13   A few months ago, Grandma traveled with me to Lafayette College, Pa., where I was invited to give a speech on the history of the gay civil-rights movement. After my talk, several students took us to dinner. As I conversed with the young women across the table from me, I overheard my grandmother talking to the student sitting next to her. She told him he was right to tell his parents he was gay, that with time and his help they would adjust. She said, "Don't underestimate their ability to change."

14   I wish Sam Nunn had called my grandmother to testify before his Senate committee. He and the other senators, as well as Defense Secretary Les Aspin and the president, could do far worse than listen to her advice.

THINKING ABOUT THE TEXT

1. What are the expressed reasons why Eric Marcus didn't tell his grandmother he is gay? What do you imagine his unexpressed concerns might be?
2. What parts of his life could Marcus not talk about with his grandmother? Why was this secret a problem for him?
3. Why does Marcus believe that the policy of "don't ask, don't tell" is not a solution for gays in the military?
4. What does Marcus show about his grandmother to illustrate her understanding and acceptance of his sexual identity?

WRITING FROM THE TEXT

1. Write an essay telling about a time that you feared a family member's response to some revelation about you—something you had done, a choice you made, or one of your beliefs or values. Show the responses to your revealing this truth.
2. Based on your own or a friend's experience in telling some important truth, argue for or against revealing the truth to others.
3. Write an analysis of your own or a friend's sexual orientation to support Marcus' view that one's sexual identity influences one's choice of friends and leisure activities.

CONNECTING WITH OTHER TEXTS

1. In "Women: Invisible Cages" (p. 94), Brigid Brophy describes the subtle pressure society places on women and men to limit their choices. Use Brophy's essay as a starting point and compare the restrictions she describes with those discussed by Marcus. Structure your paper as a comparison and/or contrast study (pp. 403–413) or problem analysis (pp. 428–434), whichever seems best to you.
2. Compare and/or contrast the behavior of the gay men described in Kimmel and Levine's essay ("A Hidden Factor in AIDS," p. 78) with Marcus' description of his activities in "Ignorance Is Not Bliss." In your essay, analyze the choices and try to come to some insightful conclusions.

YOUR PLACE IS EMPTY
Anne Tyler

Known to many as the author of *The Accidental Tourist,* Anne Tyler (b. 1941) is a critically acclaimed writer of many other novels and of short fiction. She grew up in a number of Quaker communities in the Midwest and the South. It was this "setting-apart situation" and her attempt "to fit into the outside world" that helped mold Tyler into a writer. "I don't talk well," she writes. "For me, writing something down was the only road out." A theme that runs through Tyler's work is that people cannot fully communicate with one another, and the sorrow that results creates a melancholy world in which people try to reach and love each other. Tyler lives with her Iranian-born husband and their two daughters. The following story first appeared in *The New Yorker* in 1976.

1   Early in October, Hassan Ardavi invited his mother to come from Iran for a visit. His mother accepted immediately. It wasn't clear how long the visit was to last. Hassan's wife thought three months would be a good length of time. Hassan himself had planned on six months, and said so in his letter of invitation. But his mother felt that after such a long trip six months would be too short, and she was counting on staying a year. Hassan's little girl, who wasn't yet two, had no idea of time at all. She was told that her grandmother was coming but she soon forgot about it.

2   Hassan's wife was named Elizabeth, not an easy word for Iranians to pronounce. She would have been recognized as American the world over—a blond, pretty girl with long bones and an ungraceful way of walking. One of her strong points was an ability to pick up foreign languages, and before her mother-in-law's arrival she bought a textbook and taught herself Persian. "*Salaam aleikum,*" she told the mirror every morning. Her daughter watched, startled, from her place on the potty-chair. Elizabeth ran through possible situations in her mind and looked up the words for them. "Would you like more tea? Do you take sugar?" At suppertime she spoke Persian to her husband, who looked amused at the new tone she gave his language, with her flat, factual American voice. He wrote his mother and told her Elizabeth had a surprise for her.

3   Their house was a three-story brick Colonial, but only the first two stories were in use. Now they cleared the third of its trunks and china barrels and *National Geographics,* and they moved in a few pieces of furniture. Elizabeth sewed flowered curtains for the window. She was unusually careful with them; to a foreign mother-in-law, fine seams might matter. Also, Hassan bought a pocket compass, which he placed in the top dresser drawer. "For her prayers," he said. "She'll want to face Mecca. She prays three times a day."

4   "But which direction is Mecca from here?" Elizabeth asked.

5   Hassan only shrugged. He had never said the prayers himself, not even as a child. His earliest memory was of tickling the soles of his mother's feet while she prayed steadfastly on; everyone knew it was forbidden to pause once you'd started.

6   Mrs. Ardavi felt nervous about the descent from the plane. She inched down the staircase sideways, one hand tight on the railing, the other clutching her shawl. It was night, and cold. The air seemed curiously opaque. She arrived on solid ground and stood collecting herself—a small, stocky woman in black, with a kerchief over her smooth gray hair. She held her back very straight, as if she had just had her feelings hurt. In picturing this moment she had always thought Hassan would be waiting beside the plane, but there was no sign of him. Blue lights dotted the darkness behind her, an angular terminal loomed ahead, and an official was herding the passengers toward a plate-glass door. She followed, entangled in a web of meaningless sounds such as those you might hear in a fever dream.

7   Immigration. Baggage Claims. Customs. To all she spread her hands and beamed and shrugged, showing she spoke no English. Meanwhile her fellow-passengers waved to a blur of faces beyond a glass wall. It seemed they all knew people here; she was the only one who didn't. She had issued from the plane like a newborn baby, speechless and friendless. And the customs official didn't seem pleased with her. She had brought too many gifts. She had stuffed her bags with them, discarding all but the most necessary pieces of her clothing so that she would have more room. There were silver tea sets and gold jewelry for her daughter-in-law, and for her granddaughter a doll dressed in the complicated costume of a nomad tribe, an embroidered sheepskin vest, and two religious medals on chains—one a disc inscribed with the name of Allah, the other a tiny gold Koran, with a very effective prayer for long life folded up within it. The customs official sifted gold through his fingers like sand and frowned at the Koran. "Have I done something wrong?" she asked. But of course he didn't understand her. Though you'd think, really, that if he would just *listen* hard enough, just meet her eyes once . . . it was a very simple language, there was no reason why it shouldn't come through to him.

8   For Hassan, she'd brought food. She had gathered all his favorite foods and put them in a drawstring bag embroidered with peacocks. When the official opened the bag he said something under his breath and called another man over. Together they unwrapped tiny newspaper packets and sniffed at various herbs. "Sumac," she told them. "Powder of lemons. *Shambahleh.*" They gazed at her blankly. They untied a small cloth sack and rummaged through the *kashk* she had brought for soup. It rolled beneath their fingers and across the counter—hard white balls of yogurt curd, stuck with bits of sheep hair and manure. Some peasant had labored for hours to make that *kashk*. Mrs. Ardavi picked up one piece and replaced it firmly in the sack. Maybe the official understood her meaning: she was running out of patience. He threw up his hands. He slid her belongings down the counter. She was free to go.

9   Free to go where?

10   Dazed and stumbling, a pyramid of knobby parcels and bags, scraps of velvet and brocade and tapestry, she made her way to the glass wall. A door opened out of nowhere and a stranger blocked her path. "Khanom Jun," he said. It was a name that only her children would use, but she passed him blindly and he had to touch her arm before she would look up.

11   He had put on weight. She didn't know him. The last time she'd seen him he was a thin, stoop-shouldered medical student disappearing into an Air France jet without a backward glance. "Khanom Jun, it's me," this stranger said, but she went on searching his face with cloudy eyes. No doubt he was a bearer of bad news. Was that it? A recurrent dream had warned her that she would never see her son again—that he would die on his way to the airport, or had already been dead for months but no one wanted to break the news; some second or third cousin in America had continued signing Hassan's name to his cheerful, anonymous letters. Now here was this man with graying hair and a thick mustache, his clothes American but his face Iranian, his eyes sadly familiar, as if they belonged to someone else. "Don't you believe me?" he said. He kissed her on both cheeks. It was his smell she recognized first—a pleasantly bitter, herblike smell that brought her the image of Hassan as a child, reaching thin arms around her neck. "It's you, Hassan," she said, and then she started crying against his gray tweed shoulder.

12   They were quiet during the long drive home. Once she reached over to touch his face, having wanted to do so for miles. None of the out-of-focus snapshots he'd sent had prepared her for the way he had aged. "How long has it been?" she asked. "Twelve years?" But both of them knew to the day how long it had been. All those letters of hers: "My dear Hassan, ten years now and still your place is empty." "Eleven years and still . . . "

13   Hassan squinted through the windshield at the oncoming headlights. His mother started fretting over her kerchief, which she knew she ought not to have worn. She'd been told so by her youngest sister, who had been to America twice. "It marks you," her sister had said. But that square of silk was the last, shrunken reminder of the veil she used to hide beneath, before the previous Shah had banished such things. At her age, how could she expose herself? And then her teeth; her teeth were a problem too. Her youngest sister had said, "You ought to get dentures made, I'm sure there aren't three whole teeth in your head." But Mrs. Ardavi was scared of dentists. Now she covered her mouth with one hand and looked sideways at Hassan, though so far he hadn't seemed to notice. He was busy maneuvering his car into the right-hand lane.

14   This silence was the last thing she had expected. For weeks she'd been saving up stray bits of gossip, weaving together the family stories she would tell him. There were three hundred people in her family—most of them related to each other in three or four different ways, all leading intricate and scandalous lives she had planned to discuss in detail, but instead she stared sadly out the window. You'd think Hassan would ask. You'd think they could have a better conversation than this, after such a long time. Disappointment made her cross, and now she stubbornly refused to speak even when she saw something she wanted to comment on, some imposing building or unfamiliar brand of car sliding past her into the darkness.

15   By the time they arrived it was nearly midnight. None of the houses were lit but Hassan's—worn brick, older than she would have expected. "Here we are," said Hassan. The competence with which he parked the car, fitting it neatly into a small space by the curb, put him firmly on the other side of the fence, the American side.

She would have to face her daughter-in-law alone. As they climbed the front steps she whispered, "How do you say it again?"

16   "Say what?" Hassan asked.

17   "Her name. Lizabet?"

18   "Elizabeth. Like Elizabeth Taylor. *You* know."

19   "Yes, yes, of course," said his mother. Then she lifted her chin, holding tight to the straps of her purse.

20   Elizabeth was wearing bluejeans and a pair of fluffy slippers. Her hair was blond as corn silk, cut short and straight, and her face had the grave, sleepy look of a child's. As soon as she had opened the door she said, "*Salaam aleikum.*" Mrs. Ardavi, overcome with relief at the Persian greeting, threw her arms around her and kissed both cheeks. Then they led her into the living room, which looked comfortable but a little too plain. The furniture was straight-edged, the rugs uninteresting, though the curtains had a nice figured pattern that caught her eye. In one corner sat a shiny red kiddie car complete with license plates. "Is that the child's?" she asked. "Hilary's?" She hesitated over the name. "Could I see her?"

21   "*Now?*" said Hassan.

22   But Elizabeth told him, "That's all right." (Women understood these things.) She beckoned to her mother-in-law. They climbed the stairs together, up to the second floor, into a little room that smelled of milk and rubber and talcum powder, smells she would know anywhere. Even in the half-light from the hallway, she could tell that Hilary was beautiful. She had black, tumbling hair, long black lashes, and skin of a tone they called wheat-colored, lighter than Hassan's. "There," said Elizabeth. "Thank you," said Mrs. Ardavi. Her voice was formal, but this was her first grandchild and it took her a moment to recover herself. Then they stepped back into the hallway. "I brought her some medals," she whispered. "I hope you don't mind."

23   "Medals?" said Elizabeth. She repeated the word anxiously, mispronouncing it.

24   "Only an Allah and a Koran, both very tiny. You'll hardly know they're there. I'm not used to seeing a child without a medal. It worries me."

25   Automatically her fingers traced a chain around her neck, ending in the hollow of her collarbone. Elizabeth nodded, looking relieved. "*Oh* yes. Medals," she said.

26   "Is that all right?"
    "Yes, of course."

27   Mrs. Ardavi took heart. "Hassan laughs," she said. "He doesn't believe in these things. But when he left I put a prayer in his suitcase pocket, and you see he's been protected. Now if Hilary wore a medal, I could sleep nights."

28   "Of course," Elizabeth said again.

29   When they re-entered the living room, Mrs. Ardavi was smiling, and she kissed Hassan on the top of his head before she sat down.

30   American days were tightly scheduled, divided not into morning and afternoon but into 9:00, 9:30, and so forth, each half hour possessing its own set activity. It was marvellous. Mrs. Ardavi wrote her sisters: "They're more organized here. My daughter-in-law never wastes a minute." How terrible, her sisters wrote back. They were all in Teheran, drinking cup after cup of tea and idly guessing who

might come and visit. "No, you misunderstand," Mrs. Ardavi protested. "I like it this way. I'm fitting in wonderfully." And to her youngest sister she wrote, "You'd think I was American. No one guesses otherwise." This wasn't true, of course, but she hoped it would be true in the future.

31   Hassan was a doctor. He worked long hours, from six in the morning until six at night. While she was still washing for her morning prayers she could hear him tiptoe down the stairs and out the front door. His car would start up, a distant rumble far below her, and from her bathroom window she could watch it swing out from beneath a tatter of red leaves and round the corner and disappear. Then she would sigh and return to her sink. Before prayers she had to wash her face, her hands, and the soles of her feet. She had to draw her wet fingers down the part in her hair. After that she returned to her room, where she swathed herself tightly in her long black veil and knelt on a beaded velvet prayer mat. East was where the window was, curtained by chintz and misted over. On the east wall she hung a lithograph of the Caliph Ali and a color snapshot of her third son, Babak, whose marriage she had arranged just a few months before this visit. If Babak hadn't married, she never could have come. He was the youngest, spoiled by being the only son at home. It had taken her three years to find a wife for him. (One was too modern, one too lazy, one so perfect she had been suspicious.) But finally the proper girl had turned up, modest and well-mannered and sufficiently wide of hip, and Mrs. Ardavi and the bridal couple had settled in a fine new house on the outskirts of Teheran. Now every time she prayed, she added a word of thanks that at last she had a home for her old age. After that, she unwound her veil and laid it carefully in a drawer. From another drawer she took thick cotton stockings and elastic garters; she stuffed her swollen feet into open-toed vinyl sandals. Unless she was going out, she wore a housecoat. It amazed her how wasteful Americans were with their clothing.

32   Downstairs, Elizabeth would have started her tea and buttered a piece of toast for her. Elizabeth and Hilary ate bacon and eggs, but bacon of course was unclean and Mrs. Ardavi never accepted any. Nor had it even been offered to her, except once, jokingly, by Hassan. The distinctive, smoky smell rose to meet her as she descended the stairs. "What does it taste like?" she always asked. She was dying to know. But Elizabeth's vocabulary didn't cover the taste of bacon; she only said it was salty and then laughed and gave up. They had learned very early to travel a well-worn conversational path, avoiding the dead ends caused by unfamiliar words. "Did you sleep well?" Elizabeth always asked in her funny, childish accent, and Mrs. Ardavi answered, "So-so." Then they would turn and watch Hilary, who sat on a booster seat eating scrambled eggs, a thin chain of Persian gold crossing the back of her neck. Conversation was easier, or even unnecessary, as long as Hilary was there.

33   In the mornings Elizabeth cleaned house. Mrs. Ardavi used that time for letter writing. She had dozens of letters to write, to all her aunts and uncles and her thirteen sisters. (Her father had had three wives, and a surprising number of children even for that day and age.) Then there was Babak. His wife was in her second month of pregnancy, so Mrs. Ardavi wrote long accounts of the American child-rearing methods. "There are some things I don't agree with," she wrote. "They let

Hilary play outdoors by herself, with not even a servant to keep an eye on her." Then she would trail off and gaze thoughtfully at Hilary, who sat on the floor watching a television program called "Captain Kangaroo."

34   Mrs. Ardavi's own childhood had been murky and grim. From the age of nine she was wrapped in a veil, one corner of it clenched in her teeth to hide her face whenever she appeared on the streets. Her father, a respected man high up in public life, used to chase servant girls through the halls and trap them, giggling, in vacant bedrooms. At the age of ten she was forced to watch her mother bleed to death in childbirth, and when she screamed the midwife had struck her across the face and held her down till she had properly kissed her mother goodbye. There seemed no connection at all between her and this little overalled American. At times, when Hilary had one of her temper tantrums, Mrs. Ardavi waited in horror for Elizabeth to slap her and then, when no slap came, felt a mixture of relief and anger. "In Iran—" she would begin, and if Hassan was there he always said, "But this is not Iran, remember?"

35   After lunch Hilary took a nap, and Mrs. Ardavi went upstairs to say her noontime prayers and take a nap as well. Then she might do a little laundry in her bathtub. Laundry was a problem here. Although she liked Elizabeth, the fact was that the girl was a Christian, and therefore unclean; it would never do to have a Christian wash a Moslem's clothes. The automatic dryer was also unclean, having contained, at some point, a Christian's underwear. So she had to ask Hassan to buy her a drying rack. It came unassembled. Elizabeth put it together for her, stick by stick, and then Mrs. Ardavi held it under her shower and rinsed it off, hoping that would be enough to remove any taint. The Koran didn't cover this sort of situation.

36   When Hilary was up from her nap they walked her to the park—Elizabeth in her eternal bluejeans and Mrs. Ardavi in her kerchief and shawl, taking short painful steps in small shoes that bulged over her bunions. They still hadn't seen to her teeth, although by now Hassan had noticed them. She was hoping he might forget about the dentist, but then she saw him remembering every time she laughed and revealed her five brown teeth set wide apart.

37   At the park she laughed a great deal. It was her only way of communicating with the other women. They sat on the benches ringing the playground, and while Elizabeth translated their questions Mrs. Ardavi laughed and nodded at them over and over. "They want to know if you like it here," Elizabeth said. Mrs. Ardavi answered at length, but Elizabeth's translation was very short. Then gradually the other women forgot her, and conversation rattled on while she sat silent and watched each speaker's lips. The few recognizable words—"telephone," "television," "radio"—gave her the impression that American conversations were largely technical, even among women. Their gestures were wide and slow, disproving her youngest sister's statement that in America everyone was in a hurry. On the contrary, these women were dreamlike, moving singly or in twos across wide flat spaces beneath white November skies when they departed.

38   Later, at home, Mrs. Ardavi would say, "The red-haired girl, is she pregnant? She looked it, I thought. Is the fat girl happy in her marriage?" She asked with some urgency, plucking Elizabeth's sleeve when she was slow to answer. People's

private lives fascinated her. On Saturday trips to the supermarket she liked to single out some interesting stranger. "What's the matter with that *jerky*-moving man? That girl, is she one of your dark-skinned people?" Elizabeth answered too softly, and never seemed to follow Mrs. Ardavi's pointing finger.

39   Supper was difficult; Mrs. Ardavi didn't like American food. Even when Elizabeth made something Iranian, it had an American taste to it—the vegetables still faintly crisp, the onions transparent rather than nicely blackened. "Vegetables not thoroughly cooked retain a certain acidity," Mrs. Ardavi said, laying down her fork. "This is a cause of constipation and stomach aches. At night I often have heartburn. It's been three full days since I moved my bowels." Elizabeth merely bent over her plate, offering no symptoms of her own in return. Hassan said, "At the table, Khanom? At the table?"

40   Eventually she decided to cook supper herself. Over Elizabeth's protests she began at three every afternoon, filling the house with the smell of dillweed and arranging pots on counters and cabinets and finally, when there was no more space, on the floor. She squatted on the floor with her skirt tucked between her knees and stirred great bowls of minced greens while behind her, on the gas range, four different pots of food bubbled and steamed. The kitchen was becoming more homelike, she thought. A bowl of yogurt brewed beside the stove, a kettle of rice soaked in the sink, and the top of the dishwasher was curlicued with the yellow dye from saffron. In one corner sat the pudding pan, black on the bottom from the times she had cooked down sugar to make a sweet for her intestines. "Now, this is your rest period," she always told Elizabeth. "Come to the table in three hours and be surprised." But Elizabeth only hovered around the kitchen, disturbing the serene, steam-filled air with clatter and slams as she put away pots, or pacing between stove and sink, her arms folded across her chest. At supper she ate little; Mrs. Ardavi wondered how Americans got so tall on such small suppers. Hassan, on the other hand, had second and third helpings. "I must be gaining five pounds a week," he said. "None of my clothes fit."

41   "That's good to hear," said his mother. And Elizabeth added something but in English, which Hassan answered in English also. Often now they broke into English for paragraphs at a time—Elizabeth speaking softly, looking at her plate, and Hassan answering at length and sometimes reaching across the table to cover her hand.

42   At night, after her evening prayers, Mrs. Ardavi watched television on the living-room couch. She brought her veil downstairs and wrapped it around her to keep the drafts away. Her shoes lay on the rug beneath her, and scattered down the length of the couch were her knitting bag, her sack of burned sugar, her magnifying glass, and *My First Golden Dictionary*. Elizabeth read novels in an easy chair, and Hassan watched TV so that he could translate the difficult parts of the plot. Not that Mrs. Ardavi had much trouble. American plots were easy to guess at, particularly the Westerns. And when the program was boring—a documentary or a special news feature—she could pass the time by talking to Hassan. "Your cousin Farah wrote," she said. "Do you remember her? A homely girl, too dark. She's getting a divorce and in my opinion it's fortunate; he's from a lower class. Do you remember Farah?"

43   Hassan only grunted, his eyes on the screen. He was interested in American politics. So was she, for that matter. She had wept for President Kennedy, and carried Jackie's picture in her purse. But these news programs were long and dry, and if Hassan wouldn't talk she was forced to turn at last to her *Golden Dictionary.*

44   In her childhood, she had been taught by expensive foreign tutors. Her mind was her great gift, the compensation for a large, plain face and a stocky figure. But now what she had learned seemed lost, forgotten utterly or fogged by years, so that Hassan gave a snort whenever she told him some fact that she had dredged up from her memory. It seemed that everything she studied now had to penetrate through a great thick layer before it reached her mind. "Tonk you," she practiced. "Tonk you. Tonk you." "Thank you," Hassan corrected her. He pointed out useful words in her dictionary—grocery-store words, household words—but she grew impatient with their woodenness. What she wanted was the language to display her personality, her famous courtesy, and her magical intuition about the inside lives of other people. Nightly she learned "salt," "bread," "spoon," but with an inner sense of dullness, and every morning when she woke her English was once again confined to "thank you" and "NBC."

45   Elizabeth, meanwhile, read on, finishing one book and reaching for the next without even glancing up. Hassan chewed a thumbnail and watched a senator. He shouldn't be disturbed, of course, but time after time his mother felt the silence and the whispery turning of pages stretching her nerves until she had to speak. "Hassan?"

46   "Hmm."

47   "My chest seems tight. I'm sure a cold is coming on. Don't you have a tonic?"

48   "No," said Hassan.

49   He dispensed medicines all day; he listened to complaints. Common sense told her to stop, but she persisted, encouraged by some demon that wouldn't let her tongue lie still. "Don't you have some syrup? What about that liquid you gave me for constipation? Would that help?"

50   "No, it wouldn't," said Hassan.

51   He drove her on, somehow. The less he gave, the more she had to ask. "Well, aspirin? Vitamins?" Until Hassan said, "Will you just let me *watch?*" Then she could lapse into silence again, or even gather up the clutter of her belongings and bid the two of them good night.

52   She slept badly. Often she lay awake for hours, fingering the edge of the sheet and staring at the ceiling. Memories crowded in on her, old grievances and fears, injustices that had never been righted. For the first time in years she thought of her husband, a gentle, weak man given to surprising outbursts of temper. She hadn't loved him when she married him, and at his death from a liver ailment six years later her main feeling had been resentment. Was it fair to be widowed so young, while other women were supported and protected? She had moved from her husband's home back to the old family estate, where five of her sisters still lived. There she had stayed till Babak's wedding, drinking tea all day with her sisters and pulling the strings by which the rest of the family was attached. Marriages were arranged, funerals attended, childbirth discussed in fine detail; servants' disputes were settled, and feuds patched up and then restarted. Her husband's face

had quickly faded, leaving only a vacant spot in her mind. But now she could see him so clearly—a wasted figure on his deathbed, beard untrimmed, turban coming loose, eyes imploring her for something more than an absent-minded pat on the cheek as she passed through his room on her way to check the children.

53   She saw the thin faces of her three small boys as they sat on the rug eating rice. Hassan was the stubborn, mischievous one, with perpetual scabs on his knees. Babak was the cuddly one. Ali was the oldest, who had caused so much worry—weak, like his father, demanding, but capable of turning suddenly charming. Four years ago he had died of a brain hemorrhage, slumping over a dinner table in far-away Shirāz, where he'd gone to be free of his wife, who was also his double first cousin. Ever since he was born he had disturbed his mother's sleep, first because she worried over what he would amount to and now, after his death, because she lay awake listing all she had done wrong with him. She had been too lenient. No, too harsh. There was no telling. Mistakes she had made floated on the ceiling like ghosts—allowances she'd made when she knew she shouldn't have, protections he had not deserved, blows which perhaps he had not deserved either.

54   She would have liked to talk to Hassan about it, but any time she tried he changed the subject. Maybe he was angry about the way he had heard of Ali's death. It was customary to break such news gradually. She had started a series of tactful letters, beginning by saying that Ali was seriously ill when in truth he was already buried. Something in the letter had given her away—perhaps her plans for a rest cure by the seaside, which she never would have considered if she'd had an ailing son at home. Hassan had telephoned overseas, taking three nights to reach her. "Tell me what's wrong," he said. "I know there's something." When her tears kept her from answering, he asked, "Is he dead?" His voice sounded angry, but that might have been due to a poor connection. And when he hung up, cutting her off before she could say all she wanted, she thought, I should have told him straight out. I had forgotten that about him. Now when she spoke of Ali he listened politely, with his face frozen. She would have told him anything, all about the death and burial and that witch of a wife throwing herself, too late, into the grave; but Hassan never asked.

55   Death was moving in on her. Oh, not on her personally (the women in her family lived a century or longer, burying the men one by one) but on everybody around her, all the cousins and uncles and brothers-in-law. No sooner had she laid away her mourning clothes than it was time to bring them out again. Recently she had begun to feel she would outlive her two other sons as well, and she fought off sleep because of the dreams it brought—Babak lying stiff and cold in his grave, Hassan crumpled over in some dark American alley. Terrifying images would zoom at her out of the night. In the end she had to wrap herself in her veil and sleep instead on the Persian rug, which had the dusty smell of home and was, anyway, more comfortable than her unsteady foreign mattress.

56   At Christmas time, Hassan and Elizabeth gave Mrs. Ardavi a brightly colored American dress with short sleeves. She wore it to an Iranian party, even leaving off her kerchief in a sudden fit of daring. Everyone commented on how nice she looked. "Really you fit right in," a girl told her. "May I write to my mother about

you? She was over here for a year and a half and never once stepped out of the house without her kerchief." Mrs. Ardavi beamed. It was true she would never have associated with these people at home—children of civil servants and bank clerks, newly rich now they'd finished medical school. The wives called their husbands "Doctor" even in direct address. But still it felt good to be speaking so much Persian; her tongue nearly ran away with her. "I see you're expecting a baby," she said to one of the wives. "Is it your first? I could tell by your eyes. Now don't be nervous. I had three myself; my mother had seven and never felt a pain in her life. She would squat down to serve my father's breakfast and 'Eh?' she would say. 'Aga Jun, it's the baby!' and there it would be on the floor between her feet, waiting for her to cut the cord and finish pouring the tea." She neglected to mention how her mother had died. All her natural tact came back to her, her gift with words and her knowledge of how to hold an audience. She bubbled and sparkled like a girl, and her face fell when it was time to go home.

57   After the party, she spent two or three days noticing more keenly than ever the loss of her language, and talking more feverishly when Hassan came home in the evening. This business of being a foreigner was something changeable. Boundaries kept shifting, and sometimes it was she who was the foreigner but other times Elizabeth, or even Hassan. (Wasn't it true, she often wondered, that there was a greater distance between men and women than between Americans and Iranians, or even *Eskimos* and Iranians?) Hassan was the foreigner when she and Elizabeth conspired to hide a miniature Koran in his glove compartment; he would have laughed at them. "You see," she told Elizabeth, "I know there's nothing to it, but it makes me feel better. When my sons were born I took them all to the bath attendant to have their blood let. People say it brings long life. I know that's superstition, but whenever afterward I saw those ridges down their backs I felt safe. Don't you understand?" And Elizabeth said, "Of course." She smuggled the Koran into the car herself, and hid it beneath the Texaco maps. Hassan saw nothing.

58   Hilary was a foreigner forever. She dodged her grandmother's yearning hands, and when the grownups spoke Persian she fretted and misbehaved and pulled on Elizabeth's sleeve. Mrs. Ardavi had to remind herself constantly not to kiss the child too much, not to reach out for a hug, not to offer her lap. In this country people kept more separate. They kept so separate that at times she felt hurt. They tried to be so subtle, so undemonstrative. She would never understand this place.

59   In January they took her to a dentist, who made clucking noises when he looked in her mouth. "What does he say?" she asked. "Tell me the worst." But Hassan was talking in a low voice to Elizabeth, and he waved her aside. They seemed to be having a misunderstanding of some sort. "What does he *say*, Hassan?"

60   "Just a minute."

61   She craned around in the high-backed chair, fighting off the dentist's little mirror. "I have to know," she told Hassan.

62   "He says your teeth are terrible. They have to be extracted and the gums surgically smoothed. He wants to know if you'll be here for another few months; he can't schedule you till later."

63   A cold lump of fear swelled in her stomach. Unfortunately she *would* be here; it had only been three months so far and she was planning to stay a year. So she had to watch numbly while her life was signed away, whole strings of appointments made, and little white cards filled out. And Hassan didn't even look sympathetic. He was still involved in whatever this argument was with Elizabeth. The two of them failed to notice how her hands were shaking.

64   It snowed all of January, the worst snow they had had in years. When she came downstairs in the mornings she found the kitchen icy cold, crisscrossed by drafts. "The sort of cold enters your bones," she told Elizabeth. "I'm sure to fall sick." Elizabeth only nodded. Some mornings now her face was pale and puffy, as if she had a secret worry, but Mrs. Ardavi had learned that it was better not to ask about it.

65   Early in February there was a sudden warm spell. Snow melted and all the trees dripped in the sunshine. "We're going for a walk," Elizabeth said, and Mrs. Ardavi said, "I'll come too." In spite of the warmth, she toiled upstairs for her woolen shawl. She didn't like to take chances. And she worried over Hilary's bare ears. "Won't she catch cold?" she asked. "I think we should cover her head."

66   "She'll be all right," said Elizabeth, and then shut her face in a certain stubborn way she had.

67   In the park, Elizabeth and Hilary made snowballs from the last of the snow and threw them at each other, narrowly missing Mrs. Ardavi, who stood watching with her arms folded and her hands tucked in her sleeves.

68   The next morning, something was wrong with Hilary. She sat at the breakfast table and cried steadily, refusing all food. "Now, now," her grandmother said, "won't you tell old Ka Jun what's wrong?" But when she came close Hilary screamed louder. By noon she was worse. Elizabeth called Hassan, and he came home immediately and laid a hand on Hilary's forehead and said she should go to the pediatrician. He drove them there himself. "It's her ears, I'm sure of it," Mrs. Ardavi said in the waiting room. For some reason Hassan grew angry. "Do you always know better than the experts?" he asked her. "What are we coming to the doctor for? We could have talked to you and saved the trip." His mother lowered her eyes and examined her purse straps. She understood that he was anxious, but all the same her feelings were hurt and when they rose to go into the office she stayed behind.

69   Later Hassan came back and sat down again. "There's an infection in her middle ear," he told her. "The doctor's going to give her a shot of penicillin." His mother nodded, careful not to annoy him by reminding him she had thought as much. Then Hilary started crying. She must be getting her shot now. Mrs. Ardavi herself was terrified of needles, and she sat gripping her purse until her fingers turned white, staring around the waiting room, which seemed pathetically cheerful, with its worn wooden toys and nursery-school paintings. Her own ear ached in sympathy. She thought of a time when she had boxed Ali's ears too hard and he had wept all that day and gone to sleep sucking his thumb.

70   While Hassan was there she was careful not to say anything, but the following morning at breakfast she said, "Elizabeth dear, do you remember that walk we took day before yesterday?"

71   "Yes," said Elizabeth. She was squeezing oranges for Hilary, who'd grown cheerful again and was eating a huge breakfast.

72   "Remember I said Hilary should wear a hat? Now you see you should have been more careful. Because of you she fell sick; she could have died. Do you see that now?"

73   "No," said Elizabeth.

74   Was her Persian that scanty? Lately it seemed to have shrunk and hardened, like a stale piece of bread. Mrs. Ardavi sighed and tried again. "Without a hat, you see—" she began. But Elizabeth had set down her orange, picked up Hilary, and walked out of the room. Mrs. Ardavi stared after her, wondering if she'd said something wrong.

75   For the rest of the day, Elizabeth was busy in her room. She was cleaning out bureaus and closets. A couple of times Mrs. Ardavi advanced as far as the doorway, where she stood awkwardly watching. Hilary sat on the floor playing with a discarded perfume bottle. Everything, it seemed, was about to be thrown away—buttonless blouses and stretched-out sweaters, stockings and combs and empty lipstick tubes. "Could I be of any help?" Mrs. Ardavi asked, but Elizabeth said, "Oh, no. Thank you very much." Her voice was cheerful. Yet when Hassan came home he went upstairs and stayed a long time, and the door remained shut behind him.

76   Supper that night was an especially fine stew, Hassan's favorite ever since childhood, but he didn't say a word about it. He hardly spoke at all, in fact. Then later, when Elizabeth was upstairs putting Hilary to bed, he said, "Khanom Jun, I want to talk to you."

77   "Yes, Hassan," she said, laying aside her knitting. She was frightened by his seriousness, the black weight of his mustache, and her own father's deep black eyes. But what had she done? She knotted her hands and looked up at him, swallowing.

78   "I understand you've been interfering," he said.

79   "I, Hassan?"

80   "Elizabeth isn't the kind you can do that with. And she's raising the child just fine on her own."

81   "Well, of course she is," said his mother. "Did I ever say otherwise?"

82   "Show it, then. Don't offer criticisms."

83   "Very well," she said. She picked up her knitting and began counting stitches, as if she'd forgotten the conversation entirely. But that evening she was unusually quiet, and at nine o'clock she excused herself to go to bed. "So early?" Hassan asked.

84   "I'm tired," she told him, and left with her back very straight.

85   Her room surrounded her like a nest. She had built up layers of herself on every surface—tapestries and bits of lace and lengths of paisley. The bureau was covered with gilt-framed pictures of the saints, and snapshots of her sisters at family gatherings. On the windowsill were little plants in orange and aqua plastic pots—her favorite American colors. Her bedside table held bottles of medicine, ivory

prayer beads, and a tiny brick of holy earth. The rest of the house was bare and shiny, impersonal; this room was as comforting as her shawl.

86   Still, she didn't sleep well. Ghosts rose up again, tugging at her thoughts. Why did things turn out so badly for her? Her father had preferred her brothers, a fact that crushed her even after all these years. Her husband had had three children by her and then complained that she was cold. And what comfort were children? If she had stayed in Iran any longer Babak would have asked her to move; she'd seen it coming. There'd been some disrespect creeping into his bride's behavior, some unwillingness to take advice, which Babak had overlooked even when his mother pointed it out to him. And Hassan was worse—always so stubborn, much too independent. She had offered him anything if he would just stay in Iran but he had said no; he was set on leaving her. And he had flatly refused to take along his cousin Shora as his wife, though everyone pointed out how lonely he would be. He was so anxious to break away, to get *going,* to come to this hardhearted country and take up with a Christian girl. Oh, she should have laughed when he left, and saved her tears for someone more deserving. She never should have come here, she never should have asked anything of him again. When finally she went to sleep it seemed that her eyes remained open, burning large and dry beneath her lids.

87   In the morning she had a toothache. She could hardly walk for the pain. It was only Friday (the first of her dental appointments was for Monday), but the dentist made time for her during the afternoon and pulled the tooth. Elizabeth said it wouldn't hurt, but it did. Elizabeth treated it as something insignificant, merely a small break in her schedule, which required the hiring of a babysitter. She wouldn't even call Hassan home from work. "What could he do?" she asked.

88   So when Hassan returned that evening it was all a surprise to him—the sight of his mother with a bloody cotton cylinder hanging out over her lower lip like a long tooth. "What *happened* to you?" he asked. To make it worse, Hilary was screaming and had been all afternoon. Mrs. Ardavi put her hands over her ears, wincing. "Will you make that child hush?" Hassan told Elizabeth. "I think we should get my mother to bed." He guided her toward the stairs, and she allowed herself to lean on him. "It's mainly my heart," she said. "You know how scared I am of dentists." When he had folded back her bedspread and helped her to lie down she closed her eyes gratefully, resting one arm across her forehead. Even the comfort of hot tea was denied her; she had to stay on cold foods for twelve hours. Hassan fixed her a glass of ice water. He was very considerate, she thought. He seemed as shaken at the sight of her as Hilary had been. All during the evening he kept coming to check on her, and twice in the night she heard him climbing the stairs to listen at her door. When she moaned he called, "Are you awake?"

89   "Of course," she said.

90   "Can I get you anything?"

91   "No, no."

92   In the morning she descended the stairs with slow, groping feet, keeping a tight hold on the railing. "It was a very hard night," she said. "At four my gum started throbbing. Is that normal? I think these American pain pills are constipating. Maybe a little prune juice would restore my regularity."

93   "I'll get it," Hassan said. "You sit down. Did you take the milk of magnesia?"

94   "Oh, yes, but I'm afraid it wasn't enough," she said.

95   Elizabeth handed Hassan a platter of bacon, not looking at him.

96   After breakfast, while Hassan and his mother were still sitting over their tea, Elizabeth started cleaning the kitchen. She made quite a bit of noise. She sorted the silverware and then went through a tangle of utensils, discarding bent spatulas and rusty tongs. "May I help?" asked Mrs. Ardavi. Elizabeth shook her head. She seemed to have these fits of throwing things away. Now she was standing on the counter to take everything from the upper cabinets—crackers, cereals, half-empty bottles of spices. On the very top shelf was a flowered tin confectioner's box with Persian lettering on it, forgotten since the day Mrs. Ardavi had brought it. "My!" said Mrs. Ardavi. "Won't Hilary be surprised!" Elizabeth pried the lid off. Out flew a cloud of insects, grayish-brown with V-shaped wings. They brushed past Elizabeth's face and fluttered through her hair and swarmed toward the ceiling, where they dimmed the light fixture. Elizabeth flung the box as far from her as possible and climbed down from the counter. "Goodness!" said Mrs. Ardavi. "Why, *we* have those at home!" Hassan lowered his teacup. Mixed nuts and dried currants rolled every which way on the floor; more insects swung toward the ceiling. Elizabeth sat on the nearest chair and buried her head in her hands. "Elizabeth?" said Hassan.

97   But she wouldn't look at him. In the end she simply rose and went upstairs, shutting the bedroom door with a gentle, definite click, which they heard all the way down in the kitchen because they were listening so hard.

98   "Excuse me," Hassan said to his mother.

99   She nodded and stared into her tea.

100   After he was gone she went to find Hilary, and she set her on her knee, babbling various folk rhymes to her while straining her ears toward the silence overhead. But Hilary squirmed off her lap and went to play with a truck. Then Hassan came downstairs again. He didn't say a word about Elizabeth.

101   On the following day, when Mrs. Ardavi's tooth was better, she and Hassan had a little talk upstairs in her room. They were very polite with each other. Hassan asked his mother how long they could hope for her to stay. His mother said she hadn't really thought about it. Hassan said that in America it was the custom to have house guests for three months only. After that they moved to a separate apartment nearby, which he'd be glad to provide for her as soon as he could find one, maybe next week. "Ah, an apartment," said his mother, looking impressed. But she had never lived alone a day in her life, and so after a suitable pause she said that she would hate to put him to so much expense. "Especially," she said, "when I'm going in such a short time anyway, since I'm homesick for my sisters."

102   "Well, then," said Hassan.

103   At supper that night, Hassan announced that his mother was missing her sisters and would like to leave. Elizabeth lowered her glass. "Leave?" she said.

104   Mrs. Ardavi said, "And Babak's wife, of course, will be asking for me when the baby arrives."

105   "Well . . . but what about the dentist? You were supposed to start your appointments on Monday."

106   "It's not important," Mrs. Ardavi said.

107   "But we set up all those—"

108   "There are plenty of dentists she can see at home," Hassan told Elizabeth. "We have dentists in Iran, for God's sake. Do you imagine we're barbarians?"

109   "No," Elizabeth said.

110   On the evening of the third of March, Hassan drove his mother to the airport. He was worrying about the road, which was slippery after a snowfall. He couldn't find much to say to his mother. And once they had arrived, he deliberately kept the conversation to trivia—the verifying of tickets, checking of departure times, weighing of baggage. Her baggage was fourteen pounds overweight. It didn't make sense; all she had were her clothes and a few small gifts for her sisters. "Why is it so heavy?" Hassan asked. "What have you got in there?" But his mother only said, "I don't know," and straightened her shawl, looking elsewhere. Hassan bent to open a tooled-leather suitcase. Inside he found three empty urn-shaped wine bottles, the permanent-press sheets from her bed, and a sample box of detergent that had come in yesterday's mail. "Listen," said Hassan, "do you know how much I'd have to pay to fly these things over? What's the matter with you?"

111   "I wanted to show my sisters," his mother said.

112   "Well, forget it. Now, what else have you got?"

113   But something about her—the vague, childlike eyes set upon some faraway object—made him give in. He opened no more bags. He even regretted his sharpness, and when her flight was announced he hugged her closely and kissed the top of her head. "Go with God," he said.

114   "Goodbye, Hassan."

115   She set off down the corridor by herself, straggling behind a line of businessmen. They all wore hats. His mother wore her scarf, and of all the travelers she alone, securely kerchiefed and shawled, setting her small shoes resolutely on the gleaming tiles, seemed undeniably a foreigner.

THINKING ABOUT THE TEXT

1. Discuss Mrs. Ardavi's effort to adjust to American culture. Where do you see her making a genuine effort, and where do you see her clinging to her own customs?

2. At first Elizabeth tries hard to make her mother-in-law feel at home. Discuss her efforts; then specify the signs that Elizabeth is feeling stressed by Mrs. Ardavi's prolonged stay.

3. Mrs. Ardavi notes, "Boundaries kept shifting and sometimes it was she who was the foreigner but other times Elizabeth, or even Hassan." Point out scenes where each seems the foreigner and explain why.

4. Discuss scenes where Mrs. Ardavi is "interfering." Explain each from her perspective, and then from Hassan's or Elizabeth's.

5. In what ways does the title relate to the story?

WRITING FROM THE TEXT

1. Write an essay comparing Mrs. Ardavi's beliefs and behaviors with Elizabeth's. What are the barriers between them, and which are hardest to resolve? What is Hassan's role in their relationship? Focus on an assertion or thesis you can prove about the key differences or bonds between them.

2. Rather than portraying Mrs. Ardavi as a stereotypical mother-in-law, Tyler helps us understand her as a complex and rich human, caught between worlds. Consider Mrs. Ardavi's upbringing and past as well as her current predicament in a new culture and write an analysis of her character. (See character analysis section, pp. 436–444.)

3. Write an essay focusing on an experience where you felt "undeniably a foreigner." As Tyler suggests, this alienation may happen in your own environment or your own home, as it does to Hassan and Elizabeth. Include examples that illustrate the alienation you felt.

CONNECTING WITH OTHER TEXTS

1. Using this story and any two other readings in this text, write an essay analyzing the pressure and demands of parenting. Suggested readings from this text include "The 'Perfect' Misconception" (p. 58), "My Man Bovanne" (p. 43), "Two Kinds" (p. 49), "The Writer" (p. 61), and "When Parents Don't Turn Out Right" (p. 67).

2. Intercultural marriages bring an added complexity to family relationships. Research a specific Islamic custom or belief that relates to this story (arranged marriages, Christians as unclean, the wearing of medals, carrying the Koran, etc.) and explain its origin and significance.

MY MAN BOVANNE
Toni Cade Bambara

A civil rights activist, college professor, editor, and author of short stories, a novel, and screenplays, Toni Cade Bambara (b. 1939) has also directed recreation in the psychiatry department of a metropolitan hospital. During the 1960s, Bambara became involved in urban political and cultural activities, an interest that appears in the author's work. In the *New York Times Book Review*, C. D. B. Bryan wrote that "Bambara tells . . . more about being black through her quiet, proud, silly, tender, hip, acute, loving stories than any amount of literary polemicizing could hope to do. She writes about love: a love for one's family, one's friends, one's race, one's neighborhood, and it is the sort of love that comes with maturity and inner peace." The short story included here was first published in *Gorilla, My Love* in 1971.

1   Blind people got a hummin jones if you notice. Which is understandable completely once you been around one and notice what no eyes will force you into to see people, and you get past the first time, which seems to come out of nowhere, and it's like you in church again with fat-chest ladies and old gents gruntin a hum low in the throat to whatever the preacher be saying. Shakey Bee bottom lip all swole up with Sweet Peach and me explainin how come the sweet-potato bread was a dollar-quarter this time stead of dollar regular and he say uh hunh he understand, then he break into this *thizzin* kind of hum which is quiet, but fiercesome just the same, if you ain't ready for it. Which I wasn't. But I got used to it and the onliest time I had to say somethin bout it was when he was playin checkers on the stoop one time and he commenst to hummin quite churchy seem to me. So I says, "Look here Shakey Bee, I can't beat you and Jesus too." He stop.

2   So that's how come I asked My Man Bovanne to dance. He ain't my man mind you, just a nice ole gent from the block that we all know cause he fixes things and the kids like him. Or used to fore Black Power got hold their minds and mess em around till they can't be civil to ole folks. So we at this benefit for my niece's cousin who's runnin for somethin with this Black party somethin or other behind her. And I press up close to dance with Bovanne who blind and I'm hummin and he hummin, chest to chest like talkin. Not jammin my breasts into the man. Wasn't bout tits. Was bout vibrations. And he dug it and asked me what color dress I had on and how my hair was fixed and how I was doin without a man, not nosy but nice-like, and who was at this affair and was the canapés dainty-stingy or healthy enough to get hold of proper. Comfy and cheery is what I'm tryin to get across. Touch talkin like the heel of the hand on the tambourine or on a drum.

3   But right away Joe Lee come up on us and frown for dancin so close to the man. My own son who knows what kind of *warm* I am about; and don't grown men call me long distance and in the middle of the night for a little Mama comfort? But he frown. Which ain't right since Bovanne can't see and defend himself. Just a nice old man who fixes toasters and busted irons and bicycles and things and changes the lock on my door when my men friends get messy. Nice man. Which is not why they invited him. Grass roots you see. Me and Sister Taylor and the woman who does heads at Mamies and the man from the barber shop, we all there on account of we grass roots. And I ain't never been souther than Brooklyn Battery and no more country than the window box on my fire escape. And just yesterday my kids tellin me to take them countrified rags off my head and be cool. And now can't get Black enough to suit em. So everybody passin sayin My Man Bovanne. Big deal, keep steppin and don't even stop a minute to get the man a drink or one of them cute sandwiches or tell him what's goin on. And him standin there with a smile ready case someone do speak he want to be ready. So that's how come I pull him on the dance floor and we dance squeezin past the tables and chairs and all them coats and people standin round up in each other face talkin bout this and that but got no use for this blind man who mostly fixed skates and

skooters for all these folks when they was just kids. So I'm pressed up close and we touch talkin with the hum. And here come my daughter cuttin her eye at me like she do when she tell me about my "apolitical" self like I got hoof and mouf disease and there ain't no hope at all. And I don't pay her no mind and just look up in Bovanne shadow face and tell him his stomach like a drum and he laugh. Laugh real loud. And here come my youngest. Task, with a tap on my elbow like he the third grade monitor and I'm cuttin up on the line to assembly.

4   "I was just talkin on the drums," I explained when they hauled me into the kitchen. I figured drums was my best defense. They can get ready for drums what with all this heritage business. And Bovanne stomach just like that drum Task give me when he come back from Africa. You just touch it and it hum thizzm, thizzm. So I stuck to the drum story. "Just drummin that's all."

5   "Mama, what are you talkin about?"

6   "She had too much to drink," say Elo to Task cause she don't hardly say nuthin to me direct no more since that ugly argument about my wigs.

7   "Look here Mama," say Task, the gentle one. "We just tryin to pull your coat. You were makin a spectacle of yourself out there dancing like that."

8   "Dancin like what?"

9   Task run a hand over his left ear like his father for the world and his father before that.

10   "Like a bitch in heat," say Elo.

11   "Well uhh, I was goin to say like one of them sex-starved ladies gettin on in years and not too discriminating. Know what I mean?"

12   I don't answer cause I'll cry. Terrible thing when your own children talk to you like that. Pullin me out the party and hustlin me into some stranger's kitchen in the back of a bar just like the damn police. And ain't like I'm old old. I can still wear me some sleeveless dresses without the meat hangin off my arm. And I keep up with some thangs through my kids. Who ain't kids no more. To hear them tell it. So I don't say nuthin.

13   "Dancin with that tom," say Elo to Joe Lee, who leanin on the folks' freezer. "His feet can smell a cracker a mile away and go into their shuffle number post haste. And them eyes. He could be a little considerate and put on some shades. Who wants to look into them blown-out fuses that—"

14   "Is this what they call the generation gap?" I say.

15   "Generation gap," spits Elo, like I suggested castor oil and fricassee possum in the milk-shakes or somethin. "That's a white concept for a white phenomenon. There's no generation gap among Black people. We are a col—"

16   "Yeh, well never mind," says Joe Lee. "The point is Mama . . . well, it's pride. You embarrass yourself and us too dancin like that."

17   "I wasn't shame." Then nobody say nuthin. Them standin there in they pretty clothes with drinks in they hands and gangin up on me, and me in the third-degree chair and nary a olive to my name. Felt just like the police got hold to me.

18   "First of all," Task say, holdin up his hand and tickin off the offenses, "the dress. Now that dress is too short, Mama, and too low-cut for a woman your age. And Tamu's going to make a speech tonight to kick off the campaign and will be introducin you and expecting you to organize the council of elders—"

19   "Me? Didn nobody ask me nuthin. You mean Nisi? She change her name?"

20   "Well, Norton was supposed to tell you about it. Nisi wants to introduce you and then encourage the older folks to form a Council of the Elders to act as an advisory—"

21   "And you going to be standing there with your boobs out and that wig on your head and that hem up to your ass. And people'll say, 'Ain't that the horny bitch that was grindin with the blind dude?'"

22   "Elo, be cool a minute," say Task, gettin to the next finger. "And then there's the drinkin. Mama, you know you can't drink cause next thing you know you be laughin loud and carryin on," and he grab another finger for the loudness. "And then there's the dancin. You been tattooed on the man for four records straight and slow draggin even on the fast numbers. How you think that look for a woman your age?"

23   "What's my age?"

24   "What?"

25   "I'm axin you all a simple question. You keep talkin bout what's proper for a woman my age. How old am I anyhow?" And Joe Lee slams his eyes shut and squinches up his face to figure. And Task run a hand over his ear and stare into his glass like the ice cubes goin calculate for him. And Elo just starin at the top of my head like she goin rip the wig off any minute now.

26   "Is your hair braided up under that thing? If so, why don't you take it off? You always did do a neat cornroll."

27   "Uh huh," cause I'm thinkin how she couldn't undo her hair fast enough talking bout cornroll so countrified. None of which was the subject. "How old, I say?"

28   "Sixtee-one or—"

29   "You a damn lie Joe Lee Peoples."

30   "And that's another thing," say Task on the fingers.

31   "You know what you all can kiss," I say, gettin up and brushin the wrinkles out my lap.

32   "Oh, Mama," Elo say, puttin a hand on my shoulder like she hasn't done since she left home and the hand landin light and not sure it supposed to be there. Which hurt me to my heart. Cause this was the child in our happiness fore Mr. Peoples die. And I carried that child strapped to my chest till she was nearly two. We was close is what I'm trying to tell you. Cause it was more me in the child than the others. And even after Task it was the girlchild I covered in the night and wept over for no reason at all less it was she was a chub-chub like me and not very pretty, but a warm child. And how did things get to this, that she can't put a sure hand on me and say Mama we love you and care about you and you entitled to enjoy yourself cause you a good woman?

33   "And then there's Reverend Trent," say Task, glancin from left to right like they hatchin a plot and just now lettin me in on it. "You were suppose to be talkin with him tonight, Mama, about giving us his basement for campaign headquarters and—"

34   "Didn nobody tell me nuthin. If grass roots mean you kept in the dark I can't use it. I really can't. And Reven Trent a fool anyway the way he tore into the widow man up there on Edgecomb cause he wouldn't take in three of them foster

children and the woman not even comfy in the ground yet and the man's mind messed up and—"

35   "Look here," say Task. "What we need is a family conference so we can get all this stuff cleared up and laid out on the table. In the meantime I think we better get back into the other room and tend to business. And in the meantime, Mama, see if you can't get to Reverend Trent and—"

36   "You want me to belly rub with the Reven, that it?"

37   "Oh damn," Elo say and go through the swingin door.

38   "We'll talk about all this at dinner. How's tomorrow night, Joe Lee?" While Joe Lee being self-important I'm wonderin who's doin the cookin and how come no body ax me if I'm free and do I get a corsage and things like that. Then Joe nod that it's O.K. and he go through the swingin door and just a little hubbub come through from the other room. Then Task smile his smile, lookin just like his daddy and he leave. And it just me in this stranger's kitchen, which was a mess I wouldn't never let my kitchen look like. Poison you just to look at the pots. Then the door swing the other way and it's My Man Bovanne standin there sayin Miss Hazel but lookin at the deep fry and then at the steam table, and most surprised when I come up on him from the other direction and take him on out of there. Pass the folks pushin up towards the stage where Nisi and some other people settin and ready to talk, and folks gettin to the last of the sandwiches and the booze fore they settle down in one spot and listen serious. And I'm thinkin bout tellin Bovanne what a lovely long dress Nisi got on and the earrings and her hair piled up in a cone and the people bout to hear how we all gettin screwed and gotta form our own party and everybody there listenin and lookin. But instead I just haul the man on out of there, and Joe Lee and his wife look at me like I'm terrible, but they ain't said boo to the man yet. Cause he blind and old and don't nobody there need him since they grown up and don't need they skates fixed no more.

39   "Where we goin, Miss Hazel?" Him knowin all the time.

40   "First we gonna buy you some dark sunglasses. Then you comin with me to the supermarket so I can pick up tomorrow's dinner, which is goin to be a grand thing proper and you invited. Then we goin to my house."

41   "That be fine. I surely would like to rest my feet." Bein cute, but you got to let men play out they little show, blind or not. So he chat on bout how tired he is and how he appreciate me takin him in hand this way. And I'm thinkin I'll have him change the lock on my door first thing. Then I'll give the man a nice warm bath with jasmine leaves in the water and a little Epsom salt on the sponge to do his back. And then a good rubdown with rose water and olive oil. Then a cup of lemon tea with a taste in it. And a little talcum, some of that fancy stuff Nisi mother sent over last Christmas. And then a massage, a good face massage round the forehead which is the worryin part. Cause you gots to take care of the older folks. And let them know they still needed to run the mimeo machine and keep the spark plugs clean and fix the mailboxes for folks who might help us get the breakfast program goin, and the school for the little kids and the campaign and all. Cause old folks is the nation. That what Nisi was sayin and I mean to do my part.

42   "I imagine you are a very pretty woman, Miss Hazel."

43   "I surely am," I say just like the hussy my daughter always say I was.

THINKING ABOUT THE TEXT

1. Who is the narrator of this story? What specific facts do you learn about her? What can you infer about her?
2. What are the conflicts in this story? In what ways are they typical of most "generation gaps," and in what ways are they unique to this family? Which conflicts do you imagine are related to the time period (1960–1970) in which this short story is set?
3. Ironic situations are those that are contrary to expectation. Discuss the ironic aspects of this story.
4. This story is entertaining, but it also instructs. If this short story were an essay, what might its *thesis* be?

WRITING FROM THE TEXT

1. Write about a time when one of your parents or one of your children embarrassed you. How did you respond? Create the scene so that your reader *sees* your experience. What did you learn?
2. Write an analysis of Hazel Peoples' children that uses facts and specific details from the short story for support.

CONNECTING WITH OTHER TEXTS

1. Research the Black Power movement of the 1960s and 1970s and write a paper describing the characteristics of the movement that are reflected in this story. You might consider these aspects: goals of the movement; characteristics of dress and hair style; language of the movement; the role of church in Black communities; and other characteristics you discover in your research that Bambara shows in her fiction.
2. Read Toni Cade Bambara's short story "The Lesson" and write a character analysis of Sylvia. For a character analysis of Hazel Peoples, see pages 440–442.

TWO KINDS
Amy Tan

The only daughter of Chinese immigrants, American-born Amy Tan (b. 1952) has experienced many of the cross-culture and mother-daughter conflicts that she characterizes in *The Joy Luck Club,* from which "Two Kinds" is taken. Tan's own life is a series of rebellions against her parents' high expectations. They wanted her to be a neurosurgeon and a concert pianist, but against her mother's wishes, Tan changed from a premed to an English major. She describes her assimilation into American life as "costly": "We end up deliberately choosing the American things— hot dogs and apple pie—and ignoring the Chinese offerings." Tan's most recent novel is *The Kitchen God's Wife* (1993), and *The Joy Luck Club* has been made into a feature film.

1   My mother believed you could be anything you wanted to be in America. You could open a restaurant. You could work for the government and get good retirement. You could buy a house with almost no money down. You could become rich. You could become instantly famous.

2   "Of course you can be prodigy, too," my mother told me when I was nine. "You can be best anything. What does Auntie Lindo know? Her daughter, she is only best tricky."

3   America was where all my mother's hopes lay. She had come here in 1949 after losing everything in China: her mother and father, her family home, her first husband, and two daughters, twin baby girls. But she never looked back with regret. There were so many ways for things to get better.

4   We didn't immediately pick the right kind of prodigy. At first my mother thought I could be a Chinese Shirley Temple. We'd watch Shirley's old movies on TV as though they were training films. My mother would poke my arm and say, "*Ni kan*"—You watch. And I would see Shirley tapping her feet, or singing a sailor song, or pursing her lips into a very round O while saying, "Oh my goodness."

5   "*Ni kan,*" said my mother as Shirley's eyes flooded with tears. "You already know how. Don't need talent for crying!"

6   Soon after my mother got this idea about Shirley Temple, she took me to a beauty training school in the Mission district and put me in the hands of a student who could barely hold the scissors without shaking. Instead of getting big fat curls, I emerged with an uneven mass of crinkly black fuzz. My mother dragged me off to the bathroom and tried to wet down my hair.

7   "You look like Negro Chinese," she lamented, as if I had done this on purpose.

8   The instructor of the beauty training school had to lop off these soggy clumps to make my hair even again. "Peter Pan is very popular these days," the instructor assured my mother. I now had hair the length of a boy's, with straight-across bangs that hung at a slant two inches above my eyebrows. I liked the haircut and it made me actually look forward to my future fame.

9   In fact, in the beginning, I was just as excited as my mother, maybe even more so. I pictured this prodigy part of me as many different images, trying each one on for size. I was a dainty ballerina girl standing by the curtains, waiting to hear the right music that would send me floating on my tiptoes. I was like the Christ child lifted out of the straw manger, crying with holy indignity. I was Cinderella stepping from her pumpkin carriage with sparkly cartoon music filling the air.

10   In all of my imaginings, I was filled with a sense that I would soon become *perfect*. My mother and father would adore me. I would be beyond reproach. I would never feel the need to sulk for anything.

11   But sometimes the prodigy in me became impatient. "If you don't hurry up and get me out of here, I'm disappearing for good," it warned. "And then you'll always be nothing."

12   Every night after dinner, my mother and I would sit at the Formica kitchen table. She would present new tests, taking her examples from stories of amazing children she had read in *Ripley's Believe It or Not,* or *Good Housekeeping, Reader's Digest,* and a dozen other magazines she kept in a pile in our bathroom. My mother got these magazines from people whose houses she cleaned. And since she cleaned many houses each week, we had a great assortment. She would look through them all, searching for stories about remarkable children.

13   The first night she brought out a story about a three-year-old boy who knew the capitals of all the states and even most of the European countries. A teacher was quoted as saying the little boy could also pronounce the names of the foreign cities correctly.

14   "What's the capital of Finland?" my mother asked me, looking at the magazine story.

15   All I knew was the capital of California, because Sacramento was the name of the street we lived on in Chinatown. "Nairobi!" I guessed, saying the most foreign word I could think of. She checked to see if that was possibly one way to pronounce "Helsinki" before showing me the answer.

16   The tests got harder—multiplying numbers in my head, finding the queen of hearts in a deck of cards, trying to stand on my head without using my hands, predicting the daily temperatures in Los Angeles, New York, and London.

17   One night I had to look at a page from the Bible for three minutes and then report everything I could remember. "Now Jehoshaphat had riches and honor in abundance and . . . that's all I remember, Ma," I said.

18   And after seeing my mother's disappointed face once again, something inside of me began to die. I hated the tests, the raised hopes and failed expectations. Before going to bed that night, I looked in the mirror above the bathroom sink and when I saw only my face staring back—and that it would always be this ordinary face—I began to cry. Such a sad, ugly girl! I made high-pitched noises like a crazed animal, trying to scratch out the face in the mirror.

19   And then I saw what seemed to be the prodigy side of me—because I had never seen that face before. I looked at my reflection, blinking so I could see more clearly. The girl staring back at me was angry, powerful. This girl and I

were the same. I had new thoughts, willful thoughts, or rather thoughts filled with lots of won'ts. I won't let her change me, I promised myself. I won't be what I'm not.

20   So now on nights when my mother presented her tests, I performed listlessly, my head propped on one arm. I pretended to be bored. And I was. I got so bored I started counting the bellows of the foghorns out on the bay while my mother drilled me in other areas. The sound was comforting and reminded me of the cow jumping over the moon. And the next day, I played a game with myself, seeing if my mother would give up on me before eight bellows. After a while I usually counted only one, maybe two bellows at most. At last she was beginning to give up hope.

21   Two or three months had gone by without any mention of my being a prodigy again. And then one day my mother was watching *The Ed Sullivan Show* on TV. The TV was old and the sound kept shorting out. Every time my mother got halfway up from the sofa to adjust the set, the sound would go back on and Ed would be talking. As soon as she sat down, Ed would go silent again. She got up, the TV broke into loud piano music. She sat down. Silence. Up and down, back and forth, quiet and loud. It was like a stiff embraceless dance between her and the TV set. Finally she stood by the set with her hand on the sound dial.

22   She seemed entranced by the music, a little frenzied piano piece with this mesmerizing quality, sort of quick passages and then teasing lilting ones before it returned to the quick playful parts.

23   "*Ni kan,*" my mother said, calling me over with hurried hand gestures. "Look here."

24   I could see why my mother was fascinated by the music. It was being pounded out by a little Chinese girl, about nine years old, with a Peter Pan haircut. The girl had the sauciness of a Shirley Temple. She was proudly modest like a proper Chinese child. And she also did this fancy sweep of a curtsy, so that the fluffy skirt of her white dress cascaded slowly to the floor like the petals of a large carnation.

25   In spite of these warning signs, I wasn't worried. Our family had no piano and we couldn't afford to buy one, let alone reams of sheet music and piano lessons. So I could be generous in my comments when my mother bad-mouthed the little girl on TV.

26   "Play note right, but doesn't sound good! No singing sound," complained my mother.

27   "What are you picking on her for?" I said carelessly. "She's pretty good. Maybe she's not the best, but she's trying hard." I knew almost immediately I would be sorry I said that.

28   "Just like you," she said. "Not the best. Because you not trying." She gave a little huff as she let go of the sound dial and sat down on the sofa.

29   The little Chinese girl sat down also to play an encore of "Anitra's Dance" by Grieg. I remember the song, because later on I had to learn how to play it.

30   Three days after watching *The Ed Sullivan Show,* my mother told me what my schedule would be for piano lessons and piano practice. She had talked to Mr.

Chong, who lived on the first floor of our apartment building. Mr. Chong was a retired piano teacher and my mother had traded housecleaning services for weekly lessons and a piano for me to practice on every day, two hours a day, from four until six.

31   When my mother told me this, I felt as though I had been sent to hell. I whined and then kicked my foot a little when I couldn't stand it anymore.

32   "Why don't you like me the way I am? I'm *not* a genius! I can't play the piano. And even if I could, I wouldn't go on TV if you paid me a million dollars!" I cried.

33   My mother slapped me. "Who ask you be genius?" she shouted. "Only ask you be your best. For you sake. You think I want you be genius? Hnnh! What for! Who ask you!"

34   "So ungrateful," I heard her mutter in Chinese. "If she had as much talent as she has temper, she would be famous now."

35   Mr. Chong, whom I secretly nicknamed Old Chong, was very strange, always tapping his fingers to the silent music of an invisible orchestra. He looked ancient in my eyes. He had lost most of the hair on top of his head and he wore thick glasses and had eyes that always looked tired and sleepy. But he must have been younger than I thought, since he lived with his mother and was not yet married.

36   I met Old Lady Chong once and that was enough. She had this peculiar smell like a baby that had done something in its pants. And her fingers felt like a dead person's, like an old peach I once found in the back of the refrigerator; the skin just slid off the meat when I picked it up.

37   I soon found out why Old Chong had retired from teaching piano. He was deaf. "Like Beethoven!" he shouted to me. "We're both listening only in our head!" And he would start to conduct his frantic silent sonatas.

38   Our lessons went like this. He would open the book and point to different things, explaining their purpose: "Key! Treble! Bass! No sharps or flats! So this is C major! Listen now and play after me!"

39   And then he would play the C scale a few times, a simple chord, and then, as if inspired by an old, unreachable itch, he gradually added more notes and running trills and a pounding bass until the music was really something quite grand.

40   I would play after him, the simple scale, the simple chord, and then I just played some nonsense that sounded like a cat running up and down on top of garbage cans. Old Chong smiled and applauded and then said, "Very good! But now you must learn to keep time!"

41   So that's how I discovered that Old Chong's eyes were too slow to keep up with the wrong notes I was playing. He went through the motions in half-time. To help me keep rhythm, he stood behind me, pushing down on my right shoulder for every beat. He balanced pennies on top of my wrists so I would keep them still as I slowly played scales and arpeggios. He had me curve my hand around an apple and keep that shape when playing chords. He marched stiffly to show me how to make each finger dance up and down, staccato like an obedient little soldier.

42   He taught me all these things, and that was how I also learned I could be lazy and get away with mistakes, lots of mistakes. If I hit the wrong notes because I

hadn't practiced enough, I never corrected myself. I just kept playing in rhythm. And Old Chong kept conducting his own private reverie.

43   So maybe I never really gave myself a fair chance. I did pick up the basics pretty quickly, and I might have become a good pianist at that young age. But I was so determined not to try, not to be anybody different that I learned to play only the most ear-splitting preludes, the most discordant hymns.

44   Over the next year, I practiced like this, dutifully in my own way. And then one day I heard my mother and her friend Lindo Jong both talking in a loud bragging tone of voice so others could hear. It was after church, and I was leaning against the brick wall wearing a dress with stiff white petticoats. Auntie Lindo's daughter, Waverly, who was about my age, was standing farther down the wall about five feet away. We had grown up together and shared all the closeness of two sisters squabbling over crayons and dolls. In other words, for the most part, we hated each other. I thought she was snotty. Waverly Jong had gained a certain amount of fame as "Chinatown's Littlest Chinese Chess Champion."

45   "She bring home too many trophy," lamented Auntie Lindo that Sunday. "All day she play chess. All day I have no time do nothing but dust off her winnings." She threw a scolding look at Waverly, who pretended not to see her.

46   "You lucky you don't have this problem," said Auntie Lindo with a sigh to my mother.

47   And my mother squared her shoulders and bragged: "Our problem worser than yours. If we ask Jing-mei wash dish, she hear nothing but music. It's like you can't stop this natural talent."

48   And right then, I was determined to put a stop to her foolish pride.

49   A few weeks later, Old Chong and my mother conspired to have me play in a talent show which would be held in the church hall. By then, my parents had saved up enough to buy me a secondhand piano, a black Wurlitzer spinet with a scarred bench. It was the showpiece of our living room.

50   For the talent show, I was to play a piece called "Pleading Child" from Schumann's *Scenes from Childhood.* It was a simple, moody piece that sounded more difficult than it was. I was supposed to memorize the whole thing, playing the repeat parts twice to make the piece sound longer. But I dawdled over it, playing a few bars and then cheating, looking up to see what notes followed. I never really listened to what I was playing. I daydreamed about being somewhere else, about being someone else.

51   The part I liked to practice best was the fancy curtsy: right foot out, touch the rose on the carpet with a pointed foot, sweep to the side, left leg bends, look up and smile.

52   My parents invited all the couples from the Joy Luck Club to witness my debut. Auntie Lindo and Uncle Tin were there. Waverly and her two older brothers had also come. The first two rows were filled with children both younger and older than I was. The littlest ones got to go first. They recited simple nursery rhymes, squawked out tunes on miniature violins, twirled Hula Hoops, pranced in pink ballet tutus, and when they bowed or curtsied, the audience would sigh in unison, "Awww," and then clap enthusiastically.

53   When my turn came, I was very confident. I remember my childish excitement. It was as if I knew, without a doubt, that the prodigy side of me really did exist. I had no fear whatsoever, no nervousness. I remember thinking to myself, This is it! This is it! I looked out over the audience, at my mother's blank face, my father's yawn, Auntie Lindo's stiff-lipped smile, Waverly's sulky expression. I had on a white dress layered with sheets of lace, and a pink bow in my Peter Pan haircut. As I sat down I envisioned people jumping to their feet and Ed Sullivan rushing up to introduce me to everyone on TV.

54   And I started to play. It was so beautiful. I was so caught up in how lovely I looked that at first I didn't worry how I would sound: So it was a surprise to me when I hit the first wrong note and I realized something didn't sound quite right. And then I hit another and another followed that. A chill started at the top of my head and began to trickle down. Yet I couldn't stop playing, as though my hands were bewitched. I kept thinking my fingers would adjust themselves back, like a train switching to the right track. I played this strange jumble through two repeats, the sour notes staying with me all the way to the end.

55   When I stood up, I discovered my legs were shaking. Maybe I had just been nervous and the audience, like Old Chong, had seen me go through the right motions and had not heard anything wrong at all. I swept my right foot out, went down on my knee, looked up and smiled. The room was quiet, except for Old Chong, who was beaming and shouting, "Bravo! Bravo! Well done!" But then I saw my mother's face, her stricken face. The audience clapped weakly, and as I walked back to my chair, with my whole face quivering as I tried not to cry, I heard a little boy whisper loudly to his mother, "That was awful," and the mother whispered back, "Well, she certainly tried."

56   And now I realized how many people were in the audience, the whole world it seemed. I was aware of eyes burning into my back. I felt the shame of my mother and father as they sat stiffly throughout the rest of the show.

57   We could have escaped during intermission. Pride and some strange sense of honor must have anchored my parents to their chairs. And so we watched it all: the eighteen-year-old boy with a fake mustache who did a magic show and juggled flaming hoops while riding a unicycle. The breasted girl with white makeup who sang from *Madama Butterfly* and got honorable mention. And the eleven-year-old boy who won first prize playing a tricky violin song that sounded like a busy bee.

58   After the show, the Hsus, the Jongs, and the St. Clairs from the Joy Luck Club came up to my mother and father.

59   "Lots of talented kids," Auntie Lindo said vaguely, smiling broadly.

60   "That was somethin' else," said my father, and I wondered if he was referring to me in a humorous way, or whether he even remembered what I had done.

61   Waverly looked at me and shrugged her shoulders. "You aren't a genius like me," she said matter-of-factly. And if I hadn't felt so bad, I would have pulled her braids and punched her stomach.

62.   But my mother's expression was what devastated me: a quiet, blank look that said she had lost everything. I felt the same way, and it seemed as if everybody were now coming up, like gawkers at the scene of an accident, to see what parts were

actually missing. When we got on the bus to go home, my father was humming the busy-bee tune and my mother was silent. I kept thinking she wanted to wait until we got home before shouting at me. But when my father unlocked the door to our apartment, my mother walked in and then went to the back, into the bedroom. No accusations. No blame. And in a way, I felt disappointed. I had been waiting for her to start shouting, so I could shout back and cry and blame her for all my misery.

63   I assumed my talent-show fiasco meant I never had to play the piano again. But two days later, after school, my mother came out of the kitchen and saw me watching TV.

64   "Four clock," she reminded me as if it were any other day. I was stunned, as though she were asking me to go through the talent-show torture again. I wedged myself more tightly in front of the TV.

65   "Turn off TV," she called from the kitchen five minutes later.

66   I didn't budge. And then I decided. I didn't have to do what my mother said anymore. I wasn't her slave. This wasn't China. I had listened to her before and look what happened. She was the stupid one.

67   She came out from the kitchen and stood in the arched entryway of the living room. "Four clock," she said once again, louder.

68   "I'm not going to play anymore," I said nonchalantly. "Why should I? I'm not a genius."

69   She walked over and stood in front of the TV. I saw her chest was heaving up and down in an angry way.

70   "No!" I said, and I now felt stronger, as if my true self had finally emerged. So this was what had been inside me all along.

71   "No! I won't!" I screamed.

72   She yanked me by the arm, pulled me off the floor, snapped off the TV. She was frighteningly strong, half pulling, half carrying me toward the piano as I kicked the throw rugs under my feet. She lifted me up and onto the hard bench. I was sobbing by now, looking at her bitterly. Her chest was heaving even more and her mouth was open, smiling crazily as if she were pleased I was crying.

73   "You want me to be someone that I'm not!" I sobbed. "I'll never be the kind of daughter you want me to be!"

74   "Only two kinds of daughters," she shouted in Chinese. "Those who are obedient and those who follow their own mind! Only one kind of daughter can live in this house. Obedient daughter!"

75   "Then I wish I wasn't your daughter. I wish you weren't my mother," I shouted. As I said these things I got scared. It felt like worms and toads and slimy things crawling out of my chest, but it also felt good, as if this awful side of me had surfaced, at last.

76   "Too late change this," said my mother shrilly.

77   And I could sense her anger rising to its breaking point. I wanted to see it spill over. And that's when I remembered the babies she had lost in China, the ones we never talked about. "Then I wish I'd never been born!" I shouted. "I wish I were dead! Like them."

78   It was as if I had said the magic words. Alakazam!—and her face went blank, her mouth closed, her arms went slack, and she backed out of the room, stunned, as if she were blowing away like a small brown leaf, thin, brittle, lifeless.

79   It was not the only disappointment my mother felt in me. In the years that followed, I failed her so many times, each time asserting my own will, my right to fall short of expectations. I didn't get straight As. I didn't become class president. I didn't get into Stanford. I dropped out of college.

80   For unlike my mother, I did not believe I could be anything I wanted to be. I could only be me.

81   And for all those years, we never talked about the disaster at the recital or my terrible accusations afterward at the piano bench. All that remained unchecked, like a betrayal that was now unspeakable. So I never found a way to ask her why she had hoped for something so large that failure was inevitable.

82   And even worse, I never asked her what frightened me the most: Why had she given up hope?

83   For after our struggle at the piano, she never mentioned my playing again. The lessons stopped. The lid to the piano was closed, shutting out the dust, my misery, and her dreams.

84   So she surprised me. A few years ago, she offered to give me the piano, for my thirtieth birthday. I had not played in all those years. I saw the offer as a sign of forgiveness, a tremendous burden removed.

85   "Are you sure?" I asked shyly. "I mean, won't you and Dad miss it?"

86   "No, this your piano," she said firmly. "Always your piano. You only one can play."

87   "Well, I probably can't play anymore," I said. "It's been years."

88   "You pick up fast," said my mother, as if she knew this was certain. "You have natural talent. You could been genius if you want to."

89   "No I couldn't."

90   "You just not trying," said my mother. And she was neither angry nor sad. She said it as if to announce a fact that could never be disproved. "Take it," she said.

91   But I didn't at first. It was enough that she had offered it to me. And after that, every time I saw it in my parents' living room, standing in front of the bay windows, it made me feel proud, as if it were a shiny trophy I had won back.

92   Last week I sent a tuner over to my parents' apartment and had the piano reconditioned, for purely sentimental reasons. My mother had died a few months before and I had been getting things in order for my father, a little bit at a time. I put the jewelry in special silk pouches. The sweaters she had knitted in yellow, pink, bright orange—all the colors I hated—I put those in moth-proof boxes. I found some old Chinese silk dresses, the kind with little slits up the sides. I rubbed the old silk against my skin, then wrapped them in tissue and decided to take them home with me.

93   After I had the piano tuned, I opened the lid and touched the keys. It sounded even richer than I remembered. Really, it was a very good piano. Inside the bench

were the same exercise notes with handwritten scales, the same secondhand music books with their covers held together with yellow tape.

94   I opened up the Schumann book to the dark little piece I had played at the recital. It was on the left-hand side of the page, "Pleading Child." It looked more difficult than I remembered. I played a few bars, surprised at how easily the notes came back to me.

95   And for the first time, or so it seemed, I noticed the piece on the right-hand side. It was called "Perfectly Contented." I tried to play this one as well. It had a lighter melody but the same flowing rhythm and turned out to be quite easy. "Pleading Child" was shorter but slower; "Perfectly Contented" was longer but faster. And after I played them both a few times, I realized they were two halves of the same song.

THINKING ABOUT THE TEXT

1. What are the central conflicts in this short story? In what ways are the conflicts inevitable, between-generations conflicts? In what ways might the conflicts be related to the Chinese culture? In what ways are the conflicts unique to this family? To prepare your response, list the conflicts.

2. What are the personality traits of Jing-mei Woo, the narrator of this story? What are the traits of her mother? In what ways are the mother and daughter "two kinds"?

3. What is your response to Mrs. Woo's expectations for her daughter? What do you assume to be the motivation for her goal? What are her attempts to achieve her goal?

4. Although the story is funny, it is ultimately sad because of its revelations about parent-child relationships. What are the consequences of imposing high expectations on a child?

5. How is Amy Tan using the titles of the piano pieces that the adult Jing-mei finds in her old piano book?

WRITING FROM THE TEXT

1. Write an essay arguing that an obsessive parent can damage a child. Write from an assertion that cites the specific "damage" you will discuss, and use Amy Tan's story for support.

2. Compare your experience as a child of a parent with high expectations to that of Jing-mei in "Two Kinds."

3. Contrast your experience as a child of a reasonable or indifferent parent with the experience of Jing-mei in "Two Kinds." What conclusions can you draw?

CONNECTING WITH OTHER TEXTS

1. Read interviews with Amy Tan to discover which aspects of her own life are used in "Two Kinds." Write a paper that discusses the autobiographical aspects in this story.

2. In what ways are the pressures described in David Haldane's essay "Asian Girls: A Cultural Tug of War" (p. 152) reflected in Tan's fiction? Use Haldane's research and Tan's short story to write an analysis of the conflicts facing young Asian women.

3. Read the following stories from *The Joy Luck Club:* "Rules of the Game," "Four Directions," and "Best Quality." What do these short stories reveal about the mother-daughter relationship? What do the stories reveal about how some women relate to each other?

4. In what ways are the feelings of Sherwood Anderson, expressed in "Discovery of a Father" (p. 6), analogous to the feelings expressed by Tan's character in "Two Kinds"? Focus your essay on the comparisons that you discover.

THE "PERFECT" MISCONCEPTION
Mary Miller

Having started college nearly 20 years after she graduated from high school, Mary Miller (b. 1951) certainly knows what it is like to live between worlds. Enrolled in classes with students who have recently graduated from high school, she had classmates who affectionately referred to her as "Mom" and faculty who treated her more as a peer. While Mary studied in college, she was raising her son Brian, attending all his games and school activities, caring for her ill parents, and assisting her husband with their aerospace-parts business. Because of her numerous responsibilities, Mary has had to postpone completing her college career. She continues to write poetry and essays and to live "between worlds" with her son (the product of her first, racially mixed marriage) and with her second husband, who has supported and encouraged her return to school. She wrote the following narrative for her freshman composition class in 1989 during her second semester at El Camino College.

1   A few years ago my eloquent mother told me the facts about "motherhood." She described it as a befuddled state of mind consisting of joy, pride, guilt, and fear all mixed together, creating chaos. She also compared it to a baffling yet challenging card game. "Mary dear," she stated thoughtfully, "it's just a game of chance, and if you're lucky at playing your hand, the positives just might out-

weigh the negatives. You never know." This was the first time I heard my "perfect" mother speak in uncertain terms, and I feared it was the start of senile dementia. This could not be the same confident, self-assured woman who raised me—the woman I admired so.

2   I suspect I wasn't what the psychologists now term an "easy child," although my family was loving and caring. Just because I demanded straight answers, disappeared on wash days, and refused to go to confession certainly didn't label me as difficult. No wonder Mom relished telling me stories of her youth, for there were important lessons to be learned from her examples. At the meager age of six, she picked apples all by herself in their South Dakota orchard, selling them for a nice profit to the townfolk. This taught responsibility. At age seven she could wring a chicken's neck, hack it up in the proper pieces, and cook it for dinner. Discipline and control were the lessons here. Naturally, by the time she was eight, she could design her own doll clothes and sew with ease. This taught me how terribly inept I was!

3   After all, there were no apple orchards or chickens in the city for me, and sewing held no appeal for this nine-year-old confirmed tomboy. Her tales were entertaining, for the most part, because she had a natural flair for storytelling, but often they left me feeling puzzled. My life seemed dull and meaningless compared to hers, and I couldn't imagine what important stories I would have to pass on to my own children someday. Disappointing ones, for sure.

4   My only son, Brian, is as typical and unassuming as they come. Like most ten-year-old boys, he barely tolerates homework, plays Nintendo with ease, and cleans his room bi-annually, whether it needs it or not. There are no apple trees or chickens in his life, but unlike me, it doesn't seem to bother him. I've noticed a new, serious side emerging, and recently he expressed concern about his classmates. "Why are the kids so mean to each other? The big dudes pick on the little guys, and everybody calls each other names—especially to Dave. They call him 'Dorky Dave.' It's not his fault he can't walk right!"

5   Wow, this was a part of him I hadn't witnessed before, and it sparked an old memory of my own. Perhaps I had a relevant story to tell to carry on in Mom's tradition! Knowing this was my big chance, I proceeded excitedly with my tale of Weird Harold.

6   "I was in the third grade at Prospect Heights School in Hermosa. They tore the school down some years later, but the memories survived the destruction. Anyway, the kids were a normal mixture of prissies, bullies, and underdogs. I made the decision to save the world's oppressed when Caroline and her obnoxious friends chased poor Harold home, taunting 'Weird Harold, Weird Harold with the flat head.' Something snapped in me, and somehow I rescued Harold and brought him home for cookies and milk."

7   I paused just long enough to make sure Brian was still listening, and then I continued. "Harold always looked like a lost puppy. Actually, he did have a flat head which was accentuated by a short, uneven crew-cut. Every day he wore the same old, blue-faded Pendleton, carrying the weight of the world on his sunken shoulders. When he gave in to a rare smile, he resembled the Cheshire Cat, and I had to

smile too. I would make him play Zorro with me, and he'd even let me win the swordfights! He became my best friend and purpose in life. I'm glad I stuck up for the underdog! Harold was all right!"

8   Realizing how animated I'd become in my rendition, I stopped to observe Brian staring at me as if I were some alien. "Gee, Mom," he said flatly, "too bad they tore down the school." Now it was my turn to stare. So . . . my point was missed completely. So . . . I'm ineffective as a storyteller and a mother. So . . . so what!

9   A few uneventful weeks passed in which my concerns mounted. I baked more cookies and brownies than I had in my entire lifetime, but it didn't seem to help. One dreary day after school, Brian arrived home with an unfamiliar figure by his side. "Hi, Mom. This is my new friend, Dave. How about some cookies and milk?" As they passed me in the kitchen, I noticed Dave's pronounced limp and downtrodden appearance. Suddenly I felt suspended and detached from this scene, as if I were just an observer, unable to participate. Brian brought me back with a loving pat on the rear and a rather feeble attempt at a wink. As I slowly poured their milk, my eyes filled with unexpected tears.

10   It's so odd how the smallest events can cause the greatest realizations. I understood that afternoon what my mother was trying to express a few years back. Maybe her uncertainty was always there, even though I didn't perceive it. Maybe she never was dealt the "perfect" hand, but just played it the best she could. And maybe, just maybe, my troubling obsession with apple trees and chickens will leave me forever.

THINKING ABOUT THE TEXT

1. Discuss Miller's use of a definition to open her essay. Why is it effective? How does this particular definition contribute to the tone of the narrative?

2. Describe the narrator's mother and the stories she tells. How does she make her daughter feel so "inept"?

3. Compare and contrast the narrator and her son, Brian. How are they different? What do they have in common?

4. Examine Miller's use of effective repetition throughout. (For example, apple orchards and chickens, the two parallel "outcasts," and the card-game metaphor that links the introduction and conclusion.) Discuss how such repetitions add unity to the essay.

5. What is Miller's thesis, and why does she place it where she does?

WRITING FROM THE TEXT

1. After reviewing narrative (pp. 382–389), write an essay analyzing Miller's narrative techniques and strategies that contribute to the humor and unity of this story.

2. Write an essay focusing on an anecdote once told to you by an adult. Did it have the effect that the storyteller intended? (Did it continue to haunt you? Inspire you? Misdirect you?) Try to integrate the anecdote within a central scene as Miller does.

3. Focusing on this narrative and on your own experiences, argue that parents' "stories" and lessons can sometimes be a real burden on their children and make them feel "inept" or overwhelmed.

CONNECTING WITH OTHER TEXTS

1. Examine several other stories, essays, or poems in this chapter and use details from each to support your own "definition" of motherhood or fatherhood. Focus your definition on a sharp thesis.

2. Analyze the role of parent as storyteller in this essay and in "Discovery of a Father" (p. 6). Write an essay analyzing what these narratives suggest about the potential value and risk when parents impose such stories on their children.

THE WRITER
Richard Wilbur

Educated at Amherst and Harvard, Richard Wilbur (b. 1921) has won numerous prizes for his poetry, and he was poet laureate of the United States from 1987 to 1988. Wilbur wrote editorials and stories for his college newspaper, but he attributes his earnest endeavors in poetry to his having served in World War II and the necessity to create order in his war-disordered life. In addition to his poetry, Wilbur's translations of Molière have been used on the American stage, and he was one of the lyricists for Leonard Bernstein's comic opera based on Voltaire's *Candide*. The poem printed here is from Wilbur's 1971 collection *The Mind-Reader*.

> *In her room at the prow of the house*
> *Where light breaks, and the windows are tossed with linden,*
> *My daughter is writing a story.*
>
> *I pause in the stairwell, hearing*
> *From her shut door a commotion of typewriter-keys*   5
> *Like a chain hauled over a gunwale.*
>
> *Young as she is, the stuff*
> *Of her life is a great cargo, and some of it heavy:*
> *I wish her a lucky passage.*

But now it is she who pauses,   10
As if to reject my thought and its easy figure.
A stillness greatens, in which

The whole house seems to be thinking,
And then she is at it again with a bunched clamor
Of strokes, and again is silent.   15

I remember the dazed starling
Which was trapped in that very room, two years ago;
How we stole in, lifted a sash

And retreated, not to affright it;
And how for a helpless hour, through the crack of the door,   20
We watched the sleek, wild, dark

And iridescent creature
Batter against the brilliance, drop like a glove
To the hard floor, or the desk-top,

And wait then, humped and bloody,   25
For the wits to try it again; and how our spirits
Rose when, suddenly sure,

It lifted off from a chair-back,
Beating a smooth course for the right window
And clearing the sill of the world.   30

It is always a matter, my darling,
Of life or death, as I had forgotten. I wish
What I wished you before, but harder.

THINKING ABOUT THE TEXT

1. Wilbur initially compares the daughter's writing to a sea voyage. List all images that relate to a voyage and explain each. Why does the narrator ultimately reject this "easy figure"?

2. How does the predicament of the trapped starling relate to the writer? What does this suggest about the writing process?

3. Compare the family's reaction to the starling and the father's response to his daughter's writing. Specify phrases that capture the frustration of those who long to help but cannot. Why does he wish even harder for her at the end?

WRITING FROM THE TEXT

1. Focusing on the image of "passage" and all related terms, analyze Wilbur's perception of the writer as "trapped." How does a writer get freed?

2. Write an essay analyzing the narrative point of view here. Why might Wilbur have used the father's perspective rather than the daughter's? How does this relate to the family's experience with the starling?

3. Write an essay that dramatizes specific times in your life when one of your parents might have viewed you from a perspective similar to Wilbur's. Or, as a parent, write about a time when you were concerned about your own child. Help the reader picture the incident and share your narrator's concern.

CONNECTING WITH OTHER TEXTS

1. Compare Wilbur's watchful but restrained parenting with that of the mother in "Two Kinds" (p. 49), the father in "Discovery of a Father" (p. 6), and the parents in "Where Are You Going, Where Have You Been?" (p. 124). Using details from these readings, write an essay explaining your view of parents' roles in their teenagers' lives.

2. Read the diaries, letters, or biographies of Virginia Woolf, Sylvia Plath, or Anne Sexton. Relate their experiences to Wilbur's sense of the "life and death" struggles inherent in the act of writing.

THE GIRLS' ROOM
Laura Cunningham

The author of three novels, two plays, and periodical articles, Laura Cunningham (b. 1947) has stated that she is a typical writer because she is "atypical." She has said, "I am of Jewish-Southern Baptist descent, was orphaned at age eight, and raised by two unmarried uncles (both writers). I'm a third-generation author: my grandparents also wrote stories and books. . . . I didn't know there was anything else to be. Had I known, I would have been a ballerina." The narrative included here, from the *New York Times,* September 10, 1981, has recognizable autobiographical influences.

1   When I heard she was coming to stay with us I was pleased. At age eight I thought of "grandmother" as a generic brand. My friends had grandmothers who seemed permanently bent over cookie racks. They were a source of constant treats and sweets. They were pinchers of cheeks, huggers and kissers. My own grandmother had always lived in a distant state; I had no memory of her when she decided to join the household recently established for me by my two uncles.

2   But with the example of my friends' grandmothers before me, I could hardly wait to have a grandmother of my own—and the cookies would be nice too. For while my uncles provided a cuisine that ranged from tuna croquettes to Swedish meatballs, they showed no signs of baking anything more elegant than a potato.

3   My main concern on the day of my grandmother's arrival was: How soon would she start the cookies? I remember her arrival, my uncles flanking her as they walked down the apartment corridor. She wore a hat, a tailored navy blue suit, an ermine stole. She held, tucked under her arm, the purple leather folder that contained her work in progress, a manuscript entitled "Philosophy for Women." She was preceded by her custom-made white trunk packed with purses, necklaces, earrings, dresses and more purple-inked pages that stress "the spiritual above the material."

4   She was small—at 5 feet 1 inch not much taller than I was—thin and straight, with a pug nose, one brown eye (the good eye) and one blue eye (the bad eye, frosted by cataracts). Her name was "Esther in Hebrew, Edna in English, and Etka in Russian." She preferred the Russian, referring to herself as "Etka from Minsk." It was not at once apparent that she was deaf in her left ear (the bad ear) but could hear with the right (the good ear). Because her good ear happened to be on the opposite side from the good eye, anyone who spoke to her had to run around her in circles, or sway to and fro, if eye contact and audibility were to be achieved simultaneously.

5   Etka from Minsk had arrived not directly from Minsk, as the black-eyed ermine stole seemed to suggest, but after many moves. She entered with the draft of family scandal at her back, blown out of her daughter's home after assaults upon her dignity. She held the evidence: an empty-socketed peacock pin. My cousin, an eleven-year-old boy, had surgically plucked out the rhinestone eyes. She could not be expected to stay where such acts occurred. She had to be among "human beings," among "real people" who could understand. We seemed to understand. We—my two uncles and I—encircled her, studied her vandalized peacock pin and vowed that such things would never happen with "us."

6   She patted my head—a good sign—and asked me to sing the Israeli national anthem. I did, and she handed me a dollar. My uncles went off to their jobs, leaving me alone with my grandmother for the first time. I looked at her, expecting her to start rolling out the cookie dough. Instead she suggested: "Now maybe you could fix me some lunch?"

7   It wasn't supposed to be this way, I thought, as I took her order: "toasted cheese and a sliced orange." Neither was she supposed to share my pink and orange bedroom, but she did. The bedroom soon exhibited a dual character—stuffed animals on one side, a hospital bed on the other. Within the household this chamber was soon referred to as "the girls' room." The name, given by Uncle Abe, who saw no incongruity, only the affinity of sex, turned out to be apt, for what went on in the girls' room could easily have been labeled sibling rivalry if she had not been eighty and I eight. I soon found that I had acquired not a traditional grandmother but an aged kid sister.

8   The theft and rivalry began within days. My grandmother had given me her most cherished possession, a violet beaded bag. In return I gave her my heart-shaped "ivory" pin and matching earrings. That night she stole back the purse but insisted on keeping the pin and earrings. I turned to my uncles for mediation and ran up against unforeseen resistance. They thought my grandmother should keep the beaded bag; they didn't want to upset her.

9   I burned at the injustice of it and felt the heat of an uncomfortable truth: where I once had my uncles' undivided indulgence, they were now split as my grandmother and I vied for their attention. The household, formerly geared to my little-girl needs, was rearranged to accommodate hers. I suffered serious affronts—my grandmother, in a fit of frugality, scissored all the household blankets, including what a psychiatrist would have dubbed my "security" blanket, in half. "Now," she said, her good eye gleaming, "we have twice as many." I lay under my narrow slice of blanket and stared hopelessly up at the ceiling. I thought evilly of ways of getting my grandmother out of the apartment.

10   Matters worsened, as more and more of my trinkets disappeared. One afternoon I came home from school to find her squeezed into my unbuttoned favorite blouse. Rouged and beribboned, she insisted that the size 3 blouse was hers. Meanwhile, I was forced to adapt to her idiosyncrasies: she covered everything black—from the dog to the telephone—with white doilies. She left saucers balanced on top of glasses. She sang nonstop. She tried to lock my dog out of the apartment.

11   The word that explained her behavior was "arteriosclerosis." She had forgotten so much that sometimes she would greet me with "You look familiar." At other times she'd ask, "What hotel is this?" My answer, shouted in her good ear, was: "We're not in a hotel! This is our apartment!" The response would be a hoot of laughter: "Then why are we in the ballroom?"

12   Finally we fought: arm-to-arm combat. I was shocked at her grip, steely as the bars that locked her into bed at night. Her good eye burned into mine and she said, "I'll tell." And she did. For the first time I was scolded. She had turned their love to disapproval, I thought, and how it chafed.

13   Eventually our rivalry mellowed into conspiracy. Within months we found we had uses for each other. I provided the lunches and secret, forbidden ice cream sundaes. She rewarded me with cold cash. She continued to take my clothes; I charged her competitive prices. I hated school; she paid me not to go. When I came home for lunch I usually stayed.

14   Our household endured the status quo for eight years: my uncles, my grandmother and I. Within the foursome rivalries and alliances shifted. I became my grandmother's friend and she became mine. We were the source of all the family comedy. When she said she wanted a college diploma we gave her one—with tinfoil stars and a "magna magna summa summa cum laude" inscription. We sang and performed skits. We talcum-powdered hair and wearing one of her old dresses, I would appear as her "long-lost friend." We had other themes, including a pen pal, "The Professor."

15   Of course, living with an elderly person had its raw aspects. When she was ill our girls' room took on the stark aura of a geriatrics ward. I imagined, to my shame, that neighbors could stare in through curtainless windows as I tended to my grandmother's most personal needs.

16   Yet, in these times of age segregation, with grandmothers sent off to impersonal places, I wonder if the love and the comedy weren't worth the intermittent difficulties? Certainly I learned what it might be to become old. And I took as much comfort as my grandmother did in a nightly exchange of Russian endearments— "Ya tebya lyublyu," "Ya tebya tozhe lyublyu—" "I love you," "I love you, too."

17   If I sold my grandmother blouses and baubles, maybe she gave me the truth in exchange. Once, when we were alone in the girls' room, she turned to me, suddenly lucid, her good eye as bright as it would ever be—a look I somehow recognized as her "real" gaze—and said, "My life passes like a dream."

THINKING ABOUT THE TEXT

1. Why is the granddaughter initially looking forward to her grandmother's arrival, and why is she soon disappointed?

2. List all the details Cunningham includes to bring "Etka from Minsk" to life for us. Working from this list, write a sharp assertion about her that could function as your thesis for a character analysis of the grandmother.

3. Although the granddaughter is eight and the grandmother is eighty, in what ways does their relationship resemble that of siblings?

4. How do these two roommates develop a mutual bond? What is the value of this intimacy for both of them?

WRITING FROM THE TEXT

1. Analyze how Cunningham manages to go beyond the "generic brand" of grandmother to present a character who is fresh and memorable and a relationship that enriches both lives. The list you compiled for question 2 above may help here.

2. Focusing on your own close relationship with an elderly person, help us to see an unexpected side to this person (and perhaps to yourself in that relationship). Include colorful details as Cunningham does.

3. Interview people you know who are grandparents of some of your friends. Argue that they are—or are not—happy with their present lives, whether they are living in a private home or an institution. Focus your paper on one or two qualities of the life-style of your own over-70 subjects.

CONNECTING WITH OTHER TEXTS

1. Read "Your Place Is Empty" (p. 28) and write a paper analyzing how Etka from Minsk avoids the estrangement and pain that Mrs. Ardavi experiences.

2. Research a particular program available for the elderly in your local community: a senior citizens' center, available discounts, "meals on wheels," or a program at a park or recreation center. Then write a paper evaluating the program and suggesting any ways to improve or strengthen it.

WHEN PARENTS DON'T TURN OUT RIGHT
William Aiken

A graduate of Trinity, Harvard, and Boston University, poet and essayist William Aiken (b. 1932) taught freshman composition, creative writing, and poetry for 20 years at Lowell University. His essays and poems have been widely published in such diverse publications as the *New York Times, Harvard Magazine,* the *Wall Street Journal,* and *Seventeen.* Asked why he writes, Aiken said, "I write to entertain and, in a minimal way, to inform." The essay printed here appeared on the opinion pages of the *Los Angeles Times,* May 21, 1993.

1   I was not asked to give a graduation speech this year. That makes 60 years in a row. An awkwardness has crept into my children's lives through no fault of their own. They have been watching my slow development for years and are getting pretty sick of it. Somewhere along the line, the lure to competence in a recognized field passed me by.

2   When parents don't turn out quite the way their children had hoped, there is a poignant sense of lost opportunity. They look at us and their eyes bunch up with disappointment.

3   I thought I was moving along pretty well until my daughter told me that my driving abilities had diminished greatly from when I taught her to downshift. Now when I drive her new baby around, I am nervous the whole time, worrying about corners that are too sharp and stops that are too abrupt. Also, my daughter's New Age parental monologues make me a little uncomfortable, as she talks of developing a child who is "powerful and creative," looking dubiously at my part in the gene pool.

4   I have a son, 23, whose suits are tailored in New York. He told me the other day that the buttons weren't quite right. I can hear him now, fresh from rattling the doors of investment bankers in New York and Washington, politely stifling a yawn on the telephone as he asks, "What's up with you?"

5   I think the doubts began to arise around the time my youngest daughter visited some Mennonites in Pennsylvania who had black chrome on their Mercedes so as not to be ostentatious. They also had a plane that they hid in the woods. She wanted to ask these people down to our place for the weekend. Now she wants to mandate a green revolution wherever she goes, listens only to National Public Radio and quotes Native American poetry to me. Meanwhile, a whole range of behavior I had thought perfectly reasonable has become "unacceptable." She subscribes to the Cherokee idea that whatever I do must cause no harm for seven generations.

6   I thought "appropriate" and "inappropriate" behavior was reserved for things like tea parties, but now these concepts are invading every area of my life, and the looks from my children begin to circle above me like buzzards over a fresh find.

7   Apparently I got away with a lot of stuff for years. Now I find I am not funny enough, not friendly enough, not open enough to new experiences. People of my age, they tell me, should be more commanding, more poetic, more filled with *joie de vivre*. I lack the exhilaration of the good life. And to cap things off, I am not alert to their emotional needs. There is a whole generation of older people who have not seized on the world the way they were supposed to.

8   Lately I have been reading Foucault's "Culture of the Self" in a pitifully belated attempt to fit in with new priorities and remake myself in a more tolerable parental image. But even here I have been unsuccessful, and instead of changing for the better, I stumbled upon a lame justification for my state: Some ancient philosopher was telling Foucault, "Know what is the source of your gladness."

9   Well, this I could understand. I remember I was glad the day Matthew took straight sets from me in tennis after years of throwing his racket at me. I was glad when Beth tirelessly tried to teach me the Charleston at an Iranian wedding reception, oblivious to the sorrowful gaze of bewildered onlookers. I was glad when Kathy said to me, "You know, Dad, the trouble with you is you don't take enough delight in people." My children don't realize that as they view the sick thing I have become, I approach the full flush of parental triumph.

10   They still come around, of course. I know this because after they leave I am missing my new gray T-shirts. But I think they come around mostly to talk with their mother and assess my decline. Meanwhile, I have been spending a lot of time with my granddaughter, Aisha. We talk about the circus and McDonald's. She's 6 and still views me with a certain indulgence. I also have a lot of hope for my grandson. He just turned 2.

THINKING ABOUT THE TEXT

1. List all examples that illustrate how Aiken feels he has not "turned out right" according to his children's perspective.

2. Discuss how Aiken's first two paragraphs set the humorous tone for this essay.

3. Analyze the focused sketches he creates for each of his children. How does each one provide a witty contrast with the father's self-image?

4. Why does Aiken mention he read Foucault? In what way was this reading unsuccessful? What is ironic about Aiken's "gladness"?

5. How does Aiken's conclusion maintain his humorous and ironic tone?

WRITING FROM THE TEXT

1. Based on details from this essay, write a character analysis of Aiken as a father. (See character analysis section, pp. 436–444.)

2. Write an essay examining the effectiveness of Aiken's humor and irony (presenting the opposite of what one might expect).

3. In an essay, describe how one or both of your parents did or did not "turn out right." Show examples of behavior and of your efforts to "teach." Use humor or irony, if either is appropriate.

CONNECTING WITH OTHER TEXTS

1. Although both Aiken and Sherwood Anderson (p. 6) use different points of view and tones, they both describe fathers who did not "turn out right." Write an essay comparing and contrasting Aiken's intentions with Sherwood Anderson's purpose.

2. Write an essay from the point of view of one of Hazel Peoples' children ("My Man Bovanne," p. 43) showing how Hazel did or did not "turn out right." Your vocabulary and tone will depend on which child's point of view you assume for this essay.

2

Between Genders

■ ■ ■

As you can imagine, if women and men were completely satisfied with their lives, this chapter of readings probably would be quite different. Essays would show that gender conflicts were issues of the past, poems would celebrate gender equality, and memoirs would attest to universal self-acceptance.

But as the work in this chapter reveals, many lives are still riddled with tensions related to gender. The women's movements of the last four decades have helped to identify and address these tensions, and the men's movement of the last decade has raised questions that also disturb the status quo. Some individuals embrace this disturbance, others fear it, and many feel caught in between. You and your friends may be in the process of exploring or resolving some of the same gender issues that the writers in this chapter discuss.

All of the writers show how stereotypes circumscribe the actions and thinking of women and men. Both Amy Gross and Noel Perrin argue the advantages of androgyny as they expose the limitations of the "macho" male. Conformity to "hypermasculine" behavior is also a source of problems analyzed by Michael Kimmel and Martin Levine. In his review of the issues of the men's movement, Sam Allis questions what men "really want." In one essay Armin Brott criticizes the negative depictions of men in children's books, and in another essay Warren Farrell analyzes the burden placed on men to be "success objects." Social conditioning encourages men to pursue stereotypical goals. You may have noticed the results of this conditioning in your father or uncle if not yet in your brother or yourself. You will find ideas in these essays to help you consider choices and understand what you have observed.

Clearly, women do not escape the stereotyping that limits behavior and self-acceptance. Brigid Brophy believes that women exist in "invisible cages" that thwart their vital participation in life, and Naomi Wolf's essay and the poems of May Swenson and Marge Piercy illustrate the specific myths that keep women confined. We believe that you

will find these writers addressing problems that y
ered in the last few years. Finally, several of our wri
lem affecting both genders—violence against wome.
discussed in analytical essays, a poem, and a short st
rary writers: Ellen Sweet, Ellen Goodman, Barb
Adrienne Rich, and Joyce Carol Oates.

You undoubtedly have found that gender problems ἐ ⌐ central concerns, showing up in such diverse places as the lyrics of popular music
and the feature articles of newspapers and magazines. In this chapter
our writers explore these concerns and suggest choices that may interest you. These authors reexamine gender roles, expose myths, and pose
solutions that may help both sexes reach accord between genders.

THE APPEAL OF THE ANDROGYNOUS MAN
Amy Gross

An honors graduate with a degree in zoology from Connecticut College for
Women, Amy Gross (b. 1942) has been a writer at *Glamour*, a writer and consulting editor at *Mademoiselle*, and a writer and feature editor at *Vogue*. She is currently an editor at *Mirabella* magazine. The piece included here first appeared in
Mademoiselle in 1976.

1   James Dean was my first androgynous man. I figured I could talk to him. He
was anguished and I was 12, so we had a lot in common. With only a few exceptions, all the men I have liked or loved have been a certain kind of man: a kind
who doesn't play football or watch the games on Sunday, who doesn't tell dirty
jokes featuring broads or chicks, who is not contemptuous of conversations that
are philosophically speculative, introspective, or otherwise foolish according to
the other kind of man. He is more self-amused, less inflated, more quirky, vulnerable and responsive than the other sort (the other sort, I'm visualizing as the guys
on TV who advertise deodorant in the locker room). He is more like me than the
other sort. He is what social scientists and feminists would call androgynous: having the characteristics of both male and female.

2   Now the first thing I want you to know about the androgynous man is that he is
neither effeminate nor hermaphroditic. All his primary and secondary sexual characteristics are in order and I would say he's all-man, but that is just what he is not.
He is more than all-man.

3   The merely all-man man, for one thing, never walks to the grocery store unless
the little woman is away visiting her mother with the kids, or is in the hospital
having a kid, or there is no little woman. All-men men don't know how to shop in

grocery store unless it is to buy a 6-pack and some pretzels. Their ideas of nutrition expand beyond a 6-pack and pretzels only to take in steak, potatoes, scotch or rye whiskey, and maybe a wad of cake or apple pie. All-men men have absolutely no taste in food, art, books, movies, theatre, dance, how to live, what are good questions, what is funny, or anything else I care about. It's not exactly that the all-man's man is an uncouth illiterate. He may be educated, well-mannered, and on a first-name basis with fine wines. One all-man man I knew was a handsome individual who gave the impression of being gentle, affectionate, and sensitive. He sat and ate dinner one night while I was doing something endearingly feminine at the sink. At one point, he mutely held up his glass to indicate in a primitive, even ape-like, way his need for a refill. This was in 1967, before Women's Liberation. Even so, I was disturbed. Not enough to break the glass over his handsome head, not even enough to mutely indicate the whereabouts of the refrigerator, but enough to remember that moment in all its revelatory clarity. No androgynous man would ever brutishly expect to be waited on without even a "please." (With a "please," maybe.)

4   The brute happened to be a doctor—not a hard hat—and, to all appearances, couth. But he had bought the whole superman package, complete with that fragile beast, the male ego. The androgynous man arrives with a male ego too, but his is not as imperialistic. It doesn't invade every area of his life and person. Most activities and thoughts have nothing to do with masculinity or femininity. The androgynous man knows this. The all-man man doesn't. He must keep a constant guard against anything even vaguely feminine (*i.e.,* "sissy") rising up in him. It must be a terrible strain.

5   Male chauvinism is an irritation, but the real problem I have with the all-man man is that it's hard for me to talk to him. He's alien to me, and for this I'm at least half to blame. As his interests have not carried him into the sissy, mine have never taken me very far into the typically masculine terrains of sports, business and finance, politics, cars, boats and machines. But blame or no blame, the reality is that it is almost as difficult for me to connect with him as it would be to link up with an Arab shepherd or Bolivian sandalmaker. There's a similar culture gap.

6   It seems to me that the most masculine men usually end up with the most feminine women. Maybe they like extreme polarity. I like polarity myself, but the poles have to be within earshot. As I've implied, I'm very big on talking. I fall in love for at least three hours with anyone who engages me in a real conversation. I'd rather a man point out a paragraph in a book—wanting to share it with me—than bring me flowers. I'd rather a man ask what I think than tell me I look pretty. (Women who are very pretty and accustomed to hearing that they are pretty may feel differently.) My experience is that all-men men read books I don't want to see paragraphs of, and don't really give a damn what I or any woman would think about most issues so long as she looks pretty. They have a very limited use for women. I suspect they don't really like us. The androgynous man likes women as much or as little as he likes anyone.

7   Another difference between the all-man man and the androgynous man is that the first is not a star in the creativity department. If your image of the creative

male accessorizes him with a beret, smock and artist's palette, you will not believe the all-man man has been seriously short-changed. But if you allow as how creativity is a talent for freedom, associated with imagination, wit, empathy, unpredictability, and receptivity to new impressions and connections, then you will certainly pity the dull, thick-skinned, rigid fellow in whom creativity sets no fires.

8   Nor is the all-man man so hot when it comes to sensitivity. He may be true-blue in the trenches, but if you are troubled, you'd be wasting your time trying to milk comfort from the all-man man.

9   This is not blind prejudice. It is enlightened prejudice. My biases were confirmed recently by a psychologist named Sandra Lipsetz Bem, a professor at Stanford University. She brought to attention the fact that high masculinity in males (and high femininity in females) has been "consistently correlated with lower overall intelligence and lower creativity." Another psychologist, Donald W. MacKinnon, director of the Institute of Personality Assessment and Research at the University of California in Berkeley, found that "creative males give more expression to the feminine side of their nature than do less creative men. . . . [They] score relatively high on femininity, and this despite the fact that, as a group, they do not present an effeminate appearance or give evidence of increased homosexual interests or experiences. Their elevated scores on femininity indicate rather an openness to their feelings and emotions, a sensitive intellect and understanding self-awareness and wide-ranging interests including many which in the American culture are thought of as more feminine. . . ."

10   Dr. Bem ran a series of experiments on college students who had been categorized as masculine, feminine, or androgynous. In three tests of the degree of nurturance—warmth and caring—the masculine men scored painfully low (painfully for anyone stuck with a masculine man, that is). In one of those experiments, all the students were asked to listen to a "troubled talker"—a person who was not neurotic but simply lonely, supposedly new in town and feeling like an outsider. The masculine men were the least supportive, responsive or humane. "They lacked the ability to express warmth, playfulness and concern," Bem concluded. (She's giving them the benefit of the doubt. It's possible the masculine men didn't express those qualities because they didn't possess them.)

11   The androgynous man, on the other hand, having been run through the same carnival of tests, "performs spectacularly. He shuns no behavior just because our culture happens to label it as female and his competence crosses both the instrumental (getting the job done, the problem solved) and the expressive (showing a concern for the welfare of others, the harmony of the group) domains. Thus, he stands firm in his opinion, he cuddles kittens and bounces babies and he has a sympathetic ear for someone in distress."

12   Well, a great mind, a sensitive and warm personality are fine in their place, but you are perhaps skeptical of the gut appeal of the androgynous man. As a friend, maybe, you'd like an androgynous man. For a sexual partner, though, you'd prefer a jock. There's no arguing chemistry, but consider the jock for a moment. He competes on the field, whatever his field is, and bed is just one more field to him: another opportunity to perform, another fray. Sensuality is for him candy to be

doled out as lure. It is a ration whose flow is cut off at the exact point when it has served its purpose—namely, to elicit your willingness to work out on the field with him.

13   Highly masculine men need to believe their sexual appetite is far greater than a woman's (than a nice woman's). To them, females must be seduced: Seduction is a euphemism for a power play, a con job. It pits man against woman (or woman against man). The jock believes he must win you over, incite your body to rebel against your better judgment: in other words—conquer you.

14   The androgynous man is not your opponent but your teammate. He does not seduce: he invites. Sensuality is a pleasure for him. He's not quite so goal-oriented. And to conclude, I think I need only remind you here of his greater imagination, his wit and empathy, his unpredictability, and his receptivity to new impressions and connections.

THINKING ABOUT THE TEXT

1. Prior to actually defining androgyny, Amy Gross describes the characteristics of men she likes and those that she does not like. What are those contrasting characteristics that she cites throughout her essay?

2. How does Gross' second paragraph function to "answer" her reader's unexpressed comment about androgyny?

3. Gross cites a Stanford University psychologist's experiment with masculinity and femininity. What were the discoveries of that experiment? What conclusions do you draw from the findings?

4. Gross anticipates the reader's response to her description of the androgynous man as one who lacks "gut appeal." How does she argue for the sex appeal of the androgynous man? Is she convincing?

WRITING FROM THE TEXT

1. Write an essay in which you contrast two males that you know—one "all-man man" and one androgynous man. Be *specific* in your contrasting descriptions.

2. Use Gross' essay as a model for your essay celebrating the virtues of the woman you will define and describe as more than the "all-female female"—the androgynous woman.

CONNECTING WITH OTHER TEXTS

1. Connect Gross' concept of the androgynous man with Perrin's points in his essay (p. 75). Write an extended definition of androgyny and give examples from both essays as well as your own awareness and experience to support your definition.

2. Compare Gross' concept of the ideal man with the concepts described by Allis in "What Do Men Really Want?" (p. 81).

THE ANDROGYNOUS MAN
Noel Perrin

An English professor at Dartmouth College, Noel Perrin (b. 1927) has written both scholarly and personal essays, many of which have been published in *The New Yorker*. A number of his essays have been collected and published in book form, especially those about his experiences as a part-time farmer in Vermont. Perrin's account of his discovery and preference for androgyny, included here, was first published in the *New York Times Magazine* in 1984.

1   The summer I was 16, I took a train from New York to Steamboat Springs, Colorado, where I was going to be assistant horse wrangler at a camp. The trip took three days, and since I was much too shy to talk to strangers, I had quite a lot of time for reading. I read all of "Gone With the Wind." I read all the interesting articles in a couple of magazines I had, and then I went back and read all the dull stuff. I also took all the quizzes, a thing of which magazines were even fuller then than now.

2   The one that held my undivided attention was called "How Masculine/Feminine Are You?" It consisted of a large number of inkblots. The reader was supposed to decide which of four objects each blot most resembled. The choices might be a cloud, a steam engine, a caterpillar and a sofa.

3   When I finished the test, I was shocked to find that I was barely masculine at all. On a scale of 1 to 10, I was about 1.2. Me, the horse wrangler? (And not just wrangler, either. That summer, I had to skin a couple of horses that died—the camp owner wanted the hides.)

4   The results of that test were so terrifying to me that for the first time in my life I did a piece of original analysis. Having unlimited time on the train, I looked at the "masculine" answers over and over, trying to find what it was that distinguished real men from people like me—and eventually I discovered two very simple patterns. It was "masculine" to think the blots looked like man-made objects, and "feminine" to think they looked like natural objects. It was masculine to think they looked like things capable of causing harm, and feminine to think of innocent things.

5   Even at 16, I had the sense to see that the compilers of the test were using rather limited criteria—maleness and femaleness are both more complicated than *that*—and I breathed a huge sigh of relief. I wasn't necessarily a wimp, after all.

6   That the test did reveal something other than the superficiality of its makers I realized only many years later. What it revealed was that there is a large class of men and women both, to which I belong, who are essentially androgynous. That doesn't mean we're gay, or low in the appropriate hormones, or uncomfortable performing the jobs traditionally assigned our sexes. (A few years after that summer, I was leading troops in combat and, unfashionable as it now is to admit this, having a very good time. War is exciting. What a pity the 20th century went and spoiled it with high-tech weapons.)

7   What it does mean to be spiritually androgynous is a kind of freedom. Men who are all-male, or he-man, or 100 percent red-blooded Americans, have a little

biological set that causes them to be attracted to physical power, and probably also to dominance. Maybe even to watching football. I don't say this to criticize them. Completely masculine men are quite often wonderful people: good husbands, good (though sometimes overwhelming) fathers, good members of society. Furthermore, they are often so unself-consciously at ease in the world that other men seek to imitate them. They just aren't as free as us androgynes. They pretty nearly have to be what they are; we have a range of choices open.

8   The sad part is that many of us never discover that. Men who are not 100 percent red-blooded Americans—say, those who are only 75 percent red-blooded—often fail to notice their freedom. They are too busy trying to copy the he-men ever to realize that men, like women, come in a wide variety of acceptable types. Why this frantic imitation? My answer is mere speculation, but not casual. I have speculated on this for a long time.

9   Partly they're just envious of the he-man's unconscious ease. Mostly they're terrified of finding that there may be something wrong with them deep down, some weakness at the heart. To avoid discovering that, they spend their lives acting out the role that the he-man naturally lives. Sad.

10   One thing that men owe to the women's movement is that this kind of failure is less common than it used to be. In releasing themselves from the single ideal of the dependent woman, women have more or less incidentally released a lot of men from the single ideal of the dominant male. The one mistake the feminists have made, I think, is in supposing that *all* men need this release, or that the world would be a better place if all men achieved it. It wouldn't. It would just be duller.

11   So far I have been pretty vague about just what the freedom of the androgynous man is. Obviously it varies with the case. In the case I know best, my own, I can be quite specific. It has freed me most as a parent. I am, among other things, a fairly good natural mother. I like the nurturing role. It makes me feel good to see a child eat—and it turns me to mush to see a 4-year-old holding a glass with both small hands, in order to drink. I even enjoyed sewing patches on the knees of my daughter Amy's Dr. Dentons when she was at the crawling stage. All that pleasure I would have lost if I had made myself stick to the notion of the paternal role that I started with.

12   Or take a smaller and rather ridiculous example. I feel free to kiss cats. Until recently it never occurred to me that I would want to, though my daughters have been doing it all their lives. But my elder daughter is now 22, and in London. Of course, I get to look after her cat while she is gone. He's a big, handsome farm cat named Petrushka, very unsentimental, though used from kittenhood to being kissed on the top of the head by Elizabeth. I've gotten very fond of him (he's the adventurous kind of cat who likes to climb hills with you), and one night I simply felt like kissing him on the top of the head, and did. Why did no one tell me sooner how silky cat fur is?

13   Then there's my relation to cars. I am completely unembarrassed by my inability to diagnose even minor problems in whatever object I happen to be driving, and don't have to make some insider's remark to mechanics to try to establish that I, too, am a "Man With His Machine."

14   The same ease extends to household maintenance. I do it, of course. Service people are expensive. But for the last decade my house has functioned better than it used to because I've had the aid of a volume called "Home Repairs Any Woman Can Do," which is pitched just right for people at my technical level. As a youth, I'd as soon have touched such a book as I would have become a transvestite. Even though common sense says there is really nothing sexual whatsoever about fixing sinks.

15   Or take public emotion. All my life I have easily been moved by certain kinds of voices. The actress Siobhan McKenna's, to take a notable case. Give her an emotional scene in a play, and within 10 words my eyes are full of tears. In boyhood, my great dread was that someone might notice. I struggled manfully, you might say, to suppress this weakness. Now, of course, I don't see it as a weakness at all, but as a kind of fulfillment. I even suspect that the true he-men feel the same way, or one kind of them does, at least, and it's only the poor imitators who have to struggle to repress themselves.

16   Let me come back to the inkblots, with their assumption that masculine equates with machinery and science, and feminine with art and nature. I have no idea whether the right pronoun for God is He, She or It. But this I'm pretty sure of. If God could somehow be induced to take that test, God would not come out macho, and not feminismo, either, but right in the middle. Fellow androgynes, it's a nice thought.

THINKING ABOUT THE TEXT

1. How does the magazine test reinforce stereotypes of masculine and feminine?
2. In what ways might Perrin be perceived as "all-male"?
3. According to Perrin, what are the strengths and limitations of the he-man? What does Perrin feel is so sad about those who try to imitate he-men?
4. How does Perrin define androgyny? In what specific ways has it liberated him?

WRITING FROM THE TEXT

1. Perrin notes that as a youth he would not have touched a book like "Home Repairs Any Woman Can Do," and would not have let anyone see him cry. Write an essay about certain behaviors or actions that you might have avoided or hidden in the past because of a fear of seeming not masculine or feminine enough.
2. Considering Perrin's article, write an essay describing "the androgynous female." Let us see how she differs from the "all-female" woman.

3. Write an essay arguing that it is easier for either males or females to be androgynous in our society. Support this with specific examples and illustrations.
4. Write a critique of Perrin's essay from the perspective of a he-man or an "all-female" woman.

CONNECTING WITH OTHER TEXTS

1. Using specific details from Perrin's essay as well as from "Men as Success Objects" (p. 90) and "What Do Men Really Want?" (p. 81), write about the pressures on a male to find an identity of his own.
2. Although Noel Perrin and Amy Gross (p. 71) both underscore the advantages of the androgynous man, the tone, word choices, and approaches of their essays are distinct. Write an essay comparing and contrasting the two.

A HIDDEN FACTOR IN AIDS
Michael S. Kimmel and Martin P. Levine

A specialist in the study of gender and sexuality, Michael S. Kimmel is a sociologist at the State University of New York at Stony Brook. He has written extensively on gender issues, including the books *Changing Lives: New Directions in Research on Men and Masculinity*, and *Against the Tide: Pro-Feminist Men in America, 1775 to the Present*.

A former professor of sociology at Florida Atlantic University until his AIDS-related illness forced his early retirement, Martin P. Levine (b. 1950) is the editor of *Gay Men: The Sociology of Male Homosexuality*, a collection of articles that examine the gay culture, the history of the gay rights movement, and the issue of homophobia. The book was published in 1979. The essay included here first appeared in the *Los Angeles Times* in 1991.

1   As the AIDS epidemic begins its second decade, it's time to face some unpleasant realities: AIDS is the No. 1 health problem for men in the United States; it is the leading cause of death of men aged 33 to 45; it has killed more American men than were lost in the Vietnam War.

2   No other disease that was not biologically sex-linked (like hemophilia) has ever been so associated with one gender. And yet virtually no one talks about AIDS as a men's disease. Americans generally think of it as a "gay disease," or a "drug addict" disease; some people even refuse to see it as a disease, arguing that it is "divine retribution" for "deviant behavior."

3 This dehumanizing has a lot to do with the fact that compassion and support for AIDS patients continue to be in relatively short supply among Americans. Perhaps by looking at AIDS as a "men's disease" we can put it in a more humane perspective.

4 In our society, the capacity for high-risk behavior is a prominent measure of masculinity. Men get AIDS by engaging in specific high-risk behaviors, activities that ignore potential health risks for more immediate pleasures.

5 As sociologists have long understood, stigmatized gender often leads to exaggerated forms of gender-specific behavior. Thus, those whose masculinity is least secure are precisely those most likely to follow hyper-masculine behavioral codes as well as hold fast to traditional definitions of masculinity. In social science research, hyper-masculinity as a compensation for stigmatized gender identity has been used to explain the propensity for authoritarianism and racism, homophobia, anti-Semitism, juvenile crime and gang activities.

6 Gay men and IV drug users can be seen in this light, although for different reasons. The traditional view of gay men is that they are not "real men." Most of the stereotypes revolve around effeminacy, weakness, passivity. But after the Stonewall riots in 1969, in which gay men fought back against the police raiding a gay bar, and the subsequent birth of the Gay Liberation Movement, a new gay masculinity emerged in major cities. The "clone," as he was called, dressed in hyper-masculine garb (flannel shirts, blue jeans), with short hair (not at all androgynous) and mustache; he was athletic, highly muscular. In short, the clone looked more like a "real man" than most straight men.

7 And the clones—who composed roughly one-third of all gay men living in the major urban gay enclaves in the mid-1970s—enacted a hyper-masculine sexuality in steamy back rooms, bars and bathhouses where sex was plentiful, anonymous and very hot. No unnecessary foreplay, romance or post-coital awkwardness. Sex without attachment.

8 One might say that, given the norms of masculinity (men are always supposed to want sex, seek sex and be ready for sex), for a time, gay men were the only men in our culture who were getting as much sex as they wanted.

9 Predictably, high levels of sexual activity led to high levels of sexually transmitted diseases among clones. But no one could have predicted AIDS.

10 Among IV drug users, we see a different pattern, but with some similar outcomes when seen from a gender perspective. The majority of IV drug users are African American and Latino, two groups for whom the traditional avenues of successful manhood are blocked by poverty and racism. More than half of the black men between 18 and 25 in our cities are unemployed, which means that they are structurally prevented from demonstrating masculinity as breadwinners.

11 The drug culture offers alternatives. Dealing drugs can provide an income to support a family as well as the opportunity for manly risk and adventure. The community of drug users can confirm gender identity; the sharing of needles is a demonstration of that solidarity. And the ever-present risk of death by overdose takes hyper-masculine bravado to the limit.

12 By now, most men have heard about "safer sex," the best way (short of abstinence) to reduce one's risk for contracting AIDS by sexual contact: have fewer

partners, avoid certain practices, use condoms, take the responsibility for safe behavior. In short, safer-sex programs encourage men to stop having sex like men. To men, you see, "safe sex" is an oxymoron. That which is sexy is not safe; that which is safe is not sexy. Sex is about danger, risk, excitement; safety is about comfort, softness, security.

13   Seen this way, it is not surprising to find in some research that one-fourth of urban gay men report that they have not changed their unsafe sexual behaviors. What is astonishing is that slightly more than three-fourths have changed, are practicing safer sex.

14   What heterosexual men could learn from the gay community's response to AIDS is how to eroticize responsibility—something that women have been trying to teach men for decades. And straight men could also learn a thing or two about caring for one another in illness, supporting one another in grief, and maintaining a resilience in the face of a devastating disease and the callous indifference of society.

15   In short, we must enlarge the definition of what it means to be a real man.

16   Meanwhile, AIDS is spreading, and every day there are more men who need our compassion and support. They did not contract this disease intentionally; they do not deserve blame. We must stand with them because they are our brothers. We are linked to them not through sexual orientation (although we may be) or by drug-related behavior (although we may be) but by our gender, by our masculinity.

17   They are not "perverts" or "deviants" who have strayed from the norms of masculinity. They are, if anything, over-conformists to destructive norms of male behavior. Like all real men, they have taken risks. And until daring has been eliminated from the rhetoric of masculinity, men will die as a result of risk-taking. In war. In sex. In driving fast and drunk. In shooting drugs and sharing needles.

18   Men with AIDS are real men, and when one dies, a bit of all men dies as well. Until we change what it means to be a real man, every man will die a little bit every day.

THINKING ABOUT THE TEXT

1. The authors assert that there is a relationship between the behavior of males "stigmatized" by society and the prevalence of AIDS. What is that relationship? What is the authors' thesis?

2. What are the two groups described in the essay? What factors bring them together? How do you respond to the authors' description of the dress and behavior of "real men"?

3. Do you agree that "safe sex" is an "oxymoron"?

WRITING FROM THE TEXT

1. Describe a time when your desire to prove your masculinity or femininity resulted in risk or a dangerous situation.

2. Write a short essay in which you argue that overconformity to masculine modeling—achieving a "real" male image—is destructive. Use and develop the examples cited in this essay but add others of your own.

CONNECTING WITH OTHER TEXTS

1. Amy Gross' essay "The Appeal of the Androgynous Man" (p. 71) gives a positive description of androgyny, and Noel Perrin's essay "The Androgynous Man" (p. 75) describes some freedoms androgynous men have. Write an essay in which you argue that Gross' ideal man satisfies Kimmel and Levine's plea for an "enlarg[ed] . . . definition of what it means to be a real man."
2. Enlist Farrell's "Men as Success Objects" (p. 90), Allis' "What Do Men Really Want?" (below), and Barbara Ehrenreich's "Angry Young Men" (p. 138) to write an essay in which you argue that economic factors negatively affect a male's self-concept. Use Kimmel and Levine's references to African-American and Latino males as part of your discussion, and find statistical material on unemployment to support your view.

WHAT DO MEN REALLY WANT?
Sam Allis

A student of European history who graduated from Harvard in 1969, Sam Allis (b. 1946) has worked as a writer for the *Wall Street Journal* and for the *Boston Globe*. For the last twelve years, he has worked for *Time* magazine, where he is presently the Boston bureau chief. The piece included here, a summary of the issues of the men's movement, was first published in *Time* in the fall of 1990.

1   Freud, like everyone else, forgot to ask the second question: What do *men* really want? His omission may reflect the male fascination with the enigma of woman over the mystery of man. She owns the center of his imagination, while the fate of man works the margins. Perhaps this is why so many men have taken the Mafia oath of silence about their hopes and fears. Strong and silent remain de rigueur.

2   But in the wake of the feminist movement, some men are beginning to pipe up. In the intimacy of locker rooms and the glare of large men's groups, they are

spilling their bile at the incessant criticism, much of it justified, from women about their inadequacies as husbands, lovers, fathers. They are airing their frustration with the limited roles they face today, compared with the multiple options that women seem to have won. Above all, they are groping to redefine themselves on their own terms instead of on the performance standards set by their wives or bosses or family ghosts. "We've heard all the criticism," says New York City–based television producer Tom Seligson. "Now we'll make our own decisions."

3   In many quarters there is anger. "The American man wants his manhood back. Period," snaps John Wheeler, a Washington environmentalist and former chairman of the Vietnam Veterans Memorial Fund. "New York feminists [a generic term in his lexicon] have been busy castrating American males. They poured this country's testosterone out the window in the 1960s. The men in this country have lost their boldness. To raise your voice these days is a worse offense than urinating in the subway."

4   Even more prevalent is exhaustion. "The American man wants to stop running; he wants a few moments of peace," says poet Robert Bly, one of the gurus of the nascent men's movement in the U.S. "He has a tremendous longing to get down to his own depths. Beneath the turbulence of his daily life is a beautiful crystalline infrastructure"—a kind of male bedrock.

5   Finally, there is profound confusion over what it means to be a man today. Men have faced warping changes in role models since the women's movement drove the strong, stoic John Wayne–type into the sunset. Replacing him was a new hero: the hollow-chested, sensitive, New Age man who bawls at Kodak commercials and handles a diaper the way Magic Johnson does a basketball. Enter Alan Alda.

6   But he, too, is quickly becoming outdated. As we begin the '90s, the zeitgeist has changed again. Now the sensitive male is a wimp and an object of derision to boot. In her song *Sensitive New Age Guys,* singer Christine Lavin lampoons, "Who carries the baby on his back? Who thinks Shirley MacLaine is on the inside track?" Now it's goodbye, Alan Alda; hello, Mel Gibson, with your sensitive eyes and your lethal weapon. Hi there, Arnold Schwarzenegger, the devoted family man with terrific triceps. The new surge of tempered macho is everywhere. Even the male dummies in store windows are getting tougher. Pucci Manikins is producing a more muscular model for the new decade that stands 6 ft. 2 in. instead of 6 ft. and has a 42-in. chest instead of its previous 40.

7   What's going on here? Are we looking at a backlash against the pounding men have taken? To some degree, yes. But it's more complicated than that. "The sensitive man was overplayed," explains Seattle-based lecturer Michael Meade, a colleague of Bly's in the men's movement. "There is no one quality intriguing enough to make a person interesting for a long time." More important, argues Warren Farrell, author of the 1986 best seller *Why Men Are the Way They Are,* women liked Alan Alda not because he epitomized the sensitive man but because he was a multimillionaire superstar success who also happened to be sensitive. In short, he met all their performance needs before sensitivity ever entered the pic-

ture. "We have never worshipped the soft man," says Farrell. "If Mel Gibson were a nursery school teacher, women wouldn't want him. Can you imagine a cover of TIME featuring a sensitive musician who drives a cab on the side?"

8   The women's movement sensitized many men to the problems women face in society and made them examine their own feelings in new ways. But it did not substantially alter what society expects of men. "Nothing fundamental has changed," says Farrell. Except that both John Wayne and Alan Alda have been discarded on the same cultural garbage heap. "First I learned that an erect cock was politically incorrect," complains producer Seligson. "Now it's wrong not to have one."

9   As always, men are defined by their performance in the workplace. If women don't like their jobs, they can, at least in theory, maintain legitimacy by going home and raising children. Men have no such alternative. "The options are dismal," says Meade. "You can drop out, which is an abdication of power, or take the whole cloth and lose your soul." If women have suffered from being sex objects, men have suffered as success objects, judged by the amount of money they bring home. As one young career woman in Boston puts it, "I don't want a Type A. I want an A-plus." Chilling words that make Farrell wonder, "Why do we need to earn more than you to be considered worthy of you?"

10   This imbalance can be brutal for a man whose wife tries life in the corporate world, discovers as men did decades ago that it is no day at the beach, and heads for home, leaving him the sole breadwinner. "We're seeing more of this 'You guys can have it back. It's been real,'" observes Kyle Pruett, a psychiatrist at the Yale Child Studies Center. "I have never seen a case where it has not increased anxiety for the man."

11   There has been a lot of cocktail-party talk about the need for a brave, sensitive man who will stand up to the corporate barons and take time off to watch his son play Peter Pan in his school play, the fast track be damned. This sentiment showed up in a 1989 poll, conducted by Robert Half International, in which about 45% of men surveyed said they would refuse a promotion rather than miss time at home. But when it comes to trading income for "quality time," how many fathers will actually be there at the grade-school curtain call?

12   "Is there a Daddy Track? No," says Edward Zigler, a Yale psychologist. "The message is that if a man takes paternity leave, he's a very strange person who is not committed to the corporation. It's very bleak." Says Felice Schwartz, who explored the notion of a Mommy Track in a 1989 article in the *Harvard Business Review:* "There isn't any forgiveness yet of a man who doesn't really give his all." So today's working stiff really enjoys no more meaningful options than did his father, the pathetic guy in the gray flannel suit who was pilloried as a professional hamster and an emotional cripple. You're still either a master of the universe or a wimp. It is the cognitive dissonance between the desire for change and the absence of ways to achieve it that has reduced most men who even think about the subject to tapioca.

13   Robert Rackleff, 47, is one of the rare men who have stepped off the corporate treadmill. Five years ago, after the birth of their third child, Rackleff and his wife

Jo-Ellen fled New York City, where he was a well-paid corporate speechwriter and she a radio-show producer. They moved to his native Florida, where Rackleff earns a less lavish living as a free-lance writer and helps his wife raise the kids. The drop in income, he acknowledges, "was scary. It put more pressure on me, but I wanted to spend more time with my children." Rackleff feels happy with his choice, but isolated. "I know only one other guy who left the fast track to be with his kids," he says. "Men just aren't doing it. I can still call up most of them at 8 p.m. and know they will be in the office."

14   Men have been bombarded with recipes to ripen their personal lives, if not their professional ones. They are now Lamaze-class regulars and can be found in the delivery room for the cosmic event instead of pacing the waiting-room floor. They have been instructed to bond with children, wives, colleagues and anyone else they can find. Exactly how remains unclear. Self-help books, like Twinkies, give brief highs and do not begin to address the uneven changes in their lives over the past 20 years. "Men aren't any happier in the '90s than they were in the '50s," observes Yale psychiatrist Pruett, "but their inner lives tend to be more complex. They are interested in feeling less isolated. They are stunned to find out how rich human relationships are."

15   Unfortunately, the men who attempt to explore those riches with the women in their lives often discover that their efforts are not entirely welcome. The same women who complain about male reticence can grow uncomfortable when male secrets and insecurities spill out. Says Rackleff: "I think a lot of women who want a husband to be a typical hardworking breadwinner are scared when he talks about being a sensitive father. I get cynical about that."

16   One might be equally cynical about men opening up to other men. Atlanta psychologist Augustus Napier tells of two doctors whose lockers were next to each other in the surgical dressing room of a hospital. For years they talked about sports, money and other safe "male" subjects. Then one of them learned that the other had tried to commit suicide—and had never so much as mentioned the attempt to him. So much for male bonding.

17   How can men break out of the gender stereotypes? Clearly, there is a need for some male consciousness raising, yet men have nothing to rival the giant grassroots movement that began razing female stereotypes 25 years ago. There is no male equivalent for the National Organization for Women or *Ms.* magazine. No role models, other than the usual megabillionaire success objects.

18   A minute percentage of American males are involved in the handful of organizations whose membership ranges from men who support the feminist movement to angry divorcés meeting to swap gripes about alimony and child-custody battles. There is also a group of mostly well-educated, middle-class men who sporadically participate in a kind of male spiritual quest. Anywhere from Maine to Minnesota, at male-only weekend retreats, they earnestly search for some shard of ancient masculinity culled from their souls by the Industrial Revolution. At these so-called warrior weekends, participants wrestle, beat drums and hold workshops on everything from ecology to divorce and incest. They embrace, and yes, they do cry and confide things they would never dream of saying to their wives and girlfriends. They act out emotions in a safe haven where no one will laugh at them.

19 At one drumming session in the municipal-arts center of a Boston suburb, about 50 men sit in a huge circle beating on everything from tom-toms to cowbells and sticks. Their ages range from the 20s to the 60s. A participant has brought his young son with him. Drummers nod as newcomers appear, sit down and start pounding away. Before long, a strong primal beat emerges that somehow transcends the weirdness of it all. Some men close their eyes and play in a trance. Others rise and dance around the middle of the group, chanting as they move.

20 One shudders to think what *Saturday Night Live* would do with these scenes. But there is no smirking among the participants. "When is the last time you danced with another man?" asks Paul, a family man who drove two hours from Connecticut to be there. "It tells you how many walls there are still out there for us." Los Angeles writer Michael Ventura, who has written extensively about men's issues, acknowledges the obvious: much of this seems pretty bizarre. "Some of it may look silly," he says. "But if you're afraid of looking silly, everything stops right there. In our society, men have to be contained and sure of themselves. Well, f—— that. That's not the way we feel." The goal, continues Ventura, is to rediscover the mystery of man, a creature capable of strength, spontaneity and adventure. "The male mystery is the part of us that wants to explore, that isn't afraid of the dark, that lights a fire and dances around it."

21 One thing is clear: men need the support of other men to change, which is why activities like drumming aren't as dumb as they may look. Even though no words are exchanged, the men at these sessions get something from other men that they earnestly need: understanding and acceptance. "The solitude of men is the most difficult single thing to change," says Napier. These retreats provide cover for some spiritual reconnaissance too risky to attempt in the company of women. "It's like crying," says Michael Meade. "Men are afraid that if they start, they'll cry forever."

22 Does the search for a lineal sense of masculinity have any relevance to such thorny modern dilemmas as how to balance work and family or how to talk to women? Perhaps. Men have to feel comfortable with themselves before they can successfully confront such issues. This grounding is also critical for riding out the changes in pop culture and ideals. John Wayne and Alan Alda, like violence and passivity, reflect holes in a core that needs fixing. But men can get grounded in many ways, and male retreats provide just one stylized option, though not one necessarily destined to attract most American men.

23 What do men really want? To define themselves on their own terms, just as women began to do a couple of decades ago. "Would a women's group ask men if it was O.K. to feel a certain way?" asks Jerry Johnson, host of the San Francisco–based KCBS radio talk show *Man to Man*. "No way. We're still looking for approval from women for changes, and we need to get it from the male camp."

24 That's the point. And it does not have to come at women's expense. "It is stupid to conclude that the empowerment of women means the disempowerment of men," says Robert Moore, a psychoanalyst at the C.G. Jung Institute in Chicago. "Men must also feel good about being male." Men would do well, in fact, to invite women into their lives to participate in these changes. It's no fun to face them alone. But if women can't or won't, men must act on their own and damn the torpedoes. No pain, no gain.

THINKING ABOUT THE TEXT

1. According to Sam Allis and the people he includes in his essay, what are the characteristic feelings of men today?

2. What does Allis think has happened to the sensitive, "New Age" men?

3. What does men's movement speaker Michael Meade find "dismal" about the situation for men?

4. How does the corporate world reinforce sexism in its attitude toward workers who stay home to care for young children?

5. According to Allis, how can men escape gender-based stereotypes that have burdened them?

WRITING FROM THE TEXT

1. Describe a hypothetical, end-of-the-twentieth-century male who has the strengths and foibles that Allis cites as typical of men today. Develop your description with *specific* examples.

2. What *do* men really want? Write an essay in which you focus on and develop the specific issues.

3. What do women really want in men? Write an essay in which you focus on and develop the specific qualities.

4. Argue that men should join the men's movement and give specific support for your argument.

5. Argue that men should *not* join the men's movement. Be specific in your reasoning.

CONNECTING WITH OTHER TEXTS

1. Compare Amy Gross' feelings about the androgynous man (p. 71) with what Allis and the speakers quoted in his essay believe women want. Who is right? Argue that the androgynous man is or is not a positive model. Use Allis and Gross in your essay.

2. Are Allis and the people he cites correct in saying that the problem for men is society's expectation for them to be successful in the corporate world? Use Farrell's essay "Men as Success Objects" (p. 90) for support.

3. Use the points that Allis raises and use Brophy's essay "Women: Invisible Cages" (p. 94) to argue that women *and* men are trapped in barless cages.

4. Do research on the men's movement to learn the central concerns of the men—Sam Keen, Robert Bly, Warren Farrell, Andrew Kimbrell—who are involved in it. In addition to citing the goals of the movement, evaluate the movement and its goals.

NOT ALL MEN ARE SLY FOXES
Armin A. Brott

Armin A. Brott (b. 1958) started studying the Russian language at San Francisco State and continued his studies at the American Graduate School of International Management, from which he received his M.B.A. He has worked as a commodities trader and is currently writing and consulting on business opportunities in Russia. Brott avoided all writing courses in college and believes that his parents' insistence on his reading has contributed to his ability to write. His advice is: "Find an issue and do a lot of research on it. Knowing how to use the library is vital to success." The research for this "My Turn" essay for *Newsweek* was done in the young children's section of the library. The essay was published June 1, 1992.

1   If you thought your child's bookshelves were finally free of openly (and not so openly) discriminatory materials, you'd better check again. In recent years groups of concerned parents have persuaded textbook publishers to portray more accurately the roles that women and minorities play in shaping our country's history and culture. "Little Black Sambo" has all but disappeared from library and bookstore shelves; feminist fairy tales by such authors as Jack Zipes have, in many homes, replaced the more traditional (and obviously sexist) fairy tales. Richard Scarry, one of the most popular children's writers, has reissued new versions of some of his classics; now female animals are pictured doing the same jobs as male animals. Even the terminology has changed: males and females are referred to as mail "carriers" or "firefighters."

2   There is, however, one very large group whose portrayal continues to follow the same stereotypical lines as always: fathers. The evolution of children's literature didn't end with "Goodnight Moon" and "Charlotte's Web." My local public library, for example, previews 203 new children's picture books (for the under-5 set) each *month*. Many of these books make a very conscious effort to take women characters out of the kitchen and the nursery and give them professional jobs and responsibilities.

3   Despite this shift, mothers are by and large still shown as the primary caregivers and, more important, as the primary nurturers of their children. Men in these books—if they're shown at all—still come home late after work and participate in the child rearing by bouncing baby around for five minutes before putting the child to bed.

4   In one of my 2-year-old daughter's favorite books, "Mother Goose and the Sly Fox," "retold" by Chris Conover, a single mother (Mother Goose) of seven tiny goslings is pitted against (and naturally outwits) the sly Fox. Fox, a neglectful and presumably unemployed single father, lives with his filthy, hungry pups in a grimy hovel littered with the bones of their previous meals. Mother Goose, a successful entrepreneur with a thriving lace business, still finds time to serve her goslings homemade soup in pretty porcelain cups. The story is funny and the illustrations marvelous, but the unwritten message is that women take better care of their kids and men have nothing else to do but hunt down and kill innocent, law-abiding geese.

5   The majority of other children's classics perpetuate the same negative stereotypes of fathers. Once in a great while, people complain about "Babar's" colonialist slant (little jungle-dweller finds happiness in the big city and brings civilization—and fine clothes—to his backward village). But I've never heard anyone ask why, after his mother is killed by the evil hunter, Babar is automatically an "orphan." Why can he find comfort only in the arms of another female? Why do Arthur's and Celeste's mothers come alone to the city to fetch their children? Don't the fathers care? Do they even have fathers? I need my answers ready for when my daughter asks.

6   I recently spent an entire day on the children's floor of the local library trying to find out whether these same negative stereotypes are found in the more recent classics-to-be. The librarian gave me a list of the 20 most popular contemporary picture books and I read every one of them. Of the 20, seven don't mention a parent at all. Of the remaining 13, four portray fathers as much less loving and caring than mothers. In "Little Gorilla," we are told that the little gorilla's "mother loves him" and we see Mama gorilla giving her little one a warm hug. On the next page we're also told that his "father loves him," but in the illustration, father and son aren't even touching. Six of the remaining nine books mention or portray mothers as the only parent, and only three of the 20 have what could be considered "equal" treatment of mothers and fathers.

7   The same negative stereotypes also show up in literature aimed at the *parents* of small children. In "What to Expect the First Year," the authors answer almost every question the parents of a newborn or toddler could have in the first year of their child's life. They are meticulous in alternating between references to boys and girls. At the same time, they refer almost exclusively to "mother" or "mommy." Men, and their feelings about parenting, are relegated to a nine-page chapter just before the recipe section.

8   Unfortunately, it's still true that, in our society, women do the bulk of the child care, and that thanks to men abandoning their families, there are too many single mothers out there. Nevertheless, to say that portraying fathers as unnurturing or completely absent is simply "a reflection of reality" is unacceptable. If children's literature only reflected reality, it would be like prime-time TV and we'd have books filled with child abusers, wife beaters and criminals.

9   Young children believe what they hear—especially from a parent figure. And since, for the first few years of a child's life, adults select the reading material, children's literature should be held to a high standard. Ignoring men who share equally in raising their children, and continuing to show nothing but part-time or no-time fathers is only going to create yet another generation of men who have been told since boyhood—albeit subtly—that mothers are the truer parents and that fathers play, at best, a secondary role in the home. We've taken major steps to root out discrimination in what our children read. Let's finish the job.

THINKING ABOUT THE TEXT

1. What are the specific stereotypes that Brott objects to in children's stories? What support does Brott have for his thesis?

2. What are the consequences of parenting books minimizing a father's role in child rearing?

WRITING FROM THE TEXT

1. Write an essay in which you argue from your memory of the books that you heard or read in your childhood that Brott is right or wrong in his depiction of fathers in young children's literature. You will need specific references to literature to support your view.

2. Is Brott arguing for censorship of children's literature so that only politically correct depictions of women and men are allowed? Argue one way or the other in your essay.

CONNECTING WITH OTHER TEXTS

1. In his essay "Men as Success Objects" (p. 90), Warren Farrell notes that men are often maliciously depicted in popular culture. Besides greeting cards, self-help books, and children's literature, where else are men or fathers maligned? Write an essay with the intent of describing the specific examples you cite and of proposing reform or discussing the consequences.

2. Repeat Brott's reading experience in your library with the intention of learning how *mothers* are depicted in young children's books. Write an essay like Brott's to present your focus and findings.

MEN AS SUCCESS OBJECTS
Warren Farrell

Educated at Montclair State College, UCLA, and New York University, Warren Farrell (b. 1943) has both taught and written in a variety of fields: political science, public administration, sociology, and psychology. He is presently a free-lance writer whose books treat some of the issues of the men's movement. *The Liberated Man* (1974) examines why feminism is so important to men, and *Why Men Are the Way They Are* (1986) looks at a number of gender-related issues. His most recent book is *The Myth of Male Power*. The article printed here first appeared in *Family Therapy Networker* in 1988.

1   For thousands of years, marriages were about economic security and survival. Let's call this Stage I in our culture's conception of marriage. Beginning in the 1950s, marriages became focused on personal fulfillment and we entered into the era of the Stage II relationship. In Stage II, love was redefined to include listening to each other, joint parenting, sexual fulfillment, and shared decision making. As a result, many traditional marriages consummated in Stage I failed under the new Stage II expectations. Thus we had the great surge of divorces beginning in the '60s.

2   The increasing incidence of divorce altered the fundamental relationship between women, men, and the workplace. Before divorce became common, most women's income came from men, so discrimination in favor of a woman's husband benefited her. But, as the divorce rate mushroomed, the same discrimination often hurt her. Before divorce became a common expectation, we had two types of inequality—women's experience of unequal rights in the workplace and men's experience of unequal responsibility for succeeding in the workplace. To find a woman to love him, a man had to "make his mark" in the world. As women increasingly had to provide for themselves economically, we confined our examination of inequality between the sexes to inequality in the workplace. What was ignored was the effect of inequality in the homeplace. Also ignored was a man's feeling that no woman would love him if he volunteered to be a full-time house-husband instead of a full-time provider. As a result, we falsely assumed that the experience of inequality was confined to women.

3   Because divorces led to a change in the pressures on women (should she *become* a doctor, marry a doctor, or have a career and marry a doctor?), that change became "news" and her new juggling act got attention in the media. Because the underlying pressures on men did not change (women still married men who earned more than they did), the pressure on men to succeed did not change, and, therefore, received no attention. With all the focus on discrimination against women, few understood the sexism directed against men.

4   The feminist perspective on relationships has become like fluoride in water—we drink it without being aware of its presence. The complaints about men, the

idea that "men are jerks," have become so integrated into our unconscious that even advertisers have caught on. After analyzing 1,000 commercials in 1987, researcher Fred Hayward found that when an ad called for a negative portrayal in a male-female interaction, an astonishing 100 percent of the time the "bad guy" was the man.

5   This anti-male bias isn't confined to TV commercials. A sampling of the cards in the "Love and Friendship" section of a greeting card store revealed these gems:

6   "If they can send one man to the moon, why can't they send them all?"

7   "When you unzip a man's pants . . . his brains fall out."

8   "If we can make penicillin out of moldy cheese . . . maybe we can make men out of the low-lifes in this town."

9   A visit to the bookstore turns up titles like *No Good Men.* Imagine *No Good Women* or *No Good Jews.* And what do the following titles have in common? *Men Who Can't Love; Men Who Hate Women and the Women Who Love Them; Smart Women/Foolish Choices; Successful Women, Angry Men: Peter Pan Syndrome.*

10   Feminism-as-fluoride has left us acknowledging the working mother ("Superwoman") without even being aware of the working father. It is by now well recognized that, even among men who do more housework or more childcare than their wives, almost never does the man truly share the 24-hour-a-day psychological responsibility of ministering to everyone's needs, egos, and schedules.

11   But it is not so widely recognized that, despite the impact feminism has had on the contemporary family, almost every father still retains 24-hour-a-day psychological responsibility for the family's financial well-being. Even women who earn more than their husbands tell me that they know their husbands would support their decision to earn as much or as little as they wish. If a woman marries a successful man, then she knows she will have an option to work or not, but not an obligation. Almost all men see bringing home a healthy salary as an obligation, not an option.

12   A woman today has three options:

Option 1: Full-time career.

Option 2: Full-time family.

Option 3: Some combination of career and family.

13   A man sees himself as having three "slightly different" options:

Option 1: Work full time.

Option 2: Work full time.

Option 3: Work full time.

14   The U.S. Bureau of the Census explains that full-time working males work an average of eight hours more per week on their jobs than full-time working females.

15   Since many women now earn substantial incomes, doesn't this relieve the pressure on men to be a wallet? No. Why? Because successful women do exactly what less-successful women do—"marry up," that is, marry a man whose income is greater than her own. According to statistics, if a woman cannot marry up or marry someone with a high wage-earning potential, she does not marry at all. Therefore, a man often reflexively backs away from a woman he's attracted to when he discovers she's more successful than he is because he senses he's only setting himself up for rejection. Ultimately, she'll dump him for a more successful man. She may sleep with him, or live with him, but not marry him unless she spots "potential." Thus, of top female executives, 85 percent don't get married; the remaining 15 percent almost all marry up. Even successful women have not relaxed the pressure on men to succeed.

16   Ask a girl in junior high or high school about the boy whom she would "absolutely love" to ask her out to the prom and chances are almost 100 percent that she would tell you her fantasy boy is *both* good-looking *and* successful (a jock or student leader, or someone who "has potential"). Ask a boy whom he would absolutely love to ask out to the prom and chances are almost 100 percent his fantasy girl is good-looking. Only about 25 percent will also be interested in a girl's "strong career potential" (or her being a top female jock). His invisible curriculum, then, taught him that being good-looking is not enough to attract a good-looking girl—he must be successful *in addition* to being good-looking. This was his experience of inequality: "Good-looking boy does not equal good-looking girl." Why are boys willing to consider themselves unequal to girls' attention until they hit their heads against 21 other boys on a football field?

17   In part, the answer is because boys are addicted. In all cultures, boys are addicted to the images of beautiful women. And in American culture this is enormously magnified. Boys are exposed to the images of beautiful women about 10 million times per year via television, billboards, magazines, etc. In the process, the naturally beautiful girl becomes a *genetic celebrity*. Boys become addicted to the image of the quasi-anorexic female. To be the equal of this genetic celebrity, the adolescent boy must become an *earned celebrity* (by performing, paying on dates, etc.). Until he is an earned celebrity, he feels like a groupie trying to get a celebrity's attention.

18   Is there an invisible curriculum for girls and boys growing up? Yes. For girls, "If you want to have your choice among boys, you had better be beautiful." For boys, it's "You had better be handsome *and* successful." If a boy wants a romantic relationship with a girl he must not only be successful and perform, he must pay and pursue—risk sexual rejection. Girls think of the three Ps—performing, paying, and pursuing—as male power. Boys see the three Ps as what they must do to earn their way to female love and sexuality. They see these not as power, but as compensations for powerlessness. This is the adolescent male's experience of inequality.

THINKING ABOUT THE TEXT

1. How do Farrell's historical descriptions of marriage relate to the point of his essay? What is the cause-and-effect relationship that he describes?

2. What inequalities does Farrell perceive for both genders, and how are the inequalities relevant to the men's movement? What is Farrell's thesis?

3. According to Farrell, how are men depicted in popular culture? What has the culture failed to address?

4. How do men's and women's "options" for making a living compare? Do you agree with Farrell's perceptions? What *is* the "invisible curriculum"? Does he overlook anything in his reasoning?

5. How does each gender's perceptions of a desirable date influence the perception of power or powerlessness that each gender has?

WRITING FROM THE TEXT

1. Interview male and female acquaintances of your age to see if adults' views of the desirable date or mate are consistent with the views Farrell cites for junior high and high school students. Write an essay to present your views.

2. Who has more options in the dating/mating and work worlds—women or men? Support your assertion with *specific* examples.

3. A psychological/sociological study that was done 20 years ago determined that, generally, women felt limited by what they were *allowed* to do and men felt limited by what they felt *required* to do. After discussing this perception with friends, write an essay to show what the genders feel in the last decade of the twentieth century.

CONNECTING WITH OTHER TEXTS

1. Write an analysis of the "invisible curriculum" for women and men using the essay by Brigid Brophy, "Women: Invisible Cages" (p. 94), with Farrell's work to support your points.

2. Do some research to learn more about the main grievances of the men who are in the men's movement. Write a paper in which you focus on the concerns of the movement. Use also "What Do Men Really Want?" (p. 81) for your analysis.

WOMEN: INVISIBLE CAGES
Brigid Brophy

An Anglo-Irish social critic who acknowledges her desire to promote a better world, Brigid Brophy (b. 1929) writes novels, essays, short stories, plays, and criticism. In spite of the fact that she has published widely, Brophy insists that she does not like to write. Asked during an interview what she most admires in men, Brophy replied, "Beauty." And in women? "Emancipation from domesticity." The essay printed here is from *Don't Never Forget: Collected Views and Reviews, 1963*. The problems that Brophy discusses in this essay, which was published more than 30 years ago, are still relevant issues of the women's and men's movements today.

1   All right, nobody's disputing it. Women are free. At least, they *look* free. They even feel free. But in reality women in the western, industrialised world today are like the animals in a modern zoo. There are no bars. It appears that cages have been abolished. Yet in practice women are still kept in their place just as firmly as the animals are kept in their enclosures. The barriers which keep them in now are invisible.

2   It is about forty years since the pioneer feminists, several of whom were men, raised such a rumpus by rattling the cage bars—or created such a conspicuous nuisance by chaining themselves to them—that society was at last obliged to pay attention. The result was that the bars were uprooted, the cage thrown open: whereupon the majority of the women who had been held captive decided they would rather stay inside anyway.

3   To be more precise, they *thought* they decided; and society, which can with perfect truth point out "Look, no bars," *thought* it was giving them the choice. There are no laws and very little discrimination to prevent western, industrialised women from voting, being voted for or entering the professions. If there are still comparatively few women lawyers and engineers, let alone women presidents of the United States, what are women to conclude except that this is the result either of their own free choice or of something inherent in female nature?

4   Many of them do draw just this conclusion. They have come back to the old argument of the anti-feminists, many of whom were women, that women are unfit by nature for life outside the cage. And in letting this old wheel come full cycle women have fallen victim to one of the most insidious and ingenious confidence tricks ever perpetrated.

5   In point of fact, neither female nature nor women's individual free choice has been put to the test. As American Negroes have discovered, to be officially free is by no means the same as being actually and psychologically free. A society as adept as ours has become at propaganda—whether political or commercial— should know that "persuasion," which means the art of launching myths and artificially inducing inhibitions, is every bit as effective as force of law. No doubt the reason society eventually agreed to abolish its anti-women laws was that it had become confident of commanding a battery of hidden dissuaders which would do the job just as well. Cage bars are clumsy methods of control, which excite the

more rebellious personalities inside to rattle them. Modern society, like the modern zoo, has contrived to get rid of the bars without altering the fact of imprisonment. All the zoo architect needs to do is run a zone of hot or cold air, whichever the animal concerned cannot tolerate, round the cage where the bars used to be. Human animals are not less sensitive to social climate.

6   The ingenious point about the new-model zoo is that it deceives both sides of the invisible barrier. Not only can the animal not see how it is imprisoned; the visitor's conscience is relieved of the unkindness of keeping animals shut up. He can say "Look, no bars round the animals," just as society can say "Look, no laws restricting women" even while it keeps women rigidly in place by zones of fierce social pressure.

7   There is, however, one great difference. A woman, being a thinking animal, may actually be more distressed because the bars of her cage cannot be seen. What relieves society's conscience may afflict hers. Unable to perceive what is holding her back, she may accuse herself and her whole sex of craven timidity because women have not jumped at what has the appearance of an offer of freedom. Evidently quite a lot of women have succumbed to guilt of this sort, since in recent years quite an industry has arisen to assuage it. Comforting voices make the air as thick and reassuring as cotton wool while they explain that there is nothing shameful in not wanting a career, that to be intellectually unadventurous is no sin, that taking care of home and family may be personally "fulfilling" and socially valuable.

8   This is an argument without a flaw: except that it is addressed exclusively to women. Address it to both sexes and instantly it becomes progressive and humane. As it stands, it is merely antiwoman prejudice revamped.

9   That many women would be happier not pursuing careers or intellectual adventures is only part of the truth. The whole truth is that many *people* would be. If society had the clear sight to assure men as well as women that there is no shame in preferring to stay non-competitively and non-aggressively at home, many masculine neuroses and ulcers would be avoided, and many children would enjoy the benefit of being brought up by a father with a talent for the job instead of by a mother with no talent for it but a sense of guilt about the lack.

10   But society does nothing so sensible. Blindly it goes on insisting on the tradition that men are the ones who go out to work and adventure—an arrangement which simply throws talent away. All the home-making talent which happens to be born inside male bodies is wasted; and our businesses and governments are staffed quite largely by people whose aptitude for the work consists solely of their being what is, by tradition, the right sex for it.

11   The pressures society exerts to drive men out of the house are very nearly as irrational and unjust as those by which it keeps women in. The mistake of the early reformers was to assume that men were emancipated already and that therefore reform need ask only for the emancipation of women. What we ought to do now is go right back to scratch and demand the emancipation of both sexes. It is only because men are not free themselves that they have found it necessary to cheat women by the deception which makes them appear free when they are not.

12   The zones of hot and cold air which society uses to perpetuate its uneconomic and unreasonable state of affairs are the simplest and most effective conceivable. Society is playing on our sexual vanity. Just as the sexual regions are the most vulnerable part of the body, sexuality is the most vulnerable part of the Ego. Tell a man that he is not a real man, or a woman that she is not one hundred per cent woman and you are threatening both with not being attractive to the opposite sex. No one can bear not to be attractive to the opposite sex. That is the climate which the human animal cannot tolerate.

13   So society has us all at its mercy. It has only to murmur to the man that staying at home is a feminine characteristic, and he will be out of the house like a bullet. It has only to suggest to the woman that logic and reason are the province of the masculine mind, whereas "intuition" and "feeling" are the female *forte,* and she will throw her physics textbooks out of the window, barricade herself into the house and give herself up to having wishy-washy poetical feelings while she arranges the flowers.

14   She will, incidentally, take care that her feelings *are* wishy-washy. She has been persuaded that to have cogent feelings, of the kind which really do go into great poems (most of which are by men), would make her an unfeminine woman, a woman who imitates men. In point of fact, she would not be imitating men as such, most of whom have never written a line of great poetry, but poets, most of whom so far happen to be men. But the bad logic passes muster with her because part of the mythology she has swallowed ingeniously informs her that logic is not her *forte*.

15   Should a woman's talent or intelligence be so irrepressible that she insists on producing cogent works of art or watertight meshes of argument, she will be said to have "a mind like a man's." This is simply current idiom; translated, it means "a good mind." The use of the idiom contributes to an apparently watertight proof that all good minds are masculine, since whenever they occur in women they are described as "like a man's."

16   What is more, this habit of thought actually contributes to perpetuating a state of affairs where most good minds really do belong to men. It is difficult for a woman to *want* to be intelligent when she has been told that to be so will make her like a man. She inclines to think an intelligence would be as unbecoming to her as a moustache; and many women have tried in furtive privacy to disembarrass themselves of intellect as though it were facial hair.

17   Discouraged from growing "a mind like a man's," women are encouraged to have thoughts and feelings of a specifically feminine tone. For society is cunning enough not to place its whole reliance on threatening women with blasts of icy air. It also flatters them with a zone of hot air. The most deceptive and cynical of its blandishments is the notion that women have some specifically feminine contribution to make to culture. Unfortunately, as culture had already been shaped and largely built up by men before the invitation was issued, this leaves women little to do. Culture consists of reasoned thought and works of art composed of cogent feeling and imagination. There is only one way to be reasonable, and that is to reason correctly; and the only kind of art which is any good is good art. If women are to eschew reason and artistic imagination in favour of "intuition" and "feeling," it

is pretty clear what is meant. "Intuition" is just a polite name for bad reasoning, and "feeling" for bad art.

18   In reality, the whole idea of a specifically feminine—or, for the matter of that, masculine—contribution to culture is a contradiction of culture. A contribution to culture is not something which could not have been made by the other sex—it is something which could not have been made by any other *person*. Equally, the notion that anyone, of either sex, can create good art out of simple feeling, untempered by discipline, is a philistine one. The arts are a sphere where women seem to have done well; but really they have done *too* well—too well for the good of the arts. Instead of women sharing the esteem which ought to belong to artists, art is becoming smeared with femininity. We are approaching a philistine state of affairs where the arts are something which it is nice for women to take up in their spare time—men having slammed out of the house to get on with society's "serious" business, like making money, administering the country and running the professions.

19   In that "serious" sphere it is still rare to encounter a woman. A man sentenced to prison would probably feel his punishment was redoubled by indignity if he were to be sentenced by a woman judge under a law drafted by a woman legislator—and if, on admission, he were to be examined by a woman prison doctor. If such a thing happened every day, it would be no indignity but the natural course of events. It has never been given the chance to become the natural course of events and never will be so long as women remain persuaded it would be unnatural of them to want it.

20   So brilliantly has society contrived to terrorise women with this threat that certain behaviour is unnatural and unwomanly that it has left them no time to consider—or even sheerly observe—what womanly nature really is. For centuries arrant superstitions were accepted as natural law. The physiological fact that only women can secrete milk for feeding babies was extended into the pure myth that it was women's business to cook for and wait on the entire family. The kitchen became woman's "natural" place because, for the first few months of her baby's life, the nursery really was. To this day a woman may suspect that she is unfeminine if she can discover in herself no aptitude or liking for cooking. Fright has thrown her into such a muddle that she confuses having no taste for cookery with having no breasts, and conversely assumes that nature has endowed the human female with a special handiness with frying pans.

21   Even psycho-analysis, which in general has been the greatest benefactor of civilisation since the wheel, has unwittingly reinforced the terrorisation campaign. The trouble was that it brought with it from its origin in medical therapy a criterion of normality instead of rationality. On sheer statistics every pioneer, genius and social reformer, including the first woman who demanded to be let out of the kitchen and into the polling booth, is abnormal, along with every lunatic and eccentric. What distinguishes the genius from the lunatic is that the genius's abnormality is justifiable by reason or aesthetics. If a woman who is irked by confinement to the kitchen merely looks round to see what other women are doing and finds they are accepting their kitchens, she may well conclude that she is abnormal and had better enlist her psycho-analyst's help towards "living with" her

kitchen. What she ought to ask is whether it is rational for women to be kept to the kitchen, and whether nature really does insist on that in the way it insists women have breasts. And in a far-reaching sense to ask that question is much more normal and natural than learning to "live with" the handicap of women's inferior social status. The normal and natural thing for human beings is not to tolerate handicaps but to reform society and to circumvent or supplement nature. We don't learn to live minus a leg; we devise an artificial limb.

22   That, indeed, is the crux of the matter. Not only are the distinctions we draw between male nature and female nature largely arbitrary and often pure superstition: they are completely beside the point. They ignore the essence of *human* nature. The important question is not whether women are or are not less logical by nature than men, but whether education, effort and the abolition of our illogical social pressures can improve on nature and make them (and, incidentally, men as well) *more* logical. What distinguishes human from any other animal nature is its ability to be unnatural. Logic and art are not natural or instinctive activities; but our nature includes a propensity to acquire them. It is not natural for the human body to orbit the earth; but the human mind has a natural adventurousness which enables it to invent machines whereby the body can do so. There is, in sober fact, no such creature as a natural man. Go as far back as they will, the archaeologists cannot come on a wild man in his natural habitat. At his most primitive, he has already constructed himself an artificial habitat, and decorated it not by a standardised instinctual method, as birds build nests, but by individualised—that is, abnormal—works of art or magic. And in doing so he is not limited by the fingers nature gave him; he has extended their versatility by making tools.

23   Civilisation consists not necessarily in defying nature but in making it possible for us to do so if we judge it desirable. The higher we can life our noses from the grindstone of nature, the wider the area we have of choice; and the more choices we have freely made, the more individualised we are. We are at our most civilised when nature does not dictate to us, as it does to animals and peasants, but when we can opt to fall in with it or better it. If modern civilisation has invented methods of education which make it possible for men to feed babies and for women to think logically, we are betraying civilisation itself if we do not set both sexes free to make a free choice.

THINKING ABOUT THE TEXT

1. What are the specific points of Brophy's comparisons between the modern zoo without bars and what has happened to women?

2. In what ways does Brophy argue for emancipation of both women and men?

3. How do our stereotypical views of gender and our clichés of language perpetuate the problems that Brophy discusses?

4. In spite of her title, what is Brophy advocating in her essay?

WRITING FROM THE TEXT

1. Write an essay in which you describe the "invisible cages" in which women are kept. In addition to your own points, use and appropriately document Brophy's points in your essay.

2. Compare the "invisible cages" of women *and* men.

3. Write an essay in which you focus on the "zone[s] of hot or cold air" that keep adventurous women "in their places."

4. Interview some men with the specific goal of learning if any of them would stay at home if they had mates who earned enough money to support the family. What are your subjects' responses to the idea of being "househusbands"? How many would find staying at home ego threatening? Is Brophy right or wrong? Write an essay using your collected material for specific support.

CONNECTING WITH OTHER TEXTS

1. Warren Farrell's view in "Men as Success Objects" (p. 90) is that men are required to be successful because the "hidden agenda" expects attractive dates and mates to be successful. How does Farrell's essay complement Brophy's? Write an essay from your own perspective, using these essays for support.

2. Use this essay, Swenson's poem "Women" (p. 100), and Piercy's poem "A Work of Artifice" (p. 110) to write an essay that shows the restrictions placed on women. Use these works for support of your point.

3. Brophy concludes her essay with the thought that "the more choices we have freely made, the more individualised we are." Write an analysis of the problems facing women and/or men in your generation. Propose a way that either or both genders can become free. Any of the material in this chapter will be useful to your analysis, but the work of Farrell, Allis, Wolf, and Brophy will be especially helpful in describing the problems that each gender faces.

WOMEN
May Swenson

A poet, translator, author of children's books, dramatist, and critic, Swenson (1919–1989) is noted for her perceptive insights and playful, original experimentations with poetic language. Her poems examine human concerns, scientific topics, and nature. She has said that "not only poetry, but all the arts" are humanizing, and that art "humanizes the one who makes it, as well as all the others who enjoy it." The poem printed below is from *Iconographs,* published in 1968.

```
Women        Or they
  should be      should be
    pedestals      little horses
      moving           those wooden
        pedestals          sweet
          moving             oldfashioned
            to the             painted
              motions            rocking
                of men             horses

            the gladdest things in the toyroom

                  The                    feelingly
                pegs                   and then
              of their                 unfeelingly
            ears                      To be
          so familiar               joyfully
        and dear                   ridden
      to the trusting            rockingly
    fists                       ridden until
  To be chafed              the restored

egos dismount and the legs stride away

Immobile        willing
  sweetlipped      to be set
    sturdy             into motion
      and smiling         Women
        women               should be
          should always        pedestals
            be waiting              to men
```

THINKING ABOUT THE TEXT

1. Can this poem be read in *any* direction, or does it read more smoothly and clearly one way? How does the physical shape of the poem relate to its content?

2. Using specifics from the poem, list all the qualities of a rocking horse that represent the more traditional woman.

3. May Swenson modifies the notion of putting women *on* pedestals and asserts, "Women should *be* pedestals." How is this different? How do both do a disservice to women?

4. Explain how this poem is a satire (that is, a work that uses humor, wit, exaggeration, and ridicule to make a point, or to criticize and attack). What are several targets of this satire?

WRITING FROM THE TEXT

1. Using your responses to question 2 above, write an essay focusing on Swenson's view of the "rocking horse" type of woman.

2. Using your responses to question 4 above, write an analysis of this poem as a satire.

CONNECTING WITH OTHER TEXTS

1. Read "Women: Invisible Cages" (p. 94), "The Beauty Myth" (below), and "A Work of Artifice" (p. 110), and write a paper relating these works to May Swenson's poem.

2. Read other poems by May Swenson in her collections *Iconographs* or *To Mix with Time.* Focus on several poems with a common theme and write an analysis comparing her development of that theme.

THE BEAUTY MYTH
Naomi Wolf

A graduate of Yale University, Naomi Wolf (b. 1963) was also a Rhodes Scholar at New College, Oxford. Wolf's works, including poetry, essays, and book reviews, have appeared in *Ms., Verse,* the *Iowa Review, Writing Women,* and other publications. *The Beauty Myth: How Images of Beauty Are Used Against Women* was published in 1991 to wide critical acclaim. The work included here is the first chapter of *The Beauty Myth.*

1   At last, after a long silence, women took to the streets. In the two decades of radical action that followed the rebirth of feminism in the early 1970s, Western women gained legal and reproductive rights, pursued higher education, entered the trades and the professions, and overturned ancient and revered beliefs about their social role. A generation on, do women feel free?

2   The affluent, educated, liberated women of the First World, who can enjoy freedoms unavailable to any women ever before, do not feel as free as they want to. And they can no longer restrict to the subconscious their sense that this lack of freedom has something to do with—with apparently frivolous issues, things that really should not matter. Many are ashamed to admit that such trivial concerns— to do with physical appearance, bodies, faces, hair, clothes—matter so much. But in spite of shame, guilt, and denial, more and more women are wondering if it isn't that they are entirely neurotic and alone but rather that something important is indeed at stake that has to do with the relationship between female liberation and female beauty.

3   The more legal and material hindrances women have broken through, the more strictly and heavily and cruelly images of female beauty have come to weigh upon us. Many women sense that women's collective progress has stalled; compared with the heady momentum of earlier days, there is a dispiriting climate of confusion, division, cynicism, and above all, exhaustion. After years of much struggle and little recognition, many older women feel burned out; after years of taking its light for granted, many younger women show little interest in touching new fire to the torch.

4   During the past decade, women breached the power structure; meanwhile, eating disorders rose exponentially and cosmetic surgery became the fastest-growing medical specialty. During the past five years, consumer spending doubled, pornography became the main media category, ahead of legitimate films and records combined, and thirty-three thousand American women told researchers that they would rather lose ten to fifteen pounds than achieve any other goal. More women have more money and power and scope and legal recognition than we have ever had before; but in terms of how we feel about ourselves *physically,* we may actually be worse off than our unliberated grandmothers. Recent research consistently shows that inside the majority of the West's controlled, attractive, successful working women, there is a secret "underlife" poisoning our freedom; infused with notions of beauty, it is a dark vein of self-hatred, physical obsessions, terror of aging, and dread of lost control.

5   It is no accident that so many potentially powerful women feel this way. We are in the midst of a violent backlash against feminism that uses images of female beauty as a political weapon against women's advancement: the beauty myth. It is the modern version of a social reflex that has been in force since the Industrial Revolution. As women released themselves from the feminine mystique of domesticity, the beauty myth took over its lost ground, expanding as it waned to carry on its work of social control.

6   The contemporary backlash is so violent because the ideology of beauty is the last one remaining of the old feminine ideologies that still has the power to control those women whom second wave feminism would have otherwise made relatively uncontrollable: It has grown stronger to take over the work of social coercion that myths about motherhood, domesticity, chastity, and passivity, no longer can manage. It is seeking right now to undo psychologically and covertly all the good things that feminism did for women materially and overtly.

7   This counterforce is operating to checkmate the inheritance of feminism on every level in the lives of Western women. Feminism gave us laws against job discrimination based on gender; immediately case law evolved in Britain and the United States that institutionalized job discrimination based on women's appearances. Patriarchal religion declined; new religious dogma, using some of the mind-altering techniques of older cults and sects, arose around age and weight to functionally supplant traditional ritual. Feminists, inspired by Friedan, broke the stranglehold on the women's popular press of advertisers for household products, who were promoting the feminine mystique; at once, the diet and skin care industries became the new cultural censors of women's intellectual space, and because of their pressure, the gaunt, youthful model supplanted the happy housewife as the arbiter of successful womanhood. The sexual revolution promoted the discovery of female sexuality; "beauty pornography"—which for the first time in women's history artificially links a commodified "beauty" directly and explicitly to sexuality—invaded the mainstream to undermine women's new and vulnerable sense of sexual self-worth. Reproductive rights gave Western women control over our own bodies; the weight of fashion models plummeted to 23 percent below that of ordinary women, eating disorders rose exponentially, and a mass neurosis was promoted that used food and weight to strip women of that sense of control. Women insisted on politicizing health; new technologies of invasive, potentially deadly "cosmetic" surgeries developed apace to re-exert old forms of medical control of women.

8   Every generation since about 1830 has had to fight its version of the beauty myth. "It is very little to me," said the suffragist Lucy Stone in 1855, "to have the right to vote, to own property, etcetera, if I may not keep my body, and its uses, in my absolute right." Eighty years later, after women had won the vote, and the first wave of the organized women's movement had subsided, Virginia Woolf wrote that it would still be decades before women could tell the truth about their bodies. In 1962, Betty Friedan quoted a young woman trapped in the Feminine Mystique: "Lately, I look in the mirror, and I'm so afraid I'm going to look like my mother." Eight years after that, heralding the cataclysmic second wave of feminism, Germaine Greer described "the Stereotype": "To her belongs all that is beautiful, even the very word beauty itself . . . she is a doll . . . I'm sick of the masquerade." In spite of the great revolution of the second wave, we are not exempt. Now we can look out over ruined barricades: A revolution has come upon us and changed everything in its path, enough time has passed since then for babies to have grown into women, but there still remains a final right not fully claimed.

9   The beauty myth tells a story: The quality called "beauty" objectively and universally exists. Women must want to embody it and men must want to possess women who embody it. This embodiment is an imperative for women and not for men, which situation is necessary and natural because it is biological, sexual, and evolutionary: Strong men battle for beautiful women, and beautiful women are more reproductively successful. Women's beauty must correlate to their fertility, and since this system is based on sexual selection, it is inevitable and changeless.

10   None of this is true. "Beauty" is a currency system like the gold standard. Like any economy, it is determined by politics, and in the modern age in the West it is the last, best belief system that keeps male dominance intact. In assigning value to women in a vertical hierarchy according to a culturally imposed physical standard, it is an expression of power relations in which women must unnaturally compete for resources that men have appropriated for themselves.

11   "Beauty" is not universal or changeless, though the West pretends that all ideals of female beauty stem from one Platonic Ideal Woman; the Maori admire a fat vulva, and the Padung, droopy breasts. Nor is "beauty" a function of evolution: Its ideals change at a pace far more rapid than that of the evolution of species, and Charles Darwin was himself unconvinced by his own explanation that "beauty" resulted from a "sexual selection" that deviated from the rule of natural selection; for women to compete with women through "beauty" is a reversal of the way in which natural selection affects all other mammals. Anthropology has overturned the notion that females must be "beautiful" to be selected to mate: Evelyn Reed, Elaine Morgan, and others have dismissed sociobiological assertions of innate male polygamy and female monogamy. Female higher primates are the sexual initiators; not only do they seek out and enjoy sex with many partners, but "every nonpregnant female takes her turn at being the most desirable of all her troop. And that cycle keeps turning as long as she lives." The inflamed pink sexual organs of primates are often cited by male sociobiologists as analogous to human arrangements relating to female "beauty," when in fact that is a universal, nonhierarchical female primate characteristic.

12   Nor has the beauty myth always been this way. Though the pairing of the older rich men with young, "beautiful" women is taken to be somehow inevitable, in the matriarchal Goddess religions that dominated the Mediterranean from about 25,000 B.C.E. to about 700 B.C.E., the situation was reversed: "In every culture, the Goddess has many lovers. . . . The clear pattern is of an older woman with a beautiful but expendable youth—Ishtar and Tammuz, Venus and Adonis, Cybele and Attis, Isis and Osiris . . . their only function the service of the divine 'womb.'" Nor is it something only women do and only men watch: Among the Nigerian Wodaabes, the women hold economic power and the tribe is obsessed with male beauty; Wodaabe men spend hours together in elaborate makeup sessions, and compete—provocatively painted and dressed, with swaying hips and seductive expressions—in beauty contests judged by women. There is no legitimate historical or biological justification for the beauty myth; what it is doing to women today is a result of nothing more exalted than the need of today's power structure, economy, and culture to mount a counteroffensive against women.

13   If the beauty myth is not based on evolution, sex, gender, aesthetics, or God, on what is it based? It claims to be about intimacy and sex and life, a celebration of women. It is actually composed of emotional distance, politics, finance, and sexual repression. The beauty myth is not about women at all. It is about men's institutions and institutional power.

14   The qualities that a given period calls beautiful in women are merely symbols of the female behavior that that period considers desirable: *The beauty myth is always actually prescribing behavior and not appearance.* Competition between

women has been made part of the myth so that women will be divided from one another. Youth and (until recently) virginity have been "beautiful" in women since they stand for experiential and sexual ignorance. Aging in women is "unbeautiful" since women grow more powerful with time, and since the links between generations of women must always be newly broken: Older women fear young ones, young women fear old, and the beauty myth truncates for all the female life span. Most urgently, women's identity must be premised upon our "beauty" so that we will remain vulnerable to outside approval, carrying the vital sensitive organ of self-esteem exposed to the air.

15   Though there has, of course, been a beauty myth in some form for as long as there has been patriarchy, the beauty myth in its modern form is a fairly recent invention. The myth flourishes when material constraints on women are dangerously loosened. Before the Industrial Revolution, the average woman could not have had the same feelings about "beauty" that modern women do who experience the myth as continual comparison to a mass-disseminated physical ideal. Before the development of technologies of mass production—daguerreotypes, photographs, etc.—an ordinary woman was exposed to few such images outside the Church. Since the family was a productive unit and women's work complemented men's, the value of women who were not aristocrats or prostitutes lay in their work skills, economic shrewdness, physical strength, and fertility. Physical attraction, obviously, played its part; but "beauty" as we understand it was not, for ordinary women, a serious issue in the marriage marketplace. The beauty myth in its modern form gained ground after the upheavals of industrialization, as the work unit of the family was destroyed, and urbanization and the emerging factory system demanded what social engineers of the time termed the "separate sphere" of domesticity, which supported the new labor category of the "breadwinner" who left home for the workplace during the day. The middle class expanded, the standards of living and of literacy rose, the size of families shrank; a new class of literate, idle women developed, on whose submission to enforced domesticity the evolving system of industrial capitalism depended. Most of our assumptions about the way women have always thought about "beauty" date from no earlier than the 1830s, when the cult of domesticity was first consolidated and the beauty index invented.

16   For the first time new technologies could reproduce—in fashion plates, daguerreotypes, tintypes, and rotogravures—images of how women should look. In the 1840s the first nude photographs of prostitutes were taken; advertisements using images of "beautiful" women first appeared in mid-century. Copies of classical artworks, postcards of society beauties and royal mistresses, Currier and Ives prints, and porcelain figurines flooded the separate sphere to which middle-class women were confined.

17   Since the Industrial Revolution, middle-class Western women have been controlled by ideals and stereotypes as much as by material constraints. This situation, unique to this group, means that analyses that trace "cultural conspiracies" are uniquely plausible in relation to them. The rise of the beauty myth was just one of several emerging social fictions that masqueraded as natural components of the feminine sphere, the better to enclose those women inside it. Other such fic-

tions arose contemporaneously: a version of childhood that required continual maternal supervision; a concept of female biology that required middle-class women to act out the roles of hysterics and hypochondriacs; a conviction that respectable women were sexually anesthetic; and a definition of women's work that occupied them with repetitive, time-consuming, and painstaking tasks such as needlepoint and lacemaking. All such Victorian inventions as these served a double function—that is, though they were encouraged as a means to expend female energy and intelligence in harmless ways, women often used them to express genuine creativity and passion.

18   But in spite of middle-class women's creativity with fashion and embroidery and child rearing, and, a century later, with the role of the suburban housewife that devolved from these social fictions, the fictions' main purpose was served: During a century and a half of unprecedented feminist agitation, they effectively counteracted middle-class women's dangerous new leisure, literacy, and relative freedom from material constraints.

19   Though these time- and mind-consuming fictions about women's natural role adapted themselves to resurface in the post-war Feminine Mystique, when the second wave of the women's movement took apart what women's magazines had portrayed as the "romance," "science," and "adventure" of homemaking and suburban family life, they temporarily failed. The cloying domestic fiction of "togetherness" lost its meaning and middle-class women walked out of their front doors in masses.

20   So the fictions simply transformed themselves once more: Since the women's movement had successfully taken apart most other necessary fictions of femininity, all the work of social control once spread out over the whole network of these fictions had to be reassigned to the only strand left intact, which action consequently strengthened it a hundredfold. This reimposed onto liberated women's faces and bodies all the limitations, taboos, and punishments of the repressive laws, religious injunctions and reproductive enslavement that no longer carried sufficient force. Inexhaustible but ephemeral beauty work took over from inexhaustible but ephemeral housework. As the economy, law, religion, sexual mores, education, and culture were forcibly opened up to include women more fairly, a private reality colonized female consciousness. By using ideas about "beauty," it reconstructed an alternative female world with its own laws, economy, religion, sexuality, education, and culture, each element as repressive as any that had gone before.

21   Since middle-class Western women can best be weakened psychologically now that we are stronger materially, the beauty myth, as it has resurfaced in the last generation, has had to draw on more technological sophistication and reactionary fervor than ever before. The modern arsenal of the myth is a dissemination of millions of images of the current ideal; although this barrage is generally seen as a collective sexual fantasy, there is in fact little that is sexual about it. It is summoned out of political fear on the part of male-dominated institutions threatened by women's freedom, and it exploits female guilt and apprehension about our own liberation—latent fears that we might be going too far. This frantic aggregation of imagery is a collective reactionary hallucination willed into being by both men and women stunned and disoriented by the rapidity with which gender relations

have been transformed: a bulwark of reassurance against the flood of change. The mass depiction of the modern woman as a "beauty" is a contradiction: Where modern women are growing, moving, and expressing their individuality, as the myth has it, "beauty" is by definition inert, timeless, and generic. That this hallucination is necessary and deliberate is evident in the way "beauty" so directly contradicts women's real situation.

22   And the unconscious hallucination grows ever more influential and pervasive because of what is now conscious market manipulation: powerful industries—the $33-billion-a-year diet industry, the $20-billion cosmetics industry, the $300-million cosmetic surgery industry, and the $7-billion pornography industry—have arisen from the capital made out of unconscious anxieties, and are in turn able, through their influence on mass culture, to use, stimulate, and reinforce the hallucination in a rising economic spiral.

23   This is not a conspiracy theory; it doesn't have to be. Societies tell themselves necessary fictions in the same way that individuals and families do. Henrik Ibsen called them "vital lies," and psychologist Daniel Goleman describes them working the same way on the social level that they do within families: "The collusion is maintained by directing attention away from the fearsome fact, or by repackaging its meaning in an acceptable format." The costs of these social blind spots, he writes, are destructive communal illusions. Possibilities for women have become so open-ended that they threaten to destabilize the institutions on which a male-dominated culture has depended, and a collective panic reaction on the part of both sexes has forced a demand for counterimages.

24   The resulting hallucination materializes, for women, as something all too real. No longer just an idea, it becomes three-dimensional, incorporating within itself how women live and how they do not live: It becomes the Iron Maiden. The original Iron Maiden was a medieval German instrument of torture, a body-shaped casket painted with the limbs and features of a lovely, smiling young woman. The unlucky victim was slowly enclosed inside her; the lid fell shut to immobilize the victim, who died either of starvation or, less cruelly, of the metal spikes embedded in her interior. The modern hallucination in which women are trapped or trap themselves is similarly rigid, cruel, and euphemistically painted. Contemporary culture directs attention to imagery of the Iron Maiden, while censoring real women's faces and bodies.

25   Why does the social order feel the need to defend itself by evading the fact of real women, our faces and voices and bodies, and reducing the meaning of women to these formulaic and endlessly reproduced "beautiful" images? Though unconscious personal anxieties can be a powerful force in the creation of a vital lie, economic necessity practically guarantees it. An economy that depends on slavery needs to promote images of slaves that "justify" the institution of slavery. Western economies are absolutely dependent now on the continued underpayment of women. An ideology that makes women feel "worth less" was urgently needed to counteract the way feminism had begun to make us feel worth more. This does not require a conspiracy; merely an atmosphere. The contemporary economy depends right now on the representation of women within the beauty myth. Economist John Kenneth Galbraith offers an economic explanation for "the persistence of the

view of homemaking as a 'higher calling'": the concept of women as naturally trapped within the Feminine Mystique, he feels, "has been forced on us by popular sociology, by magazines, and by fiction to disguise the fact that woman in her role of consumer has been essential to the development of our industrial society. . . . Behavior that is essential for economic reasons is transformed into a social virtue." As soon as a woman's primary social value could no longer be defined as the attainment of virtuous domesticity, the beauty myth redefined it as the attainment of virtuous beauty. It did so to substitute both a new consumer imperative and a new justification for economic unfairness in the workplace where the old ones had lost their hold over newly liberated women.

26   Another hallucination arose to accompany that of the Iron Maiden: The caricature of the Ugly Feminist was resurrected to dog the steps of the women's movement. The caricature is unoriginal; it was coined to ridicule the feminists of the nineteenth century. Lucy Stone herself, whom supporters saw as "a prototype of womanly grace . . . fresh and fair as the morning," was derided by detractors with "the usual report" about Victorian feminists: "a big masculine woman, wearing boots, smoking a cigar, swearing like a trooper." As Betty Friedan put it presciently in 1960, even before the savage revamping of that old caricature: "The unpleasant image of feminists today resembles less the feminists themselves than the image fostered by the interests who so bitterly opposed the vote for women in state after state." Thirty years on, her conclusion is more true than ever: That resurrected caricature, which sought to punish women for their public acts by going after their private sense of self, became the paradigm for new limits placed on aspiring women everywhere. After the success of the women's movement's second wave, the beauty myth was perfected to checkmate power at every level in individual women's lives. The modern neuroses of life in the female body spread to woman after woman at epidemic rates. The myth is undermining—slowly, imperceptibly, without our being aware of the real forces of erosion—the ground women have gained through long, hard, honorable struggle.

27   The beauty myth of the present is more insidious than any mystique of femininity yet: A century ago, Nora slammed the door of the doll's house; a generation ago, women turned their backs on the consumer heaven of the isolated multiapplianced home; but where women are trapped today, there is no door to slam. The contemporary ravages of the beauty backlash are destroying women physically and depleting us psychologically. If we are to free ourselves from the dead weight that has once again been made out of femaleness, it is not ballots or lobbyists or placards that women will need first; it is a new way to see.

THINKING ABOUT THE TEXT

1. According to Wolf, what prevents apparently liberated women from feeling free?

2. In this introductory chapter of her book *The Beauty Myth*, Wolf juxtaposes gains for women in the last decades of the twentieth century

with specific problems that mitigate the triumphs for women. What are the problems, and to what does she attribute their existence?

3. How does Wolf defend her assertion that "'beauty' is not universal or changeless"? Think of additional examples from your own life history or awareness of anthropology to support her point.

4. Why is the beauty myth a "fairly recent invention"?

5. What is the original Iron Maiden? How is Wolf using the term?

6. What does Wolf believe will be the only way for women to free themselves from the insidious myth?

WRITING FROM THE TEXT

1. Compare your experiences, or the experiences of a friend, with any of the specific problems that Wolf refers to in this reading.

2. Use Wolf's assertion that "'beauty' is not universal or changeless" to write your own essay. Support Wolf's statement with specific examples that you know from experience or reading.

3. What will be the "new way to see" that will liberate women from the beauty myth? Write an analysis of the problems facing women today, and propose a reform.

CONNECTING WITH OTHER TEXTS

1. In her essay "Women: Invisible Cages" (p. 94), Brigid Brophy notes that "no one can bear not to be attractive to the opposite sex" (96). Compare the points made in Brophy's essay with those made by Wolf. Have there been significant changes in the 30 years since Brophy's essay was published?

2. Take any one of the problems that Wolf discusses, and write your own researched analysis. You will find information about eating disorders, cosmetic surgery, and pornography in Wolf's book *The Beauty Myth*, as well as in popular periodicals.

3. Write an analysis of the problems that faced women in your mother's generation with those facing women in your own time. Research the different "waves" of feminism, or interview representatives of the two generations, in order to write this paper.

A WORK OF ARTIFICE
Marge Piercy

Educated at the University of Michigan and Northwestern University, Marge Piercy (b. 1936) has served as a visiting lecturer, writer in residence, and professor at many universities in the United States. She has won many prizes, awards, and honors for her novels, short stories, plays, and essays. Of her work Piercy says, "I have been particularly although not exclusively concerned with the choices open to— or perceived to be open to—women of various eras, races, and classes. I am one of the few contemporary American novelists consciously and constantly preoccupied with social class and the economic underpinnings of decision and consequence." The poem printed below is from *Circles on the Water* (published in 1969), one of Piercy's 11 collections of poetry. Her most recent, *Available Light*, was published in 1988.

> The bonsai tree
> in the attractive pot
> could have grown eighty feet tall
> on the side of a mountain
> till split by lightning.   5
> But a gardener
> carefully pruned it.
> It is nine inches high.
> Every day as he
> whittles back the branches   10
> the gardener croons,
> It is your nature
> to be small and cozy
> domestic and weak;
> how lucky, little tree,   15
> to have a pot to grow in.
> With living creatures
> one must begin very early
> to dwarf their growth:
> the bound feet,   20
> the crippled brain,
> the hair in curlers,
> the hands you
> love to touch.

THINKING ABOUT THE TEXT

1. According to the poem, how is a bonsai tree created and maintained?
2. What are the comparisons between the creation and care of a bonsai and the creation and care of a woman? Do you object to the art of bonsai? How do you feel about what happens to women?
3. Look up the word *artifice* in a dictionary and copy all of the definitions listed for the word. In what ways is each meaning of the word useful to Piercy in conveying the point of her poem? What *is* her point?

WRITING FROM THE TEXT

1. Write an essay in which you explain how Marge Piercy's title contains perfect word choice for conveying the theme of the poem. You will want to examine the multiple definitions of the word *artifice* as part of your analysis.
2. Write an essay analyzing the ways that women are "crooned" to and the resultant "cozy" and "weak" ways that they are kept. Show your attitude or stance toward this situation in your essay.

CONNECTING WITH OTHER TEXTS

1. Look up information about the art of bonsai in an encyclopedia or gardening text in your school or city library. Write about the goals of this art form, and summarize the process of maintaining a bonsai plant.
2. How has the history of keeping women "small and cozy / domestic and weak" been opposed in recent years? Use specific references to the presence of women in professional, business, or academic worlds to argue that "the crippled brain" is a metaphor of the past.
3. Compare Marge Piercy's perception about what happens to women in "A Work of Artifice" to the insights about women in the poem "Women" (p. 100).
4. Piercy's gardener has moved the tree, which might have grown to "eighty feet tall," to an attractive pot where it will stay "small and cozy." Brigid Brophy, in "Women: Invisible Cages" (p. 94), also describes forces that keep women "domestic." What are these forces? Is the agent always a *man* with an overt plan? Also consider Naomi Wolf's "The Beauty Myth" (p. 101) in writing your analysis.

DATE RAPE
Ellen Sweet

A graduate of Smith University with a master's degree in teaching from Yale, Ellen Sweet (b. 1942) has worked as a senior editor at *Ms.* magazine, where her special interest was in health-related issues. She is now an executive editor at *New Choices* magazine. The article below first appeared in *Ms.* in 1985.

1   It was the beginning of spring break when I was a junior. I was in good spirits and had been out to dinner with an old friend. We returned to his college [dorm]. There were some seniors on the ground floor, drinking beer, playing bridge. I'm an avid player, so we joined them, joked around a lot. One of them, John, wasn't playing, but he was interested in the game. I found him attractive. We talked, and it turned out we had a mutual friend, shared experiences. It was getting late, and my friend had gone up to bed, so John offered to see me safely home. We took our time, sat outside talking for a while. Then he said we could get inside one of the most beautiful campus buildings, which was usually locked at night. I went with him. Once we were inside, he kissed me. I didn't resist, I was excited. He kissed me again. But when he tried for more, I said no. He just grew completely silent. I couldn't get him to talk to me any more. He pinned me down and ripped off my pants. *I couldn't believe it was happening to me. . .*

2   Let's call this Yale graduate Judy. Her experience and her disbelief, as she describes them, are not unique. Gretchen, another student victim of date rape (or acquaintance rape, as it is also called), had known for five years the man who invited her to an isolated vacation cabin and then raped her. "I considered him my best friend," she says on a Stanford University videotape used in discussions of the problem. "I couldn't believe it. *I couldn't believe it was actually happening to me.*"

3   Such denial, the inability to believe that someone they know could have raped them, is a common reaction of victims of date rape, say psychologists and counselors who have researched the topic and treated these women. In fact, so much silence surrounds this kind of crime that many women are not even aware that they have been raped. In one study, Mary P. Koss, a psychology professor at Kent State University, Ohio, asked female students if they had had sexual intercourse against their will through use of or threat of force (the minimal legal definition of rape). Of those who answered yes, only 57 percent went on to identify their experience as rape. Koss also identified the other group (43 percent) as those who hadn't even acknowledged the rape to themselves.

4   "I can't believe it's happening on our campus," is usually the initial response to reports such as Koss's. She also found that one in eight women students had been raped, and another one in four were victims of attempted rape. Since only 4 percent of all those reported the attack, Koss concluded that "at least ten times more rapes occur among college students than are reflected in official crime statistics." (Rape is recognized to be the most underreported of all crimes, and date rape is among the least reported, least believed, and most difficult to prosecute, second only to spouse rape.)

5   Working independently of Koss, researchers at Auburn University, Alabama, and more recently, University of South Dakota and St. Cloud State University, Minnesota, all have found that one in five women students were raped by men they knew.

6   Koss also found a core group of highly sexually aggressive men (4.3 percent) who use physical force to compel women to have intercourse but who are unlikely to see their act as rape. These "hidden rapists" have "oversubscribed" to traditional male roles, she says. They believe that aggression is normal and that women don't really mean it when they say no to sexual advances. Such men answer "True" to statements like "most women are sly and manipulating when they want to attract a man," "a woman will only respect a man who will lay down the law to her," and "a man's got to show the woman who's boss right from the start or he'll end up henpecked."

7   In Koss's current study, one respondent who answered yes to a question about obtaining intercourse through physical force, wrote in the comment, "I didn't rape the chick, she was enjoying it and responding," and later, "I feel that sex is a very pleasant way to relieve stress. Especially when there are no strings attached."

8   "He acted like he had a right, like he *didn't believe me,*" says a coed from Auburn University on a videotaped dramatization of date rape experiences. And several weeks later, when she confronts him, saying he forced her, he says no, she wanted it. "You raped me," she finally tells him. And the picture freezes on his look of incredulity.

9   Barry Burkhart, a professor of psychology at Auburn, who has also studied sexual aggression among college men, found that 10 percent had used physical force to have intercourse with a woman against her will, and a large majority admitted to various other kinds of aggression. "These are ordinary males operating in an ordinary social context," he says. "So what we conclude is that there's something wrong with that social context."

10   The something wrong is that our culture fosters a "rape supportive belief system," according to social psychologist Martha Burt. She thinks that "there's a large category of 'real' rapes, and a much smaller category of what our culture is willing to call a 'real' rape. The question is, how does the culture manage to write off all those other rapes?" The way it's done, says Burt, currently director of the Social Services Research Center at the Urban Institute in Washington, D.C., is by believing in a series of myths about rape, including:

- It didn't really happen (the woman was lying);
- Women like rape (so there's no such thing as rape);
- Yes, it happened, but no harm was done (she wasn't a virgin; she wasn't white);
- Women provoke it (men can't control themselves);
- Women deserve it anyway.

11   It's easy to write off date rapes with such myths, coupled with what Burt calls our culture's "adversarial sexual beliefs": the gamesmanship theory that everybody is out for what they can get, and that all sexual relationships are basically exploitive and predatory. In fact, most victims of date rape initially blame them-

selves for what happened, and almost none report it to campus authorities. And most academic institutions prefer to keep it that way, judging from the lack of surveys on date rape—all of which makes one wonder if they don't actually blame the victim, too.

12   As long as such attacks continue to be a "hidden" campus phenomenon, unreported and unacknowledged by many college administrators, law enforcement personnel, and students, the problem will persist. Of course, the term has become much better known in the three years since *Ms.* reported on the prevalence of experiences such as Judy's and Gretchen's. (See "Date Rape: A Campus Epidemic?" September 1982.) It has been the subject of talk shows such as "The Donahue Show" and TV dramas ("Cagney and Lacey"). But for most people it remains a contradiction in terms. "Everybody has a stake in denying that it's happening so often," says Martha Burt. "For women, it's self-protective . . . if only bad girls get raped, then I'm personally safe. For men, it's the denial that 'nice' people like them do it."

13   The fault has not entirely been that of the institutions. "Ten years ago, we were telling women to look over your shoulder when you go out at night and lock your doors," says Py Bateman, director of a nationally known rape education program in Seattle, Alternatives to Fear. The prevailing myth was that most rapes were committed by strangers in dark alleys.

14   "If you have to think that sixty to eighty percent of rape is by people you know—that's hard to deal with," says Sylvia Callaway, who directed the Austin, Texas, Rape Crisis Center for more than eight years before leaving last July. "No rape center in a university community would be surprised that the university is not willing to deal with the problem."

15   Statistics alone will not solve the problem of date rape, but they could help bring it out into the open. Which is why *Ms.* undertook the first nationwide survey on college campuses. The *Ms.* Magazine Campus Project on Sexual Assault, directed by Mary P. Koss at Kent State and funded by the National Center for the Prevention and Control of Rape, reached more than seven thousand students at a nationally representative sample of thirty-five schools, to find out how often, under what circumstances, and with what aftereffects a wide range of sexual assaults, including date rape, took place.

16   Preliminary results are now ready, and the information is no surprise. Participating schools were promised anonymity, but each will receive the results applying to its student body. Our hope is that the reaction of "we can't believe it's happening on our campus" will be followed by "what can we do about it—now."

17   Just how entrenched is denial of this problem today? One gauge might be the difficulty our own researchers had in persuading schools to let us on campus. For every college that approved our study, two others rejected it. Their reasons (in writing and in telephone conversations) were themselves instructive: "we don't want to get involved," "limited foreseeable benefit," "too volatile a topic," "have not had any problems in this area," "worried about publicity," "can't allow surveys in classroom," "just can't invest the time now," "would be overintrusive," "don't want to be left holding the bag if something goes wrong."

18   Several schools rejected the study on the basis that filling out the questionnaire might upset some students, and that we were not providing adequate follow-up

counseling. (Researchers stayed on campus for at least a day after the distribution of the questionnaire, gave students listings of counselors or rape crisis centers to consult if anything upset them, and offered to meet with school personnel to brief them.) But isn't it less upsetting for a student to recognize and admit that she has been the victim of an acquaintance rape than to have buried the trauma of that rape deep inside herself?

19   "It's a Catch-22 situation. You want a survey to publicize a problem that has tremendous psychological implications. And the school says, 'Don't do it, because it will get people psychologically upset,'" admits John Jung, who heads the human subjects review committee at California State University/Long Beach (a school that declined our study).

20   One wonders just who are the "people" who will get most psychologically upset: the students, or their parents who pay for their educations, or the administrators who are concerned about the school's image. "There may have been an episode here," said John Hose, executive assistant to the president of Brandeis University, "but there is no cause célèbre surrounding the issue. In such cases, the reaction of Student Affairs is to encourage the student to be in touch with her parents and to take legal action."

21   "Student Affairs" at Brandeis is headed by Rodger Crafts, who moved to this post about a year ago from the University of Rhode Island. "I don't think we have a significant problem here because we have a sophisticated and intelligent group of students," said Dean Crafts. As for the University of Rhode Island, more students there are "first generation college attenders," as he put it, and therefore have "less respect" for other people. Vandalism and physical harm are more likely to occur with "lower educational levels." Respect for other people goes along with "intelligence level."

22   Back at the University of Rhode Island, the counseling center is sponsoring a twelve-week support and therapy group this fall for male students who are coercive and abusive in their relationships with women. Even though Nancy Carlson, director of Counseling and Career Services, is enthusiastic about such programs and workshops she notes, "the awareness about date rape has been a long time coming."

23   Another school where administrators were the last to confront the challenge to their school's self-image is Yale. Last year, two student publications reported instances of date rape on campus that surprised students, faculty, and administration. "There are no full statistics available on rape between students at Yale anywhere. . . . There is no mention of rape in the 1983–1984 Undergraduate Regulations. There is no procedure for a victim to file a formal complaint of rape with the university. But there is rape between students at Yale," wrote Sarah Oates in the *Yale Daily News*. Partly in response to such charges, current Yale undergraduate regulations now list "sexual harassment" under "offenses that are subject to disciplinary action"—but still no mention of rape.

24   Yale students brave enough to bring a charge of sexual harassment may go before the Yale College Executive Committee, a specially convened group of faculty, administrators, and students that can impose a series of penalties, graduated in severity, culminating in expulsion. All its hearings and decisions are kept secret

(but can in theory be subpoenaed in a court of law). But Michael McBride, current chair of the committee, told me that cases of date rape have come up during the past year, leading in one instance to a student being asked to "resign" from the university, and in another, the conclusion that there was not "sufficient evidence." (In Judy's case, described at the beginning of this article, the senior she charged was penalized by being denied the privilege of graduating with his class. But she claims that after he demanded that the case be reconsidered, he was fully exonerated.) Said McBride, "What surprised me the most was how complicated these cases are. It's only one person's word against another's. It's amazing how different their perceptions can be."

25   Judy chose to take her case before the Executive Committee rather than report it to the local police, because she felt she would have complete confidentiality and quick action. Actually, there were many delays. And then, because the man she accused hired a lawyer, she was forced to hire one too. As a result, the meeting felt very much like a jury trial to her, complete with cross-examinations that challenged her truthfulness and raised excruciatingly embarrassing questions.

26   Judy's lawyer felt that such painful questions were necessary. But it seems as if the lesson feminists in the sixties and seventies worked so hard and successfully to make understood—not to blame the victim for stranger rape—is one that will have to be learned all over again in the case of acquaintance rape. Only this time, the woman who reports the rape suffers a triple victimization. Not only is she attacked and then not believed, but she carries the added burden of losing faith in her own judgment and trust in other people.

27   In a recently published study of jurors in rape trials, University of Illinois sociologist Barbara Reskin found that jurors were less likely to convict a man if the victim knew him. "Consent is the preferred rape defense and gets the highest acquittal rates," Reskin observes. "In a date rape situation, I would think the jury would assume that the woman had already accepted his invitation in a romantic sense. It would be a matter of how *much* did she consent to."

28   Personal characteristics also influence jurors, Reskin says. Those she studied couldn't imagine that certain men would commit a rape: if they were attractive, had access to sexual partners such as a girlfriend or a wife. More often than not, they'd say, "But he doesn't look like a rapist." Reskin imagines that this pattern would be "magnified in date rape, because these are men who could get a date, they're not complete losers."

29   It may turn out that solutions to the problem will turn up at places with a less genteel image to protect. Jan Strout, director of Montana State, Women's Resource Center, wonders if schools such as hers, which recognize that they are dealing with a more conservative student body and a "macho cowboy image," aren't more willing to take the first step toward acknowledging the problem. A group called Students Against Sexual Assault was formed there two-and-a-half years ago after several students who were raped or resisted an attempted rape "went public." With men and women sharing leadership, this group is cosponsored by the Women's Resource Center and the student government.

30   Admitting to the problem isn't easy even when data is available, as doctoral student Genny Sandberg found at the University of South Dakota. Last spring, she

announced the results of a dating survey she coauthored with psychologists Tom Jackson and Patricia Petretic-Jackson. The most shocking statistic: 20 percent of the students (most from rural backgrounds and living in a rural campus setting) had been raped in a dating situation. The state board of regents couldn't believe it. "I just think that that's absolutely ridiculous," former regent Michael Rost said, according to the Brookings *Daily Register,* "I can't believe we would allow that to occur. If it is true, it's a very serious problem." Regent William Srstka agreed, "If this is true it's absolutely intolerable."

31   Following testimony by one of the researchers, the board changed its tune. Members are now discussing how to begin a statewide education and prevention program.

32   An inspiring example of how an administration can be led to new levels of consciousness took place at the University of Michigan earlier this year. Spurred by an article in *Metropolitan Detroit* magazine, a group of students staged a sit-in at the office of a university vice-president who had been quoted as saying that "Rape is a red flag word. . . . [The university] wants to present an image that is receptive and palatable to the potential student cohort," and also that "Rape is an issue like Alzheimer's disease or mental retardation [which] impacts on a small but sizable part of the population. . . . Perhaps it has to become a crisis that is commonly shared in order to get things done."

33   The students who spent the entire day in Vice-President Henry Johnson's office claimed that rape had already become a crisis on their campus. They presented a list of twelve demands, ranging from a rape crisis center on campus to better lighting and installation of outdoor emergency phones. By the end of the day, Johnson had started to change his mind. Although he insisted that he had been misquoted and quoted out of context in the press, he told me that "I did not realize [before that] acquaintance rape was so much of a problem, that it was the most prevalent type of rape. There is a heightened awareness now on this campus. Whether we as a faculty and administration are as sensitive as we should be is another issue—and that will take some time."

34   In the meantime, members of the Michigan Student Assembly Women's Issues Committee (one of the groups active in organizing the protest) took their demands before the school's board of regents. The result: a $75,000 program for rape prevention and education on campus, directly reporting to Johnson's office. "We'll now be in a position to document the problem and to be proactive," says Johnson. Jennifer Faigel, an organizer of the protest, acknowledges a change in the administration's awareness but says the students themselves, disappointed in the amount of funding promised for the program, have already formed a group (Students Organized Against Rape) to develop programs in the dorms.

35   In just the three years since *Ms.* first reported on date rape (in 1982), several new campus organizations have sprung up and other ongoing programs have surfaced.

36   But the real measure of a school's commitment to dealing with this problem is the range of services it provides, says Mary Harvey, who did a nationwide study of exemplary rape programs for the National Center for the Prevention and Control of Rape. "It should have preventive services, crisis intervention, possibilities for long-term treatment, advocacy, and women's studies programs that edu-

cate about violence. The quality of a university's services to rape victims can be measured by the degree to which these other things are in place."

37 Minimally, rape counselors and educators feel, students need to be exposed to information about date rape as soon as they enter college. Studies show that the group most vulnerable to acquaintance rape are college freshmen, followed by high school seniors. In Koss's original survey, for example, the average age of the victim was eighteen.

38 "I'd like a program where no first-year students could finish their starting week at college without being informed about the problem of acquaintance rape," says Andrea Parrot, a lecturer in human service studies at Cornell University, who is developing a program to train students and dorm resident advisers as date rape awareness counselors. Parrot and others admit that this would be a bare minimum. Handing out a brochure to read, even conducting a workshop on the subject during the busy orientation week and counting on students voluntarily attending, needs to be followed up with sessions in dormitories or other living units. These are the most common settings for date rapes, according to a study by Parrot and Robin Lynk.

39 So how do we go about changing attitudes? And how do we do it without "setting student against student?" asks Gretchen Mieszkowski, chair of the Sexual Assault Prevention Committee at the University of Houston/Clear Lake. Chiefly a commuter campus, with a majority of married women students, Clear Lake nevertheless had seventeen acquaintance rapes reported to the local crisis hot line last year. "We had always focused on traditional solutions like lighting and escort services at night," Mieszkowski says. "But changing lighting in the parking lot is easy; it's only money."

40 Many who have studied the problem of rape education believe it has to begin with college-age women and men talking to each other more frankly about their beliefs and expectations about sex. Py Bateman of Alternatives to Fear thinks it has to start earlier, among teenagers, by developing rudimentary dating skills at the lower end of the sexual activity scale. "We need to learn more about holding hands than about sexual intercourse."

41 Bateman continues: "We've got to work on both sides. Boys don't know what they want any more than girls do. The way our sexual interaction is set up is that boys are supposed to push. Their peers tell them that scoring is what counts. They're as divorced from intimacy as girls."

42 Gail Abarbanel of the Rape Treatment Center at Santa Monica Hospital agrees. Her center conducts educational programs for schools in Los Angeles County. In a recent survey of more than five thousand teenagers, she found a high degree of misconception and lack of information about rape: "Most boys say yes to the question, 'If a girl goes back to a guy's house when she knows no one is home, is she consenting to sex?' And most boys believe that girls don't mean no when they say it."

43 Women clearly need to get more convincing, and men clearly need to believe them more. But until that ideal time, Montana State's Jan Strout warns, "Because men have been socialized to hear yes when women say no, we have to scream it."

THINKING ABOUT THE TEXT

1. How is it possible for ambiguity to exist in defining rape? What is the social context that permits ambiguity?
2. Given the prevalence of rape on college campuses, why did many schools refuse to participate in the study conducted by *Ms?* What does Ellen Sweet imply might be the reason for their reluctance to participate?
3. Is Rodger Crafts correct in saying that physical harm is more apt to occur with "lower educational levels"? Do any of the studies noted here belie that assertion?
4. According to Sweet, what inhibits women from reporting that they have been raped? How do the cases noted here support a woman's reluctance to press charges against a rapist?
5. What specifically can schools do to help prevent rapes on campus? What is the most realistic solution to the problem?

WRITING FROM THE TEXT

1. Write an essay to persuade your reader that you understand the causes of date rape, and propose a solution to the problem.
2. Write a letter to a school newspaper—your school's paper if appropriate—arguing for a rape-prevention program on campus. Cite the benefits that you expect to come from such a program.

CONNECTING WITH OTHER TEXTS

1. Take one aspect of the problem of rape—the treatment of rape victims, the types of trials held to prosecute rapists, the jury response to alleged rapists, the ambiguity in some males' minds about what constitutes rape, the preventative education programs on campuses, or some other aspect of the problem that interests you—and do research to complement the essays by Sweet and Goodman (p. 122) and the poem by Rich (p. 120) that are in this text.
2. Learn what has been done on your campus about rape prevention and write an analysis of your school's program. If statistics are available from your counseling or health center, use them in your paper.

RAPE

Adrienne Rich

A poet, critic, essayist, and translator, Adrienne Rich (b. 1929) has changed her writing considerably from when she was an undergraduate at Radcliffe and W. H. Auden admired her poems as "neatly and modestly dressed," describing them further as poems that "speak quietly but do not mumble, respect their elders but are not cowed by them." In addition to numerous poetry collections, Rich has written *Of Woman Born: Motherhood as Experience and Institution; On Lies, Secrets, and Silence: Selected Prose, 1966–1978;* and other work that examines personal and social issues. The poem included here, originally published in 1966, is from *Poems, Selected and New, 1950–1974.* Adrienne Rich's lectures and written work today reflect her interest in the feminist movement; you can decide for yourself if her poems are still "neatly and modestly dressed." Rich is currently a professor at Stanford University.

> There is a cop who is both prowler and father:
> he comes from your block, grew up with your brothers,
> had certain ideals.
> You hardly know him in his boots and silver badge,
> on horseback, one hand touching his gun.   5
>
> You hardly know him but you have to get to know him:
> he has access to machinery that could kill you.
> He and his stallion clop like warlords among the trash,
> his ideals stand in the air, a frozen cloud
> from between his unsmiling lips.   10
>
> And so, when the time comes, you have to turn to him,
> the maniac's sperm still greasing your thighs,
> your mind whirling like crazy. You have to confess
> to him, you are guilty of the crime
> of having been forced.   15
>
> And you see his blue eyes, the blue eyes of all the family
> whom you used to know, grow narrow and glisten,
> his hand types out the details
> and he wants them all
> but the hysteria in your voice pleases him best.   20
>
> You hardly know him but now he thinks he knows you:
> he has taken down your worst moment
> on a machine and filed it in a file.
> He knows, or thinks he knows, how much you imagined;
> he knows, or thinks he knows, what you secretly wanted.   25

He has access to machinery that could get you put away;
and if, in the sickening light of the precinct,
and if, in the sickening light of the precinct,
your details sound like a portrait of your confessor,
will you swallow, will you deny them, will you lie your way home? 30

THINKING ABOUT THE TEXT

1. Using details from the poem, illustrate how the "cop" is like a "father." How is he a "prowler"? Discuss the conflict here.
2. Describe the police officer's attitude. What has caused his transformation over the years? How have his "ideals" affected him?
3. Cite all the machinery references and discuss why Rich may have chosen this image pattern.
4. Explain line 29 ("your details sound like a portrait of your confessor"). Discuss the irony here and in the phrase, "You have to confess . . . " (line 13).
5. In what ways are the police officer and rapist alike?
6. Why does Rich refer to "*you*" instead of "she" or "I"?
7. How is the title misleading, and how is it appropriate? Are males as vulnerable to this kind of rape as females are?

WRITING FROM THE TEXT

1. Using specific details from this poem, write a character analysis (pp. 436–444) of this particular police officer.
2. In an essay, explain your view of the responsibilities and rights of the police in our society. You may use details from the poem and from your own experiences.
3. If you have ever had an experience with anyone who abused a position of authority (teacher, employer, leader), describe the incident and help us see why this happened and how you reacted.

CONNECTING WITH OTHER TEXTS

1. Using "Rape," "Where Are You Going, Where Have You Been?" (p. 124), and "Date Rape" (p. 112), explain and illustrate different types of psychological abuse and explore the effect of this abuse on the victim.
2. Write your own "portrait of a rapist" based on details from "Rape," "Angry Young Men" (p. 138), "Where Are You Going, Where Have You Been?" (p. 124), "Date Rape" (p. 112), and "When a Woman Says No" (p. 122).

WHEN A WOMAN SAYS NO
Ellen Goodman

A widely syndicated columnist whose home paper is the *Boston Globe,* Ellen Good-man (b. 1941) has won the Pulitzer Prize for her outstanding journalism. Good-man believes that she writes about issues more important than politics, like the "underlying values by which this country exists . . . the vast social changes in the way men and women lead their lives and deal with each other." The essay included here, first published in the *Boston Globe* in 1984, is indicative of Goodman's con-cerns. You also may wish to read Ellen Goodman's essays "Thanksgiving" (p. 4) and "In America, Food for Thought" (p. 405).

1   There are a few times when, if you watch closely, you can actually see a change of public mind. This is one of those times.

2   For as long as I can remember, a conviction for rape depended as much on the character of the woman involved as on the action of the man. Most often the job of the defense lawyer was to prove that the woman had provoked or consented to the act, to prove that it was sex, not assault.

3   In the normal course of events the smallest blemish, misjudgment, misstep by the woman became proof that she had invited the man's attentions. Did she wear a tight sweater? Was she a "loose" woman? Was she in the wrong part of town at the wrong hour? A woman could waive her right to say no in an astonishing number of ways.

4   But in the past few weeks, in Massachusetts, three cases of multiple rape have come into court and three sets of convictions have come out of juries. These ver-dicts point to a sea change in attitudes. A simple definition seems to have seeped into the public consciousness. If she says no, it's rape.

5   The most famous of these cases is the New Bedford barroom rape. There, in two separate trials, juries cut through complicated testimony to decide the central issue within hours. Had the woman been drinking? Had she lied about that in tes-timony? Had she kissed one of the men? In the end none of these points were rel-evant. What mattered to the juries that found four of these six men guilty was that they had forced her. If she said no, it was rape.

6   The second of these cases involved a young woman soldier from Ft. Devens who accepted a ride with members of a rock band, the Grand Slamm. She was raped in the bus and left in a field hours later. Had she flirted with the band mem-bers? Had she told a friend that she intended to seduce one of the men? Had she boarded the bus willingly? The judge sentencing three of the men to jail said, "No longer will society accept the fact that a woman, even if she may initially act in a seductive or compromising manner, has waived her right to say no at any further time." If she said no, it was rape.

7   The third of these cases was in some ways the most notable. An Abington woman was driven from a bar to a parking lot where she was raped by four men, scratched with a knife, had her hair singed with a cigarette lighter and was left half-naked in the snow. The trial testimony showed that she previously had sex with three of the men, and with two of them in a group setting. Still, the jury was

able to agree with the district attorney: "Sexual consent between a woman and a man on one occasion does not mean the man has access to her whenever it strikes his fancy." If she said no, it was rape.

8   Not every community, courtroom or jury today accepts this simple standard of justice. But ten years ago, five years ago, even three years ago these women might not have even dared press charges.

9   It was the change of climate that enabled, even encouraged, the women to come forward. It was the change of attitude that framed the arguments in the courtroom. It was the change of consciousness that infiltrated the jury chambers.

10   The question now is whether that change of consciousness has become part of our own day-to-day lives. In some ways rape is the brutal, repugnant extension of an ancient ritual of pursuit and capture. It isn't just rapists who refuse to take no for an answer. It isn't just rapists who believe that a woman says one thing and means another.

11   In the confusion of adolescence, in the chase of young adulthood, the sexes were often set up to persist and to resist. Many young men were taught that "no" means "try again." Many young women were allowed to excuse their sexuality only when they were "swept away," overwhelmed.

12   The confused messages, the yes-no-maybes, the overpowered heroines and overwhelming heroes, are still common to supermarket gothic novels and *Hustler* magazine. It isn't just X-rated movies that star a resistant woman who falls in love with her sexual aggressor. It isn't just pornographic cable-TV that features the woman who really "wanted it." In as spritely a sitcom as "Cheers," Sam blithely locked a coyly ambivalent Diane into his apartment.

13   I know how many steps it is from that hint of sexual pressure to the brutality of rape. I know how far it is from lessons of sexual power plays to the violence of rape. But it's time that the verdict of those juries was fully transmitted to the culture from which violence emerges. If she says no, it means no.

THINKING ABOUT THE TEXT

1. In this essay, Goodman gives a brief history of social response to rape. In the past, how did lawyers defend alleged rapists? What seems to be the present attitude toward a charge of rape?
2. Goodman gives a summary of three different rape trials. What is the logic of her arrangement of the three examples to support her thesis?
3. Beyond what is asserted in the title of Goodman's essay, what is the important point she makes?

WRITING FROM THE TEXT

1. Describe a time when the "confused messages, the yes-no-maybes" resulted in an incomplete or erroneous understanding of a point you were trying to make.

2. Write a response to Goodman's allegation that "many young men were taught that 'no' means 'try again.'" Argue that she is correct or incorrect. Use specific examples to support your view.

CONNECTING WITH OTHER TEXTS

1. Use "Date Rape" (p. 112), "Angry Young Men" (p. 138), and "When a Woman Says No" to write an analytical essay on the causes of violence against women. What does Goodman mean about the "confused messages" in our culture? Propose a solution in your essay.

2. Read recent periodical accounts of rape trials. Is Goodman accurate in her essay that there is a "sea change" in public consciousness about rape?

3. Goodman notes that a few years ago, many women would not have dared to press rape charges. Today sexual harassment claims have become a media topic, and women are daring to charge that they are being or have been sexually harassed. Do research to learn the history of charges of sexual harassment. Focus your paper on the changes in public consciousness, and use specific examples from the reported cases to support your analysis.

WHERE ARE YOU GOING, WHERE HAVE YOU BEEN?
Joyce Carol Oates

A novelist, poet, playwright, editor, and critic, Joyce Carol Oates (b. 1938) also teaches English at Princeton University. Since her first collection of short stories appeared when she was 25, Oates has been averaging almost two books a year. Although she writes in a variety of genre and literary styles, Oates may be best known for her ability to write suspenseful tales and to create a sense of terror in an apparently ordinary situation, as the story included here illustrates. Oates has responded to critics' comments about the terror that permeates her work: "Uplifting endings and resolutely cheery world views are appropriate to television commercials but insulting elsewhere. It is not only wicked to pretend otherwise, it is futile." The story included here, from *The Wheel of Love*, has been widely anthologized since its first publication in 1965.

For Bob Dylan

1 Her name was Connie. She was fifteen and she had a quick nervous giggling habit of craning her neck to glance into mirrors or checking other people's faces to make sure her own was all right. Her mother, who noticed everything and knew

everything and who hadn't much reason any longer to look at her own face, always scolded Connie about it. "Stop gawking at yourself, who are you? You think you're so pretty?" she would say. Connie would raise her eyebrows at these familiar complaints and look right through her mother, into a shadowy vision of herself as she was right at that moment: she knew she was pretty and that was everything. Her mother had been pretty once too, if you could believe those old snapshots in the album, but now her looks were gone and that was why she was always after Connie.

2   "Why don't you keep your room clean like your sister? How've you got your hair fixed—what the hell stinks? Hair spray? You don't see your sister using that junk."

3   Her sister June was twenty-four and still lived at home. She was a secretary in the high school Connie attended, and if that wasn't bad enough—with her in the same building—she was so plain and chunky and steady that Connie had to hear her praised all the time by her mother and her mother's sisters. June did this, June did that, she saved money and helped clean the house and cooked and Connie couldn't do a thing, her mind was all filled with trashy daydreams. Their father was away at work most of the time and when he came home he wanted supper and he read the newspaper at supper and after supper he went to bed. He didn't bother talking much to them, but around his bent head Connie's mother kept picking at her until Connie wished her mother were dead and she herself were dead and it were all over. "She makes me want to throw up sometimes," she complained to her friends. She had a high, breathless, amused voice which made everything she said sound a little forced, whether it was sincere or not.

4   There was one good thing: June went places with girlfriends of hers, girls who were just as plain and steady as she, and so when Connie wanted to do that her mother had no objections. The father of Connie's best girlfriend drove the girls the three miles to town and left them off at a shopping plaza, so that they could walk through the stores or go to a movie, and when he came to pick them up again at eleven he never bothered to ask what they had done.

5   They must have been familiar sights, walking around that shopping plaza in their shorts and flat ballerina slippers that always scuffed the sidewalk, with charm bracelets jingling on their thin wrists: they would lean together to whisper and laugh secretly if someone passed by who amused or interested them. Connie had long dark blond hair that drew anyone's eye to it, and she wore part of it pulled up on her head and puffed out and the rest of it she let fall down her back. She wore a pullover jersey blouse that looked one way when she was at home and another way when she was away from home. Everything about her had two sides to it, one for home and one for anywhere that was not home: her walk that could be childlike and bobbing, or languid enough to make anyone think she was hearing music in her head, her mouth which was pale and smirking most of the time, but bright and pink on these evenings out, her laugh which was cynical and drawling at home—"Ha, ha, very funny"—but high-pitched and nervous anywhere else, like the jingling of the charms on her bracelet.

6   Sometimes they did go shopping or to a movie, but sometimes they went across the highway, ducking fast across the busy road, to a drive-in restaurant where

older kids hung out. The restaurant was shaped like a big bottle, though squatter than a real bottle, and on its cap was a revolving figure of a grinning boy who held a hamburger aloft. One night in mid-summer they ran across, breathless with daring, and right away someone leaned out a car window and invited them over, but it was just a boy from high school they didn't like. It made them feel good to be able to ignore him. They went up through the maze of parked and cruising cars to the bright-lit, fly-infested restaurant, their faces pleased and expectant as if they were entering a sacred building that loomed out of the night to give them what haven and what blessing they yearned for. They sat at the counter and crossed their legs at the ankles, their thin shoulders rigid with excitement, and listened to the music that made everything so good: the music was always in the background like music at a church service, it was something to depend upon.

7   A boy named Eddie came in to talk with them. He sat backward on his stool, turning himself jerkily around in semicircles and then stopping and turning again, and after a while he asked Connie if she would like something to eat. She said she did and so she tapped her friend's arm on her way out—her friend pulled her face up into a brave droll look—and Connie said she would meet her at eleven, across the way. "I just hate to leave her like that," Connie said earnestly, but the boy said that she wouldn't be alone for long. So they went out to his car and on the way Connie couldn't help but let her eyes wander over the windshields and faces all around her, her face gleaming with a joy that had nothing to do with Eddie or even this place; it might have been the music. She drew her shoulders up and sucked in her breath with the pure pleasure of being alive, and just at that moment she happened to glance at a face just a few feet from hers. It was a boy with shaggy black hair, in a convertible jalopy painted gold. He stared at her and then his lips widened into a grin. Connie slit her eyes at him and turned away, but she couldn't help glancing back and there he was still watching her. He wagged a finger and laughed and said, "Gonna get you, baby," and Connie turned away again without Eddie noticing anything.

8   She spent three hours with him, at the restaurant where they ate hamburgers and drank Cokes in wax cups that were always sweating, and then down an alley a mile or so away, and when he left her off at five to eleven only the movie house was still open at the plaza. Her girlfriend was there, talking with a boy. When Connie came up the two girls smiled at each other and Connie said, "How was the movie?" and the girl said, "*You* should know." They rode off with the girl's father, sleepy and pleased, and Connie couldn't help but look at the darkened shopping plaza with its big empty parking lot and its signs that were faded and ghostly now, and over at the drive-in restaurant where cars were still circling tirelessly. She couldn't hear the music at this distance.

9   Next morning June asked her how the movie was and Connie said, "So-so."

10   She and that girl and occasionally another girl went out several times a week that way, and the rest of the time Connie spent around the house—it was summer vacation—getting in her mother's way and thinking, dreaming, about the boys she met. But all the boys fell back and dissolved into a single face that was not even a face, but an idea, a feeling, mixed up with the urgent insistent pounding of the

music and the humid night air of July. Connie's mother kept dragging her back to the daylight by finding things for her to do or saying, suddenly, "What's this about the Pettinger girl?"

11   And Connie would say nervously, "Oh, her. That dope." She always drew thick clear lines between herself and such girls, and her mother was simple and kindly enough to believe her. Her mother was so simple, Connie thought, that it was maybe cruel to fool her so much. Her mother went scuffling around the house in old bedroom slippers and complained over the telephone to one sister about the other, then the other called up and the two of them complained about the third one. If June's name was mentioned her mother's tone was approving, and if Connie's name was mentioned it was disapproving. This did not really mean she disliked Connie and actually Connie thought that her mother preferred her to June because she was prettier, but the two of them kept up a pretense of exasperation, a sense that they were tugging and struggling over something of little value to either of them. Sometimes, over coffee, they were almost friends, but something would come up—some vexation that was like a fly buzzing suddenly around their heads—and their faces went hard with contempt.

12   One Sunday Connie got up at eleven—none of them bothered with church— and washed her hair so that it could dry all day long, in the sun. Her parents and sister were going to a barbecue at an aunt's house and Connie said no, she wasn't interested, rolling her eyes to let her mother know just what she thought of it. "Stay home alone then," her mother said sharply. Connie sat out back in a lawn chair and watched them drive away, her father quiet and bald, hunched around so that he could back the car out, her mother with a look that was still angry and not at all softened through the windshield, and in the back seat poor old June all dressed up as if she didn't know what a barbecue was, with all the running yelling kids and the flies. Connie sat with her eyes closed in the sun, dreaming and dazed with the warmth about her as if this were a kind of love, the caresses of love, and her mind slipped over onto thoughts of the boy she had been with the night before and how nice he had been, how sweet it always was, not the way someone like June would suppose but sweet, gentle, the way it was in movies and promised in songs; and when she opened her eyes she hardly knew where she was, the back yard ran off into weeds and a fence line of trees and behind it the sky was perfectly blue and still. The asbestos "ranch house" that was now three years old startled her—it looked small. She shook her head as if to get awake.

13   It was too hot. She went inside the house and turned on the radio to drown out the quiet. She sat on the edge of her bed, barefoot, and listened for an hour and a half to a program called XYZ Sunday Jamboree, record after record of hard, fast, shrieking songs she sang along with, interspersed by exclamations from "Bobby King": "An' look here you girls at Napoleon's—Son and Charley want you to pay real close attention to this song coming up!"

14   And Connie paid close attention herself, bathed in a glow of slow-pulsed joy that seemed to rise mysteriously out of the music itself and lay languidly about the airless little room, breathed in and breathed out with each gentle rise and fall of her chest.

15   After a while she heard a car coming up the drive. She sat up at once, startled, because it couldn't be her father so soon. The gravel kept crunching all the way in from the road—the driveway was long—and Connie ran to the window. It was a car she didn't know. It was an open jalopy, painted a bright gold that caught the sunlight opaquely. Her heart began to pound and her fingers snatched at her hair, checking it, and she whispered "Christ, Christ," wondering how bad she looked. The car came to a stop at the side door and the horn sounded four short taps as if this were a signal Connie knew.

16   She went into the kitchen and approached the door slowly, then hung out the screen door, her bare toes curling down off the step. There were two boys in the car and now she recognized the driver: he had shaggy, shabby black hair that looked crazy as a wig and he was grinning at her.

17   "I ain't late, am I?" he said.

18   "Who the hell do you think you are?" Connie said.

19   "Toldja I'd be out, didn't I?"

20   "I don't even know who you are."

21   She spoke sullenly, careful to show no interest or pleasure, and he spoke in a fast bright monotone. Connie looked past him to the other boy, taking her time. He had fair brown hair, with a lock that fell onto his forehead. His sideburns gave him a fierce, embarrassed look, but so far he hadn't even bothered to glance at her. Both boys wore sunglasses. The driver's glasses were metallic and mirrored everything in miniature.

22   "You wanta come for a ride?" he said.

23   Connie smirked and let her hair fall loose over one shoulder.

24   "Don'tcha like my car? New paint job," he said. "Hey."

25   "What?"

26   "You're cute."

27   She pretended to fidget, chasing flies away from the door.

28   "Don'tcha believe me, or what?" he said.

29   "Look, I don't even know who you are," Connie said in disgust.

30   "Hey, Ellie's got a radio, see. Mine's broke down." He lifted his friend's arm and showed her the little transistor the boy was holding, and now Connie began to hear the music. It was the same program that was playing inside the house.

31   "Bobby King?" she said.

32   "I listen to him all the time. I think he's great."

33   "He's kind of great," Connie said reluctantly.

34   "Listen, that guy's *great*. He knows where the action is."

35   Connie blushed a little, because the glasses made it impossible for her to see just what this boy was looking at. She couldn't decide if she liked him or if he was just a jerk, and so she dawdled in the doorway and wouldn't come down or go back inside. She said, "What's all that stuff painted on your car?"

36   "Can'tcha read it?" He opened the door very carefully, as if he was afraid it might fall off. He slid out just as carefully, planting his feet firmly on the ground, the tiny metallic world in his glasses slowing down like gelatine hardening and in the midst of it Connie's bright green blouse. "This here is my name, to begin

with," he said. ARNOLD FRIEND was written in tarlike black letters on the side, with a drawing of a round grinning face that reminded Connie of a pumpkin, except it wore sunglasses. "I wanta introduce myself, I'm Arnold Friend and that's my real name and I'm gonna be your friend, honey, and inside the car's Ellie Oscar, he's kinda shy." Ellie brought his transistor radio up to his shoulder and balanced it there. "Now these numbers are a secret code, honey," Arnold Friend explained. He read off the numbers, 33, 19, 17 and raised his eyebrows at her to see what she thought of that, but she didn't think much of it. The left rear fender had been smashed and around it was written, on the gleaming gold background: DONE BY CRAZY WOMAN DRIVER. Connie had to laugh at that. Arnold Friend was pleased at her laughter and looked up at her. "Around the other side's a lot more—you wanta come and see them?"

37   "No."

38   "Why not?"

39   "Why should I?"

40   "Don'tcha wanta see what's on the car? Don'tcha wanta go for a ride?"

41   "I don't know."

42   "Why not?"

43   "I got things to do."

44   "Like what?"

45   "Things."

46   He laughed as if she had said something funny. He slapped his thighs. He was standing in a strange way, leaning back against the car as if he were balancing himself. He wasn't tall, only an inch or so taller than she would be if she came down to him. Connie liked the way he was dressed, which was the way all of them dressed: tight faded jeans stuffed into black, scuffed boots, a belt that pulled his waist in and showed how lean he was, and a white pullover shirt that was a little soiled and showed the hard small muscles of his arms and shoulders. He looked as if he probably did hard work, lifting and carrying things. Even his neck looked muscular. And his face was a familiar face, somehow: the jaw and chin and cheeks slightly darkened, because he hadn't shaved for a day or two, and the nose long and hawklike, sniffing as if she were a treat he was going to gobble up and it was all a joke.

47   "Connie, you ain't telling the truth. This is your day set aside for a ride with me and you know it," he said, still laughing. The way he straightened and recovered from his fit of laughing showed that it had been all fake.

48   "How do you know what my name is?" she said suspiciously.

49   "It's Connie."

50   "Maybe and maybe not."

51   "I know my Connie," he said, wagging his finger. Now she remembered him even better, back at the restaurant, and her cheeks warmed at the thought of how she sucked in her breath just at the moment she passed him—how she must have looked at him. And he had remembered her. "Ellie and I come out here especially for you," he said. "Ellie can sit in back. How about it?"

52   "Where?"

53   "Where what?"

54   "Where're we going?"

55   He looked at her. He took off the sunglasses and she saw how pale the skin around his eyes was, like holes that were not in shadow but instead in light. His eyes were like chips of broken glass that catch the light in an amiable way. He smiled. It was as if the idea of going for a ride somewhere, to some place, was a new idea to him.

56   "Just for a ride, Connie sweetheart."

57   "I never said my name was Connie," she said.

58   "But I know what it is. I know your name and all about you, lots of things," Arnold Friend said. He had not moved yet but stood still leaning back against the side of his jalopy. "I took a special interest in you, such a pretty girl, and found out all about you like I know your parents and sister are gone somewheres and I know where and how long they're going to be gone, and I know who you were with last night, and your best girlfriend's name is Betty. Right?"

59   He spoke in a simple lilting voice, exactly as if he were reciting the words to a song. His smile assured her that everything was fine. In the car Ellie turned up the volume on his radio and did not bother to look around at them.

60   "Ellie can sit in the back seat," Arnold Friend said. He indicated his friend with a casual jerk of his chin, as if Ellie did not count and she should not bother with him.

61   "How'd you find out all that stuff?" Connie said.

62   "Listen: Betty Schultz and Tony Fitch and Jimmy Pettinger and Nancy Pettinger," he said, in a chant. "Raymond Stanley and Bob Hutter—"

63   "Do you know all those kids?"

64   "I know everybody."

65   "Look, you're kidding. You're not from around here."

66   "Sure."

67   "But—how come we never saw you before?"

68   "Sure you saw me before," he said. He looked down at his boots, as if he were a little offended. "You just don't remember."

69   "I guess I'd remember you," Connie said.

70   "Yeah?" he looked up at this, beaming. He was pleased. He began to mark time with the music from Ellie's radio, tapping his fists lightly together. Connie looked away from his smile to the car, which was painted so bright it almost hurt her eyes to look at it. She looked at that name. ARNOLD FRIEND. And up at the front fender was an expression that was familiar—MAN THE FLYING SAUCERS. It was an expression kids had used the year before, but didn't use this year. She looked at it for a while as if the words meant something to her that she did not yet know.

71   "What're you thinking about? Huh?" Arnold Friend demanded. "Not worried about your hair blowing around in the car, are you?"

72   "No."

73   "Think I maybe can't drive good?"

74   "How do I know?"

75   "You're a hard girl to handle. How come?" he said. "Don't you know I'm your friend? Didn't you see me put my sign in the air when you walked by?"

76   "What sign?"

77   "My sign." And he drew an X in the air, leaning out toward her. They were maybe ten feet apart. After his hand fell back to his side the X was still in the air, almost visible. Connie let the screen door close and stood perfectly still inside it, listening to the music from her radio and the boy's blend together. She stared at Arnold Friend. He stood there so stiffly relaxed, pretending to be relaxed, with one hand idly on the door handle as if he were keeping himself up that way and had no intention of ever moving again. She recognized most things about him, the tight jeans that showed his thighs and buttocks and the greasy leather boots and the tight shirt, and even that slippery friendly smile of his, that sleepy dreamy smile that all the boys used to get across ideas they didn't want to put into words. She recognized all this and also the singsong way he talked, slightly mocking, kidding, but serious and a little melancholy, and she recognized the way he tapped one fist against the other in homage of the perpetual music behind him. But all these things did not come together.

78   She said suddenly, "Hey, how old are you?"

79   His smile faded. She could see then that he wasn't a kid, he was much older—thirty, maybe more. At this knowledge her heart began to pound faster.

80   "That's a crazy thing to ask. Can'tcha see I'm your own age?"

81   "Like hell you are."

82   "Or maybe a coupla years older, I'm eighteen."

83   "Eighteen?" she said doubtfully.

84   He grinned to reassure her and lines appeared at the corners of his mouth. His teeth were big and white. He grinned so broadly his eyes became slits and she saw how thick the lashes were, thick and black as if painted with a black tarlike material. Then he seemed to become embarrassed, abruptly, and looked over his shoulder at Ellie. "*Him,* he's crazy," he said. "Ain't he a riot, he's a nut, a real character." Ellie was still listening to the music. His sunglasses told nothing about what he was thinking. He wore a bright orange shirt unbuttoned halfway to show his chest, which was a pale, bluish chest and not muscular like Arnold Friend's. His shirt collar was turned up all around and the very tips of the collar pointed out past his chin as if they were protecting him. He was pressing the transistor radio up against his ear and sat there in a kind of daze, right in the sun.

85   "He's kinda strange," Connie said.

86   "Hey, she says you're kinda strange! Kinda strange!" Arnold Friend cried. He pounded on the car to get Ellie's attention. Ellie turned for the first time and Connie saw with shock that he wasn't a kid either—he had a fair, hairless face, cheeks reddened slightly as if the veins grew too close to the surface of his skin, the face of a forty-year-old baby. Connie felt a wave of dizziness rise in her at this sight and she stared at him as if waiting for something to change the shock of the moment, make it all right again. Ellie's lips kept shaping words, mumbling along with the words blasting in his ear.

87   "Maybe you two better go away," Connie said faintly.

88   "What? How come?" Arnold Friend cried. "We come out here to take you for a ride. It's Sunday." He had the voice of the man on the radio now. It was the same voice, Connie thought. "Don'tcha know it's Sunday all day and honey, no matter who you were with last night today you're with Arnold Friend and don't you forget it!—Maybe you better step out here," he said, and this last was in a different voice. It was a little flatter, as if the heat was finally getting to him.

89   "No. I got things to do."

90   "Hey."

91   "You two better leave."

92   "We ain't leaving until you come with us."

93   "Like hell I am—"

94   "Connie, don't fool around with me. I mean, I mean, don't fool *around*," he said, shaking his head. He laughed incredulously. He placed his sunglasses on top of his head, carefully, as if he were indeed wearing a wig, and brought the stems down behind his ears. Connie stared at him, another wave of dizziness and fear rising in her so that for a moment he wasn't even in focus but was just a blur, standing there against his gold car, and she had the idea that he had driven up the driveway all right but had come from nowhere before that and belonged nowhere and that everything about him and even about the music that was so familiar to her was only half real.

95   "If my father comes and sees you—"

96   "He ain't coming. He's at a barbecue."

97   "How do you know that?"

98   "Aunt Tillie's. Right now they're—uh—they're drinking. Sitting around," he said vaguely, squinting as if he were staring all the way to town and over to Aunt Tillie's back yard. Then the vision seemed to get clear and he nodded energetically. "Yeah. Sitting around. There's your sister in a blue dress, huh? And high heels, the poor sad bitch—nothing like you, sweetheart! And your mother's helping some fat woman with the corn, they're cleaning the corn—husking the corn—"

99   "What fat woman?" Connie cried.

100   "How do I know what fat woman, I don't know every goddam fat woman in the world!" Arnold laughed.

101   "Oh, that's Mrs. Hornby . . . Who invited her?" Connie said. She felt a little light-headed. Her breath was coming quickly.

102   "She's too fat. I don't like them fat. I like them the way you are, honey," he said, smiling sleepily at her. They stared at each other for a while, through the screen door. He said softly, "Now what you're going to do is this: you're going to come out that door. You're going to sit up front with me and Ellie's going to sit in the back, the hell with Ellie, right? This isn't Ellie's date. You're my date. I'm your lover, honey."

103   "What? You're crazy—"

104   "Yes, I'm your lover. You don't know what that is, but you will," he said. "I know that too. I know all about you. But look: it's real nice and you couldn't ask for nobody better than me, or more polite. I always keep my word. I'll tell you

how it is. I'm always nice at first, the first time. I'll hold you so tight you won't think you have to try to get away or pretend anything because you'll know you can't. And I'll come inside you where it's all secret and you'll give in to me and you'll love me—"

105   "Shut up! You're crazy!" Connie said. She backed away from the door. She puther hands against her ears as if she'd heard something terrible, something not meant for her. "People don't talk like that, you're crazy," she muttered. Her heart was almost too big now for her chest and its pumping made sweat break out all over her. She looked out to see Arnold Friend pause and then take a step toward the porch lurching. He almost fell. But, like a clever drunken man, he managed to catch his balance. He wobbled in his high boots and grabbed hold of one of the porch posts.

106   "Honey?" he said. "You still listening?"

107   "Get the hell out of here!"

108   "Be nice, honey. Listen."

109   "I'm going to call the police—"

110   He wobbled again and out of the side of his mouth came a fast spat curse, an aside not meant for her to hear. But even this "Christ!" sounded forced. Then he began to smile again. She watched this smile come, awkward as if he were smiling from inside a mask. His whole face was a mask, she thought wildly, tanned down onto his throat but then running out as if he had plastered makeup on his face but had forgotten about his throat.

111   "Honey—? Listen, here's how it is. I always tell the truth and I promise you this: I ain't coming in that house after you."

112   "You better not! I'm going to call the police if you—if you don't—"

113   "Honey," he said, talking right through her voice, "honey, I'm not coming in there but you are coming out here. You know why?"

114   She was panting. The kitchen looked like a place she had never seen before, some room she had run inside but which wasn't good enough, wasn't going to help her. The kitchen window had never had a curtain, after three years, and there were dishes in the sink for her to do—probably—and if you ran your hand across the table you'd probably feel something sticky there.

115   "You listening, honey? Hey?"

116   "—going to call the police—"

117   "Soon as you touch the phone I don't need to keep my promise and can come inside. You won't want that."

118   She rushed forward and tried to lock the door. Her fingers were shaking. "But why lock it," Arnold Friend said gently, talking right into her face. "It's just a screen door. It's just nothing." One of his boots was at a strange angle, as if his foot wasn't in it. It pointed out to the left, bent at the ankle. "I mean, anybody can break through a screen door and glass and wood and iron or anything else if he needs to, anybody at all and specially Arnold Friend. If the place got lit up with a fire honey you'd come runnin' out into my arms, right into my arms an' safe at home—like you knew I was your lover and'd stopped fooling around. I don't mind a nice shy girl but I don't like no fooling around." Part of those words were

spoken with a slight rhythmic lilt, and Connie somehow recognized them—the echo of a song from last year, about a girl rushing into her boyfriend's arms and coming home again—

119   Connie stood barefoot on the linoleum floor, staring at him. "What do you want?" she whispered.

120   "I want you," he said.

121   "What?"

122   "Seen you that night and thought, that's the one, yes sir. I never needed to look anymore."

123   "But my father's coming back. He's coming to get me. I had to wash my hair first—" She spoke in a dry, rapid voice, hardly raising it for him to hear.

124   "No, your Daddy is not coming and yes, you had to wash your hair and you washed it for me. It's nice and shining and all for me. I thank you, sweetheart," he said, with a mock bow, but again he almost lost his balance. He had to bend and adjust his boots. Evidently his feet did not go all the way down; the boots must have been stuffed with something so that he would seem taller. Connie stared out at him and behind him Ellie in the car, who seemed to be looking off toward Connie's right into nothing. This Ellie said, pulling the words out of the air one after another as if he were just discovering them, "You want me to pull out the phone?"

125   "Shut your mouth and keep it shut," Arnold Friend said, his face red from bending over or maybe from embarrassment because Connie had seen his boots. "This ain't none of your business."

126   "What—what are you doing? What do you want?" Connie said. "If I call the police they'll get you, they'll arrest you—"

127   "Promise was not to come in unless you touch that phone, and I'll keep that promise," he said. He resumed his erect position and tried to force his shoulders back. He sounded like a hero in a movie, declaring something important. He spoke too loudly and it was as if he were speaking to someone behind Connie. "I ain't made plans for coming in that house where I don't belong but just for you to come out to me, the way you should. Don't you know who I am?"

128   "You're crazy," she whispered. She backed away from the door but did not want to go into another part of the house, as if this would give him permission to come through the door. "What do you . . . You're crazy, you . . . "

129   "Huh? What're you saying, honey?"

130   Her eyes darted everywhere in the kitchen. She could not remember what it was, this room.

131   "This is how it is, honey; you come out and we'll drive away, have a nice ride. But if you don't come out we're gonna wait till your people come home and then they're all going to get it."

132   "You want that telephone pulled out?" Ellie said. He held the radio away from his ear and grimaced, as if without the radio the air was too much for him.

133   "I toldja shut up, Ellie," Arnold Friend said, "you're deaf, get a hearing aid, right? Fix yourself up. This little girl's no trouble and's gonna be nice to me, so Ellie keep to yourself, this ain't your date—right? Don't hem in on me. Don't hog.

Don't crush. Don't bird dog. Don't trail me," he said in a rapid meaningless voice, as if he were running through all the expressions he'd learned but was no longer sure which one of them was in style, then rushing on to new ones, making them up with his eyes closed, "Don't crawl under my fence, don't squeeze in my chipmunk hole, don't sniff my glue, suck my popsicle, keep your own greasy fingers on yourself!" He shaded his eyes and peered in at Connie, who was backed against the kitchen table. "Don't mind him honey he's just a creep. He's a dope. Right? I'm the boy for you and like I said you come out here nice like a lady and give me your hand, and nobody else gets hurt, I mean, your nice old bald-headed daddy and your mummy and your sister in her high heels. Because listen: why bring them in this?"

134   "Leave me alone," Connie whispered.

135   "Hey, you know that old woman down the road, the one with the chickens and stuff—you know her?"

136   "She's dead!"

137   "Dead? What? You know her?" Arnold Friend said.

138   "She's dead—"

139   "Don't you like her?"

140   "She's dead—she's—she isn't there anymore—"

141   "But don't you like her, I mean, you got something against her? Some grudge or something?" Then his voice dipped as if he were conscious of a rudeness. He touched the sunglasses perched on top of his head as if to make sure they were still there. "Now you be a good girl."

142   "What are you going to do?"

143   "Just two things, or maybe three," Arnold Friend said. "But I promise it won't last long and you'll like me the way you get to like people you're close to. You will. It's all over for you here, so come on out. You don't want your people in any trouble, do you?"

144   She turned and bumped against a chair or something, hurting her leg, but she ran into the back room and picked up the telephone. Something roared in her ear, a tiny roaring, and she was so sick with fear that she could do nothing but listen to it—the telephone was clammy and very heavy and her fingers groped down to the dial but were too weak to touch it. She began to scream into the phone, into the roaring. She cried out, she cried for her mother, she felt her breath start jerking back and forth in her lungs as if it were something Arnold Friend were stabbing her with again and again with no tenderness. A noisy sorrowful wailing rose all about her and she was locked inside it the way she was locked inside this house.

145   After a while she could hear again. She was sitting on the floor with her wet back against the wall.

146   Arnold Friend was saying from the door, "That's a good girl. Put the phone back."

147   She kicked the phone away from her.

148   "No, honey. Pick it up. Put it back right."

149   She picked it up and put it back. The dial tone stopped.

150   "That's a good girl. Now you come outside."

151   She was hollow with what had been fear, but what was now just an emptiness. All that screaming had blasted it out of her. She sat, one leg cramped under her, and deep inside her brain was something like a pinpoint of light that kept going and would not let her relax. She thought, I'm not going to see my mother again. She thought, I'm not going to sleep in my bed again. Her bright green blouse was all wet.

152   Arnold Friend said, in a gentle-loud voice that was like a stage voice, "The place where you came from ain't there any more, and where you had in mind to go is canceled out. This place you are now—inside your daddy's house—is nothing but a cardboard box I can knock down any time. You know that and always did know it. You hear me?"

153   She thought, I have got to think. I have to know what to do.

154   "We'll go out in a nice field, out in the country here where it smells so nice and it's sunny," Arnold Friend said. "I'll have my arms tight around you so you won't need to try to get away and I'll show you what love is like, what it does. The hell with this house! It looks solid all right," he said. He ran a fingernail down the screen and the noise did not make Connie shiver, as it would have the day before. "Now put your hand on your heart, honey. Feel that? That feels solid too, but we know better, be nice to me, be sweet like you can because what else is there for a girl like you but to be sweet and pretty and give in?—and get away before her people come back?"

155   She felt her pounding heart. Her hand seemed to enclose it. She thought for the first time in her life that it was nothing that was hers, that belonged to her, but just a pounding, living thing inside this body that wasn't really hers either.

156   "You don't want them to get hurt," Arnold Friend went on. "Now get up, honey. Get up all by yourself."

157   She stood.

158   "Now turn this way. That's right. Come over here to me—Ellie, put that away, didn't I tell you? You dope. You miserable creepy dope," Arnold Friend said. His words were not angry but only part of an incantation. The incantation was kindly. "Now come out through the kitchen to me honey, and let's see a smile, try it, you're a brave sweet little girl and now they're eating corn and hot dogs cooked to bursting over an outdoor fire, and they don't know one thing about you and never did and honey you're better than them because not a one of them would have done this for you."

159   Connie felt the linoleum under her feet; it was cool. She brushed her hair back out of her eyes. Arnold Friend let go of the post tentatively and opened his arms for her, his elbows pointing in toward each other and his wrists limp, to show that this was an embarrassed embrace and a little mocking, he didn't want to make her self-conscious.

160   She put out her hand against the screen. She watched herself push the door slowly open as if she were safe back somewhere in the other doorway, watching

this body and this head of long hair moving out into the sunlight where Arnold Friend waited.

161   "My sweet little blue-eyed girl," he said, in a half-sung sigh that had nothing to do with her brown eyes but was taken up just the same by the vast sunlit reaches of the land behind him and on all sides of him, so much land that Connie had never seen before and did not recognize except to know that she was going to it.

THINKING ABOUT THE TEXT

1. Identify Connie's character traits and illustrate each. How is she a rather typical 15-year-old, and how is she unique?

2. Illustrate the various ways that Arnold Friend initially appeals to Connie.

3. Identify the numerous intimidation tactics that Friend uses to manipulate Connie.

4. Study Ellie's role in this story. How does Oates use him to illuminate Arnold Friend's character, temperament, and motives?

5. Although the ending is ambiguous, Oates has revealed that this story was based on details from actual rapes and murders committed by Charles Schmid and his accomplice John Saunders in Tucson, Arizona, during the 1960s. How do various details in the story and, particularly, in the ending suggest that a crime was committed?

6. Without reducing this story to simple morals, discuss the insights (about subjects such as adolescence, parenting, role playing, manipulation, and intimidation) that we can draw from this story.

WRITING FROM THE TEXT

1. Write a character analysis (pp. 436–444) of Arnold Friend, demonstrating how he knows and preys upon the insecurities and fantasies of a 15-year-old girl. Include details from the story to support your thesis.

2. In an essay argue that Connie does or doesn't *choose* to go with Arnold Friend at the end. Could she have resisted more than she did? Cite specific evidence from the story to support your thesis.

3. Considering Connie's character and life-style, is Oates suggesting that Connie is to be blamed for what happened to her, or does the blame fall on Arnold Friend for taking advantage of a vulnerable 15-year-old? Write an essay to support your argument.

CONNECTING WITH OTHER TEXTS

1. Read "When a Woman Says No" (p. 122) and write an essay applying Ellen Goodman's comments to Connie's experience.

2. Read "Angry Young Men" (below) and "Date Rape" (p. 112) and use ideas from these readings and from Oates' story as you consider and analyze Arnold Friend's perspective.

3. Find and read the article in *Life* magazine (March 4, 1966) about the Charles Schmid case. Then write an essay comparing the actual details of his rapes and murders with this story.

4. Joyce Chopra's 1985 feature film *Smooth Talk,* based on Oates' story, is available on video, and Oates is reported to have been pleased with this adaptation. Note the differences between the video and the story versions, and write an essay analyzing the changes made in the film.

ANGRY YOUNG MEN
Barbara Ehrenreich

Educated at Reed College and Rockefeller University, where she received her Ph.D., Barbara Ehrenreich (b. 1941) has worked as a staff member in New York City's Health Policy Advisory Center, and she has been an assistant professor of health sciences. As both a feminist and health services worker, she has written to expose the male domination of the female health care system (*Complaints and Disorders: The Sexual Politics of Sickness* and *For Her Own Good: One Hundred Fifty Years of the Experts' Advice to Women*). Ehrenreich has this to say about her life and work: "My writing is motivated by my commitment to social justice. I have been involved in the anti-war movement and the women's movement and have recently been involved in the women's health movement." Ehrenreich's work appears in many national magazines, including *Ms.* and *Mother Jones*. The essay included here appeared in *New York Woman* in 1989.

1   Recall the roar of commentary that followed the murderous 1989 assault on a 28-year-old woman jogging in Central Park. Every detail of the assailants' lives was sifted for sociological significance: Were they poor? How poor? Students or dropouts? From families with two parents or one?

2   Yet weeks before the East Harlem "posse" attacked a jogger, suburbanites in nearby Long Island were shaken by two murders that were, if anything, even more inexplicably vicious than the assault in Central Park. In early March the body of 13-year-old Kelly Tinyes was found in the basement of a house just down the

block from her own. She had been stabbed, strangled, and hit with a blunt instrument before being mutilated with a bayonet. A few weeks later 14-year-old Jessica Manners was discovered along the side of a road in East Setauket, strangled to death, apparently with her own bra, and possibly sexually assaulted.

3   Suspects have been apprehended. Their school friends, parents, and relatives have been interviewed. Their homes and cars have been searched, their photos published. We know who they hung out with and what they did in their spare time. But on the scale of large social meanings, these crimes don't rate. No one is demanding that we understand—or condemn—the white communities that nourished the killers. No one is debating the roots of violence in the land of malls and tract homes. In the city, apparently, crime is construed as something "socioeconomic." Out here it's merely "sick."

4   But East Setauket is not really all that far from East Harlem. If something is festering in the ghetto, something very similar is gnawing away in middle-income suburbs. A "way of life," as the cliché goes, is coming to an end, and in its place a mean streak is opening up and swallowing everything in its path. Economists talk about "deindustrialization" and "class polarization." I think of it as the problem of the marginal men: They are black and white, Catholic and Pentecostal, rap fans and admirers of techno-pop. What they have in common is that they are going nowhere—nowhere legal, that is.

5   Consider the suspects in the Long Island murders. Twenty-one-year-old Robert Golub, in whose basement Kelly Tinyes was killed, is described in *Newsday* as an "unemployed body-builder." When his high school friends went off to college, he stayed behind in his parents' home in Valley Stream. For a while he earned a living driving a truck for a cosmetics firm, but he lost the job, in part because of his driving record: His license has been suspended 12 times since 1985. At the time of the murder Golub had been out of work for several months, constructing a life around his weight-lifting routine and his dream of becoming an entrepreneur.

6   Christopher Loliscio, the suspect in the Manners case, is 19 and, like Golub, lives with his parents. He has been in trouble before, charged with third-degree assault and "menacing" in an altercation that took place on the campus of the State University at Stony Brook. Loliscio does not attend college himself. He is employed as a landscaper.

7   The suburbs are full of young white men like Golub and Loliscio. If they had been born 20 years earlier, they might have found steady work in decent-paying union jobs, married early, joined the volunteer fire department, and devoted their leisure to lawn maintenance. But the good blue-collar jobs are getting sparser, thanks to "deindustrialization." Much of what's left is likely to be marginal, low-paid work. Nation-wide, the earnings of young white men dropped 18 percent between 1973 and 1986, making those at the low end of the wage scale less than desirable marriage prospects.

8   Landscaping, for example—a glamorous term for raking and mowing—pays four to five dollars an hour; truck driving for a small firm is in the same range: not enough to pay for a college education, a house, or even a midsize wedding reception at the VFW hall.

9   And even those modest perquisites of life in the sub-yuppie class have become, in some sense, "not enough." On Long Island the culture that once sustained men in blue-collar occupations is crumbling as more affluent settlers move in, filling the vacant lots with their new $750,000 homes. In my town, for example, the last five years saw the bowling alley close and the blue-collar bar turn into a pricey dining spot. Even the volunteer fire department is having trouble recruiting. The prestigious thing to join is a $500-a-year racquetball club; there's just not much respect anymore for putting out fires.

10   So the marginal man lives between two worlds—one that he aspires to and one that is dying—neither of which he can afford. Take "Rick," the 22-year-old son of family friends. His father is a machinist in an aerospace plant that hasn't hired anyone above the floor-sweeping level for years now. Not that Rick has ever shown any interest in his father's trade. For one thing, he takes too much pride in his appearance to put on the dark green, company-supplied work clothes his father has worn for the past 20 years. Rick has his own kind of uniform: pleated slacks, high-tops, Italian knit cardigans, and a $300 leather jacket, accessorized with a gold chain and earring stud.

11   To his parents, Rick is a hardworking boy for whom things just don't seem to work out. Right now he has a gig doing valet parking at a country club. The tips are good, and he loves racing around the lot in the Porsches and Lamborghinis of the stockbroker members. But the linchpin of his economic strategy is living at home, with his parents and sisters, in the same room he's occupied since third grade. This arrangement is less than ideal for his social life. Besides, Rick is a long way from being able to afford even a cramped, three-bedroom house like his family home; given the choice, he'd rather have a new Camaro anyway. So Rick's girlfriends tend to move on rapidly, looking for men who might someday have a chance in the real estate market.

12   If this were the 70's, Rick might have dropped out; he might have taken up marijuana, the Grateful Dead, and vague visions of a better world. But like so many of his contemporaries in the '80's, Rick isn't rebellious. He has no problem with "the system," which, in his mind, embraces every conceivable hustle, legal or illegal. He can't imagine demanding better jobs or a living wage when there's easy money to be made elsewhere. Two years ago he made a tidy bundle dealing coke in a local dance club, bought a $20,000 car, and smashed it up. Now he spends his evenings working as a bouncer in an illegal gambling joint—his parents still think he's out "dancing"—and is proud of the handgun he's got stowed in his glove compartment.

13   Someday Rick will use that gun, and I'll probably be the first to say—like Robert Golub's friends—"but he isn't the kind of person who would hurt *anyone*." Except that even now I can sense the danger in him. He's smart enough to know he's only a cut-rate copy of the upscale young men in *GQ* ads and MTV commercials whom he is trying to emulate. Viewed from Wall Street or Southampton, he's a peon, a member of the invisible underclass that parks cars, waits on tables, and is satisfied with a $5 tip and an occasional remark about the weather.

14   He's also proud. And there's nowhere for him to put that pride except into the politics of gesture: the macho stance, the 75-mph takeoff down the expressway,

and, eventually, maybe, the drawn gun. Jobs are the liberal solution; conservatives would throw in "traditional values." But what the marginal men—from Valley Stream to Bedford-Stuyvesant—need most of all is *respect.* If they can't find that in work, or in a working-class lifestyle that is no longer honored, they'll extract it from someone weaker—a girlfriend, a random jogger, a neighbor, perhaps just any girl. They'll find a victim.

THINKING ABOUT THE TEXT

1. What is Ehrenreich's point in describing in detail the crimes that took place weeks before the infamous assault on the jogger in Central Park?

2. According to Ehrenreich, what is the common problem that prompts these vicious crimes?

3. What are the two worlds that the "marginal man" lives between? What are the consequences of his being marginal?

4. Do you agree with Ehrenreich's conclusion that the "marginal man" will find a victim—probably a female?

WRITING FROM THE TEXT

1. Write a character study of a "marginal man," using your own definition as well as Ehrenreich's observations.

2. Write your own analysis of the problems that influence the life-style and values of young men today. What can you propose to influence a positive change?

CONNECTING WITH OTHER TEXTS

1. Analyze the essays on androgyny (p. 71 and p. 75) and "Men as Success Objects" (p. 90) and relate those essays to Ehrenreich's points about angry young men. Argue that the culture that encourages a better male model (you define this) will have fewer incidences of violent crimes by men against women.

2. In what ways are the men depicted in Ellen Goodman's essay "When a Woman Says No" (p. 122) like the men described in Ehrenreich's essay? Analyze the characteristics they share. How are they different?

3. Compare the responses of the men in "What Do Men Really Want?" (p. 81) to the points Ehrenreich makes about males' anger. Focus your essay on the causes of this anger.

3

Between Cultures

■ ■ ■

Over a million people a year come from different countries to live in the United States, and your classrooms undoubtedly reflect this diversity. After classes you may find yourself enjoying sushi or tacos, digesting cultural diversity as easily as you munch a Big Mac. Or you may find yourself perplexed by cultural pluralism, unsure of its merits. The readings in this chapter illustrate the joy and stress of living with cultural differences. As you will discover, assimilation and rejection are issues not only for immigrants but for longtime residents of the United States who experience the psychological, political, and economic realities of living between cultures.

This chapter begins with an essay by someone like yourself, a college student, who describes the contrasts between his home and college environments. Marcus Mabry, an African American from New Jersey, writes of the discomfort he experiences traveling "between the two worlds" of poverty in the East and affluence in his life at Stanford in the West. In another essay, Kim Edwards describes the tensions of an American living abroad and feeling isolated from the students and faculty of her school because of political differences. Even if you have not lived in a foreign country, you may have felt like you were living in a foreign environment, and thus you will be able to understand her desire to be accepted. The young women in David Haldane's essay "Asian Girls: A Cultural Tug of War" struggle to please their immigrant parents and still fit into the dominant culture.

Cultural characteristics are important because they define who we are, but they can also lead to misunderstanding and stereotyping. The treatment of Native Americans by the dominant culture is a source of conflict and sorrow in Louise Erdrich's short story "American Horse." And the perverse use of the Native American in popular culture is criticized by Ward Churchill in his essay "Crimes Against Humanity." After you have read this essay, you may find yourself thinking differently about the displacement of Native Americans within their own homeland and about the "Indian" images that are prevalent in American life.

The stereotyping of African-American people is exposed in poems by Sharon Olds and Nikki Giovanni and a short story by Susan Straight. Finally, as a humorous response to living with stereotyping, we think you will enjoy Gary Soto's amusing essay "Like Mexicans," which recounts how he went against his family's advice and fell in love with a Japanese woman.

LIVING IN TWO WORLDS
Marcus Mabry

After completing his B.A. in English and French literature at Stanford University, Marcus Mabry (b. 1967) also earned a B.A. in international relations and an M.A. in English, all within the four years of his scholarship agreement. He was the *Newsweek* State Department correspondent from 1989 to 1992 and presently works in *Newsweek's* Paris bureau. In addition to free-lance writing for *Emerge* and *Black Collegiate,* Mabry is working with French television to produce a program on the lives of rich and poor, urban and rural African-American families. You may also be interested to read Mabry's *Newsweek* essay of May 4, 1992; in "No Father, and No Answers," Marcus Mabry addresses the concerns he has had in trying both to understand and to establish a relationship with the father he only recently met (who 20 years earlier left Mabry's unwed mother to raise her son without emotional or economic support). The work printed below also appeared in *Newsweek.*

1   A round, green cardboard sign hangs from a string proclaiming, "We built a proud new feeling," the slogan of a local supermarket. It is a souvenir from one of my brother's last jobs. In addition to being a bagger, he's worked at a fast-food restaurant, a gas station, a garage and a textile factory. Now, in the icy clutches of the Northeastern winter, he is unemployed. He will soon be a father. He is 19 years old.

2   In mid-December I was at Stanford, among the palm trees and weighty chores of academe. And all I wanted to do was get out. I joined the rest of the undergrads in a chorus of excitement, singing the praises of Christmas break. No classes, no midterms, no finals . . . and no freshmen! (I'm a resident assistant.) Awesome! I was looking forward to escaping. I never gave a thought to what I was escaping to.

3   Once I got home to New Jersey, reality returned. My dreaded freshmen had been replaced by unemployed relatives; badgering professors had been replaced by hard-working single mothers, and cold classrooms by dilapidated bedrooms and kitchens. The room in which the "proud new feeling" sign hung contained the belongings of myself, my mom and my brother. But for these two weeks it was mine. They slept downstairs on couches.

4   Most students who travel between the universes of poverty and affluence during breaks experience similar conditions, as well as the guilt, the helplessness and, sometimes, the embarrassment associated with them. Our friends are willing to listen, but most of them are unable to imagine the pain of the impoverished lives that we see every six months. Each time I return home I feel further away from the realities of poverty in America and more ashamed that they are allowed to persist. What frightens me most is not that the American socioeconomic system permits poverty to continue, but that by participating in that system I share some of the blame.

5   Last year I lived in an on-campus apartment, with a (relatively) modern bathroom, kitchen and two bedrooms. Using summer earnings, I added some expensive prints, a potted palm and some other plants, making the place look like the more-than-humble abode of a New York City Yuppie. I gave dinner parties, even a *soirée française*.

6   For my roommate, a doctor's son, this kind of life was nothing extraordinary. But my mom was struggling to provide a life for herself and my brother. In addition to working 24-hour-a-day cases as a practical nurse, she was trying to ensure that my brother would graduate from high school and have a decent life. She knew that she had to compete for his attention with drugs and other potentially dangerous things that can look attractive to a young man when he sees no better future.

7   Living in my grandmother's house this Christmas break restored all the forgotten, and the never acknowledged, guilt. I had gone to boarding school on a full scholarship since the ninth grade, so being away from poverty was not new. But my own growing affluence has increased my distance. My friends say that I should not feel guilty: what could I do substantially for my family at this age, they ask. Even though I know that education is the right thing to do, I can't help but feel, sometimes, that I have it too good. There is no reason that I deserve security and warmth, while my brother has to cope with potential unemployment and prejudice. I, too, encounter prejudice, but it is softened by my status as a student in an affluent and intellectual community.

8   More than my sense of guilt, my sense of helplessness increases each time I return home. As my success leads me further away for longer periods of time, poverty becomes harder to conceptualize and feels that much more oppressive when I visit with it. The first night of break, I lay in our bedroom, on a couch that let out into a bed that took up the whole room, except for a space heater. It was a little hard to sleep because the springs from the couch stuck through at inconvenient spots. But it would have been impossible to sleep anyway because of the groans coming from my grandmother's room next door. Only in her early 60s, she suffers from many chronic diseases and couldn't help but moan, then pray aloud, then moan, then pray aloud.

9   This wrenching of my heart was interrupted by the 3 A.M. entry of a relative who had been allowed to stay at the house despite rowdy behavior and threats toward the family in the past. As he came into the house, he slammed the door, and his heavy steps shook the second floor as he stomped into my grandmother's

room to take his place, at the foot of her bed. There he slept, without blankets on a bare mattress. This was the first night. Later in the vacation, a Christmas turkey and a Christmas ham were stolen from my aunt's refrigerator on Christmas Eve. We think the thief was a relative. My mom and I decided not to exchange gifts that year because it just didn't seem festive.

10   A few days after New Year's I returned to California. The Northeast was soon hit by a blizzard. They were there, and I was here. That was the way it had to be, for now. I haven't forgotten; the ache of knowing their suffering is always there. It has to be kept deep down, or I can't find the logic in studying and partying while people, my people, are being killed by poverty. Ironically, success drives me away from those I most want to help by getting an education.

11   Somewhere in the midst of all that misery, my family has built, within me, "a proud feeling." As I travel between the two worlds it becomes harder to remember just how proud I should be—not just because of where I have come from and where I am going, but because of where they are. The fact that they survive in the world in which they live is something to be very proud of, indeed. It inspires within me a sense of tenacity and accomplishment that I hope every college graduate will someday possess.

THINKING ABOUT THE TEXT

1. Describe Mabry's university world and his role in it. Then contrast it with details from his family's home.

2. Mabry describes living "between the universes of poverty and affluence." Detail the emotional toll this takes.

3. What happens during Christmas break to restore his sense of guilt?

4. How is the supermarket sign, hanging in the bedroom, both ironic and deeply symbolic of Mabry's life between worlds?

WRITING FROM THE TEXT

1. Using details from the story, compare and contrast Mabry's "worlds." What is ironic about the impact of success on his life?

2. For Mabry, attending college has secured him a spot in a new world vastly different from his past. Focus on your own between-worlds experience—college and home life, school and work worlds, high school and college relationships. Help the reader see each world as vividly as Mabry does; include your emotional responses, too.

3. Write about a time when you tried to escape one world and exchange it for another. How successful were you? What was your emotional toll?

CONNECTING WITH OTHER TEXTS

1. Analyze the between-worlds experiences of Mabry, the girls in "Asian Girls" (p. 152), and the teacher in "In Rooms of Women" (below). How do they compare? What conclusions can you draw about the "cultural tug of war"?

2. Write a research paper examining your college's admissions and recruiting policies, scholarship programs, dropout rate, and success record for minority students. You may want to focus your paper on what your research indicates has been the most serious obstacle or most successful accomplishment for affirmative action on your campus.

IN ROOMS OF WOMEN
Kim Edwards

After earning her B.A. in English at Colgate, Kim Edwards (b. 1958) earned her M.F.A. from the Iowa Writers' Workshop and then her M.A. in linguistics. She has taught English in Malaysia, Japan, and Cambodia. She is a free-lance writer of fiction and has had work published in the *Paris Review*. She won the Nelson Algren Award for fiction in 1990. This piece, originally published as a longer essay in the *Michigan Quarterly*, evolved from her experiences teaching in Malaysia and Japan.

1   When I lived on the East Coast of Malaysia, I used to do aerobics over a Chinese grocery store. I went there almost every afternoon, climbed up a tunnel of concrete stairs to a narrow room infused with the perfume of hair gel and perspiration, cosmetics and worn shoes. In Malaysia, where more than half the female population drifts through the tropical days beneath layers of concealing polyester, this room was an unusual domain of women. We were relaxed here, exposed in our leotards and shorts, our determination as strong as the situation was ironic. For an hour each day we stretched and ran and sweated, devoting ourselves entirely to the care of bodies which, in the outside world, we were encouraged to hide.

2   Malaysia is a multiracial country, with Islamic Malays comprising 55% of the population. Chinese and Indians make up the rest, at 35% and 10%, respectively. Though they have shared the Malay peninsula for generations, these groups maintain distinct languages and cultural traditions. They live together in uneasy proximity, with the biggest division occurring between the Malays, who follow Islam, and the other two groups, who don't. At aerobics, though, these population demographics were reversed; only one or two of the women in that room were Malay.

Their presence was an act of quiet daring. Outside, they didn't wear the polyester robes and veils. Inside, they were bold enough to appear among us in a leotard that revealed the contours of their flesh.

3   From the windows of the aerobics room we could see other Malay women as they shopped or chatted, their shiny skirts brushing their brown feet. They wore long-sleeved tunics that hung loosely to the knees, designed to hide every flux and curve of the body. On top of this most wore a *telicon,* a kind of polyester scarf that fastens beneath the chin and flows down, elbow-length, hiding the hair and curve of breasts simultaneously. Though this attire is common now, in pictures from Malaysia that are more than 15 years old, very few of the women cover their heads. Islam has been the predominant religion of the area for centuries, but traditionally it has been a gentle, even tolerant force in Malaysia, tempered by the weather and the easy-going nature of the people. In more remote villages it is still possible to see a lifestyle shaped by its quieter influence. The call to prayer comes five times a day, but little children, both boys and girls, play naked under the fruit trees. Women sit on porches, breast-feeding children. They bathe in the river together, wearing sarongs, and the most serious head-covering is a scarf draped gracefully across the hair on formal occasions. There are separate spheres here, for men and for women, but the focus is less on rules and their enforcement than it is on the harmonious flow of life from one day to another.

4   By the time I went to teach in Malaysia, however, much of the country had been profoundly influenced by the Iranian revolution. The gentle religion that had thrived in the country for centuries changed rapidly as televised images of the Middle East showed a different standard of dress and practice. This growing conservatism invaded every aspect of life, but it was most immediately visible in the dress mandated for girls and women. It began with pressure for them to discard Western clothes or sarongs in favor of the shapeless polyester dresses known as the *baju kurung.* By the time I reached Malaysia, the *baju kurung* and *telicon* were commonplace, and I watched the veils grow longer, heavier, and more somber during the two years I was there. For the more radical there was *purdah,* literally *curtain,* where a veil, usually black, hides the entire face, and dark gloves protect the fingers from view. When I first went to Malaysia, it was rare to glimpse a woman in *purdah.* By the time I left, I saw them almost every other day.

5   Yet at the same time that conservative Islam was strengthening in Malaysia, the government was sending a record number of Malay students overseas to study subjects essential to a developing country. Thus, the students were caught in two opposing forces, one that dictated a life focused solely on Islam, the other that demanded they learn technology from cultures outside of Islam. The place where these two forces met was in the preparatory schools that the students attended for two years before going overseas. Here, the stated administrative goal was to provide, as much as possible, an American style of education, in hopes of reducing culture shock and gaining transfer credit. Here too the religious teachers, alarmed by what they perceived to be a decadent influence, worked hard to ensure that the students understood the terrible evil of the West. Yet belief is an insubstantial

thing, difficult to pin down or measure, especially in a population of nearly a thousand students. And so it was the rules they turned to. The equation was a simple one: Those who followed the rules were virtuous, and those who did not were damned.

6   It was in one of these schools that I taught. My college was located in the East Coast of the peninsula, in the heart of the Islamic revival, and the religious teachers, or *ustaz,* were the most powerful men in the school. I'd had Malaysian students in the U.S., young women who appeared in class with tennis shoes poking out from beneath their polyester robes, and I'd been assured by the people who hired me that this dress code wouldn't affect my life; that, as a Westerner, I'd be outside the rules of Islam. Moreover, though I was an English teacher, it was also part of my job to *be* American, and to expose the students to other ways of living that they would encounter when they went overseas. At the time of that interview I was teaching in a major university, with students from dozens of countries in my classes. The idea of being different didn't seem particularly intimidating. I packed my most discreet Western clothes, and expected that I'd exist with the local teachers in a state of mutual tolerance and respect.

7   What I didn't fully understand, before I left America, is what it means to be different in a society where anything but conformity is greeted with unease. In Malaysia, as in many Asian cultures, there is an emphasis on the group over the individual. This focus is made stronger by Islam, which demands a structured and visible compliance to group norms, and which viewed my particular differences—American, non-Islamic, uncovered woman—as both evil and a threat. In a community of covered women, my short-sleeved blouses and calf-length skirts seemed suddenly immodest. The religious teachers made sure I understood this on my first day there, when they veered off the path—literally walking through mud—to avoid me. They couldn't keep the government from hiring me, but they could isolate me. They treated me as an unclean person, and the most devout students and teachers soon followed their example.

8   What was hardest for me, though, was the difficulty I had making connections with other women. The veils that covered them were also a kind of barrier I could not seem to cross. I suppose my skin, my hair, the obvious isolation imposed on me by the *ustaz,* seemed as unnerving to them as their veils and long skirts sometimes seemed to me. Some of the women were kind, but distant. If we talked, the subject invariably came back to Islam. Others, those who were extremely devout, were visibly unfriendly. These were the women who wore thick socks with their sandals and dressed in the most somber shades of gray and brown and black. They covered even the heads of their infant daughters, and cast disapproving glances at my exposed forearms, my calves, my toes. In this atmosphere, it was more than a year before I made any women friends at school. There were never many, and I always understood that friendship with me carried risks for them. The *ustaz* and other teachers reprimanded them often for consorting with a Westerner. One of them told me this while we were at her village, sitting on the front steps eating mangos.

9   "But it isn't true," she said, thinking. "It isn't true what they say. You are not Islam. But you are good."

10   In another situation—if I'd been a Peace Corps volunteer—I might have given in, and sought a greater harmony with this community by wearing the *baju kurung*. It would have been the easiest choice—one by one, the few uncovered women at the college were folding under the pressure and donning *telicons*—and I might have done it too, despite the fact that polyester beneath a tropical sun clings like plastic to the skin. I know this is true because I wore it once. I was in a village with my friend and I wanted to make a good impression. I remember it so clearly, the polyester slipping over my head, and the feeling of claustrophobia that accompanied it. At the school, though, wearing the *baju kurung* would have served no purpose except to mislead the students about what they could expect to find in America. Already the *ustaz* spewed a mixed and misleading propaganda: America was evil, all the people were greedy and had no morals. Though I tried to keep a low profile, and to show through my actions that different ways of dressing had very little to do with a person's character, it was clear that the *ustaz* saw my clothes, and the body they revealed, as clear manifestations of Western decadence. They did their best to isolate me, and this was more insidious than simple unfriendliness. In a society which puts its emphasis on the group, isolation is the cruelest punishment of all.

11   The longer I stayed in Malaysia, and the more friends I made, the more dangerous I became. It took my friend's comment, *you are not Islam, but you are good,* to make me realize this. Islam teaches that there is only one way. That way is strict, and tolerates no deviance. By wearing Western clothes, clothes that acknowledged waist and skin, the curve of female flesh, I was suggesting that this was not so, that there was, in fact, a choice. As long as I could be isolated, cast as a symbol of decadence and evil, the implications of my dress could be contained. But as I stayed longer, made friends, committed no evil acts, it became more difficult to cast me in the black and white terms that symbols require. I was not Islam, but neither was I evil. In essence, my presence was a kind of unspoken question, and it was seen by the devout as an act of absolute aggression. From time to time—often during moments of political tension in the Islamic world—the minimal tolerance I was granted waned. At these times I was thrust out of the middle ground with all its ambiguities and became suddenly, unwillingly, polemic.

12   There were several incidents in the two years I was there, but the one that stays most significantly in my mind occurred after the Ayatollah Khomeni called for the death of Salman Rushdie. Stirred up by the *ustaz,* the students made repeated denunciations—first against Rushdie himself, then the West in general, and finally against America and the three American teachers at the school. We watched this progression without reacting, but in the face of such anger, it was not enough to be silent. We were outside Islam, and our nonbelief, tolerated during calmer times, now evoked strong and emotional reactions. Even teachers who had seemed indifferent before soon joined in the general denunciation.

13   One day, in the worst of this, a Malay teacher who had never covered herself arrived at the college dressed in a *baju kurung* with a long black *telicon* falling over it. I remember the stir of pleasure she caused among those already covered. I remember that she passed me on the sidewalk and shot me a beatific smile. Lost, as she was, within a frame of black, I didn't recognize her at first. When I did, I understood her message immediately: *I belong, now, and I pity you, one among the damned.* She, like the more radical women in the town who donned *purdah* veils, was using her body, the negation of it, as a means of political expression. The denial of her body was a kind of aggression, and her aggression was sanctioned and supported—in this case, even demanded—by the community.

14   It is a terrible thing to hate your own body, yet in Malaysia I found that I was never far from this feeling. I was most aware of it every time I left the country, even briefly, and felt anxiety slipping from my shoulders like a heavy cloak. In Singapore I wore shorts without a stir; in Bangkok a sleeveless sundress was nothing to anyone but a sensible way of dealing with the heat. The first time it happened I was in Hong Kong, and I remember feeling light, joyously light, when the only people who followed me were the shopkeepers hoping for a sale. It is a big city, full of lovely, visible bodies. I was anonymous, and I had never felt so free.

15   In the end, of course, I left Malaysia for good. I took a job in Japan, where sometimes, at the end of a long week, I treated myself to a trip to the local hot spring. The first time I went was not long after I arrived. I remember that I felt oddly shy at the prospect of disrobing in a public area, and I realized at that moment how strongly my sense of what was appropriate had been shaped by two years in an Islamic country. Yet I made myself go. The room, at the top of an open stairway, was empty, lovely, built of pine. Moonlight flowed in through the windows and filled the wooden shelves. It was very cold. I undressed completely, as I knew was the custom, folding my clothes carefully. Wrapped in a towel, I stepped around the corner into the hot spring area.

16   At first I couldn't see much. Steam rose from the pool and caught the light, creating a kind of silver fog. Even with my closest friends in Malaysia, we had dressed and undressed discreetly, within sarongs, and the image of the body was never something that was shared. I still felt hesitant, standing on the smooth rocks with my towel clutched around me. Through the steam other women appeared, floating against the dark gray rocks, their bodies catching the light in a white and wavering contrast to the darkness below. They were all so different, women whose bodies plodded or strode or moved with grace, women whose breasts were rounded or sloped, pendulous or barely formed. I watched them all with appreciation, my body one among theirs, an individual collection of permutations and shapes, yet one of a set. In that spring, a foreigner and further isolated by my stumbling Japanese, I nonetheless felt a sense of community. For two years I'd carried, unwillingly, a sense of the body as something to hide, and a message that the flesh was an aggression, a sin, an evocation of the darker forces in human nature. In a Japanese hot spring, all this was washed away.

THINKING ABOUT THE TEXT

1. What are the contrasting cultural experiences that Kim Edwards had teaching abroad? What insight resulted from her hot spring experience in Japan?

2. What history of the coverings for women does Edwards give in her essay? Why didn't Edwards wear the *baju kurung?* Do you agree with her reasoning?

3. What personal discomfort did Edwards feel about her decision? Why was her decision interpreted as political?

4. Why did Edwards leave her teaching position in Malaysia? How did her experience in Japan confirm that her decision was a good one for her?

WRITING FROM THE TEXT

1. Describe a time in your life when the way that you were dressed separated you from people with whom you wanted to be friends. Describe specifically the way that you were dressed and how you think people perceived you. *Why* did people respond to you as they did? Like Edwards, see if you can come to some awareness in the process of writing about this experience.

2. Write an analysis of the compromises you have made in dressing to please yourself and at the same time to satisfy some explicit or understood societal "dress code." You might contrast others' expectations with your preferred style of dress.

CONNECTING WITH OTHER TEXTS

1. Women especially, although not exclusively, receive messages about their bodies and dress throughout their lives. Many of the pieces in *Between Worlds* address or refer to this issue: "On Being a Cripple" (p. 203), "A Work of Artifice" (p. 110), "Women" (p. 100), "Bodily Harm" (p. 220), and the opening chapter from *The Beauty Myth* (p. 101). Use these materials to write an analysis of one aspect of the issue of women in relation to their bodies.

2. Read Robert Heilbroner's essay "Don't Let Stereotypes Warp Your Judgments" (p. 429), and write an analysis of the problems that Edwards describes. Show in your essay that stereotyping is the source of the trouble.

ASIAN GIRLS: A CULTURAL TUG OF WAR
David Haldane

After studying psychology at UCLA, David Haldane (b. 1949) transferred to God-
dard College in Vermont, where he studied political science and then graduated
with a B.A. in creative writing. He has worked as a cab driver in New York and as
a free-lance writer for papers like the *Berkeley Barb* and the *L.A. Free Press,* as well
as for national magazines. For eight years he wrote for daily newspapers in southern California before he was hired to work full-time at the *Los Angeles Times,* where
the essay here was first published in 1988.

1   In many respects Crystal Hul, 16, is more American than Cambodian. The
daughter of a well-known leader in Southern California's Cambodian refugee
community, she has been in the United States since the age of 4. She speaks fluent
English, gets good grades, was recently nominated for sophomore princess by her
classmates and hopes to pursue a career in political science.

2   Yet when Crystal walks through the front door of her Long Beach home, she
enters a different world. Here she must never allow her head to rise above that of
her father's. She must continually refill his rice bowl until he finishes dinner and
signals that she may eat. She must never leave the house alone. She is not allowed
to date, drive a car, enter a movie theater or attend any party not also attended by
her brothers. And she fully expects her parents to eventually choose a husband for
her—with whom she is unlikely to even speak before the wedding.

3   "The rules are different at home than at school," she said. "We respect our
father and mother as gods. I could never find the heart to disobey them."

4   Meet an unusual group of immigrant Americans. They are young Asians
deeply rooted in ancient cultures that consider women subservient. And for the
girls especially, life in America can be one of stark contrasts, even two clashing
existences: life at home and life outside.

5   "I trust my parents to make the right decisions for me," Crystal said. "I feel
loved. But sometimes it's hard." So hard, according to psychologists and social
workers, that increasing numbers are breaking under the strain.

6   The story of these young women's struggle to balance two worlds has its beginnings in ancient history. Five hundred years before the birth of Christ, the Chinese
philosopher Confucius, whose teachings form the basis for much of Asian society,
preached the subservience of women and the suppression of individual needs in
favor of those of the group.

7   "It's the sense that the family is more important than the individual," said Lucie
Cheng, a professor of sociology at UCLA who is a Chinese-American and director of the university's Center for Pacific Rim Studies. "The idea that it's not individuals expressing their individualism that is important, but how everyone can
preserve the harmony within the family to keep it going and minimize conflicts."

8   While similar values prevailed to some extent in early Western societies,
experts say, the rapid technological development of the West tended to mitigate
them while the lingering agricultural life styles of the East allowed them to flour-
ish. Thus for generations, especially in East and Southeast Asian countries,

women were taught to serve their husbands without question, a role they began preparing for almost from birth.

9   And while their male siblings were also under pressure to respect and obey their elders, the girls in particular were raised as revered and protected beings who learned their proper roles at their mothers' apron strings.

10   Recent years have seen some disruptions in that tradition. In mainland China, for instance, where the Communist government has long discouraged traditional views of femininity, young people have discovered the sexual revolution with the result that as many as 30% have experienced premarital sex, according to one recent estimate.

11   Japan, strongly influenced by the West through economic and cultural ties, has also undergone some liberalization of its values regarding women.

12   And during the 1960s and '70s Southeast Asian countries such as Vietnam, Cambodia and Laos came under Communist rule, with the result that traditional family ties and gender roles there were severely challenged. It is refugees from these Southeast Asian countries—about 340,000 of whom have settled in California since 1975—who tend to cling to their traditional values most strongly.

13   "They feel guilty about leaving their countries," said Florentius Chan, a psychologist and director of the Asian Pacific Mental Health Center in Long Beach. Buffeted by media portrayals of what they perceive as an alien and dangerous American culture and wracked by uncertainties regarding their own future in it, the refugees in many cases are interpreting their own traditions more rigidly than they ever did at home. "The only thing they can control," said Chan, who was born in Taiwan, "is their value system."

14   For some families, the effort seems to be working. Crystal, for instance, says that despite occasional teasing from her friends, she is comfortable with the way she is being brought up, including the eventual selection of a mate by her parents, and intends to raise her own daughters the same way. "My husband will love me as a daughter, a little sister and a wife," the teenager says. "I know that my mom and dad will make a good decision. It's one less thing I have to worry about."

15   For others, though, the attempt to live Asian lives in a Western culture can prove devastating. One 18-year-old Cambodian student, who did not want her name used, said she became so upset at her mother's attempts at controlling her life that she ran away from home, spent several nights in a seedy hotel, got drunk and attempted suicide. "She tried to bring me up in the Cambodian way," the young woman said, "but I just didn't know how to act. I was young when we left Cambodia; it's too difficult to act like that."

16   Eventually, the youngster received counseling and returned to her Long Beach home, where she says her mother is now somewhat less restrictive.

17   Another girl, age 16, said she rebelled by moving into a Cambodian Buddhist Temple. Later she moved to a shelter, then to a foster home. "I didn't like that way I was being treated," said the girl, who continues to live in the foster home, where she says she is freer to pursue her own interests.

18   These problems are often aggravated, experts say, because many immigrant parents expect their daughters to get good educations and pursue careers as well as

behave in traditionally feminine ways. Thus, added to the pressures on Asian-American students of both genders to excel in their academic and professional pursuits is the demand that young women do so without sacrificing their traditional feminine passivity. The resulting tension has been well chronicled in the art and literature of Asian-Americans.

19   In 1976, Maxine Hong Kingston, a Chinese-American woman born and raised in Stockton, won the National Book Critics Circle Award for "Woman Warrior," a memoir of her girlhood based on stories her mother told her while working in the family laundry.

20   In the book, Kingston, who now lives in Studio City, told of purposely acting stupid and clumsy in the presence of young Chinese men chosen by her parents as potential mates. The idea, she said, was to make herself undesirable enough to be left alone.

21   "I refused to cook," Kingston wrote. "When I had to wash the dishes, I would crack one or two. 'Bad girl!' my mother yelled, and sometimes that made me gloat rather than cry. Isn't a bad girl almost a boy?"

22   Jude Narita, a young Japanese-American, presented a one-woman play last year called "Coming Into Passion/Song for a Sansei." Working through a series of vignettes, the show, which recently closed at the Fountain Theater in Hollywood, explored the lives of several Asian-American women, including an American teen-ager of Japanese descent, a Filipina mail-order bride, a Vietnamese prostitute and a grown-up who had been detained at a World War II camp for Japanese-Americans.

23   "Education changes everything," Narita said. "The benefit of coming to America is unlimited opportunity, but one of the side effects is that you lose total control of your children. That's the natural progression; the older generation tries to hold it back, but it's like trying to hold back the wind." Experts say they have no overall statistics on how many Asian girls are running away, becoming involved with drugs and prostitution or attempting suicide as a result of these cultural pressures. Most, however, say such cases are on the rise.

24   Chan's experience in Long Beach, where his agency deals primarily with Cambodians, may be instructive. Of his 30 current cases, the psychologist said, two-thirds involve girls who are having serious problems adjusting to the expectations of two cultures. Based on his experience, Chan said, he estimates that as many as half of the area's Cambodian families are encountering similar difficulties, with the number of cases requiring professional help increasing by about 20% per year. Chan attributes the increase to the continuing influx of refugees, combined with the fact that more and more girls who were very young when they arrived in the United States are reaching the rebellious teen-age years.

25   "It's getting worse and worse," Chan said. "We have parents calling us crying—they just don't know what to do." Joselyn Yap, director of the child and youth division of the Asian Pacific Counseling and Treatment Center in Los Angeles, reports an alarming increase in child-abuse cases—the majority involving girls—among clients from the Philippines, Vietnam and China, where some segments of the population consider corporal punishment acceptable. Of the 100

cases her agency sees each month, Yap said, about 20%—a twenty-fold increase since 1985—involve abused children.

26 Yap attributes the increase in reported incidents of abuse to the rising level of stress felt by immigrants dealing with the changing cultural values of their children, as well as enhanced professional awareness of the problem. One teacher was very surprised that when she said she had to discipline a child, the parents said that that was OK as long as she didn't break any of the child's bones," recalled Ben Marte, a behavioral science consultant with the agency.

27 And Johng Song, intervention program coordinator for Los Angeles' Korean Youth Center, said that about 40% of his agency's estimated 450 clients each year are girls having trouble adapting to their dual roles.

28 A smattering of academic studies have touched on various aspects of the problem. A 1980 paper done at Columbia University focused on Chinese women who had immigrated to the United States. Among its conclusions: that the earlier in their lives they emigrated, the less likely they were to suffer from serious emotional maladjustments. In 1984 a psychologist at UCLA published a paper documenting impaired motivation, increased conflict with children and a growing divorce rate among female Southeast Asian refugees.

29 One result of this attention has been a proliferation of special programs aimed at helping Asian parents and children. Yap's agency, for instance, offers classes for parents designed to improve their child-rearing skills, as well as individual and group therapy sessions for teen-age boys and girls. At Song's center, teen-agers are encouraged to discuss their culture's double standard for males and females at special workshops. The Asian Pacific Family Center in Rosemead offers therapy designed to help ease the acculturation process.

30 "Our goal is to change the conflict model into more of an integration adjustment model," said George Choi, the center's clinical director. "One can adapt by recognizing the boundaries in either world, working comfortably within those boundaries and still being comfortable with one's self. A lot of the time, [the girls] are not trying to abdicate either role as much as trying to integrate both."

31 Indeed, many young Asian women seem to be doing so. Shung Kim, a 19-year-old Korean who has been in the country since age 3 and studies psychology at UCLA, said she has learned to accept the fact that her parents expect her home by 11:30 p.m., while her 17-year-old brother is permitted to stay out until 2 a.m.

32 "For a while I challenged them," she said, "but it's pretty much instilled in me now. I'm like a combination of Korean and American; right in the middle."

33 Thuly Nguyen, 16, a Vietnamese high school student who lives in Wilmington, says she understands why her parents won't let her date. "They've been over there longer than they've been over here," she said. "I can't expect them to change that much."

34 And at 23, Vuthy Chek, a Cambodian refugee, has finally worked out an arrangement that she believes she can live with. A student at Cal State Long Beach with a full-time job, she still resides with her parents, is allowed to date only in groups and must be home by 11 p.m.

35   But when it comes time to marry, she said, her family will make a slight departure from tradition. "They would love to have an arranged marriage," Chek said,
"but they have compromised. I have the right to say no."

THINKING ABOUT THE TEXT

1. What general observations can you make about the experiences of
   the young people and the commentary by professionals presented in
   this newspaper article?
2. What are the various reasons that the older generations of Asian parents cling to the cultural patterns of "home" while they rear their
   daughters in the United States?
3. What are the various responses of the young women to their
   upbringing?

WRITING FROM THE TEXT

1. Write an analysis of the conflicts that some young Asian-American
   women face. Use the material in this essay to support your points.
2. Interview some of the Asian-American women and men at your
   school. Write an analysis of their "tug of war" experiences, but use
   many more specific details and anecdotes than Haldane uses in his
   article.
3. Write a persuasive essay, designed to appear in an Asian-American
   community newspaper, to convince parents to minimize the conflicts
   their daughters feel in living between worlds. Show from your tone
   that you realize that the parents, especially those from Southeast
   Asian countries, have experienced profound political and cultural
   changes in coming to live in the United States. But try to convince
   your readers of the advantages in considering some aspects of a new
   value system and the dangers of imposing a harsh, traditional order.

CONNECTING WITH OTHER TEXTS

1. Warren Farrell describes an "invisible curriculum" imposed on young
   American women and men in the United States (p. 92). Use Farrell's
   term as a departure point for an identification and discussion of the
   curriculum Asian-American women live with or rebel against.
2. Many of the essays in this book describe the conflicts of trying to meet
   the expectations of a former world and culture on American soil. The
   essay by Robert McKelvey, ("I Confess Some Envy," p. 399) and the

short story by Amy Tan ("Two Kinds," p. 49) address other dimensions of the problem. Do you think that the older generation feels envy
that the younger generation has been celebrated or has been given
choices the older generation never had? Use the materials in *Between
Worlds* to write an essay on cultural and generational conflicts.

AMERICAN HORSE
Louise Erdrich

A novelist, poet, and short story writer, Louise Erdrich (b. 1954) uses her
Chippewa heritage to create characters who are vivid, often eccentric, and tough
enough to struggle with the isolation, abandonment, and exploitation that threaten
them in the worlds they inhabit. Erdrich won the National Book Critics Circle
Award for *Love Medicine,* 14 interconnected stories told by seven different members of two Chippewa families. Critics praise Erdrich for her balance in portraying the struggle of Native Americans to reconcile their culture with the dominant
culture. The story included here is from *Spider Woman's Granddaughters,* published
in 1989.

1   The woman sleeping on the cot in the woodshed was Albertine American
Horse. The name was left over from her mother's short marriage. The boy was the
son of the man she had loved and let go. Buddy was on the cot, too, sitting on the
edge because he'd been awake three hours watching out for his mother and
besides, she took up the whole cot. Her feet hung over the edge, limp and brown
as two trout. Her long arms reached out and slapped at things she saw in her
dreams.

2   Buddy had been knocked awake out of hiding in a washing machine while
herds of policemen with dogs searched through a large building with many tiny
rooms. When the arm came down, Buddy screamed because it had a blue cuff and
sharp silver buttons. "Tss," his mother mumbled, half awake, "wasn't nothing."
But Buddy sat up after her breathing went deep again, and he watched.

3   There was something coming and he knew it.

4   It was coming from very far off but he had a picture of it in his mind. It was a
large thing made of metal with many barbed hooks, points, and drag chains on it,
something like a giant potato peeler that rolled out of the sky, scraping clouds
down with it and jabbing or crushing everything that lay in its path on the ground.

5   Buddy watched his mother. If he woke her up, she would know what to do
about the thing, but he thought he'd wait until he saw it for sure before he shook
her. She was pretty, sleeping, and he liked knowing he could look at her as long

and close up as he wanted. He took a strand of her hair and held it in his hands as if it was the rein to a delicate beast. She was strong enough and could pull him along like the horse their name was.

6   Buddy had his mother's and his grandmother's name because his father had been a big mistake.

7   "They're all mistakes, even your father. But *you* are the best thing that ever happened to me."

8   That was what she said when he asked.

9   Even Kadie, the boyfriend crippled from being in a car wreck, was not as good a thing that had happened to his mother as Buddy was. "He was a medium-size mistake," she said. "He's hurt and I shouldn't even say that, but it's the truth." At the moment, Buddy knew that being the best thing in his mother's life, he was also the reason they were hiding from the cops.

10   He wanted to touch the satin roses sewed on her pink tee-shirt, but he knew he shouldn't do that even in her sleep. If she woke up and found him touching the roses, she would say, "Quit that, Buddy." Sometimes she told him to stop hugging her like a gorilla. She never said that in the mean voice she used when he oppressed her, but when she said that he loosened up anyway.

11   There were times he felt like hugging her so hard and in such a special way that she would say to him, "Let's get married." There were also times he closed his eyes and wished that she would die, only a few times, but still it haunted him that his wish might come true. He and Uncle Lawrence would be left alone. Buddy wasn't worried, though, about his mother getting married to somebody else. She had said to her friend, Madonna, "All men suck," when she thought Buddy wasn't listening. He had made an uncertain sound, and when they heard him they took him in their arms.

12   "Except for you, Buddy," his mother said. "All except for you and maybe Uncle Lawrence, although he's pushing it."

13   "The cops suck the worst though," Buddy whispered to his mother's sleeping face, "because they're after us." He felt tired again, slumped down, and put his legs beneath the blanket. He closed his eyes and got the feeling that the cot was lifting up beneath him, that it was arching its canvas back and then traveling, traveling very fast and in the wrong direction for when he looked up he saw the three of them were advancing to meet the great metal thing with hooks and barbs and all sorts of sharp equipment to catch their bodies and draw their blood. He heard its insides as it rushed toward them, purring softly like a powerful motor and then they were right in its shadow. He pulled the reins as hard as he could and the beast reared, lifting him. His mother clapped her hand across his mouth.

14   "Okay," she said. "Lay low. They're outside and they're gonna hunt."

15   She touched his shoulder and Buddy leaned over with her to look through a crack in the boards.

16   They were out there all right, Albertine saw them. Two officers and that social worker woman. Vicki Koob. There had been no whistle, no dream, no voice to warn her that they were coming. There was only the crunching sound of cinders in the yard, the engine purring, the dust sifting off their car in a fine light brownish cloud and settling around them.

17   The three people came to a halt in their husk of metal—the car emblazoned with the North Dakota State Highway Patrol emblem which is the glowing profile of the Sioux policeman, Red Tomahawk, the one who killed Sitting Bull. Albertine gave Buddy the blanket and told him that he might have to wrap it around him and hide underneath the cot.

18   "We're gonna wait and see what they do." She took him in her lap and hunched her arms around him. "Don't you worry," she whispered against his ear. "Lawrence knows how to fool them."

19   Buddy didn't want to look at the car and the people. He felt his mother's heart beating beneath his ear so fast it seemed to push the satin roses in and out. He put his face to them carefully and breathed the deep, soft powdery woman smell of her. That smell was also in her little face cream bottles, in her brushes, and around the washbowl after she used it. The satin felt so unbearably smooth against his cheek that he had to press closer. She didn't push him away, like he expected, but hugged him still tighter until he felt as close as he had ever been to back inside her again where she said he came from. Within the smells of her things, her soft skin and the satin of her roses, he closed his eyes then, and took his breaths softly and quickly with her heart. They were out there, but they didn't dare get out of the car yet because of Lawrence's big, ragged dogs. Three of these dogs had loped up the dirt driveway with the car. They were rangy, alert, and bounced up and down on their cushioned paws like wolves. They didn't waste their energy barking, but positioned themselves quietly, one at either car door and the third in front of the bellied-out screen door to Uncle Lawrence's house. It was six in the morning but the wind was up already, blowing dust, ruffling their short moth-eaten coats. The big brown one on Vicki Koob's side had unusual black and white markings, stripes almost, like a hyena and he grinned at her, tongue out and teeth showing.

20   "Shoo!" Miss Koob opened her door with a quick jerk.

21   The brown dog sidestepped the door and jumped before her, tiptoeing. Its dirty white muzzle curled and its eyes crossed suddenly as if it was zeroing its cross-hair sights in on the exact place it would bite her. She ducked back and slammed the door.

22   "It's mean," she told Officer Brackett. He was printing out some type of form. The other officer, Harmony, a slow man, had not yet reacted to the car's halt. He had been sitting quietly in the back seat, but now he rolled down his window and with no change in expression unsnapped his holster and drew his pistol out and pointed it at the dog on his side. The dog smacked down on its belly, wiggled under the car and was out and around the back of the house before Harmony drew his gun back. The other dogs vanished with him. From wherever they had disappeared to they began to yap and howl, and the door to the low shoebox-style house fell open.

23   "Heya, what's going on?"

24   Uncle Lawrence put his head out the door and opened wide the one eye he had in working order. The eye bulged impossibly wider in outrage when he saw the police car. But the eyes of the two officers and Miss Vicki Koob were wide open too because they had never seen Uncle Lawrence in his sleeping getup or, indeed, witnessed anything like it. For his ribs, which were cracked from a bad fall and

still mending, Uncle Lawrence wore a thick white corset laced up the front with a striped sneakers lace. His glass eye and his set of dentures were still out for the night so his face puckered here and there, around its absences and scars, like a damaged but fierce little cake. Although he had a few gray streaks now, Uncle Lawrence's hair was still thick, and because he wore a special contraption of elastic straps around his head every night, two oiled waves always crested on either side of his middle part. All of this would have been sufficient to astonish, even without the most striking part of his outfit—the smoking jacket. It was made of black satin and hung open around his corset, dragging a tasseled belt. Gold thread dragons struggled up the lapels and blasted their furry red breath around his neck. As Lawrence walked down the steps, he put his arms up in surrender and the gold tassels in the inner seams of his sleeves dropped into view.

25   "My heavens, what a sight." Vicki Koob was impressed.

26   "A character," apologized Officer Harmony.

27   As a tribal police officer who could be counted on to help out the State Patrol, Harmony thought he always had to explain about Indians or get twice as tough to show he did not favor them. He was slow-moving and shy but two jumps ahead of other people all the same, and now, as he watched Uncle Lawrence's splendid approach, he gazed speculatively at the torn and bulging pocket of the smoking jacket. Harmony had been inside Uncle Lawrence's house before and knew that above his draped orange-crate shelf of war medals a blue-black German luger was hung carefully in a net of flat-headed nails and fishing line. Thinking of this deadly exhibition, he got out of the car and shambled toward Lawrence with a dreamy little smile of welcome on his face. But when he searched Lawrence, he found that the bulging pocket held only the lonesome-looking dentures from Lawrence's empty jaw. They were still dripping denture polish.

28   "I had been cleaning them when you arrived," Uncle Lawrence explained with acid dignity.

29   He took the toothbrush from his other pocket and aimed it like a rifle.

30   "Quit that, you old idiot." Harmony tossed the toothbrush away. "For once you ain't done nothing. We came for your nephew."

31   Lawrence looked at Harmony with a faint air of puzzlement.

32   "Ma Frere, listen," threatened Harmony amiably, "those two white people in the car came to get him for the welfare. They got papers on your nephew that give them the right to take him."

33   "Papers?" Uncle Lawrence puffed out his deeply pitted cheeks. "Let me see them papers."

34   The two of them walked over to Vicki's side of the car and she pulled a copy of the court order from her purse. Lawrence put his teeth back in and adjusted them with busy workings of his jaw.

35   "Just a minute," he reached into his breast pocket as he bent close to Miss Vicki Koob. "I can't read these without I have in my eye."

36   He took the eye from his breast pocket delicately, and as he popped it into his face the social worker's mouth fell open in a consterned O.

37   "What is this," she cried in a little voice.

38   Uncle Lawrence looked at her mildly. The white glass of the eye was cold as lard. The black iris was strangely charged and menacing.

39   "He's nuts," Brackett huffed along the side of Vicki's neck. "Never mind him."

40   Vicki's hair had sweated down her nape in tiny corkscrews and some of the hairs were so long and dangly now that they disappeared into the zippered back of her dress. Brackett noticed this as he spoke into her ear. His face grew red and the backs of his hands prickled. He slid under the steering wheel and got out of the car. He walked around the hood to stand with Leo Harmony.

41   "We could take you in too," said Brackett roughly. Lawrence eyed the officers in what was taken as defiance. "If you don't cooperate, we'll get out the hand-cuffs," they warned.

42   One of Lawrence's arms was stiff and would not move until he'd rubbed it with witch hazel in the morning. His other arm worked fine though, and he stuck it out in front of Brackett.

43   "Get them handcuffs," he urged them. "Put me in a welfare home."

44   Brackett snapped one side of the handcuffs on Lawrence's good arm and the other to the handle of the police car.

45   "That's to hold you," he said. "We're wasting our time. Harmony, you search that little shed over by the tall grass and Miss Koob and myself will search the house."

46   "My rights is violated!" Lawrence shrieked suddenly. They ignored him. He tugged at the handcuff and thought of the good heavy file he kept in his tool box and the German luger oiled and ready but never loaded, because of Buddy, over his shelf. He should have used it on these bad ones, even Harmony in his big-time white man job. He wouldn't last long in that job anyway before somebody gave him what for.

47   "It's a damn scheme," said Uncle Lawrence, rattling his chains against the car. He looked over at the shed and thought maybe Albertine and Buddy had sneaked away before the car pulled into the yard. But he sagged, seeing Albertine move like a shadow within the boards. "Oh, it's all a damn scheme," he muttered again.

48   "I want to find that boy and salvage him," Vicki Koob explained to Officer Brackett as they walked into the house. "Look at his family life—the old man crazy as a bedbug, the mother intoxicated somewhere."

49   Brackett nodded, energetic, eager. He was a short hopeful redhead who failed consistently to win the hearts of women. Vicki Koob intrigued him. Now, as he watched, she pulled a tiny pen out of an ornamental clip on her blouse. It was attached to a retractable line that would suck the pen back, like a child eating one strand of spaghetti. Something about the pen on its line excited Brackett to the point of discomfort. His hand shook as he opened the screendoor and stepped in, beckoning Miss Koob to follow.

50   They could see the house was empty at first glance. It was only one rectangular room with whitewashed walls and a little gas stove in the middle. They had already come through the cooking lean-to with the other stove and washstand and

rusty old refrigerator. That refrigerator had nothing in it but some wrinkled potatoes and a package of turkey necks. Vicki Koob noted that in her perfect-bound
notebook. The beds along the walls of the big room were covered with quilts that
Albertine's mother, Sophie, had made from bits of old wool coats and pants that
the Sisters sold in bundles at the mission. There was no one hiding beneath the
beds. No one was under the little aluminium dinette table covered with a green oil-
cloth, or the soft brown wood chairs tucked up to it. One wall of the big room was
filled with neatly stacked crates of things—old tools and springs and small half-
dismantled appliances. Five or six television sets were stacked against the wall.
Their control panels spewed colored wires and at least one was cracked all the
way across. Only the topmost set, with coat-hanger antenna angled sensitively to
catch the bounding signals around Little Shell, looked like it could possibly work.

51   Not one thing escaped Vicki Koob's trained and cataloguing gaze. She made
note of the cupboard that held only commodity flour and coffee. The unsanitary
tin oil drum beneath the kitchen window, full of empty surplus pork cans and beer
bottles, caught her eye as did Uncle Lawrence's physical and mental deteriora-
tions. She quickly described these "benchmarks of alcoholic dependency within
the extended family of Woodrow (Buddy) American Horse" as she walked around
the room with the little notebook open, pushed against her belly to steady it.
Although Vicki had been there before, Albertine's presence had always made it
difficult for her to take notes.

52   "Twice the maximum allowable space between door and threshold," she wrote
now. "Probably no insulation. 2–3 inch cracks in walls inadequately sealed with
whitewashed mud." She made a mental note but could see no point in describing
Lawrence's stuffed reclining chair that only reclined, the shadeless lamp with its
plastic orchid in the bubble glass base, or the three-dimensional picture of Jesus
that Lawrence had once demonstrated to her. When plugged in, lights rolled
behind the water the Lord stood on so that he seemed to be strolling although he
never actually went forward, of course, but only pushed the glowing waves behind
him forever like a poor tame rat in a treadmill.

53   Brackett cleared his throat with a nervous rasp and touched Vicki's shoulder.
54   "What are you writing?"
55   She moved away and continued to scribble as if thoroughly absorbed in her
work. "Officer Brackett displays an undue amount of interest in my person," she
wrote. "Perhaps?"

56   He snatched playfully at the book, but she hugged it to her chest and moved off
smiling. More curls had fallen, wetted to the base of her neck. Looking out the
window, she sighed long and loud.

57   "All night on brush rollers for this. What a joke."
58   Brackett shoved his hands in his pockets. His mouth opened slightly, then shut
with a small throttled cluck.

59   When Albertine saw Harmony ambling across the yard with his big brown
thumbs in his belt, his placid smile, and his tiny black eyes moving back and forth,

she put Buddy under the cot. Harmony stopped at the shed and stood quietly. He spread his arms wide to show her he hadn't drawn his big police gun.

60   "Ma Cousin," he said in the Michif dialect that people used if they were relatives or sometimes if they needed gas or a couple of dollars, "why don't you come out here and stop this foolishness?"

61   "I ain't your cousin," Albertine said. Anger boiled up in her suddenly. "I ain't related to no pigs."

62   She bit her lip and watched him through the cracks, circling, a big tan punching dummy with his boots full of sand so he never stayed down once he fell. He was empty inside, all stale air. But he knew how to get to her so much better than a white cop could. And now he was circling because he wasn't sure she didn't have a weapon, maybe a knife or the German luger that was the only thing that her father, Albert American Horse, had left his wife and daughter besides his name. Harmony knew that Albertine was a tall strong woman who took two big men to subdue when she didn't want to go in the drunk tank. She had hard hips, broad shoulders, and stood tall like her Sioux father, the American Horse who was killed threshing in Belle Prairie.

63   "I feel bad to have to do this," Harmony said to Albertine. "But for godsakes, let's nobody get hurt. Come on out with the boy why don't you. I know you got him in there."

64   Albertine did not give herself away this time. She let him wonder. Slowly and quietly she pulled her belt through its loops and wrapped it around and around her hand until only the big oval buckle with turquoise chunks shaped into a butterfly stuck out over her knuckles. Harmony was talking but she wasn't listening to what he said. She was listening to the pitch of his voice, the tone of it that would tighten or tremble at a certain moment when he decided to rush the shed. He kept talking slowly and reasonably, flexing the dialect from time to time, even mentioning her father.

65   "He was a damn good man. I don't care what they say, Albertine, I knew him."

66   Albertine looked at the stone butterfly that spread its wings across her fist. The wings looked light and cool, not heavy. It almost looked like it was ready to fly. Harmony wanted to get to Albertine through her father but she would not think about American Horse. She concentrated on the sky-blue stone.

67   Yet the shape of the stone, the color, betrayed her.

68   She saw her father suddenly, bending at the grille of their old grey car. She was small then. The memory came from so long ago it seemed like a dream—narrowly focused, snapshot clear. He was bending by the grille in the sun. It was hot summer. Wings of sweat, dark blue, spread across the back of his work shirt. He always wore soft blue shirts, the color of shade cloudier than this stone. His stiff hair had grown out of its short haircut and flopped over his forehead. When he stood up and turned away from the car, Albertine saw that he had a butterfly.

69   "It's dead," he told her. "Broke its wings and died on the grille."

70   She must have been five, maybe six, wearing one of the boy's tee-shirts Mama bleached in hilex-water. American Horse took the butterfly, a black and yellow

one, and rubbed it on Albertine's collarbone and chest and arms until the color and the powder of it were blended into her skin.

71   "For grace," he said.

72   And Albertine had felt a strange lightening in her arms, in her chest, when he did this and said, "For grace." The way he said it, grace meant everything the butterfly was. The sharp delicate wings. The way it floated over grass. The way its wings seemed to breathe fanning in the sun. The wisdom of the way it blended into flowers or changed into a leaf. In herself she felt the same kind of possibilities and closed her eyes almost in shock or pain, she felt so light and powerful at that moment.

73   Then her father had caught her and thrown her high into the air. She could not remember landing in his arms or landing at all. She only remembered the sun filling her eyes and the world tipping crazily behind her, out of sight.

74   "He was a damn good man," Harmony said again.

75   Albertine heard his starched uniform gathering before his boots hit the ground. Once, twice, three times. It took him four solid jumps to get right where she wanted him. She kicked the plank door open when he reached for the handle and the corner caught him on the jaw. He faltered, and Albertine hit him flat on the chin with the butterfly. She hit him so hard the shock of it went up her arm like a string pulled taut. Her fist opened, numb, and she let the belt unloop before she closed her hand on the tip end of it and sent the stone butterfly swooping out in a wide circle around her as if it was on the end of a leash. Harmony reeled backward as she walked toward him swinging the belt. She expected him to fall but he just stumbled. And then he took the gun from his hip.

76   Albertine let the belt go limp. She and Harmony stood within feet of each other, breathing. Each heard the human sound of air going in and out of the other person's lungs. Each read the face of the other as if deciphering letters carved into softly eroding veins of stone. Albertine saw the pattern of tiny arteries that age, drink, and hard living had blown to the surface of the man's face. She saw the spoked wheels of his iris and the arteries like tangled threads that sewed him up. She saw the living net of springs and tissue that held him together, and trapped him. She saw the random, intimate plan of his person.

77   She took a quick shallow breath and her face went strange and tight. She saw the black veins in the wings of the butterfly, roads burnt into a map, and then she was located somewhere in the net of veins and sinew that was the tragic complexity of the world so she did not see Officer Brackett and Vicki Koob rushing toward her, but felt them instead like flies caught in the same web, rocking it.

78   "Albertine!" Vicki Koob had stopped in the grass. Her voice was shrill and tight. "It's better this way, Albertine. We're going to help you."

79   Albertine straightened, threw her shoulders back. Her father's hand was on her chest and shoulders lightening her wonderfully. Then on wings of her father's hands, on dead butterfly wings, Albertine lifted into the air and flew toward the others. The light powerful feeling swept her up the way she had floated higher, seeing the grass below. It was her father throwing her up into the air and out of

danger. Her arms opened for bullets but no bullets came. Harmony did not shoot. Instead, he raised his fist and brought it down hard on her head.

80   Albertine did not fall immediately, but stood in his arms a moment. Perhaps she gazed still farther back behind the covering of his face. Perhaps she was completely stunned and did not think as she sagged and fell. Her face rolled forward and hair covered her features, so it was impossible for Harmony to see with just what particular expression she gazed into the head-splitting wheel of light, or blackness, that overcame her.

81   Harmony turned the vehicle onto the gravel road that led back to town. He had convinced the other two that Albertine was more trouble than she was worth, and so they left her behind, and Lawrence too. He stood swearing in his cinder driveway as the car rolled out of sight. Buddy sat between the social worker and Officer Brackett. Vicki tried to hold Buddy fast and keep her arm down at the same time, for the words she'd screamed at Albertine had broken the seal of antiperspirant beneath her arms. She was sweating now as though she'd stored an ocean up inside of her. Sweat rolled down her back in a shallow river and pooled at her waist and between her breasts. A thin sheen of water came out on her forearms, her face. Vicki gave an irritated moan but Brackett seemed not to take notice, or take offense at least. Air-conditioned breezes were sweeping over the seat anyway, and very soon they would be comfortable. She smiled at Brackett over Buddy's head. The man grinned back. Buddy stirred. Vicki remembered the emergency chocolate bar she kept in her purse, fished it out, and offered it to Buddy. He did not react, so she closed his fingers over the package and peeled the paper off one end.

82   The car accelerated. Buddy felt the road and wheels pummeling each other and the rush of the heavy motor purring in high gear. Buddy knew that what he'd seen in his mind that morning, the thing coming out of the sky with barbs and chains, had hooked him. Somehow he was caught and held in the sour tin smell of the pale woman's armpit. Somehow he was pinned between their pounds of breathless flesh. He looked at the chocolate in his hand. He was squeezing the bar so hard that a thin brown trickle had melted down his arm. Automatically, he put the bar in his mouth.

83   As he bit down he saw his mother very clearly, just as she had been when she carried him from the shed. She was stretched flat on the ground, on her stomach, and her arms were curled around her head as if in sleep. One leg was drawn up and it looked for all the world like she was running full tilt into the ground, as though she had been trying to pass into the earth, to bury herself, but at the last moment something had stopped her.

84   There was no blood on Albertine, but Buddy tasted blood now at the sight of her, for he bit down hard and cut his own lip. He ate the chocolate, every bit of it, tasting his mother's blood. And when he had the chocolate down inside him and all licked off his hands, he opened his mouth to say thank you to the woman, as his mother had taught him. But instead of a thank you coming out he was astonished

to hear a great rattling scream, and then another, rip out of him like pieces of his own body and whirl onto the sharp things all around him.

THINKING ABOUT THE TEXT

1. What are the different generations of family histories that are understood or revealed in this story? How do the contrasting histories underscore the theme of the story?
2. Why does Erdrich introduce Buddy's dream of the "giant potato peeler" so early in her story?
3. How is Albertine's view of men—except for Buddy—confirmed by the story?
4. What are the literal and symbolic roles of Uncle Lawrence, Officer Harmony, and Vicki Koob?
5. What is the "tragic complexity of the world" in which both Albertine and Buddy live? What does Albertine's family history finally have to do with this story?

WRITING FROM THE TEXT

1. Argue that Vicki Koob should not "salvage" Buddy but leave him to grow up in his own world—a world that you will describe in your essay.
2. Argue that Vicki Koob is justified in removing Buddy from Albertine and Uncle Lawrence. Describe the negative qualities of the world Buddy will leave and imagine the world he will enter.
3. Write an analysis of the "complexity" of Buddy's world. Use the text for specific details.

CONNECTING WITH OTHER TEXTS

1. Connect and analyze the detrimental effects of the Anglo culture depicted in "Proper Care and Maintenance" (p. 176) with those shown here. Analyze the impact of the dominant outside culture on the family.
2. Do some research to learn how Native American children have been educated in the United States. In your review of this history, take a stand.
3. Write a descriptive analysis of one of the problems for Native Americans in our time—unemployment, the federal government's control of their water and mineral rights, alcohol and drug abuse, media stereotyping, or a problem that you have discovered in research. How has the Native American's living between worlds created the problem?

CRIMES AGAINST HUMANITY
Ward Churchill

Creek-Cherokee métis Ward Churchill (b. 1947) is the coordinator of the American Indian Movement (AIM) for the state of Colorado. A graduate in communications from Sangamon State University, Churchill is a self-taught writer. His many publications on Native Americans include the books *Fantasies of the Master Race: Literature, Cinema, and the Colonization of American Indians; Struggle for the Land: Indigenous Resistance to Genocide, Ecocide and Expropriation in Contemporary North America;* and, most recently, *Indians Are Us.* Churchill has been a distinguished visiting scholar of the humanities at Alfred University, and he presently teaches in the Center for Studies of Ethnicity and Race in America at the University of Colorado, Boulder. Churchill is a frequent contributor to *Z Magazine*, where the essay included here was originally published in March 1993.

1   During the past couple of seasons, there has been an increasing wave of controversy regarding the names of professional sports teams like the Atlanta "Braves," Cleveland "Indians," Washington "Redskins," and Kansas City "Chiefs." The issue extends to the names of college teams like Florida State University "Seminoles," University of Illinois "Fighting Illini," and so on, right on down to high school outfits like the Lamar (Colorado) "Savages." Also involved have been team adoption of "mascots," replete with feathers, buckskins, beads, spears and "warpaint" (some fans have opted to adorn themselves in the same fashion), and nifty little "pep" gestures like the "Indian Chant" and "Tomahawk Chop."

2   A substantial number of American Indians have protested that use of native names, images and symbols as sports team mascots and the like is, by definition, a virulently racist practice. Given the historical relationship between Indians and non-Indians during what has been called the "Conquest of America," American Indian Movement leader (and American Indian Anti-Defamation Council founder) Russell Means has compared the practice to contemporary Germans naming their soccer teams the "Jews," "Hebrews," and "Yids," while adorning their uniforms with grotesque caricatures of Jewish faces taken from the Nazis' anti-Semitic propaganda of the 1930s. Numerous demonstrations have occurred in conjunction with games—most notably during the November 15, 1992 match-up between the Chiefs and Redskins in Kansas City—by angry Indians and their supporters.

3   In response, a number of players—especially African Americans and other minority athletes—have been trotted out by professional team owners like Ted Turner, as well as university and public school officials, to announce that they mean not to insult but to honor native people. They have been joined by the television networks and most major newspapers, all of which have editorialized that Indian discomfort with the situation is "no big deal," insisting that the whole thing is just "good, clean fun." The country needs more such fun, they've argued, and "a few disgruntled Native Americans" have no right to undermine the nation's enjoyment of its leisure time by complaining. This is especially the case, some have

argued, "in hard times like these." It has even been contended that Indian outrage at being systematically degraded—rather than the degradation itself—creates "a serious barrier to the sort of intergroup communication so necessary in a multicultural society such as ours."

4   Okay, let's communicate. We are frankly dubious that those advancing such positions really believe their own rhetoric, but, just for the sake of argument, let's accept the premise that they are sincere. If what they say is true, then isn't it time we spread such "inoffensiveness" and "good cheer" around among *all* groups so that *everybody* can participate *equally* in fostering the round of national laughs they call for? Sure it is—the country can't have too much fun or "intergroup involvement"—so the more, the merrier. Simple consistency demands that anyone who thinks the Tomahawk Chop is a swell pastime must be just as hearty in his or her endorsement of the following ideas. The same logic used to defend the defamation of American Indians should help us all start yukking it up.

5   First, as a counterpart to the Redskins, we need an NFL team called "Niggers" to honor Afro-Americans. Half-time festivities for fans might include a simulated stewing of the opposing coach in a large pot while players and cheerleaders dance around it, garbed in leopard skins and wearing fake bones in their noses. This concept obviously goes along with the kind of gaiety attending the Chop, but also with the actions of the Kansas City Chiefs, whose team members—prominently including black team members—lately appeared on a poster looking "fierce" and "savage" by way of wearing Indian regalia. Just a bit of harmless "morale boosting," says the Chiefs' front office. You bet.

6   So that the newly-formed Niggers sports club won't end up too out of sync while expressing the "spirit" and "identity" of Afro-Americans in the above fashion, a baseball franchise—let's call this one the "Sambos"—should be formed. How about a basketball team called the "Spearchuckers"? A hockey team called the "Jungle Bunnies"? Maybe the "essence" of these teams could be depicted by images of tiny black faces adorned with huge pairs of lips. The players could appear on TV every week or so gnawing on chicken legs and spitting watermelon seeds at one another. Catchy, eh? Well, there's "nothing to be upset about," according to those who love wearing "war bonnets" to the Super Bowl or having "Chief Illiniwik" dance around the sports arenas of Urbana, Illinois.

7   And why stop there? There are plenty of other groups to include. Hispanics? They can be "represented" by the Galveston "Greasers" and San Diego "Spics," at least until the Wisconsin "Wetbacks" and Baltimore "Beaners" get off the ground. Asian Americans? How about the "Slopes," "Dinks," "Gooks," and "Zipperheads"? Owners of the latter teams might get their logo ideas from editorial page cartoons printed in the nation's newspapers during World War II: slant-eyes, buck teeth, big glasses, but nothing racially insulting or derogatory, according to the editors and artists involved at the time. Indeed, this Second World War–vintage stuff can be seen as just another barrel of laughs, at least by what current editors say are their "local standards" concerning American Indians.

8   Let's see. Who's been left out? Teams like the Kansas City "Kikes," Hanover "Honkies," San Leandro "Shylocks," Daytona "Dagos," and Pittsburgh "Polacks"

will fill a certain social void among white folk. Have a religious belief? Let's all go for the gusto and gear up the Milwaukee "Mackerel Snappers" and Hollywood "Holy Rollers." The Fighting Irish of Notre Dame can be rechristened the "Drunken Irish" or "Papist Pigs." Issues of gender and sexual preference can be addressed through creation of teams like the St. Louis "Sluts," Boston "Bimbos," Detroit "Dykes," and the Fresno "Fags." How about the Gainesville "Gimps" and Richmond "Retards," so the physically and mentally impaired won't be excluded from our fun and games?

9   Now, don't go getting "overly sensitive" out there. None of this is demeaning or insulting, at least not when it's being done to Indians. Just ask the folks who are doing it, or their apologists like Andy Rooney in the national media. They'll tell you—as in fact they *have* been telling you—that there's been no harm done, regardless of what their victims think, feel, or say. The situation is exactly the same as when those with precisely the same mentality used to insist that Step 'n' Fetchit was okay, or Rochester on the Jack Benny Show, or Amos and Andy, Charlie Chan, the Frito Bandito, or any of the other cutesy symbols making up the lexicon of American racism. Have we communicated yet?

10   Let's get just a little bit real here. The notion of "fun" embodied in rituals like the Tomahawk Chop must be understood for what it is. There's not a single non-Indian example used above which can be considered socially acceptable in even the most marginal sense. The reasons are obvious enough. So why is it different where American Indians are concerned? One can only conclude that, in contrast to the other groups at issue, Indians are (falsely) perceived as being too few, and therefore too weak, to defend themselves effectively against racist and otherwise offensive behavior.

11   Fortunately, there are some glimmers of hope. A few teams and their fans have gotten the message and have responded appropriately. Stanford University, which opted to drop the name "Indians" from Stanford, has experienced no resulting drop-off in attendance. Meanwhile, the local newspaper in Portland, Oregon recently decided its long-standing editorial policy prohibiting use of racial epithets should include derogatory team names. The Redskins, for instance, are now referred to as "the Washington team," and will continue to be described in this way until the franchise adopts an inoffensive moniker (newspaper sales in Portland have suffered no decline as a result).

12   Such examples are to be applauded and encouraged. They stand as figurative beacons in the night, proving beyond all doubt that it is quite possible to indulge in the pleasure of athletics without accepting blatant racism into the bargain.

13   On October 16, 1946, a man named Julius Streicher mounted the steps of a gallows. Moments later he was dead, the sentence of an international tribunal composed of representatives of the United States, France, Great Britain, and the Soviet Union having been imposed. Streicher's body was then cremated, and—so horrendous were his crimes thought to have been—his ashes dumped into an unspecified German river so that "no one should ever know a particular place to go for reasons of mourning his memory."

14　　Julius Streicher had been convicted at Nuremberg, Germany of what were termed "Crimes Against Humanity." The lead prosecutor in his case—Justice Robert Jackson of the United States Supreme Court—had not argued that the defendant had killed anyone, nor that he had personally committed any especially violent act. Nor was it contended that Streicher had held any particularly important position in the German government during the period in which the so-called Third Reich had exterminated some 6,000,000 Jews, as well as several million Gypsies, Poles, Slavs, homosexuals, and other untermenschen (subhumans).

15　　The sole offense for which the accused was ordered put to death was in having served as publisher/editor of a Bavarian tabloid entitled *Der Sturmer* during the early-to-mid 1930s, years before the Nazi genocide actually began. In this capacity, he had penned a long series of virulently anti-Semitic editorials and "news" stories, usually accompanied by cartoons and other images graphically depicting Jews in extraordinarily derogatory fashion. This, the prosecution asserted, had done much to "dehumanize" the targets of his distortion in the mind of the German public. In turn, such dehumanization had made it possible—or at least easier—for average Germans to later indulge in the outright liquidation of Jewish "vermin." The tribunal agreed, holding that Streicher was therefore complicit in genocide and deserving of death by hanging.

16　　During his remarks to the Nuremberg tribunal, Justice Jackson observed that, in implementing its sentences, the participating powers were morally and legally binding themselves to adhere forever after to the same standards of conduct that were being applied to Streicher and the other Nazi leaders. In the alternative, he said, the victorious allies would have committed "pure murder" at Nuremberg—no different in substance from that carried out by those they presumed to judge—rather than establishing the "permanent bench-mark for justice" which was intended.

17　　Yet in the United States of Robert Jackson, the indigenous American Indian population had already been reduced, in a process which is ongoing to this day, from perhaps 12.5 million in the year 1500 to fewer than 250,000 by the beginning of the 20th century. This was accomplished, according to official sources, "largely through the cruelty of [Euro-American] settlers," and an informal but clear governmental policy which had made it an articulated goal to "exterminate these red vermin," or at least whole segments of them.

18　　Bounties had been placed on the scalps of Indians—any Indians—in places as diverse as Georgia, Kentucky, Texas, the Dakotas, Oregon, and California, and had been maintained until resident Indian populations were decimated or disappeared altogether. Entire peoples such as the Cherokee had been reduced to half their size through a policy of forced removal from their homelands east of the Mississippi River to what were then considered less preferable areas in the West.

19　　Others, such as the Navajo, suffered the same fate while under military guard for years on end. The United States Army had also perpetrated a long series of wholesale massacres of Indians at places like Horseshoe Bend, Bear River, Sand Creek, the Washita River, the Marias River, Camp Robinson, and Wounded Knee.

20　　Through it all, hundreds of popular novels—each competing with the next to make Indians appear more grotesque, menacing, and inhuman—were sold in the tens of millions of copies in the U.S. Plainly, the Euro-American public was being conditioned to see Indians in such a way as to allow their eradication to continue. And continue it did until the Manifest Destiny of the U.S.—a direct precursor to what Hitler would subsequently call Lebensraumpolitik (the politics of living space)—was consummated.

21   By 1900, the national project of "clearing" Native Americans from their land and replacing them with "superior" Anglo-American settlers was complete; the indigenous population had been reduced by as much as 98 percent while approximately 97.5 percent of their original territory had "passed" to the invaders. The survivors had been concentrated, out of sight and mind of the public, on scattered "reservations," all of them under the self-assigned "plenary" (full) power of the federal government. There was, of course, no Nuremberg-style tribunal passing judgment on those who had fostered such circumstances in North America. No U.S. official or private citizen was ever imprisoned—never mind hanged—for implementing or propagandizing what had been done. Nor had the process of genocide afflicting Indians been completed. Instead, it merely changed form.

22   Between the 1880s and the 1980s, nearly half of all Native American children were coercively transferred from their own families, communities, and cultures to those of the conquering society. This was done through compulsory attendance at remote boarding schools, often hundreds of miles from their homes, where native children were kept for years on end while being systematically "deculturated" (indoctrinated to think and act in the manner of Euro-Americans rather than as Indians). It was also accomplished through a pervasive foster home and adoption program—including "blind" adoptions, where children would be permanently denied information as to who they were/are and where they'd come from—placing native youths in non-Indian homes.

23   The express purpose of all this was to facilitate a U.S. governmental policy to bring about the "assimilation" (dissolution) of indigenous societies. In other words, Indian cultures as such were to be caused to disappear. Such policy objectives are directly contrary to the United Nations 1948 Convention on Punishment and Prevention of the Crime of Genocide, an element of international law arising from the Nuremberg proceedings. The forced "transfer of the children" of a targeted "racial, ethnical, or religious group" is explicitly prohibited as a genocidal activity under the Convention's second article.

24   Article II of the Genocide Convention also expressly prohibits involuntary sterilization as a means of "preventing births among" a targeted population. Yet, in 1975, it was conceded by the U.S. government that its Indian Health Service (IHS), then a subpart of the Bureau of Indian Affairs (BIA), was even then conducting a secret program of involuntary sterilization that had affected approximately 40 percent of all Indian women. The program was allegedly discontinued, and the IHS was transferred to the Public Health Service, but no one was punished. In 1990, it came out that the IHS was inoculating Inuit children in Alaska with Hepatitis-B vaccine. The vaccine had already been banned by the World Health Organization as having a demonstrated correlation with the HIV-Syndrome which is itself correlated to AIDS. As this is written, a "field test" of Hepatitis-A vaccine, also HIV-correlated, is being conducted on Indian reservations in the northern plains region.

25   The Genocide Convention makes it a "crime against humanity" to create conditions leading to the destruction of an identifiable human group, as such. Yet the BIA has utilized the government's plenary prerogatives to negotiate mineral leases "on behalf of" Indian peoples paying a fraction of standard royalty rates. The result has been "super profits" for a number of preferred U.S. corporations. Meanwhile, Indians, whose reservations ironically turned out to be in some of the most mineral-rich areas of North America, which makes us, the nominally wealthiest segment of the continent's population, live in dire poverty.

26   By the government's own data in the mid-1980s, Indians received the lowest annual and lifetime per capita incomes of any aggregate population group in the United States. Concomitantly, we suffer the highest rate of infant mortality, death by exposure and malnutrition, disease, and the like. Under such circumstances, alcoholism and other escapist forms of substance abuse are endemic in the Indian community, a situation which leads both to a general physical debilitation of the population and a catastrophic accident rate. Teen suicide among Indians is several times the national average.

27   The average life expectancy of a reservation-based Native American man is barely 45 years; women can expect to live less than three years longer.

28   Such itemizations could be continued at great length, including matters like the radioactive contamination of large portions of contemporary Indian Country, the forced relocation of traditional Navajos, and so on. But the point should be made: Genocide, as defined in international law, is a continuing fact of day-to-day life (and death) for North America's native peoples. Yet there has been—and is—only the barest flicker of public concern about, or even consciousness of, this reality. Absent any serious expression of public outrage, no one is punished and the process continues.

29   A salient reason for public acquiescence before the ongoing holocaust in Native North America has been a continuation of the popular legacy, often through more effective media. Since 1925, Hollywood has released more than 2,000 films, many of them rerun frequently on television, portraying Indians as strange, perverted, ridiculous, and often dangerous things of the past. Moreover, we are habitually presented to mass audiences one-dimensional, devoid of recognizable human motivations and emotions; Indians thus serve as props, little more. We have thus been thoroughly and systematically dehumanized.

30   Nor is this the extent of it. Everywhere, we are used as logos, as mascots, as jokes: "Big Chief" writing tablets, "Red Man" chewing tobacco, "Winnebago" campers, "Navajo" and "Cherokee" and "Pontiac" and "Cadillac" pickups and automobiles. There are the Cleveland "Indians," the Kansas City "Chiefs," the Atlanta "Braves" and the Washington "Redskins" professional sports teams—not to mention those in thousands of colleges, high schools, and elementary schools across the country—each with their own degrading caricatures and parodies of Indians and/or things Indian. Pop fiction continues in the same vein, including an unending stream of New Age manuals purporting to expose the inner works of indigenous spirituality in everything from pseudo-philosophical to do-it-yourself styles. Blond yuppies from Beverly Hills amble about the country claiming to be reincarnated 17th century Cheyenne Ushamans ready to perform previously secret ceremonies.

31   In effect, a concerted, sustained, and in some ways accelerating effort has gone into making Indians unreal. It is thus of obvious importance that the American public begin to think about the implications of such things the next time they witness a gaggle of face-painted and war-bonneted buffoons doing the "Tomahawk Chop" at a baseball or football game. It is necessary that they think about the implications of the grade-school teacher adorning their child in turkey feathers to commemorate Thanksgiving. Think about the significance of John Wayne or Charleton Heston killing a dozen "savages" with a single bullet the next time a western comes on TV. Think about why Land-o-Lakes finds it appropriate to market its butter with the stereotyped image of an "Indian princess" on the wrapper. Think about what it means when non-Indian academics profess—as they often do—to "know more about Indians than Indians do themselves." Think about the significance of charlatans like Carlos Castaneda and Jamake Highwater and Mary Summer Rain and Lynn Andrews churning out "Indian" bestsellers, one after the other, while Indians typically can't get into print.

32   Think about the real situation of American Indians. Think about Julius Streicher. Remember Justice Jackson's admonition. Understand that the treatment of Indians in American popular culture is not "cute" or "amusing" or just "good, clean fun."

33   Know that it causes real pain and real suffering to real people. Know that it threatens our very survival. And know that this is just as much a crime against humanity as anything the Nazis ever did. It is likely that the indigenous people of the United States will never demand that those guilty of such criminal activity be punished for their deeds. But the least we have the right to expect—indeed, to demand—is that such practices finally be brought to a halt.

THINKING ABOUT THE TEXT

1. What is the history of the controversy that Churchill describes?

2. What are the specific examples that Churchill proposes for other racial and ethnic groups to parallel the team names and halftime shows that refer to Native American culture? What is the effect on the reader of his examples? What is the author's intention?

3. What are the positive responses to the controversy that Churchill cites in his essay? Why does he include these two examples?

4. What is the history of the trial of Julius Streicher, and how do facts about the Nuremberg tribunal contribute to Churchill's argument?

5. What are the crimes against the American Indian that Churchill enumerates in his essay? Why does he believe that using American Indian culture for team names, logos, mascots, and advertising perpetuates the crimes against the Native American?

6. Do you perceive any flaws in Churchill's reasoning? Are you sympathetic to his point? Do you agree with his demand for change?

WRITING FROM THE TEXT

1. Write a response to Ward Churchill that agrees with his points or argues against them. Review the suggestions for writing argument (pp. 414–422) in order to write a convincing paper.

2. Recall from your childhood the images of the American Indian that appeared in books, on television, and in films. Write a descriptive analysis of a few specific examples in order to show that Churchill is correct or incorrect in his position that popular images of the Native American are "degrading caricatures" that perpetuate the crimes against them.

CONNECTING WITH OTHER TEXTS

1. In the short story "American Horse" (p. 157), Louise Erdrich shows some of the problems that Native Americans have in living between worlds. Write an essay that shows that the "crimes" against American Indians discussed by Churchill contribute to the problems that you see depicted in Erdrich's fictitious story.

2. In an analytical essay, compare the images of African Americans that have disappeared from popular culture (like Little Black Sambo or Step 'n' Fetchit) with the images of Natives Americans that still permeate popular culture in the United States. What conclusion can you draw from an analysis of these images and their presence or absence in popular culture?

3. Write an analysis of recent film depictions of the Native American in order to argue that Hollywood has or has not moved beyond caricature in its depiction of this culture.

ON THE SUBWAY
Sharon Olds

A widely anthologized poet and recipient of numerous grants and awards for her work in poetry, Sharon Olds (b. 1942) received a B.A. from Stanford University and a Ph.D. from Columbia. Olds' career has centered around the writing and teaching of poetry. She has served as lecturer in residence and visiting teacher of poetry at many colleges and universities in the United States, and she gives readings of her poems at schools, museums, and libraries. Readers find her work to be intense and moving. The poem printed here is from *The Gold Cell*, published in 1987.

The boy and I face each other.
His feet are huge, in black sneakers
laced with white in a complex pattern like a
set of intentional scars. We are stuck on
opposite sides of the car, a couple of   5
molecules stuck in a rod of light
rapidly moving through darkness. He has the
casual cold look of a mugger,
alert under hooded lids. He is wearing
red, like the inside of the body   10
exposed. I am wearing dark fur, the
whole skin of an animal taken and
used. I look at his raw face,
he looks at my fur coat, and I don't
know if I am in his power—   15
he could take my coat so easily, my
briefcase, my life—
or if he is in my power, the way I am
living off his life, eating the steak
he does not eat, as if I am taking   20
the food from his mouth. And he is black
and I am white, and without meaning or
trying to I must profit from his darkness,
the way he absorbs the murderous beams of the
nation's heart, as black cotton   25
absorbs the heat of the sun and holds it. There is
no way to know how easy this
white skin makes my life, this
life he could take so easily and
break across his knee like a stick the way his   30
own back is being broken, the
rod of his soul that at birth was dark and
fluid and rich as the heart of a seedling
ready to thrust up into any available light.

THINKING ABOUT THE TEXT

1. If the speaker initially considers this encounter a face-off, in what ways does the boy seem to be intimidating? Analyze the narrator's descriptions of him.

2. Describe the narrator's appearance. Is it consistent with her inner awareness and values? Do you think the boy on the subway would be surprised to know her thoughts?

3. In what way is she in his "power" and he in hers? Does either one of them seem to be choosing to exercise his or her power over the other? Explain the irony here.

4. Cite phrases and images that reveal the narrator's sensitivity here. How do these contribute to the tone of the poem?

5. Find images of light versus darkness throughout, and discuss how this image pattern relates to Olds' insights about racial and economic barriers.

6. Does the poem seem hopeful or bleak? Support your interpretation with details from the poem.

WRITING FROM THE TEXT

1. List several insights that can be drawn from this poem. Then focus on any one insight and analyze how the images and tone support this insight. Cite specific details as you interpret.

2. Write an essay analyzing the various stereotypes and assumptions implicit in the narrator's descriptions of the boy. Then reverse the point of view and imagine the stereotypes the boy may hold in his perception of the narrator.

3. Olds focuses on a rather commonplace situation and manages to bring exceptional sensitivity to this issue. Focus on a common encounter of your own and show how it also revealed more complex issues and emotions beneath the surface.

CONNECTING WITH OTHER TEXTS

1. Using specific details from this poem and from Marcus Mabry's "Living in Two Worlds" (p. 143) show how the privileged status in each narration is a source of guilt.

2. Write an essay analyzing how stereotyping is the source of tension in "On the Subway," "Proper Care and Maintenance" (p. 176), and "Black Men and Public Space" (p. 225). You may want to refer to Heilbroner's essay "Don't Let Stereotypes Warp Your Judgments" (p. 429).

PROPER CARE AND MAINTENANCE
Susan Straight

Except for the time when she did her M.F.A. work with James Baldwin at the University of Massachusetts, Susan Straight (b. 1960) has always lived in Riverside, California, a mile from the hospital where both she and her husband were born. Straight describes her community as a storytelling one: "Everyone tells stories, almost legends, about people and cars and events, and I've heard them for so many years that I wanted my stories to be on paper instead of only in the air." Her novel in stories, *Aquaboogie,* won a Milkweed National Fiction Prize. Her novel, *I Been in Sorrow's Kitchen and Licked Out All the Pots,* was published in 1992. True to the values of her community's oral traditions, Susan Straight is an engaging storyteller and speaker on the writing process. This short story about Darnell first appeared in the *Los Angeles Times Magazine,* June 30, 1991. Straight's novel about Darnell, *Blacker Than a Thousand Midnights,* was published in 1994.

1   "See, man, I told you she was gon do it—she pimpin' you, Darnell." Victor shook his head and watched Charolette hang out the window of the El Camino. "She pimpin' you big-time."

2   "Daddy!" she yelled, her round face bobbing furiously above the door. "I want juice! In my *mouth!*"

3   Darnell turned away from Victor and Ronnie and the other men sitting on folding chairs and boxes in the vacant lot. A blackened trash barrel breathed smoke in the early morning cool, and the pepper tree branches dangled around them. "I'm fixin' to go over my dad's," Darnell said. "He told me Sixth Avenue Baptist wants somebody to clean up that lot they got behind the church. I'll be back tomorrow, Victor."

4   He started toward the El Camino, and Victor called out, "Damn, homey, I might be a stockbroker by then." Ronnie and the others laughed.

5   He put Charolette back in her car seat and she said, "*Daddy,* I hungry. Hurry." She watched out the window, saying, "Fire, Daddy," when they circled around the lot to the street.

6   "Yeah, smoke," he said, and she looked triumphant. She was almost 2, trying to learn about a hundred words a day. She stuck out her chin and sang to herself now, while he tried not to smile.

7   He hadn't wanted a baby—Brenda had surprised him. When Brenda first brought her home from the hospital and laid her on a quilt in the living room, Charolette had spent hours sleeping on her stomach and Darnell had had all day to stare at her. The government funds had been cut off for seasonal firefighters. He stared at Charolette, but all he could think was that she looked like a horny toad, those rounded-flat lizards that ran past him when he was close to the fire: they'd streak out from the rocks, looking ridiculous. Charolette's belly was distended round and wide, far past her nonexistent butt, and her spindly arms and legs looked useless. He'd sat home watching this baby, impatient with the helpless crying and the way she lay on her back waving her limbs like a turned-over beetle.

8   Now she was old enough to talk smack, and he could jam her right back—she understood. When he pulled into the driveway at his father's house, she ran inside for his mother's hot biscuits, and then she ran back to him, hollering, "Daddy, blow on it!"

9   "You so bad, blow on it yourself," he said, and she spit rapidly at the steaming biscuit. "Yeah, right," he laughed. "Wet it up."

10   Darnell's mother came to the doorway in her robe. "Brenda restin'?"

11   "Sleepin' 24-7," Darnell said. "All day, except when she at work."

12   "That's how it is your first three months," his mother said, getting that blurry look like every woman who found out Brenda was pregnant again. "You sleep like somebody drop a rock on your chest. I remember."

13   Darnell didn't mind waking up at 6, when the curtains were just starting to hold light. Charolette called for him now. If he had a job, he had to start early anyway, before it got too hot. Brenda was a clerk for the County of Rio Seco and didn't have to go to work until 9. So Darnell left her in the warm tangle of sheets and took Charolette to his father's, where the men sat in their trucks drinking coffee before they went out. His father and Roscoe Wiley trimmed trees; Floyd King and his son Nacho hauled trash from construction sites. They all made a big deal of Charolette still in her footed sleeper, stamping from lap to lap and trying to pull dashboard knobs.

14   This morning Roscoe took her into his pickup truck and gave her a smell of his coffee. "Red Man, this girl stubborn as you," he said to Darnell's father.

15   Darnell watched Charolette poke at the glass. "Window dirty," she said.

16   "Least she look a lot better," Floyd said from his cab. "Next one gotta look like Brenda, cause this one look like Darnell spit her out his ownself."

17   Yeah. Brenda hated hearing that, Darnell thought. He remembered when the baby began to stare back at him, to crawl, and then her eyebrows grew in thick-curved like his, her teeth spaced and square like his.

18   His mother came out to the driveway for the newspaper. "Y'all need to look for a bigger place," she said. "A house, for Charolette to play in the yard. And you get a house, we can find a washer so Brenda won't drag that laundry up and down no apartment stairs."

19   "Mr. Nard rentin' out his brother's house on Pablo," Floyd called. "Got three bedrooms, and he want $625 a month."

20   "Yeah, and we can barely pay our $400 now," Darnell said.

21   "I told you get you some yards," his father said. "Steady yards, like I did."

22   "You ain't got no cleanup jobs for me next week?" Darnell said, looking at the thin chain-saw scar on his father's forearm.

23   "Yeah, Sixth Avenue Baptist wants you to do the lot—take two of you, two-day job."

24   "You gon get Victor?" Nacho said.

25   "Yeah." After Charolette, he knew he couldn't go to college for Fire Science, and he'd gotten a warehouse job, but they laid everyone off a few months later. His father had fixed up the engine on the old El Camino, which had been in the side yard since Roscoe had gotten a new truck. He lent Darnell a mower, blower, weed-whacker and rakes.

26   "Victor a stone alcoholic," Roscoe said. "Livin' at Jackson Park now."

27   Nacho said, "Shoot, he taught me how to draw, back in junior high. The broth-er was smart, too smart, started talkin' 'bout high school was boring. He just want to hang out, all day."

28   "He hangin' out now," Roscoe said, frowning. "All day."

29   Darnell said. "He just don't like nobody to tell him what to do. He don't like to answer to nobody." He'd always watched Victor, who was five years older than he

was; Victor got kicked out of school for spelling out "Superfly" in gold studs down his jeans, for outlining his fly with rhinestones. He'd quit the football team freshman year, refusing to cut off his cornrows.

30   "I'm tellin you, go door-to-door and get you some yards," Darnell's father went on, loud. "Build up a clientele." Sophia and Paula, Darnell's younger sisters, came running out in their nightgowns to see Charolette.

31   "Shoot, every dude with a truck and mower runnin' around calling himself a gardener," Roscoe said. "They want all these new houses gettin' built."

32   "Yeah, you should go see Trent," Nacho said. "He got his own business, land-scape design, and he live up there in Grayglen."

33   Floyd laughed. "With the gray men."

34   The houses were laid out in circling streets, and a sea of red-tile roofs was all that showed above miles of sandy block wall. Darnell saw crews of Mexican guys building new walls at one intersection, short Indian-looking men with bowed legs and straw hats. Two white guys with thick, sun-reddened forearms watched.

35   Trent's street was all two-story houses and lush gardens. "A brother livin' up here?" Darnell said to himself. He could tell by the yards most of these people already had gardeners. Trent was in his driveway, loading his truck with black hosing and pipes.

36   "Hey, Darnell," he said, and Darnell was surprised Trent remembered the name. Trent was Victor's age. "What's up?"

37   "Not much," Darnell said. "I heard you were livin' large with your business, and I thought maybe you had too many yards, know somebody who needs a gardener." He watched Trent count sprinkler heads.

38   "Man, I just do the planning and landscaping—I don't cut grass," Trent said, not looking up. "I ain't into maintenance. After the irrigation, I'm gone."

39   "Yeah, Nacho said you went to college for this, huh?" Darnell said, uncomfortable. "I just thought you might have some advice, 'cause I *been* knocked on doors, and that ain't workin'."

40   Trent clicked his spit against his teeth. "I heard you workin' with Victor Small and Ronnie Hunter. But you gotta buy 'em some Olde English 800 to get through the day, huh?" He coiled hosing. "They scare people off."

41   Darnell folded his arms. "Yeah. Depends." So you think you better, huh, *brotha*man? Victor and Ronnie love to talk about your ass—grinnin' and skinnin' 'til you drive down the street and shake your head.

42   "Sorry I can't help you," Trent said, reaching down awkwardly into the truck bed again. "Good luck, bro."

43   "Thanks, *brotha*man," Darnell said. Threading through the streets, he watched for shaggy grass and dandelions. Had to be a few yards let go in this maze.

44   At four lawns that looked weeks overgrown, he knocked on doors, his heart beating fast, but no one answered. Another ragged one, and a woman came to the door. He said, "Hi, I'm a gardener and I wondered if you needed your yard done today or on a regular basis." He remembered his father's words, back when Darnell had been small enough to stand on cool porches and listen.

45   "I gave you five dollars yesterday," the woman said impatiently, looking back into her house, and Darnell raised his eyes. She was about 40, her lips more invisible than most white women's—no lipstick, he realized, just when she said, "I can't afford another donation."

46   "I wasn't here yesterday," Darnell said, but she was adding loudly, "I don't need anything done today."

47   "You didn't give me five dollars," he said, finally looking at her eyes, rimmed with green shadow.

48   "Oh, I'm sorry, I—your hat," she said, fingers holding her collar. "A man came by yesterday, he said he was out of work, and I—he had a hat."

49   "Yeah," Darnell said, hard. "Another Raiders fan." He walked back down the bricks, wanting to kick apart the fancy iron mailbox exactly like Trent's.

50   He drove, swerving through the streets until he found the only opening in the block walls. Where the cops? Can't they see me? He remembered getting stopped months ago, Victor and Ronnie and him driving around up here looking for yards. The cop said, "You guys have been cruising for a while, knocking on doors. You got a reason?" Victor said, "Mowers in the back, man." He didn't care who he was talking to. "Don't you have a record, didn't you do a few weeks last year?" the cop said to Victor. "What was your first clue, Sherlock?" Victor said. "Was it my big arms?"

51   The tires slipped on loose dirt at the corner. Yeah, our marketing strategy just ain't gettin' it—door-to-door get us a sentence. If it was summer, he'd find a fire to make himself feel better, watch the flames shake up brush-covered hills, imagine himself on the line close to the roar and heat.

52   Three new houses were going up, and the bellied, blond construction workers hammering and laying brick looked up at the car. Born that way, he thought, his tongue thick and hot. Come out with hair like that, trucks with toolboxes behind the cab, stomachs already big enough—they get the job just like I can dance. Charolette's car seat rattled empty against his elbow when he scratched the tires on the asphalt, but skidding around a corner didn't make him feel any better. He looked at the crumbs crushed deep into the corduroy chair.

53   He'd used his Clark Kent voice one day on the phone, after he saw an ad for a security guard that read, "Mature white male pref." He'd made the appointment with the cheery secretary just to see if he could, and then he threw a coffee cup against the wall; the clotted breaking sound made him feel better until he heard Charolette's high-pitched screams, like a burning animal caught in dense chaparral. "That's illegal, that ad," Brenda was yelling, and he'd yelled back, "Right, let's call our lawyer immediately, baby, we'll take this all the way to the Supreme Court."

54   He pressed his fingers into the crumbs, feeling cool along his shoulders. I can't pull that act now. Driving down the hill toward the Westside, he thought about going by Jackson Park, hanging out, talking yang about anything, but he slowed at his father's street. "Daddy here!" Charolette screamed. Ain't this crazy? he thought. When he told Victor, "She my buddy now," Victor said, "You weak, nigga—you suppose to let *grown* females whip you."

55   She fell asleep when he drove around the old downtown section, with the big historic houses and huge sloping corner lawns. He and his father had cut some of these, when Darnell was 11 and just learning to mow right.

56   At one old yellow house, ivy hanging over the porch, roses thick, he saw three Mexican guys in the yard. Straightening Charolette's bent, lolling neck, he watched them ripping out a huge circle of ivy in the lawn, talking and chopping with machetes. Their radio blasted Mexican music, horns and swinging voices going so fast Darnell imagined them playing at 78 speed. He saw a shadow at the front screen: a gray-haired lady came out to watch the men, and he pulled away from the curb before she saw him.

57   All weekend, he kept hearing the music; he even turned the radio or TV to Mexican stations. "What are you trippin' about?" Brenda said, folding the laundry that lay in drifts all around the living room. Charolette threaded string into the wrought-iron balcony, the front door open so they could see her.

58   "Nothin'," Darnell said, listening to what he thought was an accordion.

59   "You really miss that firefightin' slave you had, huh?" Victor said when they'd been at the church lot for a few hours. "Crazy nigga loved bein' up there in the mountains with them cowboy white dudes."

60   "No, man," Darnell said. "It wasn't about the other guys. I just liked it up there." They pulled at the skeletal tumbleweeds and burned grass in the hard dirt, gathered bottles and disposable diapers. Darnell saw the rough brush where he'd dug firebreaks, the red-barked manzanita and tiny plants. Now and then he let his vision blur while he tore out weeds, and usually when he raised his head he was surprised to see cars rushing past him. But today he kept seeing the Mexican guys, their hats and laughing and music.

61   After they'd come down the long dirt road from the dump, Darnell gave Victor $50 and kept $75 for himself. He waited in front of Tony's Market, and when Victor came out with the big 40-ounce bottles of Olde English 800, he said, "I can't hang with you guys today; I got somethin' to do."

62   Victor unscrewed the cap. "Take me by Esther's, on your pop's street." He still wore his hair long and cornrowed neatly to his head, the tails stopped just at his neck. He let it go weeks before he could pay Esther to redo it, and today it was rough and clouded between the rows. "You go home to baby-bawlin', man, and I'll be chillin' out, eight-ballin'." He took a big swallow.

63   The next morning his father told him Mrs. Panadoukis, the doctor's wife up in Hillcrest, wanted her whole bank of ice plant cleared. When he got to Jackson Park, Darnell threw the empty car seat in the back, and Victor said, "Nigga, this the last job I want 'til next week. Don't you know black absorbs heat, man?"

64   "Shut up, Victor," Ronnie said. "You know you already broke."

65   "Hey," Victor said, "I ain't *gotta* work every day, like Darnell."

66   The ice plant had died, and the woody, tangled mesh was easy to tear from the dirt, but the piles were heavy. Ronnie and Victor took off their shirts, and Darnell remembered they didn't have anywhere to wash them. Their backs glistened in front of him. Ronnie's radio was far away, the music thumping faintly when they

clambered up the steep bank, but at lunch they unwrapped their sandwiches and turned the radio up.

67   "'I don't go nowhere without my jimhat,'" Victor sang along with Digital Underground. Then he said, "Yeah, my man Darnell ain't been usin' no jimmys—he got another one on the way."

68   Darnell said, "Least I ain't gotta worry about AIDS—you be messin' with them strawberries." He wondered how they'd gotten that name, the desperate, ashy girls who hung out at the park doing anything with anybody for some smoke.

69   "When you need some, man, you don't care," Ronnie said. Darnell heard a scraping step on the cement, and he saw Mrs. Panadoukis, her face frozen, coming around to the back door with her purse. She looked away from them, her lips tight, and fumbled with her keys. They were silent, the music loud.

70   When she'd closed the door, Victor and Ronnie busted up. Darnell saw her held-tight cheeks. He looked at Ronnie's chest, Victor's fresh braids; he remembered the Mexican guys laughing in the ivy. The Mexican guys could be saying anything, talking dirty or yanging about the lady they were working for, but it would be in Spanish and they'd sound happy—their radio was jolly, funny, that bright quick music spangled as mariachi suits. Ronnie's radio—uh-uh. The bass was low, shuffling around her, and the drums slapped her in the face.

71   "You ready?" he said, and they went back up the bank, bending and tearing, Victor making them laugh.

72   "Darnell, you just graduated a few years ago, man, you remember Mr. Rentell, that drivin' teacher? Serious redhead, always tryin' to talk hip. He came by the park the other day, talkin' 'bout, 'Victor, is that you?' He start storyin' 'bout why was I hangin' out, couldn't I do better? I told him, 'Man, I can still drive, don't worry—let me have your car, I'll show you.'" He threw ice plant down the slope to Darnell.

73   They loaded the El Camino in the front yard. Mrs. Panadoukis had paid them, her eyes averted. Darnell thought, Sorry we don't look good. He saw a Baggie on the lawn and bent to pick it up, thinking it had dropped from the car. But someone else had put it on the grass: he saw a green flier inside and a small rock. Looking down the street, he watched a silver Toyota pickup stop for a second at each lawn. A hand threw out Baggies. He saw rakes and shovels against the cab window, mower handles in the bed.

74   "Nguyen's Oriental Gardening Service," the flier read. He spread it on his lap in the car, and Victor said, "Come on, man, it's hot."

75   "Let experienced Oriental Gardeners take care of your lawn and shrubs, we will mow, edge and fertilize for only $60 a month. Weekly." The note had been printed on a computer, and a picture of a bonsai tree was in the corner, with a phone number.

76   Darnell took Victor and Ronnie to the store and then to the park, hearing Mexican music and the voices of the Asian guys he remembered from school. Tim Bui and Don Nguyen—two Vietnamese guys who wanted to be homeboys, hanging out at the picnic tables with Darnell and the brothers. They tried to imitate Darnell's voice, and after a while they could dance better than some of the crew that performed at assemblies. Nguyen—that last name was like Smith in Vietnam,

he remembered them explaining. "Like Johnson for niggas," Ronnie had laughed. Alone in the car, he drove to his mother's.

77   Charolette ran out to see him. His father and Roscoe were stacking wood from a pepper tree beside the house. "Y'all finish the doctor's-wife's job?"

78   "Yeah," Darnell said. "Ice plant was dead anyway."

79   "She pay you? She love to talk when she get started," his father said.

80   "She didn't get started with us," Darnell said, slipping the flier into his pocket.

81   "You pay off your crew?" Roscoe said. "You the big boss now—you take your cut?"

82   "What, you think I'm crazy?" All the way home, Charolette put the rock inside the Baggie and took it out. "Little rock?" she said. He looked at the stone—those guys were smart. The flier couldn't blow away, couldn't get wet.

83   He kept thinking of the Vietnamese kids at school, how the teacher had looked at them, but he saw Mexican faces for some reason. When he and Charolette made their weekend shopping trip, he tried not to stare. On the Westside, almost as many Mexican families lived on some streets as black families. He watched the men riding 10-speeds with plastic bags of laundry tied to the handlebars—guys, alone, leaving one to guard clothes in the Laundromat and going in a group to the store. They bought whole chickens, tortillas, chips, fruit, and he watched their faces, knowing that was where he was supposed to look to figure out what he was missing. On the street, he saw a mariachi band walking down the sidewalk with the huge guitars and glittering suits: they went into Our Lady of Guadalupe, where Darnell had gone to Catholic school.

84   On Monday, he drove slowly past the corners where they always gathered, crowds of Mexican men waiting for daywork. And he saw the shortest, Indian-looking guys—their eyes were slanted, their hair thick and straight, their legs bowed into curves.

85   The men shifted and scattered when a construction truck stopped at the curb, crowding around the driver. Darnell watched five guys jump in the back. Some of the disappointed ones stared at him, and he tried to recall what he could of high school Spanish. All that came to his head was *"¿Como se llama?"* and *"Hermano, hermana"*—useless stuff. He licked his lips and leaned.

86   "I need a guy who can speak English," he said, and three came over.

87   "I speak English, bro," a skinny, dark guy said, and Darnell knew he'd been in prison by the teardrops tattooed near his eyes.

88   "I'll give you 10 bucks to help here, man," Darnell said. "I need two dudes who know how to mow lawns, and I want them to look Oriental, you know, like those guys over there." He pointed to the short, slim men.

89   "He wants *los indios*," the guy said, muttering to the men. Several of the Indian men gathered around him, and he brought over four with anxious faces and small, tilted eyes under thick brows. Darnell thought of Charolette's brows suddenly, how delicate they were.

90   "You guys can do gardening?" he asked. They nodded, and he said, "But I have to be able to talk to you—who speaks English, even some?"

91   The youngest one, without a hat, said, "I try speak *pequeño*. My brother not so much." He gestured to the older one next to him, in a baseball cap.

92   "Get in," Darnell said. The two men were so small compared to Victor and Ronnie that air still flowed through to touch his shoulders. "Where you from?"

93   The young one said, "Mexico."

94   "I know—I mean where in Mexico?"

95   "Osaka," he said, and Darnell frowned. Wasn't that a city in Japan?—he'd heard the name. "Write it down, OK?" he said, and the guy wrote *Oaxaca* on the back of the green flier.

96   He watched them work at Mrs. Munson's, where his father had given him the yard. Anyone could mow, and Juan, the younger one, did the front while Jose did the back. Darnell edged and helped them blow the paths clean. It took 25 minutes.

97   "Be back on the corner next Monday," he told them. "I think I got regular work if you want it. Four bucks an hour."

98   Juan said, "All day?"

99   Darnell said, "I hope so. Where you learn English, man?"

100   "I went in college one year," Juan said. "I love English."

101   "Chill out, homey," Darnell smiled. "See you Monday."

102   He wouldn't tell Brenda what he had in mind, and when she said, "You're drivin' me crazy with that little plannin' smile and won't give up no information." Darnell just smiled it again.

103   "I gotta go see Nacho," he said. "Maybe I can make some more money."

104   "The suspense is killing me," she said, rolling her eyes, and he didn't even get angry. He went to Nacho's and said, "You the artist—can you make me a flier, one I can Xerox? I'll show you."

105   He laid out the sheet for Nacho. On it he'd written the message, and Nacho laughed. "You serious, man? You want me to print or script?"

106   "Print," Darnell said. "And put a picture in both corners—those little incense burners like you see in a Japanese garden." He thought for a minute. "Man, I hate to copy, but I bet the pine tree works."

107   He copied 300 of the sheets on light-blue paper, and then he went to the nursery for small, sparkling white rocks in bulk and bought Baggies at the store.

108   He took Charolette with him, long before dawn. She was sleepy for a few minutes, but he whispered to her, and she said, "Dark, Daddy?" He said, "We're cruisin' in the dark, baby. Watch out for trains." He remembered being angry, in a hurry, stuck behind the long trains that came through the Westside; now he tried to catch them so that she could listen in wonder to the clacking wheels and watch for the engineers.

109   "Choo-choo train!" she yelled.

110   They went to Grayglen first, Darnell driving on the wrong side of the street to drop Baggies on lawns. He pitched two onto Trent's, laughing. Charolette couldn't throw them far enough, and he gave her a pile to wreck so she wouldn't cry. "These dudes ain't even up yet, but they'll go to work soon, and then they'll find this when they get the paper," he told her.

111   "Newspaper?"

112   "You got it." They twisted through all the new streets, then went downtown and dropped more. They ended up in the university neighborhood when the sky turned gray. "We don't want nobody to see us, or we turn into pumpkins," he said, and she remembered Halloween, he could tell, because her face lit up.

113   "Cut pumpkin!" she screamed.

114   "You just like me, don't forget *nothin',*" he said, reaching over to touch her hair. "You're gonna kick some butt in school, girl."

115   His father laughed silly. "'Tuan's Oriental Landscape Maintenance Service,'" he read out loud to Roscoe. "Boy a damn gardener, talkin' 'bout maintenance. 'Expert Asian landscapers will mow, edge, fertilize and maintain your garden with weekly service for only $50 a month. Call now to keep your landscape beautiful.'" His father turned to him. "Who the hell is Tuan?"

116   Darnell said, "Nuh-uh—it's Juan. And Jose. If I get enough calls this week, I'm hirin' two Mexican dudes."

117   Roscoe said, "You know, he ain't crazy. They all want Mexican guys. But I don't know how you gon pull it off when they see your ugly face."

118   "They ain't gotta see me, just send the check here, to your address," Darnell said. "In case we move." His father raised his eyebrows. "And I'ma need to borrow some money, for a new mower. If this works, I'ma have to get a truck."

119   "You got the El Camino," his father said.

120   "Yeah, but I need that for my jobs. I need a used Toyota or Isuzu, for these dudes. Paint the name on the side."

121   The eyebrows went higher. "You serious, huh?"

122   "I want to call Mr. Nard about his house. Serious as a heart attack."

123   He practiced his voice in the bathroom. Brenda was at work. He tried to remember Tim Bui's words, which ones he left out, how he talked. He sat watching Oprah with the sound off, but no one called until the next day, and he was ready. A woman said, "Tuan's Landscape?" and he said, "Yes, ma'am. I can help you."

124   "Are you reliable?"

125   "Yes, ma'am, very reliable. We come every week, and do the best job." He chopped off the words carefully, his heart racing heat all the way to his ears.

126   He told Juan that they would have to comb their hair straight back, and no straw hats. He took them to K mart for white T-shirts, green pants and work boots. "And no talking, if the people are around to watch you," he said. "I don't want them to hear Spanish."

127   When he explained it as best he could, Juan frowned. "But if they say, speak to you? If they want different?"

128   "Just say like this—'Call my boss, he help you.'"

129   Juan looked at the flier closely and smiled. "I am Tuan, eh?"

130   "Maybe, man," Darnell said. "Maybe I am."

131   But he felt strange staying at home, waiting for the calls in the empty, tiny and stifling apartment. Summer—the shimmering bells passed on the sidewalk below,

the Mexican popsicle guys with their carts. Darnell went to the bathroom mirror, pulled at his eyes to make them long and narrow. He touched his new haircut, a fade with three lines above each ear. His father hated the razored cuts, said, "What the hell, look like a damn mower got you."

132   He stared at his face. "Homey, don'cha know me?" He'd seen Victor at a stoplight last week, near the park. Victor's eyes were half-slit and hard. "Work been *slow*, huh?"

133   "I been doin' somethin', but I got somethin' for us next week," Darnell had said. He did—his father had told someone Darnell would clean up property for the fire season.

134   He knew Nacho had told Victor about the flier, about Tuan's. He splashed water onto his face. Homey—don'cha know me? His chest was clotted with warmth when he sat on the cold edge of the bathtub. "What you gon do if somebody don't pay?" Roscoe had said.

135   "Go over there and collect."

136   "Who you—Tuan's bodyguard? His butler?" Roscoe laughed.

137   "Shit, whoever I gotta be, long as I get the cash." But he was shaking.

138   "I was just playin'," Roscoe said gently, touching his elbow. "You gon do outside jobs, get a beeper so you don't miss calls. Beepers are cheap."

139   "Yeah, and I'll look like a dope dealer," Darnell had said, turning away. "Ain't that what I'm supposed to look like anyway?"

140   He paced around the living room now, the bells fading, and he turned up the radio to pound the walls.

141   In a few weeks, he had so many yards that his father and Roscoe found a blue Toyota pickup he could buy on time. He took the El Camino to Jackson Park the next day, sweating, thinking of Victor's eyes. He'd rehearsed what he would say. Victor raised his chin half an inch when he saw Darnell. "*Brotha*man," Victor said. "What you need?"

142   "Need you guys for a job," Darnell said.

143   "Homey, don'cha know me? I'm just a nigga with an attitude."

144   "You ready?" Darnell said.

145   Victor smiled. "I heard you was hirin' illegals, man. You don't want no niggas, word is." Ronnie hovered beside him, silent.

146   "If I don't want no niggas, I better kill myself," Darnell said. "I got two Mexican guys doin' yards. Now I can do other jobs all the time. But see, Victor, man, I gotta be sweatin' every day, man, not like you. I can't wait 'til I'm in the mood."

147   "Man, you think you big shit," Victor smiled harder. "At least I ain't no strawberry."

148   Darnell breathed in through his nose. "I ain't pink." He hesitated. He had practiced this, too. "I'm just whipped, by two women. And got another one comin' to further kick my black butt. You always talkin' about 'Niggas ain't meant to be out in the sun, absorbin' that heat.' Proper maintenance keep you from shrinkin' and fadin', man, don't you know?" He waited. "You comin'?"

149   Victor ran his hands over his braids. "I'm thirsty, man."

150   When he got home, the phone rang before he could put Charolette down. He held her giggling under his arm and said, "Tuan's Landscape Maintenance."

151   A man said, "This sounds like a really great deal. I live in the Grayglen area, and your prices are reasonable compared to others."

152   "Yes, we try to make price very cheap." He was out of breath and said, "Please, can you hold, sir?" He put Charolette down. "When you like us to start?"

153   "Well, as soon as possible," the man said. "Can you come Friday?"

154   "Yes, Friday." Everybody wanted a perfect lawn for the weekend. "We come Fridays, and you send a check to Tuan's Oriental Landscape, 2498 Picasso St. Pay by mail once a month."

155   "Picasso Street?" the man said. "Isn't that on the Westside?"

156   "Yes, sir."

157   "I thought you guys were Oriental—I bet you want to get out of a minority area like that. Pretty rough in the black neighborhood."

158   Darnell's face and neck prickled. "Yes, sir, we move soon. Very soon." After he'd hung up, he saw Charolette unfolding the towels Brenda had stacked on the couch. "Daddy talking?" She imitated his clipped voice. "We move soon, sir."

159   "You ain't gotta talk like that," he said roughly. "Leave the towels alone before I get mad." He stared at the laundry, at her round face set hard. "Let's go look at a washing machine for Mama."

160   "Move, Daddy?" she asked again, since it had bothered him when she said it the first time. When he tried to take the towels away, she said angrily, "*Move, Daddy!*" and shoved him. He pretended to fall over on his back, and then he caught her on his chest to tickle her, so she couldn't get away.

THINKING ABOUT THE TEXT

1. All short stories have conflict; if there is no conflict, there is no story. But some stories do not have an obvious protagonist/antagonist conflict. What are the conflicts in Darnell's life?

2. How does Darnell resolve his problems? How does his creating a steady source of income also embroil him in another conflict?

3. Fiction and film have negatively stereotyped African-American men. Which stereotypes does this short story counter in its portrayal of Darnell?

4. What other cultural stereotypes are understood in this story?

5. The short story is positive (it has a happy ending) and humorous in tone. How is the humor achieved?

6. What are the serious issues behind this entertaining story?

WRITING FROM THE TEXT

1. Write an analysis of Darnell's character—his values, motivations, and goals—based on inferences you can draw from the text. (See character analysis section, pp. 436–444.)

2. Write a description of the conflicts in Darnell's life. In what ways is he caught between worlds? How does he resolve his problem?

3. Write a paper that illustrates how stereotyping is the underlying cause of problems for Darnell.

CONNECTING WITH OTHER TEXTS

1. Use this short story and other essays in the text—"Living in Two Worlds" (p. 143), "Black Men and Public Space" (p. 225), and "The Atlanta Riot" (p. 229)—to write an analysis of some of the problems that African Americans face.

2. Read Robert L. Heilbroner's "Don't Let Stereotypes Warp Your Judgments" (p. 429) to argue that stereotyping is a source of the problems in "Proper Care and Maintenance."

NIKKI-ROSA
Nikki Giovanni

The recipient of numerous awards, grants, and honors for her work as a poet, a writer of nonfiction, and a creator of sound recordings, Nikki Giovanni (b. 1943) has achieved international fame as an important figure in American literature. Giovanni has said, "I write out of my own experiences—which also happen to be the experiences of my people. But if I had to choose between my people's experiences and mine, I'd choose mine because that's what I know the best." In much of her work, Giovanni writes warmly of her family and childhood: "I had a really groovy childhood and I'm really pleased with my family." That pleasure is reflected in the poem included here, which was first published in *Black Judgement* in 1968.

> childhood remembrances are always a drag
> if you're Black
> you always remember things like living in Woodlawn
> with no inside toilet
> and if you become famous or something   5
> they never talk about how happy you were to have your mother
> all to yourself and

how good the water felt when you got your bath from one of those
big tubs that folk in chicago barbecue in
and somehow when you talk about home   10
it never gets across how much you
understood their feelings
as the whole family attended meetings about Hollydale
and even though you remember
your biographers never understand   15
your father's pain as he sells his stock
and another dream goes
and though you're poor it isn't poverty that
concerns you
and though they fought a lot   20
it isn't your father's drinking that makes any difference
but only that everybody is together and you
and your sister have happy birthdays and very good christmasses
and I really hope no white person ever has cause to write about me
because they never understand Black love is Black wealth and they'll 25
probably talk about my hard childhood and never understand that
all the while I was quite happy

THINKING ABOUT THE TEXT

1. Explain what you think Giovanni means when she writes "remembrances are always a drag / if you're Black."

2. Illustrate what Giovanni feels inevitably gets lost in a biography of a famous Black who was once poor.

3. How does Giovanni define "Black wealth"? Cite examples.

4. Why does she use "you" throughout? Why does she shift to "I" at the end?

5. Giovanni illustrates how easily facts about someone's life can be misinterpreted or distorted. Note how she shows this by beginning with an opening line that can easily be misunderstood and by concluding with a line that tests how well we have understood her throughout. Discuss these lines.

WRITING FROM THE TEXT

1. Write an essay contrasting Giovanni's views of her childhood with the way she is misunderstood by biographers. What may account for this misrepresentation?

2. Focus on an incident that occurred when you felt that your background (where you were born or grew up, or a family custom or practice) was misunderstood. Help your reader understand why that happened and how you handled it.

CONNECTING WITH OTHER TEXTS

1. In this poem Giovanni protests the stereotyping of Blacks by biographers. Use Heilbroner's essay (p. 429) about stereotyping to support specific observations in "Nikki-Rosa."

2. Using details from this poem, from Sharon Olds' "On the Subway" (p. 174), and from Brent Staples' "Black Men and Public Space" (p. 225), write an essay supporting the claim that Blacks are negatively stereotyped.

LIKE MEXICANS
Gary Soto

As a child, Gary Soto (b. 1952) worked as a migrant laborer in the agricultural San Joaquin Valley of California. He went to a city college, discovered poetry, and decided he would "like to do something like this." He took university classes and began meeting other writers. He describes his wanting to write poetry as "a sort of fluke" because he came from an "illiterate family," one without books and one that did not encourage the children to read. Soto teaches in the English department at Berkeley. The essay included here was first published in *Small Faces* in 1986.

1   My grandmother gave me bad advice and good advice when I was in my early teens. For the bad advice, she said that I should become a barber because they made good money and listened to the radio all day. "Honey, they don't work como burros," she would say every time I visited her. She made the sound of donkeys braying. "Like that, honey!" For the good advice, she said that I should marry a Mexican girl. "No Okies, hijo"—she would say—"Look, my son. He marry one and they fight every day about I don't know what and I don't know what." For her, everyone who wasn't Mexican, black, or Asian were Okies. The French were Okies, the Italians in suits were Okies. When I asked about Jews, whom I had read about, she asked for a picture. I rode home on my bicycle and returned with a calendar depicting the important races of the world. "Pues si, son Okies tambien!" she said, nodding her head. She waved the calendar away and we went to the liv-

ing room where she lectured me on the virtues of the Mexican girl: first, she could cook and, second, she acted like a woman, not a man, in her husband's home. She said she would tell me about a third when I got a little older.

2   I asked my mother about it—becoming a barber and marrying Mexican. She was in the kitchen. Steam curled from a pot of boiling beans, the radio was on, looking as squat as a loaf of bread. "Well, if you want to be a barber—they say they make good money." She slapped a round steak with a knife, her glasses slipping down with each strike. She stopped and looked up. "If you find a good Mexican girl, marry her of course." She returned to slapping the meat and I went to the backyard where my brother and David King were sitting on the lawn feeling the inside of their cheeks.

3   "This is what girls feel like," my brother said, rubbing the inside of his cheek. David put three fingers inside his mouth and scratched. I ignored them and climbed the back fence to see my best friend, Scott, a second-generation Okie. I called him and his mother pointed to the side of the house where his bedroom was a small aluminum trailer, the kind you gawk at when they're flipped over on the freeway, wheels spinning in the air. I went around to find Scott pitching horseshoes.

4   I picked up a set of rusty ones and joined him. While we played, we talked about school and friends and record albums. The horseshoes scuffed up dirt, sometimes ringing the iron that threw out a meager shadow like a sundial. After three argued-over games, we pulled two oranges apiece from his tree and started down the alley still talking school and friends and record albums. We pulled more oranges from the alley and talked about who we would marry. "No offense, Scott," I said with an orange slice in my mouth, "but I would never marry an Okie." We walked in step, almost touching, with a sled of shadows dragging behind us. "No offense, Gary," Scott said, "but I would *never* marry a Mexican." I looked at him: a fang of orange slice showed from his munching mouth. I didn't think anything of it. He had his girl and I had mine. But our seventh-grade vision was the same: to marry, get jobs, buy cars and maybe a house if we had money left over.

5   We talked about our future lives until, to our surprise, we were on the downtown mall, two miles from home. We bought a bag of popcorn at Penneys and sat on a bench near the fountain watching Mexican and Okie girls pass. "That one's mine," I pointed with my chin when a girl with eyebrows arched into black rainbows ambled by. "She's cute," Scott said about a girl with yellow hair and a mouthful of gum. We dreamed aloud, our chins busy pointing out girls. We agreed that we couldn't wait to become men and lift them onto our laps.

6   But the woman I married was not Mexican but Japanese. It was a surprise to me. For years, I went about wide-eyed in my search for the brown girl in a white dress at a dance. I searched the playground at the baseball diamond. When the girls raced for grounders, their hair bounced like something that couldn't be caught. When they sat together in the lunchroom, heads pressed together, I knew they were talking about us Mexican guys. I saw them and dreamed them. I threw my face into my pillow, making up sentences that were good as in the movies.

7   But when I was twenty, I fell in love with this other girl who worried my mother, who had my grandmother asking once again to see the calendar of the

Important Races of the World. I told her I had thrown it away years before. I took a much-glanced-at snapshot from my wallet. We looked at it together, in silence. Then grandma reclined in her chair, lit a cigarette, and said, "Es pretty." She blew and asked with all her worry pushed up to her forehead: "Chinese?"

8   I was in love and there was no looking back. She was the one. I told my mother who was slapping hamburger into patties. "Well, sure if you want to marry her," she said. But the more I talked, the more concerned she became. Later I began to worry. Was it all a mistake? "Marry a Mexican girl," I heard my mother say in my mind. I heard it at breakfast. I heard it over math problems, between Western Civilization and cultural geography. But then one afternoon while I was hitchhiking home from school, it struck me like a baseball in the back: my mother wanted me to marry someone of my own social class—a poor girl. I considered my fiancee, Carolyn, and she didn't look poor, though I knew she came from a family of farm workers and pull-yourself-up-by-your-bootstraps ranchers. I asked my brother, who was marrying Mexican poor that fall, if I should marry a poor girl. He screamed "Yeah" above his terrible guitar playing in his bedroom. I considered my sister who had married Mexican. Cousins were dating Mexican. Uncles were remarrying poor women. I asked Scott, who was still my best friend, and he said, "She's too good for you, so you better not."

9   I worried about it until Carolyn took me home to meet her parents. We drove in her Plymouth until the houses gave way to farms and ranches and finally her house fifty feet from the highway. When we pulled into the drive, I panicked and begged Carolyn to make a U-turn and go back so we could talk about it over a soda. She pinched my cheek, calling me a "silly boy." I felt better, though, when I got out of the car and saw the house: the chipped paint, a cracked window, boards for a walk to the back door. There were rusting cars near the barn. A tractor with a net of spiderwebs under a mulberry. A field. A bale of barbed wire like children's scribbling leaning against an empty chicken coop. Carolyn took my hand and pulled me to my future mother-in-law who was coming out to greet us.

10   We had lunch: sandwiches, potato chips, and iced tea. Carolyn and her mother talked mostly about neighbors and the congregation at the Japanese Methodist Church in West Fresno. Her father, who was in khaki work clothes, excused himself with a wave that was almost a salute and went outside. I heard a truck start, a dog bark, and then the truck rattle away.

11   Carolyn's mother offered another sandwich, but I declined with a shake of my head and a smile. I looked around when I could, when I was not saying over and over that I was a college student, hinting that I could take care of her daughter. I shifted my chair. I saw newspapers piled in corners, dusty cereal boxes and vinegar bottles in corners. The wallpaper was bubbled from rain that had come in from a bad roof. Dust. Dust lay on lamp shades and window sills. These people are just like Mexicans, I thought. Poor people.

12   Carolyn's mother asked me through Carolyn if I would like a *sushi*. A plate of black and white things were held in front of me. I took one, wide-eyed, and turned it over like a foreign coin. I was biting into one when I saw a kitten crawl up the window screen over the sink. I chewed and the kitten opened its mouth of terror as

she crawled higher, wanting in to paw the leftovers from our plates. I looked at Carolyn who said that the cat was just showing off. I looked up in time to see it fall. It crawled up, then fell again.

13   We talked for an hour and had apple pie and coffee, slowly. Finally, we got up with Carolyn taking my hand. Slightly embarrassed, I tried to pull away but her grip held me. I let her have her way as she led me down the hallway with her mother right behind me. When I opened the door, I was startled by a kitten clinging to the screen door, its mouth screaming "cat food, dog biscuits, *sushi*. . . ." I opened the door and the kitten, still holding on, whined in the language of hungry animals. When I got into Carolyn's car, I looked back: the cat was still clinging. I asked Carolyn if it were possibly hungry, but she said the cat was being silly. She started the car, waved to her mother, and bounced us over the rain-poked drive, patting my thigh for being her lover baby. Carolyn waved again. I looked back, waving, then gawking at a window screen where there were now three kittens clawing and screaming to get in. Like Mexicans, I thought. I remembered the Molinas and how the cats clung to their screens—cats they shot down with squirt guns. On the highway, I felt happy, pleased by it all. I patted Carolyn's thigh. Her people were like Mexicans, only different.

THINKING ABOUT THE TEXT

1. What is the advice that Soto's grandmother gives him? On what is her advice based? What do you imagine would be her third point—the one she will give him when he is older?

2. What is Soto's mother's position? Why does she not seem interested in his questions?

3. How does Soto characterize his seventh-grade adolescent world? Find specific *images* in the text that create pictures of this time of his life.

4. What specifically does Soto see in his girlfriend's house and family that makes him comfortable? What specifically makes them "like Mexicans"?

WRITING FROM THE TEXT

1. Write about a time in your life when you feared going to a classmate's or friend's house to meet the family. Write a narrative that focuses on this experience and what you learned.

2. Write an essay in which you argue that people ought to marry within their own ethnic or racial group *or* that marrying out of one's racial or ethnic group can be advantageous. Use specific reasons to convince your reader.

CONNECTING WITH OTHER TEXTS

1. In what ways are Soto's perceptions of his family life comparable to Nikki Giovanni's perceptions of her family as expressed in the poem "Nikki-Rosa" (p. 188)? Do these writers seem to be living between cultures, as Marcus Mabry describes in his essay "Living in Two Worlds" (p. 143)? Write an analytical study of the concept of home as these three writers experience it.

2. Read selections from Gary Soto's *Living Up the Street* or *Small Faces* and write an analysis of the characteristic subject matter or themes of his work.

3. Interview or find periodical interviews of racially or ethnically mixed marriages. What problems do these couples face that are different from those of other couples? Write from a thesis that you can support with specific data that you have read or collected from your interviews.

4

Between Perceptions

■ ■ ■

How we perceive ourselves is intrinsically related to our racial and ethnic roots, as well as to our gender. Our sense of self, however, goes beyond any definition of male or female, race or culture. Self-perception is often conditioned by the roles we assume—as students, workers, family members—but our self-image and how others see us may be distinct from the roles we play. You regard yourself as a college student, but when you are at home you might be the "baby" in the family, or the one diapering the baby. You know that your competence at work can gain you much-needed overtime pay, but your perception of yourself as an "A" student prompts you to cut back on hours instead. A woman who is physically disabled may not define herself as "handicapped," and a man who qualifies for affirmative action may not see himself as "disadvantaged." Perceiving oneself beyond labels or stereotypes is an essential process, as the readings in this chapter indicate.

Self-perception is complicated by others' images of us. If you feel that you are constantly trying to exist among worlds that perceive you differently, you will relate to the tensions described in our first selection. In this emphatic poem, Kate Rushin insists that she is "sick" of being the bridge or mediator for everyone she knows and of not finding "the bridge to [her] own power." This poem reflects a realization of how our ability to perceive ourselves may be thwarted by how others use us.

In the essay that follows, Richard Selzer prompts us to reconsider our perception of professionals in the medical world and in sports. Nancy Mairs, Ben Mattlin, and Jennifer Coleman fight stereotypes that threaten their self-perceptions. Their essays express the frustrations of productive individuals whose self-acceptance is threatened by others' delimiting views of them.

As you may realize, eating disorders often develop from our perception of what is attractive or our need to gain control of how we perceive ourselves. In "Bodily Harm," Pamela Erens chronicles the problems of many women who have eating disorders and struggle toward self-understanding and acceptance rather than perpetuate destructive behavior.

To be perceived as an individual rather than a racial or ethnic stereotype may be a challenge for you or some of your friends. Fighting stereotypes can be life-threatening, as Brent Staples and Walter White reveal in their essays, or it can be uncomfortable, as Gloria Naylor shows in hers. The essays of Richard Rodriguez and Ruben Navarrette show their conflicts in perceiving themselves in an ethnic context and rejecting the biases of ethnic identification. In a charming short story, Sandra Cisneros encourages a reexamination of what it means to perceive oneself at any given age.

Our perception of self is complicated by the multiple roles we play and our disparate self-images based on gender, social class, or ethnicity. Balancing how others see us with who we think we are is the condition of being between perceptions—and the basis of all of the writings in this chapter.

THE BRIDGE POEM
Kate Rushin

In addition to "millions of low-paying jobs"—in a factory, as a waitress, and as a live-in maid—Kate Rushin (b. 1951) has also worked in community theater, on radio, and has participated in the artist-in-residence and poet-in-the schools program for many years. She has directed the Jefferson Park Writing Center, an adult writing project, and she has been a member of the New Words Book Store Collective, a women's bookstore, for ten years. Rushin has an undergraduate degree from Oberlin College and in 1992 started an M.F.A. program at Brown University. Her most recent book is *The Black Back-Ups*. The poem printed here was first published in *This Bridge Called My Back: Writings by Radical Women of Color* in 1983.

> *I've had enough*
> *I'm sick of seeing and touching*
> *Both sides of things*
> *Sick of being the damn bridge for everybody*
>
> *Nobody*   5
> *can talk to anybody*
> *Without me*
> *Right?*

I explain my mother to my father my father to my little sister
My little sister to my brother my brother to the White Feminists   10
The White Feminists to the Black Church Folks the Black Church Folks
To the ex-Hippies the ex-Hippies to the Black Separatists the
Black Separatists to the Aritsts the Artists to my friends' parents . . .

Then
I've got to explain myself   15
To everybody

I do more translating
Than the U.N.

Forget it
I'm sick of filling in your gaps   20
Sick of being your insurance against
The isolation of your self-imposed limitations
Sick of being the crazy at your holiday dinners
The odd one at your Sunday Brunches
I am sick of being the sole Black friend to thirty-four individual White Folks 25

Find another connection to the rest of the world
Find something else to make you legitimate
Find some other way to be political and hip
I will not be the bridge to your womanhood
Your manhood   30
Your human-ness

I'm sick of reminding you not to
Close off too tight for too long

I'm sick of mediating with your worst self
On behalf of your better selves   35

Sick
of having
To remind you
To breathe
Before you   40
Suffocate
Your own
Fool self

Forget it

Stretch or drown   45
Evolve or die

You see it's like this
The bridge I must be
Is the bridge to my own power
I must translate   50
My own fears
Mediate
My own weaknesses

I must be the bridge to nowhere
But my own true self   55
It's only then
I can be
Useful

THINKING ABOUT THE TEXT

1. In what specific ways does the speaker function as a "bridge"? Why is the job frustrating?
2. What can you infer about the speaker's gender, race, education, personality? Support your inferences with information from the text.
3. What is the one bridge the speaker "must be"? In what ways does the speaker's functioning as many bridges deprive her or him of the one sought-for bridge?

WRITING FROM THE TEXT

1. Write a description of the "bridge" services you provide in your family, social, professional, and/or personal worlds.
2. Write about a time when you were seen and used as a role or as a token member of a group. How did you feel? Let your essay *show* how you felt.
3. Write an essay arguing that all gracious people assist others by helping them connect their "human-ness" to others' "human-ness." Support your assertion with specific positive descriptions of "bridging people" that you know.

CONNECTING WITH OTHER TEXTS

1. The speaker in "The Bridge Poem" vents angry frustration at being the connecting element for one person or group to another, and the token representative to make others appear "political and hip." Many readings in *Between Worlds* address the resentment people feel when they are used, their presence exploited by individuals or groups. Dis-

cuss this tokenism or exploitation and use "An Open Letter to Jerry Lewis" (p. 214), "None of This Is Fair" (p. 237), and "My Man Bovanne" (p. 43) to support your point.

THE MASKED MARVEL'S LAST TOEHOLD
Richard Selzer

The son of a family doctor, Richard Selzer (b. 1928) received his M.D. from Albany Medical College in 1953 and did his postdoctoral studies at Yale from 1957 to 1960. He is in general surgery practice and is an associate professor of surgery at Yale Medical School. He is a writer of short stories and essays and a contributor to popular magazines. Selzer's work, which raises issues about morality in medicine, is widely published. The narrative included here is from *Confessions of a Knife,* 1975.

Morning Rounds

1   On the fifth floor of the hospital, in the west wing, I know that a man is sitting up in his bed, waiting for me. Elihu Koontz is seventy-five, and he is diabetic. It is two weeks since I amputated his left leg just below the knee. I walk down the corridor, but I do not go straight into his room. Instead, I pause in the doorway. He is not yet aware of my presence, but gazes down at the place in the bed where his leg used to be, and where now there is the collapsed leg of his pajamas. He is totally absorbed, like an athlete appraising the details of his body. What is he thinking, I wonder. Is he dreaming the outline of his toes. Does he see there his foot's incandescent ghost? Could he be angry? Feel that I have taken from him something for which he yearns now with all his heart? Has he forgotten so soon the pain? It was a pain so great as to set him apart from all other men, in a red-hot place where he had no kith or kin. What of those black gorilla toes and the soupy mess that was his heel? I watch him from the doorway. It is a kind of spying, I know.

2   Save for a white fringe open at the front, Elihu Koontz is bald. The hair has grown too long and is wilted. He wears it as one would wear a day-old laurel wreath. He is naked to the waist, so that I can see his breasts. They are the breasts of Buddha, inverted triangles from which the nipples swing, dark as garnets.

3   I have seen enough. I step into the room, and he sees that I am there.

4   "How did the night go, Elihu?"

5   He looks at me for a long moment. "Shut the door," he says.

6   I do, and move to the side of the bed. He takes my left hand in both of his, gazes at it, turns it over, then back, fondling, at last holding it up to his cheek. I do not withdraw from this loving. After a while he relinquishes my hand, and looks up at me.

7   "How is the pain?" I ask.

8   He does not answer, but continues to look at me in silence. I know at once that he has made a decision.

9   "Ever hear of The Masked Marvel?" He says this in a low voice, almost a whisper.

10   "What?"

11   "The Masked Marvel," he says. "You never heard of him?"

12   "No."

13   He clucks his tongue. He is exasperated.

14   All at once there is a recollection. It is dim, distant, but coming near.

15   "Do you mean the wrestler?"

16   Eagerly, he nods, and the breasts bob. How gnomish he looks, oval as the huge helpless egg of some outlandish lizard. He has very long arms, which, now and then, he unfurls to reach for things—a carafe of water, a get-well card. He gazes up at me, urging. He *wants* me to remember.

17   "Well . . . yes," I say. I am straining backward in time. "I saw him wrestle in Toronto long ago."

18   "Ha!" He smiles. "You saw *me*." And his index finger, held rigid and upright, bounces in the air.

19   The man has said something shocking, unacceptable. It must be challenged.

20   "You?" I am trying to smile.

21   Again that jab of the finger. "You saw *me*."

22   "No," I say. But even then, something about Elihu Koontz, those prolonged arms, the shape of his head, the sudden agility with which he leans from his bed to get a large brown envelope from his nightstand, something is forcing me toward a memory. He rummages through his papers, old newspaper clippings, photographs, and I remember . . .

23   It is almost forty years ago. I am ten years old. I have been sent to Toronto to spend the summer with relatives. Uncle Max has bought two tickets to the wrestling match. He is taking me that night.

24   "He isn't allowed," says Aunt Sarah to me. Uncle Max has angina.

25   "He gets too excited," she says.

26   "I wish you wouldn't go, Max," she says.

27   "You mind your own business," he says.

28   And we go. Out into the warm Canadian evening. I am not only abroad, I am abroad in the *evening!* I have never been taken out in the evening. I am terribly excited. The trolleys, the lights, the horns. It is a bazaar. At the Maple Leaf Gardens, we sit high and near the center. The vast arena is dark except for the brilliance of the ring at the bottom.

29   It begins.

30   The wrestlers circle. They grapple. They are all haunch and paunch. I am shocked by their ugliness, but I do not show it. Uncle Max is exhilarated. He leans forward, his eyes unblinking, on his face a look of enormous happiness. One after the other, a pair of wrestlers enter the ring. The two men join, twist, jerk, tug, bend, yank, and throw. Then they leave and are replaced by another pair. At last it is the main event. "The Angel vs. The Masked Marvel."

31   On the cover of the program notes, there is a picture of The Angel hanging from the limb of a tree, a noose of thick rope around his neck. The Angel hangs just so for an hour every day, it is explained, to strengthen his neck. The Masked Marvel's trademark is a black stocking cap with holes for the eyes and mouth. He is never seen without it, states the program. No one knows who The Masked Marvel really is!

32   "Good," says Uncle Max. "Now you'll see something." He is fidgeting, waiting for them to appear. They come down separate aisles, climb into the ring from opposite sides. I have never seen anything like them. It is The Angel's neck that first captures the eye. The shaved nape rises in twin columns to puff into the white hood of a sloped and bosselated skull that is too small. As though, strangled by the sinews of that neck, the skull had long since withered and shrunk. The thing about The Angel is the absence of any mystery in his body. It is simply *there.* A monosyllabic announcement. A grunt. One looks and knows everything at once, the fat thighs, the gigantic buttocks, the great spine from which hang knotted ropes and pale aprons of beef. And that prehistoric head. He is all of a single hideous piece, The Angel is. No detachables.

33   The Masked Marvel seems dwarfish. His fingers dangle kneeward. His short legs are slightly bowed as if under the weight of the cask they are forced to heft about. He has breasts that swing when he moves! I have never seen such breasts on a man before.

34   There is a sudden ungraceful movement, and they close upon one another. The Angel stoops and hugs The Marvel about the waist, locking his hands behind The Marvel's back. Now he straightens and lifts The Marvel as though he were uprooting a tree. Thus he holds him, then stoops again, thrusts one hand through The Marvel's crotch, and with the other grabs him by the neck. He rears and . . . The Marvel is aloft! For a long moment, The Angel stands as though deciding where to make the toss. Then throws. Was that board or bone that splintered there? Again and again, The Angel hurls himself upon the body of The Masked Marvel.

35   Now The Angel rises over the fallen Marvel, picks up one foot in both of his hands, and twists the toes downward. It is far beyond the tensile strength of mere ligament, mere cartilage. The Masked Marvel does not hide his agony, but pounds and slaps the floor with his hand, now and then reaching up toward The Angel in an attitude of supplication. I have never seen such suffering. And all the while his black mask rolls from side to side, the mouth pulled to a tight slit through which issues an endless hiss that I can hear from where I sit. All at once, I hear a shouting close by.

36   "Break it off! Tear off a leg and throw it up here!"

37   It is Uncle Max. Even in the darkness I can see that he is gray. A band of sweat stands upon his upper lip. He is on his feet now, panting, one fist pressed at his chest, the other raised warlike toward the ring. For the first time I begin to think that something terrible might happen here. Aunt Sarah was right.

38   "Sit down, Uncle Max," I say. "Take a pill, please."

39   He reaches for the pillbox, gropes, and swallows without taking his gaze from the wrestlers. I wait for him to sit down.

40   "That's not fair," I say, "twisting his toes like that."

41   "It's the toehold," he explains.

42   "But it's not *fair*," I say again. The whole of the evil is laid open for me to perceive. I am trembling.

43   And now The Angel does something unspeakable. Holding the foot of The Marvel at full twist with one hand, he bends and grasps the mask where it clings to the back of The Marvel's head. And he pulls. He is going to strip it off! Lay bare an ultimate carnal mystery! Suddenly it is beyond mere physical violence. Now I am on my feet, shouting into the Maple Leaf Gardens.

44   "Watch out," I scream. "Stop him. Please, somebody, stop him."

45   Next to me, Uncle Max is chuckling.

46   Yet The Masked Marvel hears me, I know it. And rallies from his bed of pain. Thrusting with his free heel, he strikes The Angel at the back of the knee. The Angel falls. The Masked Marvel is on top of him, pinning his shoulders to the mat. One! Two! Three! And it is over. Uncle Max is strangely still. I am gasping for breath. All this I remember as I stand at the bedside of Elihu Koontz.

47   Once again, I am in the operating room. It is two years since I amputated the left leg of Elihu Koontz. Now it is his right leg which is gangrenous. I have already scrubbed. I stand to one side wearing my gown and gloves. And . . . *I am masked.* Upon the table lies Elihu Koontz, pinned in a fierce white light. Spinal anesthesia has been administered. One of his arms is taped to a board placed at a right angle to his body. Into this arm, a needle has been placed. Fluid drips here from a bottle overhead. With his other hand, Elihu Koontz beats feebly at the side of the operating table. His head rolls from side to side. His mouth is pulled into weeping. It seems to me that I have never seen such misery.

48   An orderly stands at the foot of the table, holding Elihu Koontz's leg aloft by the toes so that the intern can scrub the limb with antiseptic solutions. The intern paints the foot, ankle, leg, and thigh, both front and back, three times. From a corner of the room where I wait, I look down as from an amphitheater. Then I think of Uncle Max yelling, "Tear off a leg. Throw it up here." And I think that forty years later I am making the catch.

49   "It's not fair," I say aloud. But no one hears me. I step forward to break The Masked Marvel's last toehold.

THINKING ABOUT THE TEXT

1. Explain the significance of each physical description of The Masked Marvel. In what ways is he "between worlds"?

2. Analyze The Angel's character. What does he attempt to do to The Marvel, and why is the boy so appalled by this?

3. Contrast the behavior and attitude of Uncle Max and his nephew at the match. How is the outcome a near miracle?

4. Discuss the ironic twists or reversals at the end of the story. Specify how the narrator weaves the details of the match and the operation.

5. This essay demonstrates a number of writing techniques: the use of flashback, shifting narrative perspective (from young Richard to the adult Richard), dialogue, contrast, irony, symbolism, foreshadowing, unique characters, and pun (such as "toehold"). Discuss how each contributes to the narration.

WRITING FROM THE TEXT

1. Write an essay exploring how the narrator finds himself exposed to a world between generations, genders, perceptions, and values because of his relationship with The Masked Marvel.

2. Recall a time in your own life when you were rooting for the underdog. Show us why you chose to support an apparent "loser," how it made you feel, and what happened.

CONNECTING WITH OTHER TEXTS

1. Write an essay examining how this reading and others in this text ("On Being a Cripple," p. 203, and "An Open Letter to Jerry Lewis," p. 214) emphasize the importance of empathizing and interacting with the physically disabled rather than focusing on their differences.

2. Write an essay using Auden's essay (p. 249) to show how Selzer is a "worker" rather than a "wage slave."

ON BEING A CRIPPLE
Nancy Mairs

In spite of her multiple sclerosis, Nancy Mairs (b. 1943) is an active and productive woman, as her personal account below attests. She has been a visiting lecturer at UCLA, a teacher in women's studies and writing at the University of Arizona, and a prolific free-lance writer since 1986. Her work includes a collection of poetry—*In All the Rooms of the Yellow House*—for which she won an award, and the nonfiction, full-length works *Remembering the Bone House*, *Carnal Acts*, and *Ordinary Time*. Her most recent book, published in 1994, is *Voice Lessons*. The essay below has been widely anthologized, but first appeared in *Plaintext* in 1986.

> To escape is nothing. Not to escape is nothing.
>
> —*Louise Bogan*

1   The other day I was thinking of writing an essay on being a cripple. I was thinking hard in one of the stalls of the women's room in my office building, as I

was shoving my shirt into my jeans and tugging up my zipper. Preoccupied, I flushed, picked up my book bag, took my cane down from the hook, and unlatched the door. So many movements unbalanced me, and as I pulled the door open I fell over backward, landing fully clothed on the toilet seat with my legs splayed in front of me: the old beetle-on-its-back routine. Saturday afternoon, the building deserted, I was free to laugh aloud as I wriggled back to my feet, my voice bouncing off the yellowish tiles from all directions. Had anyone been there with me, I'd have been still and faint and hot with chagrin.

2   I decided that it was high time to write the essay.

3   First, the matter of semantics. I am a cripple. I choose this word to name me. I choose from among several possibilities, the most common of which are *handicapped* and *disabled*. I made the choice a number of years ago, without thinking, unaware of my motives for doing so. Even now, I'm not sure what those motives are, but I recognize that they are complex and not entirely flattering. People—crippled or not—wince at the word *cripple,* as they do not at *handicapped* or *disabled.* Perhaps I want them to wince. I want them to see me as a tough customer, one to whom the fates/gods/viruses have not been kind, but who can face the brutal truth of her existence squarely. As a cripple, I swagger.

4   But, to be fair to myself, a certain amount of honesty underlies my choice. *Cripple* seems to me a clean word, straightforward and precise. It has an honorable history, having made its first appearance in the Lindisfarne Gospel in the tenth century. As a lover of words, I like the accuracy with which it describes my condition: I have lost the full use of my limbs. *Disabled,* by contrast, suggests any incapacity, physical or mental. And I certainly don't like *handicapped,* which implies that I have deliberately been put at a disadvantage, by whom I can't imagine (my God is not a Handicapper General), in order to equalize chances in the great race of life. These words seem to me to be moving away from my condition, to be widening the gap between word and reality. Most remote is the recently coined euphemism *differently abled,* which partakes of the same semantic hopefulness that transformed countries from *undeveloped* to *underdeveloped,* then to *less developed,* and finally to *developing* nations. People have continued to starve in those countries during the shift. Some realities do not obey the dictates of language.

5   Mine is one of them. Whatever you call me, I remain crippled. But I don't care what I am called, as long as it isn't *differently abled,* which strikes me as pure verbal garbage designed, by its ability to describe anyone, to describe no one. I subscribe to George Orwell's thesis that "the sloppiness of our language makes it easier for us to have foolish thoughts." And I refuse to participate in the degeneration of the language to the extent that I deny that I have lost anything in the course of this calamitous disease; I refuse to pretend that the only differences between you and me are the various ordinary ones that distinguish any one person from another. But call me *disabled* or *handicapped* if you like. I have long since grown accustomed to them; and if they are vague, at least they hint at the truth. Moreover, I use them myself. Society is no readier to accept crippledness than to

accept death, war, sex, sweat, or wrinkles. I would never refer to another person as a cripple. It is the word I use to name only myself.

6   I haven't always been crippled, a fact for which I am soundly grateful. To be whole of limb is, I know from experience, infinitely more pleasant and useful than to be crippled; and if that knowledge leaves me open to bitterness at my loss, the physical soundness I once enjoyed (though I did not enjoy it half enough) is well worth the occasional stab of regret. Though never any good at sports, I was a normally active child and young adult. I climbed trees, played hopscotch, jumped rope, skated, swam, rode my bicycle, sailed. I despised team sports, spending some of the most wretched afternoons of my life, sweaty and humiliated, behind a field-hockey stick and under a basketball hoop. I tramped alone for miles along the bridle paths that webbed the woods behind the house I grew up in. I swayed through countless dim hours in the arms of one man or another under the scattered shot of light from mirrored balls, and gyrated through countless more as Tab Hunter and Johnny Mathis gave way to the Rolling Stones, Creedence Clearwater Revival, Cream. I walked down the aisle. I pushed baby carriages, changed tires in the rain, marched for peace.

7   When I was twenty-nine, I started to trip and drop things. What at first seemed my natural clumsiness soon became too pronounced to shrug off. I consulted a neurologist, who told me that I had a brain tumor. A battery of tests, increasingly disagreeable, revealed no tumor. About a year and a half later I developed a blurred spot in one eye. I had, at last, the episodes "disseminated in space and time" requisite for a diagnosis: multiple sclerosis. I have never been sorry for the doctor's initial misdiagnosis, however. For almost a week, until the negative results of the tests were in, I thought that I was going to die right away. Every day for the past nearly ten years, then, has been a kind of gift. I accept all gifts.

8   Multiple sclerosis is a chronic degenerative disease of the central nervous system, in which the myelin that sheathes the nerves is somehow eaten away and scar tissue forms in its place, interrupting the nerves' signals. During its course, which is unpredictable and uncontrollable, one may lose vision, hearing, speech, the ability to walk, control of bladder and/or bowels, strength in any or all extremities, sensitivity to touch, vibration, and/or pain, potency, coordination of movements— the list of possibilities is lengthy and horrifying. One may also lose one's sense of humor. That's the easiest to lose and the hardest to survive without.

9   In the past ten years, I have sustained some of these losses. Characteristic of MS are sudden attacks, called exacerbations, followed by remissions, and these I have not had. Instead, my disease has been slowly progressive. My left leg is now so weak that I walk with the aid of a brace and a cane; and for distances I use an Amigo, a variation on the electric wheelchair that looks rather like an electrified kiddie car. I no longer have much use of my left hand. Now my right side is weakening as well. I still have the blurred spot in my right eye. Overall, though, I've been lucky so far. My world has, of necessity, been circumscribed by my losses, but the terrain left me has been ample enough for me to continue many of the activities that absorb me: writing, teaching, raising children and cats and plants

and snakes, reading, speaking publicly about MS and depression, even playing bridge with people patient and honorable enough to let me scatter cards every which way without sneaking a peek.

10   Lest I begin to sound like Pollyanna, however, let me say that I don't like having MS. I hate it. My life holds realities—harsh ones, some of them—that no right-minded human being ought to accept without grumbling. One of them is fatigue. I know of no one with MS who does not complain of bone-weariness; in a disease that presents an astonishing variety of symptoms, fatigue seems to be a common factor. I wake up in the morning feeling the way most people do at the end of a bad day, and I take it from there. As a result, I spend a lot of time *in extremis* and, impatient with limitation, I tend to ignore my fatigue until my body breaks down in some way and forces rest. Then I miss picnics, dinner parties, poetry readings, the brief visits of old friends from out of town. The offspring of a puritanical tradition of exceptional venerability, I cannot view these lapses without shame. My life often seems a series of small failures to do as I ought.

11   I lead, on the whole, an ordinary life, probably rather like the one I would have led had I not had MS. I am lucky that my predilections were already solitary, sedentary, and bookish—unlike the world-famous French cellist I have read about, or the young woman I talked with one long afternoon who wanted only to be a jockey. I had just begun graduate school when I found out something was wrong with me, and I have remained—interminably—a graduate student. Perhaps I would not have if I'd thought I had the stamina to return to a full-time job as a technical editor; but I've enjoyed my studies.

12   In addition to studying, I teach writing courses. I also teach medical students how to give neurological examinations. I pick up free-lance editing jobs here and there. I have raised a foster son and sent him into the world, where he has made me two grandbabies, and I am still escorting my daughter and son through adolescence. I go to mass every Saturday. I am a superb, if messy, cook. I am also an enthusiastic laundress, capable of sorting a hamper full of clothes into five subtly differentiated piles, but a terrible housekeeper. I can do italic writing and, in an emergency, bathe an oil-soaked cat. I play a fiendish game of Scrabble. When I have the time and the money, I like to sit on my front steps with my husband, drinking Amaretto and smoking a cigar, as we imagine our counterparts in Leningrad and make sure that the sun gets down once more behind the sharp childish scrawl of the Tucson mountains.

13   This lively plenty has its bleak complement, of course, in all the things I can no longer do. I will never run again, except in dreams, and one day I may have to write that I will never walk again. I like to go camping, but I can't follow George and the children along the trails that wander out of a campsite through the desert or into the mountains. In fact, even on the level I've learned never to check the weather or try to hold a coherent conversation: I need all my attention for my wayward feet. Of late, I have begun to catch myself wondering how people can propel themselves without canes. With only one usable hand, I have to select my clothing with care not so much for style as for ease of ingress and egress, and even so, dressing can be laborious. I can no longer do fine stitchery, pick up babies, play the piano, braid my hair. I am immobilized by acute attacks of depression,

which may or may not be physiologically related to MS but are certainly its logical concomitant.

14   These two elements, the plenty and the privation, are never pure, nor are the delight and wretchedness that accompany them. Almost every pickle that I get into as a result of my weakness and clumsiness—and I get into plenty—is funny as well as maddening and sometimes painful. I recall one May afternoon when a friend and I were going out for a drink after finishing up at school. As we were climbing into opposite sides of my car, chatting, I tripped and fell, flat and hard, onto the asphalt parking lot, my abrupt departure interrupting him in mid-sentence. "Where'd you go?" he called as he came around the back of the car to find me hauling myself up by the door frame. "Are you all right?" Yes, I told him, I was fine, just a bit rattly, and we drove off to find a shady patio and some beer. When I got home an hour or so later, my daughter greeted me with, "What have you done to yourself?" I looked down. One elbow of my white turtleneck with the green froggies, one knee of my white trousers, one white kneesock were blood-soaked. We peeled off the clothes and inspected the damage, which was nasty enough but not alarming. That part wasn't funny: The abrasions took a long time to heal, and one got a little infected. Even so, when I think of my friend talking earnestly, suddenly, to the hot thin air while I dropped from his view as though through a trap door, I find the image as silly as something from a Marx Brothers movie.

15   I may find it easier than other cripples to amuse myself because I live propped by the acceptance and the assistance and, sometimes, the amusement of those around me. Grocery clerks tear my checks out of my checkbook for me, and sales clerks find chairs to put into dressing rooms when I want to try on clothes. The people I work with make sure I teach at times when I am least likely to be fatigued, in places I can get to, with the materials I need. My students, with one anonymous exception (in an end-of-the-semester evaluation), have been unperturbed by my disability. Some even like it. One was immensely cheered by the information that I paint my own fingernails; she decided, she told me, that if I could go to such trouble over fine details, she could keep on writing essays. I suppose I became some sort of bright-fingered muse. She wrote good essays, too.

16   The most important struts in the framework of my existence, of course, are my husband and children. Dismayingly few marriages survive the MS test, and why should they? Most twenty-two- and nineteen-year-olds, like George and me, can vow in clear conscience, after a childhood of chicken pox and summer colds, to keep one another in sickness and in health so long as they both shall live. Not many are equipped for catastrophe: the dismay, the depression, the extra work, the boredom that a degenerative disease can insinuate into a relationship. And our society, with its emphasis on fun and its association of fun with physical performance, offers little encouragement for a whole spouse to stay with a crippled partner. Children experience similar stresses when faced with a crippled parent, and they are more helpless, since parents and children can't usually get divorced. They hate, of course, to be different from their peers, and the child whose mother is tacking down the aisle of a school auditorium packed with proud parents like a Cape Cod dinghy in a stiff breeze jolly well stands out in a crowd. Deprived of

legal divorce, the child can at least deny the mother's disability, even her existence, forgetting to tell her about recitals and PTA meetings, refusing to accompany her to stores or church or the movies, never inviting friends to the house. Many do.

17   But I've been limping along for ten years now, and so far George and the children are still at my left elbow, holding tight. Anne and Matthew vacuum floors and dust furniture and haul trash and rake up dog droppings and button my cuffs and bake lasagna and Toll House cookies with just enough grumbling so I know that they don't have brain fever. And far from hiding me, they're forever dragging me by racks of fancy clothes or through teeming school corridors, or welcoming gaggles of friends while I'm wandering through the house in Anne's filmy pink babydoll pajamas. George generally calls before he brings someone home, but he does just as many dumb thankless chores as the children. And they all yell at me, laugh at some of my jokes, write me funny letters when we're apart—in short, treat me as an ordinary human being for whom they have some use. I think they like me. Unless they're faking. . . .

18   Faking. There's the rub. Tugging at the fringes of my consciousness always is the terror that people are kind to me only because I'm a cripple. My mother almost shattered me once, with that instinct mothers have—blind, I think, in this case, but unerring nonetheless—for striking blows along the fault-lines of their children's hearts, by telling me, in an attack on my selfishness, "We all have to make allowances for you, of course, because of the way you are." From the distance of a couple of years, I have to admit that I haven't any idea just what she meant, and I'm not sure that she knew either. She was awfully angry. But at the time, as the words thudded home, I felt my worst fear suddenly realized. I could bear being called selfish: I am. But I couldn't bear the corroboration that those around me were doing in fact what I'd always suspected them of doing; professing fondness while silently they put up with me because of the way I am. A cripple. I've been a little cracked ever since.

19   Along with this fear that people are secretly accepting shoddy goods comes a relentless pressure to please—to prove myself worth the burdens I impose, I guess, or to build a substantial account of good will against which I may write drafts in times of need. Part of the pressure arises from social expectations. In our society, anyone who deviates from the norm had better find some way to compensate. Like fat people, who are expected to be jolly, cripples must bear their lot meekly and cheerfully. A grumpy cripple isn't playing by the rules. And much of the pressure is self-generated. Early on I vowed that, if I had to have MS, by God I was going to do it well. This is a class act, ladies and gentlemen. No tears, no recriminations, no faintheartedness.

20   One way and another, then, I wind up feeling like Tiny Tim, peering over the edge of the table at the Christmas goose, waving my crutch, piping down God's blessing on us all. Only sometimes I don't want to play Tiny Tim. I'd rather be Caliban, a most scurvy monster. Fortunately, at home no one much cares whether I'm a good cripple or a bad cripple so long as I make vichyssoise with fair regularity. One evening several years ago, Anne was at the diningroom table reading while I cooked dinner. As I opened a can of tomatoes, the can slipped in my left

hand and juice spattered me and the counter with bloody spots. Fatigued and infuriated, I bellowed, "I'm so sick of being crippled. . . ." Anne glanced at me over the top of her book. "There now," she said, "do you feel better?" "Yes," I said, "yes I do." She went back to her reading. I felt better. That's about all the attention my scurviness ever gets.

21   Because I hate being crippled, I sometimes hate myself for being a cripple. Over the years I have come to expect—even accept—attacks of violent self-loathing. Luckily, in general our society no longer connects deformity and disease directly with evil (though a charismatic once told me that I have MS because a devil is in me) and so I am allowed to move largely at will, even among small children. But I'm not sure that this revision of attitude has been particularly helpful. Physical imperfection, even freed of moral disapprobation, still defines and violates the ideal, especially for women, whose confinement in their bodies as objects of desire is far from over. Each age, of course, has its ideal, and I doubt that ours is any better or worse than any other. Today's ideal woman, who lives on the glossy pages of dozens of magazines, seems to be between the ages of eighteen and twenty-five; her hair has body, her teeth flash white, her breath smells minty, her underarms are dry; she has a career but is still a fabulous cook, especially of meals that take less than twenty minutes to prepare; she does not ordinarily appear to have a husband or children; she is trim and deeply tanned; she jogs, swims, plays tennis, rides a bicycle, sails, but does not bowl; she travels widely, even to out-of-the-way places like Finland and Samoa, always in the company of the ideal man, who possesses a nearly identical set of characteristics. There are a few exceptions. Though usually white and often blonde, she may be black, Hispanic, oriental, or native American, so long as she is unusually sleek. She may be old, provided she is selling a laxative or is Lauren Bacall. If she is selling a detergent, she may be married and have a flock of strikingly messy children. But she is never a cripple.

22   Like many women I know, I have always had an uneasy relationship with my body. I was not a popular child, largely, I think now, because I was peculiar; intelligent, intense, moody, shy, given to unexpected actions and inexplicable notions and emotions. But as I entered adolescence, I believed myself unpopular because I was homely: my breasts too flat, my mouth too wide, my hips too narrow, my clothing never quite right in fit or style. I was not, in fact, particularly ugly, old photographs inform me, though I was well off the ideal; but I carried this sense of self-alienation with me into adulthood, where it regenerated in response to the depradations of MS. Even with my brace I walk with a limp so pronounced that, seeing myself on the videotape of a television program on the disabled, I couldn't believe that anything but an inchworm could make progress humping along like that. My shoulders droop and my pelvis thrusts forward as I try to balance myself upright, throwing my frame into a bony S. As a result of contractures, one shoulder is higher than the other and I carry one arm bent in front of me, the fingers curled into a claw. My left arm and leg have wasted into pipe-stems, and I try always to keep them covered. When I think about how my body must look to others, especially to men, to whom I have been trained to display myself, I feel ludicrous, even loathsome.

23   At my age, however, I don't spend much time thinking about my appearance. The burning egocentricity of adolescence, which assures one that all the world is looking all the time, has passed, thank God, and I'm generally too caught up in what I'm doing to step back, as I used to, and watch myself as though upon a stage. I'm also too old to believe in the accuracy of self-image. I know that I'm not a hideous crone, that in fact, when I'm rested, well dressed, and well made up, I look fine. The self-loathing I feel is neither physically nor intellectually substantial. What I hate is not me but a disease.

24   I am not a disease.

25   And a disease is not—at least not singlehandedly—going to determine who I am, though at first it seemed to be going to. Adjusting to a chronic incurable illness, I have moved through a process similar to that outlined by Elizabeth Kübler-Ross in *Death and Dying*. The major difference—and it is far more significant than most people recognize—is that I can't be sure of the outcome, as the terminally ill cancer patient can. Research studies indicate that, with proper medical care, I may achieve a "normal" life span. And in our society, with its vision of death as the ultimate evil, worse even than decrepitude, the response to such news is, "Oh, well, at least you're not going to *die*."

26   Are there worse things than dying? I think there may be.

27   I think of two women I know, both with MS, both enough older than I to have served me as models. One took to her bed several years ago and has been there ever since. Although she can sit in a high-backed wheel-chair, because she is incontinent she refuses to go out at all, even though incontinence pants, which are readily available at any pharmacy, could protect her from embarrassment. Instead, she stays at home and insists that her husband, a small quiet man, a retired civil servant, stay there with her except for a quick weekly foray to the supermarket. The other woman, whose illness was diagnosed when she was eighteen, a nursing student engaged to a young doctor, finished her training, married her doctor, accompanied him to Germany when he was in the service, bore three sons and a daughter, now grown and gone. When she can, she travels with her husband; she plays bridge, embroiders, swims regularly; she works, like me, as a symptomatic patient instructor of medical students in neurology.

28   Guess which woman I hope to be.

29   At the beginning, I thought about having MS almost incessantly. And because of the unpredictable course of the disease, my thoughts were always terrified. Each night I'd get into bed wondering whether I'd get out again the next morning, whether I'd be able to see, to speak, to hold a pen between my fingers. Knowing that the day might come when I'd be physically incapable of killing myself, I thought perhaps I ought to do so right away, while I still had the strength. Gradually I came to understand that the Nancy who might one day lie inert under a bedsheet, arms and legs paralyzed, unable to feed or bathe herself, unable to reach out for a gun, a bottle of pills, was not the Nancy I was at present, and that I could not presume to make decisions for that future Nancy, who might well not want in the least to die. Now the only provision I've made for the future Nancy is

that when the time comes—and it is likely to come in the form of pneumonia, friend to the weak and the old—I am not to be treated with machines and medications. If she is unable to communicate by then, I hope she will be satisfied with these terms.

30   Thinking all the time about having MS grew tiresome and intrusive, especially in the large and tragic mode in which I was accustomed to considering my plight. Months and even years went by without catastrophe (at least without one related to MS), and really I was awfully busy, what with George and children and snakes and students and poems, and I hadn't the time, let alone the inclination, to devote myself to being a disease. Too, the richer my life became, the funnier it seemed, as though there were some connection between largesse and laughter, and so my tragic stance began to waver until, even with the aid of a brace and a cane, I couldn't hold it for very long at a time.

31   After several years I was satisfied with my adjustment. I had suffered my grief and fury and terror, I thought, but now I was at ease with my lot. Then one summer day I set out with George and the children across the desert for a vacation in California. Part way to Yuma I became aware that my right leg felt funny. "I think I've had an exacerbation," I told George. "What shall we do?" he asked. "I think we'd better get the hell to California," I said, "because I don't know whether I'll ever make it again." So we went on to San Diego and then to Orange, up the Pacific Coast Highway to Santa Cruz, across to Yosemite, down to Sequoia and Joshua Tree, and so back over the desert to home. It was a fine two-week trip, filled with friends and fair weather, and I wouldn't have missed it for the world, though I did in fact make it back to California two years later. Nor would there have been any point in missing it, since in MS, once the symptoms have appeared, the neurological damage has been done, and there's no way to predict or prevent that damage.

32   The incident spoiled my self-satisfaction, however. I renewed my grief and fury and terror, and I learned that one never finishes adjusting to MS. I don't know now why I thought one would. One does not, after all, finish adjusting to life, and MS is simply a fact of my life—not my favorite fact, of course—but as ordinary as my nose and my tropical fish and my yellow Mazda station wagon. It may at any time get worse, but no amount of worry or anticipation can prepare me for a new loss. My life is a lesson in losses. I learn one at a time.

33   And I had best be patient in the learning, since I'll have to do it like it or not. As any rock fan knows, you can't always get what you want. Particularly when you have MS. You can't, for example, get cured. In recent years researchers and the organizations that fund research have started to pay MS some attention even though it isn't fatal; perhaps they have begun to see that life is something other than a quantitative phenomenon, that one may be very much alive for a very long time in a life that isn't worth living. The researchers have made some progress toward understanding the mechanism of the disease: It may well be an autoimmune reaction triggered by a slow-acting virus. But they are nowhere near its prevention, control, or cure. And most of us want to be cured. Some, unable to accept

incurability, grasp at one treatment after another, no matter how bizarre: megavitamin therapy, gluten-free diet, injections of cobra venom, hypothermal suits, lymphocytopharesis, hyperbaric chambers. Many treatments are probably harmless enough, but none are curative.

34   The absence of a cure often makes MS patients bitter toward their doctors. Doctors are, after all, the priests of modern society, the new shamans, whose business is to heal, and many MS patients rove from one to another, searching for the "good" doctor who will make them well. Doctors too think of themselves as healers, and for this reason many have trouble dealing with MS patients, whose disease in its intransigence defeats their aims and mocks their skills. Too few doctors, it is true, treat their patients as whole human beings, but the reverse is also true. I have always tried to be gentle with my doctors, who often have more at stake in terms of ego than I do. I may be frustrated, maddened, depressed by the incurability of my disease, but I am not diminished by it, and they are. When I push myself up from my seat in the waiting room and stumble toward them, I incarnate the limitation of their powers. The least I can do is refuse to press on their tenderest spots.

35   This gentleness is part of the reason that I'm not sorry to be a cripple. I didn't have it before. Perhaps I'd have developed it anyway—how could I know such a thing?—and I wish I had more of it, but I'm glad of what I have. It has opened and enriched my life enormously, this sense that my frailty and need must be mirrored in others, that in searching for and shaping a stable core in a life wrenched by change and loss, change and loss, I must recognize the same process, under individual conditions, in the lives around me. I do not deprecate such knowledge, however I've come by it.

36   All the same, if a cure were found, would I take it? In a minute. I may be crippled, but I'm only occasionally a loony and never a saint. Anyway, in my brand of theology God doesn't give bonus points for a limp. I'd take a cure; I just don't need one. A friend who also has MS startled me once by asking, "Do you ever say to yourself, 'Why me, Lord?'" "No, Michael, I don't," I told him, "because whenever I try, the only response I can think of is 'Why not?'" If I could make a cosmic deal, who would I put in my place? What in my life would I give up in exchange for sound limbs and a thrilling rush of energy? No one. Nothing. I might as well do the job myself. Now that I'm getting the hang of it.

THINKING ABOUT THE TEXT

1. What is Nancy Mairs' tone in this piece? How does her preference for the term "cripple" exemplify her attitude about her condition?
2. What are the activities still possible for Mairs? What can't she do? What is her attitude toward what she can't do? In what ways is her chosen life compatible with her disease?
3. According to Mairs, what is society's view of people with disabilities? What role models do these people have?

4. What support does Mairs have for maintaining her life? What elements of her personality and character help her? What has she gained as a result of her disease?

WRITING FROM THE TEXT

1. Write a character analysis of Nancy Mairs. Start from a thesis based on your perception of her character and support your thesis with details from the text. (See character analysis section, pp. 436–444.)
2. At the end of a semester, one of Mairs' students wrote a negative comment about the teacher's disability on the student evaluation form. Write an essay in which you analyze the advantages and/or disadvantages of having an instructor with a physical disability.

CONNECTING WITH OTHER TEXTS

1. If your college has a disabled student center, arrange with the director to interview one of the students willing to talk with you. Try to gain from the interview that student's feelings about the best and worst aspects of his or her condition. You might begin by asking how your campus could better meet the needs of students with disabilities.
2. Ben Mattlin ("An Open Letter to Jerry Lewis," p. 214) objects to Lewis' use of the word "cripple." Write an essay in which you argue that certain words (like "cripple," "nigger," "girl,"—you supply others) are acceptable terms, but *only* for in-group use.
3. Do research to determine what your community is doing to improve the lives of disabled people. Limit your essay to one aspect of improvement: accessibility to public buildings, improved employment possibilities, increased visibility in advertising and movies, improved educational opportunities, or any other area that interests you. (See the model research paper, pp. 460–479.)

AN OPEN LETTER TO JERRY LEWIS
Ben Mattlin

Educated in an interdisciplinary program at Harvard University, Ben Mattlin (b. 1962) claims his overall grades "weren't terrific," but he received his professors' high praise for his writing. After college he therefore decided to take the chance of supporting himself for two years as a writer. Although he received his share of rejection slips, he has continued to earn a living with his writing. He has worked as a writer of in-house publications at IBM, has published articles in business and trade journals, has sold the plot for one children's cartoon, has written a novel, and is widely published as a writer of disability-related articles, including a cover story for *Television and Families* that addresses the distorted images of the disabled in television and movies. The article included here first appeared on the opinion page of the *Los Angeles Times* in 1991.

1   Dear Jerry Lewis:

2   I was born with a muscular-dystrophy-related disease, and your Labor Day telethons have always turned my stomach. I actually appeared on one in the late 1960s, as the Muscular Dystrophy Assn. poster child for the New York metropolitan area.

3   Now I am 28, a Harvard graduate, a self-employed writer, married, still in a wheelchair. I can finally formulate what I felt as a child: Despite your undoubtedly honorable intentions, you are sadly misinformed about disabilities. Moreover, you are misleading the able-bodied population while offending the rest of us.

4   You and your organization have done much good, to be sure, and I myself have benefited from your financial resources. But people with disabilities do not need or want to be characterized as objects of pity. Last year's Americans With Disabilities Act mandates our equal participation in society, including employment. What we need is to stress competence—not outmoded notions of charity.

5   Speaking of "the dystrophic child's plight," or calling disability a "curse" reinforces the offensive stereotype that we are victims. Wheelchairs are not "steel imprisonment," nor are who use them "confined" or "bound"; they are liberating aluminum and vinyl vehicles. Similarly, phrases like "dealt a bad hand" and "got in the wrong line" are unfair. Disability is not "bad" or "wrong."

6   Other examples abound: Being dressed or fed by others is a hassle, but not an "indignity." There is no shame in needing others, no loss of dignity. Our needs are more personal and continuing than other people's—nothing to be ashamed of.

7   Saying that they are is to say our lives are somehow inferior. Is this how you feel? You have said our lives are "half"—we must learn to "do things halfway," be good at being "half a person." Even slaves in the Old South counted for three-fifths of a person.

8   Perhaps more disturbing is your use of the archaic word "cripple." While some of us have recently taken it on as a kind of hip slang among ourselves or for polit-

ical purposes—much like the gay-rights group Queer Nation—this does not mean you should.

9   Worse still may be your ubiquitous "Jerry's Kids"—never more absurd than when followed by "of all ages." Yes, a lot of MDA's clients (not necessarily, "patients") are kids, but do you know how hard it is to become, and be treated as, a self-respecting disabled adult in this society? You may argue it is a term of affection, but you wouldn't refer to your late friend Sammy Davis Jr. as your "boy."

10   What's really surprising are your inaccuracies. Your tales of disabled kids being taunted by other kids, for example, do not ring true. Most able-bodied kids whom I knew growing up couldn't wait to push my chair. They would even compete to be "chief wheeler."

11   You further allege that wheelchairs don't fit under restaurant tables, when for years they have come with "desk armrests." And what's this about their not going through metal detectors at airports? Big deal—they're metal! They go around them and are searched separately.

12   At times, you seem to understand. You talk about our right to live with dignity. What that means is access to schools and jobs, equipment like computers and vans, attendants and respect. The MDA can't be responsible for all this. But misleading people—potential employers, potential spouses, and even newly disabled people who don't know any better—only works against these goals.

13   When I was about 6 years old, I was in a full-page magazine ad for the MDA: big blue eyes peeking through blond curls. The caption read, "If I grow up, I want to be a fireman." I didn't want to be a fireman, and knew then my diagnosis called for a normal life expectancy. Confused, I decided that I wasn't really one of "them" and denied a part of my identity, my connection to the only community where I could learn to feel good about my disability. I didn't know the word "exploitation" yet.

14   I realize pity works—last year's telethon raised more money than ever before. And I know some folks think you're a saint. But I also know there were protests at last year's telethon—and will be more—asking why it has taken so long to find a cure and demanding a financial accounting.

15   Perhaps people would not be so upset if the association spoke less about finding a cure and did more to improve our lives as they are. I know MDA does buy wheelchairs and such. But what does it do to make our world more accessible and to promote employment? How many people with disabilities are employed by the organization and its corporate sponsors?

16   Don't get me wrong. Muscular dystrophy can be a killer, and we mourn our brothers and sisters who have died. Yet, despite the impression that one may get watching the telethon, we are not all terminal. And even if you whip MD, you will not end disability. It is here to stay; so are we.

17   Why not, this year, present active, well-adjusted disabled people—not superheroes but normal people—who nonetheless have used or could use financial assistance to achieve their goals of independent living?

18   The harm being done is considerable. A dynamic, young, educated, professional woman I know, who grew up with a disability similar to mine, says she cannot

watch your telethon because it makes her want to kill herself. "Is that what people think of us?" she asks.

19   Your pity campaign is so dispiriting, so destructive, that no matter how many millions you raise, the ends do not justify the means. Why not wield your sizable influence to fight our real enemies? What truly handicaps us most are the obstacles—architectural, financial and attitudinal—erected by others.

THINKING ABOUT THE TEXT

1. What are Mattlin's objections to Jerry Lewis' Labor Day telethons?
2. How has Mattlin personally benefited from the Muscular Dystrophy Association? How has he been exploited by this same group?
3. What specific changes would Mattlin like to see in the MDA and in Lewis' telethons?

WRITING FROM THE TEXT

1. Write an essay in which you define an *ideal* televised fund-raiser. Your thesis should assert what the important elements of your program would be. Reference to Mattlin's points might be part of your support.
2. Write a letter to Mattlin showing your support for his view to have a more balanced telethon, or express your concern that he has shocked a number of sensitive, charity-supporting people into skepticism about donating money to the Muscular Dystrophy Association.

CONNECTING WITH OTHER TEXTS

1. Compare points that Mattlin makes with those made by Nancy Mairs (p. 203). In your essay, show how these writers have similar views of how the disabled should be supported and represented.
2. Mattlin urges Lewis to "present active, well-adjusted disabled people—not superheroes but normal people" on his program. As if in response to the disabled person's longing for role models, advertising now features disabled people. Do research to learn something about these advertising campaigns and include an analysis of some of the specific advertisements as part of your essay.
3. Write an essay about the recent portrayals of the disabled on television and in films. Use descriptive analysis of your examples to show your reader that some portrayals are better than others.

DISCRIMINATION AT LARGE
Jennifer A. Coleman

A graduate of Boston College Law School, Jennifer A. Coleman (b. 1959) is a discrimination and civil rights lawyer in Buffalo, New York. Coleman wrote the essay printed here after seeing the film *Jurassic Park*: "The only bad person in the film is fat, and I'm tired of the stereotyping—which nobody objects to—that makes heavy people objects of ridicule and contempt." In addition to writing legal briefs, pleadings, letters, and a law review article, Coleman teaches constitutional law at Canisius College in Buffalo. The essay printed below first appeared in *Newsweek*, "My Turn," August 2, 1993.

1   Fat is the last preserve for unexamined bigotry. Fat people are lampooned without remorse or apology on television, by newspaper columnists, in cartoons, you name it. The overweight are viewed as suffering from moral turpitude and villainy, and since we are at fault for our condition, no tolerance is due. All fat people are "outed" by their appearance.

2   Weight-motivated assaults occur daily and are committed by people who would die before uttering anti-gay slogans or racial epithets. Yet these same people don't hesitate to scream "move your fat ass" when we cross in front of them.

3   Since the time I first ventured out to play with the neighborhood kids, I was told over and over that I was lazy and disgusting. Strangers, adults, classmates offered gratuitous comments with such frequency and urgency that I started to believe them. Much later I needed to prove it wasn't so. I began a regimen of swimming, cycling and jogging that put all but the most compulsive to shame. I ate only cottage cheese, brown rice, fake butter and steamed everything. I really believed I could infiltrate the ranks of the nonfat and thereby establish my worth.

4   I would prove that I was not just a slob, a blimp, a pig. I would finally escape the unsolicited remarks of strangers ranging from the "polite"—"You would really be pretty if you lost weight"—to the hostile ("Lose weight, you fat slob"). Of course, sometimes more subtle commentary sufficed: oinking, mooing, staring, laughing and pointing. Simulating a fog-horn was also popular.

5   My acute exercise phase had many positive points. I was mingling with my obsessively athletic peers. My pulse was as low as anyone's, my cholesterol levels in the basement, my respiration barely detectable. I could swap stats from my last physical with anyone. Except for weight. No matter how hard I tried to run, swim or cycle away from it, my weight found me. Oh sure, I lost weight (never enough) and it inevitably tracked me down and adhered to me more tenaciously than ever. I lived and breathed "Eat to win," "Feel the burn." But in the end I was fit and still fat.

6   I learned that by societal, moral, ethical, soap-operatical, vegetable, political definition, it was impossible to be both fit and fat. Along the way to that knowledge, what I got for my trouble was to be hit with objects from moving cars because I dared to ride my bike in public, and to be mocked by diners at outdoor

cafés who trumpeted like a herd of elephants as I jogged by. Incredibly, it was not uncommon for one of them to shout: "Lose some weight, you pig." Go figure.

7   It was confusing for awhile. How was it I was still lazy, weak, despised, a slug and a cow if I exercised every waking minute? This confusion persisted until I finally realized: it didn't matter what I did. I was and always would be the object of sport, derision, antipathy and hostility so long as I stayed in my body. I immediately signed up for a body transplant. I am still waiting for a donor.

8   Until then, I am more settled because I have learned the hard way what thin people have known for years. There simply are some things that fat people must never do. Like: riding a bike ("Hey lady, where's the seat?"), eating in a public place ("No dessert for me, I don't want to look like her"). And the most unforgivable crime: wearing a bathing suit in public ("Whale on the beach!").

9   Things are less confusing now that I know that the nonfat are superior to me, regardless of their personal habits, health, personalities, cholesterol levels or the time they log on the couch. And, as obviously superior to me as they are, it is their destiny to remark on my inferiority regardless of who I'm with, whether they know me, whether it hurts my feelings. I finally understand that the thin have a divine mandate to steal self-esteem from fat people, who have no right to it in the first place.

10   Fat people aren't really jolly. Sometimes we act that way so you will leave us alone. We pay a price for this. But at least we get to hang on to what self-respect we smuggled out of grade school and adolescence.

11   Hating fat people is not inborn; it has to be nurtured and developed. Fortunately, it's taught from the moment most of us are able to walk and speak. We learn it through Saturday-morning cartoons, prime-time TV and movies. Have you ever seen a fat person in a movie who wasn't evil, disgusting, pathetic or lampooned? Santa Claus doesn't count.

12   Kids catch on early to be sensitive to the feelings of gay, black, disabled, elderly and speech-impaired people. At the same time, they learn that fat people are fair game. That we are always available for their personal amusement.

13   The media, legal system, parents, teachers and peers respond to most types of intolerance with outrage and protest. Kids hear that employers can be sued for discriminating, that political careers can be destroyed and baseball owners can lose their teams as a consequence of racism, sexism or almost any other "ism."

14   But the fat kid is taught that she deserves to be mocked. She is not OK. Only if she loses weight will she be OK. Other kids see the response and incorporate the message. Small wonder some (usually girls) get it into their heads that they can never be thin enough.

15   I know a lot about prejudice, even though I am a white, middle-class, professional woman. The worst discrimination I have suffered because of my gender is nothing compared to what I experience daily because of my weight. I am sick of it. The jokes and attitudes are as wrong and damaging as any racial or ethnic slur. The passive acceptance of this inexcusable behavior is sometimes worse than the

initial assault. Some offensive remarks can be excused as the shortcomings of jackasses. But the tacit acceptance of their conduct by mainstream America tells the fat person that the intolerance is understandable and acceptable. Well it isn't.

THINKING ABOUT THE TEXT

1. Jennifer Coleman's focus is evident from the first paragraph of her essay. After you have read the entire essay, what do you assume is her thesis or complete assertion?
2. What is the author's personal history, and how does knowing her background contribute to your understanding of her point?
3. *Are* the jokes and slurs about overweight people "as wrong and damaging as any racial or ethnic slur"?
4. Examine Coleman's word choice in this essay. Which words and expressions specifically contribute to her making her point powerfully?
5. What are *your* feelings as you read the comments that people have made to and about Coleman?

WRITING FROM THE TEXT

1. Write an essay arguing that discrimination against the overweight is "as wrong and damaging as any racial or ethnic slur." You will want to anticipate and counter the objection that people don't *have* to be overweight.
2. Describe the character traits, habits, and values of an overweight person you know. Let the description in your essay *show* what kinds of discrimination and problems your subject has faced.

CONNECTING WITH OTHER TEXTS

1. In her essay "On Being a Cripple" (p. 203), Nancy Mairs describes some of the problems the disabled woman faces in developing self-esteem. In an analytical essay about discrimination, compare the points that Mairs and Coleman make.
2. Use Heilbroner's essay on stereotyping (p. 429) as a definitive starting point for a descriptive essay on the discrimination that overweight people experience. You might contrast specific stereotypical depictions of overweight people in films and on television with an overweight person you know.

BODILY HARM

Pamela Erens

A 1985 graduate of Yale University, Pamela Erens (b. 1963) has worked as an editor and staff writer for *Connecticut Magazine* and her reviews and articles have appeared in many magazines and newspapers. In addition to writing fiction, Erens currently is an editor at *Glamour* magazine. The essay included here was first published in *Ms.* in 1985, when Erens interned there the summer after her graduation.

1   "Before I'd even heard of bulimia," said Gloria, "I happened to read an article in *People* magazine on Cherry Boone—how she'd used laxatives and vomiting to control her weight. I thought: Wow, what a great idea! I was sure that I would never lose control of my habit."

2   Recent media attention to the binge-purge and self-starvation disorders known as bulimia and anorexia—often detailing gruesome particulars of women's eating behavior—may have exacerbated this serious problem on college campuses. But why would a woman who reads an article on eating disorders want to copy what she reads? Ruth Striegel-Moore, Ph.D., director of Yale University's Eating Disorders Clinic, suggests that eating disorders may be a way to be like other "special" women and at the same time strive to outdo them. "The pursuit of thinness is a way for women to compete with each other, a way that avoids being threatening to men," says Striegel-Moore. Eating disorders as a perverse sort of rivalry? In Carol's freshman year at SUNY-Binghamton, a roommate showed her how to make herself throw up. "Barf buddies" are notorious on many college campuses, especially in sororities and among sports teams. Eating disorders as negative bonding? Even self-help groups on campus can degenerate into the kinds of competitiveness and negative reinforcement that are among the roots of eating disorders in the first place.

3   This is not another article on how women do it. It is an article on how and why some women stopped. The decision to get help is not always an easy one. The shame and secrecy surrounding most eating disorders and the fear or being labeled "sick" may keep a woman from admitting even to herself that her behavior is hurting her. "We're not weirdos," says Nancy Gengler, a recovered bulimic and number two U.S. squash champion, who asked that I use her real name because "so much of this illness has to do with secrecy and embarrassment." In the first stages of therapy, says Nancy, much of getting better was a result of building up the strength to (literally) "sweat out" the desire to binge and to endure the discomfort of having overeaten rather than throwing up. "I learned to accept such 'failures' and moreover, that they would not make me fat. . . ."

4   Secret shame or college fad, eating disorders among college women are growing at an alarming rate: in a recent study at Wellesley College; more than half the women on campus felt they needed help to correct destructive eating patterns. These included bingeing, chronic dieting, and "aerobic nervosa," the excessive use of exercise to maintain one's body ideal—in most women, invariably five to 10 pounds less than whatever she currently weighs.

5   Why now? Wasn't the Women's Movement supposed to free women to be any body size, to explore the full range of creative and emotional possibilities?

Instead, women in epidemic numbers are developing symptoms that make them feel hopeless about the future, depleting the energy they have for schoolwork and other activities, and if serious enough, send them right back home or into the infantalizing condition of hospitalization. What has gone wrong?

6   For Brenda, college meant the freedom to question her mother's values about sex. But when she abandoned her mother's guidelines, "I went to the other extreme. I couldn't set limits about sex, food, or anything else." The pressure on college women to appear successful and in control, to know what they want among the myriad new choices they are offered, is severe. So much so that many choose internal havoc over external imperfection. Naomi, a bulimic student at Ohio State University, said she would rather be alcoholic like her father than overweight like her mother because "fat is something you can see."

7   One reason college women hesitate to enter therapy, says Stephen Zimmer, director of the Center for the Study of Anorexia and Bulimia in New York City, is that the eating disorder has become a coping mechanism. It allows the person to function when she feels rotten inside. "In the first session," says Zimmer, "I tell my patients: 'I'm not going to try to take your eating behavior away from you. Until you find something that works better, you get to keep it.' Their relief is immense."

8   Brenda at first did not even tell the counselor whom she was seeing that she was bulimic. She started therapy because of a series of affairs with abusive men. As Brenda developed the sense that she had a right to say no to harmful relationships and to make demands on others, her inability to say no to food also disappeared.

9   However, if a woman is vomiting three times a day, she may be unable to concentrate on long-term therapy. Behavioral therapy, which directly addresses the learned habit of bingeing and purging, is a more immediate alternative. For eight years, Marlene Boskind White, Ph.D., and her husband, William White, Jr., Ph.D., ran weekend workshops for bulimic women at Cornell University, usually as an adjunct to other forms of therapy. The sessions included nutritional counseling, developing techniques of dealing with binge "triggers," feminist consciousness-raising, and examining the hidden "payoffs" that keep a woman from changing her eating behavior. Boskind-White and White report that a follow-up of 300 women they had treated one to three years earlier showed that 70 percent had entirely stopped purging and drastically reduced their bingeing.

10   Group therapy (an increasingly popular resource on college campuses) may be the first time a woman realizes she is not alone with her problem. Rebecca Axelrod, who was bulimic throughout college, and now counsels bulimics herself, found that joining the Cornell workshop and meeting other bulimic women defused many of her fears about herself: "I saw ten other women who were not mentally ill, not unable to function," Axelrod says. She remembers the moment when she understood the meaning of her bingeing and purging. "Saturday afternoon, Marlene took the women off alone, and we discussed the 'superwoman syndrome'—that attempt to be the perfect friend, lover, hostess, student . . . and perfect-looking. And bingeing, I saw, was my form of *defiance*. But if you're living life as the perfect woman, you won't cuss, you won't get drunk or laid or drive too fast. No, in the privacy of your own room you'll eat yourself out of house and home. But how dare you be defiant? And so you punish yourself by throwing it up."

11   But "groups can fall into a cycle I call 'bigger and badder,'" says Axelrod. "It starts when one person comes in and says, 'I feel terrible, I binged yesterday.' Somebody else says: 'Oh, that's okay, so did I.' Then a third person says: 'That's nothing, did you know I. . . .' Pretty soon everyone is lending support to the binge instead of to the woman who needs ways of coping with it."

12   However, Axelrod feels that there is much potential for women to help one another. She encourages bulimics to ask for help from their friends, saying that while she herself was initially frightened that being open about her bulimia would alienate her friends, most were very supportive. "The important thing," says Axelrod, "is to be specific about what you need. Don't say: 'Be there for me.' Tell a friend exactly what she can do: for instance, not to urge you to go out for pizza if you tell her you're feeling vulnerable. And rely on three friends, not one."

13   One of the most important strategies in treating eating disorders, says Dr. Lee Combrinck-Graham of the newly opened Renfrew Center for anorectics and bulimics in Philadelphia, is breaking old patterns. Renfrew is a residential center that houses patients for between three weeks and two months, a period that can give women with eating disorders a respite from repetitive and destructive habits that are reinforced by the college environment. But Renfrew is not a "retreat"; its residents work hard. They participate in therapy workshops, take seminars in assertiveness-training and women's issues, and even participate in "new attitude" cooking classes. Dr. Combrinck-Graham stresses that therapy itself has often become a "pattern" for women who come to Renfrew. . . . Many of Renfrew's patients, says Dr. Combrinck-Graham, can say exactly what's "wrong" with them and why, yet are still unable to control their eating habits. Renfrew combines a philosophy that recovery is the patient's responsibility—she sets her own goals and contracts for as much supervision as she needs—with innovative art and movement therapy that may bypass some of the rationalizations that block the progress of "talking" therapies.

14   Women who live close to home and whose parents are not separated may want to try family therapy. Family therapy considers the family itself, not the daughter with an eating disorder, to be the "patient." Often, the daughter has taken on the role of diverting attention from unacknowledged conflicts within the family. Family therapists behave somewhat like manic stage managers, interrupting and quizzing various members of a family, orchestrating confrontations in an attempt to expose and demolish old, rigid patterns of relating. Ideally, family therapy benefits all the members of the family. Carol, the student at SUNY-Binghamton, said that family therapy revealed how unhappy her mother was as a homemaker in a traditional Italian family.

15   Situations like Carol's are at the heart of today's epidemic of eating disorders, argues Kim Chernin in her book *The Hungry Self: Women, Eating, and Identity.* Chernin claims that today's college woman is the heir of a particular cultural moment that turns her hunger for identity into an uncontrollable urge for bodily nourishment. Young women of an earlier generation were educated to have children and remain in the home, yet our culture devalued the work they did there. Later, the Women's Movement opened up vast new emotional and career possibil-

ities, and many daughters, on the verge of achieving their mother's suppressed dreams, are struck by panic and guilt.

16   Carol agreed: "I would try to push my mother to take classes, but my father was always against it. I was a good student, but how could I keep on getting smarter than my mother? When I was young, we'd been like one person. I wanted to be a homemaker because she was one. But when I got older, I said to myself: 'This woman has no life. She never leaves the house except to get groceries. And she's miserable.' I wanted to stop growing up, and then she would always be able to lead me and guide me." According to Chernin, an eating disorder may be a way to postpone or put an end to one's development, one's need to choose, the possibility of surpassing one's mother. In a world hostile to the values of closeness and nurturance women learn from and associate with the mother-daughter relationship, an eating disorder can disguise a desire to return to the "nourishment" of that early bond.

17   And why do the daughter's problems focus around food? As Chernin reminds us, originally with her milk, the mother *is* food. Femininity itself has historically been associated with food gathering and preparation. Food—eating it, throwing it up—can become a powerful means of expressing aspects of the mother's life or of traditionally defined femininity that the daughter is trying to ingest or reject. And relationships with other women later in life can replicate this early pattern: food mediates hostility and love.

18   Whatever forms of therapy prove most helpful for women with eating disorders, it is clear that therapy is only half the battle. The Stone Center for Developmental Services and Studies at Wellesley College recognizes the need for early prevention and is preparing a film for adolescents that will feature women and health professionals speaking about the uses and abuses of food in our culture. Janet Surrey, Ph.D., a research associate at the center, stresses the need to educate girls in the 10- to 15-year-old age bracket—66 percent of whom already diet—about the psychological, physical, and reproductive danger of dieting and excessive thinness. Nutritional counseling is another imperative. But to Kim Chernin, our first priority is outreach centers and school programs that will provide developmental counseling and feminist consciousness-raising for this crucial pre–high school group. If women could learn early on to confront their conflicts over their right to development, the use of power, and their place in a still male-dominated world, there might no longer be a need for the "silent language" of eating disorders.

THINKING ABOUT THE TEXT

1. According to Erens, how has popular press coverage of eating disorders exacerbated the problem?

2. According to Rebecca Axelrod, who is quoted in Erens' review, how does the "superwoman syndrome" contribute to the problem of recognizing and treating eating disorders?

3. How can group therapy sessions, frequently joined by people with eating disorders, actually complicate the treatment?

4. What is Kim Chernin's perception of one cause of eating disorders?

5. What is proposed to stop the increasing number of young women with eating disorders?

WRITING FROM THE TEXT

1. Do you think that women compete with each other by pursuing thinness? Do you think women bond in an effort to achieve thinness? Write an essay in which you describe and analyze the eating patterns of women you know.

2. Argue that the cause of eating disorders is not based in the mother-daughter relationship but in the superthin images in advertising. Cite and *describe* specific examples of advertising to support your view.

CONNECTING WITH OTHER TEXTS

1. Pamela Erens, Naomi Wolf ("The Beauty Myth," p. 101), and Jennifer Coleman ("Discrimination at Large," p. 217) describe the kinds of harm that can be done to women who try to conform to a standardized concept of beauty. In an analysis essay, examine the problem by connecting the ideas expressed by these three writers.

2. This article, published in 1985, gives a good review of eating problems, but new information may provide increased or different insights. Use Erens' essay as a model but use more current material to analyze the problem of eating disorders.

3. Read Kim Chernin's 1981 study of eating disorders, *The Obsession*, or at least read Chapter 9. In this chapter, Chernin argues that males' preference for "little girls" contributes to eating disorders in women. Chernin cites films like *Taxi Driver, Manhattan,* and *The Little Girl Who Lives Down the Lane* as evidence. Argue to support or refute Chernin's point about males' preference for "little girls" with your own evidence.

4. Read the chapter called "Hunger" in Naomi Wolf's *The Beauty Myth*, published in 1991. Analyze the support she offers for her thesis: "Women must claim anorexia as political damage done to us by a social order that considers our destruction insignificant because of what we are—less. We should identify it as Jews identify the death camps, as homosexuals identify AIDS: as a disgrace that is not our own, but that of an inhumane social order. . . . To be anorexic or bulimic *is* to be a political prisoner" (208).

BLACK MEN AND PUBLIC SPACE
Brent Staples

After earning his Ph.D. in psychology from the University of Chicago, Brent Staples (b. 1951) worked at the *Chicago Sun-Times* and wrote for other periodicals.
He became an assistant metropolitan editor of the *New York Times* in 1985, and he
is presently on that paper's editorial board. His book *Parallel Time: A Memoir* was
published in 1991. The essay included here was first published in the September
1986 issue of *Ms.* magazine as one article in a section on men's perspectives.

1   My first victim was a woman—white, well dressed, probably in her early twenties. I came upon her late one evening on a deserted street in Hyde Park, a relatively affluent neighborhood in an otherwise mean, impoverished section of
Chicago. As I swung onto the avenue behind her, there seemed to be a discreet,
uninflammatory distance between us. Not so. She cast back a worried glance. To
her, the youngish black man—a broad six feet two inches with a beard and billowing hair, both hands shoved into the pockets of a bulky military jacket—
seemed menacingly close. After a few more quick glimpses, she picked up her
pace and was soon running in earnest. Within seconds she disappeared into a cross
street.

2   That was more than a decade ago. I was twenty-two years old, a graduate student newly arrived at the University of Chicago. It was in the echo of that terrified
woman's footfalls that I first began to know the unwieldy inheritance I'd come
into—the ability to alter public space in ugly ways. It was clear that she thought
herself the quarry of a mugger, a rapist, or worse. Suffering a bout of insomnia,
however, I was stalking sleep, not defenseless wayfarers. As a softy who is scarcely able to take a knife to a raw chicken—let alone hold it to a person's throat—I
was surprised, embarrassed, and dismayed all at once. Her flight made me feel
like an accomplice in tyranny. It also made it clear that I was indistinguishable
from the muggers who occasionally seeped into the area from the surrounding
ghetto. That first encounter, and those that followed, signified that a vast, unnerving gulf lay between nighttime pedestrians—particularly women—and me. And I
soon gathered that being perceived as dangerous is a hazard in itself. I only needed to turn a corner into a dicey situation, or crowd some frightened, armed person
in a foyer somewhere, or make an errant move after being pulled over by a policeman. Where fear and weapons meet—and they often do in urban America—there
is always the possibility of death.

3   In that first year, my first away from my hometown, I was to become thoroughly familiar with the language of fear. At dark, shadowy intersections in Chicago, I
could cross in front of a car stopped at a traffic light and elicit the *thunk, thunk,
thunk, thunk* of the driver—black, white, male, or female—hammering down the
door locks. On less traveled streets after dark, I grew accustomed to but never
comfortable with people who crossed to the other side of the street rather than
pass me. Then there were the standard unpleasantries with police, doormen,

bouncers, cab drivers, and others whose business it is to screen out troublesome individuals *before* there is any nastiness.

4   I moved to New York nearly two years ago and I have remained an avid night walker. In central Manhattan, the near-constant crowd cover minimizes tense one-on-one street encounters. Elsewhere—visiting friends in SoHo, where sidewalks are narrow and tightly spaced buildings shut out the sky—things can get very taut indeed.

5   Black men have a firm place in New York mugging literature. Norman Podhoretz in his famed (or infamous) 1963 essay, "My Negro Problem—And Ours," recalls growing up in terror of black males, they "were tougher than we were, more ruthless," he writes—and as an adult on the Upper West Side of Manhattan, he continues, he cannot constrain his nervousness when he meets black men on certain streets. Similarly, a decade later, the essayist and novelist Edward Hoagland extols a New York where once "Negro bitterness bore down mainly on other Negroes." Where some see mere panhandlers, Hoagland sees "a mugger who is clearly screwing up his nerve to do more than just *ask* for money." But Hoagland has "the New Yorker's quick-hunch posture for broken-field maneuvering," and the bad guy swerves away.

6   I often witness that "hunch posture," from women after dark on the warrenlike streets of Brooklyn where I live. They seem to set their faces on neutral and, with their purse straps strung across their chests bandolier style, they forge ahead as though bracing themselves against being tackled. I understand, of course, that the danger they perceive is not a hallucination. Women are particularly vulnerable to street violence, and young black males are drastically overrepresented among the perpetrators of that violence. Yet these truths are no solace against the kind of alienation that comes of being ever the suspect, against being set apart, a fearsome entity with whom pedestrians avoid making eye contact.

7   It is not altogether clear to me how I reached the ripe old age of twenty-two without being conscious of the lethality nighttime pedestrians attributed to me. Perhaps it was because in Chester, Pennsylvania, the small, angry industrial town where I came of age in the 1960s, I was scarcely noticeable against a backdrop of gang warfare, street knifings, and murders. I grew up one of the good boys, had perhaps a half-dozen fist fights. In retrospect, my shyness of combat has clear sources.

8   Many things go into the making of a young thug. One of those things is the consummation of the male romance with the power to intimidate. An infant discovers that random flailings send the baby bottle flying out of the crib and crashing to the floor. Delighted, the joyful babe repeats those motions again and again, seeking to duplicate the feat. Just so, I recall the points at which some of my boyhood friends were finally seduced by the perception of themselves as tough guys. When a mark cowered and surrendered his money without resistance, myth and reality merged—and paid off. It is, after all, only manly to embrace the power to frighten and intimidate. We, as men, are not supposed to give an inch of our lane on the highway; we are to seize the fighter's edge in work and in play and even in love; we are to be valiant in the face of hostile forces.

9   Unfortunately, poor and powerless young men seem to take all this nonsense literally. As a boy, I saw countless tough guys locked away; I have since buried several, too. They were babies, really—a teenage cousin, a brother of twenty-two, a childhood friend in his mid-twenties—all gone down in episodes of bravado played out in the streets. I came to doubt the virtues of intimidation early on. I chose, perhaps even unconsciously, to remain a shadow—timid, but a survivor.

10   The fearsomeness mistakenly attributed to me in public places often has a perilous flavor. The most frightening of these confusions occurred in the late 1970s and early 1980s when I worked as a journalist in Chicago. One day, rushing into the office of a magazine I was writing for with a deadline story in hand, I was mistaken for a burglar. The office manager called security and, with an ad hoc posse, pursued me through the labyrinthine halls, nearly to my editor's door. I had no way of proving who I was. I could only move briskly toward the company of someone who knew me.

11   Another time I was on assignment for a local paper and killing time before an interview. I entered a jewelry store on the city's affluent Near North Side. The proprietor excused herself and returned with an enormous red Doberman pinscher straining at the end of a leash. She stood, the dog extended toward me, silent to my questions, her eyes bulging nearly out of her head. I took a cursory look around, nodded, and bade her good night. Relatively speaking, however, I never fared as badly as another black male journalist. He went to nearby Waukegan, Illinois, a couple of summers ago to work on a story about a murderer who was born there. Mistaking the reporter for the killer, police hauled him from his car at gunpoint and but for his press credentials would probably have tried to book him. Such episodes are not uncommon. Black men trade tales like this all the time.

12   In "My Negro Problem—And Ours," Podhoretz writes that the hatred he feels for blacks makes itself known to him through a variety of avenues—one being his discomfort with that "special brand of paranoid touchiness" to which he says blacks are prone. No doubt he is speaking here of black men. In time, I learned to smother the rage I felt at so often being taken for a criminal. Not to do so would surely have led to madness—via that special "paranoid touchiness" that so annoyed Podhoretz at the time he wrote the essay.

13   I began to take precautions to make myself less threatening. I move about with care, particularly late in the evening. I give a wide berth to nervous people on subway platforms during the wee hours, particularly when I have exchanged business clothes for jeans. If I happen to be entering a building behind some people who appear skittish, I may walk by, letting them clear the lobby before I return, so as not to seem to be following them. I have been calm and extremely congenial on those rare occasions when I've been pulled over by the police.

14   And on late-evening constitutionals along streets less traveled by, I employ what has proved to be an excellent tension-reducing measure: I whistle melodies from Beethoven and Vivaldi and the more popular classical composers. Even steely New Yorkers hunching toward nighttime destinations seem to relax, and occasionally they even join in the tune. Virtually everybody seems to sense that a

mugger wouldn't be warbling bright, sunny selections from Vivaldi's *Four Seasons.* It is my equivalent of the cowbell that hikers wear when they know they are in bear country.

THINKING ABOUT THE TEXT

1. What is the effect on the reader of Staples' opening paragraph? How does it function to underscore the point of his essay?

2. In what places is Staples' effect on people related to his being Black? Where is his maleness and/or stature a threat? Which aspect of his physiology does Staples believe is more threatening?

3. How has Staples adjusted his life to make himself less intimidating?

WRITING FROM THE TEXT

1. Write about a time when you unwittingly threatened someone. Describe the occasion using Staples' essay as a model, so that your reader can see and *hear* ("thunk, thunk, thunk, thunk") the scene.

2. Write an essay in which you describe the problems of being stereotyped as a member of a group which threatens. What, if anything, have you done to counter or handle the dangerously charged or uncomfortable environment?

3. Write an essay describing the problem of being threatened by a group or a member of a group that you perceive as intimidating. What have you done to avoid feeling intimidated or threatened?

CONNECTING WITH OTHER TEXTS

1. Compare Staples' described behavior with that of Latino, African-American, and gay men that Kimmel and Levine describe (in "A Hidden Factor in AIDS," p. 78). In your comparative essay, analyze the sources of the problem and, in your conclusion, decide if a solution is possible.

2. Find periodical articles that feature the stories of African Americans or Hispanics who have been stereotyped by the police, bouncers, or doormen as "muggers," criminals, gang members. Write an essay that uses the specific examples in the articles for support.

THE ATLANTA RIOT
Walter White

Born one of seven children to an Atlanta, Georgia, letter carrier and former teacher, the blond, blue-eyed son of light-skinned Black parents observed that people treated him in different ways, depending on what they assumed about his racial identity. An essayist, novelist, and autobiographer, Walter White (1893–1955) is noted for his portrayals of middle-class African Americans and the effects of racism on their lives. He is known for his early (1920–1950) studies of civil rights movements, and he gained a reputation as an undercover investigator and writer revealing the identity of participants in mob violence. The essay included here was published in 1948 in *A Man Called White*.

1   There were nine light-skinned Negroes in my family: mother, father, five sisters, an older brother, George, and myself. The house in which I discovered what it meant to be a Negro was located on Houston Street, three blocks from the Candler Building, Atlanta's first skyscraper, which bore the name of the ex-drug clerk who had become a millionaire from the sale of Coca-Cola. Below us lived none but Negroes; toward town all but a very few were white. Ours was an eight-room, two-story frame house which stood out in its surroundings not because of its opulence but by contrast with the drabness and unpaintedness of the other dwellings in a deteriorating neighborhood.

2   Only Father kept his house painted, the picket fence repaired, the board fence separating our place from those on either side white-washed, the grass neatly trimmed, and flower beds abloom. Mother's passion for neatness was even more pronounced and it seemed to me that I was always the victim of her determination to see no single blade of grass longer than the others or any one of the pickets in the front fence less shiny with paint than its mates. This spic-and-spanness became increasingly apparent as the rest of the neighborhood became more down-at-heel, and resulted, as we were to learn, in sullen envy among some of our white neighbors. It was the violent expression of that resentment against a Negro family neater than themselves which set the pattern of our lives.

3   On a day in September 1906, when I was thirteen, we were taught that there is no isolation from life. The unseasonably oppressive heat of an Indian summer day hung like a steaming blanket over Atlanta. My sisters and I had casually commented upon the unusual quietness. It seemed to stay Mother's volubility and reduced Father, who was more taciturn, to monosyllables. But, as I remember it, no other sense of impending trouble impinged upon our consciousness.

4   I had read the inflammatory headlines in the *Atlanta News* and the more restrained ones in the *Atlanta Constitution* which reported alleged rapes and other crimes committed by Negroes. But these were so standard and familiar that they made—as I look back on it now—little impression. The stories were more frequent, however, and consisted of eight-column streamers instead of the usual two- or four-column ones.

5   Father was a mail collector. His tour of duty was from three to eleven P.M. He made his rounds in a little cart into which one climbed from a step in the rear. I used

to drive the cart for him from two until seven, leaving him at the point nearest our home on Houston Street, to return home either for study or sleep. That day Father decided that I should not go with him. I appealed to Mother, who thought it might be all right, provided Father sent me home before dark because, she said, "I don't think they would dare start anything before nightfall." Father told me as we made the rounds that ominous rumors of a race riot that night were sweeping the town. . . .

6   During the afternoon preceding the riot little bands of sullen evil-looking men talked excitedly on street corners all over downtown Atlanta. Around seven o'clock my father and I were driving toward a mail box at the corner of Peachtree and Houston Streets when there came from near-by Pryor Street a roar the like of which I had never heard before, but which sent a sensation of mingled fear and excitement coursing through my body. I asked permission of Father to go and see what the trouble was. He bluntly ordered me to stay in the cart. A little later we drove down Atlanta's main business thoroughfare, Peachtree Street. Again we heard the terrifying cries, this time near at hand and coming toward us. We saw a lame Negro bootblack from Herndon's barber shop pathetically trying to outrun a mob of whites. Less than a hundred yards from us the chase ended. We saw clubs and fists descending to the accompaniment of savage shouting and cursing. Suddenly a voice cried, "There goes another nigger!" Its work done, the mob went after new prey. The body with the withered foot lay dead in a pool of blood on the street.

7   Father's apprehension and mine steadily increased during the evening, although the fact that our skins were white kept us from attack. Another circumstance favored us—the mob had not yet grown violent enough to attack United States government property. But I could see Father's relief when he punched the time clock at eleven P.M. and got into the cart to go home. He wanted to go the back way down Forsyth Street, but I begged him, in my childish excitement and ignorance, to drive down Marietta to Five Points, the heart of Atlanta's business district, where the crowds were densest and the yells loudest. No sooner had we turned into Marietta Street, however, than we saw careening toward us an undertaker's barouche. Crouched in the rear of the vehicle were three Negroes clinging to the sides of the carriage as it lunged and swerved. On the driver's seat crouched a white man, the reins held taut in his left hand. A huge whip was gripped in his right. Alternately he lashed the horses and, without looking backward, swung the whip in savage swoops in the faces of members of the mob as they lunged at the carriage determined to seize the three Negroes.

8   There was no time for us to get out of its path, so sudden and swift was the appearance of the vehicle. The hub cap of the right rear wheel of the barouche hit the right side of our much lighter wagon. Father and I instinctively threw our weight and kept the cart from turning completely over. Our mare was a Texas mustang which, frightened by the sudden blow, lunged in the air as Father clung to the reins. Good fortune was with us. The cart settled back on its four wheels as Father said in a voice which brooked no dissent, "We are going home the back way and not down Marietta."

9   But again on Pryor Street we heard the cry of the mob. Close to us and in our direction ran a stout and elderly woman who cooked at a downtown white hotel. Fifty yards behind, a mob which filled the street from curb to curb was closing in.

Father handed the reins to me and, though he was of slight stature, reached down and lifted the woman into the cart. I did not need to be told to lash the mare to the fastest speed she could muster.

10   The church bells tolled the next morning for Sunday service. But no one in Atlanta believed for a moment that the hatred and lust for blood had been appeased. Like skulls on a cannibal's hut the hats and caps of victims of the mob the night before had been hung on the iron hooks of telegraph poles. None could tell whether each hat represented a dead Negro. But we knew that some of those who had worn hats would never again wear any.

11   Later in the afternoon friends of my father's came to warn of more trouble that night. They told us that plans had been perfected for a mob to form on Peachtree Street just after nightfall to march down Houston Street to what the white people called "Darktown," three blocks or so below our house, to "clean out the niggers." There had never been a firearm in our house before that day. Father was reluctant even in those circumstances to violate the law, but he at last gave in at Mother's insistence.

12   We turned out the lights, as did all our neighbors. No one removed his clothes or thought of sleep. Apprehension was tangible. We could almost touch its cold and clammy surface. Toward midnight the unnatural quiet was broken by a roar that grew steadily in volume. Even today I grow tense in remembering it.

13   Father told Mother to take my sisters, the youngest of them only six, to the rear of the house, which offered more protection from stones and bullets. My brother George was away, so Father and I, the only males in the house, took our places at the front windows. The windows opened on a porch along the front side of the house, which in turn gave onto a narrow lawn that sloped down to the street and a picket fence. There was a crash as Negroes smashed the street lamp at the corner of Houston and Piedmont Avenue down the street. In a very few minutes the vanguard of the mob, some of them bearing torches, appeared. A voice which we recognized as that of the son of the grocer with whom we had traded for many years yelled, "That's where that nigger mail carrier lives! Let's burn it down! It's too nice for a nigger to live in!" In the eerie light Father turned his drawn face toward me. In a voice as quiet as though he were asking me to pass him the sugar at the breakfast table, he said, "Son, don't shoot until the first man puts his foot on the lawn and then—don't you miss!"

14   In the flickering light the mob swayed, paused, and began to flow toward us. In that instant there opened within me a great awareness; I knew then who I was. I was a Negro, a human being with an invisible pigmentation which marked me a person to be hunted, hanged, abused, discriminated against, kept in poverty and ignorance, in order that those whose skin was white would have readily at hand a proof of their superiority, a proof patent and inclusive, accessible to the moron and the idiot as well as to the wise man and the genius. No matter how low a white man fell, he could always hold fast to the smug conviction that he was superior to two-thirds of the world's population, for those two-thirds were not white.

15   It made no difference how intelligent or talented my millions of brothers and I were, or how virtuously we lived. A curse like that of Judas was upon us, a mark of degradation fashioned with heavenly authority. There were white men who said

Negroes had no souls, and who proved it by the Bible. Some of these now were approaching us, intent upon burning our house.

16   Theirs was a world of contrasts in values: superior and inferior, profit and loss, cooperative and noncooperative, civilized and aboriginal, white and black. If you were on the wrong end of the comparison, if you were inferior, if you were non-cooperative, if you were aboriginal, if you were black, then you were marked for excision, expulsion, or extinction. I was a Negro; I was therefore that part of history which opposed the good, the just, and the enlightened. I was a Persian, falling before the hordes of Alexander. I was a Carthaginian, extinguished by the Legions of Rome. I was a Frenchman at Waterloo, an Anglo-Saxon at Hastings, a Confederate at Vicksburg. I was defeated, wherever and whenever there was a defeat.

17   Yet as a boy there in the darkness amid the tightening fright, I knew the inexplicable thing—that my skin was as white as the skin of those who were coming at me.

18   The mob moved toward the lawn. I tried to aim my gun, wondering what it would feel like to kill a man. Suddenly there was a volley of shots. The mob hesitated, stopped. Some friends of my father's had barricaded themselves in a two-story brick building just below our house. It was they who had fired. Some of the mobsmen, still bloodthirsty, shouted, "Let's go get the nigger." Others, afraid now for their safety, held back. Our friends, noting the hesitation, fired another volley. The mob broke and retreated up Houston Street.

19   In the quiet that followed I put my gun aside and tried to relax. But a tension different from anything I had ever known possessed me. I was gripped by the knowledge of my identity, and in the depths of my soul I was vaguely aware that I was glad of it. I was sick with loathing for the hatred which had flared before me that night and come so close to making me a killer; but I was glad I was not one of those who hated; I was glad I was not one of those made sick and murderous by pride. I was glad I was not one of those whose story is in the history of the world, a record of bloodshed, rapine, and pillage. I was glad my mind and spirit were part of the races that had not fully awakened, and who therefore still had before them the opportunity to write a record of virtue as a memorandum to Armageddon.

20   It was all just a feeling then, inarticulate and melancholy, yet reassuring in the way that death and sleep are reassuring, and I have clung to it now for nearly half a century.

THINKING ABOUT THE TEXT

1. In the opening paragraph, White focuses on specific details about his house and its location: "Below us lived none but Negroes; toward town all but a very few were white." List other details about White's house. Then discuss the significance of the house and its location in terms of Walter White's own racial "stance" in the beginning of the story.

2. Why do Walter and his father feel less threatened than other Blacks when they are driving around town that afternoon? Discuss how they

become increasingly involved in incidents involving other Blacks: the lame bootblack, the three Blacks in the barouche, and the elderly cook.

3. Discuss different areas of this essay where White creates tension and builds suspense.

4. After the father hands his son a gun and the mob is moving toward them, White "freezes" the action for three more paragraphs and shares an epiphany (an illuminating insight) with us. Even though he has "stopped time," how does he manage to hold the reader's interest? Explain all key aspects of his realization.

5. How does White's newfound identity transcend race? Considering the trauma he has been through, why is he "glad" at the end?

WRITING FROM THE TEXT

1. Write an essay analyzing how Walter White matures and changes because of this episode. Support your claims with specific illustrations from this essay.

2. In an essay convince your reader that White's use of narration (his storytelling) helps or hinders our understanding of the actual Atlanta riots and their place in the history of humankind.

3. Analyze an episode in your own life when you could no longer remain neutral about an issue or remain "on the fence," straddling two opposed worlds. What prompted your change, and how did this new position affect you?

4. If you have ever been involved in a mob encounter, write about your experience as it relates to and contrasts with White's.

CONNECTING WITH OTHER TEXTS

1. Write a paper analyzing how White's analysis of "mob mentality" relates to "In Groups We Shrink" (p. 267) and "Why Johnny Can't Disobey" (p. 269).

2. Focusing on White's essay as well as on works by Staples (p. 225), Naylor (p. 234), Giovanni (p. 188), Olds (p. 174), or Straight (p. 176), develop an essay focusing on how difficult it is for Blacks in this culture to avoid being stereotyped.

3. Research newspaper reports of events leading up to and including the actual riots in Atlanta in 1906. Relate your findings to Walter White's account.

MOMMY, WHAT DOES "NIGGER" MEAN?

Gloria Naylor

Before starting college, Gloria Naylor (b. 1950) worked as a missionary for Jehovah's Witnesses for seven years and as a hotel telephone operator for four years. Naylor's writing career started after her graduation from the City University of New York, with a B.A., in 1981. She earned an M.A. from Yale in 1983. She has been a writer in residence at many universities and a cultural exchange lecturer to India. Naylor has said, "I wanted to become a writer because I felt that my presence as a Black woman and my perspective as a woman in general had been underrepresented in American literature." Naylor is the author of the novels *The Women of Brewster Place, Linden Hills, Mama Day,* and *Bailey's Cafe.* In her work, Naylor shows how the economic and social realities of Black lives profoundly influence and limit human beings. The essay printed here appeared in the *New York Times* in 1986.

1   Language is the subject. It is the written form with which I've managed to keep the wolf away from the door and, in diaries, to keep my sanity. In spite of this, I consider the written word inferior to the spoken, and much of the frustration experienced by novelists is the awareness that whatever we manage to capture in even the most transcendent passages falls far short of the richness of life. Dialogue achieves its power in the dynamics of a fleeting moment of sight, sound, smell and touch.

2   I'm not going to enter the debate here about whether it is language that shapes reality or vice versa. That battle is doomed to be waged whenever we seek intermittent reprieve from the chicken and egg dispute. I will simply take the position that the spoken word, like the written word, amounts to a nonsensical arrangement of sounds or letters without a consensus that assigns "meaning." And building from the meanings of what we hear, we order reality. Words themselves are innocuous; it is the consensus that gives them true power.

3   I remember the first time I heard the word nigger. In my third-grade class, our math tests were being passed down the rows, and as I handed the papers to a little boy in back of me, I remarked that once again he had received a much lower mark than I did. He snatched his test from me and spit out that word. Had he called me a nymphomaniac or a necrophiliac, I couldn't have been more puzzled. I didn't know what a nigger was, but I knew that whatever it meant, it was something he shouldn't have called me. This was verified when I raised my hand, and in a loud voice repeated what he had said and watched the teacher scold him for using a "bad" word. I was later to go home and ask the inevitable question that every black parent must face—"Mommy, what does 'nigger' mean?"

4   And what exactly did it mean? Thinking back, I realize that this could not have been the first time the word was used in my presence. I was part of a large extended family that had migrated from the rural South after World War II and formed a close-knit network that gravitated around my maternal grandparents. Their ground-floor apartment in one of the buildings they owned in Harlem was a weekend mecca for my immediate family, along with countless aunts, uncles and

cousins who brought along assorted friends. It was a bustling and open house with assorted neighbors and tenants popping in and out to exchange bits of gossip, pick up an old quarrel or referee the ongoing checkers game in which my grandmother cheated shamelessly. They were all there to let down their hair and put up their feet after a week of labor in the factories, laundries and shipyards of New York.

5   Amid the clamor, which could reach deafening proportions—two or three conversations going on simultaneously, punctuated by the sound of a baby's crying somewhere in the back rooms or out on the street—there was still a rigid set of rules about what was said and how. Older children were sent out of the living room when it was time to get into the juicy details about "you-know-who" up on the third floor who had gone and gotten herself "p-r-e-g-n-a-n-t!" But my parents, knowing that I could spell well beyond my years, always demanded that I follow the others out to play. Beyond sexual misconduct and death, everything else was considered harmless for our young ears. And so among the anecdotes of the triumphs and disappointments in the various workings of their lives, the word nigger was used in my presence, but it was set within contexts and inflections that caused it to register in my mind as something else.

6   In the singular, the word was always applied to a man who had distinguished himself in some situation that brought their approval for his strength, intelligence or drive:

7   "Did Johnny really do that?"

8   "I'm telling you, that nigger pulled in $6,000 of overtime last year. Said he got enough for a down payment on a house."

9   When used with a possessive adjective by a woman—"my nigger"—it became a term of endearment for husband or boyfriend. But it could be more than just a term applied to a man. In their mouths it became the pure essence of manhood—a disembodied force that channeled their past history of struggle and present survival against the odds into a victorious statement of being: "Yeah, that old foreman found out quick enough—you don't mess with a nigger."

10   In the plural, it became a description of some group within the community that had overstepped the bounds of decency as my family defined it: Parents who neglected their children, a drunken couple who fought in public, people who simply refused to look for work, those with excessively dirty mouths or unkempt households were all "trifling niggers." This particular circle could forgive hard times, unemployment, the occasional bout of depression—they had gone through all of that themselves—but the unforgivable sin was lack of self-respect.

11   A woman could never be a "nigger" in the singular, with its connotation of confirming worth. The noun girl was its closest equivalent in that sense, but only when used in direct address and regardless of the gender doing the addressing. "Girl" was a token of respect for a woman. The one-syllable word was drawn out to sound like three in recognition of the extra ounce of wit, nerve or daring that the woman had shown in the situation under discussion.

12   "G-i-r-l, stop. You mean you said that to his face?"

13   But if the word was used in a third-person reference or shortened so that it almost snapped out of the mouth, it always involved some element of communal disapproval. And age became an important factor in these exchanges. It was only

between individuals of the same generation, or from an older person to a younger (but never the other way around), that "girl" would be considered a compliment.

14   I don't agree with the argument that use of the word nigger at this social stratum of the black community was an internalization of racism. The dynamics were the exact opposite: the people in my grandmother's living room took a word that whites used to signify worthlessness or degradation and rendered it impotent. Gathering there together, they transformed "nigger" to signify the varied and complex human beings they knew themselves to be. If the word was to disappear totally from the mouths of even the most liberal of white society, no one in that room was naïve enough to believe it would disappear from white minds. Meeting the word head-on, they proved it had absolutely nothing to do with the way they were determined to live their lives.

15   So there must have been dozens of times that the word "nigger" was spoken in front of me before I reached the third grade. But I didn't "hear" it until it was said by a small pair of lips that had already learned it could be a way to humiliate me. That was the word I went home and asked my mother about. And since she knew that I had to grow up in America, she took me in her lap and explained.

THINKING ABOUT THE TEXT

1. What does Naylor express about the merits of written and spoken language?
2. What gives words meaning, according to Naylor? Think about an example from your own use of language to support her view.
3. How does Naylor's brief narration of her childhood family relationships and patterns prepare the reader for her defining the word "nigger"?
4. What awareness do you gain or have confirmed in print about the use of the word "nigger" and "girl" both in and outside of the Black culture?

WRITING FROM THE TEXT

1. Discuss a word that has dynamics or meaning based on the consensus of a culture rather than, or in addition to, its dictionary definition.
2. Describe the events that contributed to your understanding the full implications or dynamics of a word or phrase used to describe you. You might think about apparently innocuous words like "student," or "middle child," or "employee," or a potentially more volatile word like "tourist," "Chicano," or "foreign student."

CONNECTING WITH OTHER TEXTS

1. In this story, "An Open Letter to Jerry Lewis" (p. 214), and "On Being a Cripple" (p. 203), the authors show that the words chosen to describe an individual play an important role in self-perception. Write an essay

that shows how a term like "cripple" or "kid" can take on a pejorative consensus that harms the individual, as when a non-Black uses the term "nigger."

2. In "Discrimination at Large" (p. 217), Jennifer Coleman quotes a number of harsh words that people use to describe her. She believes that people who would never use ethnic slurs passively accept denigrating terms used on overweight people. In an essay, compare and/or contrast the effects of people using denigrating terms like "nigger" and "pig." Show in your essay the ways that language exacerbates discrimination.

NONE OF THIS IS FAIR
Richard Rodriguez

Educated at Stanford University, Columbia, and the University of California at Berkeley, Richard Rodriguez (b. 1944) has held a variety of jobs—including janitorial work—in addition to his free-lance writing. His autobiography, *Hunger of Memory: The Education of Richard Rodriguez,* is an account of how education can change a life. The son of Mexican-American immigrants, Rodriguez did not speak English when he started school, yet he won a Fulbright fellowship and earned a Ph.D. in English literature. Rodriguez has spoken out against affirmative action programs because he claims they benefit the people who are no longer disadvantaged (as he was not disadvantaged when he attended Stanford), and that these programs ignore the real problems of the genuinely disadvantaged people who cannot read or write. Rodriguez is a prolific essayist whose work appears regularly in newspapers. He is an editor at Pacific News Service in San Francisco. His most recent book, *Mexico's Children,* was published in 1992. The essay included here is from *Hunger of Memory,* which was published in 1982.

1   In 1975, I was afraid of the success I knew I would have when I looked for a permanent teaching position. I accepted another one-year appointment at Berkeley in an attempt to postpone the good fortune awaiting me and the consequent issue it would finally force. But soon it came time: September, October, November—the traditional months of academic job-searching arrived. And passed. And I hadn't written to a single English department. When one of my professors happened to learn this, late in November, he was astonished. Then furious. He yelled at me over the phone. Did I think that just because I was a minority, the jobs would come looking for me? Didn't I realize that he and several other faculty members had already written letters on my behalf to various schools? Was I going to start acting like some other minority students he knew? They struggled for academic success and then, when they almost had it made, they chickened out. Was that it? Had I decided to fail?

2   I didn't want to respond to his questions. I didn't want to admit to him—thus to myself—the reason for my delay. I agreed to write to several schools. I wrote: "I cannot claim to represent socially disadvantaged Mexican-Americans. The very fact that I am in a position to apply for this job should make that clear." After two or three days, there were telegrams and phone calls inviting me to job interviews. There followed rapid excitement: a succession of airplane trips; a blur of faces and the murmur of soft questions; and, over somebody's shoulder, the sight of campus buildings shadowing pictures I had seen, years before, when as a scholarship boy I had leafed through Ivy League catalogues with great expectations. At the end of each visit, interviewers would smile and wonder if I had any questions for *them*. I asked if they were concerned about the fact that I hadn't yet finished my dissertation. Oh no, they said. "We regularly hire junior faculty members who complete their dissertations during their first year or two here." A few times I risked asking what advantage my race had given me over other applicants. But that was an impossible question for them to answer without embarrassing me. They rushed to assure me that my ethnic identity had given me no more that a foot inside the door, at most a slight edge. "We just looked at your dossier with extra care, and frankly, we liked what we saw. There was never any question of our having to alter our standards. You can be certain of that."

3   In the first part of January their offers arrived on stiff, elegant stationery. Most schools promised terms appropriate for any new assistant professor of English. A few made matters worse by offering more: an unusually large starting salary; a reduced teaching schedule; free university housing. As their letters gathered on my desk, I delayed my decision. I started calling department chairmen to ask for another week, another ten days—"more time to reach a decision"—to avoid the decision I would have to make. (One chairman guessed my delay to be a bargaining ploy, so he increased his offer with each of my calls.)

4   At school, meanwhile, I knew graduate students who hadn't received a single job offer. One student, among the best in the department, did not get so much as a request for his dossier. He and I met outside a classroom one day, and he asked about my prospects. He seemed happy for me. Faculty members beamed at the news. They said they were not surprised. "After all, not many schools are going to pass up the chance to get a Chicano with a Ph.D. in Renaissance literature." Friends telephoned, wanting to know which of the offers I was going to take. But I wouldn't make up my mind. Couldn't do it. February came. I was running out of time and excuses. I had to promise a decision by the tenth of the month. The twelfth at the very latest. . . .

5   February 18. The secretaries in the English department kept getting phone calls; there were messages left on yellow slips of paper: Where was I? What had I decided? Have Professor Rodriguez return my call (*collect*) this evening. Please tell Richard Rodriguez that we must have a decision from him immediately because budget estimates for next year are due at the end of the week.

6   Late afternoon: In the office at Berkeley I shared with several other lecturers and teaching assistants, I was grading some papers. Another graduate student was sitting across the room at his desk. At about five, when I got up to leave, he looked

over to tell me in a weary voice that he had some very big news. (Had I heard?) He had decided to accept a position at a faraway state university. It was not the job he especially wanted, he said. But he needed to take it because there hadn't been any other offers. He felt trapped and depressed, since the job would separate him from his young daughter, who would remain in California with her mother.

7   I tried to encourage him by remarking that he was lucky at least to have found a position. So many others hadn't. . . . But before I finished, I realized that I had said the wrong thing. And I anticipated what he would say next.

8   "What are your plans?" he wanted to know. "Is it true that you've gotten an offer from Yale?"

9   I said that it was. "Only, I still haven't made up my mind."

10   He stared at me as I put on my jacket. And then stretching to yawn, but not yawning, he asked me if I knew that he too had written to Yale. In his case, however, no one had bothered to acknowledge his letter with even a postcard. What did I think of that?

11   He gave me no chance to reply.

12   "Damn!" he said, and his chair rasped the floor as he pushed himself back. Suddenly it was to *me* that he was complaining. "It's just not right, Richard. None of this is fair. You've done some good work, but so have I. I'll bet our records are just about even. But when we go looking for jobs this year, it's a very different story. You're the one who gets all the breaks."

13   To evade his criticism, I wanted to side with him. I was about to admit the injustice of affirmative action. But he continued, his voice hard with accusation. "Oh, it's all very simple this year. You're a Chicano. And I am a Jew. That's really the only difference between us."

14 . His words stung anger alive. In a voice deceptively calm, I replied that he oversimplified the whole issue. Phrases came quickly: the importance of cultural diversity; new blood; the goal of racial integration. They were all the old arguments I had proposed years before—long since abandoned. After a minute or two, as I heard myself talking, I felt self-disgust. The job offers I was receiving were indeed unjustified. I knew that. All I was saying amounted to a frantic self-defense. It all was a lie. I tried to find an end to my sentence; my voice faltered to a stop.

15   "Yeah, yeah, sure," he said. "I've heard all that stuff before. Nothing you say, though, really changes the fact that affirmative action is unfair. You can see that, can't you? There isn't any way for me to compete with you. Once there were quotas to keep my parents out of schools like Yale. Now there are quotas to get you in. And the effect on me is the same as it was for them. . . ."

16   At the edge of hearing, I listened to every word he spoke. But behind my eyes my mind reared—spooked and turning—then broke toward a reckless idea: Leave the university. Leave. Immediately the idea sprang again in my bowels and began to climb. Rent money. I pictured myself having to borrow. Get a job as a waiter somewhere? I had come to depend on the intellectual companionship of students—bright students—to relieve the scholar's loneliness. I remembered the British Museum, a year in silence. I wanted to teach; I wanted to read; I wanted

this life. But I had to protest. How? Disqualify myself from the profession as long as affirmative action continued. Romantic exile. But I had to. Yes. I found the horizon again. It was calm.

17   The graduate student across the room had stopped talking; he was staring out the window. I said nothing. My decision was final. No, I would say to them all. Finally, simply, no.

THINKING ABOUT THE TEXT

1. In what ways did Richard Rodriguez benefit from a system he now deplores? How might he have avoided the gains and guilt of a Mexican American given fellowships, grants, and assistantships?

2. What were the complicated emotions Rodriguez experienced as he neared the end of his graduate studies? What were the results of his finally applying for teaching positions?

3. How did Rodriguez's graduate school peers respond to his success? How does he respond to one student's overt complaint?

4. What is Rodriguez's thesis? Why didn't he place the thesis earlier in his essay?

5. What are Rodriguez's values? How do you feel about his stance?

WRITING FROM THE TEXT

1. Argue that Richard Rodriguez has made a mistake by not committing himself to a college teaching career.

2. Write an essay in which you show your position on affirmative action and use parts of Rodriguez's essay for support.

CONNECTING WITH OTHER TEXTS

1. Compare the views of Richard Rodriguez and Ruben Navarrette, Jr. (in "Ethnic Envidia," p. 241). Write an essay that summarizes the types of problems they describe for upwardly mobile Latinos. Propose a solution to the problems in your essay.

2. Both Carol Tavris ("In Groups We Shrink," p. 267) and Milton Mayer ("Commencement Address: What You Will Be," p. 294) describe the problems that individuals face in making morally sound decisions. Use both of these essays to write your own analysis of Richard Rodriguez's problem and decision.

ETHNIC ENVIDIA
Ruben Navarrette, Jr.

The first person in his mostly Hispanic high school to attend Harvard, Ruben Navarrette, Jr. (b. 1967) successfully completed his degree in spite of the "anguish and acute loneliness" he felt in the prestigious Ivy League school. After graduation, Navarrette taught in the Chicano studies program at California State University at Fresno. Caring deeply about where the educational system is failing Hispanic students and hoping to learn what happens to "negatively track" these young people, Navarrette substituted in kindergarten through high school classes before he became a *Los Angeles Times* free-lance writer on education and public policy issues. Navarrette is editor of *Hispanic Student Magazine,* a periodical that is distributed to over 150,000 students in 22 states. Navarrette considers Richard Rodriguez (p. 237) his friend and mentor, "the man who personally encouraged me to write." Ruben Navarrette's first book, *A Darker Shade of Crimson: Odyssey of a Harvard Chicano,* was published in 1993. The essay printed below first appeared in the *Los Angeles Times* in 1992.

1   The savaging of one by another over individual differences is learned behavior. Learned early. A friend recalls, with pain in her voice, a certain afternoon, almost 20 summers ago, in a small town in Arizona. Her mother had gone to great expense to buy her a pretty dress for school. When she arrived, she was teased by a group of Mexican children who insulted her attire for being too prim, too proper. "Aw, look at her pretty dress. She must think she's white or something." My friend ran home with tears dripping down her face and onto her blue dress.

2   Privately, I wonder where children learn to devour one another so viciously. It is, I suspect, something they learn from watching their elders.

3   As the nation's fastest growing minority group, Mexican-Americans continue to fall behind other ethnic groups economically and politically. Part of the reason may be how they relate to one another.

4   On college campuses, among shelves of Shakespeare and vaulted dining halls, we train our intra-racial assassins. There, privileged young Latinos, afraid of being found out as ethnic frauds, sharpen their skills at destroying one another, fueled by hatred and competition and intolerance of personal differences.

5   A friend remembers seeing an ambitious Mexican-American law student at Boalt Hall sternly scolded by Chicano classmates. She had announced her intention of pursuing a career in corporate law. Since the Latino left contingent at the law school—those who did not fulfill their thirst for Mexican blood in college— had decided that the *ethnically correct* career path led not to corporate America but to public service, they took it upon themselves to harass the young woman for her error. When my friend entered the room, he found her sitting on a couch in tears while a handful of Chicano brethren lectured her with pointed fingers in a spectacle resembling a feeding frenzy.

6   And, there are professionals. Grown-ups who should know better. A Latino attorney in Beverly Hills tells the tale of being an ethnic outcast since he practiced

law from what the Latino left considers the wrong side. As a federal prosecutor sending *Mexican-Americans* to jail, he was unpopular with old buddies. "Can you believe what he's doing now? Putting his own people in jail!" *Sell-out.*

7   And Latinos know well the concept of selling out, reserving for it in our collective hearts a special place. A dark, ugly place. The Latino left considers a *sell-out* someone who succeeds at the expense of his or her own cultural integrity. In Spanish, the word for such a person is an insult of particularly vicious bite. Even the angriest of Chicano activists use it sparingly. We say it with scorn: *vendido.*

8   There are more euphemisms: *Un Tio Taco,* a variation of the character of Uncle Tom in Harriet Beecher Stowe's classic; *Una Mosca En Leche,* referring to a (brown) fly in (white) milk, trying to blend in. A *coconut*—literally, brown on the outside—where it is seen, but white on the inside—where it counts. What it means to be "white on the inside" is sorted out by those who toss terms like hand grenades.

9   When the grenades miss, there is more direct action. A Latino administrator at UCLA relays to me with glee the reaction of a group of Chicano undergraduates to a conservative Latina in the Reagan Administration. Someone was incensed enough by her remarks to break into her car and defecate on the front seat.

10   I saw the same official address a group of Latino students at Harvard University. She opened the floor to questions. In the Ivy League, our intra-racial destruction is more subtle. A Latino graduate student fired away. "Isn't your reconciliatory tone influenced by the fact that your husband is white?" With that, the discourse digressed into a David Duke rally against miscegenation.

11   Harsh personal attacks between Mexican-Americans are old and tired remnants of an earlier, darker age. We accuse those fellow Chicanos with whom we disagree on political issues of somehow betraying us on a personal level.

12   There is yet another obstacle for Latinos to overcome before they may claim that elusive entity called unity. We direct it not at those who have "sold out," but rather at those with whom we would like to trade places. Those of whom we are jealous. We admit its cancer among ourselves in whispered, frustrated voices. We acknowledge it with a squinted eye and a shake of our head—*envidia.*

13   In English, the term means "envy," the green-eyed desire to have what another has. With Mexican-Americans, the term assumes a special significance. It is an emotion directed most often at those who are considered too close to positions of wealth, prestige, influence or power.

14   It is there in the heart of the teen-age girl who resents her girlfriend for being more popular. It is there in the minds of Chicano students at Stanford who wish each other well in securing that summer internship, while hoping theirs will be the juiciest plum of all. And it is there, among family (*entre familia*) who accuse the Harvard Man in their ranks of thinking himself "better than the rest of us" and secretly hope that he will not accomplish the goals he has set for himself.

15   Perhaps it is there any time that a member of a disadvantaged community strives to crawl out of the bucket and is rewarded for the effort with snide remarks from those left behind. Too intelligent. Too ambitious. Too good for the lives that others live.

16   Strangely, the one individual whom I have seen generate the greatest amount of *envidia* among some Latinos has also enjoyed the most support from others. In the 1980s, Henry G. Cisneros, the former mayor of San Antonio, became the most prominent of Latino political figures.

17   During a chat with a Chicano Studies professor from Berkeley, I cited Cisneros as my choice for a speaker for a Harvard forum. He made a snide remark about what was then the mayor's admission of marital indiscretion. Just recently, at the opening of the Republican Convention, there was another such remark following a Cisneros pledge to rally Latino support for Bill Clinton—and it was traced to U.S. Treasurer Catalina Vasquez Villalpando. To appease her party's thirst for infidelity blood, this Latina on the Bush Administration offered up one of her own.

18   In my lifetime, I may see a Latino mayor of Los Angeles or governor of California. What I have not seen, perhaps will not see, are Latino professionals holding raised hands in unity. *"You be the candidate this time, I'll go next."* Ethnic solidarity, a successful economic and political tool for American Jews and other ethnic groups, eludes Latinos.

19   I had hoped my generation could stop playing these hurtful games and, finally, respect each other's personal and ideological differences. For 50 years, the Old Guard has attributed the stagnation of the Latino population to external forces like white racism and discrimination. Yet, there are *internal* forces at work as well.

20   For Latinos, there has been little cooperation or camaraderie. And so little progress. Petty competition, personal intolerance and a refusal to let any of our own progress ahead of us make it unlikely that the *children of the sun,* however numerous, will ever inherit the earth.

THINKING ABOUT THE TEXT

1. What are the specific anecdotes that Navarrette cites as examples of Latino "envidia"? What is the *basis* of the envy?

2. Do you agree with Navarrette that "savaging" is learned early, and at home, from watching one's elders?

3. According to Navarrette, what do some Latinos perceive as the "ethnically correct" position for Latino lawyers?

4. What would Navarrette's proposal for change entail?

WRITING FROM THE TEXT

1. Describe a time when you made a decision that others thought was not "ethnically correct."

2. Write an essay to convince your reader that Navarrette is correct, or incorrect, in his belief that Latinos scorn each others' achievements.

CONNECTING WITH OTHER TEXTS

1. Use Richard Rodriguez's essay "None of This Is Fair" (p. 237) to support or refute Navarrette's argument.

2. Focus on a religious, racial, or ethnic group other than Latinos to show how some in the group feel caught in a double bind, condemned if they do achieve and condemned if they do not. Consider "The Atlanta Riot" (p. 229) and "Two Kinds" (p. 49).

ELEVEN
Sandra Cisneros

A teacher to high school dropouts, a participant in a poet-in-the-schools project, a college recruiter, and arts administrator, Sandra Cisneros was born (in 1954) to a Mexican father and a Mexican-American mother. Cisneros' work describes lives on both sides of our border with Mexico. Cisneros is the author of a collection of short stories called *The House on Mango Street* and *My Wicked Wicked Ways* (a volume of poetry), as well as *Woman Hollering Creek*, published in 1991, from which the short story included here is taken.

1   What they don't understand about birthdays and what they never tell you is that when you're eleven, you're also ten, and nine, and eight, and seven, and six, and five, and four, and three, and two, and one. And when you wake up on your eleventh birthday you expect to feel eleven, but you don't. You open your eyes and everything's just like yesterday, only it's today. And you don't feel eleven at all. You feel like you're still ten. And you are—underneath the year that makes you eleven.

2   Like some days you might say something stupid, and that's the part of you that's still ten. Or maybe some days you might need to sit on your mama's lap because you're scared, and that's the part of you that's five. And maybe one day when you're all grown up maybe you will need to cry like if you're three, and that's okay. That's what I tell Mama when she's sad and needs to cry. Maybe she's feeling three.

3   Because the way you grow old is kind of like an onion or like the rings inside a tree trunk or like my little wooden dolls that fit one inside the other, each year inside the next one. That's how being eleven years old is.

4   You don't feel eleven. Not right away. It takes a few days, weeks even, sometimes even months before you say Eleven when they ask you. And you don't feel smart eleven, not until you're almost twelve. That's the way it is.

5   Only today I wish I didn't have only eleven years rattling inside me like pennies in a tin Band-Aid box. Today I wish I was one hundred and two instead of

eleven because if I was one hundred and two I'd have known what to say when Mrs. Price put the red sweater on my desk. I would've known how to tell her it wasn't mine instead of just sitting there with that look on my face and nothing coming out of my mouth.

6   "Whose is this?" Mrs. Price says, and she holds the red sweater up in the air for all the class to see. "Whose? It's been sitting in the coatroom for a month."

7   "Not mine," says everybody. "Not me."

8   "It has to belong to somebody," Mrs. Price keeps saying, but nobody can remember. It's an ugly sweater with red plastic buttons and a collar and sleeves all stretched out like you could use it for a jump rope. It's maybe a thousand years old and even if it belonged to me I wouldn't say so.

9   Maybe because I'm skinny, maybe because she doesn't like me, that stupid Sylvia Saldívar says, "I think it belongs to Rachel." An ugly sweater like that, all raggedy and old, but Mrs. Price believes her. Mrs. Price takes the sweater and puts it right on my desk, but when I open my mouth nothing comes out.

10   "That's not, I don't, you're not. . . . Not mine," I finally say in a little voice that was maybe me when I was four.

11   "Of course it's yours," Mrs. Price says. "I remember you wearing it once." Because she's older and the teacher, she's right and I'm not.

12   Not mine, not mine, not mine, but Mrs. Price is already turning to page thirty-two, and math problem number four. I don't know why but all of a sudden I'm feeling sick inside, like the part of me that's three wants to come out of my eyes, only I squeeze them shut tight and bite down on my teeth real hard and try to remember today I am eleven, eleven. Mama is making a cake for me for tonight, and when Papa comes home everybody will sing Happy birthday, happy birthday to you.

13   But when the sick feeling goes away and I open my eyes, the red sweater's still sitting there like a big red mountain. I move the red sweater to the corner of my desk with my ruler. I move my pencil and books and eraser as far from it as possible. I even move my chair a little to the right. Not mine, not mine, not mine.

14   In my head I'm thinking how long till lunchtime, how long till I can take the red sweater and throw it over the schoolyard fence, or leave it hanging on a parking meter, or bunch it up into a little ball and toss it in the alley. Except when math period ends Mrs. Price says loud and in front of everybody, "Now, Rachel, that's enough," because she sees I've shoved the red sweater to the tippy-tip corner of my desk and it's hanging all over the edge like a waterfall, but I don't care.

15   "Rachel," Mrs. Price says. She says it like she's getting mad. "You put that sweater on right now and no more nonsense."

16   "But it's not—"

17   "Now!" Mrs. Price says.

18   This is when I wish I wasn't eleven, because all the years inside of me—ten, nine, eight, seven, six, five, four, three, two, and one—are pushing at the back of my eyes when I put one arm through one sleeve of the sweater that smells like cottage cheese, and then the other arm through the other and stand there with my arms apart like if the sweater hurts me and it does, all itchy and full of germs that aren't even mine.

19   That's when everything I've been holding in since this morning, since when Mrs. Price put the sweater on my desk, finally lets go, and all of a sudden I'm crying in front of everybody. I wish I was invisible but I'm not. I'm eleven and it's my birthday today and I'm crying like I'm three in front of everybody. I put my head down on the desk and bury my face in my stupid clown-sweater arms. My face all hot and spit coming out of my mouth because I can't stop the little animal noises from coming out of me, until there aren't any more tears left in my eyes, and it's just my body shaking like when you have the hiccups, and my whole head hurts like when you drink milk too fast.

20   But the worst part is right before the bell rings for lunch. That stupid Phyllis Lopez, who is even dumber than Sylvia Saldívar, says she remembers the red sweater is hers! I take it off right away and give it to her, only Mrs. Price pretends like everything's okay.

21   Today I'm eleven. There's a cake Mama's making for tonight, and when Papa comes home from work we'll eat it. There'll be candles and presents and everybody will sing Happy birthday, happy birthday to you, Rachel, only it's too late.

22   I'm eleven today. I'm eleven, ten, nine, eight, seven, six, five, four, three, two, and one, but I wish I was one hundred and two. I wish I was anything but eleven, because I want today to be far away already, far away like a runaway balloon, like a tiny *o* in the sky, so tiny-tiny you have to close your eyes to see it.

THINKING ABOUT THE TEXT

1. Describe the narrator's personality and "voice" here. Specify particular details that help you sympathize with the narrator, Rachel.

2. List all the similes (comparisons of unlike terms using *like* or *as*) and explain why the use of similes seems appropriate for this perspective.

3. Contrast Rachel's self-perception with Mrs. Price's attitude toward her. Use specific details to illustrate each perspective.

4. Contrast Rachel's expectations for her birthday with what really occurs on that day. What is the author suggesting about "growing up"?

WRITING FROM THE TEXT

1. Write an essay about a time in your life when an anticipated celebration did not turn out as planned. Make sure the contrast between your expectations and the reality is very vivid.

2. Using Cisneros' story as well as experiences of your own, analyze possible reasons for "humiliation in the classroom." Propose a possible solution.

3. Write an essay arguing that such "humiliation" is or is not an important learning experience. Use additional experiences of your own to support your thesis.

CONNECTING WITH OTHER TEXTS

1. Considering every child's longing to be "grown up," analyze some implicit myths about childhood and adulthood that Cisneros exposes. Relate these myths to Sanders' insights in "Under the Influence" (p. 11) or to Tan's in "Two Kinds" (p. 49).

2. Study other stories from *Woman Hollering Creek* by Sandra Cisneros. Focusing on any two stories, examine to what extent Cisneros' Chicana upbringing and culture inform her works. Analyze specifics.

5

Between Values

■ ■ ■

This final chapter of readings is necessarily a culmination of the other chapters because our age, gender, roots, and self-perceptions all influence what we value. This chapter invites you to think about work choices, group dynamics, and the problem of maintaining your individualism in a social context.

Your various work experiences may have prompted you to think about the advantages and disadvantages of different jobs. An essay by W. H. Auden makes an important distinction between working and laboring, and Jim Daniels' exuberant poem exemplifies one of Auden's definitions. Barbara Brandt contends that workers in the United States spend too much of their lives at the grindstone, and Robert Moog argues that we need to improve the quality of products made in the United States rather than blindly "buy American." These readings may prompt you to consider the importance of work in your life and ask you to think about whether your jobs will provide satisfaction and self-definition along with a paycheck.

Working and living in any society requires us to balance social pressures and individual needs. Carol Tavris argues that in groups we "shrink" from right actions that we would not hesitate to execute as individuals, and Sara McCarthy and William Kowinski analyze the sources of group conformity in places as diverse as schools and shopping malls. Both Shirley Jackson's disturbing short story "The Lottery" and a nonfiction account of "Stone-throwing in India" illustrate the consequences of going along with a group.

Milton Mayer concludes our chapter with an argument essay set in the context of a "Commencement Address." Like all of the writers in this chapter, Mayer asks you to consider "What You Will Be." The question is as valid for a graduating student as a continuing one. You already have a strong sense of who you are and what you value; the authors in this chapter invite you to confirm your convictions while they ask you to examine the values of others.

WORK, LABOR AND PLAY
W. H. Auden

Poet, critic, essayist, dramatist, editor, translator, and librettist W. H. Auden (1907–1973) was raised in the industrial north of England but became an American citizen in 1939. Auden's father was a prominent physician who may have influenced Auden's early interest in science and engineering. On a scholarship, Auden attended Oxford, but his interest in English prompted his academic move from science to letters. Critics find Auden's work powerful for his strong interest in moral issues and political, social, and psychological preoccupations. The essay included here is from A Certain World, which was published in 1970.

1   So far as I know, Miss Hannah Arendt was the first person to define the essential difference between work and labor. To be happy, a man must feel, firstly, free and, secondly, important. He cannot be really happy if he is compelled by society to do what he does not enjoy doing, or if what he enjoys doing is ignored by society as of no value or importance. In a society where slavery in the strict sense has been abolished, the sign that what a man does is of social value is that he is paid money to do it, but a laborer today can rightly be called a wage slave. A man is a laborer if the job society offers him is of no interest to himself but he is compelled to take it by the necessity of earning a living and supporting his family.

2   The antithesis to labor is play. When we play a game, we enjoy what we are doing, otherwise we should not play it, but it is a purely private activity; society could not care less whether we play it or not.

3   Between labor and play stands work. A man is a worker if he is personally interested in the job which society pays him to do; what from the point of view of society is necessary labor is from his own point of view voluntary play. Whether a job is to be classified as labor or work depends, not on the job itself, but on the tastes of the individual who undertakes it. The difference does not, for example, coincide with the difference between a manual and a mental job; a gardener or a cobbler may be a worker, a bank clerk a laborer. Which a man is can be seen from his attitude toward leisure. To a worker, leisure means simply the hours he needs to relax and rest in order to work efficiently. He is therefore more likely to take too little leisure than too much; workers die of coronaries and forget their wives' birthdays. To the laborer, on the other hand, leisure means freedom from compulsion, so that it is natural for him to imagine that the fewer hours he has to spend laboring, and the more hours he is free to play, the better.

4   What percentage of the population in a modern technological society are, like myself, in the fortunate position of being workers? At a guess I would say sixteen per cent, and I do not think that figure is likely to get bigger in the future.

5   Technology and the division of labor have done two things: by eliminating in many fields the need for special strength or skill, they have made a very large number of paid occupations which formerly were enjoyable work into boring labor; and by increasing productivity they have reduced the number of necessary

laboring hours. It is already possible to imagine a society in which the majority of the population, that is to say, its laborers, will have almost as much leisure as in earlier times was enjoyed by the aristocracy. When one recalls how aristocracies in the past actually behaved, the prospect is not cheerful. Indeed, the problem of dealing with boredom may be even more difficult for such a future mass society than it was for aristocracies. The latter, for example, ritualized their time; there was a season to shoot grouse, a season to spend in town, etc. The masses are more likely to replace an unchanging ritual by fashion which it will be in the economic interest of certain people to change as often as possible. Again, the masses cannot go in for hunting, for very soon there would be no animals left to hunt. For other aristocratic amusements like gambling, dueling, and warfare, it may be only too easy to find equivalents in dangerous driving, drug-taking, and senseless acts of violence. Workers seldom commit acts of violence, because they can put their aggression into their work, be it physical like the work of a smith, or mental like the work of a scientist or an artist. The role of aggression in mental work is aptly expressed by the phrase "getting one's teeth into a problem."

THINKING ABOUT THE TEXT

1. How does the "laborer" contrast with the "worker," according to Auden?
2. How does "play" figure in his contrast study? How much validity do you find in his prediction of how the unhappy masses will use their new leisure?
3. How reliable do you find Auden's figure of workers numbering only 16 percent of the work force? To what does Auden attribute the unhappiness in the workplace?

WRITING FROM THE TEXT

1. Write an essay in which you analyze happy workers, using your observations of family and friends for support. Organize your support around a thesis that asserts something about worker happiness and use a variety of supporting examples, as if to acknowledge Auden's view that satisfaction is unrelated to status or paycheck.
2. Write an analysis of unhappy workers, using your observations of family and friends for supporting examples. Proceed as in the above topic.

CONNECTING WITH OTHER TEXTS

1. Use "Less Is More: A Call for Shorter Work Hours" (p. 253) to argue that the issue facing the employed is not Auden's view of work but how much *time* they need to spend at work.

2. The July/August 1991 issue of the *Utne Reader* is devoted to "Making a Living Versus Making a Life." Use the articles collected in this issue to support an essay in which you argue for an alternative to the usual postcollege career.

3. Do research, including interviews, with people who work in your future occupation. Write a paper in which you argue that it will be possible to be a "worker" in this field.

SHORT-ORDER COOK
Jim Daniels

A contributor of poems to magazines and literary journals, Jim Daniels (b. 1956) is also a teacher and has been a visiting writer in residence. He judges poetry competitions, and he gives readings at schools and libraries and on National Public Radio. Daniels says, "Though I am currently teaching, much of my poetry focuses on the factory life of my native Detroit. My grandfather, brothers, and I have all worked in the auto industry. . . . I feel that there is little poetry being written about the world that I come from and the people that I care about. If nothing else, I'm trying to say that these people are important, that their lives have value and meaning." The poem included here is from *Places/Everyone*, published in 1985.

> An average joe comes in
> and orders thirty cheeseburgers and thirty fries.
>
> I wait for him to pay before I start cooking.
> He pays.
> He ain't no average joe.   5
>
> The grill is just big enough for ten rows of three.
> I slap the burgers down
> throw two buckets of fries in the deep frier
> and they pop pop spit spit . . .
> psss . . .   10
> The counter girls laugh.
> I concentrate.
> It is the crucial point—
> they are ready for the cheese:
> my fingers shake as I tear off slices   15
> toss them on the burgers/fries done/dump/
> refill buckets/burgers ready/flip into buns/
> beat that melting cheese/wrap burgers in plastic/
> into paper bags/fries done/dump/fill thirty bags/

> *bring them to the counter/wipe sweat on sleeve*   20
> *and smile at the counter girls.*
> *I puff my chest out and bellow:*
> *"Thirty cheeseburgers, thirty fries!"*
> *They look at me funny.*
> *I grab a handful of ice, toss it in my mouth*   25
> *do a little dance and walk back to the grill.*
> *Pressure, responsibility, success,*
> *thirty cheeseburgers, thirty fries.*

THINKING ABOUT THE TEXT

1. What do you think is the point of this exuberant poem?
2. How does the speaker in Daniels' poem specifically exemplify Auden's view of the "worker"? Cite specific examples from the poem to show the cook's attitude toward his work.

WRITING FROM THE TEXT

1. Write about a job that you have enjoyed. Start from a thesis that asserts what you found good about the job, and support your thesis with specific and vivid examples.

2. Write about a job that you have disliked. Start from a thesis that asserts why you did not like the job, and support your thesis with specific examples.

3. Write an essay in which you argue that a definition of ideal work must be developed to satisfy workers at all levels of employment. Set up the "ideals" in your thesis.

4. Interview restaurant workers to learn how many have the job satisfactions described in Daniels' poem. What provides satisfaction to the workers you have interviewed? What keeps them from "success" at work? Write from a thesis that you can support with your collected responses.

CONNECTING WITH OTHER TEXTS

1. People who work in restaurants often complain about long daily shifts, weekends without time off, and stress. Write an analysis of restaurant satisfaction or dissatisfaction with the purpose of confirming or refuting Brandt's views in "Less Is More: A Call for Shorter Work Hours" (p. 253).

2. Write an analysis of "Short-order Cook" to show that the speaker is a "worker," not a "wage slave." Use Auden's essay as part of your definition essay.

LESS IS MORE: A CALL FOR SHORTER WORK HOURS
Barbara Brandt

A community organizer and political activist in the Boston area, Barbara Brandt (b. 1943) considers her academic background—in philosophy, sociology, and psychology—unimportant in describing who she is. Brandt helped put together the 1988 and 1990 conferences for The Other Economic Summit (TOES). Her most recent book, *Whole Life Economics,* was published in the summer of 1993. The book is about how to build an economy that meets both human and environmental needs. The article included here is excerpted from a paper prepared by the Shorter Work-Time Group of Boston.

1   America is suffering from overwork. Too many of us are too busy, trying to squeeze more into each day while having less to show for it. Although our growing time crunch is often portrayed as a personal dilemma, it is in fact a major social problem that has reached crisis proportions over the past 20 years.

2   The simple fact is that Americans today—both women and men—are spending too much time at work, to the detriment of their homes, their families, their personal lives, and their communities. The American Dream promised that our individual hard work paired with the advances of modern technology would bring about the good life for all. Glorious visions of the leisure society were touted throughout the '50s and '60s. But now most people are working more than ever before, while still struggling to meet their economic commitments. Ironically, the many advances in technology, such as computers and fax machines, rather than reducing our workload, seem to have speeded up our lives at work. At the same time, technology has equipped us with "conveniences" like microwave ovens and frozen dinners that merely enable us to adopt a similar frantic pace in our home lives so we can cope with more hours at paid work.

3   A recent spate of articles in the mainstream media has focused on the new problems of overwork and lack of time. Unfortunately, overwork is often portrayed as a special problem of yuppies and professionals on the fast track. In reality, the unequal distribution of work and time in America today reflects the decline in both standard of living and quality of life for most Americans. Families whose members never see each other, women who work a double shift (first on the job, then at home), workers who need more flexible work schedules, and unemployed and underemployed people who need more work are all casualties of the crisis of overwork.

4   Americans often assume that overwork is an inevitable fact of life—like death and taxes. Yet a closer look at other times and other nations offers some startling surprises.

5   Anthropologists have observed that in pre-industrial (particularly hunting and gathering) societies, people generally spend 3 to 4 hours a day, 15 to 20 hours a week, doing the work necessary to maintain life. The rest of the time is spent in socializing, partying, playing, storytelling, and artistic or religious activities. The ancient Romans celebrated 175 public festivals a year in which everyone participated, and people in the Middle Ages had at least 115.

6   In our era, almost every other industrialized nation (except Japan) has fewer annual working hours and longer vacations than the United States. This includes all of Western Europe, where many nations enjoy thriving economies and standards of living equal to or higher than ours. Jeremy Brecher and Tim Costello, writing in Z Magazine (Oct. 1990), note that "European unions during the 1980s made a powerful and largely successful push to cut working hours. In 1987 German metalworkers struck and won a 37.5-hour week; many are now winning a 35-hour week. In 1990, hundreds of thousands of British workers have won a 37-hour week."

7   In an article about work-time in the *Boston Globe*, Suzanne Gordon notes that workers in other industrialized countries "enjoy—as a statutory right—longer vacations [than in the U.S.] from the moment they enter the work force. In Canada, workers are legally entitled to two weeks off their first year on the job. After two or three years of employment, most get three weeks of vacation. After 10 years, it's up to four, and by 20 years, Canadian workers are off for five weeks. In Germany, statutes guarantee 18 days minimum for everyone, but most workers get five or six weeks. The same is true in Scandinavian countries, and in France."

8   In contrast to the extreme American emphasis on productivity and commitment, which results in many workers, especially in professional-level jobs, not taking the vacations coming to them, Gordon notes that "in countries that are America's most successful competitors in the global marketplace, all working people, whether lawyers or teachers, CEOs or janitors, take the vacations to which they are entitled by law. 'No one in West Germany,' a West German embassy's officer explains, 'no matter how high up they are, would ever say they couldn't afford to take a vacation. Everyone takes their vacation.'"

9   And in Japan, where dedication to the job is legendary, Gordon notes that the Japanese themselves are beginning to consider their national workaholism a serious social problem leading to stress-related illnesses and even death. As a result, the Japanese government recently established a commission whose goal is to promote shorter working hours and more leisure time.

10   Most other industrialized nations also have better family-leave policies than the United States, and in a number of other countries workers benefit from innovative time-scheduling opportunities such as sabbaticals.

11   While the idea of a shorter workweek and longer vacations sounds appealing to most people, any movement to enact shorter work-time as a public policy will

encounter surprising pockets of resistance, not just from business leaders but even from some workers. Perhaps the most formidable barrier to more free time for Americans is the widespread mind-set that the 40-hour workweek, 8 hours a day, 5 days a week, 50 weeks a year, is a natural rhythm of the universe. This view is reinforced by the media's complete silence regarding the shorter work-time and more favorable vacation and family-leave policies of other countries. This lack of information, and our leaders' reluctance to suggest that the United States can learn from any other nation (except workaholic Japan) is one reason why more Americans don't identify overwork as a major problem or clamor for fewer hours and more vacation. Monika Bauerlein, a journalist originally from Germany now living in Minneapolis, exclaims, "I can't believe that people here aren't rioting in the streets over having only two weeks of vacation a year."

12   A second obstacle to launching a powerful shorter work-time movement is America's deeply ingrained work ethic, or its modern incarnation, the workaholic syndrome. The work ethic fosters the widely held belief that people's work is their most important activity and that people who do not work long and hard are lazy, unproductive, and worthless.

13   For many Americans today, paid work is not just a way to make money but is a crucial source of their self-worth. Many of us identify ourselves almost entirely by the kind of work we do. Work still has a powerful psychological and spiritual hold over our lives—and talk of shorter work-time may seem somehow morally suspicious.

14   Because we are so deeply a work-oriented society, leisure-time activities— such as play, relaxation, engaging in cultural and artistic pursuits, or just quiet contemplation and "doing nothing"—are not looked on as essential and worthwhile components of life. Of course, for the majority of working women who must work a second shift at home, much of the time spent outside of paid work is not leisure anyway. Also much of our non-work time is spent not just in personal renewal, but in building and maintaining essential social ties—with family, friends, and the larger community.

15   Today, as mothers and fathers spend more and more time on the job, we are beginning to recognize the deleterious effects—especially on our young people— of the breakdown of social ties and community in American life. But unfortunately, our nation reacts to these problems by calling for more paid professionals—more police, more psychiatrists, more experts—without recognizing the possibility that shorter work hours and more free time could enable us to do much of the necessary rebuilding and healing, with much more gratifying and longer-lasting results.

16   Of course, the stiffest opposition to cutting work hours comes not from citizens but from business. Employers are reluctant to alter the 8-hour day, 40-hour workweek, 50 weeks a year because it seems easier and more profitable for employers to hire fewer employees for longer hours rather than more employees—each of whom would also require health insurance and other benefits—with flexible schedules and work arrangements.

17   Harvard University economist Juliet B. Schor, who has been studying issues of work and leisure in America, reminds us that we cannot ignore the larger relationship between unemployment and overwork: While many of us work too much, others are unable to find paid work at all. Schor points out that "workers who work longer hours lose more income when they lose their jobs. The threat of job loss is an important determinant of management's power on the shop floor." A system that offers only two options—long work hours or unemployment—serves as both a carrot and a stick. Those lucky enough to get full-time jobs are bribed into docile compliance with the boss, while the spectre of unemployment always looms as the ultimate punishment for the unruly.

18   Some observers suggest that keeping people divided into "the employed" and "the unemployed" creates feelings of resentment and inferiority/superiority between the two groups, thus focusing their discontent and blame on each other rather than on the corporations and political figures who actually dictate our nation's economic policies.

19   Our role as consumers contributes to keeping the average work week from falling. In an economic system in which addictive buying is the basis of corporate profits, working a full 40 hours or more each week for 50 weeks a year gives us just enough time to stumble home and dazedly—almost automatically—shop; but not enough time to think about deeper issues or to work effectively for social change. From the point of view of corporations and policymakers, shorter work-time may be bad for the economy, because people with enhanced free time may begin to find other things to do with it besides mindlessly buying products. It takes more free time to grow vegetables, cook meals from scratch, sew clothes, or repair broken items than it does to just buy these things at the mall.

20   Any serious proposal to give employed Americans a break by cutting into the eight-hour work day is certain to be met with anguished cries about international competitiveness. The United States seems gripped by the fear that our nation has lost its economic dominance, and pundits, policymakers, and business leaders tell us that no sacrifice is too great if it puts America on top again.

21   As arguments like this are put forward (and we can expect them to increase in the years to come), we need to remember two things. First, even if America maintained its dominance (whatever that means) and the economy were booming again, this would be no guarantee that the gains—be they in wages, in employment opportunities, or in leisure—would be distributed equitably between upper management and everyone else. Second, the entire issue of competitiveness is suspect when it pits poorly treated workers in one country against poorly treated workers in another; and when the vast majority of economic power, anyway, is in the control of enormous multinational corporations that have no loyalty to the people of any land.

22   Many people are experimenting with all sorts of ways to cope with grueling work schedules. Those with enough money use it to "buy time." They find child care, order take-out meals, and hire people to pick their children up from school and do the family shopping. Other options being pursued by both men and women

include actively looking for good part-time jobs; sharing jobs; arranging more flexible work schedules; going into business for themselves; working at home; and scaling back on consumption in order to work fewer hours for lower pay. While these ideas work in some cases, they are often stymied by a lack of support from employers, and they aren't available to many people, especially those with lower incomes.

23   But perhaps the major shortcoming of all these individual responses is precisely that: They are individual. The problem of overwork is a broad problem of our economic system. It cannot be solved by just one individual, family, or business. Individual approaches ignore the many larger causes of the problem.

24   A number of solutions now discussed for the overwork crisis are actually steps in the wrong direction.

25   The conservative climate of the '80s and '90s has spawned a neotraditional cultural movement that holds up the 1950s as a golden age from which we have unwisely strayed. Their simplistic solution to the complex set of social issues involved with overwork is to force women back into the home. While we all should support the right of any woman to freely choose home and family as her primary responsibility and source of fulfillment, we need to oppose social and economic policies that either seek to keep women at home or offer them only limited opportunity—low-paying, low-status, part-time jobs—outside the home. Such policies are not only unfair to women themselves, they are economically harmful to the many families supported by working women.

26   The idea of a four-day, 10-hour-a-day workweek has frequently been suggested as a superior alternative to the current five-day workweek. But this is no shortening of work hours, and it ignores the fact that many people who do paid work also need to care for home and family when they get home. Lengthening the workday would add considerably to the burden these people already carry.

27   Finally, we should be wary of programs supposedly aimed at helping working parents and their families when the ultimate outcome is to keep parents at work longer—day care for sick children and corporate day care centers open on weekends to accommodate parents who want to work extended hours, for example.

28   Now that public attention is beginning to take note of the mounting personal, economic, and social toll of overwork, it is time to treat overwork as a major political and social issue. To accomplish this, the Shorter Work-Time Group of Boston—a multicultural group of women's and labor activists—proposes a national campaign for shorter work hours that could foster a formidable alliance of unions, community groups, women's groups, and workers in all fields. To begin this campaign, we propose a 10-point plan that could help heal the problems of overwork in its many forms and enhance the quality of all our lives—at home, on the job, and in the community.

29   **1. Establish a 6-hour day/30-hour week**

30   We propose that a 6-hour day/30-hour week be made the new standard for "full-time work." This new policy would not only give America's workers more time to devote to our families, friends, and personal and community lives, but

would also provide benefits to employers in increased efficiency and productivity, reduced accidents and absenteeism, improved morale, lower turnover, and retention of valuable employees.

31   So that workers do not suffer financially from reduction of their work-time, we also propose that any reduction in hours be accompanied by a corresponding increase in hourly income—that the six-hour day be compensated by what was formerly eight-hour pay. Since numerous studies have shown shortened workdays improve productivity, this would not be economically unrealistic.

32   **2. Extend paid vacations for all American workers**

33   American workers should enjoy what their counterparts around the world take for granted—four to six weeks of paid vacation each year. Vacation should be based on overall years in the work force rather than tied to the number of years a person has been employed in a particular firm.

34   **3. Improve family-leave policies**

35   The Family and Medical Leave Act . . . needs broad national support so that politicians would fear reprisals from an angry public if they did not support it. This bill would provide job security for people who have to leave work for extended periods in order to care for newborn children or seriously ill family members. Although it does not provide for pay during such leaves, paid leave should be an eventual goal.

36   **4. Establish benefits for all workers**

37   At present, employers of part-time and temporary workers are not legally required to provide health insurance, vacations, pensions, or any other benefits. This is especially insidious because women and many low-income workers are most likely to hold part-time and temporary jobs. Congresswoman Pat Schroeder has introduced HR 2575, the Part-Time and Temporary Workers Protection Act, to rectify this situation at the national level.

38   **5. Discourage overtime work**

39   Since overtime is detrimental to workers, their families, and the other workers it replaces, we would like to see it eliminated as much as possible. This can be done by mandating the elimination of compulsory overtime and raising the pay rate to double time for voluntary overtime.

40   **6. Support alternative working arrangements**

41   We encourage business to increase flex-time and other innovative work-time arrangements that enable employees to better meet their personal and family needs.

42   **7. Acknowledge workaholism as a social disorder**

43   In Japan, they even coined a word—*karoshi* (death from overwork)—to show this is a serious disease.

44   **8. Promote awareness that our citizens and our nation as a whole will benefit from shorter work-time**

45   We need a public education campaign to raise public consciousness about the devastating effects that overwork is having on our health, our families, our communities, and especially on our young people. American workers must have more time to care for their families and restore their communities. This does not mean

sending women back home. It means giving all people the time and resources to create their own solutions. If we had more time for ourselves, for example, we would probably see a wide variety of child-care options. In some families, women would do this exclusively; in others, women and men would share child-care responsibilities; some people would hire paid help; and others would develop cooperative or community-based programs for their children; many people would take advantage of a mix of options. The same would probably occur with regard to a wide range of family and community issues.

46   **9. Look at how the issue of overwork influences the problems of underemployment and unemployment**

47   Because of increasing economic pressures, many corporations are developing a two-tier work force: a core of workers who enjoy good salaries, job security, and full benefits, and another group of lower paid part-time and temporary workers who have no benefits or job security.

48   **10. Challenge the assertion that we have to enslave ourselves to our jobs in order to keep America competitive**

49   Germany, for example, has mandated shortened work hours, and clearly has not lost its competitive edge in the world economy.

ANNUAL VACATION TIME (in weeks)

	By law	By bargaining agreement
Austria	4	4–5
Denmark	—	5
Finland	5	5–6
France	5	5–6
Germany	3	4–6
Greece	4	—
Ireland	3	4
Italy	—	4–6
Netherlands	3	4–5
Portugal	4	—
Spain	5	5
Sweden	5	5–8
Switzerland	4	4–5
United States	—	2–4
United Kingdom	—	4–6

Source: "Reduction of Working Time in Europe," European Industrial Relations Review, No. 127, August 1984:9–13.

THINKING ABOUT THE TEXT

1. What is Barbara Brandt's complete thesis? How does she support her assertions?

2. What are the contrasting habits of people in preindustrial and industrial nations?

3. Brandt cites a number of obstacles to correcting overwork in the United States. What are they, and how do you feel about her discussion of the problems? How much validity do you find in Brandt's suggestion of the "deleterious effects" of absent parents?

4. What "corrections" of labor problems in the United States does Brandt caution against? What are Brandt's specific suggestions for improving life in the United States?

WRITING FROM THE TEXT

1. In an essay, analyze Brandt's 10-point plan. Start with an assertion that reflects your view of her program and then look carefully at each point, analyzing the merits or drawbacks of each.

2. Take any "obstacle" Brandt cites—such as the amount of self-identity and esteem Americans derive from productive work—and argue that a reduction in work time conflicts with this deeply held value.

CONNECTING WITH OTHER TEXTS

1. Review Auden's essay on "Work, Labor and Play" (p. 249), and write an essay in which you focus on "leisure use" or play as it is understood in relation to work in both Brandt's and Auden's essays.

2. The problems Brandt cites are not related to one gender or the other, but men and women have responded differently to the problem of making a living. Use Warren Farrell's essay "Men as Success Objects" (p. 90), Barbara Ehrenrich's essay "Angry Young Men" (p. 138), and Sam Allis' "What Do Men Really Want?" (p. 81) to argue that men have the more difficult problems in deciding the value of work in their lives.

3. Argue that women have the more difficult problem in deciding the importance of work in their lives. Learn how women balance careers and child rearing, or careers and leisure, and integrate Brandt's report with what you have found in your research.

WHO'S NOT SUPPORTING WHOM?
Robert Moog

Credited with designing the first widely used electronic music synthesizers, Robert Moog (b. 1934) is not only president of his own music equipment company, but he continues to write and lecture on music technology. In spite of his extensive technical background—he has a Ph.D. in engineering physics from Cornell—Moog believes *writing* is a critical skill, especially for those in science, business, and computers: "In this post-industrial era, it's easy to push buttons, but if you want to convey information or convince people of your views, you have to either talk or write well. I prefer to write." Drawing on his experience developing products, managing companies, and having his own business fold, Moog challenges the "buy American" trend. The following article appeared as a guest editorial in *Keyboard* magazine in September 1992.

1   Two years ago here in North Carolina, Harvey Gantt was running for the U.S. Senate against incumbent Jesse Helms. It was a heated campaign, with Helms, perhaps the most reactionary senator ever, accusing Gantt of favoring minorities, welfare cheaters, gays, and immoral musicians and artists at the expense of the moral white majority. Those of us who had Gantt bumper stickers on our cars could depend on hearing nasty remarks from some of our fellow citizens.

2   One day back then, I was filling the tank of my Toyota when another customer at the gas station came up to me and asked, "Why is it that all you Gantt people have Jap cars?" For an instant, the question made no sense to me, so I said to him, "I give up. Why is it that all us Gantt people have Jap cars?" With steam coming out of his ears, he sputtered, "Well, you're all so goddamn patriotic!" Then he turned, bolted to his shiny new Chevy, slammed the door, and varoomed off in a cloud of smoke.

3   If my mind was quicker, I could have told him why I have a "Jap" car. Since 1950 I'd been trying to buy a small, well-made car—one in which the gas mileage was good, the doors didn't leak, and the frequency-of-repair records were favorable. Such cars were simply not made in the United States. From my perspective it appeared that Detroit was so busy building land-going versions of the Queen Mary, changing model years, fighting with their unions, voting themselves obscene salaries, and making sure that their stockholders got their dividends every quarter, that they did not have time to find out what kinds of cars people like me wanted. And the automotive unions seemed to be too busy negotiating big fat wage and benefit packages for their members to worry about the unseemly number of "Monday cars" (*i.e.,* lemons) that were populating the highways of our country.

4   So I did what any good patriotic American would do. Believing in the free enterprise system and in the benefits of vigorous competition, I did the only thing that made sense—I bought a superior competitive product, one that met my needs. That, I thought, would certainly help stimulate some action in the marketing

american need to make better products

departments of the Detroit establishment. That's how progress happens in a free market. Companies that are <u>truly customer-oriented thrive, and the less able com</u>panies—those that are burdened with inflexible or incompetent management . . . well, too bad, that's how our system works.

5   During the past two decades, millions of Americans like me have opted for Japanese cars, and Detroit is beginning to get the message. American cars being made today are smaller, more reliable, and more fuel-efficient than the wheeled dream-boats of the '50s and '60s. Our free market system is working. In the meantime, I have my Toyota, which still gets 35 miles per gallon and runs like a top after seven years, and has cost me a total of $200 in repair bills. It's all part of our capitalist system; my car is an ongoing reminder to Detroit of what they have to do in order to get my business.

6   That's what I would have told the man with the Chevy at the gas station—if my mind had been quicker.

7   I remembered that gas station incident when I read Richard Marshall's letter in the June '92 issue of *Keyboard*. Like my Chevy-driver acquaintance, Marshall was off on a be-patriotic-and-buy-American rant. Marshall's nuggets of protectionist wisdom rang familiar: "Every time we purchase an instrument, we vote with our wallet, either to keep our neighbors employed and off welfare or to fill the bank accounts of those wonderful people who brought us Pearl Harbor. Going out of one's way to buy American is neither paranoid nor racist, as some have accused, but rather <u>economic common sense</u>," intoned Marshall, as if his logic were irrefutable.

To support our ctry

8   Well, I, for one, don't buy any of this patriotism-through-purchase logic. I'll tell you why, from the perspective of a person who has been deep in the electronic musical instrument business for nearly 30 years.

9   Under the free market system, which is certainly a cornerstone of American capitalism, producers are free to make and sell any products they choose, and consumers are free to buy any products they choose. <u>Under this system, producers who offer desirable products at the right prices thrive, and those who don't must either improve their products' desirability or fail. This system has been the engine of genuine economic progress in our society. Under this system, the United States has become the wealthiest and most powerful nation on Earth.</u>

thesis?

10   Now, when some foreign producers enter our free market and offer more desirable products than some domestic producers, how does it suddenly become the patriotic duty of consumers to abandon their role of free-market buyer and "go out of their way" to buy American? Buying a less desirable product in order to "help keep our neighbors employed and off welfare" is <u>not</u> "economic common sense" at all. It's <u>charity</u>. It's short-term humanitarian aid, a form of middle-class welfare that subverts our cherished free-market economy and hurts our national strength in the long run.

11   So who's not being patriotic and supporting their fellow countrymen when American musicians buy Japanese instruments in ever-increasing numbers? I'll tell you who. It's us instrument builders whose instruments you're not buying, that's who! Somewhere along the line, each of us has neglected to build desirable

instruments at the right price, or we've neglected to manage our businesses so they are profitable and financially sound. Many of us have faltered or failed, and in doing so we've taken a toll on our national economic vitality.

12   When I began studying electrical engineering at Columbia University, our Dean of Students gave us a definition of an engineer: "An engineer is someone who can do for two cents what any damn fool can do for three cents." This should be the golden rule of engineering. But we seemed to lose sight of this wisdom as we worked through courses in circuit theory, solid state electronics, and advanced mathematics. We were taken with how clever we were becoming, and sneered at those of our fellow students who were majoring in mere industrial engineering. Those were the guys who would be running the factories while we would be sitting in our air-conditioned offices, designing one clever circuit after another. By the time we graduated from Columbia, we'd forgotten about our Dean's advice to be better than a damn fool when it came to making things at the best price.

13   Thus, when I started Moog Music (called R. A. Moog, Inc. back then), I had little understanding of how to manage manufacturing. But what's worse, I had no understanding at all of how to manage a business. I hired several electrical engineers like me, and together we managed to build a lot of synthesizers in the 1960s. But we wasted a lot of effort and money, and when our market became saturated and the first serious competition came, we simply ran out of money. The company eventually became a division of Norlin Music and, after being mishandled by a string of managers with more testosterone than management smarts, dropped out of the musical instrument manufacturing business about eight years ago.

14   At its peak, Moog Music had about 300 employees. How many overpriced, underfeatured instruments would have to have been sold to well-meaning musicians who wanted to "keep our neighbors employed and off welfare," even for one year? Well, at an average salary of, say, $15,000 a year (back then), and manufacturing labor being about 20% of an instrument's retail price, you musicians would have had to cough up about $22 million just to keep Moog Music's employees off welfare for one year! For sure, everybody was better off with the forces of competition pushing my old company swiftly and mercifully into the ground.

15   An unusual story? Not at all. Moog's chief competitor, ARP Instruments, was riding high during the early '70s. But by the late '70s, a combination of mismanagement, bad product development decisions, and really nasty infighting in the front office propelled the company into involuntary bankruptcy (the worst kind). Lots of people were laid off. Should musicians have done their patriotic duty and come to ARP's rescue by buying carloads of poorly conceived, overpriced products? Are you kidding?

16   Another example is an Italian electronic keyboard manufacturer that I did some work for about ten years ago. It was a well-established company, originally an accordion manufacturer. But as electronic instruments increased in complexity, the sophistication of their management still remained geared to the labor-intensive practices of their earlier days. Shortly before its demise, the company was shipping instruments that had a mean time between failures of three weeks!

Still, the head of the company would go on his daily rounds to turn out lights to save electricity, and to belittle the men and harass the women to remind everybody who was boss. So how many Italians do you think stepped forward to buy the company's instruments "to keep their neighbors off welfare"? None that I know of.

17   Space limitations prevent me from regaling you with more stories of instrument manufacturers who are no longer in business. Like Moog Music, most of these companies did enjoy a few years of successful, profitable operation, but then failed because of a combination of inadequate marketing, manufacturing control, and financing. Most had been founded by engineers who were not trained managers. And more to the point of this editorial, no amount of "going out of one's way to buy American" would have saved any of these companies.

18   To be sure, there are many American instrument companies that have operated successfully for many years, who have grown, and who have consistently offered successful, desirable products. My hat is off in admiration to Peavey, E-mu, and Ensoniq, to name three companies who are doing the right kind of job for their employees, their customers, and their country.

19   Let me put down a few words about global competitiveness. Much of what we buy and use in our daily lives comes from outside our borders, because the production capacity to meet our needs does not exist here. Let's not get into why it doesn't exist, but merely note that if our supply of foreign petroleum, TV sets, sport shirts, computer printers, paper clips, rum, cheap shoes, expensive brandy, and thousands upon thousands of other items were to be cut off tomorrow, our domestic producers of these items could not keep up with our needs, and the conduct of our daily lives would be severely curtailed. To pay for all these foreign-made items, we have to export stuff that people in foreign countries want to buy. The more we export, the more foreign currency we have and the easier it is for us as a nation to afford the foreign goods that we need. This means that companies that make products that foreigners are willing to buy are helping us all to have foreign goods that we need.

20   Now, how do you help a company to be competitive in the world market? By saying that you'll buy its products just because they're made in America? No way! Any time a company perceives that it has a captive, unquestioning market, it becomes less competitive. I've seen it happen many times, especially in the early days of synthesizers. To take an extreme case, look what happened in the former Soviet Union and the Eastern bloc countries. They went one step beyond asking their citizens to give preference to their domestic goods. Through their import restrictions, they made it virtually impossible for their citizens to buy foreign goods. The result: Has anybody ever seen a Soviet consumer product that's competitive in the world market (except maybe for vodka and caviar)? What Soviet car would you buy? How about a nice Soviet jacket or portable stereo? None of these things exist as world-marketable products, because the manufacturers of these products, having a captive domestic market, grew inefficient and unresponsive.

21   Here's my answer to how to help your fellow American instrument builders: The next time you need an instrument, buy the best one for your needs that you

can afford. If it happens to be an American product, great! Write to the marketing department of the instrument manufacturer, and tell them why you like their instrument. If they're on the ball (and they probably are if they got as far as making instruments that you like), they'll use your letter to fine-tune their product development program.

22   On the other hand, if you wind up buying a foreign-made instrument, it's your patriotic duty to write to the American manufacturers whose products you didn't buy, tell them whose product you bought, and tell them why. If a company reads your letter and acts on it, then you have helped them to improve their product line, thereby helping them to be more competitive worldwide. The day's pay or so that you denied some worker in that company because you bought a competitive product should be more than offset by the increased business that the company will enjoy because of the information you gave it. Or, if some company receives your letter and ignores it, then it won't last long anyhow, and the sooner its employees find employment elsewhere, the better it will be for them.

23   I'll close with a response to Marshall's crack about "the folks that gave us Pearl Harbor." Yes, Japan gave us Pearl Harbor, no doubt about it. They were able to do it because their country was under the control of an imperialist, warmongering regime. As it turns out, the Japanese people paid dearly for their military adventures. Today, the political climate in Japan is decidedly pacifist. The Japanese people have directed their energies and their intelligence to economic, rather than military, achievements.

24   In our free market economy, playing our free market game, the Japanese have made dramatic progress. In many cases, especially consumer electronics, they've gone far beyond us. They started out with the same technology that we had, but while we were keeping hundreds of thousands of people busy designing Star Wars Space Zappers and stockpiling nuclear weapons like so many bales of hay, Japanese engineers developed the technologies for portable DATs, professional-quality hand-held video cameras, and, yes, digital keyboards. The Japanese nation has become wealthy by designing and making these things, and their products have given millions of people around the world great pleasure and enjoyment.

25   As a nation, we no longer need Space Zappers and thousands of nuclear weapons. We no longer need a military-industrial complex of the size that has developed over the past 40 years. Now, for our own safety as well as our own economic well-being, we have to put a stop to being the world's arms purveyor and start designing and building products that people at peace want to buy.

THINKING ABOUT THE TEXT

1. Moog opens his argument with a narrative about a time when he was criticized for supporting a liberal senatorial candidate (instead of Jesse Helms) and for driving a "Jap car." Discuss how this personal anecdote helps Moog identify his narrator, establish his focus, and build to his thesis. What is his thesis?

2. What does Moog feel is wrong with keeping neighbors off welfare by buying a less desirable product? Why is this not "economic common sense"? How is this "patriotism-through-purchase" logic flawed?

3. How does the author's experience with Moog Music support his claims?

4. How can we help an American company be competitive in the world market? What should we do if we buy a foreign-made product?

5. What does Moog suggest that the American government can learn from the Japanese?

WRITING FROM THE TEXT

1. Focus on a Japanese-made product that you have purchased (for example, one made by Toyota, Honda, Mitsubishi, Nissan, Sony, Panasonic, Casio, Minolta, or Yamaha) and write a letter to the American competitor explaining whose product you bought and why. Be detailed, offer suggestions, and explain what it will take to get you to "buy American."

2. Moog identifies himself as "a good patriotic American." Write an essay focusing on Moog's implicit definition of "patriotism" and contrast it with the Chevy driver and with Richard Marshall, whose letter triggered this article.

3. Write an analysis of Moog's argument. Consider his thesis, supporting points, tone, use of narrative, definition, and contrast. Where does he anticipate and counter possible objections? (See "Argument," pp. 414–422.)

CONNECTING WITH OTHER TEXTS

1. Write an essay analyzing the importance of pride in one's work by relating Moog's argument to Auden's definition of workers and laborers (p. 249).

2. Focusing on a particular high-tech product (automobile, VCR, CD player, microwave), research the latest *Consumer Reports* evaluation of the various competitors. Then write a paper supporting or opposing the buy-American trend, based on your findings. Be careful that the American products you consider are indeed American and not just foreign products with American brand names on them.

IN GROUPS WE SHRINK
Carol Tavris

After studying sociology and comparative literature at Brandeis University, Carol Tavris (b. 1944) earned her Ph.D. in social psychology at the University of Michigan. Tavris has worked as a free-lance writer, taught in UCLA's psychology department, and served as both a writer and editor for *Psychology Today*. She has published extensively in the field of psychology, with emphasis on emotions, anger, sexuality, and gender issues. Her most recent book, *The Mismeasure of Woman*, was published in 1992. The essay printed here appeared in the *Los Angeles Times* in 1991.

1   The ghost of Kitty Genovese would sympathize with Rodney King. Genovese, you may remember, is the symbol of bystander apathy in America. Screaming for help, she was stabbed repeatedly and killed in front of her New York apartment, and not one of the 38 neighbors who heard her, including those who came to their windows to watch, even called for help.

2   One of the things we find appalling in the videotape of King's assault is the image of at least 11 police officers watching four of their colleagues administer the savage beating and doing nothing to intervene. Whatever is the matter with them, we wonder.

3   Something happens to individuals when they collect in a group. They think and act differently than they would on their own. Most people, if they observe some disaster or danger on their own—a woman being stabbed, a pedestrian slammed by a hit-and-run driver—will at least call for help; many will even risk their own safety to intervene. But if they are in a group observing the same danger, they hold back. The reason is not necessarily that they are lazy, cowardly or have 50 other personality deficiencies; it has more to do with the nature of groups than the nature of individuals.

4   In one experiment in behavioral psychology, students were seated in a room, either alone or in groups of three, as a staged emergency occurred: Smoke began pouring through the vents. Students who were on their own usually hesitated a minute, got up, checked the vents and then went out to report what certainly seemed like fire. But the students who were sitting in groups of three did not move. They sat there for six minutes, with smoke so thick they could barely see, rubbing their eyes and coughing.

5   In another experiment, psychologists staged a situation in which people overheard a loud crash, a scream and a woman in pain, moaning that her ankle was broken. Seventy percent of those who were alone when the "accident" occurred went to her aid, compared with only 40% of those who heard her in the presence of another person.

6   For victims, obviously, there is no safety in numbers. Why? One reason is that if other people aren't doing anything, the individual assumes that nothing needs to be done. In the smoke-filled room study, the students in groups said they thought

that the smoke was caused by "steam pipes," "truth gas" or "leaks in the air conditioning"; not one said what the students on their own did: "I thought it was fire." In the lady-in-distress study, some of those who failed to offer help said, "I didn't want to embarrass her."

7. Often, observers think nothing needs to be done because someone else has already taken care of it, and the more observers there are, the less likely any one person is to call for help. In Albuquerque, N.M., 30 people watched for an hour and a half as a building burned to the ground before they realized that no one had called the fire department. Psychologists call this process "diffusion of responsibility" or "social loafing": The more people in a group, the lazier each individual in it becomes.

8. But there was no mistaking what those officers were doing to Rodney King. There was no way for those observers to discount the severity of the beating King was getting. What kept them silent?

9. One explanation, of course, is that they approved. They may have identified with the abusers, vicariously participating in a beating they rationalized as justified. The widespread racism in the Los Angeles Police Department and the unprovoked abuse of black people is now undeniable. A friend who runs a trucking company told me recently that one of her drivers, a 50-year-old black man, is routinely pulled over by Los Angeles cops for the flimsiest of reasons "and made to lie down on the street like a dog." None of her white drivers has been treated this way.

10. Or the observers may have hated what was happening and been caught in the oldest of human dilemmas: Do the moral thing and be disliked, humiliated, embarrassed and rejected. Our nation, for all its celebration of the Lone Ranger and the independent pioneer, does not really value the individual—at least not when the person is behaving individually and standing up to the group. (We like dissenters, but only when they are dissenting in Russia or China.) Again and again, countless studies have shown that people will go along rather than risk the embarrassment of being disobedient, rude or disloyal.

11. And so the banality of evil is once again confirmed. Most people do not behave badly because they are inherently bad. They behave badly because they aren't paying attention, or they leave it to Harry, or they don't want to rock the boat, or they don't want to embarrass themselves or others if they're wrong.

12. Every time the news reports another story of a group that has behaved mindlessly, violently and stupidly, including the inevitable members who are just "going along," many people shake their heads in shock and anger at the failings of "human nature." But the findings of behavioral research can direct us instead to appreciate the conditions under which individuals in groups will behave morally or not. Once we know the conditions, we can begin to prescribe antidotes. By understanding the impulse to diffuse responsibility, perhaps as individuals we will be more likely to act. By understanding the social pressures that reward groupthink, loyalty and obedience, we can foster those that reward whistle-blowing and moral courage. And, as a society, we can reinforce the belief that they also sin who only stand and watch.

THINKING ABOUT THE TEXT

1. What is Tavris' thesis? How does she support her position?
2. How does the psychologist's term for the behavior Tavris describes explain what actually happens?
3. How does Tavris imagine this condition will right itself?

WRITING FROM THE TEXT

1. Write about an incident that you observed or were a part of that confirms Carol Tavris' point.
2. Write about an incident that you observed or were a part of that shows an exception to Tavris' point.

CONNECTING WITH OTHER TEXTS

1. Research the Rodney King incident of 1991 to find interviews and court testimony from the police officers involved as participants or observers of the beating. Do their own words and feelings confirm or refute Tavris' thesis?
2. Compare the views of Milton Mayer (p. 294) with the observations made in Tavris' essay.
3. Analyze the activity described in "Stone-throwing in India" (p. 290), and the short story "The Lottery" (p. 283), in terms of Tavris' description of group behavior.

WHY JOHNNY CAN'T DISOBEY
Sarah J. McCarthy

A graduate of Duquesne University, Sarah J. McCarthy (b. 1942) is an owner of Amel's Restaurant, in Pittsburgh, Pennsylvania, and a free-lance writer. McCarthy has written "Pornography, Rape, and The Cult of Macho," and "Cultural Fascism," for *Forbes* magazine. The essay printed here appeared first in *The Humanist* in 1979.

1   Few people are too concerned about whether Johnny can disobey. There is no furor or frantic calls to the PTA, as when it is discovered that he can't read or does poorly on his S.A.T. scores. Even to consider the question is at first laughable. Parents and teachers, after all, are systematically working at developing the virtue

of obedience. To my knowledge, no one as yet has opened a remedial disobedience school for overly compliant children, and probably no one ever will. And that in itself is a major problem.

2   Patricia Hearst recently said that the mindless state of obedience which enveloped her at the hands of the Symbionese Liberation Army could happen to anyone. Jumping to a tentative conclusion from a tip-of-the-iceberg perspective, it looks as though it already has happened to many, and that it has required nothing so dramatic as a kidnapping to bring it about.

3   Given our experience with various malevolent authority figures such as Adolph Hitler, Charles Manson, Lieutenant Calley, and Jim Jones, it is unfortunately no longer surprising that there are leaders who are capable of wholesale cruelty to the point of directing mass killings. What remains shocking, however, is that they are so often successful in recruiting followers. There seems to be no shortage of individuals who will offer their hearts and minds on a silver platter to feed the egos of the power-hungry. This becomes even more disturbing when one ponders the truism that society's neurotics are often its cultural caricatures, displaying exaggerated manifestations of its collective neuroses. There are enough examples of obedience to horrendous commands for us to ask if and how a particular culture sows the seeds of dangerous conformity.

4   Political platitudes and lip service to the contrary, obedience is highly encouraged in matters petty as well as profound. Linda Eton, an Iowa firefighter, was suspended from her job and catapulted to national fame for the radical act of breast-feeding at work. A dehumanized, compartmentalized society finds little room for spontaneity, and a blatantly natural act like breast-feeding is viewed as a preposterous interruption of the status quo.

5   Pettiness abounds in our social relationships, ensuring compliance through peer pressure and disapproval, and enforced by economic sanctions at the workplace. A friend of mine, a construction worker, reported to his job one rainy day carrying an umbrella. The foreman was outraged by this break from the norm, and demanded that the guy never again carry an umbrella to the construction site, even if the umbrella was black, since it "caused his whole crew to look like a bunch of faggots."

6   Another friend, though less scandalizingly visible in his job as a security guard during the wee hours for a multinational corporation, was caught redhanded playing a harmonica. Mercifully, he was given another chance, only to be later fired for not wearing regulation shoes.

7   Ostensibly, such firings and threats are deemed necessary to prevent inefficiency and rampant chaos at the workplace. But if employers were merely concerned about productivity and efficiency, it certainly is disputable that "yes-people" are more productive and beneficial than "no-people." Harmonicas may even increase efficiency by keeping security guards sane, alert, and awake by staving off sensory deprivation. A dripping-wet construction worker could conceivably be less productive than a dry one. And the Adidas being worn by the errant security guard could certainly have contributed to his fleetness and agility as opposed to the cumbersome regulation shoes. The *real* issues here have nothing to do with productivity. What is really involved is an irrational fear of the mildly unusual, a pervasive

attitude held by authorities that their subordinates are about to run amok and need constant control.

8   These little assaults on our freedom prepare us for the big ones. Having long suspected that a huge iceberg of mindless obedience existed beneath our cultural surface, I was not particularly surprised when I heard that nine hundred people followed their leader to mass suicide. For some time we have lived with the realization that people are capable of killing six million of their fellow citizens on command. Jonestown took us one step further. People will kill themselves on command.

9   In matters ridiculous and sublime, this culture and the world at large clearly exhibit symptoms of pathological obedience. Each time one of the more sensational incidents occurs—Jonestown, the Mai Lai massacre, Nazi Germany, the Manson murders—we attribute its occurrence to factors unique to it, trying to deny any similarities to anything close to us, tossing it about like a philosophical hot potato. We prefer to view such events as anomalies, isolated in time and space, associated with faraway jungles, exotic cults, drugged hippies, and outside agitators. However, as the frequency of such happenings increases, there is the realization that it is relatively easy to seduce some people into brainwashed states of obedience.

10   Too much energy and time have been spent on trying to understand the alleged compelling traits and mystical powers of charismatic leaders, and not enough in an attempt to understand their fellow travelers—the obedient ones. We need to look deeper into those who *elected* Hitler, and all those followers of Jim Jones who went to Guyana *voluntarily*. We must ask how many of us are also inclined toward hyperobedience. Are we significantly different, capable of resisting malevolent authority, or have we simply had the good fortune never to have met a Jim Jones of our own?

11   Social psychologist Stanley Milgram, in his book *Obedience to Authority,* is convinced that:

> In growing up, the normal individual has learned to check the expression of aggressive impulses. But the culture has failed, almost entirely, in inculcating internal controls on actions that have their origin in authority. For this reason, the latter constitutes a far greater danger to human survival.

12   Vince Bugliosi, prosecutor of Charles Manson and author of *Helter Skelter,* commented on the Jonestown suicides:

> Education of the public is the only answer. If young people could be taught what can happen to them—that they may be zombies a year after talking to that smiling person who stops them on a city street—they may be prepared.

Presumably, most young cult converts have spent most of their days in our educational system, yet are vulnerable to the beguiling smile or evil eye of a Charles Manson. If there is any lesson to be learned from the obedience-related holocausts, it must be that we can never underestimate the power of education and the socialization process.

13   Contrary to our belief that the survival instinct is predominant over all other drives, the Jonestown suicides offer testimony to the power of cultural indoctrination. Significantly, the greatest life force at the People's Temple came from the children. Acting on their survival instincts, they went kicking and screaming to their deaths in an "immature" display of disobedience. The adults, civilized and educated people that they were, lined up with "stiff upper lips" and took their medicine like the followers they were trained to be—a training that didn't begin at Jonestown.

14   When something so horrible as Jonestown happens, people draw metaphors about the nearness of the jungle and the beast that lurks within us. It seems that a more appropriate metaphor would be our proximity to an Orwellian civilization with its antiseptic removal of our human rough edges and "animal" instincts. On close scrutiny, the beast within us looks suspiciously like a sheep.

15   Despite our rich literature of freedom, a pervasive value instilled in our society is obedience to authority. Unquestioning obedience is perceived to be in the best interests of the schools, churches, families, and political institutions. Nationalism, patriotism, and religious ardor are its psychological vehicles.

16   Disobedience is the original sin, as all of the religions have stated in one way or another. Given the obedience training in organized religions that claim to possess mystical powers and extrarational knowledge and extoll the glories of self-sacrifice, what is so bizarre about the teachings of Jim Jones? If we arm our children with the rationality and independent thought necessary to resist the cultist, can we be sure that our own creeds and proclamations will meet the criteria of reason? The spotlight of reason which exposes the charlatan may next shine on some glaring inconsistencies in the "legitimate" religions. Religions, which are often nothing more than cults that grew, set the stage for the credulity and gullibility required for membership in cults.

17   A witch hunt is now brewing to exorcise the exotic cults, but what is the dividing line between a cult and a legitimate religion? Is there a qualitative difference between the actions of some venerated Biblical saints and martyrs and the martyrs of Jonestown? If the Bible contained a Parable of Guyana, the churches would regularly extoll it as a courageous act of self-sacrifice. Evidently saints and martyrs are only palatable when separated by the chasm of a few centuries. To enforce their beliefs, the major religions use nothing so crass as automatic weapons, of course, but instead fall back on automatic sentences to eternal damnation.

18   Certainly there must be an optimal level of obedience and cooperation in a reasonable society, but obedience, as any other virtue that is carried to an extreme, may become a vice. It is obvious that Nazi Germany and Jonestown went too far on the obedience continuum. In more mundane times and places the appropriate level of obedience is more difficult to discover.

19   We must ask if our society is part of the problem, part of the solution, or wholly irrelevant to the incidents of over-obedience exhibited at Jonestown and Mai Lai. Reviewing social psychologists' attempts to take our psychic temperatures through empirical measurements of our conformity and obedience behavior in experimental situations, our vital signs do not look good.

20   In 1951 Solomon Asch conducted an experiment on conformity, which is similar to obedience behavior in that it subverts one's will to that of peers or an

authority. This study, as reported in the textbook *Social Psychology* by Freedman, Sears, and Carlsmith, involved college students who were asked to estimate lines of equal and differing lengths. Some of the lines were obviously equal, but if subjects heard others before them unanimously give the wrong answer, they would also answer incorrectly. Asch had reasoned that people would be rational enough to choose the evidence of their own eyes over the disagreeing "perceptions" of others. He found that he was wrong.

21   When subjects were asked to estimate the length of a line after confederates of the experimenter had given obviously wrong answers, the subjects gave wrong answers about 35 percent of the time. Authors Freedman, Sears, and Carlsmith stress:

> It is important to keep the unambiguousness of the situations in mind if we are to understand this phenomenon. There is a tendency to think that the conforming subjects are uncertain of the correct choice and therefore are swayed by the majority. This is not always the case. In many instances subjects are quite certain of the correct choice and, in the absence of group pressure, would choose correctly 100 percent of the time. When they conform, they are conforming despite the fact that they know the correct answer.

22   If 35 percent of those students conformed to group opinion in unambiguous matters and in direct contradiction of the evidence of their own eyes, how much more must we fear blind following in *ambiguous* circumstances or in circumstances where there exists a legitimate authority?

23   In the early sixties, Yale social psychologist Stanley Milgram devised an experiment to put acts of obedience and disobedience under close scrutiny. Milgram attempted to understand why thousands of "civilized" people had engaged in an extreme and immoral act—that of the wholesale extermination of Jews—in the name of obedience. He devised a learning task in which subjects of the experiment were instructed to act as teachers. They were told to "shock" learners for their mistakes. The learners were actually confederates of the experimenter and were feigning their reactions. When a mistake was made, the experimenter would instruct the teacher to administer an ever-increasing voltage from a shock machine which read "Extreme Danger," "Severe Shock," and "XXX." Although the machine was unconnected, the subject-teachers believed that they were actually giving shocks. They were themselves given a real sample shock before the experiment began.

24   Milgram asked his Yale colleagues to make a guess as to what proportion of subjects would proceed to shock all the way to the presumed lethal end of the shock-board. Their estimates hovered around 1 or 2 percent. No one was prepared for what happened. All were amazed that twenty-six out of forty subjects obeyed the experimenter's instruction to press levers that supposedly administered severely dangerous levels of shock. After this, Milgram regularly obtained results showing that 62 to 65 percent of people would shock to the end of the board. He tried several variations on the experiment, one of which was to set it up outside of Yale University so that the prestige of the University would not be an overriding factor in causing subjects to obey. He found that people were just as likely to administer severe shock, whether the experiments occurred within the hallowed halls of Yale

or in a three-room walk-up storefront in which the experiments spoke of themselves as "scientific researchers."

25   In another variation of the experiment, Milgram found that aggression—latent or otherwise—was not a significant factor in causing the teacher-subjects to shock the learners. When the experimenter left the room, thus permitting the subjects to choose the level of shock themselves, almost none administered more than the lowest voltage. Milgram concluded that obedience, not aggression, was the problem. He states:

> I must conclude that [Hannah] Arendt's conception of the *banality of evil* comes closer to the truth than one might dare imagine. The ordinary person who shocked the victim did so out of a sense of obligation—a conception of his duties as a subject—and not from any peculiarly aggressive tendencies.
>
> This is, perhaps, the most fundamental lesson of our study: ordinary people, simply doing their jobs, and without any particular hostility on their part, can become agents in a terrible destructive process. Moreover, even when the destructive effects of their work become patently clear, and they are asked to carry out actions incompatible with fundamental standards of morality, relatively few people have the resources needed to resist authority. A variety of inhibitions against disobeying authority come into play and successfully keep the person in his place.

A lack of compassion was not a particularly salient personality factor in the acts of obedience performed by the follows of Hitler, Jim Jones, and the subjects in the Milgram experiments. Nazi soldiers were capable of decent human behavior toward their friends and family. Some, too, see an irony in that Hitler himself was a vegetarian. The People's Temple members seemed more compassionate and humanitarian than many, and yet they forced their own children to partake of a drink laced with cyanide. Those shocking the victims in the Milgram experiments exhibited signs of compassion both toward the experimenter and to the persons that they thought were receiving the shocks. In fact, Milgram finds that:

> It is a curious thing that a measure of compassion on the part of the subject, an unwillingness to "hurt" the experimenter's feelings, are part of those binding forces inhibiting disobedience . . . only obedience can preserve the experimenter's status and dignity.

26   Milgram's subjects showed signs of severe physiological tension and internal conflict when instructed to shock. Presumably, these signs of psychic pain and tortured indecision were a manifestation of an underlying attitude of compassion for the victim, but it was not sufficient to impel them to openly break with, and therefore embarrass, the experimenter, even though this experimenter had no real authority over them. One of Milgram's subjects expressed this dilemma succinctly:

I'll go through with anything they tell me to do. . . . They know more than I do. . . . I know when I was in the service [if I was told] "You go over the hill and we're going to attack," we attacked. So I think it's all based on the way a man was brought up . . . in his background. Well, I faithfully believed the man [whom he thought he had shocked] was dead until we opened the door. When I saw him, I said: "Great, this is great!" But it didn't bother me even to find that he was dead. I did a job.

27   The experiments continued with thousands of people—students and nonstudents, here and abroad—often demonstrating obedience behavior in 60 to 65 percent of the subjects. When the experiments were done in Munich, obedience often reached 85 percent. Incidentally, Milgram found no sex differences in obedience behavior. Though his sample of women shockers was small, their level of obedience was identical to that of the men. But they did exhibit more symptoms of internal conflict. Milgram concluded that "there is probably nothing the victim can say that will uniformly generate disobedience," since it is not the victim who is controlling the shocker's behavior. Even when one of the experimental variations included a victim who cried out that he had a heart condition, this did not lead to significantly greater disobedience. In such situations, the experimenter-authority figure dominates the subject's social field, while the pleading cries of the victim are for the most part ignored.

28   Milgram found that the authority's power had to be somehow undermined before there was widespread disobedience, as when the experimenter was not physically present, when his orders came over the telephone, or when his orders were challenged by another authority. Most importantly, subjects became disobedient in large numbers only when others rebelled, dissented, or argued with the experimenter. When a subject witnessed another subject defying or arguing with the experimenter, thirty-six out of forty also rebelled, demonstrating that peer rebellion was the most effective experimental variation in undercutting authority.

29   This social orientation in which the authority dominates one's psyche is attributed by Milgram to a state of mind which he terms "the agentic state." A person makes a critical shift from a relatively autonomous state into this agentic state when she or he enters a situation in which "he defines himself in a manner that renders him open to regulation by a person of higher status."

30   An extreme agentic state is a likely explanation for the scenario at Jonestown, where even the cries of their own children were not sufficient to dissuade parents from serving cyanide. Despite some ambiguity as to how many Jonestown residents were murdered and how many committed suicide, there remains the fact that these victims had participated in previous suicide rehearsals. Jim Jones, assured of their loyalty and of their critical shift into an agentic state, then had the power to orchestrate the real thing. The supreme irony, the likes of which could only be imagined as appearing in the *Tralfamadore Tribune* with a byline by Kurt Vonnegut, was the picture of the Guyana death scene. Bodies were strewn about beneath the throne of Jones and a banner which proclaimed that those who failed to learn from the lessons of history were doomed to repeat them.

31   How many of us have made the critical shift into an agentic state regarding international relations, assuming that our leaders know best, even though they have repeatedly demonstrated that they do not? Stanley Milgram predicts that "for the man who sits in front of the button that will release Armageddon, depressing it will have about the same emotional force as calling for an elevator . . . evolution has not had a chance to build inhibitors against such remote forms of aggression."

32   We should recognize that our human nature renders us somewhat vulnerable. For one thing, our own mortality and that of our loved ones is an unavoidable fact underlying our lives. In the face of it, we are powerless; and in our insecurity, many reach out for sure answers. Few choose to believe, along with Clarence Darrow, that not only are we not the captains of our fate, but that we are not even "deckhands on a rudderless dinghy." Or, as someone else has stated: "There are no answers. Be brave and face up to it." Most of us won't face up to it. We want our answers, solutions to our plight, and we want them now. Too often truth and rational thought are the first casualties of this desperate reach for security. We embrace answers from charlatans, false prophets, charismatic leaders, and assorted demagogues. Given these realities of our nature, how can we avoid these authority traps to which we are so prone? By what criteria do we teach our children to distinguish between the charlatan and the prophet?

33   It seems that the best armor is the rational mind. We must insist that all authorities account for themselves, and we need to be as wary of false prophets as we are of false advertising. Leaders, political and spiritual, must be subjected to intense scrutiny, and we must insist that their thought processes and proclamations measure up to reasonable standards of rational thought. Above all, we must become skilled in activating our inner resources toward rebellion and disobedience, when this seems reasonable.

34   The power of socialization can conceivably be harnessed so as to develop individuals who are rational and skeptical, capable of independent thought, and who can disobey or disagree at the critical moment. Our society, however, continues systematically to instill exactly the opposite. The educational system pays considerable lip service to the development of self-reliance, and places huge emphasis on lofty concepts of individual differences. Little notice is taken of the legions of overly obedient children in the schools; yet, for every overly disobedient child, there are probably twenty who are obeying too much. There is little motivation to encourage the unsqueaky wheels to develop as noisy, creative, independent thinkers who may become bold enough to disagree. Conceivably, we could administer modified Milgram obedience tests in the schools which detect hyperobedience, just as we test for intelligence, visual function, vocational attributes and tuberculosis. When a child is found to be too obedient, the schools should mobilize against this psychological crippler with the zeal by which they would react to an epidemic of smallpox. In alcoholism and other mental disturbances, the first major step toward a reversal of the pathology is recognition of the severity of the problem. Obedience should be added to the list of emotional disturbances requiring therapy. Disobedience schools should be at least as common as military schools and reform schools.

35   The chains on us are not legal or political, but the invisible chains of the agentic state. We have all gotten the message that it is dangerous and requires exceptional courage to be different.

36   If we are to gain control of our lives and minds, we must first acknowledge the degree to which we are not now in control. We must become reasonable and skeptical. Reason is no panacea, but, at the moment, it is all that we have. Yet many in our society seem to have the same attitude about rationality and reason that they do about the poverty program—that is, we've tried it and it doesn't work.

37   Along with worrying about the S.A.T. scores and whether or not Johnny can read, we must begin to seriously question whether Johnny is capable of disobedience. The churches and cults, while retaining their constitutional right to free expression, must be more regularly criticized. The legitimate religions have been treated as sacred cows. Too often, criticism of them is met with accusations of religious bigotry, or the implications that one is taking candy from a baby or a crutch from a cripple. The concept of religious tolerance has been stretched to its outer limits, implying freedom from criticism and the nonpayment of taxes. Neither patriotism nor religion should be justification for the suspension of reason.

38   And, on a personal level, we must stop equating sanity with conformity, eccentricity with craziness, and normalcy with numbers. We must get in touch with our own liberating ludicrousness and practice being harmlessly deviant. We must, in fact, cease to use props or other people to affirm our normalcy. With sufficient practice, perhaps, when the need arises, we may have the strength to force a moment to its crisis.

THINKING ABOUT THE TEXT

1. What do the infamous authority figures like Charles Manson and Jim Jones have to do with McCarthy's point in this essay?

2. What cases of failure to comply with workplace norms does McCarthy cite to support her assertion that we are petty in enforcing conformity? How does she anticipate and meet the reader's possible objections that regulations may increase efficiency?

3. McCarthy says that we spend too much time trying to figure out the malevolent, charismatic leaders like Hitler. Where, instead, should our contemplative energies be used?

4. Which institutions in our culture inculcate the need for obedience to authority? Give specific examples of expected conformity for each of the institutions that you discuss.

5. What psychology experiments does McCarthy cite to support her view that as a nation we lack "the resources needed to resist authority"?

6. If the subjects in the studies reflect social norms, how do people who comply with authority figures feel about their obedience? What are

the reactions of both women and men during and after the test? Under what conditions *will* people resist authority?

7. What does the author predict as a possible reality for people who live in an "agentic state"? What does she insist we do to protect ourselves? How do you respond to her proposals for changes in the education of children?

WRITING FROM THE TEXT

1. Write an analysis of the conformity or obedience expectations of the institutions with which you have been identified. What was expected of you? What were your feelings then, and how do you feel now?

2. Write to persuade your reader that a particular authority figure you know expects specific obedience that is unnecessary or dangerous.

CONNECTING WITH OTHER TEXTS

1. Carol Tavris (p. 267) describes our "shrinking" from doing what we know is right when we are in groups. How does her analysis of human behavior relate to Milgrim's findings, reported in McCarthy's essay? Write an essay that shows the relationship.

2. How would McCarthy's "disobedience school" influence some of the gender-related problems expressed in the essays in this text? Consider Brophy's analysis of women in "invisible cages" (p. 94), for example, or Farrell's anger that men are expected to be "success objects" (p. 90). Propose a program for a disobedience school to liberate human beings from gender role conformity.

KIDS IN THE MALL: GROWING UP CONTROLLED
William Severini Kowinski

A free-lance writer who lives in Greensburg, Pennsylvania, William Kowinski (b. 1946) has been the book review editor and managing arts editor of the *Boston Phoenix* and has written for many national newspapers and magazines. In *The Malling of America*, his first book, Kowinski notes that the mall is "where all the postwar changes were tied together. It was the culmination of all the American dreams, both decent and demented; the fulfillment, the model of the postwar paradise." The book was published in 1985. The essay included here is a part of one chapter.

Butch heaved himself up and loomed over the group. "Like it was different for me," he piped. "My folks used to drop me off at the shopping mall every morning and leave me all day. It was like a big free baby-sitter, you know? One night they never came back for me. Maybe they moved away. Maybe there's some kind of a Bureau of Missing Parents I could check with."

—*Richard Peck*
Secrets of the Shopping Mall,
a novel for teenagers

1   From his sister at Swarthmore, I'd heard about a kid in Florida whose mother picked him up after school every day, drove him straight to the mall, and left him there until it closed—all at his insistence. I'd heard about a boy in Washington who, when his family moved from one suburb to another, pedaled his bicycle five miles every day to get back to his old mall, where he once belonged.

2   These stories aren't unusual. The mall is a common experience for the majority of American youth; they have probably been going there all their lives. Some ran within their first large open space, saw their first fountain, bought their first toy, and read their first book in a mall. They may have smoked their first cigarette or first joint, or turned them down, had their first kiss or lost their virginity in the mall parking lot. Teenagers in America now spend more time in the mall than anywhere else but home and school. Mostly it is their choice, but some of that mall time is put in as the result of two-paycheck and single-parent households, and the lack of other viable alternatives. But are these kids being harmed by the mall?

3   I wondered first of all what difference it makes for adolescents to experience so many important moments in the mall. They are, after all, at play in the fields of its little world and they learn its ways; they adapt to it and make it adapt to them. It's here that these kids get their street sense, only it's mall sense. They are learning the ways of a large-scale, artificial environment; its subtleties and flexibilities, its particular pleasures and resonances, and the attitudes it fosters.

4   The presence of so many teenagers for so much time was not something mall developers planned on. In fact, it came as a big surprise. But kids became a fact of mall life very easily, and the International Council of Shopping Centers found it necessary to commission a study, which they published along with a guide to mall managers on how to handle the teenage incursion.

5   The study found that "teenagers in suburban centers are bored and come to the shopping centers mainly as a place to go. Teenagers in suburban centers spent more time fighting, drinking, littering and walking than did their urban counterparts, but presented fewer overall problems." The report observed that "adolescents congregated in groups of two to four and predominantly at locations selected by them rather than management." This probably had something to do with the decision to install game arcades, which allow management to channel these restless adolescents into naturally contained areas away from major traffic points of adult shoppers.

6   The guide concluded that mall management should tolerate and even encourage the teenage presence because, in the words of the report, "The vast majority support the same set of values as does shopping center management." *The same set of values* means simply that mall kids are already preprogrammed to be consumers and that the mall can put the finishing touches to them as hard-core, lifelong shoppers just like everybody else. That, after all, is what the mall is about. So it shouldn't be surprising that in spending a lot of time there, adolescents find little that challenges the assumption that the goal of life is to make money and buy products, or that just about everything else in life is to be used to serve those ends.

7   Growing up in a high-consumption society already adds inestimable pressure to kids' lives. Clothes consciousness has invaded the grade schools, and popularity is linked with having the best, newest clothes in the currently acceptable styles. Even what they read has been affected. "Miss [Nancy] Drew wasn't obsessed with her wardrobe," noted the *Wall Street Journal.* "But today the mystery in teen fiction for girls is what outfit the heroine will wear next." Shopping has become a survival skill and there is certainly no better place to learn it than the mall, where its importance is powerfully reinforced and certainly never questioned.

8   The mall as a university of suburban materialism, where Valley Girls and Boys from coast to coast are educated in consumption, has its other lessons in this era of change in family life and sexual mores and their economic and social ramifications. The plethora of products in the mall, plus the pressure on teens to buy them, may contribute to the phenomenon that psychologist David Elkind calls "the hurried child": kids who are exposed to too much of the adult world too quickly and must respond with a sophistication that belies their still-tender emotional development. Certainly the adult products marketed for children—form-fitting designer jeans, sexy tops for preteen girls—add to the social pressure to look like an adult, along with the home-grown need to understand adult finances (why mothers must work) and adult emotions (when parents divorce).

9   Kids spend so much time at the mall partly because their parents allow it and even encourage it. The mall is safe, doesn't seem to harbor any unsavory activities, and there is adult supervision; it is, after all, a controlled environment. So the temptation, especially for working parents, is to let the mall be their baby-sitter. At least the kids aren't watching TV. But the mall's role as a surrogate mother may be more extensive and more profound.

10   Karen Lansky, a writer living in Los Angeles, has looked into the subject, and she told me some of her conclusions about the effects on its teenaged denizens of the mall's controlled and controlling environment. "Structure is the dominant idea, since true 'mall rats' lack just that in their home lives," she said, "and adolescents about to make the big leap into growing up crave more structure than our modern society cares to acknowledge." Karen pointed out some of the elements malls supply that kids used to get from their families, like warmth (Strawberry Shortcake dolls and similar cute and cuddly merchandise), old-fashioned mothering ("We do it all for you," the fast-food slogan), and even home cooking (the "homemade" treats at the food court).

11   The problem in all this, as Karen Lansky sees it, is that while families nurture children by encouraging growth through the assumption of responsibility and then by letting them rest in the bosom of the family from the rigors of growing up, the mall as a structural mother encourages passivity and consumption, as long as the kid doesn't make trouble. Therefore all they learn about becoming adults is how to act and how to consume.

12   Kids are in the mall not only in the passive role of shoppers—they also work there, especially as fast-food outlets infiltrate the mall's enclosure. There they learn how to hold a job and take responsibility, but still within the same value context. When *CBS Reports* went to Oak Park Mall in suburban Kansas City, Kansas, to tape part of their hour-long consideration of malls, "After the Dream Comes True," they interviewed a teenaged girl who worked in a fast-food outlet there. In a sequence that didn't make the final program, she described the major goal of her present life, which was to perfect the curl on top of the ice-cream cones that were her store's specialty. If she could do that, she would be moved from the lowly soft-drink dispenser to the more prestigious ice-cream division, the curl on top of the status ladder at her restaurant. These are the achievements that are important at the mall.

13   Other benefits of such jobs may also be overrated, according to Laurence D. Steinberg of the University of California at Irvine's social ecology department, who did a study on teenage employment. Their jobs, he found, are generally simple, mindlessly repetitive and boring. They don't really learn anything, and the jobs don't lead anywhere. Teenagers also work primarily with other teenagers; even their supervisors are often just a little older than they are. "Kids need to spend time with adults," Steinberg told me. "Although they get benefits from peer relationships, without parents and other adults it's one-sided socialization. They hang out with each other, have age-segregated jobs, and watch TV."

14   Perhaps much of this is not so terrible or even so terribly different. Now that they have so much more to contend with in their lives, adolescents probably need more time to spend with other adolescents without adult impositions, just to sort things out. Though it is more concentrated in the mall (and therefore perhaps a clearer target), the value system there is really the dominant one of the whole society. Attitudes about curiosity, initiative, self-expression, empathy, and disinterested learning aren't necessarily made in the mall; they are mirrored there, perhaps a bit more intensely—as through a glass brightly.

15   Besides, the mall is not without its educational opportunities. There are bookstores, where there is at least a short shelf of classics at great prices, and other books from which it is possible to learn more than how to do sit-ups. There are tools, from hammers to VCRs, and products, from clothes to records, that can help the young find and express themselves. There are older people with stories, and places to be alone or to talk one-on-one with a kindred spirit. And there is always the passing show.

16   The mall itself may very well be an education about the future. I was struck with the realization, as early as my first forays into Greengate, that the mall is only one of a number of enclosed and controlled environments that are part of the lives

of today's young. The mall is just an extension, say, of those large suburban schools—only there's Karmelkorn instead of chem lab, the ice rink instead of the gym: It's high school without the impertinence of classes.

17   Growing up, moving from home to school to the mall—from enclosure to enclosure, transported in cars—is a curiously continuous process, without much in the way of contrast or contact with unenclosed reality. Places must tend to blur into one another. But whatever differences and dangers there are in this, the skills these adolescents are learning may turn out to be useful in their later lives. For we seem to be moving inexorably into an age of preplanned and regulated environments, and this is the world they will inherit.

18   Still, it might be better if they had more of a choice. One teenaged girl confessed to *CBS Reports* that she sometimes felt she was missing something by hanging out at the mall so much. "But I'm here," she said, "and this is what I have."

THINKING ABOUT THE TEXT

1. Kowinski observes that the shopping mall has been the site of many rites of passage. Where have these "firsts" occurred in previous generations?

2. What are the learning potentials for adolescents who spend time in the mall? In what specific ways is the mall an advantage for teenagers and their parents, and in what ways is it a disadvantage?

3. In what ways do the mall managers and teens form a symbiotic relationship?

4. What do you consider the most negative effects of young people growing up in the mall?

WRITING FROM THE TEXT

1. Write about some of your experiences in the shopping mall, perhaps rites of passage, or specific events that directed growth or maturity. Focus your paper to support the positive or negative effects of the mall or to show both aspects, as Kowinski does.

2. Interview people in their sixties and seventies to learn how they spent time when they were not in school. What were their leisure activities? What kind of jobs did they have? In a paper, describe and evaluate this generation's free-time experiences. If it makes sense to do so, compare or contrast those experiences with the mall kids' experiences.

3. Write an essay to convince your reader that predominantly bad values and habits are inculcated in the young who spend too much time in malls.

4. Write to convince your reader that growing up in the mall is a positive experience for young people. Be specific in your support.

CONNECTING WITH OTHER TEXTS

1. In "Why Johnny Can't Disobey" (p. 269), "Commencement Address" (p. 294), "In Groups We Shrink" (p. 267), and this essay, the authors point out the insidious expectations for conformity in American culture. Write an essay in which you show that growing up in a shopping mall prepares young people for a life of conformity (you'll need plenty of specific mall examples) and that conformity results in the character defects that McCarthy, Mayer, and Tavris discuss.

2. Read Kowinski's book *The Malling of America: An Inside Look at the Great Consumer Paradise* (1985), from which this essay is taken. Write about another dimension of mall life that the author explores.

THE LOTTERY
Shirley Jackson

A graduate of Syracuse University, Shirley Jackson (1919–1965) lived in a large nineteenth-century house in Bennington, Vermont. There she deliberately required herself to write a fixed number of words each day. She wrote light articles about rearing four children and her life as a housewife for *Good Housekeeping*, but she also produced a number of novels: *The Road Through the Wall, Hangsamen, The Haunting of Hill House*, and *We Have Always Lived in the Castle*. In 1948, "The Lottery" was published in *The New Yorker* and received immediate acclaim. She has said that her purpose in writing the story was "to shock the story's readers with a graphic demonstration of the pointless violence and general inhumanity in their own lives."

1   The morning of June 27th was clear and sunny, with the fresh warmth of a full-summer day; the flowers were blossoming profusely and the grass was richly green. The people of the village began to gather in the square, between the post office and the bank, around ten o'clock; in some towns there were so many people that the lottery took two days and had to be started on June 26th, but in this village, where there were only about three hundred people, the whole lottery took less than two hours, so it could begin at ten o'clock in the morning and still be through in time to allow the villagers to get home for noon dinner.

2   The children assembled first, of course. School was recently over for the summer, and the feeling of liberty sat uneasily on most of them; they tended to gather together quietly for a while before they broke into boisterous play, and their talk was still of the classroom and the teacher, of books and reprimands. Bobby Martin had already stuffed his pockets full of stones, and the other boys soon followed his example, selecting the smoothest and roundest stones; Bobby and Harry Jones and

Dickie Delacroix—the villagers pronounced this name "Dellacroy"—eventually made a great pile of stones in one corner of the square and guarded it against the raids of the other boys. The girls stood aside, talking among themselves, looking over their shoulders at the boys, and the very small children rolled in the dust or clung to the hands of their older brothers or sisters.

3   Soon the men began to gather, surveying their own children, speaking of planting and rain, tractors and taxes. They stood together, away from the pile of stones in the corner, and their jokes were quiet and they smiled rather than laughed. The women, wearing faded house dresses and sweaters, came shortly after their menfolk. They greeted one another and exchanged bits of gossip as they went to join their husbands. Soon the women, standing by their husbands, began to call to their children, and the children came reluctantly, having to be called four or five times. Bobby Martin ducked under his mother's grasping hand and ran, laughing, back to the pile of stones. His father spoke up sharply, and Bobby came quickly and took his place between his father and his oldest brother.

4   The lottery was conducted—as were the square dances, the teen-age club, the Halloween program—by Mr. Summers, who had time and energy to devote to civic activities. He was a round-faced, jovial man and he ran the coal business, and people were sorry for him, because he had no children and his wife was a scold. When he arrived in the square, carrying the black wooden box, there was a murmur of conversation among the villagers, and he waved and called, "Little late today, folks." The postmaster, Mr. Graves, followed him, carrying a three-legged stool, and the stool was put in the center of the square and Mr. Summers set the black box down on it. The villagers kept their distance, leaving a space between themselves and the stool, and when Mr. Summers said, "Some of you fellows want to give me a hand?" there was a hesitation before two men, Mr. Martin and his oldest son, Baxter, came forward to hold the box steady on the stool while Mr. Summers stirred up the papers inside it.

5   The original paraphernalia for the lottery had been lost long ago, and the black box now resting on the stool had been put into use even before Old Man Warner, the oldest man in town, was born. Mr. Summers spoke frequently to the villagers about making a new box, but no one liked to upset even as much tradition as was represented by the black box. There was a story that the present box had been made with some pieces of the box that had preceded it, the one that had been constructed when the first people settled down to make a village here. Every year, after the lottery, Mr. Summers began talking again about a new box, but every year the subject was allowed to fade off without anything's being done. The black box grew shabbier each year; by now it was no longer completely black but splintered badly along one side to show the original wood color, and in some places faded or stained.

6   Mr. Martin and his oldest son, Baxter, held the black box securely on the stool until Mr. Summers had stirred the papers thoroughly with his hand. Because so much of the ritual had been forgotten or discarded, Mr. Summers had been successful in having slips of paper substituted for the chips of wood that had been used for generations. Chips of wood, Mr. Summers had argued, had been all very

well when the village was tiny, but now that the population was more than three hundred and likely to keep on growing, it was necessary to use something that would fit more easily into the black box. The night before the lottery, Mr. Summers and Mr. Graves made up the slips of paper and put them in the box, and it was then taken to the safe of Mr. Summers' coal company and locked up until Mr. Summers was ready to take it to the square next morning. The rest of the year, the box was put away, sometimes one place, sometimes another; it had spent one year in Mr. Graves's barn and another year underfoot in the post office, and sometimes it was set on a shelf in the Martin grocery and left there.

7   There was a great deal of fussing to be done before Mr. Summers declared the lottery open. There were the lists to make up—of heads of families, heads of households in each family, members of each household in each family. There was the proper swearing-in of Mr. Summers by the postmaster, as the official of the lottery; at one time, some people remembered, there had been a recital of some sort, performed by the official of the lottery, a perfunctory, tuneless chant that had been rattled off duly each year; some people believed that the official of the lottery used to stand just so when he said or sang it, others believed that he was supposed to walk among the people, but years and years ago this part of the ritual had been allowed to lapse. There had been, also, a ritual salute, which the official of the lottery had had to use in addressing each person who came up to draw from the box, but this also had changed with time, until now it was felt necessary only for the official to speak to each person approaching. Mr. Summers was very good at all this; in his clean white shirt and blue jeans, with one hand resting carelessly on the black box, he seemed very proper and important as he talked interminably to Mr. Graves and the Martins.

Ritual is military

8   Just as Mr. Summers finally left off talking and turned to the assembled villagers, Mrs. Hutchinson came hurriedly along the path to the square, her sweater thrown over her shoulders, and slid into place in the back of the crowd. "Clean forgot what day it was," she said to Mrs. Delacroix, who stood next to her, and they both laughed softly. "Thought my old man was out back stacking wood," Mrs. Hutchinson went on, "and then I looked out the window and the kids was gone, and then I remembered it was the twenty-seventh and came a-running." She dried her hands on her apron, and Mrs. Delacroix said, "You're in time, though. They're still talking away up there."

9   Mrs. Hutchinson craned her neck to see through the crowd and found her husband and children standing near the front. She tapped Mrs. Delacroix on the arm as a farewell and began to make her way through the crowd. The people separated good-humoredly to let her through; two or three people said, in voices just loud enough to be heard across the crowd, "Here comes your Missus, Hutchinson," and "Bill, she made it after all." Mrs. Hutchinson reached her husband, and Mr. Summers, who had been waiting, said cheerfully, "Thought we were going to have to get on without you, Tessie." Mrs. Hutchinson said, grinning, "Wouldn't have me leave m'dishes in the sink, now, would you, Joe?," and soft laughter ran through the crowd as the people stirred back into position after Mrs. Hutchinson's arrival.

10   "Well, now," Mr. Summers said soberly, "guess we better get started, get this over with, so's we can go back to work. Anybody ain't here?"

11   "Dunbar," several people said. "Dunbar, Dunbar."

12   Mr. Summers consulted his list. "Clyde Dunbar," he said. "That's right. He's broke his leg, hasn't he? Who's drawing for him?"

13   "Me, I guess," a woman said, and Mr. Summers turned to look at her. "Wife draws for her husband," Mr. Summers said. "Don't you have a grown boy to do it for you, Janey?" Although Mr. Summers and everyone else in the village knew the answer perfectly well, it was the business of the official of the lottery to ask such questions formally. Mr. Summers waited with an expression of polite interest while Mrs. Dunbar answered.

14   "Horace's not but sixteen yet," Mrs. Dunbar said regretfully. "Guess I gotta fill in for the old man this year."

15   "Right," Mr. Summers said. He made a note on the list he was holding. Then he asked, "Watson boy drawing this year?"

16   A tall boy in the crowd raised his hand. "Here," he said. "I'm drawing for m'mother and me." He blinked his eyes nervously and ducked his head as several voices in the crowd said things like "Good fellow, Jack," and "Glad to see your mother's got a man to do it."

17   "Well," Mr. Summers said, "guess that's everyone. Old Man Warner make it?"

18   "Here," a voice said, and Mr. Summers nodded.

19   A sudden hush fell on the crowd as Mr. Summers cleared his throat and looked at the list. "All ready?" he called. "Now, I'll read the names—heads of families first—and the men come up and take a paper out of the box. Keep the paper folded in your hand without looking at it until everyone has had a turn. Everything clear?"

20   The people had done it so many times that they only half listened to the directions; most of them were quiet, wetting their lips, not looking around. Then Mr. Summers raised one hand high and said, "Adams." A man disengaged himself from the crowd and came forward. "Hi, Steve," Mr. Summers said, and Mr. Adams said, "Hi, Joe." They grinned at one another humorlessly and nervously. Then Mr. Adams reached into the black box and took out a folded paper. He held it firmly by one corner as he turned and went hastily back to his place in the crowd, where he stood a little apart from his family, not looking down at his hand.

21   "Allen," Mr. Summers said. "Anderson. . . . Bentham."

22   "Seems like there's no time at all between lotteries any more," Mrs. Delacroix said to Mrs. Graves in the back row. "Seems like we got through with the last one only last week."

23   "Time sure goes fast," Mrs. Graves said.

24   "Clark. . . . Delacroix."

25   "There goes my old man," Mrs. Delacroix said. She held her breath while her husband went forward.

26   "Dunbar," Mr. Summers said, and Mrs. Dunbar went steadily to the box while one of the women said, "Go on, Janey," and another said, "There she goes."

27   "We're next," Mrs. Graves said. She watched while Mr. Graves came around from the side of the box, greeted Mr. Summers gravely, and selected a slip of paper

from the box. By now, all through the crowd there were men holding the small folded papers in their large hands, turning them over and over nervously. Mrs. Dunbar and her two sons stood together, Mrs. Dunbar holding the slip of paper.

28   "Harburt. . . . Hutchinson."

29   "Get up there, Bill," Mrs. Hutchinson said, and the people near her laughed.

30   "Jones."

31   "They do say," Mr. Adams said to Old Man Warner, who stood next to him, "that over in the north village they're talking of giving up the lottery."

32   Old Man Warner snorted. "Pack of crazy fools," he said. "Listening to the young folks, nothing's good enough for *them*. Next thing you know, they'll be wanting to go back to living in caves, nobody work any more, live *that* way for a while. Used to be a saying about 'Lottery in June, corn be heavy soon.' First thing you know, we'd all be eating stewed chickweed and acorns. There's *always* been a lottery," he added petulantly. "Bad enough to see young Joe Summers up there joking with everybody."

33   "Some places have already quit lotteries," Mrs. Adams said.

34   "Nothing but trouble in *that*," Old Man Warner said stoutly. "Pack of young fools."

35   "Martin." And Bobby Martin watched his father go forward. "Overdyke. . . . Percy."

36   "I wish they'd hurry," Mrs. Dunbar said to her older son. "I wish they'd hurry."

37   "They're almost through," her son said.

38   "You get ready to run tell Dad," Mrs. Dunbar said.

39   Mr. Summers called his own name and then stepped forward precisely and selected a slip from the box. Then he called, "Warner."

40   "Seventy-seventh year I been in the lottery," Old Man Warner said as he went through the crowd. "Seventy-seventh time."

41   "Watson." The tall boy came awkwardly through the crowd. Someone said, "Don't be nervous, Jack," and Mr. Summers said, "Take your time, son."

42   "Zanini."

43   After that, there was a long pause, a breathless pause, until Mr. Summers, holding his slip of paper in the air, said, "All right, fellows." For a minute, no one moved, and then all the slips of paper were opened. Suddenly, all the women began to speak at once, saying, "Who is it?," "Who's got it?," "Is it the Dunbars?," "Is it the Watsons?" Then the voices began to say, "It's Hutchinson. It's Bill," "Bill Hutchinson's got it."

44   "Go tell your father," Mrs. Dunbar said to her older son.

45   People began to look around to see the Hutchinsons. Bill Hutchinson was standing quiet, staring down at the paper in his hand. Suddenly, Tessie Hutchinson shouted to Mr. Summers, "You didn't give him time enough to take any paper he wanted. I saw you. It wasn't fair!"

46   "Be a good sport, Tessie," Mrs. Delacroix called, and Mrs. Graves said, "All of us took the same chance."

47   "Shut up, Tessie," Bill Hutchinson said.

48   "Well, everyone," Mr. Summers said, "that was done pretty fast, and now we've got to be hurrying a little more to get done in time." He consulted his next list.

"Bill," he said, "you draw for the Hutchinson family. You got any other house-holds in the Hutchinsons?"

49   "There's Don and Eva," Mrs. Hutchinson yelled. "Make *them* take their chance!"

50   "Daughters draw with their husbands' families, Tessie," Mr. Summers said gently. "You know that as well as anyone else."

51   "It wasn't *fair*," Tessie said.

52   "I guess not, Joe," Bill Hutchinson said regretfully. "My daughter draws with her husband's family, that's only fair. And I've got no other family except the kids."

53   "Then, as far as drawing for families is concerned, it's you," Mr. Summers said in explanation, "and as far as drawing for households is concerned, that's you, too. Right?"

54   "Right," Bill Hutchinson said.

55   "How many kids, Bill?" Mr. Summers asked formally.

56   "Three," Bill Hutchinson said. "There's Bill, Jr., and Nancy, and little Dave. And Tessie and me."

57   "All right, then," Mr. Summers said. "Harry, you got their tickets back?"

58   Mr. Graves nodded and held up the slips of paper. "Put them in the box, then," Mr. Summers directed. "Take Bill's and put it in."

59   "I think we ought to start over," Mrs. Hutchinson said, as quietly as she could. "I tell you it wasn't *fair*. You didn't give him time enough to choose. *Every*body saw that."

60   Mr. Graves had selected the five slips and put them in the box, and he dropped all the papers but those onto the ground, where the breeze caught them and lifted them off.

61   "Listen, everybody," Mrs. Hutchinson was saying to the people around her.

62   "Ready, Bill?" Mr. Summers asked, and Bill Hutchinson, with one quick glance around at his wife and children, nodded.

63   "Remember," Mr. Summers said, "take the slips and keep them folded until each person has taken one. Harry, you help little Dave." Mr. Graves took the hand of the little boy, who came willingly with him up to the box. "Take a paper out of the box, Davy," Mr. Summers said. Davy put his hand into the box and laughed. "Take just *one* paper," Mr. Summers said. "Harry, you hold it for him." Mr. Graves took the child's hand and removed the folded paper from the tight fist and held it while little Dave stood next to him and looked at him wonderingly.

64   "Nancy next," Mr. Summers said. Nancy was twelve, and her school friends breathed heavily as she went forward, switching her skirt, and took a slip daintily from the box. "Bill, Jr.," Mr. Summers said, and Billy, his face red and his feet overlarge, nearly knocked the box over as he got a paper out. "Tessie," Mr. Summers said. She hesitated for a minute, looking around defiantly, and then set her lips and went up to the box. She snatched a paper out and held it behind her.

65   "Bill," Mr. Summers said, and Bill Hutchinson reached into the box and felt around, bringing his hand out at last with the slip of paper in it.

66   The crowd was quiet. A girl whispered, "I hope it's not Nancy," and the sound of the whisper reached the edges of the crowd.

67   "It's not the way it used to be," Old Man Warner said clearly. "People ain't the way they used to be."

68   "All right," Mr. Summers said. "Open the papers. Harry, you open little Dave's."

69   Mr. Graves opened the slip of paper and there was a general sigh through the crowd as he held it up and everyone could see that it was blank. Nancy and Bill, Jr., opened theirs at the same time, and both beamed and laughed, turning around to the crowd and holding their slips of paper above their heads.

70   "Tessie," Mr. Summers said. There was a pause, and then Mr. Summers looked at Bill Hutchinson, and Bill unfolded his paper and showed it. It was blank.

71   "It's Tessie," Mr. Summers said, and his voice was hushed. "Show us her paper, Bill."

72   Bill Hutchinson went over to his wife and forced the slip of paper out of her hand. It had a black spot on it, the black spot Mr. Summers had made the night before with the heavy pencil in the coal-company office. Bill Hutchinson held it up, and there was a stir in the crowd.

73   "All right, folks," Mr. Summers said. "Let's finish quickly."

74   Although the villagers had forgotten the ritual and lost the original black box, they still remembered to use stones. The pile of stones the boys had made earlier was ready; there were stones on the ground with the blowing scraps of paper that had come out of the box. Mrs. Delacroix selected a stone so large she had to pick it up with both hands and turned to Mrs. Dunbar. "Come on," she said. "Hurry up."

75   Mrs. Dunbar had small stones in both hands, and she said, gasping for breath, "I can't run at all. You'll have to go ahead and I'll catch up with you."

76   The children had stones already, and someone gave little Davy Hutchinson a few pebbles.

77   Tessie Hutchinson was in the center of a cleared space by now, and she held her hands out desperately as the villagers moved in on her. "It isn't fair," she said. A stone hit her on the side of the head.

78   Old Man Warner was saying, "Come on, come on, everyone." Steve Adams was in the front of the crowd of villagers, with Mrs. Graves beside him.

79   "It isn't fair, it isn't right," Mrs. Hutchinson screamed, and then they were upon her.

THINKING ABOUT THE TEXT

1. To understand Jackson's use of understatement (a weaker description than the circumstances warrant), cite all of the details in the opening paragraphs that seem contrary to the real nature of this lottery.

2. Describe Mr. Summers. Discuss the significance of Mr. Summers and Mr. Graves conducting this lottery.

3. What are the earliest signs that people are anxious about this lottery?

4. How does Old Man Warner defend the lottery tradition?

5. What is Tessie Hutchinson's initial attitude toward the lottery? How do each of the Hutchinsons react to Tessie "winning" the lottery? Use these details and others to demonstrate that this lottery seems to be perverting more noble human instincts even before the actual stoning.

6. The story is narrated objectively, or dramatically, without revealing the thoughts or feelings of the characters. Why does Jackson choose this point of view?

7. List numerous insights that this story suggests about humanity, the individual and society, tradition, conservative societies, and conformity.

WRITING FROM THE TEXT

1. Using details from the story as well as from your own experience, explore why conventional, close-knit societies are not always as safe as they seem.

2. Adding to your answers for question 1 above, list all examples of understatement and of irony (a discrepancy between appearance and reality) in this story. Then write a paper analyzing Jackson's use of irony in "The Lottery."

CONNECTING WITH OTHER TEXTS

1. Write an essay relating "The Lottery" to theories discussed in "Why Johnny Can't Disobey" (p. 269).

2. Using Tavris' essay "In Groups We Shrink," write an analysis of "groupthink" or "mob mentality" as it is demonstrated in "The Lottery" and in "The Atlanta Riot" (p. 229).

3. Write an essay comparing Jackson's fictional treatment of group conformity with what actually happens in the Indian town of Pandhurna, as described in "Stone-throwing in India.".

STONE-THROWING IN INDIA
Mark Fineman

Since receiving his B.A. in journalism from the University of Syracuse in 1974, Mark Fineman (b. 1952) has had a varied writing career. He has been a staff writer for the *Chicago Sun-Times* and the Allentown, Pennsylvania, *Call-Chronicle*, and Asian correspondent for the *Philadelphia Inquirer*. He has been the bureau chief for the *Los Angeles Times* in Manila and New Delhi, and, currently, in Cyprus. Fineman's report on an Indian village tradition, included here, first appeared in the *Los Angeles Times* in 1989.

1   PANDHURNA, India—To most of the 45,000 seemingly normal residents of this sleepy little town on the banks of the River Jam, Anil Sambare is nothing more than a spoilsport.

2   To some, he is something worse. A troublemaker, some say. An idealistic radical, according to others. Some even think him a traitor to his hometown.

3   And all because the 27-year-old high school teacher has dedicated his life to stopping his entire town from going completely berserk once a year in a frenzied festival of destruction—a daylong event in which thousands of people try to stone each other to death in the name of fun, tradition and, now, stardom.

4   The annual event is called the Gotmaar Festival—literally, "stone-hitting"—and it is an ancient Pandhurna tradition, unique and brutal even by Indian standards.

5   No one here remembers exactly how ancient it is, although older people say that it dates back at least three centuries. And no one knows exactly why they do it every year, year after year, despite scores of deaths and thousands of injuries, although the myth behind it is a compelling one.

6   All the Pandhurnans really know for sure is that once a year, on the day of the new moon in the Hindu month of Sharawan, when the drums start beating along the River Jam, the time for the madness has begun again.

7   Within minutes, thousands of male Pandhurnans, ranging in age from 6 to 60, many of them deeply scarred or limping from festivals of years past, divide into two groups, gather their huge piles of stones on opposite sides of the river and, for the next $6^1/_2$ hours, try to kill, maim and mangle as many fellow townsfolk as they can.

8   When sunset comes, and the drumbeat stops, the two sides drop their rocks, come together, shake hands, nurse each other's wounds and return to the peaceful monotony of rural Indian life.

9   This year, the Gotmaar carnage, which took place two weeks ago, left four dead and 612 injured. But there were a few new twists this year that speak volumes about India's struggle to enter the modern age.

10   First, there was Anil Sambare and his signature drive to end the carnage, which drew the ire of almost everyone. Second, this is an election year in India, which meant that Sambare's signature campaign was doomed to failure. And finally, there was the introduction of a new evil, videotape equipment, which is likely to ensure that Pandhurna's sadomasochistic ritual will continue for many years to come.

11   The story of the Pandhurnans and their bizarre, ancient rite of stoning is a living illustration of the paradoxes of a modern-day India, as well as a freeze-frame glimpse at the ironies and distortions resulting from Indian Prime Minister Rajiv Gandhi's five-year-old pledge to modernize rural India.

12   Pandhurna, in central Madhya Pradesh state, is hardly what one would call a backwater. In many ways it is a model of Rajiv Gandhi's rural modernization plan.

13   There are 10,000 television sets in Pandhurna, 340 telephones and even 100 videocassette players. More than 90% of the homes have electricity. Everyone has access to clean drinking water. Unemployment is under 5%, and there are even beauty parlors doing booming business.

14   "There is just this one little thing that sets us apart," said Bhargao Pandurang Bhagwatkar, who has taught in the local high school for the last 41 years. "We all know it is barbaric. It is a kind of madness. And it has no reason at all. But it has been with us since Day 1, and, on that day every year, we just cannot help ourselves."

15   Day 1, as myth has it, was sometime in the 1600s, according to local historians, police and other local officials, who say they and their predecessors have been trying to stop it every year for the last half-century.

16   On Day 1, it seems, Pandhurna's brutal battle began as a love story.

17   "The way the old ones tell it," town official M. M. Singh explained, "a boy from the Pandhurna side of the river eloped with a girl from the village on the other side, which was then known as Sawargaon but since has merged into Pandhurna.

18   "As the amorous young couple was trying to flee across the river, the Sawargaon people began throwing stones at them. The Pandhurnans heard about this and quickly ran to the river bank, where they began stoning the Sawargaons.

19   "The couple, of course, died in the cross-fire. And it's on the spot where they died that the people now put the tree every year."

20   "The tree?" the stranger asked.

21   "Oh, the tree. The tree is the main object of the game."

22   The Pandhurnans who actually play "the game," which is what everyone here except Sambare calls the annual stoning battle, explained that the tree is cut the day before the festival from a special grove of flame trees beside a temple to the Hindu god of destruction, which is where legend states that the mythical young couple first met.

23   The tree is then "planted" in the middle of the River Jam, and the object of "the game" is to chop down the tree with an ax, without, of course, getting stoned to death in the process.

24   Enter the videotape.

25   Unlike previous years, in which an average of two or three Pandhurnans were stoned to death during the festival, the four deaths this year were from drowning.

26   "These boys had climbed the tree, and were posing for the camera," Sambare explained. "They were so preoccupied with the video camera, they didn't see the stones coming. They got hit in the head, fell into the river and drowned."

27   Sambare knows what he's talking about. He lives on Stone-hitting Road, in a riverfront house with a view of the battle zone. And he jumped into the river and saved four other "players" from the same fate this year, getting hit in the back with stones in the process.

28   But that's not why Sambare is so committed to ending the carnage of Gotmaar. It's not even because his uncle was stoned to death 27 years ago, or because he cannot stop his own younger brother from joining in—"imagine, my own brother

bought five different outfits and changed clothes five times during the stone-hitting this year because he wanted to look good for the camera.

29   "No, I am fighting this because it is a perversion, because it is barbaric and because it puts all of India in a very poor light," said Sambare, who has a masters degree in mathematics.

30   "This is not a game. This is madness. And now, with this videotape, there is all of a sudden a renewed interest in joining in. Everyone wants to show off their bravado."

31   Enter Rajiv Gandhi's high-tech revolution.

32   The videotape was the government's idea. And the local police actually paid 5,000 rupees (about $300) in government funds to a local video contractor to film the festival this year.

33   "The idea was to minimize the killing," said Krishna Kohle, the enterprising Pandhurnan who got the video contract. "It was, how do you call it, a compromise."

34   For decades, local officials said, the authorities have attempted to end the festival. Two years ago, the police even opened fire on the festival, killing two Pandhurnans, in an attempt to end it after a passing constable was accidentally stoned to death.

35   "I myself have seen too many deaths and very much want this madness to end," said Dr. Ratan Singhvi, a local physician who is Pandhurna's equivalent of mayor and the local head of Gandhi's ruling Congress-I party.

36   "I have seen people with eyes bulging out, ears sheared off, noses broken, teeth shattered, skulls and legs fractured to bits. But we've never been able to stop it. My God, the people like it.

37   "Of course, an additional problem is these people are all dead drunk when they're playing the game, and the game gives them a good excuse to get drunk. They look forward to it all year long."

38   Enter politics.

39   "The people of Pandhurna, you see, are very sentimental about this festival," Singhvi said. "And such things are very important to our local voters. Had we stopped the Gotmaar this year, for example, the Congress Party definitely would be sent away in the next elections. So what we did instead was try to cut down on the deaths—we banned the slingshot."

40   Called *gofans,* the handmade slingshots came into vogue two years ago and clearly escalated the conflict. They turned the stones into speeding bullets, tripling the death toll and ultimately forcing the police to step in. The *gofan* was outlawed. And, in an effort to enforce that ban, police hired the video man to film violators for prosecution.

41   "I guess it backfired," said Kohle, who conceded he is now making a tidy profit renting out copies of the Gotmaar video to townspeople who want to relive their moments of bravery and endurance.

THINKING ABOUT THE TEXT

1. What is the myth that prompts the Indian town's "game"? What does the tree represent?

2. Why did the officials of the town decide to videotape the event? How has the camera influenced the yearly activity?

3. Why does Anil Sambare fight the town's tradition?

WRITING FROM THE TEXT

1. Is the behavior in this community different from the behavior in cities where gang members shoot at each other and innocent bystanders? Write an analysis of this community's behavior that the details in Fineman's article can support, and compare the behavior here with that in urban areas in the United States.

2. Write a letter to the Pandhurna newspaper to convince the population of the "barbarity" of their actions. Propose a plan for a change.

CONNECTING WITH OTHER TEXTS

1. Read Shirley Jackson's short story "The Lottery" (p. 283) and show how Fineman's news article eerily parallels Jackson's fictitious account.

2. In Tavris' essay "In Groups We Shrink" (p. 267) and in McCarthy's "Why Johnny Can't Disobey" (p. 269), we learn that groups and cultural inhibitors influence how people behave. Try to explain what happens in Pandhurna from your understanding of the analysis of human behavior in Tavris' and McCarthy's work.

COMMENCEMENT ADDRESS: WHAT YOU WILL BE
Milton Mayer

An educator, journalist, editor, and author, Milton Mayer (1908–1986) is known for his introspective examination of the individual in relation to politics and religion. His work includes *They Thought They Were Free: The Germans, 1933–1945; What Can a Man Do?; If Men Were Angels;* and *The Nature of the Beast.* The essay below is from *What Can a Man Do?* published in 1969.

1   As you are now, so I once was; as I am now, so you will be. You will be tempted to smile when I tell you that I am middle-aged and corrupt. You should resist the temptation. Twenty-five years from now you will be ineluctably middle-aged and, unless you hear and heed what I say today, just as ineluctably corrupt. You will not believe me, and you should not, because what I say at my age should be unbelievable at yours. But you should hear me out because I know more than you do in one respect: you know only what it is to be young, while I know what it is to be both

young and old. In any case, I will not lie to you in order to make you feel good. You will be old much longer than you are young, and I would rather that you believed me the longer time than the shorter.

2   I tell you today that instantly is not a moment too soon if you are going to escape the fate I predict for you and embody myself. For what was said long ago is still true, that corruption runs faster than death and the faster runner overtakes the slower. It may indeed be too late already, unless you mend your ways this least of all likely moments. I once heard Robert Hutchins tell a graduating class that they were closer to the truth that day than they would ever be again. I did not believe him. But I have seen most of the members of that class since, and I regret to inform you that Hutchins was right. Mind you, he did not say that they were close to the truth; he only said that they would never be so close again. They had been taught what right and wrong were and had not yet had a chance to do what e. e. cummings calls "up grow and down forget." If my own history and the history of the race is instructive, this commencement is for nearly every last one of you the commencement of disintegration. A cynic once said that he would not give a hang for a man who wasn't a socialist before he was twenty or who was one after that. I do not know if socialism is a good ideal, but I know that it is an ideal and I know that the cynic was confident that you would lose your ideals. You may even have trifled, in your springtime, with such radical aberrations as pacifism. But you will soon stop trifling; and when, at thirty, you have already begun to molder, your friends will tell you that you have mellowed.

3   All societies are deplorable, and history indicates that they always will be. You have lived twenty years in a deplorable society. You have lived sheltered lives, but you have had no one to shelter you from your parents and teachers. Your parents have done what they could to adjust you to the deplorable society to which they, as their advanced age testifies, have successfully adjusted themselves. When they said you were improving, they meant that you were getting to be like them. When they said they hoped you would keep out of trouble, they meant that you should not do anything that they wouldn't do. But some of the things that they wouldn't do should have been done. The condition of the society to which they have accommodated their lives is the proof of their criminal negligence. Your teachers have been no better, and no better an influence on you, than your parents. They may have had higher ideals; it takes higher ideals to teach children than to have them. But your teachers' survival (like your parents') testifies to their adjustability. They have done as they were told, and in a deplorable society there are some things that men are told to do that no man should do. A high-school teacher in California told me that not one of his colleagues wanted to take the anti-Communist oath required of teachers in that state, and neither did he; but every one of them took it in order to hold his job and escape the national black list. As they are now, so you will be.

4   Like your teachers and your parents before you, you will be told to do bad things in order to hold your job. In college you may have quit the campus daily or defied the old fraternity on principle. It will be harder to quit the metropolitan daily or defy the old country on principle; it will be easier to forget the principle. And if, in addition to holding your job, you want to be promoted, you will think of

bad things to do on your own. And you will have good reasons for doing them. You will have wives (at least one apiece) and children to maintain. You will have a home and mortgage to enlarge. And life insurance, purchased against the certainty of death, dread of which in turn adds preciousness to staying alive at any price. And neighbors who are having their children's teeth straightened. Your dentists' bills alone will corrupt you. You will have doctors' bills to pay, and they will increase as you grow older, becoming extremely heavy when you are moribund and powerless to earn money. You will have lusts, as you have now, to gratify, but the lusts you have now are relatively inexpensive and they will give way to more expensive if less gratifying lusts. You will have worthy philanthropies to support and the respect of people whose respect depends on your supporting those philanthropies. You will have an automobile (if you are so wretched as to be a one-car family), and you might as well turn it in every year because the new model will be so revolutionary that it will depreciate the old one to the point where there's no point in keeping it.

5   Some of the things you will be expected to do (or will expect yourself to do) for the sake of your wife and children, your community, your health, or your burial are bad things. You will have to have good reasons for doing them; and, thanks to your education, you will have them. The trouble with education is that it teaches you rhetoric while you are young. When, for rhetorical purposes, you embrace the doctrine of the lesser evil, you ignore its fatal flaw of present certainty and future contingency; being young, you think you will live forever, so that you may do bad things today in order to do good things tomorrow. But today is certain, tomorrow contingent; and this night an old man's soul may be required of him. When you are old, and too tired to embrace doctrines for rhetorical purposes, you will find that the doctrine of the lesser evil has embraced you and destroyed you. You protest my melancholy prediction, but the Great Actuarial Table is against you. Twenty-five years from now nine out of ten of you (or all ten) will tolerate an existence which, if you could foresee it now, you would call intolerable. If such an existence has any virtue at all, it has only one: it will give you a wistful old age. You will look back to your springtime, fifty years gone, and say, "Those were the days." And you will be right.

6   The only thing that will save you from wistfulness is the one talent whose lack now redeems you—the talent for self-deception. You won't even know that you are corrupt. You will be no worse than your neighbors, and you will be sure to have some that you won't be as bad as. You will have friends who praise in you the characteristics you have in common with them. They will persuade you that there is nothing wrong with either hoarding or squandering as much money as you can get legally. And if, some sudden night, you go berserk and bawl out that life is a sell, they will put you to bed with the assurance that you will be all right in the morning. And you will be. Worse than being corrupt, you will be contented in your corruption.

7   Twenty-five years from now you will celebrate your twentieth wedding anniversary. Because you love your wife—still more if you don't—you will want to celebrate it in style. You will reserve a window table for two at the choicest restaurant

in town, and the champagne bucket will be at the table when you arrive. You will not be the cynosure of all eyes, but you will think you are. The head waiter (or maitre de, as he is known here) will address you by name. As your eye travels down the menu it will be distracted by something outside the window, which will prove to be a hungry man. What will you do? Do you know what you will do then, twenty-five years from now? You will call the maitre de and tell him to have the drapes pulled, and he will tell the waiter, and he will tell the bus boy, who will do it.

8   Your table, even before you have ordered, will be laden with rolls and crackers (of several sorts) and butter pats on butter plates. Hungry, and a little nervous, as you should be, you will break up a roll and butter it and eat it as you wait for your wife to make up her confounded mind. The waiter will ask you if you want the champagne poured, and you will say yes; and he will open it with a pop which, beneath the dinner din, will be unheard by the rest of the diners (but you won't know that). Thirsty, and a little nervous still, you will sip your glass, forgetting to toast your wife, and resume your study of the menu. And then, for the first time, you will see, in fine italic print at the bottom, the words "The Management reserves the right to refuse service to anyone." And then you will know (for you will be an educated man) that you are sitting in a Jim Crow restaurant—that being the meaning of the words "The Management, etc."

9   Now the country in which you were raised calls itself a Christian country, and the parents who raised you up called themselves Christian people, and the church whose vestry has just elected you calls itself a Christian church, and you call yourself a Christian. Jim Crowism is un-Christian. It is also un-American, and you call yourself an American. What will you do? What will you do then, twenty-five years from now?

10   The champagne is open and sipped. The roll is buttered, half-eaten. Will you get up from the table and tell your wife to get up and tell her why, and tell the waiter and the maitre de, and maybe the management, that you are leaving the restaurant and why, and pay for the champagne and the rolls and the butter pats and, if necessary, for the dinner, but refuse to eat there? Or will you pretend, as the management (by printing the notice in fine italic type) intended you to pretend, that you did not see the notice. You will stay at the table and order your dinner and eat it.

11   You will have been measured for corruption and found to fit. You may be the man who raised the flag on Iwo Jima—a hero abroad but not at home, where it's harder to be a hero. At Iwo Jima you had either to raise the flag or drop it. It was publicly shameful to drop it. But the night of your anniversary dinner it would have been publicly shameful to *raise* the flag by leaving the restaurant. And public shame was what you could not bear, either at Iwo Jima or in the restaurant.

12   There are a lot of involuntary, non-voluntary or reflexive heroes. I am one myself. I do not doubt that I would have raised the flag at Iwo Jima rather than let it drop in public. But I was the man who took his wife to dinner at the Jim Crow restaurant. Believe me, there is no contradiction between the corruption which will consume you, day by day, in the face of unpopularity or public shame and the heroism of the moment accompanied by public praise. And when you have been measured often enough and long enough for corruption, you will like what you

see in the mirror. I don't mean that you won't continue to have good impulses. You will. But you will have persuasive reasons for suppressing them. From time to time, as the vestige of your springtime idealism stirs you, you will want to do the right thing. But you will have to put off doing it until you have buried your father, and then your mother, your brother, your children, and your grandchildren. You may live to be very old, but you will not outlive the last descendant for whose sake you will suppress your good impulses.

13   What life did to me, because there was no one to tell me what I am telling you now, it will do to you if you do not at once adopt *Principiis obsta* as your motto and spurn every other. "Resist the beginnings." At twenty I was what you are; I had had all the middle-class care that a middle-class society and a middle-class home could provide. My parents wanted me to have what they took to be advantages, and I had them. But my advantages were of no use to me at all when life came down on me, as it will upon you, like a ton of bricks. I had studied morality, just as you have, but it was the easy morality designed to sustain my character in an easy world. I would not steal another man's watch unless my children were starving, and my children would never be starving. Nor will yours if, with what your parents call your advantages, you do as you are told and get to the top. The reason your children will not be starving is that you will have been corrupted. Your corruption will save you from having to decide whether to steal another man's watch. I was prepared, like you, to be a hero the instant heroism was required of me. I saw myself at Iwo Jima, at Gettysburg, at Concord. But I did not see myself at home, so weakened by the corrosive years ahead that I would not be able to stand up on my hind legs and say no when I had to do it alone. Never knowing—as you do not know—that my needs would be limitless, I never imagined that my surrender would be complete.

14   My education prepared me to say no to my enemies. It did not prepare me to say no to my friends, still less to myself, to my own limitless need for a little more status, a little more security, and a little more of the immediate pleasure that status and security provide. Corruption is accompanied by immediate pleasure. When you feel good, you are probably, if not necessarily, doing bad. But happiness is activity in accordance with virtue, and the practice of virtue is painful. The pursuit of happiness requires a man to undertake suffering. Your intelligence, or your psychiatrist's, will tell you whether you are suffering for the right reason. But it will not move you to undertake the suffering.

15   God is said to come to us in little things. The Devil is no fool: he comes that way too. The Devil has only one objective, and if he can persuade you to justify your derelictions by saying "I'm only human," he has achieved it. He will have got you to deny the Christ within you, and that is all he wants. If you are only human you are his. The Devil will keep you quiet when you ought to talk by reminding you that nobody asked you to say anything. He will keep you in your chair when you ought to get up and out by reminding you that you love your wife and it's your twentieth anniversary. He will give you the oath to take and say, "As long as you're loyal, why not say so?" He will tell you that the beggar outside the restaurant would only spend the money on whiskey. The Devil has come to me in little

things for twenty-five years—and now I say and do the things in which, when he first began coming, he had to instruct me.

16   I tell you that you are in mortal jeopardy today, and anyone who tells you differently is selling you to the Devil. It is written on Plato's ring that it is easier to form good habits than to break bad ones. Your habits are not yet fully formed. You are, in some measure still, only potentially corrupt. Life will actualize and habitualize every bit of your corruptibility. If you do not begin to cultivate the habit of heroism today—and habits are formed by acts—you never will. You may delude yourselves, as I did, by setting about to change the world. But for all that you do or do not do, you will leave the world, as I do, no better than you found it and yourselves considerably worse. For the world will change you faster, more easily, and more durably than you will change it. If you undertake only to keep the world from changing you—not to lick 'em but to avoid j'ining 'em—you will have your hands full.

17   Other, more agreeable commencement orators have warned you of life's pitfalls. I tell you that you are marked for them. I believe you will not escape them because I see nothing in your environment that has prepared you even to recognize them. Your elders tell you to compare yourselves with the Russians and see how much worse the Russians are; this is not the way to prepare you to recognize pitfalls. Your elders tell you to be technologists because the Russians are technologists and your country is technologically backward; this is no way to prepare you to recognize pitfalls. You are marked for the pit. The Great Actuarial Table is against you.

18   What you need (and the Russians with you) is neither pharisaism nor technology. What you need is what the psalmist knew he needed—a heart, not a head, of wisdom. What you need is what Bismarck said was the only thing the Germans needed—civilian courage. I do not know where you will get it. If I did, I would get it myself. You were divinely endowed to know right and to do right, and you have before you, in the tradition of your country and of human history, the vision to help you if you will turn to it. But no one will compel you to turn to it, and no one can. The dictates of your society, of any society, will not serve you. They are dictates that corrupted your parents and your teachers. If Socrates did not know where virtue came from—and he didn't—neither do I. He pursued it earlier and harder than anyone else and concluded that it was the gift of God. In despair of your parents and your society, of your teachers and your studies, of your neighbors and your friends, and above all of your fallen nature and the Old Adam in you, I bespeak for you the gift of God.

THINKING ABOUT THE TEXT

1. What is Milton Mayer's point in his address to college graduates? If he could achieve his goal, what would it be?

2. Mayer states that twenty-five years after their graduation, "nine out of ten" of the graduates "will tolerate an existence" which they would at their graduations call "intolerable." What *specifically* does he cite

to support this assertion? What else do you imagine Mayer believes will happen to the average graduate?

3. What does Mayer mean by "public shame"?

4. Do you agree with Mayer that "corruption is accompanied by immediate pleasure," and that "when you feel good, you are probably, if not necessarily, doing bad"? What examples does he give to support his point?

WRITING FROM THE TEXT

1. Write about specific examples from your own experience that confirm Mayer's view that "corruption is accompanied by immediate pleasure."

2. Write about an experience or experiences that you have had that refute Mayer's argument that growing older is concurrent with growing more corrupt.

3. Imagine yourself 10 or 15 years from now, a college graduate with a job that provides an income that keeps you and your family comfortable. Write an essay from the perspective that Mayer is right, that moral corruption is a reality in your life.

4. Imagine yourself 10 or 15 years from now, a college graduate with a job that provides an income that keeps you and your family comfortable. Write an essay from the perspective that, as a result of Mayer's commencement address, you have gone off into the world determined to resist corruption. Describe everything that you do to avoid the pitfalls and to achieve some virtue.

CONNECTING WITH OTHER TEXTS

1. Mayer writes that his middle-class parents wanted him to have "what they took to be advantages." What are the specific "advantages" that parents want their children to have? What is the cost of this affluence if Mayer is correct? Consider "Men as Success Objects" (p. 90), "Kids in the Mall: Growing Up Controlled" (p. 278), or "Less Is More: A Call for Shorter Work Hours" (p. 253) to use with Mayer's essay to support your analysis of one issue raised here.

2. Write an essay in which you compare the issues Mayer raises with those considered by Richard Rodriguez ("None of This Is Fair," p. 237) and Ruben Navarrette, Jr. ("Ethnic Envidia," p. 241).

2

THE RHETORIC

■   ■   ■

This rhetoric is designed for you to use easily and constantly, not only in class with your instructor but also at home when you are on your own. Therefore the instruction is deliberately focused and practical, with plenty of suggestions and illustrations. The rhetoric begins by demonstrating many prewriting techniques to help you move quickly beyond the blank page or computer screen. We are convinced that you will only learn to write better by actually writing, and our prewriting exercises prompt you to do just that. We guide you through the entire process, from discovering a topic and writing a draft to supporting a thesis and revising the essay.

In order to demonstrate the stages of an actual writing assignment, we trace one student's progress from prewriting and information gathering through organizing, outlining, drafting, revising, documenting, and editing the essay. This assignment typifies the writing that you will be asked to do in college; it begins with responses to readings and shows you how to meld your experience with other writers' ideas. This short project will also teach you how to paraphrase, quote, and document material responsibly.

Throughout this rhetoric, then, you will gain skills to craft the varied types of papers that you will need to write. We provide instruction, examples, and discussions of particular methods for developing essays, and we show you how to draft these essays, too. We offer opportunities for you to practice active reading, note taking, incorporating quotations, and interviewing—all important skills to help you write successful papers. We show how important it is to consider audience and style. In addition to the many shorter assignments, we provide instruction for all stages of a longer research paper, with guides to both MLA and APA documentation forms.

6

Prewriting as Discovery

■ ■ ■

Because writing involves discovery, we are eager to help you find ways to explore the ideas, experiences, and information that you bring to the composition class. We want you to understand the discovery process because that process has so much to do with your finished product.

Let's think for a few moments about how you will begin your assignments—about strategies that will encourage you to become involved in your subject and discover what you want to write about it. The practice exercises in this section are related to issues about family and generations, but even if you have not read the readings in Chapter 1, you can practice most of these prewriting exercises.

It seems paradoxical to suggest that you will discover what you want to write by writing. But students frequently tell us—and our own writing habits confirm—that the very act of working with words, ideas, or feelings on a page or computer screen will help you learn what you want to express about a topic.

Conversations with friends, too, can help you mull over your ideas. Sometimes a spirited exchange with a classmate or roommate will help you "get going" on a writing topic because you start to reconsider and refine your ideas as you discuss them, and you start to care if your ideas have been communicated or accepted. If your perceptions are questioned, you may want to present your point more convincingly in written form. In fact, the best thing you can do when you are assigned a writing task is immediately to jot down any responses and ideas. Consider this initial, quick writing as a conversation with yourself, because that is what it is. It is also like the stretching exercises or warm-ups that runners, dancers, and musicians do.

To help you get moving, here are some prewriting exercises that come from the reading and writing topics in this book. Try these different methods; you may find a few that help you get beyond the blank page or screen.

FREEWRITING

As the term implies, **freewriting** involves jotting down uncensored thoughts as quickly as you can. Don't concern yourself with form or correctness. Write whatever comes into your mind without rejecting ideas because they may seem silly or irrelevant. In freewriting, one thought might trigger a more intriguing or significant one, so anything that comes into your head may be valuable. Here is one student's freewriting response to the topic of stereotyping:

> Stereotyping? I don't think I stereotype--maybe I do.
> But I sure have had it done to me. When people see my tatoo
> they seem to think I'm in Hell's Angels or a skinhead. Talk
> about prejudgements! It's as if the snake coiling up my arm
> is going to get them, the way they look at it and pull back
> from me. I remember once, in a campground in Alaska, a
> bunch of us campers were stranded when the road washed out.
> As food and supplies dwindled, people started borrowing
> from each other. In the john one morning I asked this guy
> if I could borrow a razor blade and he jumped back. Not
> till he looked away from my arm and into my eyes did he
> relax. He gave me a blade, we talked, later shared some
> campfires together. . . . I could write about that experi-
> ence, a good story. I wonder if people with tatooes have
> always been connected with trouble--pirates maybe, sailors
> and gang members today anyhow. It could be interesting to
> find out if the negative stereotypes about tatooes have
> always been there. Now that's some research I could get
> into.

Ryan's response to the topic of stereotyping starts with his personal feeling that the subject doesn't really relate to him. But then he thinks about the fact that he has been stereotyped by others. As he considers how people react to his tattoo, he recalls an incident he thinks he could write about as a narrative. As he thinks more about the nature of tattoos, he finds an aspect of stereotyping that concerns him and that he might like to research. If he had not written down his feelings about stereotyping, he might have settled for a more predictable response to the assignment.

Notice that Ryan's freewriting starts with a question that he asks himself about the topic—a perfect way to get himself warmed up and moving. He's not worried about checking his spelling. He can consult a dictionary when he is drafting his paper to learn that *tattoos* and *prejudgments* are the correct spellings. Ryan also uses language in his prewriting that might not be appropriate in his essays: "guy," "bunch," "john," "anyhow," and "get into." Most important is that Ryan got started on his assignment without procrastinating and that he explored his own unique thoughts and feelings. He found a personal experience he might relate and discovered research that he would like to do.

■ PRACTICING FREEWRITING

To help you see how freewriting can lead to discovery, write for 15 minutes, without stopping, on one of the topics below. Do not worry about form and do not censor any idea, fact, picture, or feeling that comes to you. Freewrite about the following:

1. One of your parents or one of your children
2. A time spent with a grandparent
3. A particular family occasion when you learned something
4. Your response to "Thanksgiving" (p. 4)
5. Your response to "When Parents Don't Turn Out Right" (p. 67)

Your freewriting may be written on a sheet of paper, composed at a computer, or jotted down in your journal.

JOURNAL WRITING

Journals may be used to record your feelings or respond to others' ideas, including material that you have read. As a conversation with yourself, journal writing may also help you warm up before writing a paper. It will give you another way to discover your ideas; in fact, many professional writers rely on journals to store ideas for future stories, articles, editorials, and poems.

Your professor may ask you to keep a journal just so that you will have additional writing practice while you are in a composition course. Nearly all of the "Thinking About the Text" questions and many of the "Writing from the Text" assignments in the reader make ideal topics for a journal. If you use your journal to write responses to assigned readings, you will:

- be better prepared for class discussions,
- retain more material from the readings, and
- gain more writing practice.

For your journal, you can use a notebook of any size. Some writers prefer ones that are thin enough to fit into a purse or a full backpack. That way, they can pull out their journals whenever the inspiration strikes them, such as on a bus or while waiting for someone. Others prefer binders so that they can add or delete loose-leaf pages as needed. It helps to date each entry so that you can trace the development of your thoughts and your writing.

Using a Journal for Active Reading

One type of assigned active reading is a *dialectical journal*. In this journal you write down specific phrases from your readings and then record thoughts that are evoked by these phrases—in effect, having a conversation with your reading material. You may find yourself jotting down questions you would like to ask the writer, or words and terms you looked up in a dictionary. Include specific details that you want to interpret or analyze. You will find yourself discovering feelings about particular topics related to the reading.

Imagine Ryan, the student who did freewriting about stereotypes, responding specifically to the essay "Don't Let Stereotypes Warp Your Judgments" (p. 429). His journal response to the essay might look like this:

```
     "Are criminals more likely to be dark than blond?"

That's a provocative question the author asks. It makes me

think about all the bad guys in movies. Aren't they always

dark? You never see Robert Redford playing a villain--or do

you? I think some of our stereotyping comes from film,

which is Heilbroner's point when he writes about "type-

casts." Maybe only bad films use "types." I like what the

author says about stereotypes making us "mentally lazy." I

can see what he means when he says there are two people

hurt in stereotyping--the person who is unjustly lumped

into some category and the person who is "impoverished" by

his laziness. Heilbroner says that a person can't "see the

world in his own absolutely unique, inimitable and indepen-

dent fashion." That makes sense about being independent.

But I wonder what "inimitable" means?
```

Notice that Ryan begins his journal entry with a question from the essay itself; he also might have started with his own question about the work. Ryan jots down ideas that come to him as he responds to the assigned reading. It is important that he puts quotation marks around any words, phrases, or sentences from the text: in case he uses these later, Ryan wants to remember that the ideas and language belong to the author of the essay.

In addition to moving Ryan into his assigned topic, his journal writing lets him record his responses to parts of Heilbroner's essay. He is practicing finding the essence of the essay, as well as parts that he might want to quote in his own work. Further, if Ryan reads "Proper Care and Maintenance" (p. 176) and "Black Men and Public Space" (p. 225), he will have relevant material in his journal that he can connect to these other readings, either for his own interest or for other writing assignments.

■ PRACTICING JOURNAL WRITING

Respond to any of the following topics by conversing with yourself in an uncensored dialogue. Start with the question or topic, but permit your mind to wander around the block and down some alleys.

1. Sibling rivalry—does it relate to me?

2. How have my parents changed since I've been in college?

3. Do I agree with Ellen Goodman when she writes in "Thanksgiving" (p. 4), "We don't have to achieve to be accepted by our families. We just have to be."

4. Are any of the generational conflicts in "Two Kinds" (p. 49) ones that I also have?

CLUSTERING

Clustering is a more visual grouping of ideas on a page. It is the perfect prewriting exercise for students who tend to see ideas or concepts in spatial relationships. We have found that many students use clustering for in-class writing assignments, including essay exams, where the object is not to discover a topic but to organize information that they already have. For these writers, clustering is the best way to see the assigned question in terms of main topics and subtopics, and thus the organization of content is quickly perceived.

One student used clustering in response to an assignment to discover some "between-worlds" topics in her own life. Rachel wrote the assignment as a question in the middle of the page. Then she drew lines from the topics to several subtopics, which she placed in boxes. As you can see below, her subtopics are the chapter titles in the reader portion of this text. She placed "perceptions" and "genders" in the same box because, for her, these areas were closely related. Next to each subtopic, she then wrote down a brief phrase or reference to experiences and concerns that related to it. By clustering her responses, Rachel discovered topics that were important to her.

She was also able to group related issues—an immediate advantage of clustering. You may want to read the paper (p. 357) that came from this prewriting discovery work. But first look at Rachel's clustering exercise, which is reproduced below:

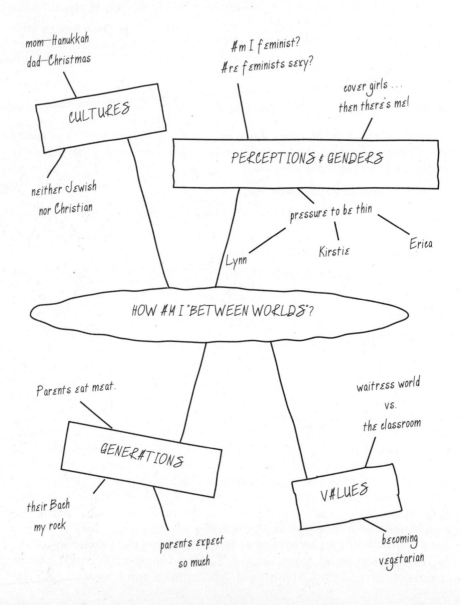

Notice that Rachel started with the assigned question of how she was "between worlds" and used that as a center or starting point for her personal inquiry into specific areas where she felt "betweenness." You can respond graphically to the topics below by clustering.

■ PRACTICING CLUSTERING

1. Center "self and family" in a box on a page. As you cluster, consider how you are "a part of" your family and how you are "apart from" your family.

2. Center "incidents that united my family" in a box on a page. Draw lines to other boxes that will include specific outings, celebrations, crises, customs, and events that have united your family. Don't forget the surprising or unlikely incidents that no one expected would draw you together.

Clustering may help you discover topics that interest you, as well as find relationships between ideas that you have written on your page.

LISTING

You can use listing as a way of making a quick inventory of thoughts, ideas, feelings, or facts about a topic. The object is to list everything, again without censoring any notion that comes to you. In addition to clustering her "between-worlds" experiences as shown (p. 308), Rachel listed her ideas after she discovered a topic for her paper. (You can see her listing on pp. 328–329.)

If you are answering a specific question or know what your topic is, you can also use listing to collect from your reading the data that will be useful in your paper. Listing will help you see ways to group and to arrange the material that you have found.

For example, a student who is assigned a character analysis based on a particular reading may list details from the text that indicate the character's traits. In order to write a character analysis of Hazel Peoples, the speaker and central character in the short story "My Man Bovanne" (p. 43), student Tim Hogan wrote a list that you can see on page 437. Notice how Tim's list helps him find important details and then organize those details for his essay.

■ PRACTICING LISTING

1. Write a list of options or advantages your parents or grandparents had that you feel you do not have. List options or advantages you have that they did not.

2. List the tensions that occur between generations in your family.

3. List the customs, habits, and values in your family that are transmitted between generations.

4. List the behavior traits of Sanders' father in "Under the Influence" (p. 11).

ACTIVE READING

Active reading is an appropriate prewriting strategy when you are asked to write a specific response to something that you have read, or when you know that your own experience and knowledge provide insufficient information for a meaningful essay. A great deal of college writing—in every course—fits these circumstances, so it is important that you either learn active reading or perfect the skills that you already have.

Active reading involves reading with a pen in your hand. *If* you are using your own book, you can read and mark directly in the copy. If you are using a library book, you will need to photocopy the pages you intend to read actively. As you read your own text or the photocopied pages, make the following markings:

- *Underline* key points and supporting details
- *Place checkmarks* and *asterisks* next to important lines
- *Jot* brief summary or commentary *notes* in the margins
- *Circle* unfamiliar words and references to look up later
- *Ask questions* as you read
- *Seek answers* to those questions
- *Question* the writer's *assumptions* and assertions as well as your own.

Reading actively allows you to enter into a conversation with your authors where you examine and challenge their ideas. Active reading will also help you find important lines more easily so that you don't have to reread the entire work each time that you refer to it during class discussions or in your essays. Don't underline or highlight *everything*, however, or you will defeat your purpose of finding just the important points.

If you have a writing assignment that requires you to use information from readings in addition to your own experience, you will profit from learning how to read actively and how to incorporate information that you have read into your own work. Rachel, the student who used clustering to discover her concern about the pressure among her friends to be thin, decided to do some reading about eating disorders. The excerpt on the facing page from "Bodily Harm" (p. 220), illustrates her active reading.

Check specific definitions

Recent media attention to the binge-purge and self-starvation disorders known as <u>bulimia</u> and <u>anorexia</u>—often detailing gruesome particulars of women's eating behaviors—may have exacerbated this serious problem on college campuses. But why would a woman who reads an article on eating disorders want to copy what she reads? Ruth Striegel-Moore, Ph.D., director of Yale University's Eating Disorders Clinic, suggests that <u>eating disorders</u> may be a way to be like other "<u>special</u>" <u>women</u> and at the same time strive to outdo them. "The pursuit of thinness is a way for women to compete with each other, a way that <u>avoids</u> <u>being threatening to men</u>," says Striegel-Moore. Eating disorders as a <u>perverse sort of rivalry</u>? In Carol's freshman year at SUNY-Binghamton, a roommate <u>showed</u> her how to make herself throw up. ("Barf buddies") are notorious on many college campuses, especially in sororities and among sports teams. Eating disorders as <u>negative bonding</u>? Even self-help groups on campus can degenerate into the kinds of competitiveness and negative reinforcement that are among the roots of eating disorders in the first place.

Media may exacerbate the problem

general term

"special" = how to be unique?

thinness as competition— without threatening men.

How ironic!

Self-help groups as negative reinforcement

This is not another <u>article on how women do it</u>. It is an article on <u>how and why some women stopped</u>. The decision to get help is not always an easy one. The shame and secrecy surrounding most eating disorders and the fear of being labeled "<u>sick</u>" may keep a woman from admitting even to herself that her behavior is hurting her. "We're not weirdos," says Nancy Gengler, a recovered bulimic and number two U.S. squash champion, who asked that I use her real name because "so much of this illness has to do with <u>secrecy and embarrassment</u>." In the first stages of therapy, says Nancy, much of getting better was a result of building up the strength to (literally) "sweat out" the desire to binge and to <u>endure the discomfort of having overeaten</u> rather than throwing up. "I learned to accept such 'failures' and moreover, <u>that they would not make me fat</u>."

the focus:

labeled "sick"

secrecy is part of the problem.

Need to accept our "failures"

Writing notes in the margins helped Rachel to stay involved as she read and to remember details from the essay. Like Rachel, you can better understand and retain what you read if you practice active reading.

■ PRACTICING ACTIVE READING

1. Practice the steps listed on page 310 and actively read the next work that you have been assigned in this course. Do you feel better prepared for class discussion? Did you find the central point or thesis of the essay as a result of your active reading? Was the author's organization scheme apparent to you?

2. Actively read "The Only Child" (p. 22), "I Confess Some Envy" (p. 399), or "When Parents Don't Turn Out Right" (p. 67). After you have actively read one of these essays, join a small group of others who have read the same essay. Compare your active-reading notes with the markings of others in your group.

GROUP BRAINSTORMING—COLLABORATIVE LEARNING

Writing doesn't have to be a lonely activity, with the writer isolated from the world. In fact, much professional writing is a collaborative effort in which writers work together or consult editors. Corporations, educational institutes, and governmental organizations hold regular "brainstorming" sessions so that everyone can offer ideas, consider options, and exchange opinions. Reporters often work together on a story, business experts pool ideas to draft a proposal, and lawyers work as a team on a brief. Many of your textbooks—including this one—are the result of extensive collaboration.

Your college writing classes may offer you opportunities to work together in small groups, brainstorm for paper topics or supporting details, and critique and edit your classmates' writing. Just as freewriting is a conversation with yourself, group brainstorming provides a conversation with others. These small groups can provide new thoughts, multiple perspectives, and critical questions. Small-group discussion can prompt you to consider others' ideas, as well as help free you from the fear that you have nothing to say. You may find you are more comfortable sharing ideas with a few classmates rather than the entire class.

In the classroom, groups of four or five work well, with each person recording the different comments and key ideas for an assigned question and then sharing these responses with the entire class. Students in your group can decide who will explain each response so that the burden for reporting the discussion does not fall on any one group member. Your instructor, however, may ask that someone from each group serve as "group secretary," recording responses and then reading them. Either way, the goal is to generate as many different responses as possible to a given topic or question. Your group may need to be reminded that everyone's ideas are welcome and needed

and that even seemingly farfetched comments can trigger very productive discussions. As in all of the prewriting activities, no idea or
comment should be censored.

Let's assume you have been assigned a paper about growing up
with or without siblings. Each group can take a different aspect of
this topic:

- The advantages of growing up with siblings
- The advantages of growing up as an only child
- The ways that only children find "substitutes" for siblings
- The reasons for sibling rivalry and competition, and the solutions
  to these problems
- The unexpected bonds that develop between siblings
- The reasons that sibling friendships often outlast other friendships

After 10 to 15 minutes of discussion, you should each make sure your
group has recorded the key points so they can be shared with the
class as a whole. After each report by a group, all students should be
invited to add comments or insights on that topic. Students who are
listening to a group should take notes to supplement their own essay
ideas.

Group brainstorming is an ideal way to discuss reading assignments, and most of the "Thinking About the Text" questions in the
reader are designed for collaborative work. Any of those questions
may be used for this exercise. Below you will find brainstorming
exercises for both general topics and specific readings.

■ PRACTICING BRAINSTORMING IN SMALL GROUPS

1. Brainstorm about the forces threatening the family unit today, and consider
   ways of preventing or solving particular conflicts. (All groups can do this, since
   the responses will be so varied.)

2. Discuss the extent to which grandparents are or are not valued by families.
   Support the discussion with your own experience.

3. Discuss the various types of families currently portrayed on television. One
   group can analyze the impact of the media on the family. Other groups can compare sitcoms with family dramas or PBS specials on the family. Another group
   can contrast portraits of more conventional families with those of less conventional ones. A final group can suggest programs that could help or support the
   family.

4. Read "The Girls' Room" (p. 63) and discuss specific ways that the two generations live in harmony and in discord. You may add your own experiences to this
   discussion.

5. Read "Discovery of a Father" (p. 6) and "When Parents Don't Turn Out Right" (p. 67) and discuss the expectations that children have for their parents.

Brainstorming lets you see others' perspectives and consider their views in relation to your own—an awareness you will need when you are writing for an audience. Collaborative work gets you away from the isolation of your own desk or computer screen and into a social context.

INCUBATION

After you have done one or more of the prewriting responses to an assignment, allow yourself time to think about your topic before you begin to draft the paper. Rather than being a way to avoid the writing assignment, the incubation period lets you subconsciously make connections and respond to your focus. Students often comment on experiencing flashes of insight about their papers while in the shower, falling asleep, or doing some physical activity.

You, too, will find that your brain will continue to "work" on your paper if you are preoccupied with it, and productive insights can occur during this incubation period. If you do some prewriting on your paper when it is first assigned, your early thoughts and ideas may develop during incubation. Clearly, though, if you have waited until the night before the assignment is due, you aren't going to enjoy much of an incubation period!

The need for incubation continues throughout the drafting process. While you are away from your desk or computer screen, you can still be thinking about ways to hone your topic, increase support of your points, discover links between ideas in your paper, and recall words that will sharpen your meaning. This is also an ideal time to remind yourself that you are writing for readers and to consider their expectations.

CONSIDERING AUDIENCE

Identifying Your Audience

All writing is intended for an audience. Except for personal journal writers, who may be able to understand their own notes to themselves, writers have certain responsibilities to meet the needs and expectations of a reader. But who *is* the reader?

In some specific writing situations, you can easily define the audience for your work: for example, your reader may be a friend or family member who will receive your letter. You are surely aware that your writing tone—the voice that you use that affects your word choice and emphasis—will differ if you are writing to your lover, brother, elderly aunt, or mother. However, you may be less able to define the audience for other writing situations. You might assume that for papers assigned in your college classes, your reader is a classmate or an instructor, a thoughtful person who may know something about the subject of your writing and who is very willing (indeed, eager) to learn more.

In general, you should not assume that your only reader is your composition instructor, for that conclusion will prompt you to write for a very small audience. Further, your English teacher may be your easiest audience, because he or she is *required* to read what you have written, comment on your thinking and writing skills, and then perhaps place a grade on your work. In the real world, when you are writing for a boss, readers of a newspaper, or a community organization member, your easily distracted or unwilling reader may lack the empathy an academic instructor has for the effort you have put into your writing, which may be ignored or tossed into the trash rather than honored with comments or praise. The skills that you learn in your composition class, however, will prepare you for your broader college and "real-world" writing requirements.

Academic Audiences

Academic readers (your instructors and classmates) will assume that you have carefully considered the assigned topic. This means that you understand what is expected of you and that you are writing to satisfy that assignment. This may require finding out what other people know or believe, collecting specific data, or sorting through your own thoughts and information on the subject. Your audience will expect a certain depth of response, even for a short paper. The reader will expect to learn specific facts, find actual examples, discover important insights, or see particular relationships that she or he was not aware of prior to reading your paper. The paper's required length may define how many dimensions of the subject you can explore to satisfy the assignment.

An academic audience will also expect you to have worked with integrity if you incorporate the ideas, facts, or words of another writer. (See the discussions of plagiarism on p. 342 and on pp. 454–456.) Your reader will assume that you have understood any material that you have brought in from another source, that you have not distorted the material in any way, and that you have given credit to the writer whose words or ideas you have used.

An academic audience will expect you to make some point and to support that point logically and with sufficient details (of description, fact, or example) to be convincing. Such readers will expect that you know what you are writing about and that your work has not just been assembled from other people's work—that your treatment or perspective is fresh.

Academic readers will expect your material to be presented in an orderly way, so that a lack of organization does not obscure the points you are making. They will expect your points to cohere. Finally, they will expect the language of your work to be appropriate: standard English and well-chosen words, edited to remove errors in grammar, spelling, and mechanics.

Nonacademic Audiences

For writing outside the classroom—for example, a letter to the newspaper, a report for your boss, or an analysis for a community project—it is vital for you to engage an audience that is not required to read your writing. What are the expectations of this audience?

To start, you may need to convince those readers that your subject and the way you have treated it are worth their time. Depending on the attention span of your reader, you may have to establish the value of your subject and the quality of your writing in the first few sentences! Developing an engaging style will help keep your reader interested.

Voice

Most instructors will tell you to "write in your own voice." That means that they want you to write using the vocabulary, sentence structure, and style that you use for communicating as an adult. You do not want to use pretentious words or artificial language, nor do you want to use diction that is more appropriate for talking with a friend. Often your intention in writing and the position you take on your subject will help you determine how emphatic your stance and your language will be. In any case, though, you will write in your own voice.

Stance and Tone

To engage your audience quickly, you may want to assume a stance and tone that is positive for all readers, even those who are disinterested or hostile to the topic you are writing about. You may want to anticipate possible objections, doubts, or lack of interest by writing in a tone that does not put off any reader. Consider these two opening sentences:

Only someone ignorant of contract law will find ambiguity in the handling of surrogate parenting disputes.

Surrogate parenting disputes may occur because the parties involved have unrealistic expectations about surrogate parenting agreements and because the legal world has not yet found a clear way to judge these cases of ethical dilemma.

The tone of the first sentence is bold, the assertion straightforward. Some readers will be put off by the claim that "only someone ignorant of contract law will find ambiguity" because some of the audience may be ignorant of contract law, and the "will" suggests no room for consideration. The use of "ignorant" will be offensive to some readers and perhaps compelling to others. Some readers may continue to read in spite of the brash voice, or even because of it. But others may conclude that the tone is too hostile to tolerate, and those readers will stop reading.

In contrast, the tone of the second sentence is cautious ("may occur") and contemplative: perhaps "unrealistic expectations" are a reason, or perhaps "the legal world" is unable to rule clearly. By suggesting that there is room for discussion, the writer may win the reader who is interested in an unbiased exploration of surrogate parenting disputes. The writer of the second sentence has tried to create a reasonable and informing relationship between writer and reader, one that should attract readers.

You will need to choose the tone that you want to use for your particular writing assignment. The subject matter of your work and the *audience* for whom you are writing will help you determine whether a neutral tone will keep your audience engaged.

Style

Style is conscious use of language, and good style will help assure the attention of the audience. This means considering everything from your choice of words to your construction of sentences. Style includes the following elements:

- Word choice—precisely chosen words, wordplay, and level of diction (formal, conversational, or slang); see also pp. 551–566
- Sentence structure—length, types, and variety
- Voice—real, rather than artificial or pretentious
- Tone—your intention, attitude, and relationship with the reader

Consider the opening line below from the *Harvard Health Letter*. The topic is controversial, and the reader may have opinions about the subject. Notice that the style of the author, Ruth Papazian, is apparent to the reader in her first sentence.

A Hot Issue

In January, 1992, when Florida shoppers bought strawberries that had been treated with gamma rays, food irradiation moved from the realm of theory to America's kitchen tables.

First, the author uses wit and wordplay in writing her title. There's nothing wrong with evoking a chuckle from a reader, even when the subject matter is serious or scientific. (An academic in the scientific fields may object to humor in formal papers. You will need to learn from your instructors the style requirements of specific disciplines.) Further, the writer creates an immediate and natural bond with any reader who has bought strawberries; that reader would wonder, "Hey! Do my strawberries get zapped?" The writer assures that bond by further noting that the issue moved from "theory"—which some readers may not care about—to "America's kitchen tables." Notice that the writer does not write "dining room tables." This writing is clearly directed toward general readers, all of whom eat, and the kitchen image evokes a folksiness that engages the audience.

In the rest of the article, the author uses sentences that further win the reader. For example, after establishing the topic, she writes in her seventh paragraph, "Since a caveperson first tossed a chunk of mastodon onto glowing embers, humans have been cooking with infrared radiation." Notice the gender-neutral *caveperson* instead of the sexist term *caveman,* and notice the diction of *chunk,* the humorous specificity of *mastodon,* and the effective imagery of *glowing embers.* Who wouldn't want to read this entire essay? (It's in the August 1992 issue, volume 17, number 10 if you're really engaged in the topic or want to see more of this author's style.)

An academic reader who is required to read your writing may not insist on lively style, wit, or exquisite word choice. And she or he may tolerate a brash tone or hostile stance. Nevertheless, ideas about engaging an audience are as applicable to writing done for academics as it is to the writing done for a nonacademic reader.

■ PRACTICING STYLE

1. Write two letters—one to your best friend, and one to your parents or children—describing a party that you recently attended. (Your letters probably will vary in vocabulary, kinds of details, sentence structure, and tone.)

2. Write two memos—one to a coworker who is a friend, and one to your boss—arguing for a particular change at work.

Analyzing Audience Awareness

Clearly, professional writers have an understanding of audience when they direct their texts for publication. We can profit from a study of the techniques that they use to engage and hold their particular audiences.

Ellen Sweet

In her informative essay on date rape, "Date Rape" (p. 112), Ellen Sweet begins her study of the "epidemic" with first-person accounts from women who have been raped by dates or acquaintances. Each woman's narrative has a similar theme: because of her friendship with the rapist, she could not believe what was happening to her.

Sweet does not retreat from the burden of exposing shocking data—for example, the statistic that 60 to 80 percent of all rapes are done by a person the victim knows. Sweet presents her data almost entirely through interviews, so her own voice is absent or controlled rather than inflammatory. The author wants her selected subjects' voices to reveal the problems of date rape: the victims reveal their shock that a friend would abuse them, the school officials reveal their refusal to acknowledge a pervasive campus problem, and the psychologists show the denial pattern of aggressive men who force women to have intercourse but believe their behavior is acceptable. After quoting one school official who refused to involve his campus in the survey because he feared people would become "psychologically upset," Sweet coolly but pointedly writes, "One wonders just who are the 'people' who will get most psychologically upset: the students, or their parents who pay for their educations, or the administrators who are concerned about the school's image."

Sweet's intention is to stir her audience—originally, readers of *Ms.* magazine—to an awareness *and* a constructive course of action. Sweet wants readers to pressure their colleges' educators, administrators, and counselors to implement the sort of rape prevention programs that she discusses in her report. An audience that is merely angry will not do what the author wants done; hence her voice is modulated to inform and provide a course of action rather than to blame and enrage. Her conclusion is a controlled call to action: "Women clearly need to get more convincing, and men clearly need to believe them more. But until that ideal time, Montana State's Jan Strout warns, 'Because men have been socialized to hear yes when women say no, we have to scream it.'" Sweet lets her interviewed subjects "scream" for her. It is not surprising that this essay has been widely reprinted in the decade since its initial publication.

Michael Kimmel and Martin Levine

In their essay "A Hidden Factor in AIDS" (p. 78), Michael Kimmel and Martin Levine also have unpleasant and controversial material to present to their audience—readers of the opinion section of the *Los Angeles Times,* where their essay first appeared. The authors' intention is to increase both the awareness and compassion level of this general reader.

Their first method to engage the reader is to assert that AIDS has killed more American men than were "lost" in Vietnam, a startling statistic that must jolt *many* readers. Their next intention is to show that certain men—gay men and IV drug users—are more at risk for AIDS because they engage in high-risk behavior in order to demonstrate their masculinity. The authors reason that threatened men need to demonstrate hypermasculinity to counter the general social perception that they are "perverts" or "deviants" from normal masculinity. The writers must employ a stance that will appeal to a broader audience than might initially read this essay, and they accomplish this by insisting that these men are "over-conformists" who deserve our understanding of the sociological forces that condition their behavior, an interesting perception the reader might be intrigued to consider.

The authors further argue that these men at risk for AIDS deserve our respect for the way they have rallied to support each other in this crisis—a point that the general reader might favorably consider—and they deserve our compassion for what they are suffering. It is worth noting that only after Kimmel and Levine have gained a general audience willing to follow their intellectual suppositions that they appeal in their emotional conclusion to a gender-specific brotherhood that would have lost them part of their audience had they employed the stance earlier.

The authors attract their general audience with statistical data, keep the audience by positing and supporting an interesting argument, involve the audience by suggesting its responsibility for the AIDS crisis, and risk limiting their audience only at the conclusion of their essay, when the reader has been engaged entirely in the work.

In your own writing, you should consider the assumptions about audience that professional writers make and employ the techniques that they use to engage and keep their readers. You can do this by assuming a stance that will be attractive to your audience and maintaining a voice that will keep your reader interested in your work.

■ PRACTICING AUDIENCE AWARENESS

1. Write a short essay for a men's magazine, such as *Esquire* or *Playboy*, using some of the data in Ellen Sweet's essay "Date Rape" (p. 112).

2. Write a letter to your college president or dean of student affairs to convince the administrator that your college needs better education, security, and counseling for rape prevention. Use the material in Sweet's essay for your letter.

Good style—achieved with deliberately chosen vocabulary, sentence structure, and tone—can engage your reader immediately. With a realistic understanding of your audience in mind, you are ready to begin organizing and drafting your essay. You will gain an understanding of that aspect of the writing process in the next chapter of the rhetoric.

7

Organizing and Drafting an Essay

■ ■ ■

DISCOVERING A THESIS

From Prewriting to Working Thesis

The prewriting experiences described in the previous chapter should have helped you discover focus points and different ways that you might respond to your writing assignment. You were also given some ideas about considering the audience for your writing. It is now important that you determine your specific approach for your paper. All essays require a focus—a controlling idea for both the writer and the reader. So after doing some prewriting activities, thinking about your topic, considering your audience, and writing an initial draft, you should be able to construct at least a tentative or working thesis that will help you direct your writing. That thesis may change a number of times as you draft and revise your paper. Let's think about how the controlling idea for your paper might be expressed.

Developing a Thesis

A thesis is an assertion about a limited subject that will be supported, proven, or described by the writer of the essay. Often, but not always, the view of the writer shows in the language of the thesis. Sometimes the writer constructs a thesis to forecast the plan or organization of the paper. The thesis will reflect the aim or intention of the paper.

Let's imagine that Ryan is deciding from his prewriting experiences (pp. 304–307) how to respond to his assignment on stereotyping. His particular interest has to do with his tattoo and how he is stereotyped because of it, an awareness he gained in freewriting. Ryan realized that he had a good focus for a story he could narrate. He also discovered that he was interested in doing some reading about the history of tattoos to learn whether they always were regarded negatively.

If Ryan's assignment had been to write about a personal experience involving stereotyping, he probably would have written about the incident in the Alaskan campground. Had he been asked to define stereotyping or show its consequences, Ryan might have recalled his dialectical journal prewriting (p. 306) on the essay "Don't Let Stereotypes Warp Your Judgments," and he may have developed his paper in a different way. Ryan may have used any of the following for a working thesis, depending on his purpose in writing the paper:

- An experience in Alaska showed me how uncomfortable stereotyping can be for the person stereotyped.
- Stereotyping, or prejudgments based on "standardized pictures" in our heads, can create unnecessary anxiety and deprive us of worthwhile experiences.
- Because tattoos have been worn by the lower classes and fringe members of various cultures throughout history, there has been prejudice against them.
- Because prominent citizens of the world have started to wear tattoos, earlier prejudice against tattoos has diminished.

Each of these assertions requires Ryan to develop his paper in a slightly different way. The first thesis can be supported with his own experience. The second statement requires some incorporation of definitive and appropriately documented material from Heilbroner's essay on stereotyping, as well as personal experience. The third and fourth thesis statements will require Ryan to research material in order to support his assertions. Like Ryan, your personal interests, as well as the aim of the assignment itself, will help you decide on a suitable thesis.

Recognizing a Thesis

If a thesis is a complete sentence that makes an assertion about a limited subject, which of the following are supportable thesis statements? Which are not? Which statements forecast a plan or direction for the paper?

1. Sexism in college courses.
2. Sexist language in college textbooks can be eliminated with the right attitude and language awareness.

3. I think the school's cafeteria should post a nutritional analysis of every meal it offers.

4. When grandparents live with two younger generations, everyone learns flexibility and new reasons to laugh.

5. Should Americans buy only American-made products?

6. Siblings can remind us of our family's history and values and can provide physical and emotional support as we age.

The first example may be a suitable subject or topic for an essay, but it is not a thesis. As the absence of a verb indicates, the example lacks an assertion that makes a claim about sexism. The second example does make a claim about sexist language and is a reasonable thesis. It has a limited subject (sexist language in college textbooks), and it forecasts that "attitude" and "language awareness" will be the subtopics discussed to support the thesis. Example three contains a clear assertion, but "I think" is unnecessary. The thesis should directly express this conviction: The school's cafeteria should post a nutritional analysis of every meal it offers. The fourth example is an effective thesis that forecasts two benefits of generations living together. A question like that in the fifth example may be a good way to engage a reader in an introduction, but it is not an assertion, so it is not a suitable thesis. The question encourages an unfocused, disorganized response. Contrast the direction implicit in the statements of examples two, four, or six with this question, and you will see why it is not effective. Six is a very explicit thesis statement. It cites exactly the areas of support that will come in the paper: the "family's history and values" and "physical and emotional support." Writers who write from a strong thesis will know where they are going, and so will their readers.

Changing the Thesis

Before we discuss thesis statements any further, it is important to acknowledge some qualities about the thesis. For one thing, the thesis can undergo many changes in the course of drafting and rewriting a paper. Everyone has had the experience of finishing a draft only to discover that her or his feelings about the subject have changed. In order to reflect that new awareness in the paper, the writer will want to return to the thesis, revise it, and then reshape the points in the paper so they will adequately support the new assertion. Perhaps it is best to consider any thesis as only a working thesis until you are about to edit your final draft. (See Rachel's work on developing a thesis, pp. 328–334.)

The "Missing" Thesis

Although the final draft of a well-written essay will be clearly focused and will support a central point, some writers do not explicitly state their thesis, and some instructors do not demand one. Sometimes the overt assertion may spoil the sense of discovery that the writer intends for the reader. But even if a thesis is implied rather than stated, in a well-structured essay you should be able to articulate the writer's fundamental assertion.

Positioning the Thesis

If you are going to state a thesis in your essay, you need to consider where you will place it. For many writers, and for many essays, placing the thesis at the conclusion of the introduction makes sense. The thesis follows logically from the introductory materials used to engage the audience, and the plan or direction of the paper is set forth so that the reader knows not only what is coming, but in what order the support will be presented. This forecasting also helps you, the writer of the essay, to stay organized and on target.

Although it may seem natural to place the thesis at the end of the introductory paragraph, not all writers do this. Essays that are tightly written, with very well-organized support, may conclude with the thesis to bring an inevitable (if not predictable) sense of closure. The reader will perceive where the writer is headed, so the assertion at the end of the paper will not come as a surprise.

Many writing instructors will require that you place your thesis within the first few paragraphs of your essay. Tired of wondering and writing "Where is all of this going?" in the margins of student papers, some instructors favor the clearly stated thesis that forecasts the subtopics and their order of presentation. In any case, a strong focus—whether stated in a thesis or implied—contributes to good writing, and you will want to perfect your ability to focus your work.

Sample Thesis Statements

The chart below shows how writers work from a limited subject to write a thesis that their experience or information can support.

Limited Subject	Focus	Thesis
College students	Commuting students	College students who live at home know the problems of living between worlds.
Native Americans	Popular depictions	The Native American is stereotyped and denigrated in American popular culture.
TV for children	Improved programming	In contrast to ten years ago, television programs designed for elementary-age children today are multi-cultural and interracial.
The men's movement	Is it necessary?	The men's movement is needed to create a social connection between men. The movement can rectify divorce and paternity inequities.

■ PRACTICING THESIS WRITING

Although seeing other writers' thesis statements will help you gain awareness of the thesis, you need to practice writing your own assertions for your own papers. You also need to have readers critique the thesis statements that you have written.

1. Return to one of your prewriting exercises or freewrite here on the subject of a parent's ability or inability to be open to new and possibly controversial ideas. Freewrite for 15 minutes without censoring any thought that comes to you. Then reread what you have written. Find an aspect of that material that interests you. Limit your focus and write two or three different thesis statements that you can support with the ideas in your freewriting. Type or write these assertions neatly on a sheet of paper and make three copies prior to your next class session.

2. In the first few minutes of class time, work in groups of four students to comment on each other's assertions. Let each student in the group make comments about one thesis statement before you go on to look at each person's second assertion. Determine which statements are true assertions that can be support-

ed. Then predict the type of support that is necessary (narrative of personal experience, definition, or examples from research material) for each thesis. If you are having trouble seeing what is lacking in your thesis statements, talk with your instructor or writing assistant.

Critical Thinking and the "So What?" Response

After you have a tentative assertion around which to direct your support, ask yourself, "So what?" A sure way to realize that your assumed assertion isn't headed anywhere meaningful is to discover yourself shrugging indifferently at your own claim. And as you jot down answers to this question, you will start to see what you are actually claiming. For example, imagine what would happen if you started with this assertion:

Thesis: Many people in the world are victims of stereotyping.

"So what?"
Some people have preconceived ideas about others.
"So what?"
It's unfair. People see them as types, not individuals.
"So what?"
These prejudgments limit the people who are stereotyped *and* the people doing the stereotyping.

As you continue to answer the "So what?" questions, you may discover a way to state your assertion that makes your reader more eager to read your paper. Compare the following assertion with the first one above. In what way is it better?

Thesis: Prejudgments limit the lives of the stereotyped individual and the person doing the stereotyping.

Notice how this statement conforms to the requirements of a thesis. It is a complete sentence, not a question or a phrase, and it articulates a definite opinion or assertion. Unlike the first attempt at a thesis, this statement establishes a definite focus on prejudgments (they "limit . . . lives"), and it suggests an order for the analysis ("the stereotyped individual" and "the person doing the stereotyping").

By asking yourself "So what?" *throughout* your writing, you will not only sharpen your thesis but also help yourself discover points and insights worth sharing with readers. If you continue to ask this question, you will prompt yourself to think more critically about each claim as you make it. You also will ensure that you are writing from a worthwhile assertion and that you are explaining your points to your reader.

SUPPORTING A THESIS

Drafting

Once you have done some prewriting, you are ready to begin the drafting process. No one writer drafts the same way; in fact, there are as many methods (and "nonmethods") for drafting as there are writers. But there are lots of strategies and approaches that help writers organize, develop, and support their ideas and assertions.

In the next pages, we will trace how one student, Rachel, drafted her paper. Look back to page 308 to see Rachel's clustering exercise where she discovered a topic related to living "between worlds." From this initial prewriting, she perceived that recurrent topics of interest were related to food: her vegetarianism, her friends' preoccupation with slimness, her awareness that her body does not fit the cover-girl mold, and even her job as a waitress.

Developing Support

Reviewing all of these food-related topics, Rachel realized she was most interested in her friends' eating problems. She decided to pursue the topic; because her instructor had required her to incorporate readings from this textbook in her paper, she started by actively reading "Bodily Harm." You can read an excerpt from this prewriting exercise on page 311. This active reading helped stimulate Rachel's thinking and helped her understand her friends' experiences.

Listing

After her prewriting activities, Rachel started to list more specific ideas and experiences that related to eating disorders:

- My friend, Lynn, hospitalized for anorexia, nearly died
- Another friend, Kirstie, was proud she could vomit automatically every time she ate
- My friend, Erica, in a treatment program, was shocked by the number of women over thirty still plagued by eating disorders
- Binge-and-purge syndrome
- Ads depict tall models in size 3 bikinis
- "Bodily Harm" examines psychological motives, "barf buddies," and "aerobic nervosa"

- "The Beauty Myth" continues to imprison women
- Jane Fonda, once bulimic, hooked so many on her "Work Out" videos
- Princess Di—bulimic and suicidal—the myth collapses
- My own insecurity about weight
- My cousin spent weeks in a hospital program for anorexics
- Weight loss—the ultimate "control" mechanism?
- Women's movement trying to free women from such images
- Young women torn between being feminist or sexy—why either/or?
- Sexy women are always pictured as thin
- Women competing without threatening men

Working Thesis

From this list, Rachel linked certain topics: friends' experiences, celebrities with serious eating disorders, advertising images of women, psychological motives, the women's movement, and dieting as a control mechanism. These groupings helped her draft a working thesis so she could start planning her paper.

Working Thesis: Many women suffer from eating disorders.

Using this preliminary thesis as a guide, Rachel started to write.

First Draft

In this day and age many women suffer from eating disorders. Influenced by television commercials and movies, most women have been conditioned to believe they must be thin to be beautiful. Who wouldn't want to hear friends whisper, "What a body! She really knows how to stay in shape!" or "Don't you hate some-one who looks that good?" Either way, the sense of envy is clear. A thin girl has something that others don't--and this gives her power and control. She can make herself in the image of the cover girls. "The pursuit of thinness is a way for women to compete with each other, a way that avoids being threatening to men" (Erens 220).

Unfortunately, this competition keeps women from seeking or obtaining the help they might otherwise get from close friends. Many bulimics keep their secret as guarded as they can. For example, my friend Kirstie did this. She waited for years before she told friends (and later, her family) that she was bulimic. At first, only her "barf buddy" (from Erens?) knew.

Kirstie seemed to have a good life with her family and friends. But years later, she revealed to me that her greatest pride was when she discovered that she was now vomiting automatically after eating, without needing to use a finger or spoon.

Erica was another friend who needed help. In fact, her situation was so bad that she needed to go into a hospital. And my friend Lynn would have died had she not entered the hospital when she did. She had to drop out of Berkeley immediately and get prolonged therapy for herself and her family. As Erens notes, "Family therapy considers the family itself, not the daughter with the eating disorder, to be the 'patient.' Often the daughter has taken on the role of diverting atten- tion from unacknowledged conflicts within the family."

One problem Lynn had was conforming to her par- ents' expectations. Lynn decided to major in art even though her parents wanted her to get a degree in com- puter science so she would have a job when she gradu- ated. There was so much stress in that house every

time Lynn enrolled in another art class. Maybe she
felt that the only thing she could control in her life
was how thin she could get.

The message to be thin comes from popular role
models. Actress Jane Fonda has sold many on the value
of her "Work Out" and has helped spawn "aerobic nervosa" (Erens 220). Many women who admire her shape may
not know that Fonda was once bulimic. And no one
watching the televised spectacle of Prince Charles and
Princess Diana's wedding could have predicted that
years later biographers would be discussing "Di's
bulimia."

Not just the superstars but all models seem
incredibly thin today. Wolf contends: "the weight of
fashion models plummeted to 23 percent below that of
ordinary women, eating disorders rose exponentially,
and a mass neurosis was promoted that used food and
weight to strip women of that sense of control" (103).
It seems that many women--celebrities, models, and my
friends--have not escaped this curse.

Evaluating the First Draft

As Rachel was writing this draft she found herself crossing out occasional words and adding phrases, but her main concern was getting
her ideas down on the page. She remembered relevant ideas from
some assigned readings in *Between Worlds,* and she put some of the
quoted material in her draft. She didn't worry about the form of her
quotes, but she was careful to copy the page numbers correctly so she
wouldn't have to waste time searching for them later. Once she had
written this rough draft, she reread it with a pen in hand, spotting
weak areas and making quick notes to herself. Her critique of her
first draft is shown on pages 332–333.

cliché?

dull!

(In this day and age) many women suffer from eating disorders. Influenced by television commercials and movies, most women have been conditioned to believe they must be thin to be beautiful. Who wouldn't want to hear friends whisper, "What a body! She really knows how to stay in shape!" or "Don't you hate someone who looks that good?" Either way, the sense of envy is clear. A thin girl has something that others

maybe save...

don't--and this gives her power and control. She can make herself in the image of the cover girls. "The

put thesis here?

pursuit of thinness is a way for women to compete with each other, a way that avoids being threatening to men" (Erens 220).

Unfortunately, this competition keeps women from seeking or obtaining the help they might otherwise get from close friends. Many bulimics keep their secret as guarded as they can. For example, my friend Kirstie did this. She waited for years before she told friends (and later, her family) that she was bulimic. At

page?

first, only her "barf buddy" (from Erens?) knew.

Kirstie seemed to have a good life with her family

illustrate

and friends. But years later, she revealed to me that

develop

her greatest pride was when she discovered that she was now vomiting automatically after eating, without

too gross?

needing to use a finger or spoon.

better link here?

or OK?

Erica was another friend who needed help. In fact,

develop

her situation was so bad that she needed to go into a hospital. And my friend Lynn would have died had she not entered the hospital when she did. She had to drop out of Berkeley immediately and get prolonged therapy for herself and her family. As Erens notes, "Family therapy considers the family itself, not the daughter with the eating disorder, to be the 'patient.' Often the daughter has taken on the role of diverting attention from unacknowledged conflicts within the family."

One problem Lynn had was conforming to her par- *discuss & link better* ents' expectations. Lynn decided to major in art even though her parents wanted her to get a degree in computer science so she would have a job when she graduated. There was so much stress in that house every time Lynn enrolled in another art class. Maybe she felt that the only thing she could control in her life was how thin she could get. *)link?*

The message to be thin comes from popular role models. Actress Jane Fonda has sold many on the value of her "Work Out" and has helped spawn "aerobic nervosa" (Erens 220). Many women who admire her shape may not know that Fonda was once bulimic. And no one watching the televised spectacle of Prince Charles and Princess Diana's wedding could have predicted that years later biographers would be discussing "Di's bulimia."

Put earlier

Not just the superstars but all models seem *lead in?* incredibly thin today. Wolf contends: "the weight of fashion models plummeted to 23 percent below that of ordinary women, eating disorders rose exponentially, and a mass neurosis was promoted that used food and weight to strip women of that sense of control" (103). It seems that many women--celebrities, models, and my friends--have not escaped this curse. *OK for thesis?*

Revising the Thesis

Writing the draft helped Rachel realize the link between her friends' experiences and the influence of the media. She decided to revise her thesis to reflect this connection between the media and eating disorders.

New Working Thesis: Magazine ads and commercials influence how women see themselves and how they behave.

Rachel felt that her material—both her personal experiences and readings—would support her new thesis. She also realized that this thesis helped her link the influence of the media on women's actions and behavior. Rachel showed her thesis to her instructor, who suggested she apply the "So what?" response to this assertion:

Ads and commercials influence women's self-perceptions.
"So what?"
Women try to look like the skinny models.
"So what?"
It's dangerous! Women are starving themselves.
"So what?"
The media has to change—they are responsible for programming
    women this way.

After thinking about this conversation with herself, Rachel revised her working thesis again:

Revised Working Thesis: The media must be forced to stop programming young women to believe skeletal models are the ideal.

Rachel's revised thesis more accurately reflected her view that the media must change what they are doing to women. Her reference to the "skeletal models" would permit her to discuss her friends' experiences. A friend in her English class who knew her topic recommended she look at a book, *The Obsession: Reflections on the Tyranny of Slenderness* by Kim Chernin. Rachel found a page with pertinent information supporting her criticism of the media; she photocopied the page in case she wanted to use it later.

WRITING AN OUTLINE

Organizing to Highlight Key Points

Excellent ideas and interesting information can get lost or buried in a paper that is not carefully arranged and organized. After collecting your thoughts and materials during the prewriting exercises, you need to present these materials in a logical and effective order. You may decide to arrange your thesis to reflect your organization scheme and help you draft your essay.

Notice how Rachel's thesis forecasts her essay's key points:

> The media must be forced to stop programming young women to believe skeletal models are the ideal.

Rachel's thesis suggests that she will first look at how the media is "programming" women, and then she will show how specific women become "skeletal" victims of the advertising that they see. Further, her assertion that the media "must be forced to stop" this practice invites her to propose a solution. Although Rachel devised a general scheme for organizing her paper, she knew she needed a more detailed outline.

To Outline or Not to Outline

By helping you arrange your materials effectively, <u>an outline can save you time and frustration.</u> It can keep you from going around in circles and never arriving at your destination. Just as most drivers need a map to direct them through unfamiliar territory, most writers need outlines in order to draft their papers.

You probably have had the experience of being in a car without a map, however, when someone could intuit the right direction and get you where you needed to be. Some writers have that intuition and therefore find detailed outlines unnecessary. But these writers will still craft a strong thesis and rely on their intrinsic sense of organization to guide them as they write.

Most of us also have been in cars with drivers who were convinced they could manage without a map, but couldn't. All that aimless driving and backtracking should prove the value of maps and directions! Such indirection or "backtracking" in papers prompts instructors to note in the margins: "Order?" "Repetitious," "Organization needs work," "Relevant?" "Transition needed," or "Where is this going?" If you see these indicators on your papers, you know your intuition is failing you. Outline before you write! Unless your instructor requires a particular outline form, your outline may be an informal "map" of key points and ideas in whatever order seems both logical and effective.

Ordering Ideas

You have a number of options for effective organization, and your purpose in writing will help you determine your arrangement. For example, Rachel's purpose was to convince readers that the media must stop promoting thinness as an ideal. Because this was the most important part of her argument, she saved it until the end, building support for it as she wrote. Rachel thus chose an emphatic arrangement scheme.

In an *emphatic* or *dramatic* organization, you arrange your material so that the most important, significant, worthy, or interesting material (for which you generally have the most information) is at the end of the paper. The virtue of this type of organization is that it permits you to end your paper in a dramatic way, using the most vital material or the bulk of your support for a concluding impression.

Some papers, however, invite a *spatial* arrangement. Often used in description, this kind of arrangement permits you to present your points in a systematic movement through space. Walter White uses a spatial arrangement in "The Atlanta Riot" (p. 229) when he initially describes from a distance the mob attacking victims. Then, like a zoom lens, he moves closer to each incident until he is inevitably involved.

Because White is narrating an episode, he also uses a *chronological* arrangement. White begins his story with an afternoon ride through town and ends with the evening attack on his house. Like White, you may use a chronological arrangement to narrate a story, tell historical detail, or contrast past and present. But variations in the chronology of a story add interest, especially when you can incorporate the values of *emphatic* ordering as White does.

After you have chosen a particular pattern of organization, you are ready to order your points further. Outlining can help.

An Informal Outline

Because Rachel found it was difficult to focus her initial draft and order her supporting details, she decided to write an informal outline: a list of points, written in a logical order, that she planned to cover in her essay. She knew this outline would simply be a personal guide to help her stay focused and to make sure she included all relevant materials. Therefore she didn't spend hours on the outline or concern herself with its wording.

Rachel wrote her working thesis first and then listed her key points in the order she planned to cover them. She knew that she might add other points or modify this order as she wrote the paper, but at least she would have a map to help keep her on track.

Thesis: The media must be forced to stop programming young women to believe skeletal models are the ideal.

Introduction
— Typical ad described: model in bikini
— Models as unhealthy and obsessed with being thin

— The horror: skinny models seem "right"
— Thesis

Anorexia and bulimia as epidemics
— Jane Fonda and her "Work Out"
— Princess Di, reputed bulimic
— Women competing with each other (use Erens)

My friend Kirstie, bulimic
— Kept this secret; only her "barf buddy" and I knew
— Obsessed with food
— Outpatient counseling didn't really work
— I didn't know how to help her

My friend Erica, anorexic
— Enrolled in in-hospital program
— Shocked by number of older women in program
— Received nutritional and emotional help

My friend Lynn, anorexic, almost died
— Dropped out of Berkeley, enrolled in hospital
— Family received treatment too (use Erens)
— These friends felt programmed by the media to be thin
— Child models made to look like women (use Chernin)
— Model Christine Olman is only 12 (use Chernin)
— Ad photographer finds this deception disgusting
— Diet industry undermines women's control (use Wolf)

Conclusion
— A time for shock *and* action
— Refuse to support products that promote these images

In an informal outline like this, the ideas that you loosely group as "information blocs" may become paragraphs. In some cases, your grouping or bloc may end up being split into two or more paragraphs. This outline includes supporting details, but the topic sentences are not written out; therefore the outline is still rather sketchy. In Rachel's case, she didn't feel she needed more elaboration because she had already done some prewriting and initial drafting. Like Rachel, you may find that an outline will help you write stronger, more focused essays and ultimately save you time by organizing your ideas.

WRITING A PARAGRAPH

Focusing the Paragraph

Once you have done some prewriting and have written a working thesis, you are ready to draft your essay. Your thesis has made an assertion you need to support, and the body of your essay consists of paragraphs that build this support. Each of those paragraphs may include a *topic sentence*—a sentence that expresses the central idea of that paragraph. The topic sentences emerge naturally from the groupings discovered in prewriting and from the subtopics of the outline.

Not all paragraphs in an essay will have a topic sentence, but all paragraphs must have a focus. The value of a topic sentence is analogous to the value of a thesis: both keep the writer and reader on track. Again, like the thesis, the topic sentence should be deliberately placed to help the reader understand the focus of the paragraph.

Let's look at some short paragraphs that lack topic sentences.

Writing Topic Sentences

Practice writing your own topic sentence (the central idea) for each of these paragraphs:

1. Registration lines extend beyond the walls of the gymnasium. Because the health service requires proof of insurance, students wait in long lines to argue for exemptions. The financial aid office assigns appointment times, but invariably lines form there, too. At the bookstore, students wait 20 minutes at a register, and I need to have my out-of-state check verified in a separate line. Even before classes begin, I'm exhausted.

2. A great amount of corn is used as feed for cattle, poultry, and hogs. Corn is also distilled into ethanol—a fuel for cars and a component in bourbon. Corn is made into a sweetener used in snacks and soft drinks and a thickener for foods and industrial products. A small amount of corn is consumed at dining tables in kernel or processed form.

Although each paragraph is clearly focused, each would profit from an explicit assertion. Compare your topic sentences with your classmates' assertions before reading the possibilities below. Although topic sentences may be placed anywhere in the paragraph, the topic sentences here seem to be most effective as the first or last sentence in these paragraphs.

Some possibilities for the first example include the following:

- Going back to school means going back to lines.
- Lines are an inevitability at my college.
- Lines are the worst aspect of returning to school.

Some possibilities for the second example are as follows:

- Corn is used for extraordinarily diverse purposes.
- Humans, animals, and machines profit from products made of corn.
- Corn is a remarkably useful grain.

In addition to evaluating your classmates' topic sentences, it may be worthwhile to evaluate the relative strengths of the sentences above. Which are stronger, and why?

Analyzing an Effective Paragraph

In the following paragraph, notice how Rachel includes very good supporting details but lacks a topic sentence that expresses the central idea of the paragraph:

> During Kirstie's senior year in high school, she was dating a college guy, was enrolled in college prep classes, jogged religiously every morning and every evening, and loved to ski with her family and beat her brothers down the slope. She seemed to crave the compliments she received from her brothers and their friends because of her good looks, and she received plenty! But years later, she revealed to me that her greatest pride at that time was when she discovered that she could vomit automatically after eating, without needing to use a finger or spoon.

Rachel realized that she had not articulated the focus of her paragraph. She went back to clarify her point—that "Kirstie had it all." But Rachel also realized that her perception of her friend was an illusion. Rachel brought the two ideas together to form a topic sentence:

> Few of us ever suspected that Kirstie was in trouble, because she seemed to have it all.

Rachel asserts that Kirstie "seemed to have it all," but was really "in trouble." First Rachel shows specific examples of Kirstie's seem-

ingly happy life: "dating a college guy," being in "college prep classes," jogging "religiously," and skiing with her family. Then Rachel
supports the fact that Kirstie was really a troubled young woman.

It is important that you use very specific examples to support your
topic sentence. It would not have been enough for Rachel to claim
that Kirstie had "everything" without showing specifically what that
meant. She doesn't just mention that Kirstie had a boyfriend, but that
he was a "college guy." Kirstie doesn't simply have a close family; they
go skiing together, and she spends time with her brothers' friends.
Rachel's support is vivid, visual, and specific. Her shocking last sentence
is graphic and unforgettable because it is so detailed in its description.

Unifying the Paragraph

This last sentence also contributes to paragraph coherence and unity.
Rachel's opening sentence suggests Kirstie was in trouble, even
though she did not appear to be. Subtle references to this trouble
appear in the paragraph: Kirstie seems obsessed with exercise, and
she craves compliments. Finally, after enumerating Kirstie's apparent
successes—what she *should* be proud of—Rachel stuns the reader
with the irony of Kirstie's "greatest pride," her ability to vomit automatically. Thus the concept of pride unites the paragraph. The key
word in the topic sentence, "seemed," predicts the illusions that permeate and unite the paragraph. (For more on paragraph unity and
coherence, see pp. 363–370.)

Developing a Paragraph

When you have a topic sentence or controlling idea for a paragraph,
it is essential to support it with examples and any necessary explanation. Try to anticipate questions or objections your reader may have;
you can use the "So what?" response here to make sure the significance of your idea is clear. Support for your topic sentences can be
drawn from your own ideas, experiences, and observations, as well as
from your readings. If you are using material that does not belong to
you, you may find it easier to photocopy pages so that you can mark
comments directly on the source.

USING SOURCES FOR SUPPORT

Using Photocopied Pages

Although in a formal research paper you may be required (or prefer)
to use notecards for recording data, for a short paper with few

sources, you might choose to work from books or periodicals photocopied at the library. Here is Rachel's photocopied excerpt from *The Obsession* by Kim Chernin. Notice the quick notes she made as she read the photocopy:

Consider then the case of Christine Olman, one of the leading fashion models of our time. Her picture can be seen in *Vogue*, in *Bazaar*, in all the leading fashion magazines; she is photographed by the leading photographers, posing in the traditional seductive postures that sell consumer goods in our culture. Nothing unusual about all this we say? But then we look further. A newspaper article appears and then a television program[8], both talking about a new wave of young models. Suddenly, we are given a look behind the scenes, before the spotlights and cameras have begun to work. We are shown a room filled with people at work on the model, *media* combing her, clothing her, making her up. But this time the labor of these illusion-makers is expended to its uttermost. For the model they are preparing is modeling clothes intended for mature women and she is twelve years old. This roomful of people is at work to *121* transform a little girl into the illusion of a woman.

But what sort of figure in fact emerges when this labor of transformation has been accomplished? Is it a precociously full-bodied girl who actually looks like a mature woman? Not at all. What emerges is a preadolescent girl, with slender arms and shoulders, undeveloped breasts and hips and thighs, whose body has been covered in sexy clothes, whose face has been painted with a false *anorexic* allure and whose eyes imitate a sexuality she has, by her own confession, never experienced. And this, says fashion, is what a mature woman should attempt to look like.

"It's disgusting," says the photographer who makes his livelihood recording the ideal form of a woman in this land. "It's not necessary," he says, "to have a twelve-year-old look. But that's the *Use!* look that's selling right now. And Christine is one of the hottest young models around."

It might be redundant to spell out the implicit message in all this, but it can't hurt to state, with all the literalness possible in language, the lesson we are meant to learn as women studying the fashions deemed appropriate for us. According to fashion, large size, maturity, voluptuousness, massiveness, strength, and power are not permitted if we wish to conform to our culture's ideal. Our bodies, which have knowledge of life, must undo this fullness of knowing and make themselves look like the body of a precocious child if we wish to win the approval of our culture. *from The Obsession p. 94*

Giving Credit and Avoiding Plagiarism

No matter what method you use to record supporting material from readings—on notecards or photocopies—you must give proper credit for borrowed ideas and put quotation marks around the quoted words that you use in your paper. By including the author's name and a page number after every idea or quotation that she used, Rachel avoided *plagiarism:* using someone else's words or ideas without giving them credit.

Even if she *paraphrased* the material—put the ideas in her own words—Rachel knew she had to give the author credit for the idea or concept. Had she neglected to do this, she would have inadvertently plagiarized those ideas. (For more discussion of inadvertent plagiarism, see pp. 454–456.)

Rachel's instructor required her to use MLA documentation form. Therefore she gave credit by either citing the author's name before the material and then giving the source's page number in parentheses afterward or by including both the author and page citations in parentheses immediately following the quotation. Two popularly used documentation forms (MLA and APA) are described in detail on pages 480–497.

Remember, giving credit means the following:

- Using quotation marks around borrowed words or phrases
- Acknowledging the source and page number of any borrowed words or paraphrased ideas immediately afterward
- Including the complete source—author, title, and publishing information—in the list of works at the end of the paper.

Incorporating Quoted Material

Quoted material may support your ideas and may be a vital component of your paper. If the original material is particularly well written or precise, or if the material is bold or controversial, it makes sense to quote the author's words so you can examine them in detail.

All quoted material needs to be introduced in some way. It is a mistake to think that quoted material can stand on its own, no matter how incisive it is. Often, in fact, it is vital to introduce and also to comment on the quoted material. Let's look at an example from Rachel's paper:

```
    Lynn's family became involved in her therapy, too.

Erens emphasizes the importance of the family in any treat-

ment plan: "Often, the daughter has taken on the role of
```

diverting attention from unacknowledged confl.
the family" (222). In therapy, Lynn and her fa
ly learned that her parents' "unacknowledged (
over Lynn's choice of art as a major instead of computer
science contributed to Lynn's stress. Therapy involved
acknowledging these internalized conflicts as well as seeing a relationship between her eating disorder and that
stress.

In this passage, Rachel uses Lynn's experience to lead into the
quoted material. The quote provides an explanation of family dynamics that reflects Lynn's situation. Rather than letting the quotation
stand by itself, Rachel *uses* it by discussing the connection between
the quoted material and her friend's specific experience.

The "Sandwich"

Just as bread holds the contents of a sandwich together, Rachel uses
the introduction and the discussion about the quotation to hold the
quoted material together. The introduction, the top slice of bread,
gives the reader enough of a context for the quoted material to make
sense. The quote itself—the "meat" of the sandwich—comes next.
Finally the sandwich needs that bottom slice of bread—a line or two
of clarification or interpretation after the quote. Rachel integrated key
words from the quote into her discussion. Depending on the quote
and the purpose of your paper, you may need to discuss, clarify, analyze, or interpret the quoted material. In all cases, your commentary
after the quote will demonstrate the importance of that quotation.

It may help you to visualize that the sandwich consists of the following:

- Lead-in
- Quotation
- Analysis

The lead-in needs to be informative without duplicating the material
in the quotation. In the following example from the page Rachel photocopied (p. 341), notice how she leads in to her quote and then comments on it afterward without being redundant:

In The Obsession Kim Chernin claims that today's ideal
model excludes many women: "According to fashion, large
size, maturity, voluptuousness, massiveness, strength, and

power are not permitted if we wish to conform to our culture's ideal" (94). Such conformity spells self-destruction
and is threatening to reduce women to mere skeletons.

■ PRACTICING THE "SANDWICH"

1. Using the essay assigned for your next class session, find a memorable line that you deem worthy of use in a paper. Write a lead-in to that line, quote it exactly, and then analyze or comment on it so that any reader would see the quotation's importance to the work as a whole.

2. Compare the following two uses of quoted material. Which one is better? In what specific ways? Rewrite the weaker example to make the quotation more effective:

   a. How can one see the world for what it really is, if one's vision is obscured by prejudgment? Heilbroner quotes Walter Lippmann as saying "For the most part we do not first see, and then define; we define first, and then we see" (430). Prejudging is a bad idea.

   b. In "Black Men and Public Space," Brent Staples describes the posture of women who walk at night: "They seem to set their faces on neutral and, with their purse straps strung across their chests bandolier style, they forge ahead as though bracing themselves against being tackled" (226). Staples suggests that these women need to play multiple roles. They must appear to be indifferent to their environment and not make eye contact as they "set their faces on neutral." Further, they become soldiers with bandoliers and defensive football players guarding themselves against being attacked.

Paraphrasing

Paraphrasing a writer's ideas makes that information available to the reader in a condensed form. Sometimes you will want to put into your own words the essence of an entire piece that you have read; other times you will want to paraphrase just one section of the work. If the author's idea is useful but the material is wordy, filled with jargon, or contains information you do not need, you will want to paraphrase rather than quote the text.

Here we will examine how to paraphrase one section of given works. Assume that you have been asked to write an essay in which you respond to Carol Tavris' "In Groups We Shrink" (p. 267) by comparing or contrasting Tavris' reported observations with experiences of your own. First, you may want to summarize the main point of her essay. Active reading of the piece probably will lead you to the third paragraph of Tavris' essay, where part of her focus is located.

Something happens to individuals when they collect in a group. They think and act differently than they would on their own. Most people, if they observe some disaster or danger on their own—a woman being stabbed, a pedestrian slammed by a hit-and-run driver—will at least call for help; many will even risk their own safety to intervene. But if they are in a group observing the same danger, they hold back. The reason is not necessarily that they are lazy, cowardly or have 50 other personality deficiencies; it has more to do with the nature of groups than the nature of individuals.

The point of this section might be paraphrased like this:

Although most individuals will help someone who is hurt or in danger, when they are in a group they think and act differently and may disregard a plea for assistance.

The important aspects of Tavris' original point are retained: that people alone act differently than they do when they are in groups. Notice that Tavris' finding that "most" people will help someone in need is part of the paraphrased thesis, an important detail that would be distorted if the summary writer indifferently wrote "some" or "many." Later in her essay, Tavris identifies the group's failure to respond to an emergency as "diffusion of responsibility" or "social loafing." In responding to her essay, it might be useful to quote those terms specifically to describe the apparent indifference of individuals in groups.

Analyzing Paraphrasing

Original from "A Hidden Factor in AIDS" (p. 78):

As sociologists have long understood, stigmatized gender often leads to exaggerated forms of gender-specific behavior. Thus, those whose masculinity is least secure are precisely those most likely to follow hyper-masculine behavioral codes as well as hold fast to traditional definitions of masculinity.

Paraphrase:

Men who feel least manly are most apt to perpetuate "macho" behavior and stereotypes.

The paraphrase above may be particularly helpful in removing the sociological jargon of "stigmatized gender" and "hyper-masculine behavioral codes" and writing in language any reader can understand.

Original from "Women: Invisible Cages" (p. 94):

The pressures society exerts to drive men out of the house are nearly as irrational and unjust as those by which it keeps women in. The mistake of the early reformers was to assume that men were emancipated already and that therefore reform need ask only for the emancipation of women. What we ought to do now is go right back to scratch and demand the emancipation of both sexes. It is only because men are not free themselves that they have found it necessary to cheat women by the deception which makes them appear free when they are not.

Paraphrase:

Society puts pressure on both men and women, so neither gender is actually free. We will have to rethink the irrational and unfair demands that are made on us if we really want to be emancipated.

The paraphrase above condenses Brophy's point by removing what may be unnecessary information—that early reformers made mistakes in their analyses. Further, the paraphrase emphasizes the fact that neither gender is free.

Combining Paraphrase and Quotation

Most often, the material you use to support your points will be a blend of paraphrase and direct quotation. You can capture the essence of an author's idea by paraphrasing it, but there will be well-crafted phrases and key ideas that need to be quoted to convey the flavor of the original work. When you combine paraphrase and direct quotation, you still need to be careful to give credit for both.

Rachel decided to paraphrase most of the material that she photocopied at the library (see p. 341), but then she found a choice quotation that succinctly expressed what she wanted to say. Here is how Rachel used the material from her photocopied page:

> In The Obsession Kim Chernin refers to the ideal model
> today as a "woman-child." She notes that one of the current
> top models, featured in Vogue and Bazaar, is twelve-year-
> old Christine Olman and that even professionals in the
> advertising industry are appalled by this: "'It's disgust-
> ing,' says the photographer who makes his livelihood
> recording the ideal form of a woman in this land. 'It's not
> necessary,' he says, 'to have a twelve-year-old look. But
> that's the look that's selling right now.'" (Chernin 94)

Rachel introduces her quotation by referring to the title and author of this important study of women's eating habits. Rachel thus gains credibility by showing that she has consulted a respected writer on this subject. After identifying the source of her material, Rachel uses a key term from Chernin, "woman-child." This term must be quoted because it is from Chernin's book.

Rachel first summarizes Chernin's point about the current top models being children and then narrows her focus to the photographer, one of the "professionals" who is "appalled" by this practice. This serves as her lead-in to the specific quotation from the photographer in Chernin's text.

■ PRACTICING COMBINING PARAPHRASE AND QUOTATION

Practice incorporating choice quotations into your paraphrased versions of the following passages. In your lead-in, you may want to include the author's name and the source of the material. Compare your paraphrases with those written by your classmates. The page numbers given are from the essays as they appear in this textbook.

1. From "Women: Invisible Cages" (p. 94): "That many women would be happier not pursuing careers or intellectual adventures is only part of the truth. The whole truth is that many *people* would be. If society had the clear sight to assure men as well as women that there is no shame in preferring to stay non-competitively and non-aggressively at home, many masculine neuroses and ulcers would be avoided, and many children would enjoy the benefit of being brought up by a father with a talent for the job instead of by a mother with no talent for it but a sense of guilt about the lack."

2. From "The Beauty Myth" (p. 101): "And the unconscious hallucination grows ever more influential and pervasive because of what is now conscious market manipulation: powerful industries—the $33-billion-a-year diet industry, the $20-billion cosmetics industry, the $300-million cosmetic surgery industry, and the $7-billion pornography industry—have arisen from the capital made out of unconscious anxieties, and are in turn able, through their influence on mass culture, to use, stimulate, and reinforce the hallucination in a rising economic spiral."

3. From "What Do Men Really Want?" (p. 81): "Finally, there is profound confusion over what it means to be a man today. Men have faced warping changes in role models since the women's movement drove the strong, stoic John Wayne–type into the sunset. Replacing him was a new hero: the hollow-chested, sensitive, New Age man who bawls at Kodak commercials and handles a diaper the way Magic Johnson does a basketball. Enter Alan Alda."

4. From "Why Johnny Can't Disobey" (p. 269): "It seems that the best armor is the rational mind. We must insist that all authorities account for themselves, and

we need to be as wary of false prophets as we are of false advertising. Leaders, political and spiritual, must be subjected to intense scrutiny, and we must insist that their thought processes and proclamations measure up to reasonable standards of rational thought. Above all, we must become skilled in activating our inner resources toward rebellion and disobedience, when this seems reasonable."

As you work on refining your incorporation of paraphrased and quoted material, you also will be revising your essay. Rewriting is such a critical activity in preparing an essay that we have devoted the entire next chapter to various aspects of revision.

8

Revising an Essay

■ ■ ■

REWRITING AND REWRITING

As we have already noted, rewriting may occur during all stages of the writing process. But it is essential that you give yourself time to reconsider your rough draft and make some necessary changes. Usually these changes involve sharpening the thesis, reorganizing ideas, developing sketchy points, adding new material for support, removing irrelevant material, improving transitions between ideas, strengthening the introduction and conclusion, and editing for word choice, mechanics, and spelling.

Thinking Critically for an Audience

Every phase of the writing process involves thinking critically—reasoning, analyzing, and assessing so that your points are clear and your audience understands your points. The act of revision depends on good critical thinking.

Even during prewriting, which invites creativity and experimentation, you are evaluating your topic in relationship to your readers. In clustering and listing your ideas, you are discerning features in order to sort out your uncensored thoughts. In this way you are using critical thinking to group compatible ideas for presentation to a reader. In collaborative brainstorming, you have an opportunity to assess your ideas in light of your peers' views and to question others' assumptions as well as your own.

You use critical thinking to impose order on your material, and you assess your organization plan to ascertain if your reader can follow your logic. Both logic and aesthetic considerations govern your judgment about which section of support belongs before another. Your decision to remove irrelevant details reflects your awareness that irrelevant points not only weaken your support but also confuse your readers.

The need for clarity and precision continues throughout drafting and revision. Even as you are revising, you continue to determine whether your depth of analysis has been sufficient and whether you have fully supported your assertions. You reconsider your focus, the logic of your organization, and the strength of your conclusion. As you edit, you scrutinize your word choice, sentence structure, grammar, and mechanics so that surface flaws do not frustrate your reader.

Thinking critically mandates that you recognize that your audience does not necessarily share your views. Thus the writing process forces you to challenge your own assertions and consider the readers' perspectives. Although it may appear that these stages of writing a paper involve a step-by-step process, all of these writing activities occur concurrently.

Revision may occur while you are drafting your paper, and editing may occur from the early drafts until the moment you hand the paper to your instructor. As noted in the last chapter, Rachel started revising her draft as soon as she had a printout from her computer. Thinking critically about her aim in writing this essay—to persuade readers of the media's role in fostering eating disorders—Rachel made substantial changes as she revised her rough draft.

Revising a Rough Draft

Working from her own evaluation of her rough draft (see pp. 332–333), Rachel rewrote her draft and, as required by the assignment, showed it to her instructor for comments. Rachel's paper had started out very rough, as most first drafts do, but she continued to develop her ideas and rearrange them. She felt that her second draft was stronger than the first but still could be improved. Her instructor helped her by identifying weak areas and suggesting improvements.

Example: Draft with Instructor's Comments

more striking or suggestive title?

Eating Disorders and the Media

except for ?

Bare, [with the exception of] a bikini, the
deep-tanned model poses at a beach. She is surrounded by five adoring guys. She is sipping a
frothy soda and inviting all of us to do the same
. . . if we want to get the guys . . . if we want
to be the envy of our friends. She is thin but
tall. Viewers don't notice the bony ribs, [how hungry she is,] and all the "diet pills" she popped to
stay that thin. A picture doesn't reveal the vomit
on her breath or the spearmint gum used to mask
it. In fact, our magazines and T.V. commercials
present us with these ads until such girls don't
seem skinny any more--they seem right.

Tighten — avoid repeating "she is"

How thin?

How tall?

not //

✔ very graphic

stronger verb?

✔ clear point

It doesn't seem to matter that, for some years
now, the media has been reporting the epidemic
among college "coeds" of eating disorders, anorexia
and bulimia. It doesn't seem to matter that the
Women's Movement has tried to free women from
being so caught up on the way they look. Despite
the varied opportunities now available to women,
"thirty-three thousand American women told
researchers that they would rather lose ten to
fifteen pounds than achieve any other goal" (Wolf 102).
In the last decade, actress Jane Fonda has sold
many on the value of her "Work Out" and has helped
spawn "aerobic nervosa" (Erens 220). Many women
who admire Jane Fonda's shape may not know that
Fonda was once a bulimic. And no one watching the

diction (old-fashioned?)

briefly distinguish

What is?

televised spectacle of Prince Charles and Princess Diana's wedding could have predicted that years later, biographers would be discussing "Di's bulimia." *> transition?*

necessary?

Who wouldn't want to hear friends whisper, "What a body! She really knows how to stay in shape!" or "Don't you hate someone who looks that good?" Either way, the sense of admiration and affirmation is clear. A thin girl has something *specify* that others don't--and this gives her power and *You need* *what* control. She can make herself in the image of the *Erens'* *is* cover girls. In "Bodily Harm," the author quotes *name* *wrong* Ruth Striegel: "The pursuit of thinness is a way *here or in* *with* for women to compete with each other, a way that *your ( ) at* *this* avoids being threatening to men" (220). *end of* *this line.*

Unfortunately, this competition keeps women from seeking or obtaining the help they might otherwise get from close friends. Many bulimics keep their secret as guarded as their mothers might *tighten* have kept their sex life. My friend Kirstie ~~did~~ ~~this. She~~ waited for years before she told friends (and later, her family) that she was bulimic. At first, only her "barf buddy" (Erens 220)--a cousin *awk* who had initially introduced her to this "great *split* diet plan"--knew. Gradually, their friendship *of subj/* revolved exclusively around this dark secret and *verb* was eroded by their unacknowledged rivalry.

develop

Few of us ever suspected Kirstie was in trouble: she seemed to have it all. *illustrate* But years later, she revealed to me that her greatest pride at that

time was when she discovered that she was now vomiting automatically after eating, without needing
to use a finger or spoon.

Even when Kirstie received out-patient counseling and her family thought she was "cured," she
How could you tell?
wasn't. For her it was either fasting or bingeing--
there was no in-between. As her friend, I often
felt trapped between either respecting her confidence or letting some adult know so she might get
the help she needed. While encouraging her to find
other interests and to be open with her therapist,
I felt quite helpless. I didn't want to betray her
confidence and tell her parents, but I worried
that my silence was betraying our friendship. *transition?*

According to another friend, many young women
continue to have obsessions with food for years
afterwards. My friend Erica was shocked by the
number of women over thirty ~~who were~~ in her hospital treatment program for anorexics. She admitted
that (this) is what made her decide she needed help *?*
while she was still in college. Unlike Kirstie,
Erica decided she needed an in-hospital treatment
program that cut her off from her old habits and
helped her deal with her emotions and learn better
nutritional habits. Erica managed to enter the
program as soon as her finals were over and therefore she didn't jeopardize her schooling. *good transition*

But some don't have that choice. My friend
Lynn would have died had she not entered the hospital when she did. She had to drop out of

Berkeley immediately and get prolonged therapy before she could be released to her parents and begin her recovery. Her family became involved in her therapy too. As Erens notes, "Family therapy considers the family itself, not the daughter with the eating disorder, to be the 'patient.' Often, the daughter has taken on the role of diverting attention from unacknowledged conflicts within the family" (222). In therapy, Lynn and her family gradually learned that her parents' "unacknowl-edged conflicts" over her mother's return to work and over Lynn's choice of art instead of computer science as a major contributed to Lynn's stress. Therapy involved acknowledging these internalized conflicts as well as examining the pressure to be thin.

tighten this discussion?

In addition to absorbing family conflicts, each of these friends felt that they were pro-grammed by advertisers to accept and seek a lean look as the ideal. In <u>The Obsession</u> Kim Chernin refers to the ideal model today as a "woman-child." She points out that one of the current top models, featured in <u>Vogue</u> and <u>Bazaar</u>, is twelve-year-old Christine Olman and that even profession-als in the advertising industry are appalled by this: "'It's disgusting,' says the photographer who makes his livelihood recording the ideal form of a woman in this land. 'It's not necessary,' he says, 'to have a twelve-year-old look. But that's the look that's selling right now'" (Chernin 94).

effective link between personal experience & reading

ideal support for your thesis!

better lead-in?

Chernin adds: "According to fashion, large size, *review* maturity, voluptuousness, massiveness, strength, *"sandwich"* and power are not permitted if we wish to conform to our culture's ideal" (94). *comment or expand*

Such conformity threatens women today. It is *Be* ironic that this should happen at a time when *specific. How?* women have more freedom to control their lives and their bodies. In "The Beauty Myth" Naomi Wolf notes that "the $33-billion-a-year diet industry" has undermined women's control over their bodies (107). "Reproductive rights gave Western

Shorten quote or indent 10 spaces & delete "marks women control over our own bodies; the weight of fashion models plummeted to 23 percent below that of ordinary women, eating disorders rose exponentially, and a mass neurosis was promoted that used food and weight to strip women of that sense of control" (103).

It is time to let ourselves become shocked again. And then we need to move beyond shock and take action. Those who make the images will only change when those of us who support them stop buying products and tuning in on shows that continue to impose "bodily harm" on us. *Return to your opening image, if you can, and sharpen your thesis. Don't forget "Works Cited".*

Revising Can Make the Difference

Every paper can benefit from careful revision and editing, but many students do not have the opportunity to get their instructors' comments on their drafts before they revise. Occasionally students can find trained tutors and willing peers who will provide feedback and make suggestions. The resulting comments may not be as thorough as those Rachel received, but they can help the writer see the essay from another perspective.

Some instructors may even spend time helping students serve as "peer editors" who critique each other's papers. A good peer editor need not excel at grammar or be an excellent writer. An effective editor needs to be a careful *reader,* one who is sensitive to the writer's main point and supporting details.

A Checklist for Revising and Editing Papers

Whether you are revising your own essay or commenting on a class-mate's, the following checklist should help:

- *Focus:* Is the thesis clear? Provocative? Convincing?
- *Support:* Are all points illustrated and supported?
- *Organization:* Is the order logical? Are there smooth transitions?
- *Paragraphs:* Is each paragraph well focused? Well developed?
- *Sentences:* Are all sentences coherent? Are the sentences varied in type?
- *Wording:* Any unnecessary/confusing words? Diction problems?
- *Introduction:* Is it captivating? developed? Does it set the right tone?
- *Conclusion:* Is there a sense of resolution? Does it return to the thesis?
- *Style:* Does the essay read well? Are there any stumbling blocks?
- *Mechanics:* Correct punctuation? Grammar? Spelling?

These questions will help you determine the strengths of the essay, as well as any areas that need improvement. If you are editing a class-mate's essay, you do not have to be able to correct the errors. A peer editor only needs to point out areas that seem flawed or confusing; it is then the writer's responsibility to use a handbook (like the one in this book) and correct the errors.

After studying the instructor's comments and corrections, Rachel continued modifying her draft. She rewrote certain phrases and para-graphs a number of times, shifted words and sentences, and found ways to "tighten" her prose by eliminating unnecessary words. Most of all, she tried to replace sluggish words with more precise and specific details. Notice below how her title gained more punch and how the opening is tighter and less repetitive. She also took the time to develop certain thoughts and paragraphs and to clarify her points. The following version is her final essay.

Student Example: Final Essay

Krell 1

Dieting Daze: No In-Between

Bare, except for a bikini, the deep-tanned model poses at a beach surrounded by five adoring and adorable guys. She is sipping a frothy diet drink and inviting us to do the same, if we want to get the guys and be the envy of our friends. She stands 5'10" and wears a size 3. Viewers don't notice the bony ribs, the hunger pangs, and the "diet pills" she popped to stay that thin. A picture doesn't reveal the vomit on her breath or the spearmint gum used to mask it. In fact, our magazines and TV commercials bombard us with these ads until such girls don't seem skinny any more--they seem right.

It doesn't seem to matter that, for years now, the media has been reporting the epidemic among college women of eating disorders, anorexia (self-starvation) and bulimia (binge and purge). It doesn't seem to matter that the women's movement has tried to free women from bondage to their bodies. Despite the varied opportunities now available to women, "thirty-three thousand American

Krell 2

women told researchers that they would rather lose
ten to fifteen pounds than achieve any other goal"
(Wolf 102). In the last decade, actress Jane Fonda
has sold many on the value of her "Work Out" and
has helped spawn "aerobic nervosa"--the excessive
use of exercise to maintain an ideal weight (Erens
220). Many women who admire Jane Fonda's shape may
not know that Fonda was once bulimic. And no one
watching the televised spectacle of Prince Charles
and Princess Diana's wedding could have predicted
that years later, biographers would be discussing
"Di's bulimia."

    Such celebrities, and those females in the ads,
are held up as models for all of us to mirror. A
thin girl has something that others don't--and
this gives her power and control. She can make her
body resemble a cover girl's. In "Bodily Harm,"
Pamela Erens quotes Ruth Striegel, Ph.D., director
of Yale University's Eating Disorders Clinic: "The
pursuit of thinness is a way for women to compete
with each other, a way that avoids being threatening to men" (220). But this competition threatens
and endangers the women's well-being because it
keeps women from seeking the help they might otherwise get from close friends.

    In fact, many bulimics keep their secret as
guarded as their mothers might have kept their sex
life. My friend Kirstie waited for years before
she told friends (and later, her family) that she
was bulimic. At first the only one who knew about
her bulimia was her cousin who had initially

Krell 3

introduced her to "this great diet plan." This
cousin became Kirstie's "barf buddy" (Erens 220).
Gradually, their friendship revolved exclusively
around this dark secret and was eroded by their
unacknowledged rivalry.

Few of us ever suspected Kirstie was in trouble, because she seemed to have it all. During her
senior year in high school, she was dating a college guy, was enrolled in college prep classes,
jogged religiously every morning and every evening,
and loved to ski with her family and beat her
brothers down the slope. She seemed to crave the
compliments she received from her brothers and
their friends because of her good looks--and she
received plenty! But years later, she revealed to
me that her greatest pride at that time was when
she discovered she could vomit automatically after
eating, without needing to use a finger or spoon.

Even when Kirstie received out-patient counseling and her family thought she was "cured," she
would still binge and purge at will. Every conversation with Kirstie inevitably returned to the
subject of food--fasting or bingeing--there was no
in-between. As her close friend, I often felt
helpless, trapped between either respecting her
confidence and keeping her dark secret or letting
an adult know and perhaps getting her more help. I
didn't want to betray her confidence and tell her
parents, but I worried that my silence was betraying our friendship. Even though we each went to
different colleges and gradually lost touch, I

Krell 4

find myself wondering if Kirstie ever got the help she needed.

According to another friend, even mature women continue to have obsessions with food. My friend Erica was shocked by the number of women over thirty in her hospital treatment program for anorexics. She admitted that seeing these older women is what convinced her she needed help while she was still in college. Unlike Kirstie, Erica decided she needed an in-hospital treatment program that cut her off from her old habits and helped her deal with her emotions and learn better nutritional habits. Erica managed to enter the program as soon as her finals were over, and therefore she didn't jeopardize her schooling.

But some don't have that choice. My friend Lynn would have died had she not entered the hospital when she did. She had to drop out of Berkeley immediately and get prolonged therapy before she could be released to her parents and begin her recovery. Lynn's family became involved in her therapy, too. Erens emphasizes the importance of the family in any treatment plan: "Often, the daughter has taken on the role of diverting attention from unacknowledged conflicts within the family" (222). In therapy Lynn and her family gradually learned that her parents' "unacknowledged conflicts" over Lynn's choice of art as a major instead of computer science contributed to her stress. Therapy involved acknowledging these

internalized conflicts as well as seeing a relationship between her eating disorder and that
stress.

In addition to absorbing family conflicts,
each of these friends felt that she was programmed
by advertisers to accept a lean look as the ideal.
In The Obsession Kim Chernin refers to the ideal
model today as a "woman-child." She notes that one
of the current top models, featured in Vogue and
Bazaar, is twelve-year-old Christine Olman and
that even professionals in the advertising industry are appalled by this: "'It's disgusting,' says
the photographer who makes his livelihood recording the ideal form of a woman in this land. 'It's
not necessary,' he says, 'to have a twelve-year-
old look. But that's the look that's selling right
now'" (Chernin 94). Chernin adds that this ideal
excludes many women: "According to fashion, large
size, maturity, voluptuousness, massiveness,
strength, and power are not permitted if we wish
to conform to our culture's ideal" (94). Such conformity spells self-destruction and is threatening
to reduce women to mere skeletons.

It is ironic that this should happen at a
time when women have more freedom to control their
lives and their bodies. In "The Beauty Myth,"
Naomi Wolf notes that the "$33-billion-a-year diet
industry" has undermined women's control over
their bodies (107). Within a generation, "the
weight of fashion models plummeted to 23 percent

Krell 6

below that of ordinary women, eating disorders
rose exponentially, and a mass neurosis was promoted that used food and weight to strip women of
that sense of control" (103). Stripped of control,
many women feel compelled to diet constantly;
images of emaciated models that were once so
shocking have now become commonplace.

It is time to let ourselves become shocked
again--shocked by an epidemic that is destroying
women's lives. And then we need to move beyond
shock and take action. Insisting that our television sponsors, magazines, and video artists stop
perpetrating such deadly images of women is something we can all do. A letter from one viewer carries clout because stations often assume that each
letter represents many who didn't take the time to
write. Ten letters from ten viewers wield even
more power. It is time to protest the images of
bikini-clad models parading before us and demand
images that reflect the emotional and intellectual
scope and diversity among women in our society.
With some of our best and brightest dying among
us, there is no in-between position any more.
Those who make the images will only change when
those of us who support them stop buying products
and stop tuning in on programs that continue to
impose "bodily harm" on us.

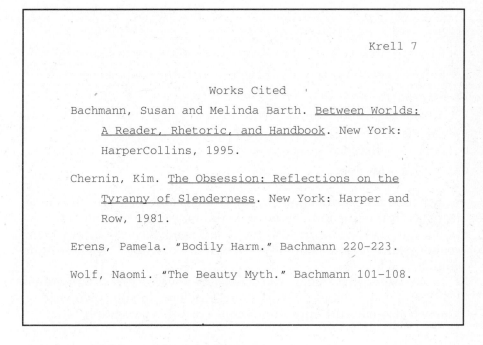

```
                                          Krell 7


                       Works Cited
Bachmann, Susan and Melinda Barth. Between Worlds:
     A Reader, Rhetoric, and Handbook. New York:
     HarperCollins, 1995.

Chernin, Kim. The Obsession: Reflections on the
     Tyranny of Slenderness. New York: Harper and
     Row, 1981.

Erens, Pamela. "Bodily Harm." Bachmann 220-223.

Wolf, Naomi. "The Beauty Myth." Bachmann 101-108.
```

REWRITING FOR COHERENCE

As you may have noticed, Rachel devoted considerable attention to the way she linked information and ideas within and between her paragraphs. The goal, of course, is to ensure that all parts of the paper cohere (that is, hold together).

To sustain your readers' interest and ensure their comprehension of your work, you will want to examine the drafts of your essays to see if your ideas hold together. Each idea should follow logically from the one before, and all of your points must support your focus. That logical connection must be clear to the reader—not just you, the writer of the essay, who may gloss over a link that is not obvious. All readers value clear connections between phrases, sentences, and paragraphs.

A Paragraph That Lacks Coherence

If the writing is carefully organized, the reader will not stumble over irrelevant chunks of material or hesitate at unbridged gaps. Let's examine an incoherent paragraph:

```
    Students who commute to campus suffer indignities that
 dorm students can't imagine. Parking is expensive and lots
```

```
are jammed. It is embarrassing to walk into class late.
Often it takes over a half hour to find a spot. Commuters
feel cut off from students who can return to the dorm to
eat or rest. Commuters seldom have a telephone number to
get missed lecture notes. Study groups readily form in
dorms. Dorm students have a sense of independence and free-
dom. Commuters need to conform to old family rules and
schedules, to say nothing of the need to babysit or cook
for younger siblings and drive grandparents to the bank.
```

Although this paragraph has a clear focus and the ideas all belong, its coherence needs to be improved. You may sense that the information is out of order, the logic of the writer is not always obvious to the reader, sentences do not flow together, words are repeated, and emphasis is lost.

In the pages that follow, you will learn how to correct paragraphs like the one above and to avoid these problems in your own writing. You will also have the opportunity to correct this paragraph.

Using Transitions

Even when material is carefully organized, well-chosen transition words and devices will help you connect sentences and paragraphs and will help your points cohere. You are familiar with most of these words and expressions. But if you have been trying for more than five minutes to find a specific word to connect two ideas or sentences in your essay, the partial list of particular terms shown below may be useful. The principal organization or development method of your essay often will suggest the specific transition terms that will be useful to you for gaining unity in that essay. All will be useful at some time or another to help your reader see the connections that you intend.

Transition Terms

- *time relationship:* first, second, before, then, next, meantime, meanwhile, finally, at last, eventually, later, afterwards, frequently, often, occasionally, during, now, subsequently, concurrently
- *spatial relationship:* above, below, inside, outside, across, along, in front of, behind, beyond, there, here, in the distance, alongside, near, next to, close to, adjacent, within

- *to contrast:* in contrast, on the contrary, on the other hand, still, however, yet, but, nevertheless, despite, even so, even though, whereas
- *to compare:* similarly, in the same way
- *to give examples or illustrations:* for example, for instance, to illustrate, to show, in particular, specifically, that is, in addition, moreover
- *to show a cause or an effect:* as a result, accordingly, therefore, then, because, so, thus, consequently, hence, since
- *to conclude or to summarize:* in conclusion, finally, in summary, evidently, clearly, of course, to sum up, therefore

Noticing Transitions

If you are writing a narrative, some part of your essay—if not the entire work—probably will be arranged chronologically. See if you can spot the *time signals* in the following excerpt from Bruce Halling's narrative "A Bully's Unjust Deserts" and underline them.

> One day as I crossed the street, I heard something hit the ground near me. Then I felt the sting of a dirt clod hitting me in the head. I stopped and looked in the direction of Ricky's house, but I couldn't see where he was hiding. I brushed most of the dirt out of my hair and kept walking, trying to ignore being hit several more times before I made it home.

Can you see how "one day," "then," and "before" are transitions used to help the reader connect the actions in the narrative?

With three or four of your classmates, read the next two paragraphs of this narrative (which appears in complete form on pp. 385–387) and underline the transition words that have to do with the essay's chronological connections.

Chronological concepts may also be important for gaining transition and coherence in nonnarrative essays. Look at this paragraph from "Discrimination at Large" (p. 217) to see if you can identify the time concept around which this paragraph is structured.

> Since the time I first ventured out to play with the neighborhood kids, I was told over and over that I was lazy and disgusting. Strangers, adults, classmates offered gratuitous comments with such frequency and urgency that I started to believe them. Much later I needed to prove it wasn't so. I began a regimen of swimming, cycling and jogging that put all but the most compulsive to shame. I ate only cottage

cheese, brown rice, fake butter and steamed everything. I really believed I could infiltrate the ranks of the nonfat and thereby establish my worth.

You may rightly perceive that "since the time I first," "I began" and "much later" are the three terms that denote the passage of time within this paragraph. But you may also note that the writer uses the past tense, as if what Jennifer Coleman "really believed" at one time is different from what she believes now. The chronological ordering of the essay emphasizes this fact. Read the rest of the essay to observe how Coleman uses these time-relationship transitions— "along the way," "for awhile," "still," "until," "until then," and "now" and "finally"—to emphasize the history that led to her change in self-perception.

Essays that include description often require terms that connect sentences or paragraphs in *spatial relationship*. Notice the spatial concepts that connect the descriptions in this paragraph from "The Only Child" (the complete essay appears on p. 22).

> The room is a slum, and it stinks. It is wall-to-wall beer cans, hundreds of them, under a film of ash. He lights cigarettes and leaves them burning on the windowsill or the edge of the dresser or the lip of the sink, while he thinks of something else—Gupta sculpture, maybe, or the Sephiroth Tree of the Kabbalah. The sink is filthy, and so is the toilet. Holes have been burnt in the sheet on the bed, where he sits. He likes to crush the beer cans after he has emptied them, then toss them aside.

Do you see this paragraph, as we do, as a movement from the periphery to the interior? We sense that the author moves from broad description—"wall-to-wall beer cans" around the room—to smaller, interior descriptions—"holes [that] have been burnt in the sheet on the bed, where he sits." The outside-to-inside movement of this description parallels the author's description of elements outside of his brother (in his room) to his observation of what is closer and more central to him (his thoughts, his talk, his gestures). The arrangement also complements the author's argument that his brother's life and mind were destroyed by drugs—the external environment destroying the interior.

Using Transitions Effectively

The placement of the transition words listed on pages 364–365 will seem contrived if you use them too often in any one essay, or if you use the same ones in every essay you write. You also have other, more subtle ways to gain connections between sentences and paragraphs in your essays.

Key Word Repetition

In some cases you will want to repeat an important word, one that emphasizes the point that you are making. Its repetition will reinforce the focus point of your paragraph and essay.

In another paragraph from "The Only Child," the author emphasizes his disdain for his brother's living conditions by repeating his brother's explanation. Can you hear the irony or sarcasm in the author's repetition?

> He tells me that he is making a statement, that this room is a statement, that the landlord will understand the meaning of his statement. In a week or so, according to the pattern, they will evict him, and someone will find him another room, which he will turn into another statement, with the help of the welfare checks he receives on account of his disability, which is the static in his head.

Notice that the repetition of "statement" is very deliberate and strategic, rather than boring for the reader, because it emphasizes the nonreasoning to which the brother's mind has been reduced.

Synonyms or Key Word Substitutions

Synonyms are words that have the same or similar meanings, and you can connect ideas or concepts within your paragraphs and throughout your essay by skillfully using synonyms—or key word substitutions—to emphasize your focus. Notice how Jennifer Coleman in "Discrimination at Large" piles word substitutions into her sentences to simulate for her reader the effect of being assaulted, as fat people are, by denigrating words:

> It was confusing for awhile. How was it I was still lazy, weak, despised, a slug and a cow if I exercised every waking minute? This confusion persisted until I finally realized: it didn't matter what I did. I was and always would be the object of sport, derision, antipathy and hostility so long as I stayed in my body. I immediately signed up for a body transplant. I am still waiting for a donor.

How many substitutions for "lazy" did you find? How many implied substitutions for "contempt"? Coleman cites many specific terms for how she has been perceived and treated to make clear to the reader that these attacks come under many names, but the intention to denigrate is always the same.

Pronouns

Pronouns, words substituting for nouns that clearly precede or follow them, can effectively connect parts of a paragraph. By prompting the reader to mentally supply the missing noun or see the relationship the pronouns imply, the writer also has a way to engage the reader. To emphasize the contrast between people who are fat and those who are not, Coleman uses pronoun substitutions to unite her paragraphs:

> Things are less confusing now that I know that the nonfat are super-ior to me regardless of their personal habits, health personalities, cho-lesterol levels or the time they log on the couch. And, as obviously supe-rior to me as they are, it is their destiny to remark on my inferiority regardless of who I'm with, whether they know me, whether it hurts my feelings. I finally understand that the thin have a divine mandate to steal self-esteem from fat people, who have no right to it in the first place.
>
> Fat people aren't really jolly. Sometimes we act that way so you will leave us alone. We pay a price for this. But at least we get to hang on to what self-respect we smuggled out of grade school and adolescence.

In the first paragraph above, *I* and *me* contrast with *they* and *their* to emphasize the separation between the author and the "nonfat" and "superior" other people. In the second paragraph the author unites herself with "fat people," repeatedly saying "we" to emphasize their unity. Coleman's entire essay coheres because she skillfully employs numerous unifying devices in and between her paragraphs. Read the essay in its entirety to see how key word repetition, syn-onyms, and transitions between sentences and paragraphs create coherence within an essay. A discussion of transitions between para-graphs follows.

Transitions Between Paragraphs

Key word repetition is also one important way to achieve the impor-tant goal of *connection between paragraphs*. While your reader may be able to follow your movement and sustain your ideas within a para-graph, coherence within your essay as a whole requires transition sentences and, in longer essays, entire paragraphs of transitions.

One device that works well is to pick up a key concept or word from the end of the earlier paragraph and use it toward the beginning of the new paragraph. Notice the following excerpts from Shannon Paaske's research paper, which appears on pages 460–478. What moves the reader between paragraphs?

The Americans With Disabilities Act, signed in 1990, reinforced the legislation that was not earlier implemented. But because the law takes effect in gradual stages, the results of all of its provisions have not yet been fully realized. However, as each stipulation is introduced, its impact on the whole of American society is undeniable.

Equally undeniable is the fact that laws such as these, together with the flourishing of adaptive technology, have created greater awareness in our communities.

By repeating the key phrase "equally undeniable" and the concept of "laws," the author is able to connect the ideas in the earlier paragraph (the impact of laws) to her new material in the next paragraph (the impact of technology).

In another section of her research paper, Shannon uses a question to help her reader move from one paragraph to another:

Rebecca Acuirre, 16, who has cerebral palsy, says that she recently asked a stranger what time it was and he kept walking as though he didn't hear her. "Some people are prejudiced and ignore us. That makes me angry," she says.

How can these prejudices be abolished? "We need more exposure," says DeVries.

The repetition of the word "prejudice" helps these paragraphs cohere. The question engages the reader because most of us feel obliged to think about answers to questions. And this rhetorical question does not merely repeat the word. Instead, it moves the reader beyond the previous aspect of prejudice to the solution Paaske will discuss in the next section.

Although all paragraphs in your essay should hold together, the device of repeating key words should not be overused or strained. If your "technique" is perceived as a formula, that awareness can irritate your reader. For example, let's imagine you have written a paragraph that ended with the sentence "These are rationalizations, not reasons." Avoid merely repeating the exact phrasing, like "Although these are rationalizations, not reasons," at the start of your next paragraph. Instead, you might want to begin with something like this: "Such rationalizations are understandable if one considers the. . . ." With conscious practice of the technique, you'll improve your skills.

Avoiding Gaps

Transition terms and devices will help you achieve coherence in your work, but they can't fill in for gaps in logic—sentences or paragraphs that just don't go together, or that are out of order. You can't expect your readers to move from one point to another if you have failed to write into your work the sense that you perceive. For example, in the incoherent paragraph on pages 363–364, the writer places the following two sentences together:

```
Parking is expensive and lots are jammed. It is embarrass-
ing to walk into class late.
```

In the writer's mind, there is a logical connection between these two thoughts. That link is not at all apparent to readers, and a transition term like *and* or *therefore* will not bridge that gap. The writer must write something to express the connection between the two sentences so there is no gap and no need for the readers to invent their own bridge.

■ PRACTICING COHERENCE

In small groups, return to the incoherent paragraph on pages 363–364 and discuss its problems. As a group, rewrite the paragraph so that all information is included, but also so that the ideas are logically linked. As you fill in the gaps in logic, practice using the transition terms and devices that will ensure coherence in this paragraph. Here is one solution to improve the coherence of the paragraph.

Students who commute to campus suffer indignities that dorm students can't imagine. Even before commuting students get to classes they have a problem. Parking on campus is expensive and hard to find because the lots are jammed. Often it takes over half an hour to find a spot. By then class has started, and it is embarrassing to walk into class late. Commuters also feel cut off from those students who can return to the dorm to eat or rest. And while study groups readily form in dorms, commuting students seldom have even a telephone number to get missed lecture notes. Dorm students have a sense of independence and freedom from their families, but commuters need to conform to old family rules and schedules. Often the indignities of living at home include doing those tasks the students did through high school, like baby sitting or cooking for younger siblings, or driving grandparents to the bank.

In addition to considering the links between ideas in the body of your essay, you will want to refine your introduction and conclusion to frame your essay and to achieve coherence.

WRITING INTRODUCTIONS AND CONCLUSIONS

Introductions and Audience

Typically, a strong introduction "hooks" the reader and then expands on the hook while building to the thesis statement, which often concludes the introduction. The introduction to an essay has two obligations: to attract the reader to the subject of the essay, and to establish for the reader the particular focus of the writer. The focus of the writer—the assertion he or she is making about a limited subject—is contained in the thesis statement. The thesis statement does not have to be at the end of the introduction, but that is often a natural place for it because both the writer and reader are then immediately aware of the key assertion that will be supported in the essay. The concept of the thesis is discussed in more detail on pages 322–334.

If you have not discovered in your prewriting activities a useful way to lead to your thesis, you may find the ideas below helpful. Some subjects will seem best introduced by one type of introduction rather than another, and it's a good idea to keep your audience in mind as you draft possible "hooks" to your topic. Clearly, a reader would be confused and find inappropriate an amusing anecdote used as an introduction to a study of AIDS, unemployment, or infant mortality in Third World countries. Your introduction should anticipate the intention and tone of the paper that will follow.

Often you will have a working thesis before you write your first draft, but the idea for your introduction—the first words in the essay—will not come until you have worked extensively with your material. You may find that if you deliberately vary your introductions, perhaps trying each of the methods suggested here, you will not be intimidated by that blank sheet of paper or empty computer screen each time you start to write.

Types of Introductions

Direct Quotation

An essay that begins with the words of another person, especially a well-known person, should help convince your reader that you are a prepared writer who has researched others' views on the subject and found relevance in their words. When we were writing the introduction to Chapter 1 of the reader, we realized that one author in the chapter, Ellen Goodman, had incorporated into her essay a number of interesting comments from André Malraux. We found one of his comments so compelling that we used the quotation in our chapter introduction. André Malraux, a French novelist, political activist, and social and art critic, is not a noted authority on the sociology or psychology of family life. Nevertheless, his mildly philosophical statements about the family interested us, and we found his thoughts relevant for our introduction. Notice how we use Malraux's words throughout our introduction.

> In our opening essay, Ellen Goodman quotes André Malraux's belief that "without a family" the individual "alone in the world trembles with the cold" (qtd. in Goodman 4). The family often nurtures its members and tolerates differences and failings that friends and lovers cannot accept. But as you may realize from your own experiences and observations, people also tremble with fear or anxiety even within the family unit. The writers in this chapter show the family as a source of both nurturing and trembling.

Description

Whether it presents a vivid picture of nature or of a person, an introduction using description can appeal to the imagination and the senses simultaneously. The power of the opening can be enhanced if the writer also postpones specific identification of the subject, place, or person until the reader is engaged. In the following paragraph, notice that John Leonard does not reveal his subject. In fact, the reader of "The Only Child" (p. 22) does not know that he or she is reading about Leonard's brother until the last line of the essay.

> He is big. He always has been, over six feet, with that slump of the shoulders and tuck in the neck big men in this country often affect, as if to apologize for being above the democratic norm in size. (In high school and at college he played varsity basketball. In high school he was senior class president.) And he looks healthy enough, blue-eyed behind his beard, like a trapper or a mountain man, acquainted with silences. He also grins a lot.

Question

The psychology behind a question probably lies in the fact that most of us feel obliged to at least *consider* answering when someone asks us something. If we don't have an immediate answer, we consider the subject and then continue with the reading—exactly what the writer wants us to do. But readers may find questions irritating if they seem silly or contrived, like "What is capital punishment?" Notice your own interest as you read the questions in the introduction to Robert Heilbroner's essay "Don't Let Stereotypes Warp Your Judgments" (p. 429).

Is a girl called Gloria apt to be better-looking than one called Bertha? Are criminals more likely to be dark than blond? Can you tell a good deal about someone's personality from hearing his voice briefly over the phone? Can a person's nationality be pretty accurately guessed from his photograph? Does the fact that someone wears glasses imply that he is intelligent?

Anecdote or Illustration

Just as listeners look up attentively when a speaker begins a speech with a story, all readers are engaged by an anecdote. If the story opens dramatically, the involvement of the reader is assured. In the following example, from Brent Staples' essay "Black Men and Public Space" (p. 225), the author initially misleads the reader into thinking the writer has malicious intentions—exactly the misconception that is the subject matter of his essay.

My first victim was a woman—white, well dressed, probably in her early twenties. I came upon her late one evening on a deserted street in Hyde Park, a relatively affluent neighborhood in an otherwise mean, impoverished section of Chicago. As I swung onto the avenue behind her, there seemed to be a discreet, uninflammatory distance between us. Not so. She cast back a worried glance. To her, the youngish black man—broad six feet two inches with a beard and billowing hair, both hands shoved into the pockets of a bulky military jacket—seemed menacingly close. After a few more quick glimpses, she picked up her pace and was soon running in earnest. Within seconds she disappeared into a cross street.

Definition

Often the definition of a term is a necessary element of an essay, and a definition may interest the reader in the subject (if the writer does not resort to that boring and cliché opener, "According to Webster's Dictionary. . . "). Notice how Amy Gross uses her term, then gives many vivid examples before she gives an actual definition, in her essay "The Appeal of the Androgynous Man" (p. 71).

James Dean was my first androgynous man. I figured I could talk to him. He was anguished and I was 12, so we had a lot in common. With only a few exceptions, all the men I have liked or loved have been a certain kind of man: a kind who doesn't play football or watch the games on Sunday, who doesn't tell dirty jokes featuring broads or chicks, who is not contemptuous of conversations that are philosophically speculative, introspective, or otherwise foolish according to the other kind of man. He is more self-amused, less inflated, more quirky, vulnerable and responsive than the other sort (the other sort, I'm visualizing as the guys on TV who advertise deodorant in the locker room). He is more like me than the other sort. He is what social scientists and feminists would call androgynous: having the characteristics of both male and female.

Deliberate Contradiction

Sometimes the writer can start the paper with a view or statement that will be contradicted or contrasted with the subject matter of the essay. Brigid Brophy, in her essay "Women: Invisible Cages" (p. 94), does just that in her introduction:

> All right, nobody's disputing it. Women are free. At least, they look free. They even feel free. But in reality women in the western, industrialised world today are like the animals in a modern zoo. There are no bars. It appears that cages have been abolished. Yet in practice women are still kept in their place just as firmly as the animals are kept in their enclosures. The barriers which keep them in now are invisible.

Statistic or Startling Fact or Idea

An essay that starts with a dramatic statistic or idea engages the reader at once. Notice how the following introduction from Michael S. Kimmel and Martin P. Levine's essay "A Hidden Factor in AIDS" (p. 78) uses three statistics together to interest the reader in their essay:

> As the AIDS epidemic begins its second decade, it's time to face some unpleasant realities: AIDS is the No. 1 health problem for men in the United States; it is the leading cause of death of men aged 33 to 45; it has killed more American men than were lost in the Vietnam War.

Mixture of Methods

Many enticing introductions will combine the approaches described above. For example, Laura Cunningham employs narration, specific illustrations, and definition to entice the reader to her account of living with her grandmother. In addition, in the third paragraph of "The Girls' Room" (p. 63), Cunningham uses question and description, and it is clear that Cunningham's introduction has described an expectation that is a contradiction to the reality of her grandmother:

> When I heard she was coming to stay with us I was pleased. At age eight I thought of "grandmother" as a generic brand. My friends had grandmothers who seemed permanently bent over cookie racks. They were a source of constant treats and sweets. They were pinchers of cheeks, huggers and kissers. My own grandmother had always lived in a distant state; I had no memory of her when she decided to join the household recently established for me by my two uncles.

But with the example of my friends' grandmothers before me, I could hardly wait to have a grandmother of my own—and cookies would be nice too. For while my uncles provided a cuisine that ranged from tuna croquettes to Swedish meatballs, they showed no signs of baking anything more elegant than a potato.

A Few Final Words on Introductions

In your prewriting activities, if you have not found a way to lead your reader into your paper, try one of the types of introductions defined and exemplified here. Those first few words can attract your reader, set the tone for your essay, and predict the focus of your study. Ideally, the introduction will also anticipate your conclusion.

WRITING CONCLUSIONS

The conclusion of an essay should bring closure to the reader, a feeling of completion or satisfaction. Ideally, the conclusion will fit like the lid on a box. You might return to your introduction and thesis, select key images or phrases that you used, and reflect them in your conclusion. This return to the start of the paper assures your reader that all aspects of your assertion have been met in the essay. An effective conclusion is one that echoes the tone of the introduction without merely repeating the exact words of the thesis (a type of closure that is contrived and dull). Although your conclusion may be weakened by "tacking on" a new topic or concept without sufficient explanation and development, you may want to suggest that there is some broader issue to think about, or some additional goal that might be achieved if the situation you have discussed were satisfied.

For his conclusion to the essay "Don't Let Stereotypes Warp Your Judgments," Robert Heilbroner returns to the images of the pictures in our mind, the ideas stirred by the questions he uses in his introduction given on page 429:

> Most of the time, when we type-cast the world, we are not in fact generalizing about people at all. We are only revealing the embarrassing facts about the pictures that hang in the gallery of stereotypes in our own heads.

Another effective conclusion appears in Carol Tavris' essay "In Groups We Shrink" (p. 267). After describing specific real and test situations in which people in groups failed to respond to an obvious problem, Tavris concludes with a social psychologist's hope for improving behavior. She also plays with a line from the poet John Milton ("They also serve who only stand and wait"), a reference that the reader will enjoy if he or she knows Milton's poem "On His Blindness."

By understanding the social pressures that reward groupthink, loyalty and obedience, we can foster those that reward whistle-blowing and moral courage. And, as a society, we can reinforce the belief that they also sin who only stand and watch.

The student papers in this book also show effective techniques in their conclusions. Rachel, who wrote the paper on eating disorders (pp. 357–363), was advised by her instructor to strengthen the conclusion of her rough draft (p. 355) by returning to the images and key words of her introduction. Rachel did this in her final paper. She also was able to echo the title of a source that she used in her essay. The part of her conclusion that mirrors her introduction looks like this:

```
It is time to protest the images of bikini-clad models
parading before us and demand images that reflect the emo-
tional and intellectual scope and diversity among women in
our society. With some of our best and brightest dying
among us, there is no in-between position any more. Those
who make the images will only change when those of us who
support them stop buying products and stop tuning in on
programs that continue to impose "bodily harm" on us.
```

Shannon Paaske also returned to her introduction to conclude her research paper on the disabled, "From Access to Acceptance: Enabling America's Largest Minority." Her thesis and conclusion are printed below, but you can read her entire essay on pages 460–478.

Thesis:

```
     Although combinations of technological advances,
equality-promoting legislation, and increasing media expo-
sure have worked as a collective force in bringing about
improvements in the lives of the people who make up what is
sometimes termed "America's largest minority" (Davidson
61), ignorance and prejudice continue to plague the dis-
abled.
```

Conclusion:

```
     The legislation and technology that have developed at
the end of this century will continue to make new worlds
accessible to the disabled. Ideally, these developments
```

will permit the disabled to be viewed in terms of their
capabilities rather than their disabilities. In that climate, the disabled can gain acceptance in the worlds to
which they have access. With the steps being taken by government, science, and the media, individuals alone are
needed to make the dream of acceptance a reality for the
disabled.

Notice that the title of Shannon's essay also is echoed in her conclusion.

Final Tips for Writing Conclusions

To draft a good conclusion, try the following:

- Return to your thesis and restate it in different words. Incorporate that restatement into your conclusion.
- Examine your introduction and try to incorporate the key words, images, description, anecdote, or response to the question into your conclusion.
- Consider your reader: Have you brought a sense of significant closure to your topic?

You have been considering your reader and the aim of your paper throughout as you have rewritten your rough drafts, verified the logic of your organization, strengthened the introduction and conclusion, and edited for surface errors. These essential revision strategies can help you with any paper that you write.

In the next chapter of the rhetoric, we will show you ways to develop essays using specific methods or modes. Whether you are assigned a particular type of essay or you choose to use these methods of development within your papers, you will find the instructions, illustrations, and exercises pertinent for a variety of writing assignments.

9

Methods for Developing Essays

■ ■ ■

Your instructor may ask you to write a paper using a particular method of development for presenting your support. For example, your instructor may ask you to write a narrative, or a comparison and/or contrast study. In order to help you understand how papers develop with one type of support or another, we have isolated these forms as models for discussion. In doing this, we do not mean to suggest that all paper topics will fit precisely into one of these categories. Nothing could be further from our experience as students, teachers, and publishing writers.

In fact, you may recall that our first student essay, Rachel's "Dieting Daze," incorporates narrative, definition, description, comparison–contrast and research in a problem analysis paper that argues for a change. These multiple approaches are ideal complements, and together they help the writer thoroughly address the topic.

Because you may be asked to develop a paper with a single and particular strategy, we have included in this chapter models of the methods most often assigned. But because we believe that most essays are developed with combined modes, we will start our analysis with an essay that combines multiple strategies. You will find "The Appeal of the Androgynous Man," by Amy Gross, on page 71. Please read or review the essay before you read the commentary below.

COMBINING MULTIPLE STRATEGIES

If you read "The Appeal of the Androgynous Man" with the intention of determining what kinds of support the author used, you may have noticed that she employs definitions, narration, comparison and contrast, characterization, and summary writing in order to argue her point and defend her thesis—that the androgynous man is more than an "all-man man."

Analyzing Mixed Methods

Definition and Characterization Through Comparison and Contrast

The author's first obligation is to define *androgyny,* a word that might be unfamiliar to her reader. She does this through a *comparison–contrast* mode by first describing what the androgynous man is not. He is a man who "doesn't play football or watch the games on Sunday, who doesn't tell dirty jokes featuring broads or chicks, who is not contemptuous of conversations that are philosophically speculative, [or] introspective." She then describes what the androgynous man is— "more self amused, less inflated, more quirky, vulnerable and responsive" than the other type of man. Gross then gives an actual definition of androgyny: "having the characteristics of both male and female." The definition serves as a concluding sentence to the exemplifications in her comparison–contrast descriptions. This timely placement of a definition shows Gross' awareness of audience.

Audience Awareness

In our discussion of audience (pp. 315–321), we noted that the writer must be aware of the reader's responses to the text. Gross is especially aware of her audience, and even addresses the reader, something usually considered bad style in formal writing ("Now the first thing I want you to know . . . "). Gross must meet her reader's possible objections to the androgynous man in order to keep her audience. She states that the androgynous man is "neither effeminate nor hermaphroditic." After insisting that "all his primary and secondary sexual characteristics are in order," Gross notes that she would call the androgynous man "all-man," but that term wouldn't be correct because he is *more* than all-man. Her thesis comes as a natural assertion from the descriptions, characterizations, definitions, comparisons, and contrasts that started her essay.

Argument Strategy

Gross' first goal after defining her terms is to disparage the opponent, the "all-man man." Our experience in teaching this work is that this section of her essay is the one that prompts the most bitter retorts from students. Gross is merciless in describing the all-man's grocery shopping habits, inspired only by the "little woman's" temporary absence from the kitchen. Our male students protest that they know how to cook, and that their shopping is of necessity more than pretzels and a six-pack, steak and potatoes, and a "wad" of cake or apple pie. Gross' word choice is both inflammatory and humorous. She creates a negative caricature of the "all-man man" because the negative image is an important part of her argument.

Narration

Notice that part of the author's development includes a *narrative*, a very short but stinging anecdote to describe an evening she endured with an all-man man. Placed where it is, the humor in the narrative may soften the harshness of Gross' previous negativity. We all like stories, and a personal anecdote can't be too offensive; after all, the author might have reasoned, this nasty experience happened to *me!* In addition to supporting her points about this type of man, the narrative also contributes an additional aspect to her characterization of the androgynous man. He may be a hard-hat or well educated, but he will not be a "brute" with a "superman package" that includes an "imperialistic" ego. By showing that the androgynous man—as well as the "brute"—comes in varying social classes, she does not alienate any reader sensitive to class distinctions.

More Definition

As part of her argument that the androgynous man is creative, Gross is compelled to *define* this term. She does this by insisting on what creativity is not—a cliché cartoon in beret and artist's smock. She contrasts this image with an actual definition: creativity is "a talent for freedom, associated with imagination, wit, empathy, unpredictability, and receptivity to new impressions and connections."

Expert Sources to Help an Argument

To convince her reader that her personal preference for the androgynous man is more than "prejudice," Gross relies on experts to help her prove that the androgynous man really is more sensitive and creative. To do this, Gross uses a *summary* of two psychological studies of high masculinity in males and high femininity in females. Gross shows that the psychologists' findings support her "prejudice" that creative males—synonymous now with androgynous males—are more open "in their feelings and emotions" and have "a sensitive intellect and understanding self-awareness," as well as "wide-ranging interests." The androgynous man "shuns no behavior" because our culture would "label it as female," and even while he gets problems solved, he expresses concern for others. Gross uses a summary of another psychologist's findings to present a contrast with the androgynous man's characteristics, stating that highly masculine men lack "the ability to express warmth, playfulness and concern." Gross lets quoted summaries from the experts at reputable institutions help her convince any reader that nobody would want to try to have a relationship with an "all-man man."

More Audience Awareness

Gross anticipates her reader's possible objection once again when she agrees that "gut appeal" and "chemistry" have something to do with a woman's selection of a partner. She again contrasts the qualities of the "all-man man"—described in her conclusion as a competitive jock whose idea of sex is to conquer—with the characteristics of the androgynous man. Her conclusion relies on a return to the terms that she has used throughout the essay to define androgyny. Gross reminds the reader of the androgynous man's "greater imagination, his wit and empathy, his unpredictability, and his receptivity to new impressions and connections." Because she has created a sexual scenario where these androgynous character traits would be played out, she has a suggestive, amusing, and cleverly emphatic recapitulation of her argument.

Why This Analysis?

The purpose of this analysis of "The Appeal of the Androgynous Man" is to encourage you to recognize the multiple modes and devices that professional writers use to engage and persuade their readers. This recognition can have a positive effect on your own writing. By practicing the single-development assignments given in the writing topics and described in the rhetoric—narration, definition, cause and effect, comparison and contrast, argument, and analysis (process, problem, subject)—you will learn to employ multiple methods confidently to write an engaging and convincing paper.

NARRATION

Everyone loves a good story, and most people enjoy telling them. Narration is telling a single story or several related ones. It is often associated with fiction—with myths, fairy tales, short stories, and novels—but writers of all types of essays use narrative strategies.

When to Use Narration

Narration can be used to argue a point, define a concept, or reveal a truth. Writers in all disciplines have discovered the power of the narrative. Journalists, historians, sociologists, and essayists often "hook" their readers by opening with a personal anecdote or a human interest story to capture the reader and illustrate points. In fact, many writers use narration to persuade their audiences to a course of action. For example, George Orwell's famous narrative "Shooting an Elephant" is a compelling indictment of imperialism.

Personal narratives can be powerful if they focus on a provocative insight and if the details are carefully selected and shaped. Therefore narratives are more than mere diary entries, because certain details may be omitted while others may be altered. Narratives may help the writer better understand the significance of an experience, and they help readers "see for themselves." Typically narratives require no library research (our lives are rich with resources for this type of essay), but often writers may choose to supplement personal narration with research and outside sources to move beyond their own experience.

How to Write a Narrative

Narratives typically focus on an incident involving a conflict, whether it is between opposing people, values, or perceptions. This incident is then dramatized so the reader can picture what happened and can hear what was said. Such incidents often involve some aspect of change—a contrast between "before" and "after"—even though the change may be internal (a change in awareness) rather than external or physical.

Narratives do not have to feature life-shattering incidents; in fact, many of the best narratives involve profound changes that are not always obvious to others. In "Discovery of a Father" (see p. 6), the son's attitude toward his father changes from one of hatred to one of respect, yet neither his father nor his mother may realize this change.

Brainstorming for a Subject

Writers usually need to dig deep to find those buried experiences that have changed their attitudes and views. To help generate ideas, you will find specific narrative assignments at the end of many poems and essays in the "Writing from the Text" sections. If your assignment is more general—to write about any significant moment or change in your life—it will help to consider these questions.

What Are My Most Vivid Memories Of:

Kindergarten? first grade? 2nd? 3rd? 4th? 5th? 6th?
Junior high? high school? college?
Team sports? living in another culture?
Staying with friends or relatives?
Getting a job or working?

When Did I First:

Feel ashamed (or proud) of myself
Stand up to my parents
Realize teachers make mistakes
Give in to peer pressure
Pressure another to go against authority
Wish I had different parents
Wish someone would disappear from my life

What One Incident Showed Me:

What living between two worlds really means
How it feels to be alone
Why conformity isn't always best
How stereotyping has affected me
How different I am from my sister/brother/friend
Why we have a certain law
How it feels to live with a physical disability

Additional Prewriting

If you prefer a visual strategy, you might try clustering or mapping your ideas. One method is to write your topic—for example, "significant changes"—in a circle in the center of your page and then draw spokes outward from it. At the end of each spoke, write down a specific incident that triggered important changes in your life. Write the incident in a box and then use more spokes, radiating from the box, to specify all the changes that resulted. (For an illustration of cluster-ing, see p. 308.)

After you have brainstormed about all possible changes, choose the incident that seems most vivid and worth narrating. Then use anoth-er sheet of paper and write about specific change in a circle at the center and write down all the details that relate to it. After you have lots of details, you are ready to focus these thoughts and draft your paper.

From Brainstorming to Drafting a Paper

In a narrative essay, the thesis is not always articulated in the essay itself because it can ruin the sense of surprise or discovery often asso-ciated with narratives. In fact, an explicit thesis can slow the momen-tum of the story or spoil the ending. Whether it is articulated or implied, however, a thesis is still essential in order to keep the writer focused and to ensure that the story has a point or insight to share.

Beginning with a Working Thesis

For example, in the student essay that follows, Bruce Halling focuses on a time when he was intimidated by a bully, Ricky. His idea of writ-ing about being intimidated is not yet a thesis because the insight, focus, or assertion is not at first clear. At the start of his writing, Halling had only a topic. But after he clustered or listed his details, he probably wrote a *working thesis*—a preliminary assertion that could be changed and refined as the narrative took shape.

Working Thesis: Being plagued by a bully can make one yearn for revenge.

Discovering the Real Thesis

Most writers aren't lucky enough to identify the thesis immediately. Often, particularly in a narrative, it takes considerable writing before the best thesis is discovered. Therefore writers typically continue sharpening their thesis throughout the writing process as they, too, discover the point of their story. As Bruce narrated this experience, it developed as a genuine "between worlds" experience.

Discovered Thesis: As a child, I found myself caught between an intense wish for revenge and extreme guilt when this wish came true.

Once the thesis becomes clear to the writer, the rough draft needs to be revised so that all the details relate to this new thesis. Notice, however, that the thesis statement does not need to be specified in the actual essay.

Student Example: Narrative

The following essay by student Bruce Halling demonstrates a narrative focusing on a significant change in the narrator's life:

A Bully's Unjust Deserts

Bruce Halling

A young boy sits alone, admiring his father's gun. Ricky knows he's not supposed to play with the gun, but his father never keeps it loaded, so Ricky isn't afraid. Perhaps he imagines he hears a strange noise in his house and wants to investigate. Perhaps he imagines he's a private detective or a criminal. He might have pointed the gun at himself as if he were captured by the enemy. Or he might have been looking down the barrel at the darkness inside. But we'll never know what Ricky was imagining.

Ricky was in my sixth grade class, and almost every day after lunch we would have to wait by the door to our room until the teacher returned. And almost every day Ricky would find some way to amuse himself, at my expense.

"Oops! Sorry, Bruce," Ricky lied after he bumped into me from behind. I turned and looked at him. Couldn't he see I wasn't going to be any fun? He slapped me in the face and then stuck his bottom lip out in an exaggerated pout. "Is Brucie gonna cry?"

"No," I said as I turned my back on him and walked a few steps away. I wanted so badly to knock him down on the ground and have the other kids laugh at him as they were laughing at me. Not all of the kids were laughing, though. My friends weren't laughing. They were admiring their shoes. I walked away from my friends to make it easier for them to ignore me. I didn't need their help, and I was glad they didn't offer it. I was prepared to take anything Ricky could give me, but no matter how much I wanted to, I could never bring myself to hit him. I always felt it was wrong to fight.

Ricky's house was on my street, and I had to pass it on my way home from school. Walking home from school should have been a nice stroll for a ten year old. I know that was what I had always wished my walks home would be. It wasn't a long walk--just three blocks, and the weather is always nice in the South Bay. But even in those few blocks, I had an obstacle, and it presented itself in the form of a young boy.

Some days I would stay after school to practice in the choir or to help the teacher. For my reward on those days, Ricky would be waiting for me on my way home. My house was on the other side of the street, and I always made sure to cross before I came to his house.

One day as I crossed the street, I heard something hit the ground near me. Then I felt the sting of a dirt clod hitting me in the head. I stopped and looked in the direction of Ricky's house, but I couldn't see where he was hiding. I brushed most of the dirt out of my hair and kept walking, try-ing to ignore being hit several more times before I made it home.

I stood in the shower, holding the valves to the hot and cold water as the dirt was washed out of my hair. Every time I thought about Ricky, I turned down the cold water until it was uncomfortably hot. As my skin turned red from the heat, I closed my eyes and wished for his death. I imagined it. Sometimes I would kill him. Other times he died in an acci-dent. But always I was a witness. Always I would be free from his torment.

Unfortunately, later that year, my wish came true. I remember when I heard about Ricky's death. I was in an eleva-tor with two of my friends who had also known Ricky. After I stepped into the elevator, I pushed the button for the third floor.

"Did you hear what happened to Ricky Liverpool?" one friend asked.

"Yeah," sighed the other friend as the door started closing.

"What happened?" I asked, feigning moderate interest.

"He shot himself in the head," one friend replied. The elevator gave a slight jerk upwards. I saw it in the way my friends bounced slightly, but I didn't feel it. I only felt the rigid walls of the elevator as my friends' polite lamentations seemed to punctuate my silence. The doors finally opened, and I followed my friends into the dim hallway.

I wasn't glad my wish came true. I wanted to feel happy. I wanted to feel freed. I could only feel sad. I felt sad because Ricky had died . . . and I had wanted it to happen. All of the hate I had built up inside for Ricky only brought me a tremendous amount of guilt. I realized then I had to be careful of what I wished for in the future. Because sometimes wishes do come true.

Analyzing Narrative Strategy: Show Rather Than Tell

When writers narrate a story, they try to recreate scenes so that the reader can experience the moment as they did. Rather than simply telling us what they felt, they try to *show* us. For example, in the student model, Halling could have simply told us that Ricky would often deliberately ridicule him. Instead, he lets us hear this, see it, and feel it with him as Ricky bumped him from behind:

I turned around and looked at him. Couldn't he see I wasn't going to be any fun? He slapped me in the face and then stuck his bottom lip out in an exaggerated pout. "Is Brucie gonna cry?"

Such a scene draws in the reader because each of us can empathize with this moment of humiliation. The writer doesn't need to write, "I felt humiliated," because he has *shown* this more vividly than any claim he could make. Halling's use of dialogue, action, and vivid details (the exaggerated pout) makes Ricky seem real to the reader.

Selecting Telling Details

The key to describing scenes and characters is to make sure each detail is revealing. It is not important to know the narrator's hair color or height, so such details would not be relevant or "telling." But the fact that he is in the choir and stays after to help the teacher reveals that he is not a trouble maker, not one who would typically want to kill a classmate. Such details help us to understand better the narrator's character as well as the extent of his hatred of Ricky.

Similarly, the setting can be revealing. Although the weather is not always important in a story, here an afternoon stroll on a sunny day becomes darkened by the bully's attacks. In this scene the pleasant weather is juxtaposed against the narrator's pain as the clods of mud strike his head. The choice of setting itself can automatically reveal qualities about both character and conflict.

■ PRACTICING WRITING ESSAYS WITH NARRATION

Many of the topics in the "Writing from the Text" sections of the reader invite you to relate your own experience to the particular readings and to respond with a narrative. Here are some additional assignments:

1. Write an essay describing one school experience that taught you an unexpected lesson. Show us the incident as it happened, and describe what you learned and why it was unexpected.

2. Write an essay focusing on a time when you bullied or were bullied by someone else. Let us see what happened and what you discovered about yourself and others.

3. Write about a time when one of your peers, parents, or children embarrassed you. Was the situation funny or painful, or a little of both? Recreate the moment of embarrassment so that your reader sees and hears what happened.

4. Write about an incident when you felt that your cultural or family background was incorrectly prejudged. Describe what happened so that your reader can understand the event and your response to it. Did you make any discoveries as a result of this experience?

5. Write about an event that revealed that something you once believed or thought was important had lost its validity or importance. Dramatize the revelation as vividly as you can.

Readings in Part I That Use Narration

Examples of works in this text that are predominantly narration include the following:

"My Man Bovanne," p. 43

"Two Kinds," p. 49

"The 'Perfect' Misconception," p. 58

"The Girls' Room," p. 63

"The Appeal of the Androgynous Man," p. 71

"The Androgynous Man," p. 75

"Where Are You Going, Where Have You Been?" p. 124

"Living in Two Worlds," p. 143

"American Horse," p. 157

"Proper Care and Maintenance," p. 176

"The Masked Marvel's Last Toehold," p. 199

"On Being a Cripple," p. 203

"Black Men and Public Space," p. 225

"The Atlanta Riot," p. 229

"Eleven," p. 244

"The Lottery," p. 283

"I Confess Some Envy," p. 399 (in the rhetoric)

Final Tips for a Narrative

- Focus your story on a provocative insight so that your story reflects some real thought.
- Continue sharpening your thesis as your narrative develops. Remember, the thesis does not need to be explicitly stated in the essay.
- Dramatize a scene or two, using action and dialogue. Don't just tell the reader; show the scene.
- Include telling details that reveal relevant character traits. Have your characters interact with each other.
- Rewrite sentences and revise paragraphs to eliminate wordiness and generalizations.
- Study other narratives in the text, looking for techniques and strategies. Experiment!

DEFINITION

Whether your entire essay is a definition or you have incorporated a definition into your essay to clarify a term or concept for your reader, explaining what a term means is an integral part of writing. Knowing your intended audience will help you determine which words you need to define. For example, in a paper for a psychology class, you would not need to define terms generally used in that field. But when you write for a general reader and use language unfamiliar to most people—a technical or foreign term, or a word peculiar to an academic discipline—you will need to define the term so your reader can understand it. Even if you are using a familiar word, you need to explain its meaning if you or an author you are quoting use it in a unique way.

Sometimes a brief definition is all that you need. In that case, a few words of clarification, or even a synonym, may be incorporated into your text quite easily:

> *Los Vendidos*, or "The Sellouts," is the Spanish-language title of Luis Valdez's play.

> Achondroplasia—a type of dwarfism—may affect overall bone structure and cause arms and legs to be disproportionately smaller than the rest of the body.

> A classic glaze for porcelain tea sets is celadon—a French name given in the seventeenth century to gray-green Chinese glazes.

Whenever possible, incorporate into your text the necessary clarification of a term. As the above examples show, such incorporation is unobtrusive and therefore superior to writing a separate sentence to define the term.

A formal definition may be required for some writing situations. In that case, you will need to follow the dictionary model of establishing the term in a *class* and then distinguishing the term from its class by citing its difference, or *differentia:*

> Haiku is a form of poetry composed of seventeen syllables in a 5-7-5 pattern of three lines.

> A paring chisel is a woodworking tool with a knife-sharp edge, pushed by hand and used to finish a rough cut of wood.

> "Multiple sclerosis is a chronic degenerative disease of the central nervous system, in which the myelin that sheathes the nerves is . . . eaten away and scar tissue forms in its place, interrupting the nerves' signals" (Mairs 205).

When to Use Definition

You may be asked to write a "definition essay," a paper that develops with the primary intention of increasing the reader's understanding of a term. This type of paper topic might be assigned in a psychology, sociology, history, philosophy, or English course. Usually, however, your goal will be something else. You may be attempting to convince your reader to consider the explained term in a positive light, or to compare it—even to prefer it—to something else. Sometimes the persuasive aspect of the essay relies on the reader understanding the definition of a word.

Strategies for Incorporating Definitions

When an assignment calls for an extended definition of a concept or term, the following methods may be used alone or in combination:

- *Comparison–contrast:* You may want to contrast your definition of the word with the way it is typically used, or with a more conventional definition of the term. If the term is unfamiliar, you might show how it is similar to another concept.
- *Description:* You can define a term by describing its characteristics: size, shape, texture, color, noise, and other telling traits.
- *Exemplification:* Giving examples and illustrations of a concept can help your reader to understand it better, but examples are rather specific and therefore should help supplement a definition rather than be used by themselves.
- *Negation:* Understanding what something is *not* can help limit the definition and eliminate misconceptions.

Example: An In-Class Writing Assignment

The following definition reflects a brief in-class writing assignment in which the student was asked to explain Robert Moog's definition of a patriotic American in "Who's Not Supporting Whom?" (p. 261). The student, Adam Kiefer, had read Moog's article and had a time limit to write this response.

Patriotism Re-examined

Adam Kiefer

In "Who's Not Supporting Whom?" Robert Moog defies the
prevalent definition of a patriotic American as one who only

"buys American." Instead, he defines a "good patriotic American" as one who believes in the free enterprise system and in the benefits of vigorous competition. Convinced that such competition is best for America, Moog argues that patriotic Americans are those who buy the best product, no matter what country produces it. He feels that such competition is best for this country because it will force Americans to make a better product, one that is efficient and cost-effective.

In the long run, this alone will save American businesses and ensure employment for all--patriotic goals, for sure. Moreover, he claims that whenever Americans buy foreign-made products, it is their patriotic duty to write to American manufacturers and explain why. According to Moog, the patriotic American should not coddle American companies because ultimately this weakens and undermines the entire country and its economy.

Analysis of the Definition Essay

Because this essay had to be written during class, the time was limited. Therefore Adam immediately focused on a succinct definition of a "patriotic American"—one who believes in the free enterprise system and therefore buys the best product, not necessarily an American-made one. The remaining definition attempts to explain and justify this controversial definition. Adam used negation when he claimed that the patriotic American is not one who simply "buys American." He also supported his definition with some specific quotations from the article.

■ PRACTICING WRITING DEFINITION ESSAYS

1. In your college papers, you will most frequently incorporate short definitions to clarify terms. In small groups, armed with dictionaries, practice writing single sentences that define the following terms:

    a. schizophrenia

    b. satire

    c. Marxist

    d. interface

   e. Cubist

   f. picaresque

2. Although you will use definition most often as a component of your papers, it is useful to practice writing short definition essays. In small groups, collaborate with your classmates to write a short essay that defines one of the following:

   a. power

   b. "between worlds"

   c. artifice

   d. witty

   e. unconditional love

   f. disabled

Readings in Part 1 That Use Definition

Each of the following works requires definition to achieve its goal:

"The Appeal of the Androgynous Man," p. 71

"The Androgynous Man," p. 75

"A Hidden Factor in AIDS," p. 78

"A Work of Artifice," p. 110

"Date Rape," p. 112

"Rape," p. 120

"When a Woman Says No," p. 122

"Crimes Against Humanity," p. 167

"Like Mexicans," p. 190

"On Being a Cripple," p. 203

"An Open Letter to Jerry Lewis," p. 214

"Discrimination at Large," p. 217

"The Atlanta Riot," p. 229

"Mommy, What Does 'Nigger' Mean?" p. 234

"Ethnic Envidia," p. 241

"Eleven," p. 244

"Work, Labor and Play," p. 249

"Who's Not Supporting Whom?" p. 261

"Don't Let Stereotypes Warp Your Judgments," p. 429 (in the rhetoric)

Final Tips for Writing Definitions

- Consider your audience and define any terms that your readers can't be expected to know.
- Whenever possible, incorporate into your text the necessary clarification of a term. Avoid writing a separate sentence to define the term.
- For a formal definition, first establish the term in a class and then distinguish it from this class by citing its difference.
- Remember that definitions can also be developed by comparing and contrasting that word with other terms, by describing the characteristics of a term, by presenting examples, and by illustrating what the term is not.

CAUSE AND EFFECT

All your life you have been made aware of the consequences of your behavior: not getting your allowance because you didn't keep your room clean; winning a class election because you ran a vigorous campaign; getting a C on an exam because you didn't review all of the material; earning a friend's trust because you kept a confidence. In all of these cases, a particular behavior seems to *cause* or result in a certain *effect*. In the case of the denied allowance, for example, your parents may have identified the cause: not keeping your room clean.

Causes are not always so easy to identify, however, for there may be a number of indirect causes of an action or inaction. For example, you may have won an election because of your reputation as a leader, your popularity, your opponent's inadequacies, your vigorous campaign, or even a cause that you may not have known about or been able to control. Effects usually are more evident: homeless families, few jobs for college graduates, small businesses failing, and houses remaining on the market for years are all obvious effects of a recession. What has caused the recession typically is more difficult to discern, but good critical thinking involves speculating about possible causes and their effects. And good writing can come from such cause-and-effect thinking.

When to Use Cause and Effect

Cause-and-effect development can be used in diverse writing situations. For example, you will use this strategy when you trace the reasons for a historical event, such as the causes for American entry into World War II and the results of that entry. You perceive cause-and-effect relationships when you analyze and write about broad social problems (like runaway teens) or more personal concerns (such as why you and your siblings are risk takers). You may rely on cause-and-effect description to discuss a small town's abandoned shopping district, or to compare the aspirations of college graduates in 1968 and those today. All of these thinking and writing tasks invite you to examine the apparent effects and to question what has caused them. This questioning inevitably involves speculation about causes rather than absolute answers, but this speculation can lead to fruitful analysis and provocative papers.

Brainstorming to Find Causes or Effects

In order to speculate about causes for an effect that you have perceived, you will want to brainstorm freely and let all of your hunches emerge. In fact, a lively prewriting session is the key to a lively cause-

and-effect paper. To produce a paper that goes beyond predictable or obvious discussion, take time to think about diverse causes for an effect you have observed and to contemplate plausible effects of situations that you perceive.

For example, you may have noticed that your downtown area is no longer attracting people as it once did. Instead of stopping at the family-owned clothing store or the donut shop next to the downtown movie theater, you and your family and friends go out to suburban malls for shopping, dining, and movies. Consider the causes for this phenomenon.

You can brainstorm this perceived problem by writing a list of every possible cause that comes to you. After you have written your own list, you might look at this one:

WHY AREN'T WE GOING DOWNTOWN ANYMORE?

STORES

1. Limited stock—embarrassing, never have my size
2. Only carry expensive brands
3. Prices higher than the mall, too few sales
4. Old-fashioned, dull window displays, ugly mannequins
5. Clerks are old ladies who've been around forever

RESTAURANTS

6. Have boring menus: vegetable soup and bacon and eggs
7. Decorating is still very 1960s—pink and gray
8. Plastic plants
9. My favorite donut shop has closed
10. No inexpensive quick foods or snacks
11. Slow-moving waitresses

MOVIE THEATERS

12. Seats have broken springs and torn upholstery
13. Warped screen, bad sound system
14. Musty smell, no air conditioning
15. Same features play for weeks

OVERALL DOWNTOWN

16. Only old people shop downtown
17. I never meet any of my friends down there
18. Lots of homeless people, gangs

19. Dusty window-fronts of abandoned shops are demoralizing

20. Need to pay to park in city lots or need to feed meters

If you give some energy to the prewriting, you will undoubtedly come up with more causes than we have, and the paper that you write will have interesting explanations for a problem threatening nearly every community. You might not have the sophistication of a city planner or the statistics and research of your city hall, but your insights are bound to create a provocative paper worth reading. And we think you will find that creative speculation is useful for any cause-and-effect brainstorming that you do.

Drafting a Paper

After you have listed causes and/or effects, your next drafting step is to discover ideas that logically connect. As you link points, evaluate them to make sure your reasoning is clear and that your points are plausible and logical.

For example, the fact that the donut shop has closed is not *why* you have stopped shopping for clothing in the downtown area. That point would seem illogical to your reader without your developing a connection—perhaps that empty shops are disheartening reminders of the economic recession, or that a particular cruller the shop made provided a tasty, quick, and inexpensive snack during a shopping trip. Or you might see, as you draft, that some "causes" on your list are not worth developing.

In addition to developing plausible explanations for the points you do want to use, you need to consider organization. In your brainstorming, you may have perceived a natural grouping that worked well to get ideas down on paper. We answered our question about what was wrong with the downtown area by listing what was wrong with the stores, restaurants, movie theaters, and general atmosphere there. Suppose we realized that we could provide a better answer to the question if we organized around *issues* rather than grouped examples. Here is the revised list that might result:

WHY WE AREN'T GOING DOWNTOWN ANYMORE

ECONOMIC ISSUES:
   points 2, 3, 10, 20

AESTHETIC ISSUES:
   points 4, 6, 7, 8, 9, 12, 13, 14, 19

SOCIAL ISSUES:
   points 1, 5, 11, 15, 16, 17, 18

You will also need to decide the order of the grouped points that you will include in your paper. We decided that the social causes of not going downtown were more significant than the aesthetic or economic issues, so we decided we would conclude our paper by discussing social issues. (For more about ordering ideas, see pp. 335–336.)

Throughout your drafting, continue evaluating your points. Remove any points that are implausible or cannot be supported by the information you have, or do some research to find more convincing data. Continue to apply the "So what?" standard to ensure that you are developing a worthwhile paper. By this time in your drafting, it would help you to formulate a working thesis—in this case, an assertion that establishes the cause and/or effect relationship you perceive.

■ PRACTICING FINDING CAUSES AND EFFECTS

In small groups or individually, list multiple causes for the following effects:

1. Prevalence of two-income families
2. Increased number of comic book and sports card stores
3. Trend toward instructors assigning collaborative projects
4. Popularity of high-risk sports
5. Resurgence of rock music from the late 1950s and the 1960s

Now list the effects of these realities:

1. Prevalence of single-parent families
2. Increase in multicultural materials in education
3. More women in the professions
4. More people from all economic classes attending college
5. City-sponsored recycling projects

Any one of these brainstorming exercises could lead to a paper based on cause-and-effect development.

Example: Cause-and-Effect Essay

An analysis of a social issue is Robert McKelvey's goal in "I Confess Some Envy." In it McKelvey, a Bronze Star recipient in Vietnam and now a child psychiatrist and professor at Baylor University, analyzes the causes of the envy he felt while watching the Desert Storm troops receive public acclaim. He cites the reasons that his generation of soldiers failed to gain support and the effects of this failure on him and his peers. This essay first appeared in the *Los Angeles Times* on June 16, 1991, shortly after the return of American troops from Kuwait.

I CONFESS SOME ENVY
Robert McKelvey

Every year on the Marine Corps' birthday, the commandant sends a message to all Marine units world-wide commemorating the event. On Nov. 10, 1969, I was stationed with the 11th Marine Regiment northwest of Da Nang in Vietnam. It was my task to read the commandant's message to the Marines of our unit.

One sentence, in particular, caught my attention: "Here's to our wives and loved ones supporting us at home." Ironically, that week my wife had joined tens of thousands of others marching on the nation's capital to protest U.S. involvement in Vietnam.

It was a divisive, unhappy time. Few people believed the war could be won or that we had any right to interfere in Vietnam's internal affairs. However, for those of us "in country," there was a more pressing issue. Our lives were on the line. Even though our family and friends meant us no harm by protesting our efforts, and probably believed they were speeding our return, their actions had a demoralizing effect.

Couldn't they at least wait until we were safely home before expressing their distaste for what we were doing? But by then, the military had become scapegoats for the nation's loathing of its war, a war where draft dodgers were cast as heroes and soldiers as villains.

Watching the Desert Storm victory parades on television, I was struck by the contrast between this grand and glorious homecoming and the sad, silent and shameful return of so many of us 20-odd years ago. Disembarking from a troop ship in Long Beach, my contingent of Marines was greeted at the pier by a general and a brass band. There were no family, friends, well-wishers, representatives of the Veterans of Foreign Wars or children waving American flags.

We were bused to Camp Pendleton, quickly processed and sent our separate ways. After a two-week wait for my orders to be cut, during which time I spent most days at the San Diego Zoo, I was discharged from active duty. I packed up and flew home to begin pre-medical studies.

As the plane landed in Detroit, the on-board classical music channel happened to be playing Charles Ives' "America." The piece's ironic, teasing variations on the theme, "My Country 'Tis of Thee," seemed a fitting end to my military service.

My wife met me at the airport and drove me directly to Ann Arbor for a job interview. We were candidates for a job as house parents for the Religious Society of Friends (Quakers) International Co-op. Face to face with these sincere, fervent pacifists, I felt almost ashamed of the uniform I was still wearing with its ribbons and insignia.

I recalled stories of comrades who had been spat upon in airports and called "baby killers." The Friends, however, were exceptionally gentle and kind. They, at least, seemed able to see beyond the symbols of the war they hated to the individual human being beneath the paraphernalia. Much to my surprise, we got the job.

I took off my uniform that day, put it away and tried to resume the camouflage of student life. I seldom spoke of my service in Vietnam. It was somehow not a topic for polite conversation, and when it did come up the discussion seemed always to become angry and polarized.

Like many other Vietnam veterans, I began to feel as if I had done something terribly wrong in serving my country in Vietnam, and that I had better try to hush it up. I joined no veterans' organizations and, on those rare times when I encountered men who had served with me in Vietnam, I felt embarrassed and eager to get away. We never made plans to get together and reminisce. The past was buried deep within us, and that is where we wanted it to stay.

The feelings aroused in me by the sight of our victorious troops marching across the television screen are mixed and unsettling. There is pride, of course, at their stunning achievement. Certainly they deserve their victory parade. But there is also envy. Were we so much different from them?

Soldiers do not choose the wars they fight. Theirs happened to be short and sweet, ours long and bitter. Yet we were all young men and women doing what our country had asked us. Seeing my fellow Vietnam veterans marching with the Desert Storm troops, watching them try, at last, to be recognized and applauded for their now-distant sacrifices, is poignant and sad.

We have come out of hiding in recent years as the war's pain has receded. It has become almost fashionable to be a veteran and sport one's jungle fatigues. Still, a sense of hurt lingers and, with it, a touch of anger. Anger that the country we loved, and continue to love, could use us, abuse us, discard and then try to forget us, as if we were the authors of her misery rather than her loyal sons and daughters. It was our curious, sad fate to be blamed for the war we had not chosen to fight, when in reality we were among its victims.

Small-Group Discussion

1. After reading McKelvey's essay, meet in small groups to develop a list of the *causes* of the Vietnam soldiers' unhappiness during the war and afterwards. What are the *effects* of this unhappiness on McKelvey and his peers?

2. Discuss these questions in your small groups:

    a. What is the effect on McKelvey of his reading the commandant's message to the Marines in his unit?

    b. What is the effect the protesters at home intended by marching on the nation's capital? What may have been the effect of this march on the troops in Vietnam?

   c. What caused McKelvey to refrain from discussing his service experience with friends or from joining veterans' organizations after he returned?

   d. What has caused changes in attitudes toward Vietnam veterans?

■ PRACTICING WRITING ESSAYS ABOUT CAUSES AND EFFECTS

Write an essay that focuses on the causes and/or effects of one of the following:

1. Your having revealed an important truth about yourself to a member of your family

2. A friend or family member abusing alcohol or using drugs

3. Your family getting together for a holiday occasion

4. Your feeling trapped in the "invisible cages" described by Brigid Brophy (p. 94)

5. Your sense of being caught living between two worlds, as Marcus Mabry (p. 143) or Kim Edwards (p. 146) depicts

6. Your discovery that you are unwillingly intimidating others, as Brent Staples describes (p. 225)

7. Your need to conform to gender roles as discussed by Warren Farrell (p. 90), Brigid Brophy (p. 94), Naomi Wolf (p. 101), Michael Kimmel and Martin Levine (p. 78)

Readings in Part 1 That Use Cause and Effect

A number of essays in this textbook use cause and effect as a significant part of their development. You may be interested in reading some of these essays:

"Discovery of a Father," p. 6

"The Only Child," p. 22

"Ignorance Is Not Bliss," p. 25

"A Hidden Factor in AIDS," p. 78

"Men as Success Objects," p. 90

"Women: Invisible Cages," p. 94

"The Beauty Myth," p. 101

"Angry Young Men," p. 138

"Living in Two Worlds," p. 143

"In Rooms of Women," p. 146

Final Tips for Cause and Effect Development

- Brainstorm energetically in order to come up with every possible cause and/or effect for your particular topic.

- Go over your list of causes and effects to determine that each point is reasonable and supportable. Eliminate any which are illogical or for which you lack data. Do research if additional evidence is needed.

- Apply the "So what?" standard. Will this cause or effect analysis make worthwhile reading?

- Group ideas that belong together and order your evidence to conclude with your most emphatic and well-developed support.

- Develop your explanations fully so that your reader doesn't need to guess your assumptions or suppose your connection between points.

- Whether you have a stated or implied thesis, assure yourself that the assertion of your paper is both clear and worth supporting.

- Listen to the voice you have used throughout your essay. If your purpose in writing is to consider possible cause and effect relationships, don't feign a voice that purports to know all the answers.

COMPARISON AND CONTRAST

Whether you are examining your own experiences or responding to texts, you will inevitably rely on comparison and contrast thinking. To realize how two people, places, works of art, films, economic plans, laboratory procedures or aspects of literature—or anything else—may be alike or different is to perceive important distinctions between them.

While we may start an analysis process believing that two subjects are remarkably different (how they *contrast*), after thoughtful scrutiny we may see that there are important similarities between them. Conversely, although we may have detected clear similarities in two subjects (how they *compare*), the complete analysis may reveal surprising differences. Therefore, while **comparison** implies similarity and **contrast** implies difference, these two thinking processes work together to enhance perception.

When to Use Comparison and Contrast Development

Subtle comparison–contrast cues are embedded in writing assignments, both in-class exams and out-of-class papers. For example, an economics instructor may ask for a study of prewar and postwar inflation; a philosophy instructor may want the student to show how one philosophical system departs from another; a psychology instructor may require an explanation of how two different psychologists interpret dreams; or a literature instructor may assign an analysis of how a character changes within a certain novel.

The prevalence of such assignments in all disciplines underscores the importance of comparison–contrast in many experiences and learning situations. Assignments that ask writers to explain the unfamiliar, evaluate certain choices, analyze how someone or something has changed, establish distinction, discover similarities, and propose a compromise all require some degree of comparison and contrast.

For example, a writer responding to the readings in Chapter 2 may initially believe that women and men have quite different complaints about their lives. Women feel that they need to be attractive; they feel limited in their choice of career, and restricted by the career heights and pay they may attain; and they feel obligated to be domestic (good mothers, cooks, and housekeepers). Men feel they need to be successful at work to be attractive to women; they feel burdened to select high-status, high-paying jobs regardless of their real interests, and they must work continuously; and they feel precluded from domestic life—cut off from their children and home life.

At first, the complaints of each gender appear to be quite different. But the writer examining these complaints may perceive that they have something in common: that women *and* men suffer from "an invisible curriculum," a series of social expectations that deprive human beings of choice. A thesis for this study might look like this:

> **Thesis:** Although women and men seem to have different problems, both genders feel hampered by an "invisible curriculum" that affects their self-esteem and limits their choices at work and in their families.

How to Compare and Contrast

There are two basic methods for organizing data to compare or contrast. In the *block* method, the writer would organize the material for a study of conflicts affecting gender like this:

BLOCK 1. WOMEN

1. Need to feel attractive to be successful
2. Feel limited in workplace choices, level, pay
3. Feel obligated to be mothers, domestic successes

BLOCK 2. MEN

1. Need to feel successful at work to feel attractive
2. Feel burdened to achieve high position, work continuously
3. Feel cut off from children and domestic choices

In the *point-by-point* method, the writer would organize the material like this:

POINT 1. FACTORS THAT GOVERN SELF-ESTEEM

a. Women need to feel attractive
b. Men need to feel successful at work

POINT 2. RELATIONSHIP TO WORK

a. Women feel restricted in choice, level, pay
b. Men feel burdened to achieve high position, work continuously

POINT 3. RELATIONSHIP TO FAMILY

a. Women feel obligated to be mothers, domestic successes
b. Men feel cut off from children, domestic choices

Notice that in the block method, each point in the second block appears in the same order as the points in the first block. In the point-by-point method of arrangement, the first subject (in this case, women) will precede the second in each point of comparative analysis.

Although you may be wise to follow one of these methods quite deliberately, professional writers do not always adhere to this somewhat rigid form. Consider, for example, the following essay by Ellen Goodman.

Example: Comparison and Contrast Essay

IN AMERICA, FOOD FOR THOUGHT
Ellen Goodman

I once knew a thin sociologist who believed that people were obsessed by food only when they were chronically hungry. Even Freud described "oral" as a stage that adults (and perhaps cultures) would grow out of, with no more than an occasional regression for, say, weddings or Thanksgiving.

But today we live in a country where most of us are on demand feeding. The average American doesn't have to stalk the wild hamburger or gather ice cream in the woods. But it seems that much of the time that we used to spend on the basic problem of food—getting enough—has simply been transferred to the more elaborate food problems.

Recently I read not only Julia Child's delightful new cookbook but also an intriguing group of articles in the latest *Psychology Today* magazine on the new food consciousness. These readings reminded me that we have developed two major alternatives to the meat-and-potatoes mainstream: the "gourmet-food" culture and the "health-food" culture.

On one level, the two food "regimens" seem wildly disparate. Gourmet food is a response to our fantasies about what tastes good, while health food is a response to our fears about what's bad for you. Moreover, as alternative menus to the burger bourgeoise, the first group offers Turkey Orloff, while the second group offers Tofu with bean sprouts. One group is "into" a fish mousse en croute, while the other is high on brown rice. It's a matter of vintage wine versus fresh carrot juice.

Yet I think they have more in common than meets the mouth. The most extreme devotees of both the sensible Julia Child and late Adelle Davis demonstrate, at times, a moral elitism that is both righteous and intimidating. Many of the gourmet set are convinced that anyone who doesn't make his or her own mayonnaise is hopelessly gauche. Others among the health contingents look on a beefeater with as much horror as if they'd caught him biting the left leg off their dog.

These two alternative groups often share another characteristic. They are the oral equivalent of joggers. Conversation among the most committed Cordon Bleu crowd runs the gamut from artichoke to zabaglione, with arguments about preserving the balance of the elusive hollandaise. Dinner among the food cultists concerns the organic growth of vegetables, and the best way to maintain harmony between the yin and the yang on the serving platter. No Twinkie would darken the lips of either group. Instant coffee is taboo, although for different reasons. And Wonder bread is to both an unspeakable obscenity: the kidporn of the food fetishists.

But the appeal of both of these groups is enormous, for another reason. These advocates of the good life share something significant with the rest of us: the need to pay attention to food every day. The easy, fast-food mainstream of America, the simple three-meal culture, may satisfy our hunger pangs, but not some kind of innate need for allotting to food and eating an important place in our lives.

It may be that our current attraction to the alternative food cultures is more than the allure of the perfect pate or the sirens of guilt and sensible warnings of the natural-food advocates. It may be that part of our current fascination with analyzing and preparing "health foods" and concocting gourmet dinners is a rebellion against easy eating.

Analyzing Comparison and Contrast Strategy

In this essay, Goodman seems to be contrasting the "two major alternatives to the meat-and-potatoes mainstream: the 'gourmet-food' culture and the 'health-food' culture." Goodman acknowledges that these "two food 'regimens' seem wildly disparate." To show the apparent *contrasts* between the two eating habits, Goodman concentrates on one focal point at a time. Here she states why people are attracted to gourmet or health foods:

> Gourmet food is a response to our fantasies about what tastes good, while health food is a response to our fears about what's bad for you.

Then Goodman gives specific examples to support her point:

> [The] first group offers Turkey Orloff, while the second group offers Tofu with bean sprouts. One group is 'into' a fish mousse en croute, while the other is high on brown rice. It's a matter of vintage wine versus fresh carrot juice.

But after establishing the obvious differences in what these groups eat, Goodman notes that they have similarities, that "they have more in common than meets the mouth." To emphasize what they share, she continues to use the **point-by-point method,** moving back and forth between the two eating preferences, treating one focus point at a time and specifically showing how each habit relates to the point that she has made:

- Both groups demonstrate "a moral elitism that is both righteous and intimidating":
  — Gourmets insist everyone makes mayonnaise
  — Health food eaters deplore beef eaters

- Both groups are preoccupied with and talk about foods:
  — Gourmets' talk ranges from artichokes to zabaglione, how to maintain a hollandaise
  — Health food eaters discuss organic vegetables, plan plates to preserve yin/yang

- Both groups share the same taboos, if for different reasons:
  — Twinkies, instant coffee, Wonder bread

Finally, Goodman concludes that these apparently different groups share something more significant than their differences: "the need to pay attention to food every day." The focus of Goodman's essay, then, turns out to be the *comparison* between the two food "regimens," and the essay develops with wonderful style and wit to show the subtle but significant perceptions of the author.

Which Method to Use: Block or Point by Point?

Goodman used a point-by-point method to compare and contrast her two subjects. She might have chosen the block method, writing first on every aspect of the gourmet culture and then, in the second block, on every aspect of the health food regimen. Although the block method seems easier, it may let the writer ramble vaguely about each subject without concentrating on specific points of comparison or contrast. The resulting essay may resemble two separate discussions that could be cut apart with scissors. Imagine how much verve Goodman's essay would have lost had she looked first at the health food culture and then the gourmet culture. The dramatic speed of her delivery—"vintage wine versus fresh carrot juice"—would have been lost in the block method, and the *real* point of her essay (that the regimens share "a rebellion against easy eating" would have been buried in a conclusion following the two blocks of discussion of the different eating habits. Whenever it seems reasonable, use the point-by-point method to arrange your comparison and contrast material.

Ellen Goodman's essay is arranged *inductively;* that is, her thesis is "discovered" by the reader in the middle of her essay. If you place your thesis at the beginning of your essay—and many instructors in freshman composition courses prefer that you do—it may be important to forecast the way or ways in which the subjects compare or contrast. But remember that a weak thesis is worse than no thesis. For example, a weak thesis for the study of conflicts in the lives of women and men might be "Although women and men have different problems, they also share a social concern." Such a thesis is weak because it doesn't say anything specific. Furthermore, it doesn't help the writer focus on the basis for the study, and focus for the writer (as well as the reader) is one function of the thesis.

Writers do not always announce their intention to compare and contrast in their thesis, even though comparison and contrast elements predominate in the development of their thinking and writing. Consider the essay below, which James Seilsopour wrote when he was a student at Riverside City College in Riverside, California, in 1984.

Student Example: Comparison and Contrast Essay

I Forgot the Words to the National Anthem

James Seilsopour

The bumper sticker read, "Piss on Iran."

To me, a fourteen-year-old living in Teheran, the Iranian revolution was nothing more than an inconvenience. Although the riots were just around the corner, although the tanks lined the streets, although a stray bullet went through my sister's bedroom window, I was upset because I could not ride at the Royal Stable as often as I used to. In the summer of 1979 my family--father, mother, brothers, sister, aunt, and two cousins--were forced into exile. We came to Norco, California.

In Iran, I was an American citizen and considered myself an American, even though my father was Iranian. I loved baseball and apple pie and knew the words to the "Star-Spangled Banner." That summer before high school, I was like any other kid my age; I listened to rock'n'roll, liked fast cars, and thought Farrah Fawcett was a fox. Excited about going to high school, I was looking forward to football games and school dances. But I learned that it was not meant to be. I was not like other kids, and it was a long, painful road I traveled as I found this out.

The American embassy in Iran was seized the fall I started high school. I did not realize my life would be affected until I read that bumper sticker in the high school parking lot which read, "Piss on Iran." At that moment I knew there would be no football games or school dances. For me, Norco High consisted of the goat ropers, the dopers, the jocks, the brains, and one quiet Iranian.

I was sitting in my photography class after the hostages were taken. The photography teacher was fond of showing travel films. On this particular day, he decided to show a film about Iran, knowing full well that my father was Iranian and that I grew up in Iran. During the movie, this teacher encouraged the students to make comments. Around the room, I could hear "Drop the bomb" and "Deport the mothers." Those words hurt. I felt dirty, guilty. However, I managed to laugh and assure the students I realized they were just joking. I went home that afternoon and cried. I have long since forgiven those students, but I have not and can never forgive that teacher. Paranoia set in. From then on, every whisper was about me: "You see that lousy son of a bitch? He's Iranian." When I was not looking, I could feel their pointing fingers in my back like arrows. Because I was absent one day, the next day I brought a note to the attendance office. The secretary read the note, then looked at me. "So you're Jim Seilsopour?" I couldn't answer. As I walked away, I thought I heard her whisper to her co-worker, "You see that lousy son of a bitch? He's Iranian." I missed thirty-five days of school that year.

My problems were small compared to those of my parents. In Teheran, my mother had been a lady of society. We had a palatial house and a maid. Belonging to the women's club, she collected clothes for the poor and arranged Christmas parties for the young American kids'. She and my father dined with high government officials. But back in the States, when my father could not find a job, she had to work at a fast-food restaurant. She was the proverbial pillar of strength. My mother worked seventy hours a week for two years. I never heard her complain. I could see the toll the entire situation was taking on her. One day my mother and I went grocery shopping at Stater Brothers Market. After an hour of carefully picking our food, we proceeded to the cashier. The cashier was friendly and began a conversation with my mother. They spoke briefly of the weather as my mother wrote the check. The cashier looked at the check and casually asked, "What kind of name is that?" My mother said, "Italian." We exchanged glances for just a second. I could see the pain in her eyes. She offered no excuses; I asked for none.

Because of my father's birthplace, he was unable to obtain a job. A naturalized American citizen with a master's degree in aircraft maintenance engineering from the Northrop Institute of Technology, he had never been out of work in his life. My father had worked for Bell Helicopter International, Flying Tigers, and McDonnell Douglas. Suddenly, a man who literally was at the top of his field was unemployable. There is one incident that haunts me even today. My mother had gone to work, and all the kids had gone to school except me. I was in the bathroom washing my face. The door was open, and I could see my father's reflection in the mirror. For no particular reason I watched him. He was glancing at a newspaper. He carefully folded the paper and set it aside. For several long moments he stared blankly into space. With a resigned sigh, he got up, went into the kitchen, and began doing the dishes. On that day, I know I watched a part of my father die.

My father did get a job. However, he was forced to leave the country. He is a quality control inspector for Saudi Arabian Airlines in Jeddah, Saudi Arabia. My mother works only forty hours a week now. My family has survived, financially and emotionally. I am not bitter, but the memories are. I have not recovered totally; I can never do that.

And no, I have never been to a high school football game or dance. The strike really turned me off to baseball. I have been on a diet for the last year, so I don't eat apple pie much anymore. And I have forgotten the words to the national anthem.

Discussing a Student's Comparison and Contrast Strategy

Seilsopour's intention is to contrast his expectations as a teenager with a reality imposed by political events. He develops his contrast by showing his home life in Iran, and his feelings about America at that time, with his family's way of life and his feelings about America after the family moved to the United States.

Seilsopour makes it clear that when he lived in Iran he was not only an American citizen, but he had "typical" traits of an American teenager. He knew the words to the "Star-Spangled Banner"; he loved baseball, apple pie, rock music, fast cars, and Farrah Fawcett. He states that he anticipated starting high school and going to football games and dances. He also suggests atypical aspects of his life in Iran when he alludes to riding horses at "the Royal Stable," an activity curtailed by the revolution in Iran, which otherwise had little impact on his life.

Seilsopour's move to the United States occurred shortly before the American embassy in Teheran was seized and hostages were taken. Seilsopour notes that seeing the bumper sticker—"Piss on Iran"—and feeling victimized by an insensitive high school teacher were the turning points in his perception of his life. He says, "I knew there would be no football games or school dances." The reality of his life at Norco High became isolation, paranoia, and absence from school—points that he develops as contrasts with his earlier anticipation.

Seilsopour also contrasts his family's past in Iran with their reality in the United States. His family had lived in a "palatial house," had a maid, and his parents had associated with "high government officials." His mother may have been a typical woman of leisure, enjoying women's club activities and doing charity work. Because of anti-

Iranian feelings, after Seilsopour's family moved to the United States, his Iranian father was unemployable in the defense industries where he had previously held good jobs. His mother supported the family by working 70 hours a week in a fast-food restaurant. The contrast between her former way of life and her life in the United States is *shown* rather than stated. Similarly, the contrast between his father's former high political status and his reduced self-esteem in the United States is *shown* rather than overtly summarized.

Seilsopour brings closure to his personal story by acknowledging his bitter memories and by specifically citing his former anticipations that were never met: "I have never been to a high school football game or dance." He notes that he has been "turned . . . off to baseball," and because of a diet he does not "eat apple pie much anymore." His conclusion pointedly sums up his attitude about being an American citizen whose youthful aspirations were crushed by political exigencies and adult insensitivity: "I have forgotten the words to the national anthem." Each point in his former catalog of preferences for American things is countered by his specific concluding denials.

Seilsopour's unstated thesis might have been something like this: "My expectations for being a typical American high school student were thwarted by the reality I met at Norco High." But Seilsopour's essay is much more dramatic and compelling because his essay *lacks* this obvious comparison–contrast set up. Notice that even though Seilsopour does not announce his intention of contrasting "expectations" with "reality," each of the points in his study is deliberately and specifically contrasted.

■ PRACTICING WRITING ESSAYS THAT USE COMPARISON AND CONTRAST

Select one topic below to write an essay that compares or contrasts:

1. A family member's response to an important decision with how you expected that person to respond

2. A perception of a family member that you held in your youth with a view of that person that you have today

3. Your understanding or interpretation of a particular movie, song, or event with a friend's view

4. Your concept of ideal employment with a job you have held or hold now

5. Brigid Brophy's understanding of the social climate that influences women (p. 94) with Naomi Wolf's view (p. 101)

6. Carol Tavris' analysis of how people in groups behave (p. 267) with what happens in "The Lottery" (p. 283)

Readings in Part I That Use Comparison and Contrast

The works in this text that use comparison and/or contrast strategies for development include the following:

Final Tips for Comparison and Contrast

- Make sure that your thesis includes both subjects that are being compared and contrasted, and that the wording is specific. *Avoid a thesis that simply claims they are both alike and different.*
- Consider using the *point-by-point* method of comparison–contrast for a more emphatic delivery of information.
- Continue *interrelating* the two subjects so that you never make a point about one without showing how it relates to the other.
- Search for *subtle links and distinctions* as well as for the obvious ones. Then analyze the *reasons* for those differences.

ARGUMENT

Convincing others that your beliefs and perspectives are worth understanding, and perhaps even supporting, can be a definite challenge.
Sometimes one must counter both preconceptions and convictions in
order to get readers to modify their beliefs or change their behavior.
In fact, persuasion is a part of many writing situations, and to convince a reader that a certain assertion or opinion is supportable is the
heart of argument.

Arguments and Proposals

A distinction can be made between two types of writing that attempt
to convince readers to reconsider their views and beliefs:

An *argument* employs logic to *reason* a point and get the reader to
   think

A *proposal* employs logic to *influence* others and get the reader to
   think and act

Although these types of writing often overlap, some assignments
seem to fit more in one category than the other. If you are asked to
analyze an essay and argue for or against the writer's views, your
essay will involve *argumentation*. You will be expected to focus on a
thesis that can provoke the reader's thoughts and to use supporting
evidence that is logically presented and carefully analyzed.

If you are asked to offer a solution to a problem or to persuade
others to modify or change their behavior, your essay will need to
include a *proposal* in addition to argumentation. You will be expected to focus on a thesis that provokes a response. Therefore you will
also need to suggest a reasonable plan of action or activities for your
reader.

Presenting a logical argument or proposal does not exclude appealing to your reader's emotions. For example, an essay may propose
that the school district establish more bilingual education programs
to help Hispanic students become assimilated into American culture.
To appeal to readers emotionally, a Hispanic writer may decide to
begin by illustrating the isolation she felt when she was enrolled in an
English-speaking kindergarten but spoke no English. Another writer
may start with research that demonstrates how bright Hispanic students are failing and dropping out before they finish high school.
Both introductions would be designed to arouse an emotional
response, yet both would need to be supported by logical evidence
and analysis.

When and How to Use Argument

Argument strategies may be used in all types of essays. Whenever you are attempting to convince a reader that one course of action is superior to another (comparison–contrast), that a particular behavior caused a certain consequence (cause and effect), or that one interpretation of a reading has validity (analysis), you will need to employ argument strategies. Because you are attempting to convince readers of a view that may be different from their own, it often helps to begin by illustrating what is wrong with the current thinking or practice on this issue.

For example, if a writer is arguing that female students in the early grades need greater encouragement to succeed in math and science classes, then it would make sense to establish the need first. The introduction and part of the body of the essay might demonstrate how females are discouraged from pursuing math and science majors and how few women today excel in these fields, even though studies indicate females are no less capable of succeeding in science and math than males are.

Audience and Argument

It is critical to identify one's *audience* and to find an approach that would best appeal to them. Identification of the audience may include asking these questions:

- Is the reader aware that the problem exists?
- Will the reader find the problem sufficiently important?
- Is the reader affected by the problem?
- Do any readers have special interests or biases that will cause them to resist the information? The proposal? The essay?

If you are arguing for increased bilingual education programs, you may design your paper differently if your audience is predominantly Hispanic or Anglo, or if it is predominantly educators or parents. If the writer can determine whether the audience is likely to be sympathetic, neutral, or hostile, the approach can then be designed with this in mind.

Organizing an Argument

In order to keep the argument focused and organized, an *outline* can be critical. Often this involves an informal list of points, written in a logical order, that the writer plans to cover. The outline functions as a map to keep the writer on track. It may also help your instructor to follow the argument and to detect any flaws or gaps before the essay is actually written. In such cases, a more formal outline may be required. (For an illustration of an informal outline for an argument, see pp. 334–337.)

Avoiding Logical Fallacies

Just as the argument must be presented in logical order, the thinking and analysis must be logical, too. Name-calling and personal attacks only weaken an argument because they suggest that the writer is desperate and has no other support or logical reasoning to defend the argument. Moreover, such devices are *logical fallacies,* having no basis or foundation in reason. These tactics discredit the argument and erode the readers' trust.

Illogical claims, whether intentional or not, are often associated with advertisers and politicians, whose careers may depend on their power to manipulate and mislead the public. Calling someone a "liberal" or a "redneck" is intended to get the audience to respond emotionally to a prejudice rather than to think rationally about an issue. Often these attacks are designed to divert attention from the issue to the opponent's personal traits or associates, in order to cast doubt on his character or expertise.

Besides smearing or ridiculing the opponent, the following logical fallacies may involve manipulating the argument itself:

A *circular argument* does not prove anything because it simply restates the assertion ("Instructors who teach writing are better teachers because good instructors teach writing").

An *either/or* argument sets up a false black-and-white dilemma, assuming that a particular viewpoint or course of action can only have two diametrically opposed outcomes ("College professors either require writing assignments or they are poor teachers").

A *hasty generalization* consists of drawing a broad conclusion from a few unrepresentative generalizations ("Math teachers use Scantron tests; math teachers don't teach students to think critically").

A *false analogy* compares two things that aren't really comparable and therefore results in a false conclusion ("If developmental math classes can be taught effectively in a large lecture hall, developmental English classes can be, too").

A *bandwagon* appeal suggests that "everyone is doing this—why don't you?" This pressures the reader to conform whether or not the view or action seems logical or right ("All good teachers are dividing students into small-group workshops in their classes today").

These are only some of the many logical fallacies that can weaken an argument. Instead of relying on illogical attacks and charges, writers must seek logical support for their positions and seek legitimate flaws in their opponent's argument.

Conceding and Refuting

Rather than twisting facts or attacking the person, it is best to anticipate the opponent's objections and refute them, logically and directly, before the reader can even utter "But . . . " Overlooking or ignoring potential holes in an argument can render your argument vulnerable to attack. It doesn't necessarily weaken your argument to recognize what may appear to be a weakness in your plan, provided you can refute it and show that it doesn't really undermine your argument.

Another effective strategy is to acknowledge conflicting viewpoints and perhaps even admit they have merit, but then show how your solution or viewpoint is still superior. Such a strategy suggests that you are informed, open-minded, and reasonable—qualities that will make the reader more receptive to your argument.

Evaluating an Argument

Arguments and proposals written by students can be more than mere classroom exercises. They can be sent to newspapers, television stations, corporations, and government boards. Several of the argument assignments in the "Writing from the Text" and "Connecting with Other Texts" sections of the reader involve college-related issues and may be appropriate for the editorial or opinion page of your campus or local newspaper.

The following proposal was written by Joe Goodwin, a high school student, and printed in the "Campus Correspondence" section of the *Los Angeles Times* on August 9, 1992. As you read his argument, consider these questions in order to evaluate its effectiveness:

- Who is the targeted audience, and how does the writer appeal to this audience?
- What is the problem? What is the thesis?
- What are the supporting points?
- What are the strengths of the argument?
- What are the weaknesses? Are there any logical fallacies?
- How does the ending bring satisfying closure to the essay?

Student Example: An Argument Essay

My Favorite School Class: Involuntary Servitude

Joe Goodwin

Like most teen-agers, I hate to be told what to do. I chafe at curfews, refuse to patronize restaurants that tell me what to wear, and complain daily about the braces my parents and dentist want me to have.

Yet, I look forward to the "forced opportunity" for community service my high school requires. While criticism mounts against Maryland's action in becoming the first state to mandate students to perform 75 hours of community service over seven years, it is well to look at the experience of local school districts that have instituted similar programs.

For five years, every student at the Concord-Carlisle Regional High School in Massachusetts has been required to perform 40 hours of community service in order to graduate. Conventional wisdom would have us believe that this would be an especially burdensome task, perhaps an impossible one, for students who hold outside paying jobs. But the graduation requirement may be satisfied within the school by working as teacher's aides, library assistants or tutors. Outside school, the requirement may be met by working at hospitals, nursing homes, senior citizens' centers, soup kitchens or for the town's park service or recreational department.

To be sure, it would be wonderful if students volunteered such service. But the great benefit of the mandated program is the responsibility it places on the school to work with community leaders to locate the places where students can best make a solid contribution. It is unrealistic to expect students to roam from place to place in search of service opportunities. Once the arrangements for those opportunities are made, the student needs only to decide which kind of service best fits his or her personality.

Those who oppose the community-service mandate fear it will interfere with the regular school curriculum. But what more important class can a student take than one that teaches values and responsibility? Is it better to require students to listen to long lectures about the plight of the elderly and homeless, or to have them provide hours of warmth merely by reading the newspaper to a senior citizen?

Some say that schools should not be in the business of fostering civic concerns among its youth. But what more important role can a school play than in shaping values—respect for the elderly, patience for those younger, compassion for those less fortunate—among its young? These and related values used to be taught in the home. Now, they must be learned elsewhere, since we live in a world in which many families have two parents working long hours every day and many more have just a single parent.

There has been much talk about the decline of American society, about the disintegration of the American family. Yet, when those who find pleasure in lecturing about this decline are faced with a solution that would help strengthen society, they fall back on the past. It is this negative attitude toward change that has caused the country to reach the point of such neglect.

Today, the passion and commitment that marked my parents' generation—the 1960's—is gone, replaced by an ominous silence. I listen to my parents talk of their experiences with the civil-rights movement, the sit-ins, the war on poverty, and I am impatient for the time when my own generation is similarly involved in the great public events of our day. Though 40 hours of community service is not very much, it is a beginning.

My interest in community service was heightened last spring. While on a class trip to the Science Museum in Boston, a group of students in my 8th-grade class were involved in an altercation with another group of students from a largely black school in Roxbury, a neighborhood near downtown. Taunts were exchanged, a fight broke out. It was unsettling.

The following week, teachers from both schools arranged a daylong meeting of a representative sampling of students at each school. The discussion that resulted was an extraordinary experience. As I listened to black students describe their stereotypes of whites in the suburbs, as I heard one black girl say she cried herself to sleep the night of the fight in fear and frustration that racial relations would never improve, I realized how far America was from the ideals of equality and justice. If community service could help to bridge the gap between ideal and reality, I will feel happy indeed.

Analyzing Argument Strategy

Even as Goodwin begins his essay, he seems to be anticipating a possible objection against mandating community service for high school students. He admits that he, like most teenagers, "hate[s] to be told what to do," yet this is one "forced opportunity" that he supports. Then, one by one, he raises and refutes certain objections:

- Doing community service is a burden for students who hold outside paying jobs. (Students can choose to work on-campus or off.)

- Students should volunteer for such service. (He concedes that they should volunteer, but feels it is unrealistic to expect students to search for such opportunities on their own.)

- Community service will interfere with regular curriculum. (He feels community service is as important as any class, and that it teaches students to apply what they are learning in the classroom.)

- Schools should not be in the business of fostering civic concerns among students. (He argues that schools must help shape values, especially since many children are not getting such training at home.)

After anticipating and countering these objections, Goodwin notes that many critics relish *lecturing* about the decline of American society and the disintegration of the family but are not willing to implement the necessary changes. He contrasts their reluctance with the passion and commitment that characterized his parents' generation during the 1960s, and he asks for opportunities for his generation to become more involved and concerned.

Throughout his essay, Goodwin's tone is restrained and reasonable. His writing reflects a healthy balance between idealism (free choice) and realism (mandatory service). He might have been tempted to resort to name-calling or offensive attacks, but instead he relies on facts and evidence to support his case. Finally, he ends his argument with a brief narrative to remind us of the need to merge the realms of the inner city and the suburbs. He acknowledges that his proposal is only a beginning but suggests that it is long overdue.

■ PRACTICING WRITING ARGUMENT ESSAYS

Write an essay to convince your reader of one of the following assertions:

1. All college students, regardless of age, ethnicity, or status, are (or are not) caught "between worlds"

2. Graffiti taggers should (or should not) be prosecuted for leaving their marks around the community

3. Year-round school is (or is not) a viable solution to overcrowding

4. The lyrics in contemporary music reflect (or incite) societal tension

5. Robert Moog (p. 261) is correct (or incorrect) in his position that "buying American" ultimately hurts American industry

6. Ward Churchill (p. 167) is (or is not) correct that using Native American names for sport teams is a crime against the humanity of Native Americans

7. Date rape (p. 112) is (or is not) a significant problem that warrants an education program on your campus

8. The work week and vacation allowances for Americans should (or should not) emulate the European pattern (p. 253)

Readings in Part I That Use Argument

Essays in this text that are primarily argumentative in their intention include the following:

"The Only Child," p. 22
"Ignorance Is Not Bliss," p. 25
"The Appeal of the Androgynous Man," p. 71

Final Tips for Argument

- Recognize your purpose (argument or proposal).
- Identify your audience, consider their perspective, and prepare your appeal. Avoid insulting or attacking them.
- Word your thesis carefully to provoke thought or action.
- Outline your argument so it is focused and organized.
- Support all claims with convincing evidence and reasoned analysis.
- Anticipate objections and differing viewpoints, and show why your argument is stronger even if the others have some merit.
- Guard against logical fallacies; they weaken any argument.
- Make sure your conclusion brings satisfying closure to your argument. Avoid tacking on any new points.

ANALYSIS: PROCESS, PROBLEM, SUBJECT

When you analyze anything—a film, an instructor's performance, an experiment in a chemistry lab, or even your roommate's mysterious casserole—you are taking the whole apart to examine its components. This, in turn, lets you understand how the parts contribute to the entire work. The purpose of an analysis is not merely to take the process, problem, or subject apart, but to see the value of the individual parts and to appreciate their interaction in creating the whole.

When to Use Analysis

You analyze constantly, perhaps without knowing you are going through any formal steps. For example, if you are giving a party, you may have an unconscious order or process. You will wait to hear who is coming before you shop for food, clean before you decorate, and stock the coolers before your friends arrive. The order of these steps is important. Further, you know that each individual step is important to achieving a successful whole—a great party—and that if any step is neglected (like no ice for the cooler), the party may flop.

Written analysis involves the same attention to order and details, regardless of the academic field. In fact, you will find that written analysis is assigned in every academic discipline. Whether you are dissecting a frog in biology, interpreting a painting in art history, examining a poem in English, reviewing curriculum in education, exploring a management problem in business, or studying a discrimination problem in law, you will be expected to write analytical papers.

These papers will be specifically targeted to the subject you are studying, but three basic types of analytical assignments predominate: analysis of a process, a problem, or a subject. Sometimes these distinctions blur, depending on the writer's purpose and audience. For example, you might write a set of directions about how to dissect a frog, describe how frogs are usually dissected, or write about the problems that students have in biology courses. All of these papers involve breaking the whole into parts and examining the parts to show a reader their importance to the whole.

Analysis of a Process

A paper that examines a process explains how to do something or how the process itself is done: for example, perform a swimming pool rescue, get a classmate to ask you out, train for a marathon, cook in a wok, avoid loaning your favorite jacket, tune up a 1957 Chevy, pay car insurance while earning minimum wage, or get a roommate's friend to move out.

Brainstorming for a Topic

If a topic has not been assigned, brainstorm for possibilities. Consider what you know how to do that others don't (such as how to make a perfect quiche) or what you would like to learn in order to explain that process to a reader (such as how to create a bonsai arrangement). Don't overlook the unusual: how to wallpaper the inside of your car, how to chart a cross-country flight for the least amount of money, or how to get your little brother to do your chores. You might also want to research how other people do things: how communities implement recycling projects, how bills are passed in Congress, how a new course becomes part of your college's curriculum, or how marketing firms predict consumers' willingness to try new products. Remember that a process analysis paper doesn't need to be dull or tedious. These papers can be lively if you use ingenuity and a little prewriting energy.

How to Write a Process Analysis

If you are writing a paper that tells your reader how to do something, or one that describes how something happens, these tips will help:

1. Determine whether or not the chronology is important. For some processes the sequence of the steps is critical (performing a swimming pool rescue), while for others it isn't as important (getting a classmate to ask you out).

2. If the chronology is important, list the steps and reexamine your list to make sure any reader can follow the logic of your arrangement.

3. Write each step completely, including all of the necessary information and removing confusing or irrelevant details. Imagine yourself in your readers' position, trying to follow your instructions for something they have never done.

4. Write a thesis that clearly asserts your point:

   Thesis: Creating bonsai arrangements is satisfying and lucrative.

   Thesis: Following the proper sequence of steps will facilitate a swimming pool rescue.

5. Draft your essay by linking each step with appropriate transitions to move your reader smoothly through this process.

6. Rewrite and edit your essay so that the language is vivid and the directions are precise.

■ PRACTICING THE STEPS OF A PROCESS

In small groups, write down the steps explaining how to do the following:

1. Find summer employment
2. Balance a diet to achieve good nutrition
3. Prepare a 3-year-old for a romp in the snow
4. Stay awake in a dull lecture
5. Convince an unwilling landlord to make a repair
6. Use library computers to find a book or an article on immigrants seeking political asylum

Spend time reaching accord within your group to ensure that all steps follow logically and that no necessary steps are left out. Aim for clarity and precision; remove words that obscure your directions. Any one of these analyses could be drafted into a collaborative paper.

Throughout this textbook you will notice a number of sections that explain various processes like how to conduct an interview; how to cluster, list, and read actively; how to incorporate quoted material; and how to write a thesis or an outline. These sections of this textbook may be useful to you as models of process analysis, and they also underscore how important process is to teaching and learning.

■ PRACTICING DESCRIBING A PROCESS

Select and describe a process that you know well from the list below:

1. How social cliques form
2. How a camera or videocamera works
3. How a college orients its freshmen
4. How glaciers form
5. How Olympic teams are created
6. How a batik is made
7. How pool, backgammon, or your favorite game or sport is played
8. How a music piece is practiced for performance

Write your description as precisely as you can so that a reader can learn the process. Does your interest in the topic show in your description?

Example: Process Analysis Essay

In the following essay, Walter Gajewski, Instructional Lab Coordinator of Academic Computing Services at California State University, Long

Beach, describes the process of using electronic mail (or "e-mail," as it is popularly termed).

E PLURIBUS E-MAIL
Walter Gajewski

Communicating with colleagues worldwide is no longer the exclusive tool of the "mad hacker." Students and faculty at many colleges now have access to e-mail—electronic mail—which combines the capabilities of the computer with those of the telephone line. Text, sound, and video movies can be transmitted, by way of phone lines, from one computer address to another.

To contact colleagues at distant locations, you must either subscribe to a commercial service such as Compuserve, Genie, America Online, MCI Mail or Prodigy, or you need to have an account on a mainframe computer that is connected to the Internet. The Internet is a complex, worldwide network of thousands of computers that are accessible to university professors, government researchers, the military—and you, if your school has access to the Internet. Over the Internet, talk is cheap. No matter how many messages you send or how far you send them, your college or university does not pay anything beyond the fixed amount required to maintain its own portion of the Internet.

When you use e-mail, you need to have a specific account name which is your e-mail "address." Before you can log on to your computer account, the computer will ask you to enter your secret password. (No one else should know or needs to know this password to send you mail.) Next, call up the mail utility software and wait to be asked for the "address" of the person or persons you are contacting. This could be one address or it could be a word (an "alias") that represents a mailing list of thousands of addresses that you compiled ahead of time. After you enter the address, the computer will request the subject of your communication, followed by the body of your message. This message may be any length.

When you are finished, you simply give the command that indicates you are done. (This command varies depending on your software package.) The computer will ask if you want to send copies to anyone else. The computer then sends off your message. In a matter of seconds, your mail arrives at its destination anywhere in the world.

As important as speed is the fact that documents traveling directly from computer to computer remain as computer files rather than as a fixed printed page. Therefore, this document can be immediately edited without needing to be retyped into the computer. The ease and versatility of this process has made e-mail very popular today. But the possibilities for e-mail are just emerging. If you are interested in the future of interpersonal communication, make sure you check in the mail—the e-mail, that is.   :-)

Small-Group Discussion

In small groups, discuss Gajewski's strategy:

1. How does Gajewski attract the reader to his subject? Who is his intended audience?
2. Why does Gajewski incorporate definition in this analysis?
3. What is the process described? In what ways is chronology important to this analysis?
4. Cite specific details that Gajewski includes to encourage the reader to consider using e-mail.
5. If you are computer literate, can you follow the description of this process to use e-mail? Are there any steps that need to be expanded or removed?

Final Tips for Analyzing a Process

- Review the order of the steps you have written to determine that your reader can follow your instructions or description.
- Examine the details you have given to remove any confusing instructions or irrelevant details.
- Put yourself in your reader's position to see if you have defined necessary terms and provided necessary details.
- Reread your work to see if appropriate transitions link the steps or the parts of your analysis.

Analysis of a Problem

Another kind of analysis paper describes a problem; it may or may not offer a solution. The writer may trace the history of the problem, but chronology is not as vital to this type of analysis as it is in a step-by-step process analysis. What is critical in this type of analysis is that the writer establishes the problem, examines its parts, and shows how the parts are related to the problem as a whole.

When to Use Problem Analysis

More than any other single type of writing, problem analysis appears in every academic field and profession. Our daily newspapers, weekly newsmagazines, monthly periodicals, and scholarly journals all feature essays analyzing issues. The writers of the readings in this textbook analyze a variety of problems: alcoholism, drug abuse, irresponsible parenting, closeted homosexuals, living between two cultures, stereotyping, isolation of the disabled, group conformity, work patterns, and racial, ethnic, and gender discrimination. In spite of the wide range of issues, writers of problem analysis share similar strategies when they examine an issue.

How to Write Problem Analysis

Your initial job in any writing situation is to engage your readers, and nowhere is this more important than in problem analysis. Why should your readers care about stereotypes, ethnic bias, the rights of the disabled, or any other subject that doesn't directly relate to them? It is your job to create reader interest, and you can do this in a number of ways. Sometimes historical review of the problem will intrigue readers. Startling statistics or a bold anecdote should jar complacent readers out of apathy. Sometimes posing a direct question to the readers prompts them to consider their responses and become involved in the topic—at least enough to read the work. After you have engaged your readers, decide how much background information they require in order to understand the problem. For example, if you are writing an analysis of changing interest rates, you will include less background material if you are writing the paper for your business class than for your English class.

Then, as in all analysis papers, you will need to decide the parts of the problem that you want to examine. You must describe the problem so that any reader can understand it. This might include a discussion of the severity of the problem, the numbers affected by it, which population is most affected, and the consequences if this problem is uncorrected. A detailed study about each aspect of the problem and how it relates to the other parts will constitute the body of your paper. If it is relevant to your analysis, you might speculate about the barriers to solving this problem (such as cost, social bias, frustration with earlier failures, indifference, or denial).

It is important that this analysis has a focus and a clear point or assertion. For example, if you are concerned about the fact that Americans are on the job more than workers in other countries, it is not enough merely to identify the number of hours that American employees work each week. Nor is it enough to show that they work more hours per week and more weeks per year than their European counterparts, or that they are not routinely given flexible work schedules so they can coordinate their family's needs with their work responsibilities. All of these important facts could support a point, but the point must be made.

You will need to clarify, in the form of a thesis or assertion, why the analysis of these facts is important: that American workers are overworked, that Americans have insufficient leisure time, that American children grow up deprived of their parents, or any other point that you deem significant as a result of your analysis. But without a point, you have no paper.

Once you have determined your assertion, you are ready to outline, draft, and revise your paper. (See the student example of a problem analysis on eating disorders, pp. 328–363, for specific suggestions about outlining, drafting, and revising.)

Example: Problem Analysis Essay

The following analysis was written by a Harvard-educated economist, Robert L. Heilbroner, who has written extensively on economics and business. This essay, originally published in *Reader's Digest,* contains a unique perception of a common problem.

DON'T LET STEREOTYPES WARP YOUR JUDGMENTS
Robert L. Heilbroner

Is a girl called Gloria apt to be better-looking than one called Bertha? Are criminals more likely to be dark than blond? Can you tell a good deal about someone's personality from hearing his voice briefly over the phone? Can a person's nationality be pretty accurately guessed from his photograph? Does the fact that someone wears glasses imply that he is intelligent?

The answer to all these questions is obviously, "No."

Yet, from all the evidence at hand, most of us believe these things. Ask any college boy if he'd rather take his chances with a Gloria or a Bertha, or ask a college girl if she'd rather blind-date a Richard or a Cuthbert. In fact, you don't have to ask: college students in questionnaires have revealed that names conjure up the same images in their minds as they do in yours—and for as little reason.

Look into the favorite suspects of persons who report "suspicious characters" and you will find a large percentage of them to be "swarthy" or "dark and foreign-looking"—despite the testimony of criminologists that criminals do not tend to be dark, foreign or "wild-eyed." Delve into the main asset of a telephone stock swindler and you will find it to be a marvelously confidence-inspiring telephone "personality." And whereas we all think we know what an Italian or a Swede looks like, it is the sad fact that when a group of Nebraska students sought to match faces and nationalities of 15 European countries, they were scored wrong in 93 percent of their identifications. Finally, for all the fact that horn-rimmed glasses have now become the standard television sign of an "intellectual," optometrists know that the main thing that distinguishes people with glasses is just bad eyes.

Stereotypes are a kind of gossip about the world, a gossip that makes us pre-judge people before we ever lay eyes on them. Hence it is not surprising that stereotypes have something to do with the dark world of prejudice. Explore most prejudices (note that the word means prejudgment) and you will find a cruel stereotype at the core of each one.

For it is the extraordinary fact that once we have typecast the world, we tend to see people in terms of our standardized pictures. In another demonstra-tion of the power of stereotypes to affect our vision, a number of Columbia and Barnard students were shown 30 photographs of pretty but unidentified girls, and asked to rate each in terms of "general liking," "intelligence," "beauty" and so on. Two months later, the same group were shown the same pho-tographs, this time with fictitious Irish, Italian, Jewish and "American" names attached to the pictures. Right away the ratings changed. Faces which were now seen as representing a national group went down in looks and still farther down in likability, while the "American" girls suddenly looked decidedly prettier and nicer.

Why is it that we stereotype the world in such irrational and harmful fashion? In part, we begin to type-cast people in our childhood years. Early in life, as every parent whose child has watched a TV Western knows, we learn to spot the Good Guys from the Bad Guys. Some years ago, a social psychologist showed very clearly how powerful these stereotypes of childhood vision are. He secretly asked the most popular youngsters in an elementary school to make errors in their morning gym exercises. Afterwards, he asked the class if anyone had noticed any mistakes during gym period. Oh, yes, said the children. But it was the unpopular members of the class—the "bad guys"—they remembered as being out of step.

We not only grow up with standardized pictures forming inside of us, but as grown-ups we are constantly having them thrust upon us. Some of them, like the half-joking, half-serious stereotypes of mothers-in-law, or country yokels, or psychiatrists, are dinned into us by the stock jokes we hear and repeat. In fact, without such stereotypes, there would be a lot fewer jokes. Still other stereo-types are perpetuated by the advertisements we read, the movies we see, the books we read.

And finally, we tend to stereotype because it helps us make sense out of a highly confusing world, a world which William James once described as "one great, blooming, buzzing confusion." It is a curious fact that if we don't know what we're looking at, we are often quite literally unable to see what we're look-ing at. People who recover their sight after a lifetime of blindness actually can-not at first tell a triangle from a square. A visitor to a factory sees only noisy chaos where the superintendent sees a perfectly synchronized flow of work. As Walter Lippmann has said, "For the most part we do not first see, and then define; we define first, and then we see."

Stereotypes are one way in which we "define" the world in order to see it. They classify the infinite variety of human beings into a convenient handful of "types" towards whom we learn to act in stereotyped fashion. Life would be a wearing process if we had to start from scratch with each and every human contact. Stereotypes economize on our mental effort by covering up the blooming, buzzing confusion with big recognizable cut-outs. They save us the "trouble" of finding out what the world is like—they give it its accustomed look.

Thus the trouble is that stereotypes make us mentally lazy. As S. I. Hayakawa, the authority on semantics, has written: "The danger of stereotypes lies not in their existence, but in the fact that they become for all people some of the time, and for some people all the time, substitutes for observation." Worse yet, stereotypes get in the way of our judgment, even when we do observe the world. Someone who has formed rigid preconceptions of all Latins as "excitable," or all teenagers as "wild," doesn't alter his point of view when he meets a calm and deliberate Genoese, or a serious-minded high school student. He brushes them aside as "exceptions that prove the rule." And, of course, if he meets someone true to type, he stands triumphantly vindicated. "They're all like that," he proclaims, having encountered an excited Latin, an ill-behaved adolescent.

Hence, quite aside from the injustice which stereotypes do to others, they impoverish ourselves. A person who lumps the world into simple categories, who type-casts all labor leaders as "racketeers," all businessmen as "reactionaries," all Harvard men as "snobs," and all Frenchmen as "sexy," is in danger of becoming a stereotype himself. He loses his capacity to be himself—which is to say, to see the world in his own absolutely unique, inimitable and independent fashion.

Instead, he votes for the man who fits his standardized picture of what a candidate "should" look like or sound like, buys the goods that someone in his "situation" in life "should" own, lives the life that others define for him. The mark of the stereotyped person is that he never surprises us, that we do indeed have him "typed." And no one fits this strait-jacket so perfectly as someone whose opinions about other people are fixed and inflexible.

Impoverishing as they are, stereotypes are not easy to get rid of. The world we type-cast may be no better than a Grade B movie, but at least we know what to expect of our stock characters. When we let them act for themselves in the strangely unpredictable way that people do act, who knows but that many of our fondest convictions will be proved wrong?

Nor do we suddenly drop our standardized pictures for a blinding vision of the Truth. Sharp swings of ideas about people often just substitute one stereotype for another. The true process of change is a slow one that adds bits and pieces of reality to the pictures in our heads, until gradually they take on some of the blurriness of life itself. Little by little, we learn not that Jews and Negroes and Catholics and Puerto Ricans are "just like everybody else"—for that, too, is a stereotype—but that each and every one of them is unique, special, different and individual. Often we do not even know that we have let a stereotype lapse until we hear someone saying, "all so-and-so's are like such-and-such," and we hear ourselves saying, "Well—maybe."

Can we speed the process along? Of course we can.

First, we can become aware of the standardized pictures in our heads, in other peoples' heads, in the world around us.

Second, we can become suspicious of all judgments that we allow exceptions to "prove." There is no more chastening thought than that in the vast intellectual adventure of science, it takes but one tiny exception to topple a whole edifice of ideas.

Third, we can learn to be chary of generalizations about people. As F. Scott Fitzgerald once wrote: "Begin with an individual, and before you know it you have created a type; begin with a type, and you find you have created—nothing."

Most of the time, when we type-cast the world, we are not in fact generalizing about people at all. We are only revealing the embarrassing facts about the pictures that hang in the gallery of stereotypes in our own heads.

Small-Group Discussion

In small groups, discuss Heilbroner's strategy:

1. How does Heilbroner attract the reader? What is his introduction technique?

2. What does Heilbroner perceive as the *real* problem of stereotyping? Where does his assertion appear? How does Heilbroner convince a reader that stereotyping is a problem if that person has never felt victimized by stereotyping?

3. How does Heilbroner analyze the severity of the problem? According to Heilbroner's analysis of the problem, which populations are engaged in stereotyping, and how widespread is this? Evaluate the quality of his support and how he uses it.

4. Explain why Heilbroner moves into a process analysis mode to propose a solution to the problem of stereotyping.

■ PRACTICING PROBLEM ANALYSIS

Problem analysis assignments appear after many of the works in the reader. In addition to those that reflect the theme of being "between worlds," you might write an analysis of any of these problems:

1. Limited inexpensive housing available for college students

2. Policies at work or school that seem poorly conceived

3. A family's inability to communicate

4. Athletes' use of drugs

5. Unnecessary packaging of everyday products

6. Overdrinking and overeating in our society

Readings in Part I That Use Problem Analysis

Essays in this book that are examples of a problem analysis include the following:

Final Tips for Analyzing a Problem

- Engage your readers to convince them of the importance of the problem.

- Provide sufficient background information for your intended audience.

- Make sure that your thesis expresses why your analysis of the problem is important.

- Reread and revise to ascertain that you have adequately discussed the parts of the problem that require analysis, and that you have related those parts to the problem as a whole.

Analysis of a Subject

Another type of analysis paper is one that examines a subject—a painting, poem, sculpture, car, contract, course, or short story. An analysis paper may also focus on a particular aspect of the subject—the composition of a painting, an image in a poem, the proportions of a sculpture, the motor of a car, the exceptions of a contract, the requirements of a course, or a character in a short story. These papers, too, involve breaking the subject into parts and closely examining its parts to show the reader their importance to the subject as a whole.

Brainstorming for a Topic

If a topic has not been assigned, brainstorm to find a subject that interests you or for which you have some information. While it might not make sense for someone without mechanical aptitude to decide to analyze what is under the hood of a Volkswagen Jetta or for a mechanical engineering student to analyze "The Love Song of J. Alfred Prufrock," don't select a subject that is too familiar. The purpose of any writing assignment is discovery, and nothing will help you understand a subject better than careful analysis.

When to Use Subject Analysis

Instructors expect analysis when their assignments and exam questions contain words like *explain, interpret, describe, explore why, show how, explicate, discuss, relate,* or *trace.* If you have been asked to examine an art object, explain an economic plan, explicate a particular work of literature, explore why a company's health plan needs review, show how a historical treatise influenced a movement, trace a legal decision, analyze a candidate's platform, or describe a community's park system, you are required to examine the parts—or a part that has been assigned—and show how that part or those parts relate to the whole.

How to Write a Subject Analysis

Examine carefully the subject that you have selected or that has been assigned. Question the significance of the work, responding to it freshly. Don't assume that because it is a famous work of art or literature, it is therefore worthy of analysis. Determine for yourself why the subject is worth the time that you will devote to examining it.

If you have not been assigned a particular part to analyze, make a list of as many aspects or parts of the subject as you can. Then consider which parts are most significant and which you can most productively examine. In some cases, the success of your paper and how you will be evaluated will be determined by your ability to limit your selection to particularly provocative or relevant aspects. Ultimately, your job will be to show the significance of the parts or a particular part in relation to the entire work.

As introductory material, before you begin your analysis of the parts, describe the whole subject *briefly*. Remember that description is not the same thing as analysis, but realize also that your reader can't care about the parts without knowing something about the whole. Depending on the subject of your analysis, this introductory description might involve a historical context (of a treatise, bill, contract), an overall physical description (of a sculpture, painting, motor, person), or a summary (of a novel, short story, play, poem, bill, contract).

Write your minute description and detailed perception of the parts that you perceive to be the most significant for an understanding of the work. As you write an analysis of each part, keep your eye on the whole. Whether you are analyzing an art form, literary work, or object, you will need to return to your subject repeatedly to be sure that you are seeing or reading it thoroughly and carefully. You will not be able to write an analysis of a painting quickly glimpsed or a poem read only once.

Focus your paper with an assertion that shows your perception of the parts in relation to the subject that you are analyzing. Expressing your perception in the form of a thesis will keep both you and your reader on target.

When to Use Character Analysis

Because literary analysis is frequently assigned in English courses, and because narratives often are read in freshman composition classes, we include here a character analysis to demonstrate the process of analyzing a subject. Character analysis can be used to study someone you know or someone in a text—a narrative, a poem, a short story, a novel, a play, or a biography. In history, psychology, art, and education courses, you may be asked to analyze the traits of a particular person in order to understand the time period, the created work, or the behavior of important figures.

How to Write a Character Analysis

Whether you are examining a subject from life or print, you will want to observe and record telling details—those that reveal something significant about the person. As you study a character, you will accumulate lots of facts, some that you will discard as irrelevant and others that you will decide are indicative of the person's character. From these facts you will be able to make assumptions about your subject's personality and character. In fact, the heart of your analysis will depend on inference—that is, a hypothesis that you formulate about character based on the facts that you have observed.

Prewriting for a Text-Based Character Study

As you actively read the narrative or biography, list specific examples of speech, behavior, and thought that reveal the character. Read the text with an alert eye, pulling examples, important phrases, and key lines for your list. Mix facts and your responses or inferences about them as you go along. You do not need to evaluate each example as you write your list; you will sort, eliminate, and reword examples later.

Listing Information from a Book

If you are keeping notes for a biographical study and are using a full-length book, you might find it useful to keep separate index cards for each character trait that you observe while you are reading. Record the page numbers each time you see that trait reappearing. By the time that you have completed a 300- or 400-page biography, you may have 15 or 20 different "inference cards," each with a different trait written at the top and each with many recorded page numbers. The cards that have similar traits can be grouped, the traits with few page numbers can be ignored, and the traits that look most useful for a character study can then be shaped into focus points for the paper.

The page numbers on the cards that will form the focus points for the paper should be written into paraphrased and quoted note cards. These cards can then be arranged for a draft. This system of note taking, a variation of listing, is especially useful for longer texts.

Listing Information from a Short Story

If you are taking notes from a short text—a poem, play, or short story—you can use lined paper for your list. Here is how a list of character traits describing Hazel Peoples, the speaker and central character in Toni Cade Bambara's short story "My Man Bovanne" (p. 43), might look:

Plays checkers with a blind man—Shakey Bee
Dances close with a blind man—Bovanne
Talks late at night with men who call for "mama comfort"
Laughs "real loud"
Argued with Elo about wigs
Sensitive—afraid she'll cry when children indict her dancing
Wears "short" dress
Wears "low-cut" dress
Thinks she can still wear sleeveless dresses
Gets loud when she drinks (her children's complaint)
Observant—notices Task's gesture is like his father's and grand-
        father's
Notices nobody got Bovanne a sandwich or talked with him
Outspoken—"You know what you all can kiss"
Hurt—when Elo's hand "landin light," like it didn't belong on her
        shoulder
"A chub-chub" and "not very pretty"—says about herself
Plans to buy Bovanne sunglasses—responsive to her children
Plans to make dinner for the family's organizational meeting
Plans to give Bovanne a bath, herb tea, massage
Will tell Bovanne he's needed to fix mailboxes and mimeo
Sees herself as a "hussy," as Elo always says she is

Grouping and Arranging

The grouping of like ideas on the list may be the next step in the prewriting of your character analysis. Find examples that belong together—usually because they support the trait that you have inferred about the person—and rewrite your list or number the examples on your list to reflect the commonality that prompts you to place the details together. If the reason the details belong together comes to you, or you realize that the details support a character inference, write down your idea.

Here is how the grouped list of details about Hazel Peoples might look:

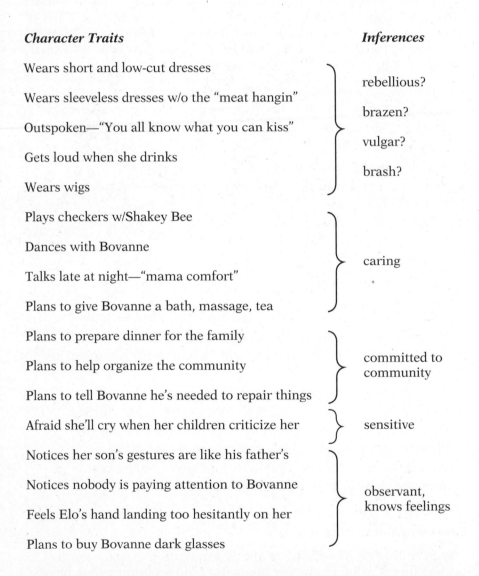

Character Traits	*Inferences*
Wears short and low-cut dresses	rebellious?
Wears sleeveless dresses w/o the "meat hangin"	brazen?
Outspoken—"You all know what you can kiss"	vulgar?
Gets loud when she drinks	brash?
Wears wigs	
Plays checkers w/Shakey Bee	
Dances with Bovanne	
Talks late at night—"mama comfort"	caring
Plans to give Bovanne a bath, massage, tea	
Plans to prepare dinner for the family	
Plans to help organize the community	committed to community
Plans to tell Bovanne he's needed to repair things	
Afraid she'll cry when her children criticize her	sensitive
Notices her son's gestures are like his father's	
Notices nobody is paying attention to Bovanne	observant, knows feelings
Feels Elo's hand landing too hesitantly on her	
Plans to buy Bovanne dark glasses	

Listing and grouping may take some time, but by listing the details of character that are important, and by grouping items on the list that are analogous, you will have done a considerable amount of preparation for your paper.

Arranging and Thesis Construction

Consider how you will arrange your character traits and the specific examples that support the traits. What do you want to emphasize in your analysis? Consider ending your character analysis with the trait that you find most significant or most indicative of character. By using your most emphatic point in the terminal spot in your paper, you will have a natural conclusion—one that gets at both the heart of your subject and the theme of the short story.

Perhaps the place to start is with the most obvious feature of the subject for analysis, because it will take less effort to convince your audience of your perception if your reader shares your perception. In the case of Hazel Peoples, her flamboyant exterior and behavior are probably the dramatic starting points for the analysis.

Determining a Thesis

You need to have a thesis for your character study, whether or not you include it in your paper. You can determine one by using the character traits that you perceived during grouping. Remember that your thesis expresses a view about a limited subject, such as Hazel Peoples' character. If you have many observations on your prewriting list, you know you have good support ready.

Possible Thesis Statements

Here are some possibilities for thesis statements for the character analysis of Hazel Peoples. Remember, each writer's perceptions and preferences will determine the thesis and the order in which the information will be presented.

1. Hazel Peoples appears to be a brash woman, but she is also sensitive and caring about her family and community.
2. Because Hazel Peoples is so flamboyant, it is possible to miss the sensitive, caring qualities in her character.
3. Hazel Peoples is a sensitive woman whose caring commitment to her family and community is masked by her outrageous exterior.
4. Hazel Peoples appears to be a rebellious woman, indifferent to her children and their values, but she is actually a caring, sensitive woman, committed to her family and culture.
5. Although Hazel Peoples looks like the "hussy" her daughter says she is, beneath that vulgar exterior exists a sensitive, caring woman.

Student Example: Character Analysis

As you read this character analysis, notice that in addition to a thorough examination of the separate qualities of his subject's character, Hogan returns to the essence of the entire work to bring closure to his study.

Truth Beneath the Surface

Timothy Hogan

The old expression, "You can't judge a book by its cover," definitely applies to the character of Hazel Peoples in the short story "My Man Bovanne" by Toni Cade Bambara (43). Hazel Peoples dances with the blind man Bovanne, and then is scolded by her children because they judge her dress and manner as inappropriate and lewd. She is deeply hurt by her children's attack on her character, yet she still complies with their request to take charge of a political dinner the next night. However, Hazel plans on defying their wishes by bringing Bovanne to dinner. Although her exterior traits are viewed by her children as vile, Hazel Peoples is a truly liberated, empathetic and nurturing woman.

The picture of Hazel Peoples the reader sees is not at all flattering from an external point of view. She shows herself as a slightly inebriated, older woman who dances in an inti-mate way with a blind man--not just any blind man, but Bovanne, a man described by her children as a tom who "can smell a cracker a mile away" (45). Hazel's children criticize her manner of dress and her choice to wear a wig over her cornroll, something they had originally encouraged her to do. They chastize her for dancing so closely with Bovanne. Mrs. Peoples, at first glance and without further examination of her character, appears to be overtly flirtatious and in her children's view "a bitch in heat" (45). This brazen hussy most assuredly appears to be nothing more than a sleazy slut.

But then first impressions are often misleading, and it is on deeper exploration into her character that we realize Hazel is far more liberated than her apparently liberal children. Though her children are members of the Black Power Movement for civil rights, they choose to deny their mother the very right to be herself. Hazel Peoples is not at all a hussy; she is simply a sexually liberated woman. She has men folk calling her at night, for "mama comfort" she calls it, and when they get "messy," she changes the lock on her door. Her motivation for dancing with Bovanne has little to do with sexual advance; as she says, "Wasn't bout tits. Was bout vibrations" (44). Mrs. Peoples certainly understands the necessity to fight for liberties. And she defends her actions as her right to "enjoy [herself] cause [she's] a good woman" (46). Hazel intuitively understands the essence of what it is her children are striving for, even beyond their own comprehension of liberty and rights.

Hazel has a deep, empathetic understanding of human beings and their mannerisms, an ability to see beyond the surface of a person and into the truth of a person's character. Her account of the behavior of her blind friend Shakey Bee relates this empathy: "Blind people got a hummin jones if you notice. Which is understandable completely once you been around one and notice what no eyes will force you into to see people" (44). Hazel doesn't write off Shakey Bee because he is humming and grunting low. She has the compassion to adapt to this sound and even to grow to appreciate it--"it's like you in church"--except, of course, when she's playing checkers with him and wants to win! And while others forget about the goodness of Bovanne's nature, Hazel remembers and cares about this "nice man" who used to fix things for the very people who now cast discerning looks at him. Hazel sees Bovanne not as some old, useless blind man, but as someone who is overlooked despite all of his contributions to the community. Hazel relates her deep comprehension of human need when she comments to her children about the Reverend Trent. She says, "Reverend

Trent a fool . . . the way he tore into the widow man up there on Edgecomb because he wouldn't take in three of them foster children and [his dead wife] not even comfy in the ground yet" (46). Hazel empathizes with people; she understands the need to look beyond surface impressions.

Hazel Peoples may not have the exterior qualities of the stereotypical mother, but her ability to nurture easily meets or exceeds expectation. Hazel cares; she is sensitive to the needs of people and meets needs where she can. Hazel chooses not to retaliate against her children's attacks on her. She organizes the family dinner for the political group because she realizes that others are in need of the benefits. This dinner can "get the breakfast program goin, and the school for the little kids," and she wants the older folk to know that they are still needed to "run the mimeo machine . . . and fix mailboxes" (47). Hazel's reason for asking Bovanne to dance comes out of her need to nurture, not because he is blind but because he is being overlooked and passed by. She plans on taking Bovanne home, to give him a bath and massage, and some herb tea. "Cause you gots to take care of the older folks. And let them know they still needed . . . " (47). Hazel values and understands people and their needs; she's a nurturing mother to more people than her ungrateful children.

Hazel Peoples reveals a truth that her children are unable to see: ". . . old folks is the nation." The value of a person is not measured by something as superficial as age or dress. The value of a person is measured in terms of good character, an ability to empathize and nurture. Hazel Peoples has that character.

Work Cited

Bambara, Toni Cade. "My Man Bovanne." <u>Between Worlds: A Reader, Rhetoric, and Handbook</u>. Ed. Susan Bachmann and Melinda Barth. New York: HarperCollins. 43-47.

Small-Group Discussion

In small groups, discuss the strategies Hogan employs in his character analysis. Consider these questions:

1. What is the strategy of Hogan's introductory paragraph?
2. What is the thesis of this character study?
3. How does Hogan convince you that his character inferences are sound?
4. How is each paragraph individually focused? How is each paragraph related to the essay as a whole?
5. How does Hogan give his reader both an understanding of the parts of Hazel's character and their relationship to her as a whole? How does Hogan's character analysis contribute to your understanding of the short story as a whole?

■ PRACTICING CHARACTER ANALYSIS

In small groups, select one of the following:

1. Write a list of character traits that describe Darnell, from "Proper Care and Maintenance" (p. 176). Group the details that belong together, arrange the details, and write an assertion—a thesis—that would be workable for a character analysis.
2. Write a list of character traits that describe Nancy Mairs, the author of "On Being a Cripple" (p. 203). Group the details that belong together, arrange the details, and write an assertion—a thesis—that would be workable for a character analysis.

Essay Assignments for Subject Analysis

Practice writing an analysis of one of the topics below:

1. A favorite painting or a photo from a magazine
2. The lyrics to a piece of music
3. Arnold Friend in "Where Are You Going, Where Have You Been?" (p. 124)
4. A piece of laboratory, electronic, or exercise equipment
5. The setting or music in a particular film
6. The bonsai image in "A Work of Artifice" (p. 110)
7. A controversial campus policy
8. Mrs. Ardavi in "Your Place Is Empty" (p. 28)

Readings in Part I That Use Subject Analysis

Works in this text that analyze a subject include the following:

Final Tips for Subject Analysis

- Study your subject thoroughly so that you understand how and why it is a worthwhile topic for analysis.

- Choose the most significant parts of the subject to analyze. List specific details and group qualities that belong together.

- Examine those parts in considerable detail, showing how they are both discrete and interrelated.

- Focus on an assertion that needs to be proven by analysis.

- In your introduction, *briefly* describe the whole so that your reader has some context for your study.

- Throughout your essay, stay aware of the whole as you discuss the separate parts.

WRITING AN ESSAY EXAM

An in-class essay exam will require you to retrieve information that you know and to present it in an orderly way and with sufficient development that your instructor will be convinced that you know the material. Here is a six-step strategy that will help you present information that you know:

A Six-Step Strategy

1. Read the question more than once.

2. Determine what the question specifically requires you to do. Have you been asked to *define, list, summarize, compare or contrast, explain,* or *analyze?* See the list on page 446 for definitions of words that are commonly used on essay exams.

3. Briefly outline the material that will satisfy the question you were asked. Do not spend much time on this step; the outline can be brief, with only key words or phrases to remind you of material that you need to include.

4. Write a thesis that will focus your answer and possibly forecast the areas you will develop in your response to the question.

5. Write the essay.

6. Reread your answer to correct errors in spelling and grammar. Use a dictionary if you are permitted to bring one to the exam. Do *not* plan to rewrite; you will seldom have sufficient time. If you recall material that would improve your essay, indicate that you have an insertion and write the added material on another sheet of paper.

It is most important that you understand exactly what the question requires you to do. For example, if the test question asks you to *list* the chemical elements commonly called salts, you are to enumerate—present in a list or outline form—the specific chemical elements called salts. An essay is not required, would be inappropriate, and might cost you points. If the question asks you to *compare and contrast* two subjects, and you only show how the subjects contrast, you have missed part of the question—how the subjects compare. The chart on the next page will help you understand what is expected on exams.

Key Words Used on Exams

Word Used	Meaning and Example
analyze	Break into elements or parts and examine ("Analyze the job of the Attorney General of the United States," or "Analyze Piercy's use of 'artifice' in the poem 'A Work of Artifice' ").
compare	Look for and bring out points of similarity, qualities that resemble each other ("Compare the legislative branches of the state and national governments").
contrast	Stress the dissimilarities, differences ("Contrast the roles of Jim and the Duke and Dauphin as father figures for Huck Finn").
define	Give the meaning of a word or concept ("Define the term 'archetype' ").
describe	Give an account, word picture, or narration ("Describe the Aztec civilization at Teotihuacan," or "Describe the method for providing emergency first aid to an accident victim").
discuss	Examine, and consider from different points of view ("Discuss the use of pesticides in controlling mosquitoes").
explain	Make clear, interpret, tell the meaning of, tell how ("Explain how man can, at times, trigger a rainstorm").
justify	Show good reason for, give evidence to support your position ("Justify the American bombing of Iraq").
relate	Show correlation, how things are connected ("Show the relationship of early childhood education to elementary school academic success").
summarize	Give the main points or facts in condensed form, omitting details ("Summarize the plot of *Othello*").
trace	In narrative form, describe the progress, development, or history of events ("Trace the opening of the American West through the development of wagon-train trails").

If you understand the meaning of words used in exams, you will not lose points or time by pursuing a direction that will fail to give you full credit for the information that you know.

An Outline for an In-Class Essay

Any of the practice assignments on page 448 could be posed as in-class essay exams. First we present a brief sample outline that would lead to a focused in-class essay. Try outlining answers to the practice assignments to improve your skills and as a study review of the essays that you have read.

Summarize and *discuss* the important issues raised in Ben Mattlin's "An Open Letter to Jerry Lewis" (p. 214).

1. Lewis' language is offensive
   — Stereotypes of "victims"
     ex. plight, curse, confined, bound
     ex. "dealt a bad hand" or "got in the wrong line"
     ex. needing help isn't an "indignity"
     ex. "kids" — offensive to adults!
     ex. "cripple" is in-group slang only
2. Lewis' inaccuracies are offensive, mislead, exploit
     ex. disabled kids aren't taunted by other kids
     ex. airports accommodate wheelchair passengers
     ex. life-expectancy is normal, not "if"
   — pity brings in money but depresses disabled
3. Dignity is needed, not pity
   — What is MDA really doing to help?
        employment?
   — Is MDA reducing obstacles: architectural,
        financial, attitudinal?
4. Show well-adjusted, active, normal disabled people

Each of the four areas contributes to the *summary* of Mattlin's issues. Each of the numbered points would be treated in a separate paragraph, with the key words noted in each section to become part of the specific development and exemplification in the *discussion* of Mattlin's grievances against Lewis and his telethons. Point number four would probably be an effective conclusion to the in-class essay. The thesis might forecast that *language, inaccuracies,* and *the question about what the MDA really does to help the disabled* are the central issues in Mattlin's letter to Jerry Lewis.

■ PRACTICING OUTLINING FOR IN-CLASS ESSAYS

1. Define irony and describe three specific examples of irony in Bambara's short story "My Man Bovanne" (p. 43).

2. Summarize and discuss Armin Brott's point in "Not All Men Are Sly Foxes" (p. 87).

3. Based on Auden's essay "Work, Labor and Play" (p. 249), write an essay in which you contrast his descriptions of a "laborer" and a "worker."

4. Analyze the poem "Short-order Cook" (p. 251) to show that the speaker is a worker by Auden's definition.

10

Writing the Research Paper

■ ■ ■

Assigned by most freshman composition instructors and loved by few freshman composition students, the research paper has a worse reputation than it deserves. Like most tasks that at first seem overwhelming—packing the car to go away to school, or preparing for a party—the research paper needs time and organization. The steps suggested here, and the model of a student paper in this section, should help you handle the project.

PLANNING THE RESEARCH PAPER

Time Schedule for the Research Paper

Even if you had outstanding luck in high school and welded a research paper together in an amazing overnight session, your college professor probably won't be forgiving of the "solder drips" of hasty welding, and you may find your course grade threatened by a poorly prepared research paper. Instead, admit to yourself that the research paper requires your attention through a number of steps, all of which you can handle.

Further, the paper may allow you to experience the pleasure of discovering some new interest and information. If your instructor gives you some choice in your topic, take advantage of this opportunity to find out more about something that you really *do* want to learn more about. Instead of selecting a topic that is familiar or seems easy, pursue one that intrigues you, one that is worth the time and energy that you will devote to the investigation.

Some instructors assign due dates for the various stages of the paper. If yours does not, try dividing the time between the assigned date and the due date into four approximately equal parts. For example, if you have two months for the preparation of this paper, each stage will have two weeks. If you have one month, you can give each stage a week of your time.

STAGE 1

—*Determine the topic* that interests you and satisfies the paper assigned. Allow a few days for this, but do not let yourself postpone that first decision for longer than a few days.

—Go to the library and begin your search for materials. Use the computers and *meet the reference room librarian*—the researcher's best friend. Ask the librarian if your topic has additional subject headings that you should be aware of so that you can do a *complete* search while you are in the library. Make bibliography note cards for each source. (See the model note cards on p. 453.)

STAGE 2

—*Read and take notes* on the material that you have found. If you take notes in the library on material that you do not intend to photocopy and take home with you, write direct quotations and paraphrase these later, when you know how much material you want to use. Keep accurate records of titles, authors, and page numbers so that you do not need to return to the sources to find information that you need for correct documentation. (This step will be discussed more completely on pp. 452–453.) As you take notes, think about how you might focus your paper.

STAGE 3

—*Determine a working thesis* and write an outline for the paper.

—*Write a draft* of your paper and meet with your instructor or writing center staff for feedback before you begin the revision.

—*Revise* your manuscript, strengthening the thesis, improving the arrangement, using more emphatic support, improving word choice and transitions, and clarifying any writing that your reader found ambiguous or weak.

STAGE 4

—*Type* your paper, the works-cited page, and, if your instructor prefers one, a cover sheet with the title and your name, section, professor's name, and date. (See the MLA model on pp. 460–478.)

—*Proofread your manuscript* from cover page through the works-cited page. Neatly correct *all* typing and other errors that you discover. If you have a major correction—for example, an entire sentence omitted when you typed from your draft—you may need to retype the page or edit on your computer.

If you divide the research paper assignment into parts, you will not be overwhelmed by the task. You may discover that the time allotted for a certain stage is not realistic for you. For example, you may realize that you need longer to draft and revise your paper and less time for stage 4; this may be true if you are working on a word processor. But think how comfortable you will be if you still have 25 percent of your time for that final preparation of your manuscript.

GATHERING LIBRARY MATERIAL

Getting Started

Shannon Paaske's instructor required a research paper that was more developed, and used more sources, than the shorter documented papers that had been assigned in her composition course. In addition to the length and source requirements, Shannon's assignment was to respond more fully to one of the subjects included in the reader of *Between Worlds*. Shannon considered the topics that had been discussed in class, and she realized that she wanted to learn more about the world of the disabled.

Her initial response to the research paper may have been posed in the form of *questions:* What are the problems the disabled have in attending classes? In working? In their social lives? There appears to be interesting technology for the disabled on my campus; what *is* available to help the disabled? What kind of legislation exists to help the disabled? How do the disabled feel about their conditions? Are the attitudes of Mairs and Mattlin characteristic of the disabled? Have they written any other articles that aren't in this text?

With these questions in mind, Shannon went to her college library.

Meet the Librarian

The week before the longer research paper was assigned, Shannon's composition instructor arranged a class library tour. The reference librarian showed the students how to use the computers and indexed guides for book and periodical searches.

The librarian will show you how to find books in the stacks and how to find and use the microfilm machines. All libraries have trained assistants whose job it is to show you how to find the microfilm reels and how to thread the film into the machine. You should never feel embarrassed to ask for help and instruction. Even professors who have used microfilm numerous times will ask for help when they haven't used the machines for a semester or two.

Finding Information

Before you begin *your* search for materials, ask a librarian for information about the library that you are using and anything about the computers that you do not understand. Each library has its own computer system with particular choices for you to make about the type of search that you can conduct (such as "keyword" or "browse"). Every time you use a new library or begin a different research project, ask the librarian which type of search he or she would recommend for the books that you need, and which type of search for the periodicals. Many students leave libraries empty-handed or with few sources because they have not used the correct search, or because they have not entered in all of the appropriate headings.

The reference librarian should not be expected to do your work for you, but you will find that reference librarians know more ways to discover material than you can imagine. For example, a student's search for information on the men's movement yielded nothing when "Men's Movement" was entered into the computer. The reference librarian knew to use "Psychology—Men" to find that material. The student who tries to find information about the "Elephant Man's disease" will be thwarted, but the reference librarian knows to put "Neurofibromatosis" into the computer to start the research.

Your library has information on just about every topic; if you are not finding what you need, you may be using an incorrect heading or misspelling a term. Computers are helpful, but it often takes a human being—a librarian—to show you how to access that help. Better than always giving you the answers, most librarians will also show you the *process* for finding the information for your research.

Evaluating Sources

Your topic will determine the kinds of supporting material you will need in your paper. If your topic requires up-to-date information (news events, current legislation, technological or medical data, or recent statistics), you will want to consult periodicals. As the term implies, they are issued periodically, and therefore they are timely. If your writing does not require current information, or if it necessitates an overview (or legislative changes, economic patterns, fashion trends, art, or political movements), you may want the depth and perspective that books provide. In addition to periodicals and books, don't neglect videos, films, and interviews as potential sources of information.

Sample Bibliography Cards

Shannon started by recording on index cards the bibliographic information that she would need to document her sources. Because she used cards instead of a sheet of paper, Shannon would be able to arrange the cards alphabetically when the time came to type her works-cited page. If your library provides you a printed copy of the bibliographic information of books and periodicals that you are using for your essay, you may decide to use those sheets, arranging them in alphabetical order by author's last name when you write your works-cited page.

Here are *sample bibliography cards* for the note-taking phase:

For a book

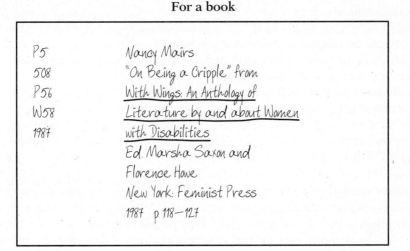

```
P5              Nancy Mairs
508             "On Being a Cripple" from
P56             With Wings: An Anthology of
W58             Literature by and about Women
1987            with Disabilities
                Ed. Marsha Saxon and
                Florence Howe
                New York: Feminist Press
                1987   p 118–127
```

For a periodical

```
Rab, Victoria Y. and Geraldine Youcha. "Body." Omni
     June 1990: 22+.
```

Shannon began the reading and note-taking process after she had collected the books and had photocopied the pages of the periodical articles that were available and seemed most relevant to her subject. On earlier class assignments, Shannon had practiced summarizing and paraphrasing the main ideas of work that she used. She also had practiced finding and extracting the best parts of a writer's work to use in quoted form in her own writing. Because Shannon had worked with incorporating other writers' ideas and language into her material, she understood the problem of *plagiarism*.

Plagiarism

Using someone else's ideas or language as your own, accidentally *or* deliberately, is a serious offense that schools may punish with expulsion. If you are desperate to complete an assigned paper, using somebody else's work may seem like a good idea to you. *Don't do it.* Failing a course or risking expulsion from school cannot be a sensible decision. Talk to your instructor about your anxieties, then determine that you will do the work with integrity.

Plagiarism most often occurs inadvertently. Often it occurs because of sloppy note taking, poor record keeping, or even ignorance. You can avoid this problem by assiduously recording, from your earliest notes on, the source of every idea—even in summary or paraphrased form—and of every key word or phrase of another writer that you are using. Plagiarism also occurs if you incorrectly begin or end the quotation marks that designate the quote you are incorporating into your text. Further, if you change or omit *anything* in the text that you are quoting, you need to use brackets (see p. 546) and ellipses (see p. 544) to signify to your reader that you have made a change. Plagiarism also occurs if you incompletely or inaccurately cite the source of material that you have used. Make certain, even from the first note-taking sessions, that you have correctly recorded *all* of the information that you will need for your works-cited page. Examples of inadvertent plagiarism are shown below, so that you can avoid this error in your own work.

Inadvertent Plagiarism

Plagiarism occurs if a quotation is not used or documented correctly. Read the original, from Marcus Mabry's "Living in Two Worlds" (p. 143) and the incorrect uses of the quotation on page 455:

Original:

Most students who travel between the universes of poverty and affluence during breaks experience similar conditions, as well as the guilt, the helplessness and, sometimes, the embarrassment associated with them. Our friends are willing to listen, but most of them are unable to imagine the pain of the impoverished lives that we see every six months. Each time I return home I feel further away from the realities of poverty in America and more ashamed that they are allowed to persist. What frightens me most is not that the American socioeconomic system permits poverty to continue, but that by participating in that system I share some of the blame.

Identify the incorrect uses of the material in each of the examples below:

1. Marcus Mabry talks about the student who travels between the universes of poverty and affluence during school breaks.

2. Mabry is frightened by the fact that "the American socio-economic system permits poverty to continue" and that "by participating in that system" he shares some of the blame (144).

3. One student who was studying at Stanford describes the guilt, helplessness and the embarrassment that he and other students feel when they move between their school lives and their home lives when they return home for vacation.

4. Mabry is concerned not that "the American socioeconomic system permits poverty to continue, but that by participating in that system he shares some of the blame" (144).

Explanation of Errors

1. In his mistaken notion that he has "only paraphrased," this writer has failed to place quotation marks around Mabry's words "who travel between the universes of poverty and affluence." Additionally, the student has not documented with parenthetical information the source of the material that he has taken from Marcus Mabry. Even if the student were to use only the image of the "universes of poverty and affluence," the image is Mabry's and must be documented.

2. This writer has misrepresented Mabry. The original expresses the idea that it is *not* America's "socioeconomic system" that frightens him but his fear that "by participating in that system" he "shares some of the blame." The writer has written a combination of paraphrase and quotation that does not correctly express Mabry's point.

3. The writer here has attempted a paraphrase of Mabry's words that stays too close to the original in repeating "guilt," "helplessness," and "embarrassment," without using quotation marks and which fails, in any case, to attribute and document the source of the idea.

4. This writer has made a change in Mabry's quoted material in order to merge his or her text smoothly with Mabry's words. But the writer has failed to use brackets to inform the reader that there is a change in the quoted material. This is how the quotation should look: "'The American socioeconomic system permits poverty to continue, but that by participating in that [he shares] some of the blame.'"

You may feel that there are too many ways for you to make mistakes when you use another writer's ideas or words in your essays. But if you carefully copy material from another source, double-check your paraphrases, and inspect your quoted material and compare it to the original to verify that you have been accurate in your sense as well as in the use of quotation marks, brackets, and parentheses, you will avoid the inadvertent plagiarism that threatens your integrity as a writer and flaws the writing that you produce.

With the goal in mind of paraphrasing and quoting carefully those relevant sections of her collected texts, Shannon began making note cards for her paper.

Sample Note Cards

The note cards that Shannon wrote during stage 2 of her paper preparation looked like these:

Original text:

"People without the use of their arms or legs can now rely on computerized 'sip and puff' machines. With light puffs into a plastic straw, users can switch on the TV and change its channels, telephone a friend and play computer games."

Paraphrased note card

> "Machines — Miracles"
>
> Ann Blackman p. 70
>
> Other developments include computerized "sip and puff" machines which enable people without the use of their arms or legs to change television channels, talk on the phone, and play computer games by inhaling or exhaling into a plastic straw.

Original text:

"We used to look at people who were disabled as shut-ins," [Jan Galvin] says. "Not anymore. Computers, new materials and new attitudes have revolutionized our industry. If you can move one muscle in your body, wiggle a pinkie or twitch an eyebrow, we can design a switch to allow you to operate in your environment."

Quotation note card

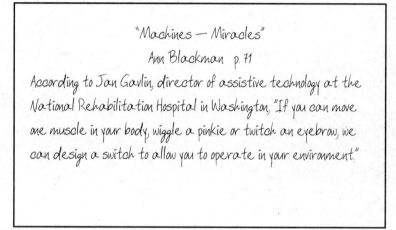

"Machines — Miracles"
Ann Blackman p. 71
According to Jan Gavlin, director of assistive technology at the National Rehabilitation Hospital in Washington, "If you can move one muscle in your body, wiggle a pinkie or twitch an eyebrow, we can design a switch to allow you to operate in your environment."

Developing a Working Thesis

While she read from her collection of materials and took notes, Shannon began to focus on her subject in a sharper way. She realized that there were a number of ways to approach the subject of the disabled, but that she was especially interested in three: technology that equips the disabled to leave home and enter the outside world, the media's recent interest in depicting the disabled, and the attitudes of the nondisabled person toward the disabled. Her working thesis looked something like this:

> Technology and the media have improved life for the disabled, but they still suffer social isolation and indignities.

Shannon talked with her instructor about her working thesis and the rough outline of the three parts that she planned to write. (For a complete discussion of outlining and for illustrations, see pp. 334–337.) After discussing her plan and what she had found in her research, Shannon and her instructor concluded that she did not have enough information about the social isolation of the disabled, and that her own casual observations would be insufficient for a well-developed research paper. The instructor suggested that Shannon approach the special resources center on the campus to arrange interviews with disabled students who would be willing to talk about their social situations. Further, both the instructor and Shannon concluded that they knew very little about legislation that gave rights to the disabled, and both realized that any reader would want to know something about this legislation.

Gathering Additional Information, the Interview

Before she started the first draft of her paper, Shannon returned to the library to collect information on the legislation that gives the disabled access and assures their rights. She made summary note cards of the legislation that had been passed. She discovered some old laws that were so ridiculous that they could provide a dramatic introduction for her paper.

Shannon also contacted the director of her campus special resources center and collected names and telephone numbers of students that he thought would enjoy talking with her. She needed an extra few days to arrange to meet and talk with these students. Shannon conducted three interviews with disabled individuals to use their experiences to support her research. More than reflecting their perspectives, she was able to catch their actual voices in print.

Preparing for the Interview

In order to "catch" voices to use in your paper, you need to do some prior work. You will want to think through exactly what additional support you hope to gain from the interview. It helps to prepare an "icebreaker" question or two to put your interviewees at ease. If you suspect they may be guarded or unwilling to reveal the information you need—particularly for an argument essay, where they may represent the opposing position—you should order your questions so that the milder ones come first. Once the interviewees are engaged in conversation, it will be easier to get them to answer more hard-hitting questions.

Your questions should be written down in the order that you plan to ask them. If you number each, you can use these same numbers as you record the answers during the interview so you don't have to rewrite the question, or even the topic, when you are taking notes.

Conducting the Interview

Although you have prepared questions and ordered them, you may find that the answers cause you to skip to another question or to think up a question on the spot. Your ability to respond with follow-up questions and encouragement ("Why do you think that happened?" "How did you respond?") may determine the depth of the interview. Such follow-up questions may prompt the subjects to move from predictable responses to ones that are fresh and candid.

As you take notes, concentrate on getting down key phrases and controversial claims. Shannon recorded this from one of her interviewees: "Some people are prejudiced and ignore us. That makes me angry." Shannon put quotation marks around exact words so she could remember which words were her subject's and which she added or paraphrased. As you interview your subjects, don't hesitate to ask them to clarify points or expand on ideas so you can get the necessary information.

Some interviewers use portable tape recorders as a backup to capture precise words, but tape recorders haven't replaced notebooks. Relying on tape recorders can be disastrous if the machine is malfunctioning or the tape turns out to be inaudible. Even if the tape is clear, it is tedious to sit through an hour or two of taped conversation in order to transcribe the key quotations. Before you leave, remember to ask about additional sources or reference materials (reading materials, brochures, and names of other specialists).

Because these people are giving you some valuable time for the interview, it is essential that you offer to meet where and when it is convenient for *them*. Arrive on time, don't overstay your welcome, and prepare your questions before the meeting. Remember to be exceptionally courteous and to show appreciation for their time and help.

Recording the Interview

Immediately after the interview, write out or type up the questions and answers while the session is still fresh in your mind. If you discover you have missed any important material or may have misunderstood a point, call back your interviewee immediately for a clarification.

When you integrate the interviewees' comments into your paper, be careful to quote exactly and to represent the context of the statement accurately. Misusing quotations or distorting their intended meaning destroys your integrity as a writer. Shannon found that her conversations with the disabled provided insights that her readings could not. The strength of her argument, however, could not rely only on interviews and personal experiences. She used seven printed sources, including an article from *Scientific American*, to develop her argument.

Sample Student Paper

Shannon Paaske's full paper is included here. The numbers on the manuscript correspond to the numbers of the explanations on the facing page. These explanations will guide you through the rhetorical and form considerations for your own paper.

3.

1.

Shannon Paaske

2. English 1A Sec. 6336

Prof. Douglas

November 17, 1993

From Access to Acceptance:

4.

Enabling America's Largest Minority

In the early 1900's, a Chicago city ordinance
stated that no "unsightly, deformed or maimed person
can appear on the public thoroughfares" (Davidson

5.

62). A court case in Wisconsin in 1919 upheld the
expulsion from school of a twelve-year-old boy with
cerebral palsy because his teachers and fellow students regarded him as "depressing and nauseating"
(62). In contrast to these limiting laws of the
first half of the 20th century, the second half has

6.

drafted legislation and designed equipment to
improve life for the disabled. In 1990, the
Americans with Disabilities Act was passed by
Congress. This enormous piece of legislation, among
other things, requires both public buildings and
private businesses to provide architectural access
for disabled persons and it prohibits discrimination
against them in the workplace. In 1991, a cus-
tomized, computerized van allows a man paralyzed
from the chest down to operate a motor vehicle by
himself. And as this century concludes, major network television shows such as <u>Life Goes On</u>, <u>L.A.
Law</u>, and <u>Star Trek: The Next Generation</u> regularly
feature people with all types of disabilities.

Explanatory Notes for the Research Paper

The numbers on these explanatory notes correspond to the numbers in the margin of the research paper.

1. *Form.* Shannon types her last name and the page number of her manuscript in the upper right corner of *each* page of her paper. She leaves a one-inch margin on the sides, top, and bottom of each page of her paper.

2. *Heading.* According to the MLA, you do not need to use a separate sheet of paper for a title page. If your instructor prefers one, include the information required here and print it on the lower right corner or centered on a plain sheet of typing paper that will precede the first page of your manuscript.

   To follow the MLA form, begin your *heading* on the first page of your manuscript, one inch from the top of the first page and flush with the left margin. Include your name, the course number and section, your instructor's name, and the date on separate lines, double-spacing between them. Double-space again and center your title and then double-space between your title and the first line of your manuscript. Do *not* put quotation marks around or underline your title.

3. *Holding the paper together.* Secure the pages of your paper with *one* paper clip, as MLA advises, or with a staple, as many instructors prefer. If you have the choice, use the staple because it will keep the pages together better than a paper clip. Either the staple or the paper clip is less expensive, more ecologically sound, and holds the manuscript together better than a plastic slide-on binder.

4. Your *title* should engage your reader by establishing an appropriate expectation for what the paper is about, and it should please your reader's ears as well as eyes. If your reader "stumbles" while reading your title, you need to work on it. Shannon establishes the focus of her paper, the disabled person's wish for "access" *and* "acceptance." Notice that she uses the strong verb "enabling," and she raises a possible question in her reader's mind about America's "largest minority." That question can be an effective way to engage the reader.

5. *Citations.* Shannon's opening sentence includes a quotation, so she must document the source. She ends her quotation and, without other punctuation, uses parentheses to enclose the last name of the author of the article and the page number where she found the ordinance that she quotes. Any reader who wants more information about the article will find complete information on Shannon's works-cited page at the end of the manuscript. The second time that Shannon quotes material from Davidson's article she uses only the page number; the reader understands that quoted language from the case study is also from Davidson, noted in the parenthetical citation above. Notice that the terminal punctuation, a period, appears outside the closing parenthesis.

6. *Introduction.* Shannon's introduction is a dramatic, abbreviated history of the legislation, equipment changes, and media responses to the disabled in this century. She cites two remarkable examples from the beginning of the century to engage her reader, and she concludes her first paragraph with the evidence of profound change in the last decade of the century. She chose to use the exact language of the ordinances, rather than paraphrasing their content, because the language is pointed and emphasizes the history that Shannon is writing about in her analysis.

Paaske 2

Clearly, America's institutions have come a
long way in acknowledging the 43 million people in
this country with disabilities (Blackman 70).
Although combinations of technological advances,
equality-promoting legislation, and increasing media
exposure have worked as a collective force in bringing about improvements in the lives of the people
who make up what is sometimes termed "America's
largest minority" (Davidson 61), ignorance and prejudice continue to plague the disabled.

Technological developments, almost exclusively
computer-oriented, have revolutionized the world of
the disabled person. Citizens who were once confined to home, forbidden to travel by air, and
unable to attend classes or enter businesses have
been liberated by recent inventions that encourage
independence as well as allow for enriching life
experiences. Just how extensive is the new technology? According to Jan Gavlin, director of assistive
technology at the National Rehabilitation Hospital
in Washington, "If you can move one muscle in your
body, wiggle a pinkie or twitch an eyebrow, we can
design a switch to allow you to operate in your
environment" (qtd. in Blackman 71).

An example of one such device is the Eyegaze
Response Interface Computer Aid (ERICA), developed
by biomedical engineer Thomas Hutchinson at the
University of Virginia. This eye-controlled computer empowers severely disabled yet bright people
with the ability to learn and communicate. Ten

7.

8.

9.

10.

11.

7. *Statistic acknowledgment.* Shannon notes that there are "43 million" disabled people in the United States. She documents this figure with a reference to her source, Blackman, and the page of the article where she located this figure.

8. *Thesis.* Shannon's thesis, which begins with "although," prepares the reader for the problem that her paper will explore. Her intention is to forecast: to look at the technical and legislative changes, and increased media exposure, as improvements for the disabled. But she will also examine the problems that "plague" the disabled and prevent their full "acceptance."

9. *Uncommon knowledge quoted.* It is not common knowledge that the disabled are "America's largest minority," so Shannon documents the source of this statement with a parenthetical reference to Davidson's article and the page where this statement was made.

10. *Summarized material.* In this section of her paper, Shannon summarizes the technological developments that illustrate positive steps that are being taken to "enable" the disabled. Shannon notes the previous limitations for the disabled before she cites specific equipment changes that have "revolutionized" their lives.

11. *Quotation within the article.* Shannon quotes a knowledgeable source, the director of assistive technology at the National Rehabilitation Hospital in Washington, Jan Gavlin, as he is quoted in Blackman's article. Because she wisely has used Gavlin's name in her paper, Shannon needs only to note that he is "quoted" in Blackman and give the page number where his quoted comment appears. If she had not used Gavlin's name in her text, her in-text citation would have looked like this: (Gavlin qtd. in Blackman 71).

Paaske 3

years ago these people would have been misdiagnosed
as mentally retarded by traditional tests that are
unable to correctly measure their intelligence.
Originally designed for children who previously
might have been misdiagnosed, ERICA and other sys-
tems like it instead "create pathways for kids to
express themselves and for teachers to engage their
minds" (Rab and Youcha 22).   **12.**

Other developments include computerized "sip
and puff" machines which enable people without the
use of their arms or legs to change television
channels, talk on the phone, and play computer   **13.**
games simply by inhaling or exhaling into a plastic
straw (Blackman 70). A system called DragonDictate
is a computer program that prints dictation onto a
monitor when the user speaks into a microphone
(70). This type of program is especially useful to
people who are unable to type because of poor muscle control (a characteristic of cerebral palsy) or
who have various types of paralysis. The system
even comes with a spell-check mode that responds to
the incorrect word with an "oops."

Modern wheelchair designs also reflect the
recent advancements that permit the disabled to
leave home and enter the world. Robert Cushmac, 16,
who was paralyzed from the neck down in a car accident when he was 10, gets from class to class at
his Virginia high school, where he is an honors
student, in a wheelchair activated by a chin-con-
trolled joystick (Blackman 71). The Hi-Rider is a

12.   *Two-author citation.* The quoted comment from an article written by two authors is used to conclude one section of the material on technological advancements. In the parenthetical reference is the last name of each author, connected with "and" and the page number of the article where the quotation appears.

13.   *Paraphrased material.* Shannon describes in her own words how the "sip and puff" machine is used. She documents the source of her information first with the author's last name and page number of the article where she found the information, and then with the page number only. If Shannon had felt there would be any confusion in her reader's mind about the source of her information in this section of her paper, she would have repeated Blackman's name (as she does in the next paragraph) in addition to giving the page number of the article.

Paaske 4

"standing wheelchair" that was designed by Tom
Houston who is paralyzed from the waist down. His
design makes it possible for him to perform tasks
previously impossible, such as reaching an object
on an overhead shelf, or greeting someone face to
face (Blackman 70).

   As these examples show, the continuous headway
being made in adaptive technology has considerably
altered the way of life for many disabled people.   **14.**
However, it is highly unlikely that much of this
progress could have been accomplished without the
help of a sympathetic political climate. Federal
Disability Laws passed by Congress since 1968
addressed the environmental needs of the disabled
and particularly focused on independent living as a
goal. This goal expressed the desire of people with
disabilities to view themselves and be viewed "no
longer as passive victims deserving of charitable
intervention but as self-directed individuals seeking to remove environmental barriers that preclude
their full participation in society" (DeJong and
Lifchez 45).

   Laws such as the Architectural Barriers Act of
1968 required buildings built with federal funds or
leased by the federal government to be made accessible, and the Urban Mass Transportation Act and   **15.**
Federal Aid Highway Act of 1970 and 1973 worked to
make transportation a reality for the disabled
(DeJong and Lifchez 42). Later laws were created to
achieve the attitudinal changes implicit in the

14.   *Transition.* Shannon moves from her review of the technological advancements designed to enhance the lives of the disabled to a review of legislation that has given them rights. Notice that her transition establishes that the technological advancements would not have occurred without the legislative changes. This is a more critically perceptive transition, showing a cause and effect relationship, than one that suggests merely "another change for the disabled is in the area of legislation."

15.   *Paraphrased and quoted material.* Shannon summarizes the various laws and acts and documents her source of information, the *Scientific American* article written by the two authors noted in her parenthetical references throughout this portion of her text. Her review of this legislation is historical, and it is chronologically arranged.

Paaske 5

objectives of the independent living movement. One
law is The Rehabilitation Act of 1973, which prohibits discrimination against disabled people in
programs, services, and benefits that are federally
funded. The Rehabilitation Comprehensive Services
and Developmental Disability Amendments of 1978
established independent living as a priority for
state vocational programs and provided federal
funding for independent living centers (DeJong and
Lifchez 42). The Social Security Disability
Amendments of 1980 gave disabled people more incen-
tives to work by letting them deduct independent-
living expenses from their taxes (42). The
Americans With Disabilities Act, signed in 1990,
reinforced the legislation that was not earlier
implemented. But because the law takes effect in
gradual stages, the result of all of its provisions
have not yet been fully realized. However, as each
stipulation is introduced, its impact on the whole
of American society will be undeniable.   16.

Equally undeniable is the fact that laws such
as these, together with the flourishing of adaptive
technology, have created greater awareness of the
disabled in our communities. The increasing number   17.
of disabled characters in movies and television
reflect that awareness. Deaf actress Marlee Matlin,
for example, has enjoyed success, starring in the
Academy award-winning <u>Children of a Lesser God</u> in
1986, and currently in the television series
<u>Reasonable Doubts</u>. In assessing Matlin's character

16.   *Conclusion to one section and transition to the next.* Shannon concludes her
      review of the legislation with a statement that the provisions of the most
      recent act for which she has information have not yet been fully implement-
      ed. She believes the impact will be "undeniable" when the act is fully in
      effect.

17.   *New focus point.* Again, Shannon relates the next section of her paper to the
      previous sections by asserting that technology and legislation have made the
      disabled visible citizens in our communities. The media have reflected this
      visibility by increasing the number of disabled employed in film, television,
      and advertising.

Paaske 6

in <u>Reasonable Doubts</u>, Ben Mattlin (no relation), a 18.
writer with a muscular dystrophy-related disease,
says he "can't say enough good things about working
a highly visible disability into a major character"
(Mattlin 8). Ben Mattlin also finds it significant 19.
that this character is portrayed as both intelligent and sexy. In addition, on ABC's <u>Life Goes On</u>,
Christopher Burke, an actor who has Down's Syndrome,
plays Corky, a "competent, high-functioning integral
part of his family" (Mattlin 8). Because Matlin and
Burke are disabled actors who portray disabled
characters--in contrast to the many able-bodied
actors who play disabled roles--they have helped
mark a path of new acceptance for the disabled.

Progressing along that path are retail stores
that employ the disabled to model in their advertising. In 1991, retail store Kids R Us hired disabled children from hospital pediatric wards to
work as professional models for their catalogues
and circulars. Some of the store's executives got
the idea while watching these kids play. Vice
President Ernie Speranza reasoned, "They think of
themselves as average kids, so we decided we should
too" (Speranza qtd. in Yorks 1). Kids R Us was not 20.
the first retail store to make this move, and since
1990, Target and Nordstrom's--representing both
ends of the economic spectrum--have hired disabled
people of all ages as models in an effort to better
represent the diversity of its clientele (Yorks 1).

Although efforts such as these indicate that
the media have "started to get a broader perspec-

18.   *Parenthetical explanation.* Shannon makes a point of noting that the media critic, Ben Mattlin, is no relation to Marlee Matlin. She is then free to use Mattlin's name in parenthetical documentation without concern that her reader will be perplexed.

19.   *Summary and direct quotation.* In a combination of summarized information and direct quotation, Shannon uses Ben Mattlin's article about the depictions of disabled actors in various media. She was tempted to use Mattlin's critical comments about the "distorted images" of the disabled in particular films, but she realized that this digression would change the balance and focus of her paper. From Mattlin's article, she used only what was relevant to her essay—brief references to actual programs and actors, and the appreciation of a disabled writer for positive portrayals of the disabled in film.

20.   *Quotation within the article.* The vice president of a retail store is quoted within an article that Shannon read about the use of the disabled as models in advertising. She quotes him in her text and notes his name and the page of the quotation in her parenthetical reference.

tive on real life" (Olson), people with disabilities have yet to enjoy full acceptance by American
society. Nancy Mairs, a woman with multiple sclerosis who balances a college teaching and lecturing
career with the demands of a marriage and motherhood, finds that while her family and the people
she works with have accepted her disability, she
still has had to endure an end-of-the-semester
evaluation by a student who was perturbed by her
disability (122).

While no longer blatantly discriminated
against, the disabled often continue to suffer the
burden of social bias. Even those remarkable individuals who are able to triumph over physical barriers have trouble surmounting social barriers.
Post-polio actor Henry Holden relates his own experience with social discrimination:

> A guy with paralyzed legs is not sup-
> posed to be able to sell insurance, but I
> did very well at it in New Jersey before I
> became an actor. A guy with paralyzed legs
> is not supposed to climb mountains, but I
> made the trek up the cliff at Masada in
> Israel at four o'clock in the morning. A
> guy with paralyzed legs is not supposed to
> ride horses, but I rode in an exhibition
> in Madison Square Garden. Yet I am not
> generally accepted by nondisabled people
> in social situations. The attitude in the
> country is that, if you have a disability,
> you should stay home. (Holden qtd. in
> Davidson 63)

21.

22.

23.

21.   *Quotation from an interview.* Because there are no page numbers associated with interviews, only the last name of the subject interviewed is enclosed in the parentheses. Shannon uses Steve Olson's comment about the value of images of the disabled in advertising as a transition to the final section of her paper. This section focuses on the feelings the disabled have about nondisabled people's perceptions of them. Shannon gained these insights in interviews as well as readings.

22.   *Paraphrased and summarized material.* An experience noted by an author in her essay is summarized and paraphrased by Shannon, and the source of the material is documented.

23.   *Long quotations.* Because the experience of the actor Henry Holden is especially revealing, Shannon decided to include the long quotation in her paper. Because the quotation is longer than four typed lines, it cannot be incorporated within the manuscript. Instead, the longer quotation is set off from the rest of the paper with double-spacing at the top and bottom of the quotation, and it is indented ten spaces from the left margin. The quotation itself is double-spaced, and the final period *precedes* the parenthetical information.

Paaske 8

Susan Rodde, who has cerebral palsy, confirms
that in most social situations, "we, the physically
challenged, have to be the icebreakers." At parties
and social gatherings, the disabled person is often
isolated or ignored. Having used a wheelchair since
a surfing accident, Berkeley student Steve Olson
confirms this experience: "Sometimes I meet people
at parties who feel uncomfortable about [my dis-   24.
ability]. I talk and tell jokes to break the ice,
and soon no one realizes there's a disabled person--
me--sitting in the room with them." Unfortunately,
the "ice" does need to be broken because many people feel uncomfortable around disabled or disfig-
ured people, and so far, the responsibility of making social contact lies with the disabled person.

But many of the disabled report that fully
abled people have a hard time "respecting the fact   25.
that we're the same as they are," says Diane
DeVries, who was born with no legs and only partial
arms. Perhaps because of ignorance or fear, our
disabilities "remind people of their own vulnera-
bilities" (DeVries). As Nancy Mairs says, "Society   26.
is no readier to accept crippledness than to accept
death, war, sex, sweat, or wrinkles" (119).   27.

Because they may feel vulnerable, able-bodied
people tend not to form close relationships with
disabled people, and some even refuse casual contact. Rebecca Acuirre, 16, who has cerebral palsy,
says that she recently asked a stranger what time
it was and he kept walking as though he didn't hear

24.   *Brackets.* Shannon has enclosed in brackets a change that she has made in material from an interview. It is possible that her subject used a pronoun that would have been ambiguous to the reader; Shannon substituted the noun and placed the clarifying term in brackets. The reader understands that the brackets are used to clarify or change tense or other language forms to permit easy reading of the quoted material as it is integrated with the writer's text. No changes may be made and put into brackets that would alter the meaning of the material quoted. (See p. 546 for more information about brackets.)

25.   *Incorporating short quotations.* Shannon incorporates into her text the specific quoted material from her reading and interviews. When the subject of an interview is named in the text, there is no need for additional documentation.

26.   *Interview subject quoted.* Because Shannon does not reuse Diane DeVries' name in her text, she documents the source of the quotation by using DeVries' last name in parentheses.

27.   *Documentation from a book.* Nancy Mairs' name is used in Shannon's text, so only the page number of the book is cited in parentheses.

her. "Some people are prejudiced and ignore us.
That makes me angry," she says.

How can these prejudices be abolished? "We
need more exposure," says DeVries. Acuirre con-
curs, saying the media should do more to educate
the public. On a personal level, Bill Davidson, in
"Our Largest Minority, Americans with Handicaps,"   **28.**
recommends the nondisabled public "help reverse
centuries of discrimination" by getting to know
disabled people "at work, in the marketplace, at
school" and by making "contact that is real--not
just casual" (63). Able-bodied people can help
overcome their own preconceived notions and realize that if disabled people seem bitter, "it's not
because of their disability . . . but because of
society's attitude toward them." Prejudices can be
stopped before they start by encouraging children
"not to shun and fear" the disabled (63).

The legislation and technology that have developed at the end of this century will continue to   **29.**
make new worlds accessible to the disabled.
Ideally, these developments will permit the disabled to be viewed in terms of their capabilities
rather than their disabilities. In that climate,
the disabled can gain acceptance in the worlds to
which they have access. With the steps being taken
by government, science, and the media, individuals
alone are needed to make the dream of acceptance a
reality for the disabled.

28.   *Incorporating summary and quotations.* Shannon introduces the author and title of the article in her text. This attribution within her text facilitates Shannon's documentation; she only needs to note the page number within the parentheses. Her citations document the specific quoted material as well as the paraphrased content of Davidson's article.

29.   *Conclusion.* In her conclusion, Shannon reviews the relationship between the points she has made in her paper. She concludes by asserting that the advancements for the disabled lie in the hands of individuals, not only institutions. She uses the language of her title to bring a more dramatic closure to her analysis.

Paaske 10

WORKS CITED

Acuirre, Rebecca. Personal interview. 23 Sept. 1992.

Blackman, Ann. "Machines That Work Miracles." <u>Time</u>
18 Feb. 1991: 70-71.

Davidson, Bill. "Our Largest Minority: Americans
with Handicaps." <u>McCall's</u> Sept. 1987: 61-68.

Dejong, Gerben and Raymond Lifchez. "Physical
Disability and Public Policy." <u>Scientific
American</u> June 1983: 40-49.

DeVries, Diane. Telephone interview. 22 Sept. 1992.

Mairs, Nancy. "On Being a Cripple." <u>With Wings: An
Anthology of Literature by and about Women with
Disabilities</u>. Ed. Marsha Saxon and Florence
Howe. New York: Feminist Press, 1987. 118-127.

Mattlin, Ben. "Beyond <u>Reasonable Doubts</u>: The Media
and People with Disabilities." <u>Television and
Families</u> 13.3 (1991): 4-8.

Olson, Steve. Telephone interview. 18 Sept. 1992.

Rab, Victoria Y. and Geraldine Youcha. "Body." <u>Omni</u>
June 1990: 22+

Yorks, Cindy LaFavre. "Challenging Images." <u>Los
Angeles Times</u>. 22 Nov. 1991: E1-2.

30.

31.

32.

33.

34.

35.

36.

37.

38.

39.

40.

30.   *The form for the list of sources used in the text.* The heading "Works Cited" is centered on the line that is one inch from the top of the page. The first cited work is typed two lines beneath the heading. The entire list is double-spaced. The list is alphabetically arranged by the author or speaker's last name or by the first word in the title of an unsigned article. The entry begins at the left margin. If it is longer than one line, its second line begins five spaces indented from the left margin. (More complete information on MLA form is on pp. 480–491.)

31.   Entry for a personal interview. The date of the interview is noted.

32.   Entry for a signed article in a weekly periodical.

33.   Entry for a signed article in a monthly magazine.

34.   Entry for a magazine article written by two authors.

35.   Entry for a telephone interview. The date of the interview is noted.

36.   Entry for a chapter within an anthology with two editors. Notice that the name of the author of the chapter Shannon used is listed first.

37.   Entry for a signed article in a periodical with volume and number.

38.   Entry for a telephone interview.

39.   Entry for two authors of an article within a monthly periodical. Notice that the article started on page 22 but did not appear on continuous pages. The "+" symbol indicates that the pages were not consecutive.

40.   Entry for a signed article in a daily newspaper. Notice the "E" prior to the page number to indicate the section of the newspaper in which the article appeared.

DOCUMENTING THE RESEARCH PAPER: MODERN LANGUAGE ASSOCIATION (MLA) STYLE

Whenever you use the words, information, or ideas of another writer—*even if in your own words* as a summary or paraphrase—you must credit the *source*. Prior to 1984, writers gave credit to their sources by using numbers that referred to notes at the bottom of the page, or at the end of the manuscript on a separate sheet of paper. In contrast to this older method, the new MLA style guide liberates the writer from hours of tedious work. Instead of using footnote numbers, you will place the necessary information in parentheses immediately following the quoted or paraphrased passage.

The forms illustrated below will show you exactly how to provide the necessary information for documenting your sources. The third edition (1988) of the *MLA Handbook for Writers of Research Papers* is the source of this guide, and it is certainly the form that your college English instructors will want you to use.

Writing Parenthetical Citations

Your in-text citation should give just enough information so that your reader can find the origin of your material on the works-cited page (your bibliography) at the end of your paper. Here are sample parenthetical citations to illustrate MLA format:

Author Not Named in the Text

When you haven't included the author's name in your text, you must note in parentheses the *author's last name* and the *page* or pages of your source.

> "The first steps toward the mechanical measurement of time, the beginnings of the modern clock in Europe, came not from farmers or shepherds, nor from merchants or craftsmen, but from religious persons anxious to perform promptly and regularly their duties to God" (Boorstin 36).

Author Named in the Text

It is often advantageous to introduce your paraphrased or quoted material by noting the author's name within your text, especially if your author is an authority on the subject. If you do include the author's name in the text, your parenthetical citation will be brief and less intrusive, containing only the page number by itself.

According to Daniel Boorstin, the senior historian of
the Smithsonian Institute, "the first steps toward the
mechanical measurement of time, the beginnings of the modern clock in Europe, came not from farmers or shepherds,
nor from merchants or craftsmen, but from religious persons
anxious to perform promptly and regularly their duties to
God" (36).

Two Books by the Same Author

If your paper contains two different works by the same author, your
parenthetical reference will need to give an abbreviated form of the
title, with the page number, so that your reader will know which work
you are using in that particular section of your paper.

Ben Mattlin deplores the pity for the disabled that
Jerry Lewis' yearly telethon evokes ("Open Letter" 6).
Mattlin also exposes the hypocrisy in depicting the dis-
abled as superheroes. His point is that "courage and deter-
mination are often necessary when living with a disability.
But there's nothing special in that, because there's no
choice. Flattering appraisals sound patronizing. . . "
("Beyond Reasonable Doubts" 5).

A Work with Two or Three Authors

If the work was written by two or three authors, use each of their
names in your text or in the parenthetical citations.

In their study of John Irving's The World According to
Garp, Janice Doane and Devon Hodges analyze the author's
attitude toward female authority: "Even novels that contain
sympathetic female characters, as Irving's novel does, may
still be oppressive to women" (11).

Critics have charged that John Irving's The World
According to Garp doesn't really support female authority:
"Even novels that contain sympathetic female characters, as
Irving's does, may still be oppressive to women" (Doane and
Hodges 11).

A Work with More Than Three Authors

If your source was written by more than three authors, you may use only the first author's last name, followed by "et al." and the page number, in parentheses or you may list all of the authors' last names in the text or with the page number in parentheses.

> In <u>Women's Ways of Knowing: The Development of Self,</u> <u>Voice, and Mind</u>, the authors note that there are many women who "believed they were stupid and helpless. They had grown up either in actual physical danger or in such intimidating circumstances that they feared being wrong, revealing their ignorance, being laughed at" (Belenky et al. 57).

> In <u>Women's Ways of Knowing: The Development of Self,</u> <u>Voice, and Mind</u>, the authors note that there are many women who "believed they were stupid and helpless. They had grown up either in actual physical danger or in such intimidating circumstances that they feared being wrong, revealing their ignorance, being laughed at" (Belenky, Clinchy, Goldberger, and Tarule 57).

> In <u>Women's Ways of Knowing: The Development of Self,</u> <u>Voice, and Mind</u>, Belenky, Clinchy, Goldberger, and Tarule note that there are many women who "believed they were stupid and helpless. They had grown up either in actual physical danger or in such intimidating circumstances that they feared being wrong, revealing their ignorance, being laughed at" (57).

Author's Name Not Given

If the author is anonymous, use the complete title in your text or an abbreviated form of the title with the page number in the parentheses.

> The obituary for Allan Bloom in <u>Newsweek</u> describes him as the man who "ignited a national debate on higher education" and "defended the classics of Western Culture and excoriated what he saw as the intellectual and moral relativism of the modern academy" ("Transition" 73).

Corporate Author or Government Publication

Either name the corporate author in your text or include an abbreviated form in the parentheses. If the name is long, try to work it into your text to avoid an intrusive citation.

> Southern California Edison, in a reminder to customers to "Conserve and Recycle," gives the shocking statistic that "every hour, Americans go through 2.5 million plastic bottles, only a small percentage of which are now recycled" (Customer Update 4).

Literature: Novel, Play, Poem

Because works appear in various editions, it is best to give the chapter number or part in addition to the page number to help your reader find the reference you are citing.

Novel

> In the novel Invisible Man, Ralph Ellison uses a grotesque comparison to describe eyes: "A pair of eyes peered down through lenses as thick as the bottom of a Coca-Cola bottle, eyes protruding, luminous and veined, like an old biology specimen preserved in alcohol" (230; ch. 11).

Play

> In William Shakespeare's Othello, Emilia sounds like a twentieth-century feminist when she claims that "it is their husbands' faults" if their wives have affairs (4.3.89–90).

Poem

> Poet Robert Hass, in "Misery and Splendor," describes the frustration of lovers longing to be completely united: "They are trying to become one creature, / and something will not have it" (13–14).

Indirect Source

When you use the words of a writer who is quoted in another author's work, begin the citation with the abbreviation "qtd. in" and both writers' names if you have not used them in your text.

> Women and men both cite increased "freedom" as a bene-
> fit of divorce. But Riessman discovered that women meant
> that they "gained independence and autonomy" while men
> meant that they felt "less confined," "less claustropho-
> bic," and had "fewer responsibilities" (Catherine Kohler
> Riessman qtd. in Tanner 40-41).

More Than One Work

If you want to show that two works are the sources of your information, separate the references with a semicolon.

> Two recent writers concerned with men's issues observe
> that many women have options to work full time or part
> time, stay at home, or combine staying at home with a
> career. On the other hand, men need to stay in the corpo-
> rate world and provide for the family full time (Allis 81;
> Farrell 90).

Preparing the Works-Cited Page

Whenever you note in parentheses that you have used someone else's
material, you will need to explain that source completely in the
works-cited list (the bibliography) at the end of your manuscript. To
see how this page will look, refer to the student research paper on
page 460.

Because the complete source is only listed in the works cited, *it is
essential that each entry conform exactly to standard form* so that the
reader can easily locate your source. Most of the forms that you will
need are illustrated below.

Elements of a Citation

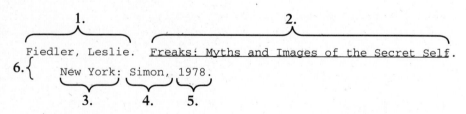

1. Use the author's full name—last name first—followed by a comma
   and then the first name and any middle name or initial. Omit any
   titles (Dr., Ph.D., Rev.). End with a period and two spaces.

2. Print the book's full title including any subtitles. Underline the title and capitalize the first and last words as well as all important words. If there is a subtitle, separate the main title and the subtitle with a colon and one space. Place a period after the title and leave two spaces.

3. Type the publication information beginning with the city of publication, followed by a colon and one space.

4. Print the name of the publisher, followed by a comma. Shorten the name to remove "and Co." or "Inc." Abbreviate multiple names to include only the first name. (The "Simon" in the above example refers to Simon and Schuster.)

5. Include the date of publication and end with a period.

6. Any line after the first line is double-spaced and indented five spaces.

Sample MLA Entries

Books

One Author

Fiedler, Leslie. Freaks: <u>Myths and Images of the Secret Self</u>. New York: Simon, 1978.

Two or Three Authors

Doane, Janice and Devon Hodges. <u>Nostalgia and Sexual Difference: The Resistance to Contemporary Feminism</u>. New York: Methuen, 1987.

Notice that any authors' names *after the first author* are written with the first name before the last name.

More Than Three Authors or Editors

Boardman, John et al., eds. <u>The Oxford History of the Classical World</u>. New York: Oxford University Press, 1986.

or

Boardman, John, Jasper Griffin, and Oswyn Murray, eds. <u>The Oxford History of the Classical World</u>. New York: Oxford University Press, 1986.

With more than three authors, you have the choice of shortening the entry to provide only the first author's name, followed by the Latin abbreviation "et al." (which means "and others"), *or* you may provide all of the names.

Author with an Editor

```
Shakespeare, William.  King Lear.  Ed. Alfred Harbage.
     Baltimore: Penguin, 1969.
```

Cite the name of the author first and then, after the title of the work, give the editor's name, preceded by "Ed."

Book with an Editor and No Author Cited

```
Allen, Donald M., ed.  The New American Poetry.  New York:
     Grove, 1960.
```

If the book does not have an author, cite the editor's name, followed by "ed."

Selection from an Anthology or Collection

```
Roethke, Theodore.  "I Knew A Woman." The Collected Poems of
     Theodore Roethke.  New York: Doubleday, 1975.  122.
```

```
Mairs, Nancy. "On Being a Cripple."  With Wings: An
     Anthology of Literature by and about Women with
     Disabilities.  Ed. Marsha Saxton and Florence Howe. New
     York: Feminist P at City U NY, 1987.  118-127.
```

Give the author and title of the selection, using quotation marks around the title. Then give the underlined title of the anthology. If the anthology has an editor, note the name or names after the "Ed." Give the page numbers for the entire selection as shown above.

Two or More Selections from the Same Anthology

```
Anderson, Sherwood. "Discovery of a Father." Bachmann 6-10.

Bachmann, Susan and Melinda Barth.  Between Worlds: A Reader,
     Rhetoric, and Handbook.  New York: HarperCollins, 1995.

Olds, Sharon. "On the Subway." Bachmann 174-75.
```

To avoid repetition, give the full citation for the book *once*, under the editor's last name. Then all articles are listed under the individual authors' names, followed by the title of the work. After each title, put the editor's name as a cross-reference to the complete citation.

Two or More Books by the Same Author(s)

```
Olsen, Tillie.  Silences.  New York: Dell, 1979.

---.  Tell Me a Riddle.  New York: Dell, 1985.
```

Give the name(s) for the first entry only. After that, in place of the name(s), type three hyphens, followed by a period and two spaces and then the next title. The three hyphens always stand for exactly the same name(s) as in the preceding entry. The titles of the author's works should be listed alphabetically.

Corporate Author

```
National Council of Teachers of English.  "Guidelines for
     Nonsexist Use of Language in NCTE Publications."
     Urbana, Illinois: NCTE, 1975.
```

Use the name of the institution or corporation as the author even if it is also the name of the publisher.

Author Not Named

```
The Oxford Dictionary of Quotations.  2nd ed.  New York:
     Oxford UP, 1964.
```

If a book has no author noted on the title page, begin the entry with the title and alphabetize according to the first word other than "a," "an," or "the."

Other Than First Edition

If you are citing an edition other than the first, place the edition number between the title and the publication information. (See above.)

Republication

```
Melville, Herman.  Billy Budd, Sailor (An Inside Narrative).
     1924.  Chicago: U Chicago P, 1962.
```

If you are citing a work that has been published by different publishers, place the original date of publication (but not the place or publisher's name) after the title. Then provide the complete information for the source you are using.

Book Title Within the Title

Gilbert, Stuart. <u>James Joyce's</u> Ulysses. New York: Vintage,
    1955.

If the title of the work that you are using contains another *book* title, do not underline or place the original book title in quotation marks.

Story or Poem Title Within the Title

Lessing, Doris. <u>"The Temptation of Jack Orkney" and Other</u>
    <u>Stories</u>. New York: Knopf, 1972.

If the title of the work that you are using contains a title that is normally enclosed in quotation marks (a short story or poem), keep the quotation marks and underline the entire title, extending the underlining to include the final period and closing quotation mark: *Dare to Eat a Peach: A Study of "The Love Song of J. Alfred Prufrock."*

Multivolume Work

Raine, Kathleen. <u>Blake and Tradition</u>. 2 vols. Princeton:
    Princeton UP, 1968.

If you have used two or more volumes of a multivolume work, state the total number of volumes in the work. Place this information ("2 vols.") between the title and publishing information.

Malone, Dumas. <u>The Sage of Monticello</u>. Boston: Little,
    Brown, 1981. Vol. 6 of <u>Jefferson and His Time</u>. 6 vols.
    1943-1981.

If you are using only one volume of a multivolume work, give the title of that volume after the author's name and then give the publishing information. After the publishing date, note the volume number, the title, and the number of volumes in the collection. If the volumes were published over a period of years, indicate the dates.

Translation

Ibsen, Henrik. <u>A Doll's House and Other Plays</u>. Trans.
    Peter Watts. New York: Penguin, 1965.

When citing a work that has been translated, give the author's name. After the title, give the translator's name, preceded by "Trans."

Introduction, Preface, Foreword, or Afterword

Grumbach, Doris. Foreword. <u>Aquaboogie</u>. By Susan Straight.

Minneapolis: Milkweed, 1990.

If you are citing material from an introduction, preface, foreword, or afterword written by someone other than the author of the book, give the name of the writer and designate the section she or he wrote. Notice also that "Foreword" above is without underlining or quotation marks. After the title of the work, "By" precedes the author's name.

If the author of the introduction or preface is the same as the author of the book, give only the last name after the title:

Conrad, Joseph. Author's Note. <u>Youth: A Narrative; and Two</u>

<u>Other Stories</u>. By Conrad. New York: Heinemann, 1917.

3-5.

Article in an Encyclopedia or Other Reference Books

Benet, William Rose. "Courtly Love." <u>The Reader's</u>

<u>Encyclopedia</u>. 1965 ed.

"Hodgkin's Disease." <u>The New Columbia Encyclopedia</u>. 1975 ed.

If there is an author of the edition or article, alphabetize by last name. Otherwise, alphabetize in the works-cited page by the title of the entry.

Periodicals: Journals, Magazines, and Newspapers

Journal with Continuous Pagination

Culp, Mary Beth. "Religion in the Poetry of Langston

Hughes." <u>Phylon</u> 48 (1983): 240-45.

Journals sometimes paginate consecutively throughout a year. Each issue, after the first one, continues numbering from where the previous issue ended. After the title, give the volume number and the publication date in parentheses, followed by a colon and the page numbers.

Journal That Paginates Each Issue Separately

Hardwick, Julie. "Widowhood and Patriarchy in Seventeenth-
     Century France." <u>Journal of Social History</u> 26.1 (1992):
     133-48.

If the journal numbers each issue separately, give the volume number, a period, and the issue number (as in "26.1" above) after the title of the journal.

Monthly or Bimonthly Periodical

Mazzatenta, O. Louis. "A Chinese Emperor's Army for
     Eternity." <u>National Geographic</u> Aug. 1992: 114-30.

Notice that in a monthly or bimonthly periodical, the month of publication is abbreviated, and no volume or issue numbers are given.

Weekly or Biweekly Periodical

Fotos, Christopher. "Right-to-Fly Law Spurs Operators to
     Provide Access for Disabled." <u>Aviation Week & Space</u>
     <u>Technology</u> 8 June 1992: 58-60.

Daily Newspaper, Signed Article

Soto, Onell R. "Putting the Tag on Graffiti-Smearers."
     <u>Press Telegram</u> 28 Jan. 1992: B-3.

Daily Newspaper, Unsigned Article or Editorial

"Back to Future: The Nation's Cities." Editorial. <u>Los</u>
     <u>Angeles Times</u> 3 May 1992: M-4.

If the newspaper is divided into numbered or lettered sections, give the section designation before the page number, as in "M-4" above.

Titled Review

Ansa, Tina McElroy. "Taboo Territory." Rev. of <u>Possessing</u>
     <u>the Secret of Joy</u>, by Alice Walker. <u>Los Angeles Times</u> 5
     July 1992: 4+.

The page number "4+" in the citation on page 490 indicates that the article starts on page 4 but does not continue on consecutive pages.

Untitled Review

> Shore, Paul.   Rev. of <u>Backlash: The Undeclared War Against</u>
> <u>American Women</u>, by Susan Faludi. <u>The Humanist</u> Sept.-Oct.
> 1992: 47-48.

Other Sources
Interview

> Acuirre, Rebecca. Personal interview.   23 Sept. 1992.
>
> Olson, Steve. Telephone interview. 18 Sept. 1992.

Film or Television Programs

> <u>Children of a Lesser God</u>. Dir. Randa Haines. With William
> Hurt, Marlee Matlin, Piper Laurie, and Phillip Bosco.
> Paramount, 1986.

If you want to refer to a particular individual involved with the film, cite that person's name first:

> Matlin, Marlee, actress. <u>Children of a Lesser God</u>. Dir.
> Randa Haines. With William Hurt, Piper Laurie, and
> Phillip Bosco. Paramount, 1986.

Organizing the Works Cited

The works cited are always arranged alphabetically, according to authors' last names. If there are no authors named, then the works are listed according to title. If the title begins with "A" or "The," keep the article where it is but alphabetize the title according to the second word.

All sources—whether book or article—are arranged together in one list. Do not have a list of books and then a list of articles. *Do not number the sources in your bibliography*. Double-space between all lines; after the first line of each entry extends to the right-hand margin, the second line is indented five spaces. See the works-cited page in the model student research paper (p. 478).

DOCUMENTING THE RESEARCH PAPER: AMERICAN PSYCHOLOGICAL ASSOCIATION (APA) STYLE

Although most English instructors will require MLA form for documenting sources, instructors from other disciplines may prefer APA form. Check with your instructors to see which of the two forms they prefer. *These two styles are very different; don't confuse them.*

Writing Parenthetical Citations

The main difference between MLA and APA forms is that in APA parenthetical citations, the date of publication and sometimes the page number of the source are included. The punctuation, therefore, is also different.

Using APA form, *if you introduce quoted material with the author's name,* follow the author's name with the date of publication in parentheses. Then, at the end of the quotation, include the page number in parentheses.

> In Ben Mattlin's recent study (1991) of the media and
> people with disabilities, he approves Christopher Burke's
> role as a "competent, high-functioning, integral part of
> his family" (p. 8).

Notice that the date of the study is included within the introduction to the quotation, and then the page number is abbreviated as "p." within the final parentheses.

If you do not use the author's name when you introduce the quoted material, place the author's name, the date, and the page number in parentheses at the end of the quoted material. Use commas between the items in the parentheses.

> One critic approves Christopher Burke's role as a
> "competent, high-functioning, integral part of his family"
> (Mattlin, 1991, p. 8).

If you paraphrase the material rather than quoting it specifically, include the author's last name and the date of publication either in your text or in the parentheses at the end of the summarized material. Do not include the page number.

> According to Ben Mattlin (1991), disabled actors are
> playing important roles in television dramas.

One writer who has examined the media's treatment of
the disabled reports some positive changes in television
(Mattlin, 1991).

Specific Examples of APA Form

Below are specific examples of common situations you may need to
document in APA form:

A Work with Two Authors

If your material was written by two authors, name both in the introduction to the material or in the final parentheses each time you cite
the work. In the parentheses, use "&" rather than "and."

DeJong and Lifchez (1983) examine state and federal
funding for vocational programs and independent living centers provided for disabled citizens.

Two writers have reported on The Rehabilitation
Comprehensive Services and Developmental Disability
Amendments (DeJong & Lifchez, 1983).

Author's Name Not Given

If the author of the material that you are using is not given, either use
the complete title in your introduction to the material or use the first
few words of the title in the parenthetical citation with the date.

Retired Supreme Court Justice Thurgood Marshall graduated first in his class at Howard Law School and then sued
the University of Maryland Law School, which had rejected
him because he was black ("Milestones," 1993).

One obituary ("Milestones," 1993) noted that Thurgood
Marshall graduated first in his class at Howard Law School
and then sued the University of Maryland Law School, which
had rejected him because he was black.

Corporate Author

If you are using a work with a corporate or group author that is
particularly long, write out the full name the first time you use it,

followed by an abbreviation in brackets. In later citations, use just the abbreviation.

> The American Philosophical Association has prepared
> "Guidelines for Non-Sexist Use of Language" because
> philosophers are "attuned to the emotive force of words and
> to the ways in which language influences thought and behav-
> ior" (American Philosophical Association [APA], 1978).

Indirect Source

If you use work that is borrowed from another source, you need to acknowledge that you did not use the original source.

> Actor Henry Holden relates his own experience with
> social discrimination by noting that he is "not generally
> accepted by nondisabled people in social situations" (cited
> in Davidson, 1987).

Preparing the References Page

In APA form, the alphabetical listing of works used in the manuscript is entitled "References." (In MLA form, this listing is called the "Works Cited.") Here are some general guidelines for the references page.

- Double-space the entries. The first line should start at the left margin, and all subsequent lines should be indented *three* spaces.
- Alphabetize the list by the last name of the author or editor. If the work is anonymous, alphabetize by the first name of the title other than "a," "an," or "the."
- All authors' names should be listed last name first, with the parts of names separated with commas. Do not use "et al." Use initials for first and middle names. Use an ampersand ("&") rather than the word "and."
- For the titles of books and articles, capitalize only the first word of the title and of the subtitle, as well as all proper nouns.
- Underline the titles of books and journals. Do not underline or use quotations marks around the titles of articles. Capitalize the names of periodicals as they are normally written. Underline the volume number of periodicals.

- Give the full names of publishers, excluding "Inc." and "Co."
- Use the abbreviation "p." or "pp." before page numbers in books, magazines, and newspapers, but not for scholarly journals. For inclusive page numbers, include all figures ("365–370," not "365–70").

Sample APA Entries

Books

One Author

Fiedler, L. (1978). <u>Freaks: Myths and images of the secret self</u>. New York: Simon & Schuster.

Two or More Authors

Doane, J., & Hodges, D. (1987). <u>Nostalgia and sexual difference: The resistance to contemporary feminism</u>. New York: Methuen.

Editor

Allen, D. M. (Ed.). (1960). <u>The new American poetry</u>. New York: Grove Press.

Translator

Ibsen, H. (1965). <u>A doll's house and other plays</u>. (P. Watts, Trans.). New York: Penguin Books.

Author Not Named

<u>The Oxford dictionary of quotations</u>. (1964). New York: Oxford University Press.

Later Edition

Fowler, R. H., & Aaron, J. E (1992). <u>The Little, Brown handbook</u>. (5th ed.). New York: HarperCollins Publishers.

Multivolume Work

Raine, K. (1968). <u>Blake and tradition</u> (Vol. 2). Princeton: Princeton University Press.

Malone, D. (1943–1981). <u>Jefferson and his time</u> (Vols. 1–6). Boston: Little, Brown.

Work in an Anthology

Mairs, N. On being a cripple. (1987). In M. Saxton & F. Howe (Eds.), <u>With wings: An anthology of literature by and about women with disabilities</u> (pp. 118–127). New York: Feminist Press at City University of New York.

Two or More Books by the Same Author

Olsen, T. (1979). <u>Silences</u>. New York: Dell Publishing.

Olsen, T. (1985). <u>Tell me a riddle</u>. New York: Dell Publishing.

Periodicals: Journals, Magazines, and Newspapers

Journal with Continuous Pagination

Culp, M. B. (1983). Religion in the poetry of Langston Hughes. <u>Phylon</u>, <u>48</u>, 240–245.

Journal That Paginates Each Issue Separately

Hardwick, J. (1992). Widowhood and patriarchy in seventeenth-century France. <u>Journal of Social History</u>, <u>26</u>(1), 133–148.

Article in a Magazine

Mazzatenta, O. L. (1992, August). A Chinese emperor's army for eternity. <u>National Geographic</u>, pp. 114–130.

Article in a Daily Newspaper, Signed

Soto, O. R. (1992, January 28). Putting the tag on graffiti-smearers. <u>Press Telegram</u>, sec. B, p. 3.

Article in a Daily Newspaper, Unsigned or Editorial

Back to Future. (1992, May 3). <u>Los Angeles Times</u>, p. M-4.

Titled Review

Ansa, T. M. (1992, July 5). Taboo territory [Review of <u>Possessing the secret of joy</u>]. <u>Los Angeles Times Book Review</u>, pp. 4, 8.

Personal Interview

Interviews that you conduct yourself are not listed in APA references. Instead, use an in-text parenthetical citation. If the subject's name is in your text, use this form: "(personal communication, June 23, 1992)." If the subject's name is not in your text, use this form: "(S. Olson, personal communication, June 23, 1992)."

3

THE HANDBOOK

■ ■ ■

This handbook is designed to help you use words and control sentences in order to write convincing, error-free papers. You can use this handbook while you are drafting and revising your essays, as well as to understand the comments that your instructors write in the margins of your papers.

We do not believe that you need an extensive background in grammar in order to write clearly or well. But we are convinced that control of grammar and punctuation will give you power over both your ideas *and* your readers.

You may believe that you make numerous mistakes on your papers; indeed, the prevalence of circled words and margin notes on some may seem overwhelming. If you and your friends were to examine all of your papers, however, you would discover that you do not make a great number of *different* errors so much as you repeat the same kind of error many times. For that reason, we have isolated those recurrent errors for discussion and correction.

This handbook begins with a short chapter on "Understanding How Sentences Work." This chapter is deliberately succinct; in it we try to meet your needs without telling you more than you ever wanted (or needed) to know about the elements of a sentence. The next chapter, "Understanding Common Errors," precisely identifies and describes those recurrent errors—the "terrible ten"—that typically appear in student papers. The following chapter, "Understanding Punctuation," will help you eliminate guesswork and punctuate accurately. In "Understanding Faulty Word Choice," you will learn how well-chosen words can strengthen your essays. To determine quickly whether your word choice is sound, you can use the alphabetical list of troublesome words in the last chapter, "Understanding Commonly Confused Words."

As you are revising your drafts, you can use this handbook whenever you feel uncertain about your grammar or mechanics. When your papers are returned, you can use it as a guide to error correction by matching your instructor's margin notes to the symbols used in this book. Ultimately, this handbook is designed to empower you without overwhelming you.

EDITING SYMBOLS

The following symbols may be used by your instructor to indicate errors in your paper. You may also use these symbols when you proofread a paper to denote changes you will want to make in your drafts or to mark errors in your classmates' papers.

∧	insert (such as a missing word or punctuation)
∧	insert comma
∼	reverse (such as letters or words)
ℓ	delete (such as punctuation or word)
#	add a space
⊂	close up space
⌗	new paragraph
no⌗	no paragraph
≡	capitalize
/	use lower case

Sentence errors, discussed in Chapter 12, are commonly indicated by the following symbols:

frag	fragment
ros. or *r–o*	run-on sentence
fs	fused sentence
cs	comma splice
ref	pronoun reference
agr	agreement

shift	inconsistency in text
mixed	mixed construction
mm	misplaced modifier
//	faulty parallelism
P	faulty punctuation

Symbols used to correct word choice errors, discussed in Chapters 14 and 15, and other symbols to designate common errors include:

cliché	cliché, an overused or trite expression
dialect	not standard English usage, or a regional, occupational, or ethnic word not appropriate in the context used
d or *dic*	diction, inappropriate level
id	idiomatic, not standard American usage; the problem often appears in preposition use
jarg	jargon, or an occupational word inappropriate for formal writing
nonst.	nonstandard; may indicate idiomatic use, jargon, or slang
sl or *slang*	the level of the word choice is inappropriate
trite	overused expression, as a cliché
wd ch	word choice; a general term that may indicate any of the more definitively marked errors on this list
w/w	wrong word; a general term that may indicate a word confused with another word, slang, jargon, improper word, or idiom
X	obvious error; may refer to any of the above
awk	awkward
coh	lacks coherence
?	confused meaning
red	redundant

sp	spelling error
trans	stronger transition needed
wdy	wordy

In addition to denoting errors, your instructor may indicate strong writing and good points by using this symbol:

✓	excellent point and word choice

11

Understanding How Sentences Work

■ ■ ■

Understanding how sentences work will give you the vocabulary you need to discuss your writing, as well as to correct errors that have been noted in your papers. Such knowledge will also increase your power and versatility as a writer. By eliminating some of the guesswork that can hamper student writers, this handbook can help give you the tools and confidence to write with conviction.

As you probably know, every sentence must contain a **subject** and a **verb.** This basic unit is called a **clause.** (For more on clauses, see pp. 509–510.) In key examples throughout this section, we often have underlined the subject once and the verb twice to help you identify them quickly.

SUBJECTS

A **subject** is who or what a clause is about.

    Ryan draws constantly.

[Subjects may precede verbs.]

    There is a grin on Adam's face.

[Subjects may follow verbs.]

Noun as Subject

The subject of the clause may be a **noun** or a **pronoun.** A **noun** can be a

person: athlete, Whitney Houston, veterinarian

place: Lake Erie, bike path, the Acropolis

thing: computer, hammock, Harley-Davidson

quality/idea/activity: wit, peace, dancing

Pronoun as Subject

A **pronoun** takes the place of a noun and can also function as the subject of a clause. Pronouns can be

personal: I, you, he, she, it, we, they

> <u>They</u> reviewed their lecture notes.

indefinite: all, any, anybody, anything, each, either, everybody, everyone, neither, nobody, none, no one, nothing, one, some, somebody, someone, something

> <u>Everybody</u> needs to recycle.

demonstrative: that, this, such, these, those

> <u>Those</u> are the sale items.

relative: who, whom, whoever, whomever, whose, which, whichever, that, what

> The order <u>that</u> is ready is the deluxe pizza.

[In this example, that is the subject of the dependent or relative clause. The subject of the independent clause is <u>order</u>.] (For more about clauses, see pp. 509–510.)

interrogative: who, whom, whoever, whomever, whose, which, that, what

> <u>Who</u> recommended this awful film?

Compound Subject

Subjects may be *compound,* as in these sentences:

> <u>Julie</u> and <u>Joe</u> restore old automobiles.
>
> <u>Books</u> and <u>papers</u> collected on his desk.
>
> Here are <u>questions</u> and <u>assignments</u> for each reading.
>
> The <u>dietician</u> and <u>nurses</u> gave the patients new menus.

OBJECTS

Direct Object

Not all nouns function as the subject of a clause. A noun that receives the action of the verb is called a **direct object.** In the sentence "Julie and Joe restore old automobiles," the noun *automobiles* answers the question, "What do Julie and Joe restore?" *Automobiles* is thus the direct object of the verb *restore.*

Indirect Object

A noun that identifies to or for whom or what the action of the verb is performed is the **indirect object.** In the sentence "The dietician and nurses gave the patients new menus," the noun *patients* answers the question, "To whom were the menus given?"

Object of the Preposition

A noun that follows a preposition (see list on p. 507) is called the **object of the preposition.** In the sentence "Books and papers collected on his desk," the noun *desk* is the object of the preposition *on.*

Objects may provide important information in a sentence, but they are not necessary in order to have a clause. **Verbs,** however, are essential.

VERBS

A **verb** is what the subject does, is, has, or has done to it. The verb may be more than one word (<u>may be coming</u>). The verb also changes form to agree with the subject (he <u>drives</u>; they <u>drive</u>) and to indicate time (he <u>drove</u>, he <u>has driven</u>). Regular verbs form their past tense by adding *-ed,* but there are a number of irregular forms like *drive* that have special forms.

Action Verbs

An **action verb** specifies what the subject does, has, or has done to it. The action does not have to be physical in any sense: *meditate* is an action verb. Other action verbs include *dance, think, laugh, provoke, erupt,* and *suggest:*

Wally's humor <u>relaxes</u> everyone.

Dr. Sanders <u>wrote</u> an insightful study of Oates' work.

State-of-Being Verbs

A **state-of-being** or **linking verb** specifies what the subject is. State-of-being verbs include the following: *is, are, was, were, am, feel, seem, be, being, been, do, does, did, have, has, had*. These can be main verbs or helping verbs. For more on helping verbs, see the following section.

```
Dylan is interested in American history.
```

[<u>is</u> as main verb.]

```
Evan is playing volleyball this year.
```

[<u>is</u> as a helping verb.]

Note: Words ending in *-ing* need a helping verb in order to function as the main verb of a sentence. The *-ing* form of the verb can also function as a noun: <u>Playing</u> is a form of <u>learning</u> for small children. Here *playing* is the subject, and *learning* is the object of the preposition *of*. Thus, just because there is an *-ing* word in a word group, there is not necessarily a verb.

Helping Verbs

The **helping verb** is always used with a main verb. Helping verbs include *can, will, shall, should, could, would, may, might,* and *must*.

```
The designated driver will get everyone home safely.
```

```
They should have requested assistance.
```

ADJECTIVES AND ADVERBS

Many sentences contain modifying words that describe the nouns and verbs. **Adjectives** modify nouns (*corroded* pipes, *hectic* schedule) and pronouns (the *curious* one). **Adverbs** modify verbs (*cautiously* responded), adjectives (*truly* generous), adverbs (*very* slowly), and word groups (*Eventually*, he entered the room.) Adverbs answer the questions *how? when? where?* and *why?* They often end in *-ly*, but not always.

The following sentence contains both adjectives and adverbs. Can you identify each?

```
According to Barbara Ehrenreich, angry young men often
will vent their frustrations on vulnerable, weaker beings--
typically children or women.
```

The adjectives *angry* and *young* modify the noun *men;* the adjectives *vulnerable* and *weaker* modify the noun *beings.* The adverbs *often* and *typically* modify the verb *will vent.*

Adjectives and adverbs can provide valuable details, but they can be overused. Being descriptive doesn't require a string of adjectives and adverbs. Often a strong verb gives a more precise picture in fewer words:

```
The drunken man walked unsteadily and unevenly from the bar.

The drunken man staggered from the bar.
```

The verb *staggered* is vivid and precise. The pile-up of adverbs in the first sentence is wordy and imprecise. Such tightening often improves writing and saves space for more necessary depth and development.

PHRASES

Just as clauses do not necessarily have objects, adjectives, and adverbs, they also do not necessarily have any phrases. Because, typically, the subject and verb must be elsewhere in the sentence. This is particularly helpful to know in order to avoid fragments.

A **phrase** is a group of words forming part of a sentence. There are many types of phrases, but below we discuss two of the most common.

Prepositional Phrases

A **prepositional phrase** always starts with a **preposition** (a word that shows relationships in time and space) and ends with the **object** of the preposition. The most common prepositions are listed below.

about	beside	from	outside	toward
above	besides	in	over	under
across	between	inside	past	underneath
after	beyond	into	plus	unlike
against	but	like	regarding	until
along	by	near	respecting	unto
among	concerning	next	round	up
around	considering	of	since	upon
as	despite	off	than	with
at	down	on	through	without
before	during	onto	throughout	
behind	except	opposite	till	
below	for	out	to	

Some prepositions, such as *along with, as well as, in addition to, next to,* and *up to* are more than one word long.

The object of the preposition is always a noun or pronoun:

<u>Elaine</u> <u>finds</u> the best deals **at yard sales.**

During intermission <u>Becky</u> and <u>Joey</u> <u>went</u> **for popcorn.**

At home, <u>Anne</u> <u>babysits</u> **for her daughter during the day.**

[In the last sentence, *at home, for her daughter,* and *during the day* are all prepositional phrases. Note how much easier it is to locate the subject and verb when the prepositional phrases are eliminated.]

Verbal Phrases

These phrases look like verbs, but they do not function as the main verb of the clause. Verbal phrases may serve as subjects, objects, adjectives, and adverbs. Two main types of verbal phrases are **infinitive phrases** and **-*ing* phrases.**

Infinitive Phrases

If the verb is preceded by *to* (*to ski*), the verb is in the **infinitive** form. It helps to recognize infinitives because they cannot be the main verbs.

Most <u>professors</u> <u>like</u> **to challenge** students.

To think <u>is</u> **to question.**

[Infinitives can function as subjects.]

-ing Phrases

A word ending in *-ing* may look like a verb, but it needs a helping verb or a main verb elsewhere in the sentence. Notice how *working* serves a different function in each of the following sentences (only in the first sentence is it part of the main verb):

<u>Rise Daniels</u> <u>is</u> **working** as an art director.

Working as an art director <u>requires</u> overtime hours.

[When *-ing* words function as subjects, they are called **gerunds.**]

The **working** <u>artist</u> exhibited her paintings.

[When *-ing* words function as adjectives, they are called **participles.**]

-*ing* words and phrases can often lead writers to believe they have a complete sentence—that is, at least one independent clause—when they may have only a fragment. For example, "In the evening after arriving home from work" is not an independent clause; it simply consists of three phrases.

One way to determine if there is an independent clause, and therefore a sentence, is to draw a line through each phrase:

~~In the evening~~ ~~after arriving home from work,~~ <u>Bill</u> <u>retreats</u>

~~to his studio~~ ~~for hours~~ ~~to play piano~~ and ~~to compose new~~

~~songs~~.

Now that you can recognize the most important parts of a sentence, you can better understand how clauses work and how they can be combined.

CLAUSES

A **clause** is a group of words with a subject and main verb. The two basic types of clauses are discussed below.

Independent (or Main) Clauses

The **independent clause** has a subject and main verb and can stand alone:

<u>Daniel</u> <u>is remodeling</u> his apartment.

<u>Alyssa</u> <u>loves</u> singing with Robert and Susie.

The <u>poet</u> <u>invited</u> Gigi and Keith backstage.

Dependent (or Subordinate) Clauses

The **dependent clause** has a subject and main verb but cannot stand alone. Dependent clauses begin with one of these **subordinate conjunctions:**

after	that, so that
although	unless
as, as if	until
because	what, whatever
before	when, whenever
how	whether
if, even if	which, whichever
in order that	while
since	who, whom, whose

Whenever a clause begins with one of these words (unless it is a question), it is a dependent clause. If we take an independent clause such as

```
We jogged
```

and put one of the subordinate conjunctions in front of it, it becomes dependent (and therefore a fragment):

```
After we jogged

Because we jogged
```

To make a complete sentence, we need to add an independent clause (or delete the subordinate conjunction):

```
After we jogged, we went for a swim.

Because we jogged, we justified eating brownies.
```

Every sentence must have at least one independent clause in it.

SENTENCE VARIATION

If you know how to control and combine clauses, you can vary your sentences for greater emphasis, more clarity, and less monotony. The four basic sentence types are illustrated below.

Simple Sentences

Simple sentences contain one independent clause:

```
Ron's support delighted us.

Despite his busy schedule, Walter spent hours with his sons
each night.
```

Compound Sentences

Compound sentences contain two independent clauses. There are only two ways to punctuate a compound sentence:

1. A **comma** followed by a coordinating conjunction (*and, but, for, or, nor, yet, so*):

```
We arrived at the cabin, so they left.
```

2. A **semicolon** by itself (or it may be followed by a word like *nevertheless* or *however*):

```
We arrived; they left.

We arrived; therefore, they left.
```

Notice that the writer's decision to use a coordinate conjunction or a semicolon is not arbitrary. If the writer wishes to clarify or emphasize the relationship between the two clauses, he or she will use a coordinate conjunction (such as *so*) or a conjunctive adverb (such as *therefore*). If the writer prefers not to define the relationship between the clauses, then the semicolon by itself is more appropriate.

Complex Sentences

Complex sentences contain one independent clause and one or more dependent clauses. Below, the dependent clauses are underscored with a broken underline.

```
When the dependent clause comes first in the sentence,
a comma is necessary.

A comma isn't necessary when the dependent clause comes
at the end.
```

Compound-Complex Sentences

Compound-complex sentences contain two or more independent clauses and one or more dependent clauses. The dependent clause or clauses may be at the beginning, at the end, or between the independent clauses. Here one dependent clause begins the sentence, and another ends the sentence:

```
Although Jane is a senior citizen, she swims competitively,
and we are all impressed that she has won so many medals.
```

In the following sentence, the dependent clause is between the two independent clauses:

```
Tammy studied before she went to work each night, but she
still felt anxious about the exam.
```

Student Assignment

Using details from the last essay that you discussed in class, write your own sentences to illustrate each sentence type: simple, compound, complex, and compound-complex. Then underline all <u>subjects</u> once and all <u>verbs</u> twice to make sure you have the necessary clauses. Manipulating these sentence types will help you vary your sentences and combine your ideas more smoothly.

12

Understanding Common Errors

■ ■ ■

In the next three chapters, we examine the ten common errors that appear most frequently in student papers. These errors are listed below, with the symbols instructors use to note these errors in the margins of your papers:

frag	fragment
ros/fs	run-on sentence or fused sentence
ref	pronoun reference
agr	agreement
shift	inconsistency in text
mixed	mixed construction
mm	misplaced modifier
//	faulty parallelism
P	faulty punctuation
wd ch	faulty word choice

FRAGMENTS

Although sentence fragments are used frequently in fiction and advertising copy to simulate spoken English, the sentence fragment is considered nonstandard in formal writing. Fragments may confuse the reader, and they make your writing seem choppy and your ideas disconnected.

frag   A **fragment** is a group of words that, for some reason, cannot stand alone as a complete sentence. The reason may be any one of the following:

1. The word group may lack a subject.

frag
```
While the students prepared their finals, they sunbathed at
the same time. Became involved in discussions that distract-
ed them from their studies.
```
[Add a subject.]
```
While the students prepared their finals, they sunbathed at
the same time. Soon they became involved in discussions that
distracted them from their studies.
```

2. The word group may lack a complete verb.

frag
```
Arriving before the concert began, we enjoyed the excitement
in the air. The band tuning up before their opening song.
```
[Add a helping verb.]
```
Arriving before the concert began, we enjoyed the excitement
in the air. The band was tuning up before their opening
song.
```

3. The word group may lack both a subject and a verb.

frag
```
I value my piano teacher. A bright and patient woman. She
encourages perfection even while she tolerates my mistakes.
```
[Attach the phrase *a bright and patient woman* to the independent clause before or after it.]
```
I value my piano teacher, a bright and patient woman. She
encourages perfection even while she tolerates my mistakes.
```
or

```
I value my piano teacher. A bright and patient woman, she
encourages perfection even while she tolerates my mistakes.
```

4. The word group may contain both a subject and a verb but be simply a dependent clause.

frag

Native American music and dances are national treasures.
Which is why our dance company performs them regularly.

[Avoid starting any sentence with *which* unless you are asking a question.]

Native American music and dances are national treasures.
<u>This</u> <u>is</u> why our dance company performs them regularly.

or

Because Native American music and dances are national treasures, our dance company performs them regularly.

Another example of such a fragment is the following:

frag

Although rap music has been criticized for its violence and
harsh language. Rap really reflects the tension in the cities
rather than causes it.

Although rap music has been criticized for its violence and
harsh language, rap really reflects the tension in the
cities rather than causes it.

As noted earlier, writers may deliberately use a fragment for
emphasis or to mimic conversation, but these uses are always controlled and planned. Otherwise, fragments make an essay confusing or choppy. Sometimes the simplest solution is to connect the
fragment to an independent clause that is either right before or
after it.

RUN-ON OR FUSED SENTENCES

ros
fs

Run-on or **fused sentences,** or sentences flawed with a **comma
splice,** occur when a writer perceives that the thoughts in two complete sentences are related but fails to join the thoughts appropriately.
Sometimes the writer makes the mistake of inserting a comma

cs

between the independent clauses, creating a comma splice. No punctuation at all between the independent clauses creates a run-on or
fused sentence. Both errors occur because the writer sees a relationship between sentences and isn't sure what to do to show the relationship.

The "sentence" that follows is one anyone might say, and a writer
might be tempted to write:

ros

It snowed for days the skiers were ecstatic.

The writer has clearly perceived a relationship between the joy of the skiers and the weather conditions. But the word group is incorrectly punctuated and is a run-on or fused sentence.

Comma Splice

The writer may decide to "correct" the error by inserting a comma between the two independent clauses:

CS

```
It snowed for days, the skiers were ecstatic.
```

The comma is inadequate punctuation, however, for separating the independent clauses. That "correction" results in the sentence fault called a **comma splice,** which is noted as "**CS**" in the margin of a paper.

Correcting Run-on Sentences

The methods below illustrate alternatives for correcting run-on sentences. Notice that the five choices are all grammatically correct, but each places different emphasis on the two clauses and may change the meaning of the sentence.

1. Separate each independent clause with a period.

```
It snowed for days. The skiers were ecstatic.
```

2. Use a comma plus a coordinating conjunction (*and, but, for, or, nor, yet, so*) between the independent clauses.

```
It snowed for days, and the skiers were ecstatic.
```
or

```
It snowed for days, yet the skiers were ecstatic.
```
or

```
It snowed for days, so the skiers were ecstatic.
```

3. Use a semicolon between the independent clauses.

```
It snowed for days; the skiers were ecstatic.
```

4. Change one independent clause into a dependent clause.

```
Because it snowed for days, the skiers were ecstatic.
```
or

```
The skiers were ecstatic because it snowed for days.
```

Notice that when the dependent clause begins the sentence, a comma separates it from the main clause. Conversely, when the independent clause begins the sentence, there is no comma before the dependent clause that concludes the sentence. See page 509 for a list of words that begin dependent clauses.

5. Use a semicolon after the first independent clause, and then a conjunctive adverb (see below) followed by a comma:

```
It snowed for days; consequently, the skiers were ecstatic.
```

or

```
It snowed for days; nevertheless, the skiers were ecstatic.
```

Conjunctive Adverbs

Conjunctive adverbs include: *accordingly, also, anyway, besides, certainly, consequently, conversely, finally, furthermore, hence, however, incidentally, indeed, instead, likewise, meanwhile, moreover, nevertheless, next, nonetheless, otherwise, similarly, specifically, still, subsequently, then, therefore,* and *thus.*

Style and Meaning

Grammatical correction of a run-on-sentence is not the only concern of the writer. Style, emphasis, and meaning also should be considered when you are deciding which conjunction to use. Notice the difference in emphasis in the following examples:

```
It snowed for days. The skiers were ecstatic.
```

```
Because it snowed for days, the skiers were ecstatic.
```

In the first correction, the writer asks the reader to infer the relationship between the skiers' being "ecstatic" and the fact that "it snowed for days." In the second example, the cause-and-effect relationship is defined clearly. Take the following simple sentences, also fused, and notice what happens to the meaning, emphasis, or relationship between the independent clauses when different corrections are employed:

ros

```
Renée pitched the team won.
```

1. ```
Renée pitched. The team won.
```

There is not a relationship that the writer has defined between the facts stated in the two sentences.
```

2. Renée pitched, and the team won.

A mild relationship is suggested by connecting the two events with *and*.

Renée pitched, so the team won.

The relationship between the team's victory and the person who pitched is defined in this construction using *so*.

Renée pitched, yet the team won.

The use of *yet*, which signals something contrary to expectation, changes the relationship between the independent clauses in this example. The word *yet* tells the reader that in spite of the fact that Renée pitched, the team won.

3. Renée pitched; the team won.

The semicolon does not define the relationship between the two independent clauses although a subtle relationship *is* suggested by the writer's using a semicolon instead of a period. The semicolon is a compromise punctuation symbol. It is stronger than a comma, but it is not as complete a stop as a period.

4. Whenever Renée pitched, the team won.

The team won because Renée pitched.

Although Renée pitched, the team won.

The team won unless Renée pitched.

The dependent clause, whether it begins or ends the sentence, defines the exact relationship between the two clauses in the sentence. Clearly, the subordinate conjunction chosen has everything to do with the meaning of the sentence.

5. Renée pitched; therefore, the team won.

Renée pitched; nevertheless, the team won.

Again, the conjunctive adverb defines the precise relationship between the two clauses of the sentence. For the purpose of connecting two short independent clauses, most writers would find the combination of semicolon and conjunctive adverb and comma too cumbersome. A coordinating conjunction with a comma would probably be a better method of linking the two clauses.

PRONOUN REFERENCE

ref

Pronouns are words that take the place of nouns. In most cases, pronouns are an advantage to the writer because they permit reference to nouns named without the writer's having to repeat the noun or finding a clear substitute (or synonym) for it. Ambiguity, vagueness, or confusion can result, however, if the writer has not used pronouns responsibly. The margin symbol "**ref**" indicates a problem with the pronoun reference.

This chart shows the form personal pronouns take:

	Singular	
Subjective	*Possessive*	*Objective*
I	my, mine	me
you	your, yours	you
he	his	him
she	her, hers	her
it	its	it
	Plural	
we	our, ours	us
you	your, yours	you
they	their, theirs	them

Indefinite pronouns include *all, any, anybody, anything, each, either, everybody, everyone, everything, neither, nobody, none, no one, nothing, one, some, somebody, someone,* and *something.*

Pronoun problems occur when the reader does not know what noun is referred to by the noun substitute, the pronoun.

1. Sometimes the pronoun used could refer to either of two nouns:

ref

When Karen told Pat the news, she burst into tears.

She can refer to either Karen or Pat. The ambiguity must be resolved for the reader:

Pat burst into tears when Karen told her the news.

or

Karen burst into tears when she told Pat the news.

2. Sometimes the subject is implied by the writer but is not stated in the sentence. The pronoun does not clearly refer to any given noun, and confusion results for the reader:

ref

```
For years, Pete carried rocks from the quarry, and it
strained his back.
```

It cannot refer to the plural *rocks,* and the singular noun *quarry* didn't "strain his back." The writer probably means "this work" or "the constant hauling of heavy rocks." The writer needs to make that clarification in the sentence:

```
For years, Pete carried rocks from the quarry, and this work
strained his back.
```

3. Indefinite pronouns can also pose a problem for writer and reader if the singular form of the indefinite pronoun is inconsistent with the meaning of the sentence or the gender of the pronoun is assumed by the writer to be a generic *he.* Generally, a singular pronoun should be used with an indefinite pronoun:

```
Each boy on the football team has his own locker.

Anybody who has her doubts about the value of natural child-
birth should take a Lamaze course.
```

If the writer is certain of the singular intention and gender of the subject, no problems arise in determining the form of the possessive pronoun and no reader will be offended. If the indefinite pronoun has a plural meaning, however, the grammatical necessity of a singular possessive pronoun may result in an inappropriate use of a generic *his,* or an awkward, repetitive use of *his or her,* or the temptation to use the incorrect form *his/her.*

Here is an example of the problem:

ref

```
Everybody running for class office should report to his
counselor.
```

Everybody is a singular pronoun and requires a singular possessive pronoun: *his* or *her. Their* is plural and can't be used in this sentence. But should the writer assume the generic *his?* A reader might object that the implication of the sentence is that only males may run for class office. A similar misunderstanding would occur if the writer opted for *her* as the singular possessive pronoun. If this were a single-sentence statement, as in a school bulletin, the writer might choose *his or her* for a correct and clear mandate. But the repetitive use of *his or her* can be a burden in a lengthy manuscript.

Learn to find alternatives. A plural noun and plural possessive pronoun will take care of the problem, so rewrite the sentence:

```
All of the candidates for class office should report to
their counselors.
```

You may also want to see "Sexist Language" (pp. 553–554) in Chapter 14 for further discussion of pronoun choices.

AGREEMENT

agr The margin note **"agr"** means that there is an agreement problem; the subject and the verb do not agree in number. Both subject and verb should be singular or both should be plural. Speakers who are comfortable with standard English usually will not have trouble selecting the correct verb form for the subject of sentences. But some sentences, especially those that have groups of words separating the subject and verb, may offer a temporary problem for any writer. Some conditions to be aware of are listed below.

1. A prepositional phrase does not influence the verb of the sentence:

```
The birds in the nest need food from the mother bird.

Our first five days of vacation are going to be in New York
City.

Her secretary, in addition to her staff, prefers the new
computer.
```

Notice that by removing the prepositional phrases from your consideration, you will use the correct verb form for the subject of the sentence.

2. Subjects connected by *and* usually have a plural verb:

```
The student's academic load and work time keep him busy.
```

a. When the compound subject (nouns connected by *and*) is regarded as a unit, the subject is regarded as singular and has a singular verb:

```
Peanut butter and jelly remains Raul's favorite lunch.
```

b. If the double nouns refer to the same person or thing, the verb is singular:

```
Bill's home and studio is 215 Thompson Street.
```

   c. When *each* or *every* precedes the multiple nouns, use a singular verb:

<u>Each</u> instructor, student, and staff member <u>prefers</u> the

new insurance plan.

   d. When nouns are connected by *or* or *nor*, the verb agrees with the noun closer to it:

Your student ID or room <u>key</u> <u>guarantees</u> the loan of a

beach chair.

Your student ID or room <u>keys</u> <u>guarantee</u> the loan of a

beach chair.

Neither the police officer nor his <u>cadets</u> <u>were attending</u>

the lecture.

Either the band or the <u>comedian</u> <u>provides</u> the program notes.

3. Most indefinite pronouns have a singular verb, even if the pronoun seems to convey a plural sense. Indefinite pronouns include *anybody, anyone, each, either, everybody, everyone, everything, neither, none, no one, someone,* and *something.* Notice how each indefinite pronoun is used in the following sentences:

<u>Each</u> of the band members <u>has</u> two free tickets.

<u>Everybody</u> <u>endures</u> the stress of two finals a day.

<u>Everyone</u> on the school board <u>votes</u> at each meeting.

All, any, or *some,* however, may be singular or plural depending on what the pronoun refers to:

<u>All</u> of the pizza <u>is gone</u>.

<u>All</u> of the books <u>are shelved</u>.

4. Collective nouns (like *band, family, committee, class, jury,* and *audience*) require a singular verb unless the meaning of the noun is plural, or individuality is to be emphasized:

The <u>jury</u> <u>presents</u> its decision today.

The <u>jury</u> <u>are</u> undecided about a verdict.

5. Even when the subject follows the verb, the verb must be in the correct form:

There <u>remains</u> too little <u>time</u> to organize the campaign.

6. Titles require singular verbs:

<u>Roots</u> <u>is</u> the book we will read next.

<u>Jacoby and Associates</u> <u>is</u> the law firm on the corner.

<u>Succulents</u> <u>is</u> the section of the nursery Carlos prefers.

7. Nouns describing academic disciplines—like *economics, statistics,* or *physics*—and diseases that end in an *s*—like *mumps* and *measles*— and *news*—are treated as singular nouns:

<u>Physics</u> <u>challenges</u> Maria, but she does well in the course.

<u>Measles</u> usually <u>attacks</u> only the children who have not been inoculated.

SHIFTS

shift The margin note **"shift"** marks an inconsistency in the text in person, number, or verb tense.

Shifts in Person and Number

Shifts in person and number sometimes occur because you are not certain from what point of view to write or because you move from one perspective to another without being conscious of the change. You may begin with the idea of addressing a general audience— "someone"—and then decide to address the reader as "you." Or you may begin with a singular reader in mind and switch to a plural sense of "all readers." If you start to write from one perspective and switch to another, a distracting shift occurs:

shift   If <u>someone</u> in the group writes a paper, <u>they</u> may present it.

Corrections:

If a <u>person</u> writes a paper, <u>he or she</u> may present it.

or, better:

If <u>people</u> write papers, <u>they</u> may present them.

shift

The vegetarian learns to prepare interesting and nutritious
meals with vegetables and grains, but then you have to
assure your friends that you're getting enough protein.

Corrections:

If you are a vegetarian, you learn to prepare interesting
and nutritious meals with vegetables and grains, but then
you have to assure your friends that you're getting enough
protein.

or

Vegetarians learn to prepare interesting and nutritious
meals with vegetables and grains, but then they have to
assure their friends that they are getting enough protein.

Shifts in Verb Tense

Shifts in verb tense will confuse a reader about the time the action of
your sentence takes place. You have probably heard oral story-tellers
shift from one tense to another. Eventually you may have figured out
the course of the narration, perhaps by asking the speaker to clarify
the time of the action. But a shift in tense is particularly distracting
in writing because you can't ask a writer for a clarification of the text.
Notice how the verb tense in the following example shifts from the
past to the present:

shift

Shortly after we arrived at the picnic site, it started to
rain. So we pack up the bread, salami, and fruit and rush to
the cars.

Correction for verb tense consistency:

Shortly after we arrived at the picnic site, it started to
rain. So we packed up the bread, salami, and fruit and
rushed to the cars.

Use the present tense throughout to write a summary or a description of a literary work:

shift

Daisy Miller first meets Winterbourne in Geneva, and she later
met him in Rome where she is dating the charming Giovanelli.

Winterbourne <u>was</u> furious that Daisy <u>does</u>n't <u>realize</u> that
Giovanelli <u>was</u>n't a "real" gentleman.

Correction for verb tense consistency:

Daisy Miller first <u>meets</u> Winterbourne in Geneva, and she
later <u>meets</u> him in Rome where she <u>is dating</u> the charming
Giovanelli. Winterbourne <u>is</u> furious that Daisy <u>does</u>n't
<u>realize</u> that Giovanelli <u>is</u>n't a "real" gentleman.

Shifts in Voice

Just as a shift in number or tense can be distracting, a shift from one
voice to another can confuse or distract your reader. Use the active
voice or passive voice consistently.

When the subject of a sentence does the action, the sentence is in
the **active voice**:

<u>Lester</u> <u>brought</u> the tossed salad.

When the subject *receives* the action, the verb is in the **passive
voice**. Notice that the passive voice is less effective than the active
voice because it is less direct:

The tossed <u>salad</u> <u>was brought</u> by Lester.

When the active and passive voice are combined, the sentence is
inconsistent in voice and would be marked with a "shift" in the margin of the paper:

shift   <u>Lester</u> <u>brought</u> the tossed salad, and the soft <u>drinks</u> <u>were</u>
<u>brought</u> by Mike.

Correction:

<u>Lester</u> <u>brought</u> the tossed salad, and Mike brought the soft
drinks.

In some cases, the passive voice is necessary because what might
be the subject of the sentence is unknown or unimportant:

The <u>car</u> <u>was hijacked</u> last week.

Because the hijacker is apparently unknown, the sentence is in the
passive voice, with the action being done to the car, the subject of the
sentence.

```
NASA was granted additional funds to complete the study for
the space station.
```

The name of the agency that granted NASA the funds for the study may be unimportant to the writer of this sentence; the important point is that NASA has the funds for the project.

Passive voice constructions may create suspicion that the writer is deliberately hiding information:

```
The city council was voted unlimited travel funds.
```

Clearly, the city resident who reads that sentence in the local paper would want to know *who* did the voting, and why the newspaper failed to name the subject of the verb *voted*. Use the active voice whenever you know and wish to identify the "doer" of a particular act.

MIXED SENTENCES

mixed The margin note **"mixed"** indicates that there are sentence parts that don't go together. The sentence may start with one subject and shift to another, or the verb may not fit the true subject of the sentence. The sentence also may begin with one grammatical construction and end with another. The problem, then, is a misfit in grammar or in logic, so the sentence is confusing to the reader:

mixed
```
Although he is active in the men's movement doesn't mean he
is a misogynist.
```

In this sentence the writer tries to make the dependent clause *Although he is active in the men's movement* the subject of the sentence. The writer probably intends *he* to be the subject of the sentence; rewriting the sentence to show this *and* selecting a correct verb for the subject will eliminate the confusion:

```
Although he is active in the men's movement, he is not a
misogynist.
```

Confused Sentence Parts

Each of the mixed sentences on page 527 contains a confusion between sentence parts. In some cases, the writer has started with one subject in mind and has ended the sentence with a different or implied subject. In other cases, the grammatical form of the first part of the sentence is inconsistent with the end of the sentence. Most often the revision involves correct identification of the true subject of the sentence and then the selection of an appropriate verb.

mixed   Among those women suffering with eating disorders, they are not always bulimic.

Not all women with eating disorders are bulimic.

mixed   By prewriting, outlining, drafting, and revising is how he wrote good papers.

He wrote good papers by prewriting, outlining, drafting, and revising his work.

mixed   The subject of ecology involves controversy.

Ecology involves controversy.

Faulty Verb Choice

In some sentences with mixed meaning, the fault occurs because the subject is said to do or to be something that is illogical.

mixed   A realization between the academic senate and the dean would be the ideal policy on plagiarism.

The sentence says that "a realization" would be "the ideal policy," which is not exactly what the writer means. Correction of the faulty use of the verb *would be* will clarify the sentence.

Ideally, a policy on plagiarism would be decided between the academic senate and the dean.

or

Ideally, the academic senate and the dean would realize the necessity for a policy on plagiarism.

In speech, *is when* and *is where* are common constructions for defining words, but these are mixed constructions and should be corrected in writing.

mixed   Acquiescence is when you give in to your oppressor.

Acquiescence means to give in to an oppressor.

mixed   A final exam is where you show comprehensive knowledge.

On a final exam you show comprehensive knowledge.

MISPLACED (AND DANGLING) MODIFIERS

mm   The margin note "**MM**" means misplaced modifier. A **modifier** is a word, phrase, or clause used to describe another word in the sentence. The modifier should be as close to that word as possible, or the meaning can be confusing or unintentionally humorous.

mm   Attacking our canary, I caught the cat.

Written this way, *attacking the canary* appears to describe *I* rather than *cat*. Such a misplaced modifier can be easily corrected by rearranging the phrase so it describes *cat:*

   I caught the cat attacking our canary.

Sometimes there may not be a word for the modifier to describe. In these cases, the sentence needs to be rewritten:

mm   At the age of 12, my family hiked into the Grand Canyon.

Here the writer probably does not mean that his or her family was 12 years old, but this sentence does not contain a word for the opening phrase to describe. Therefore, *at the age of 12* is called a **dangling modifier** because it fails to refer logically to any word in the sentence. Dangling modifiers can be corrected by the following methods:

1. Keeping the modifier as it is and adding a word for the modifier to describe.

mm   At the age of 12, I hiked into the Grand Canyon with my
   family.

2. Turning the modifier into a dependent clause so that the meaning is clear.

   When I was 12, my family hiked into the Grand Canyon.

Often the modifier is not simply "dangling" but is oddly placed in the sentence so that the meaning is absurd:

mm   You will value the difficult classes you took semesters
   from now.

   Semesters from now, you will value the difficult classes
   you took.

mm   Yuko's blind date was described as a six-foot-tall musician
   with a long ponytail weighing only 160 pounds.

```
Yuko's blind date was described as a 160-pound, six-foot-
tall musician with a long ponytail.
```

Misplaced words can turn even the most serious dissertation into a comedy of errors! Occasionally an instructor may simply write "awk" (awkward) or "confusing" or "reword" in the margins when the error is actually a misplaced modifier. Becoming aware of the importance of the *placement* of each word or phrase in a sentence can help you detect and prevent such comical and confusing meanings before you type your final draft.

FAULTY PARALLELISM

To achieve clarity, emphasis, and harmony in writing, use **parallel construction** for parts of sentences that you repeat. The "parts" may be single words, phrases, or clauses. Therefore, when you write any kind of list, put the items in similar grammatical form (all *-ing* words, all infinitives, and so on). Instead of writing "He likes hiking and to ski," you should write "He likes hiking and skiing" or "He likes to hike and to ski."

// If **faulty parallelism** is noted in the margin of your paper, you have not kept the parts of your sentence in the same grammatical form.

Single Words

//
```
The movie entertained and was enlightening.
```
```
The movie was entertaining and enlightening.
```

Phrases

//
```
Jane enjoys telling complicated jokes, performing the latest
dances, and exotic food.
```
```
Jane enjoys telling complicated jokes, performing the latest
dances, and eating exotic food.
```

Dependent Clauses

//
```
The instructor reminded the students that papers must be
submitted on time and to prepare reading assignments before
class.
```

The instructor reminded the students **that papers must be submitted on time** and **that reading assignments must be prepared before class.**

Independent Clauses

// "I came, I did some learning, and I triumphed," announced the jubilant graduate.

"I came, I learned, and I triumphed," announced the jubilant graduate.

You can also achieve greater clarity, emphasis, and balance by using parallel constructions with correlative conjunctions (paired terms such as *not only . . . but also; either . . . or;* and *neither . . . nor*):

// We discovered fast walking is good for health and also for friendship.

We discovered that fast walking is good **not only for health but also for friendship.**

// Fran doesn't work as a waitress any longer, and neither does Donna.

Neither Fran nor Donna works as a waitress any longer.

13

Understanding Punctuation

■ ■ ■

P A **"P"** in the margin of an essay indicates some sort of error in punctuation. Because the comma is the most frequently used punctuation symbol, most errors occur in comma use. Commas usually function to separate elements within a sentence, but they also have standard uses in dates, addresses, and in multiple-digit numbers. Below are models of the standard uses of the comma, with brief explanations to help you avoid comma errors.

THE COMMA

1. Use a comma *before a coordinating conjunction* joining independent clauses. (Coordinating conjunctions are *and, but, for, or, nor, yet,* and *so.* See also p. 510.)

   ```
   The school board has slashed the budget, so activity fees
   will increase this year.
   ```

   ```
   Many men want to take paternity leave when their babies are
   born, but most companies are not prepared for the requests.
   ```

   Short independent clauses may not need a comma with the conjunction, but if there is any doubt about the need or clarity, use the comma.

   ```
   He arrived so I left.
   ```

   ```
   He arrived, so I left.
   ```

2. Use a comma *to separate introductory elements* from the rest of the sentence:

   ```
   To register for classes, bring your advisor's signature
   card.
   ```

If elementary schools continue to close, increased bus service will be necessary.

Exhilarated, the climber reached the summit.

By the next century, most college graduates will be in
service-related careers.

3. Use a comma *to separate items* in a series.

The campus bookstore has been criticized for selling sexist
magazines, cigarettes, and greeting cards of questionable
taste.

Triathlons require quick running, swimming, and cycling.

The requirements for ownership of the condominium include
a bank-approved loan, a satisfactory security rating, and
a willingness to comply with the homeowners' rules and
procedures.

4. Use a comma *between coordinate adjectives* if there is not a conjunction. Coordinate adjectives are adjectives that modify the same
word equally.

The shady, blooming, fragrant garden welcomed the walkers.

A shady and fragrant garden welcomed the walkers.

If the first adjective modifies the second adjective, do *not* use a
comma.

That mansion's most interesting feature is a white oak
staircase.

Professor Pierce's exams require complicated mathematical
computations.

5. Use commas *to set off nonrestrictive word groups.* Nonrestrictive
elements describe nouns or pronouns by giving extra or nonessen-
tial information. The nonrestrictive element could be removed
from the sentence without sacrificing the accuracy of the sentence.

Walden Pond, which is located outside of Concord, was the
site of Thoreau's one-room shelter and bean field.

Amy Tan's first novel, <u>The Joy Luck Club,</u> was written in a
few months.

The Rolls Royce, its silver hood ornament gleaming in the
sun, was completely out of gas.

6. Do *not* use commas with restrictive word groups. Restrictive elements limit the meaning of words or provide vital (or restricting) information.

The entrees on the left side of the menu are suitable for
diners who prefer low-cholesterol diets.

The sentence gives the information that only the entrees on the left side of the menu are low in cholesterol. Presumably, the other items on the menu are not especially for clients who prefer low cholesterol.

Our son who lived in Maryland studies American History.

For a family with sons residing in different states, the restrictive clause is essential and commas should not be used.

Customers using credit cards collect free airline mileage.

Again, the lack of commas shows that the information is restrictive. Only those customers who use credit cards will collect airline mileage; customers who pay by check or cash do not.

7. Use commas to separate transitional or parenthetical expressions, conjunctive adverbs, contrasting elements, and most phrases from the main part of the sentence.

Silk, for example, can be washed by hand.

Joseph Heller, as the story goes, wanted to call his novel
Catch-18 instead of Catch-22.

A medium avocado contains 324 calories; therefore, it is not
an ideal fruit for people watching their weight.

Darren, unlike his brother Stephen, can be reasonable.

Her medical studies completed, Nancy started a practice in
Fresno.

8. Use commas to set off expressions and questions of direct address, the words *yes* or *no*, and interjections.

Sorry, Professor Rigid, only two of those books are in the
stacks.

You will complete the immigration papers, won't you?

Yes, most readers prefer the new MLA documentation form.

Oh, I can't decide if we really need an attorney.

9. Use commas for dates, addresses, and titles.

James Joyce was born on February 2, 1882, St. Bridget's Day and Groundhog Day, too.

The special delivery letter was sent to 1010 Oak Street, Champaign, Illinois.

Will Wood, Ph.D., begins his new research at Duke University.

10. Use commas to set off direct quotations.

As Richard Ellman notes, "Stephen Dedalus said the family was a net which he would fly past."

"I too believe in Taos, without having seen it. I also believe in Indians. But they must do <u>half</u> the believing: in me as well as in the sun," wrote D. H. Lawrence to Mabel Luhan.

11. Do *not* use a comma to separate a verb from its subject or object. The following examples all show **incorrect** uses of the comma:

P   Fast walking around a track, can be painless but effective exercise.

P   Christine explained to Mario, that law school studying had precedence over dining and dancing.

12. Do *not* use a comma between compound elements if the word groups are not independent clauses. The following examples show **incorrect** uses of the comma:

P   Frank can prepare a multi-course meal, and bake bread on the same day.

P   Sara understands that the conference is in June, and that she will need to grade finals while she is attending it.

13. A comma should not be used to separate an adjective from the
noun that follows it. The following examples are **incorrect** uses of
the comma:

P

It was a sunny, warm, and windless, day.

P

A massive, polished, ornately carved, buffet stood in the
dining room.

THE APOSTROPHE

An **apostrophe** is used most frequently to form **contractions** and
possessives.

Contractions

When two words are merged into one, the apostrophe takes the place
of any missing letters:

does n<u>o</u>t	doesn'␣t
it <u>is</u>	it'␣s
should <u>have</u>	should'␣ve
I <u>would</u>	I'␣d

Contractions tend to make writing seem more conversational and
informal; therefore, contractions are often avoided in formal writing
and in research papers. Remember that the apostrophe takes the
place of the missing letter and does not ever belong in the break
between the two words:

couldn't [*not* could'nt]

Other instances where apostrophes indicate a missing letter or letters
are commonly found in informal writing and speech, particularly in
dialogues from narratives and fiction:

<u>a</u>round	'␣round
<u>un</u>til	'␣til
<u>19</u>50's	'␣50's
playi<u>ng</u>	playin'␣

Again, such forms are typically reserved for writing that is intended
to sound conversational.

Possessives

Possessive nouns indicate belonging or ownership and are typically placed immediately before whatever is owned. Rather than write "the trumpet of Jason" or "the office of his doctor," we eliminate the *of* and move the owner in front of the possession:

```
Jason's trumpet

his doctor's office
```

Sometimes such ownership is loosely implied:

```
tonight's party

Thursday's test

one day's sick leave

two weeks' vacation
```

But, in a sense, the party really does "belong" to tonight (not tomorrow) and the test "belongs" to Thursday (not Friday). Similarly, the sick leave is "of one day" and the vacation is "of two weeks." Clearly, the possessive form here makes the writing smoother and less wordy.

To indicate possession, obey the following guidelines:

1. Add -'s if the possessive noun does not end in *s* (whether it is singular or plural):

```
Sarah's jokes

Ben's request

the men's movement

the children's enthusiasm
```

2. Add an apostrophe at the end of the word if the possessive noun ends in an *s* (whether it is singular or plural):

```
those actors' salaries

five students' projects

the Knights' generosity

James' routine

Yeats' poetry
```

You may find a variation of this second rule so that "Yeats' poetry" may be written "Yeats's poetry." It is correct either way.

Joint Possession

When two or more people possess the same thing, show joint possession by using -'s (or -s') with the last noun only:

```
We relaxed at Al and Helen's cabin.

Nate and Jess' help was appreciated.
```

Individual Possession

When two or more people possess distinct things, show individual possession by using -'s (or -s') with both nouns:

```
Andy's and Beth's summer projects aren't completed yet.

Luis' and Charles' questions were both fascinating.
```

Compound Nouns

If a noun is compound, use -'s (or -s') with the last component of that noun term:

```
My brother-in-law's woodworking is very professional.

Barbara and Joe took their sisters-in-laws' advice.
```

Indefinite Pronouns

Indefinite pronouns are those that refer to no specific person or thing: *everyone, anyone, no one,* and *something.* These pronouns also need an apostrophe to indicate possession:

```
We asked everybody's opinion of the film.

Is someone's safety in jeopardy?
```

Possessive Pronouns

Possessive pronouns are already possessive and need no apostrophes:

> my, mine
>
> you, yours
>
> her, hers
>
> his,
>
> its
>
> our, ours
>
> their, theirs
>
> whose

Whose car should we drive?

I would prefer to ride in **yours** rather than **theirs.**

Plurals of Numbers, Letters, Words, and Abbreviations

Use -'s to pluralize numbers mentioned as numbers, letters mentioned as letters, words mentioned as words, and abbreviations:

They all marched in two's.

He earned three A's this term.

Their hurray's were all we needed to hear.

All candidates must have earned their B.A.'s.

Some reminders:

1. Make sure a noun is possessive (and not merely plural) before you use an apostrophe. The noun *passengers* does not "own" anything in the following sentence; therefore it is a simple plural.

   passengers
   The ~~passenger's~~ were not allowed to smoke.

2. Possessive pronouns need no apostrophes.

   its
   The crowd expressed ~~it's~~ pleasure.

   hers
   That responsibility is ~~her's~~.

3. Many instructors prefer that their students not use contractions in formal writing and research papers.

THE PERIOD, QUESTION MARK, AND EXCLAMATION POINT

The most obvious use of the period is to mark the end of a sentence—unless the sentence is a direct question or needs an exclamation point:

Do you remember learning punctuation symbols in elementary school?

Yes, and it all seemed so easy then!

Because the exclamation point is used for strong commands and emphatic statements, it should not be overused. Further, an exclamation mark is never used with a period, a comma, or another exclamation point.

Don't use a question mark for an indirect or implied question:

```
I wonder if I ever had trouble with punctuation in elemen-
tary school.
```

Use the period for abbreviations:

```
Mr. Mrs. Ms.        Dr. Rev. Capt.        B.S. M.A. Ph.D.
B.C. A.D.           A.M. P.M.             i.e. e.g. etc.
```

Use only one period if the abbreviation falls at the end of a sentence:

```
Most archaeologists believe that Mayans were living in the
area of Tikal by 600 B.C.
```

Notice that *no* period is used with postal abbreviations:

```
CA    NY    TX    IL
```

Do *not* use periods with acronyms (words that are made from the first letters of many words and are pronounced as words):

```
NATO    UNICEF
```

Usually no period is used in abbreviations of the names of organizations or schools:

```
NBC    NATO    UN    NBA    NYU
```

THE SEMICOLON

The semicolon is most often used to connect two independent clauses:

```
Students with an advisor's signature card register in their
division office; students without a signature must register
in the gym.
```

Notice that the semicolon is used in place of a period to show that the two independent ideas—clauses that could stand alone as separate sentences—are *related*. The semicolon suggests the relationship without defining it.

The semicolon is also used after an independent clause and before some transitional phrases (like *on the other hand* or *in contrast*) and after conjunctive adverbs (such as *therefore, however,* and *furthermore;* see the complete list on p. 517).

Newcomers to the United States often enjoy material advantages that they lacked in their native lands; on the other hand, they often feel spiritually deprived in their new country.

Professor Smiley will accept late papers; however, he reduces the grade for each day the paper is late.

The semicolon is used for separating items in a list if the punctuation within the list includes commas. Notice Naomi Wolf's use of the semicolon in this example from *The Beauty Myth:*

In 1984, in the United States, "male lawyers aged 25-34 earn $27,563, but female lawyers the same age, $20,573; retail salesmen earn $13,002 to retail saleswomen's $7,479; male bus drivers make $15,611 and female bus drivers $9,903; female hairdressers earn $7,603 less than male hairdressers" (49).

THE COLON

A colon is used to introduce and call attention to a statement, to introduce a list, to introduce a quotation if the quotation is at the end of a sentence, in bibliographic forms, in reporting time, for separating main titles from subtitles, and in distinguishing chapters from verses in the Bible. A colon is usually preceded by a main clause (a word group containing a subject and verb). The main clause does not need to be followed by a complete clause.

The candidates need to realize that women form a significant majority in this country: six million more potential votes.

The application form requires the following: a final transcript, a housing request, a medical report, and the first tuition check.

Women do not expect promotions or high salaries: "[Women] are often unsure of their intrinsic worth in the marketplace" (Sidel qtd. in Wolf 49).

New York: HarperCollins

Between Worlds: A Reader, Rhetoric, and Handbook

The train departs at 5:30 in the morning.

John 11:25

In some cases, a colon should not be used. For example, do *not* place a colon between a subject and a verb, between a verb and its complements, or between a preposition and its object:

P
> The animals in that section of the zoo include: panthers, leopards, lions, and tigers.

P
> The courses he needs to take are: biology, chemistry, physics, and calculus.

P
> Don't put luggage on: the bed, the desk, or the reading chair.

THE DASH

The dash (which is sometimes created by typing two hyphens with no spaces around or between them) is used sparingly for dramatic emphasis, to call attention to material the dash sets off. Sometimes the dash is used in places where a colon could also be used, but the dash is considered more informal. Because the dash indicates a sudden shift in thought and is used for dramatic emphasis, it should not be overused. In formal writing a comma, colon, or period may be more appropriate punctuation symbols.

> We all believe that environmental protection is an obligation of our era--but we still use toxic cleaners in our homes.

Here the dash is used to emphasize the contrast between what "we all believe" and what we do. A comma could also be used in this sentence.

> Both successful women and less-successful women have the same goal--to "marry up"--so men still have a constant psychological need to be successful at work.

The dash is used here to set off the definitive information, the "same goal" the writer believes women have. A comma could have been used, but the dash achieves more emphasis.

The dash may also be used in the same manner as the colon to announce a dramatic point:

> The candidates need to realize that women form a significant majority in this country--six million more potential votes.

QUOTATION MARKS

Quotation marks are used to enclose direct quotations, some titles, and occasionally words defined or used in a special way. Quotation marks are used in pairs.

A *direct quotation* is noted with quotation marks. A direct quotation states in exact words what someone has said or written:

> Brigid Brophy insists, "If modern civilisation has invented
> methods of education which make it possible for men to feed
> babies and for women to think logically, we are betraying
> civilisation itself if we do not set both sexes free to make
> a free choice" (98).

Notice that Brophy's spelling of *civilisation* is British, and that the writer quoting her is not permitted to change her spelling without indicating the change in brackets: "civili[z]ation." See more on brackets on pages 546–547.

An *indirect quotation* notes what has been said in a paraphrased or indirect way. No quotation marks are needed:

> Brigid Brophy believes that men and women should be free to
> make the choices that education and technology have made
> possible.

A *quotation within a quotation* requires the use of standard quotation marks around the outside quotation and single quotation marks around the interior quotation:

> According to Naomi Wolf, "Every generation since about 1830
> has had to fight its version of the beauty myth. 'It is very
> little to me' said the suffragist Lucy Stone in 1855, 'to
> have the right to vote, to own property, etcetera, if I may
> not keep my body, and its uses, in my absolute right'" (103).

Commas and periods are placed inside quotation marks:

> Brigid Brophy thinks that both genders should be "free to
> make a free choice."

> If we do not let men and women make choices, "we are betray-
> ing civilisation itself," believes Brigid Brophy.

Semicolons and colons are placed outside quotation marks:

> Brophy says we are all "free to make a free choice"; in
> fact, we let convention limit our awareness of choice.

```
Brophy says we are all "free to make a free choice": about
our educations, our careers, our domesticity.
```

Question marks go inside quotation marks if they are part of the quotation but belong outside of quotation marks if the quoted statement is being used as a question by the writer quoting the material:

```
The professor asked, "Who agrees with Brigid Brophy's
thesis?"
```

```
Does Brophy think we "should be free to make a free choice"?
```

If you are quoting a conversation, begin a new paragraph for each speaker. Notice the punctuation of the quoted conversation in this excerpt from Bruce Halling's narrative, that appears on pages 385–387.

```
  "Did you hear what happened to Ricky Liverpool?" one
friend asked.

  "Yeah," sighed the other friend as the door started
closing.

  "What happened?" I asked, feigning moderate interest.
```

If you are quoting poetry, integrate into your own text quoted single lines of poetry. Two or three lines of poetry may be brought into your text and enclosed in quotation marks, or they may be set off from your text, without quotation marks but indented ten spaces from the left margin:

```
  The gardener in Marge Piercy's poem "A Work of Artifice"
"croons" to the plant as he "whittles" it into his desired
shape. He says:

        It is your nature

        To be small and cozy

        domestic and weak;
```

or

```
  The gardener in Marge Piercy's poem "A Work of Artifice"
"croons" to the plant as he "whittles" it into his desired
shape. He says, "It is your nature / To be small and cozy /
domestic and weak."
```

The slash (/) is used when poetry lines are incorporated into a text to indicate the end of a poetry line. (The use of the slash is described further on pp. 547–548.) Set off poetry quotations of more than three lines and prose quotations of more than four lines.

Titles of short stories, songs, essays, poems, articles, parts of books, and the titles of episodes on television and radio are enclosed in quotation marks:

"My Man Bovanne"

"Chicago"

"Don't Let Stereotypes Warp Your Judgments"

"A Work of Artifice"

"A Hidden Factor in AIDS"

"Tracks" in *Aquaboogie*

"After the Trial" on *Which Way L.A.?*

In special instances, quotation marks can be used to enclose words that are defined or used in a special way:

```
The "artifice" is not so much the "skill or ingenuity" used
to shape women but the "trickery or craft" that keeps them
dependent.
```

Do not use quotation marks around a word that you feel self-conscious about using. Instead, change the word:

```
The morning meeting is held to give the staff the "rundown"
on the advertising goals for the day.

The morning meeting is held to explain that day's advertis-
ing goals to the staff.
```

THE ELLIPSIS

The ellipsis, a set of three spaced periods (. . .), informs the reader that something has been left out of a quotation. For example, a writer quoting material from Naomi Wolf's book *The Beauty Myth* might decide to leave out some material unnecessary to the text he or she is writing. Here Wolf writes about the phenomenon of eating disorders in countries other than the United States:

```
It is spreading to other industrialized nations: The United
Kingdom now has 3.5 million anorexics or bulimics (95 per-
cent of them female), with 6,000 new cases yearly (183).
```

Here the passage is revised using an ellipsis:

> It is spreading to other industrialized nations: The United
> Kingdom now has 3.5 million anorexics or bulimics . . . with
> 6,000 new cases yearly (183).

The decision to remove material and use the ellipsis must be governed by the writer's intent. But the ellipsis may not be used to remove anything that would change the meaning of the section that the writer is quoting. The fact that 95 percent of the eating disorders in the United Kingdom are women may not be relevant to the writer of the revised text, so the ellipsis is used as a convenient tool to shorten the quoted material and keep the emphasis where the writer wants it. The missing words in this case do not change the meaning of the original.

If you remove material from the quoted material at the end of the sentence, use a period before the three periods of the ellipsis. Notice this example of quoted material from H. Patricia Hynes' 1990 edition of *Earth Right:*

> The United States creates about 450,000 tons of residential
> and commercial solid waste every day. By the year 2000, this
> amount is expected to reach 530,000 tons per day. . . . The
> Environmental Protection Agency estimates that in the next
> five to ten years more than twenty-seven states and half of
> the country's cities will run out of landfill space (47).

If a parenthetical reference follows an ellipsis at the end of a sentence, use three spaced periods and then place the period to conclude the sentence after the final parenthesis:

> As Lisa Appignanesi records in her biography <u>Simone de</u>
> <u>Beauvoir</u>, Beauvoir believed that "the genuinely moral person
> can never have an easy conscience. . . " (79).

To avoid using the ellipsis too often, integrate carefully selected parts of quoted material into your text:

> As Carol Tavris notes, people respond "in shock and anger at
> the failings of 'human nature'" (268).

By paraphrasing part of the quotation and integrating the author's text with your own, you can avoid both using lengthy quotations *and* overusing the ellipsis.

PARENTHESES

Use parentheses to separate from the main material a digression or aside:

> Their house number (usually painted on the curb) was on the mail box.

> Because an increasing number of women (and men) are suffering from eating disorders, we must address the problem at our next NOW conference.

Rules govern the use of punctuation within and outside of parentheses. If a sentence requires a comma in addition to parentheses, use the comma after the second or closing parenthesis:

> During the Civil War (1861–65), African Americans were trained for active duty and fought in segregated units.

If the information within the parentheses is a complete sentence, the final punctuation is enclosed within the parentheses:

> More information on gardens that require little water appears throughout the book. (See the chapters on cactus and native plants, especially.)

Parentheses also are used in documentation to enclose the source of paraphrased or quoted information. In these cases, the terminal punctuation appears outside the parentheses:

> As Virginia Woolf says in <u>Orlando</u>, "Clothes have . . . more important offices than merely to keep us warm. They change our view of the world and the world's view of us" (187).

(For a more complete discussion of how parentheses are used in MLA documentation, see pp. 480–484, and for their use in APA documentation, see pp. 492–494.)

BRACKETS

Use brackets to enclose words or phrases that you have added to a quotation, to show any changes that you have made in quoted material, or to record your own comments about quoted material:

> Today, more attention is being paid "to the relationship between eating disorders [anorexia and bulimia] and the compulsive eating of many women."

In the preceding example, the writer has clarified a point for the reader by defining within the quotation types of eating disorders. The brackets indicate that the words are not part of the original quotation.

> The Duke of Ferrara, in Robert Browning's poem "My Last
> Duchess," is disturbed that the Duchess "ranked [his] gift
> of a nine-hundred-years-old name / With anybody's gift."

In this example, the writer changed the original "my gift of a nine-hundred-years-old name" to fit into a text. To show the change from *my* to *his*, the writer placed brackets around the change. The diagonal line (or slash) between "name" and "With" indicates the end of the line in the poem.

> The "Poison Pen Letters" greeting card says, "Everything has
> it's [sic] price . . . but I didn't know you came so cheap!"

This use of the brackets is to enclose *sic*, a Latin word meaning "in this manner." The [sic] used after *it's* in the above example indicates that the error of not using *its* is in the original, and is not an error written by the person quoting the original.

THE SLASH

The slash may be used sparingly to show options, like pass/fail or Dean/Department Head. Notice that there is no space between the words and the slash when the slash is used to show options.

The slash is also used to define the end of a line of poetry if the line is incorporated into a text. For example, notice how the writer incorporates into a poetry explication some words from Kate Rushin's poem "The Bridge":

> The speaker in the poem observes that "Nobody / can talk to
> anybody," and the narrator resents the fact that she or he
> must function as a "connection to the rest of the world."

The slash indicates where the line ends in the original work (which appears on p. 196). Notice that a space appears on either side of the slash when it is used to indicate the end of a line of poetry.

In bulletins, reports, and some business correspondence, the slash is used in the form *he/she*, as in this sentence:

> The person who lost a ring in the library may claim it after
> he/she describes it to campus police.

In formal writing, you should avoid the form *he/she* by writing *he or she*, as in this sentence:

> The student who aspires to a law degree may attain it if he
>
> or she is willing to work hard.

Both *he/she* and *he or she* can be avoided by rewriting the sentence:

> The person who lost a ring in the library may claim it by
>
> describing it to campus police.

> The student who aspires to a law degree may attain it by
>
> working hard.

THE HYPHEN

The hyphen is used to divide a word or to form a compound word. To divide a word that will not fit on the typed or written line, separate the part of the word that will fit on the line with a hyphen at a syllable break, then conclude the word on the next line. The break must occur only between syllables and should not leave fewer than two letters at the end of the line or fewer than three letters at the beginning of the next line. The hyphen appears at the end of the first line, *not* at the beginning of the next line.

Notice how each error is corrected:

P

> Of all of the applicants for the job, she was the best te-
>
> acher for the class.

> Of all of the applicants for the job, she was the best
>
> teacher for the class.

A word can be broken between syllables if the break will leave at least two letters at the end of the line and three or more letters at the beginning of the next line. Because the syllables of *teach-* and *-er* will not fit that rule, the entire word must be moved to the next line.

P

> After his paper was completed, the frustrated student fo-
>
> und another critical article.

> After his paper was completed, the frustrated student
>
> found another critical article.

> [A one-syllable word cannot be broken, so *found* must be moved to the next line.]

P

Since the 1993 Presidential inauguration, interest in the po-
-etry of Maya Angelou has increased.

Since the 1993 Presidential inauguration, interest in the poetry of Maya Angelou has increased.

[The hyphen is used *only* at the end of the first line.]

Divide compound words only where the hyphen already exists:

P

He gave the family heirloom to his sis-
ter-in-law.

He gave the family heirloom to his sister-
in-law.

P

Histories of popular music describe the heart-throb-
bing gestures of Elvis Presley.

Histories of popular music describe the heart-
throbbing gestures of Elvis Presley.

Hyphens are also used to form compound words that modify a noun:

The grade-conscious students knew the best sequence for the
courses.

The award-winning play went on to Broadway.

If the modifiers follow the noun, the hyphens are usually left out.

The students are grade conscious.

The play was award winning and went on to Broadway.

Hyphens are used in spelled-out fractions and compound whole numbers from twenty-one to ninety-nine:

Over one-half of the voters will stay home election day.

Everyone hates that old school-bus song, "Ninety-Nine
Bottles of Beer on the Wall."

Hyphens are used to attach some prefixes and suffixes. Usually, prefixes are attached to a word without a hyphen: *preconceived, disinterested, unhappy.* But prefixes such as *ex-, self-,* and *all-,* prefixes that precede a capitalized word, or prefixes that are a capitalized letter usually require a hyphen; for example, *self-supporting, ex-champion, anti-European,* and *U-boat.* Sometimes, to prevent confusion, a hyphen is necessary to separate a prefix ending in a vowel and a main word that starts with a vowel; for example, *de-escalate, re-invent,* and *pre-advise.*

14

Understanding Faulty Word Choice

■ ■ ■

wd ch Poor word choice will weaken writing, and instructors will note these errors in the margins of papers. Specific examples are cited in the alphabetically arranged list of commonly confused words (pp. 555–556); the types of word choice problems are defined and exemplified here.

CLICHÉS

Clichés, or overused words or expressions, should be avoided because predictable language is stale. Expressions that were once novel and even colorful have lost their descriptive quality through overuse. Like a faded carpet, clichés no longer add color to the space they occupy. If you can complete the following expression automatically, you know that you have an example of a cliché:

```
The bread was hard as a_____.

We searched all day, but it was like looking for a needle

_____.
```

Good writing is clear, fresh, and vivid:

```
The bread was as hard as aged camel dung and about as tasty.

We searched all day, but it was like looking for a button in
my mother's tool drawer.
```

SLANG, JARGON, AND COLLOQUIAL WORDS

Some of our most vivid language is considered **slang** (highly informal, often coined words used in speaking) or **jargon** (the special vocabulary of people who have the same job, interest, or way of life). In fact, in conversation, if pretentious language were substituted for some of the commonly used colloquial words—*intoxicated* for *drunk* or *children* for *kids*—our conversations would sound stuffy or silly. Slang is often vigorous and colorful, but it is nonstandard and therefore unacceptable in most formal writing. And the jargon that is acceptable in conversation or memos at work may be unintelligible to the general reader. If you think your "funky," "laid-back," or "awesome" word choice is going to influence negatively your reader's feelings about your integrity as a writer, elevate your language and remove the inappropriate word.

ARCHAIC WORDS, EUPHEMISMS, AND PRETENTIOUS WORDS

Some words that appear in literature, especially poetry, may not be appropriate for expository writing:

wd ch   Marcus Mabry was amongst the minority students accepted at Stanford.

Marcus Mabry was among the minority students accepted at Stanford.

The word *amongst,* used in poetry, sounds inflated in expository texts.
Writers sometimes use **euphemisms**—substitutes for words perceived as offensive. One problem with euphemisms is they are often imprecise, as in this sentence: "We lost our grandmother last week." The reader might wonder if she is still wandering in the parking lot of the local mall. Use direct and precise language to communicate accurately.
Pretentious language is used by writers who believe it will make their work appear more refined or elegant. Avoid words like *facilitate* or *utilize* when *help* and *use* are adequate. Some *pretentious words* have persisted and reached *cliché* status: *viable* and *parameters,* for example.

REDUNDANCIES

The legal profession has contributed some double-talk like *aid and abet* to our language, and some other redundancies have persisted even though they are bulky or inane: *each and every, revert back, end result, temporary respite,* or *true fact.* You can see that *each* and *every* mean the same thing, so the words should not be used together. To revert means "to go back." And what is a fact if it isn't true? If you regard these redundancies as you would clichés—language that is predictable and imprecise—you will eliminate them from your writing.

SEXIST LANGUAGE

Language that demeans women or men is **sexist.** Most writers would know not to use *chick* or *broad* or *stud* or *hunk* in papers. More subtle but equally insidious sexist language also needs to be avoided:

wd ch   The professor uses his wisdom to remain objective.

wd ch   Each nurse is required to store her lunch in a locker.

wd ch   A clever lawyer parks his car in the free lot.

wd ch   The competent PTA president uses her gavel rarely.

Even a superficial look at job and life-style choices in the last decades would confirm the necessity of unbiased language in print. Nurses and lawyers are both female and male; nowhere is it prescribed that only women will be PTA presidents. Consider the choices illustrated below for freeing your papers of sexist language:

A professor uses wisdom to remain objective.

Professors use their wisdom to remain objective.

Nurses are required to store their lunches in lockers.

Each nurse is required to store his or her lunch in a locker.

Clever lawyers park their cars in the free lot.

A clever lawyer parks her or his car in the free lot.

Vary using *his or her* pattern with *her or his,* but avoid this very awkward construction as often as possible by using the article instead of a possessive pronoun, or by using a plural noun as the subject:

The competent PTA president uses the gavel rarely.

Competent PTA presidents use their gavels rarely.

Do not assume any job is gender specific. *Fireman* should be *firefighter, clergyman* should be *minister* or *member of the clergy,* and *mailman* should be *letter carrier* or *mail carrier.* Do not add *lady* to job titles; "She is a lady doctor" is as inane as "He is a male artist."

You can further free your writing from sexism by eliminating the generic use of *man* in examples like the following:

wd ch

Mankind is more aware of stereotypes than it was a decade ago.

Humanity is more aware of stereotypes than it was a decade ago.

People are more aware of stereotypes than they were a decade ago.

15

Understanding Commonly
Confused Words

■ ■ ■

There are a number of words that are often confused or misused by many writers, not just college students. Each of your authors learned something from the other about word choice as we compiled this list. Your audience and your intention will govern your word choice, but if you have an error noted in the margin of one of your papers, look here for an explanation in order to revise the language you used.

An examination of many different college handbooks shows us that instructors use a remarkable number and variety of possible marginal symbols to alert students to errors or confusion in word choice. Any of the following symbols may appear in the margin of a paper to alert the student to an incorrect word:

cliché	an overused or trite expression
dialect	not standard English usage, or a regional, occupational, or ethnic word not appropriate in the context used
d or *dic*	diction, an inappropriate level of language use, inappropriate word or slang
id	idiomatic, not standard American usage; the problem often appears in preposition use
jarg	jargon, or an occupational word inappropriate for formal writing

nonst.	nonstandard; may indicate idiomatic use, jargon, or slang
sl or *slang*	the level of the word choice is inappropriate
trite	overused expression, such as a cliché
wd ch	word choice; a general term that may indicate any of the more definitively marked errors on this list
w/w	wrong word; a general term that may indicate a word confused with another word, slang, jargon, improper word, or idiom
X	obvious error; may refer to *any* of the above

It is important for you to ask your instructor for a clarification of a margin symbol if one is used that you do not understand. If one of your words is marked as a poor choice or an error, we believe that you will find the explanation here, and then you can easily revise your work.

COMMONLY CONFUSED WORDS

a, an Use *a* before words beginning with consonant sounds, including those spelled with an initial pronounced *h* (*a* horse) and those spelled with vowels that are sounded as consonants (*a* one-hour final, *a* university). Use *an* before words beginning with vowel sounds, including those spelled with an initial *h* (*an* igloo, *an* hour).

accept, except *Accept* is a verb meaning "to receive." *Except* is a preposition meaning "excluding" or "but."

> I *accept* your plan to tour New York City *except* for the concert in Central Park.

advice, advise *Advice* is the noun meaning "opinion of what to do." *Advise* is the verb meaning "to give opinion or counsel."

> I *advise* you to follow your counselor's *advice*.

affect, effect *Affect* is usually a verb meaning "to influence." *Effect* is a noun meaning "result." In psychology, *affect* is used as a noun meaning "a feeling or emotion." *Effect* can be used as a verb meaning "to implement, or to bring about."

> The eyedrops do not *affect* his driving.

> Candles create a romantic *effect* in the dining room.

An examination of *affect* is critical in understanding personality.

Congress must *effect* a change in the tax laws.

all ready, already *All ready* means "completely prepared." *Already* means "by now" or "before now."

We were *all ready* for the trip, but the bus had *already* left.

a lot *A lot* is always two words, never *alot*.

all right *All right* is standardly spelled as two words. (*Alright* appears in some dictionaries, but most readers still consider it a misspelling.)

all together, altogether *All together* means "in a common location," "in unison," or "as a group." *Altogether* means "completely" or "entirely."

We are *altogether* certain that caging the rabbits *all together* is a mistake.

allusion, illusion An *allusion* is an "indirect reference"; an *illusion* is a "a deceptive appearance" or "a fantasy that may be confused with reality."

Julie's use of biblical *allusions* gave the *illusion* that she was religious.

among, between Use *between* when referring to two; use *among* for three or more.

Between you and me, he is *among* the most creative students in the class.

amount, number *Amount* refers to a quantity of something that cannot be counted. *Number* refers to items that can be counted.

The *amount* of flour used depends on the *number* of cookies you want to bake.

anxious *Anxious* means "apprehensive" or "worried." Often it is confused with the word *eager,* which means "anticipating" or "looking forward to."

Yumiko was *anxious* about her tax refund because she was *eager* to buy a CD player.

a while, awhile *a while* is an article and a noun; *awhile* is an adverb.

We spoke for *a while* and then parted.

Wait *awhile* before you swim.

being as, being that These terms should not be used for *because* or *since.*

Because the lot is full, I parked on the street.

beside, besides *Beside* is a preposition meaning "next to." *Besides* is a preposition meaning "except," as well as an adverb meaning "in addition to."

> The secretary sat *beside* his dean.
>
> Everyone *besides* the team rides the school bus to each game.
>
> Your expertise is needed; *besides,* you know how to have fun!

can, may *Can* means "is able to." "May" indicates permission.

> You *can* talk on the telephone for three hours, but you *may* not in my house!

capital, capitol *Capital* refers to the city and is the word to describe an upper case letter. *Capitol* indicates the building where government meets.

> The *capital* is the destination for the class trip, but a visit to the *capitol* is impossible because the ceiling is under repair.

censor, censure *Censor* as a verb means "to suppress or remove objectionable material." *Censor* as a noun is "the person who suppresses the objectionable material." *Censure* means "to criticize severely."

> The librarian refused to work with citizens who *censor* the classics.
>
> The *censor* of a few decades ago *censored The Adventures of Huckleberry Finn!*
>
> The city council needs to *censure* neon signs in "Old Town."

cite, site, sight *Cite* means "to quote by way of example, authority, or proof." *Site* is "the location of." *Sight* is a "spectacle or view."

> The tourist *sights* were on the *site* of an ancient village as *cited* in the Fodor's Guide.

complement, compliment *Complement* means "to complete" or "something that completes or supplements another." *Compliment* is a noun or verb that means "to praise."

> His sensitivity *complements* her assertiveness.
>
> Most people see through false *compliments.*

conscience, conscious *Conscience* refers to one's sense of right and wrong. *Conscious* is an adjective that means "alert to or aware of."

> The jury member was *conscious* of his nagging *conscience.*

could of, should of, would of These are incorrect forms for *could have, should have,* and *would have. Of* is a preposition, not a part of a verb.

> The trainer *should have* exercised his horse today.

double negative Double negatives to emphasize negativity are non-standard in English.

> I didn't see anything [not *nothing*].

> The child could hardly control [not *couldn't hardly control*] his tears.

due to *Due to* is acceptable following a linking verb but is considered less acceptable at the beginning of a sentence.

> Most minor injuries during earthquakes are *due to* panic.

> Because of [not *due to*] rain, the beach party was canceled.

due to the fact that Use *because* to avoid wordiness.

each *Each* is singular (see p. 519).

effect See **affect**

e.g. This is a Latin abbreviation meaning "for example." It is sometimes confused with *i.e.,* which means "that is." Neither of these abbreviations should be used in the text of a manuscript, but they can be used in parenthetical expressions.

either *Either* is singular (see p. 519).

elicit, illicit *Elicit* is a verb meaning "to evoke." *Illicit* is an adjective meaning "illegal or unlawful."

> The attorney was unable to *elicit* any information from her client about *illicit* drug sales in the neighborhood.

emigrate from, immigrate to *Emigrate* means "to leave a country or region to settle elsewhere." *Immigrate* means "to enter another country and live there."

> When Pano *emigrated* from Turkey, he missed living near the sea.

> After the Revolution, many Cubans *immigrated* to the United States.

eminent, imminent *Eminent* means "celebrated" or "exalted." *Imminent* means "about to happen."

> The *eminent* seismologist predicted that an earthquake was *imminent*.

especially, specially *Especially* means "particularly" or "more than other things." *Specially* means "for a specific reason."

> Ryder *especially* values working on cabinets. He's known for *specially* ordered fine pieces of exotic woods.

etc. Avoid ending a list with the abbreviation *etc*. Writers often overuse it to suggest they have more information than they do. The Latin expression is *et cetera,* which means "and others" or "and other things." The expression is best avoided because it is vague. It is also often misspelled as "ect."

everybody, everyone *Everybody* and *everyone* are singular (see p. 519).

except See **accept**

farther, further *Farther* refers to distance. *Further* implies quantity or degree. *Further* is now widely accepted for both meanings.

> We drifted *farther* out to sea.
>
> He is *further* along in his dissertation than his advisor expected.

fewer, less *Fewer* refers to items that can be counted. *Less* refers to measurable amounts.

> Nathan does *fewer* chores and therefore earns *less* money than his brother.

firstly *Firstly* is pretentious. Use *first.*

fun *Fun* is colloquial when used as an adjective and should be avoided.

> It was an amusing [not *fun*] movie.

further See **farther**

good, well *Good* is an adjective; *well* is usually an adverb.

> *Good* work is almost always *well* rewarded.

hanged, hung *Hanged* refers to people. *Hung* refers to pictures and things that can be suspended.

> The criminal was *hanged* from the tree.
>
> The Walshes *hung* Debbie's recent paintings in the living room.

he, he/she, his/her The writer should no longer assume that *he* is an acceptable pronoun for all nouns. Further, *he/she or his/her* are awkward. To avoid this construction, use the plural or a specific noun instead of the pronoun. (See also p. 520.)

> When a student works in a small group, he/she participates more.
>
> When students work in small groups, they participate more.

hisself *Hisself* is nonstandard. Use *himself.*

hung See **hanged**

i.e. This Latin abbreviation should be replaced by the English *that is.*

illusion See **allusion**

imminent See **eminent**

imply, infer *Imply* means "to state indirectly or to suggest." *Infer* means "to come to a conclusion based on the evidence given."

> By covering his ears, he *implied* that he no longer wanted to listen.

> We can *infer* that the Duke of Ferrara is an arrogant man because he refused to "stoop" to speak to his wife.

irregardless *Irregardless* is nonstandard. Use *regardless*.

its, it's *Its* is the possessive form. *It's* is the contraction for *it is* or *it has* (see p. 535).

> *It's* too bad that Dick and Jean's cat has injured *its* tail.

> *It's* been a bad day for Jacoby's cat.

later, latter *Later* refers to time. *Latter* refers to the second of two things named.

> Initially many southern European immigrants came to this country, but *later* the immigration policy restricted the numbers.

> Both Diego Rivera and his wife Frida Kahlo painted, but the *latter* has gained more public recognition in the last few years.

lay, lie *Lay* means "to place or put" and requires an object. (The past tense is *laid*.) *Lie* means "to rest or recline." (The past tense of *lie* is *lay*, and so the two words are sometimes confused.)

> Evan *lay* the piano music on the bench before he left.

> The dog will *lie* down exactly where he *lay* yesterday.

less See **fewer**

lie See **lay**

loose, lose *Loose* is an adjective meaning "unrestrained or unfastened." *Lose* is a verb meaning "to misplace" or "to be defeated."

> If his bathing suit is too *loose*, Lester will *lose* it in the next wave.

lots, lots of Avoid these constructions in formal writing. Elevate the diction to *many* or *much*.

mankind Avoid this term, as its sexism offends many readers. Use *humans* or *humanity* or *humankind* instead.

> It was one small step for the man who walked on the moon, but it was a giant step for *humanity*.

maybe, may be *Maybe* is an adverb that means "perhaps." *May be* is a verb.

> *Maybe* the community will improve its social services, but that *may be* the only benefit of the turmoil.

may of, might of These are nonstandard forms of *may have* and *might have.*

media, medium *Media* is the plural of *medium.*

> Pablo Picasso created clay forms and sculptures in wood and wire, but paint is the *medium* for which he is best known. Perhaps the *media* should review his other art forms.

myself *Myself* is a reflexive or intensive pronoun and, like the other *-self* pronouns, should not be used in place of personal pronouns.

> I drove *myself* to the hospital because no one else was home.
>
> "I can do it *myself!*" the toddler protested.
>
> Juan ladled the chili for his father and me [not *myself*].

neither *Neither* is singular (see p. 519).

> *Neither* of us is available to babysit tonight.

nohow *Nohow* is nonstandard for *in any way.*

none *None* is singular.

> *None* of the alternatives seems reasonable.

nowheres *Nowheres* is nonstandard for *nowhere.*

number See **amount**

of *Of* should not be used in constructions like *should have* or *would have. Of* is a preposition.

off of *Of* is not necessary with *off.* Use *off* alone or use *from.*

> The marbles rolled *off* the table and continued rolling around Monahan's room.

O.K., OK, okay All three forms are acceptable, but in formal writing these expressions are inappropriate.

on account of A wordy way to write *because.*

owing to the fact that A wordy way to write *because.*

plus *Plus* is not appropriately used as a conjunction to join independent clauses. Use a standard coordinating or adverbial conjunction.

> We celebrated the Fourth of July with hot dogs, corn on the cob, potato salad, and watermelon; in addition, [not *plus*] we enjoyed the firework display at Zaca Lake.

precede, proceed The verb *precede* means "come before" (note the prefix *pre-*). The verb *proceed* means "go forward" or "move on."

> Spanish 4 *precedes* Spanish 5, "Literature of Mexico."
>
> To *proceed* without a contract would be foolish.

prejudice, prejudiced *Prejudice* is a noun; *prejudiced* is an adjective. Do not leave out the -*d* from the adjective.

> *Prejudice* that starts in childhood is difficult to obliterate, and he was distinctly *prejudiced* against working mothers.

principal, principle *Principal* is a noun for the "chief official" or, in finance, the "capital sum." As an adjective, *principal* means "major" or "most important." *Principle* is a noun meaning "a law or truth, rule, or axiom."

> The school's *principal* uses two *principles* for deciding the graduation speakers: which students have the best grades, and which students have the best *principles* to share with classmates.

proceed, precede See **precede**

raise, rise *Raise* is a verb meaning "to move or cause to move up," and it takes an object. *Rise* is a verb meaning "to go up," and it does not take a direct object.

> The farmers who *raise* cows are concerned about the disease.
>
> They *rise* early to attend to the livestock.

reason is because In speech, this expression is common. In formal writing, it is not appropriate. A clause using *that* is the preferred form:

> The *reason* he paid his rent early was *that* [not *because*] he intended to be out of town on the first of the month.

reason why The expression *reason why* is redundant. *Reason* is sufficient.

> The *reason* [not *reason why*] Jorge attends law school at night is not obvious to anyone but his family.

rise, raise See **raise, rise**

should of *Should of* is nonstandard; use *should have*.

> He *should have* [not *should of*] known not to build a campfire on that windy hill.

since *Since* is sometimes used to mean *because,* but it is only clear as a conjunction in constructions having to do with time.

> Andy has been waiting *since* January for his tax forms.
>
> *Since* [or *because*?] you left, I've been dating others.

sit, set *Sit* means "to rest the weight of the body" as on a chair. *Set* means "to place."

> Dorothy wants you to *sit* on the black leather sofa.
>
> Tom would rather you not *set* stoneware dishes on his cherry-wood table.

site, cite, sight See **cite, site, sight**

somebody, someone *Somebody* and *someone* are singular (see p. 519).

sometime, some time, sometimes *Sometime* means "at an indefinite time." *Some time* is the adjective *some* modifying the noun *time*. *Sometimes* means "now and then."

> *Sometime* we should get together and play tennis.
>
> Raul devoted *some time* to perfecting his pronunciation.
>
> *Sometimes* Ken discards every yolk from the eggs as he prepares his omelette.

supposed to, used to Don't neglect to use the *-d* ending on these often used and often misspelled words!

> He is *supposed to* [not *suppose to*] bring the wine for the dinner.
>
> Ariane became *used to* [not *use to*] Dee's indifferent housekeeping.

than, then *Than* is used in comparisons. *Then* is an adverb denoting time.

> There are many more calories in avocados *than* in apples.
>
> First Sylvia Plath attended the school, and *then* she taught there.

their, there, they're *Their* is a possessive pronoun. *There* is an adverb denoting place. *They're* is a contraction meaning *they are.*

> *Their* plans for hang gliding *there* in the park are apt to be postponed because *they're* not ready to pass the safety test.

then, than See **than, then.**

this here, these here, that there, them there Nonstandard for *this, these, that,* or *those.*

till, until, 'til *Till* and *until* have the same meaning and both are used. *'Til* is an unnecessary contraction of *until.*

thru *Thru* is a nonstandard spelling of *through* that should be avoided in all formal writing.

thusly Use *thus,* which is less pretentious.

to, too, two *To* is a preposition meaning "toward" and is part of the infinitive form of the verb (for example, *to run*). *Too* is an adverb meaning "overly." *Two* is a number.

> *Two* trips *to* the market in one day are not *too* many for a fine cook like Mike.

toward, towards Either form is acceptable, but *toward* is preferred.

try and *Try and* is nonstandard; *try to* is preferred.

> *Try to* [not *try and*] meet Ryan before he locks up his bike.

unique *Unique* means "distinctively characteristic." It is an absolute adjective that shouldn't be modified by "most" or "very."

> A tuxedo shirt and jacket, bow tie, and Bermuda shorts create a *unique* [not *most unique*] style for a hot-weather prom.

until See **till, until, 'til**

usage The noun *use* should be used whenever possible. *Usage* refers only to convention, as in *language usage*.

> The *use* [not *usage*] of computers has facilitated essay writing, but papers with proper *usage* have not increased because of expensive equipment.

used to See **supposed to, used to**

well See **good, well**

which, who *Which* is used for a thing or things, not for people. Use *who* for people.

> Martin Luther King, the American *who* defined civil disobedience for his generation, was a theologian as well as a political figure. His letter from Birmingham, *which* he wrote in jail, defines his position.

which, in which Writers occasionally use *in which* in places where *which* is sufficient. Read work carefully to eliminate the unnecessary preposition.

> Salma grabbed the gray cape, *which* [not *in which*] had been left on the sofa.

while Do not use *while* to mean *although* if there is a chance of confusion for the reader. Like *since, while* should be reserved for time sense. Unless the point is to show that the actions occur at the same time, *although* is the better word.

> Nero fiddled *while* Rome burned.
>
> *Although* [not *while*] Elizabeth continues to invest her small savings, Bill never resists a shoe sale.

who's, whose *Who's* is the contraction for *who is* or *who has*. *Whose* is a possessive pronoun.

> *Who's* going to return the library books?
>
> *Who's* been reading *Aquaboogie?*
>
> That depends on *whose* book is due.

would of *would of* is nonstandard for the complete verb *would have.*

> *Los Vendidos would have* [not *would of*] been a perfect theater experience for Cinco de Mayo.

you The indefinite use of *you,* or even its use to mean "you the reader," can be incongruous or offensive and can be avoided:

> A decade ago, the fit hiker [rather than *you*] could camp on the beach with the seals at Pt. Sal, but now even the poor trail has eroded.

> It is common practice in some African tribes for prepubescent females [rather than *you*] to be scarified.

your, you're *Your* is a possessive pronoun. *You're* is the contraction of *you are.*

> *Your* savings will disappear if *you're* not careful.

Acknowledgments

■ ■ ■

p. 4 "Thanksgiving" by Ellen Goodman. Copyright © 1993 by Boston Globe Company. Reprinted by permission.

p. 6 "Discovery of a Father" by Sherwood Anderson, originally appeared in *Reader's Digest*, 1939. Reprinted by permission of Harold Ober Associates Incorporated. Copyright © 1939 by the Reader's Digest. Copyright renewed 1966 by Eleanor Copenhaver Anderson.

p. 11 "Under the Influence" by Scott Russell Sanders. Copyright © 1987 by *Harper's* magazine. All rights reserved. Reprinted from the November issue by special permission.

p. 22 "The Only Child" from *Private Lives in the Imperial City* by John Leonard. Reprinted by permission.

p. 25 "Ignorance Is Not Bliss" by Eric Marcus. *Newsweek*, July 5, 1993. Copyright © 1993 by Newsweek, Inc. All rights reserved. Reprinted by permission.

p. 28 "Your Place Is Empty" by Anne Tyler, originally appeared in *The New Yorker*, November 22, 1976. Reprinted by permission of Russell & Volkening as agents for the author. Copyright © 1976 by Anne Tyler.

p. 43 "My Man Bovanne" from *Gorilla, My Love* by Toni Cade Bambara. Copyright © 1971 by Toni Cade Bambara. Reprinted by permission of Random House, Inc.

p. 49 "Two Kinds" from *The Joy Luck Club* by Amy Tan. Copyright © 1989 by Amy Tan. Reprinted by permission of The Putnam Publishing Group.

p. 58 "The 'Perfect' Misconception" by Mary Miller. Used by permission of Mary Miller.

p. 61 "The Writer" from *The Mind-Reader*. Copyright © 1971 by Richard Wilbur, reprinted by permission of Harcourt Brace & Company.

p. 63 "The Girls' Room" by Laura Cunningham. Reprinted by permission of The William Morris Agency, Inc., on behalf of the author. Copyright © 1981 by Laura Cunningham. Originally published in *The New York Times*.

p. 67 "When Parents Don't Turn Out Right" by William Aiken. Reprinted by permission of William Aiken.

p. 71 "The Appeal of the Androgynous Man" by Amy Gross (appeared in *Mademoiselle*, May 1976). Copyright © 1976 by Amy Gross. Used by permission of the Wallace Literary Agency, Inc.

p. 75 "The Androgynous Man" by Noel Perrin from *The New York Times Magazine*, February 5, 1984. Copyright © 1984 by The New York Times Company. Reprinted by permission.

p. 78 "A Hidden Factor in AIDS: 'Real' Men's Hypersexuality" by Michael S. Kimmel and Martin P. Levine as originally appeared in *The Los Angeles Times*, June 3, 1991. Reprinted by permission of Michael S. Kimmel.

p. 81 "What Do Men Really Want?" by Sam Allis from *Time* magazine, Fall 1990. Copyright © 1990 Time, Inc. Reprinted by permission.

p. 87 "Not All Men Are Sly Foxes" by Armin A. Brott from *Newsweek*, June 1, 1992. Reprinted by permission of Armin A. Brott.

p. 90 "Men as Success Objects" by Warren Farrell. Warren Farrell, Ph. D., is the author of the best-sellers *Why Men Are the Way They Are* and *The Myth of Male Power* (both in paperback by Berkley Books). Reprinted by permission of Warren Farrell.

p. 94 "Women: Invisible Cages" by Brigid Brophy. Copyright © 1953 by Brigid Brophy. Published by Virago Press, 1991. Reprinted by permission.

p. 100 "Women" from *Iconographs* by May Swenson. Reprinted by permission of The Literary Estate of May Swenson.

p. 101 Excerpt from *The Beauty Myth* by Naomi Wolf. Copyright © 1991 by Naomi Wolf. Reprinted by permission of Willliam Morrow & Company, Inc., and Random House of Canada Limited.

p. 110 "A Work of Artifice" from *Circles on the Water* by Marge Piercy. Copyright © 1982 by Marge Piercy. Reprinted by permission of Alfred A. Knopf, Inc.

p. 112 "Date Rape: The Story of an Epidemic and Those Who Deny It" by Ellen Sweet. Reprinted by permission of Ellen Sweet.

p. 120 "Rape" is reprinted from *The Fact of a Doorframe, Poems Selected and New, 1950–1984*, by Adrienne Rich, by permission of W. W. Norton & Company, Inc. Copyright © 1984 by Adrienne Rich. Copyright © 1975, 1978 by W. W. Norton & Company, Inc. Copyright © 1981 by Adrienne Rich.

p. 122 "When a Woman Says No" by Ellen Goodman. Copyright © 1993, The Boston Globe Company. Reprinted by permission.

p. 124 "Where Are You Going, Where Have You Been?" by Joyce Carol Oates, in *The Wheel of Love and Other Stories* of 1970, published by Vanguard. Copyright © 1970 by Joyce Carol Oates. Reprinted by permission of John Hawkins & Associates, Inc.

p. 138 Excerpt from "Angry Young Men" by Barbara Ehrenreich. Reprinted by permission of Barbara Ehrenreich.

p. 143 "Living in Two Worlds" by Marcus Mabry from *Newsweek on Campus*. Reprinted by permission of *Newsweek*. All rights reserved.

p. 146 "In Rooms of Women" by Kim Edwards. Reprinted by permission of Kim Edwards.

p. 152 "Asian Girls: A Cultural Tug of War" by David Haldane from *The Los Angeles Times*, September 1, 1991. Copyright © 1991 The Los Angeles Times. Reprinted by permission.

p. 157 "American Horse" by Louise Erdrich from *Spider Woman's Granddaughters*. Copyright © 1989, introduction by Paula Gunn Allen. Reprinted by permission of Beacon Press.

p. 167 "Crimes Against Humanity" by Ward Churchill. Reprinted by permission of Ward Churchill.

p. 174 "On the Subway" from *The Gold Cell* by Sharon Olds. Copyright © 1987 by Sharon Olds. Reprinted by permission of Alfred A. Knopf, Inc.

p. 176 "Proper Care and Maintenance" by Susan Straight. Reprinted by permission of The Richard Parks Agency. Copyright © 1991 by Susan Straight.

p. 188 "Nikki-Rosa" from *Black Feeling, Black Talk, Black Judgment* by Nikki Giovanni. Copyright © 1968, 1970 by Nikki Giovanni. Reprinted by permission of William Morrow & Company, Inc.

p. 190 "Like Mexicans," from *Small Faces* by Gary Soto. Copyright © 1986 by Gary Soto. Used by permission of Delacorte Press, a division of Bantam Doubleday Dell Publishing Group, Inc.

p. 196 "The Bridge Poem" from *This Bridge Called My Back* by Kate Rushin. Copyright © 1983. Used by permission of the author and of Kitchen Table: Women of Color Press, P. O. Box 908, Latham, NY 12110.

p. 199 "The Masked Marvel's Last Toehold" by Richard Selzer from *Confessions of a Knife*, published by Simon & Schuster in 1979. Copyright © 1979 by Richard Selzer. Reprinted by permission of John Hawkins & Associates, Inc.

p. 203 "On Being a Cripple" by Nancy Mairs. Reprinted from *Plaintext* by Nancy Mairs by permission of the University of Arizona Press. Copyright © 1986. All rights reserved.

p. 214 "An Open Letter to Jerry Lewis" by Ben Mattlin as appeared originally in *The Los Angeles Times*, September 1, 1991. Reprinted by permission of Ben Mattlin.

p. 217 "Discrimination at Large" by Jennifer A. Coleman from *Newsweek*, August 2, 1993. Reprinted by permission of Jennifer A. Coleman.

p. 220 "Bodily Harm" by Pamela Erens. Reprinted by permission of the author.

p. 225 "Just Walk On By: A Black Man Ponders His Power to Alter Public Space" by Brent Staples. Brent Staples writes on politics and culture for *The New York Times* Editorial Board and is author of a memoir, *Parallel Time: Growing Up in Black and White*, Pantheon Books, 1994. Reprinted by permission.

p. 229 "The Atlanta Riot" from *A Man Called White* by Walter White. Copyright © 1948 by Walter White, renewed © 1976 by the Estate of Walter White. Used by permission of Viking Penguin, a division of Penguin Books USA Inc.

p. 234 "Mommy, What Does 'Nigger' Mean?" by Gloria Naylor from *The New York Times Magazine*, 1986. Reprinted by permission of Sterling Lord Literistics, Inc. Copyright © 1986 by Gloria Naylor.

p. 237 "None of This Is Fair" from *Hunger of Memory* by Richard Rodriguez. Copyright © 1982 by Richard Rodriguez. Reprinted by permission of David R. Godine Publishers, Inc.

p. 241 "Ethnic Envidia" by Ruben Navarrette, Jr. Reprinted by permission of Ruben Navarrette, Jr.

p. 244 "Eleven" from *Woman Hollering Creek* by Sandra Cisneros. Copyright © 1991 by Sandra Cisneros. Published in the United States by Vintage Books, a division of Random House, Inc., New York. First published in hardcover by Random House, Inc., New York in 1991. Reprinted by permission of Susan Bergholz Literary Services, New York.

p. 249 "Work, Labor and Play" from *A Certain World* by W. H. Auden. Reprinted by permission of Curtis Brown, Ltd. Copyright © 1970 by W. H. Auden.

p. 251 "Short-order Cook" by Jim Daniels from *Places/Everyone,* 1985, Board of Regents of The University of Wisconsin. Reprinted by permission of The University of Wisconsin Press.

p. 253 "Less Is More: A Call for Shorter Work Hours" by Barbara Brandt from *Shorter Work Time Group of Boston.* Reprinted by permission of the author.

p. 261 "Who's Not Supporting Whom?" by Bob Moog from *Keyboard* magazine, September 1992, p. 13. Reprinted by permission of *Keyboard* magazine.

p. 267 "In Groups, We Shrink From Loner's Heroics" by Carol Tavris. Copyright © 1991 by Carol Tavris. Reprinted by permission of Lescher & Lescher, Ltd.

p. 269 "Why Johnny Can't Disobey" from Sarah J. McCarthy as first appeared in *The Humanist* magazine, September/October 1979. Reprinted by permission of the author.

p. 278 "Kids in the Mall: Growing Up Controlled" from *The Malling of America* by William S. Kowinski.

p. 283 "The Lottery" from *The Lottery* by Shirley Jackson. Copyright © 1948, 1949 by Shirley Jackson. Copyright renewed © 1976, 1977 by Laurence Hyman, Barry Hyman, Mrs. Sarah Webster, and Mrs. Joanne Schnurer. Reprinted by permission of Farrar, Straus & Giroux, Inc.

p. 290 "Stone-throwing an Annual Bash in India Town" by Mark Fineman from *The Los Angeles Times,* September 24, 1989. Copyright © 1989, *Los Angeles Times.* Reprinted by permission.

p. 294 "Commencement Address: What You Will Be" by Milton Mayer. Copyright © 1958 by Christian Century Foundation. Reprinted by permission from the May 14, 1958, issue of *The Christian Century.*

p. 341 Brief excerpt from *The Obsession: Reflections of the Tyranny of Slenderness* by Kim Chernin. Copyright © 1981 by Kim Chernin. Reprinted by permission of HarperCollins Publishers, Inc.

p. 385 "A Bully's Unjust Deserts" by Bruce Halling. Used by permission of the author.

p. 399 "I Confess Some Envy" by Robert McKelvey. Reprinted by permission of the author.

p. 405 "Food for Thought" by Ellen Goodman. Copyright © 1994, The Boston Globe Company. Reprinted with permission.

p. 408 "I Forgot the Words to the National Anthem" by James Seilsopour. Copyright © 1984 from *Student Writers at Work/The Bedford Prizes* by Nancy Sommers and Donald McQuade, editors. Reprinted with permission of St. Martin's Press, Incorporated.

p. 418 "My Favorite School Class: Involuntary Servitude" by Joe Goodwin as appeared in *The Los Angeles Times,* August 9, 1992. Reprinted by permission of Joe Goodwin.

p. 426 "E Pluribus E-Mail" by Walter J. Gajewski. Used by permission of Walter J. Gajewski.

p. 429 "Don't Let Stereotypes Warp Your Judgments" by Robert L. Heilbroner. Reprinted by permission of Robert L. Heilbroner.

p. 440 "Truth Beneath the Surface" by Tim Hogan. Used by permission of the author.

p. 460 "From Access to Acceptance: Enabling America's Largest Minority" by Shannon Paaske. Used by permission of the author.

Author Index

■ ■ ■

Subject and Title Index